UNION BY LAW

The Chicago Series in Law and Society
Edited by John M. Conley, Charles Epp, and Lynn Mather

Also in the series:

SPEAKING FOR THE DYING: LIFE-AND-DEATH DECISIONS IN INTENSIVE CARE *by Susan P. Shapiro*

JUST WORDS, THIRD EDITION: LAW, LANGUAGE, AND POWER *by John M. Conley, William M. O'Barr, and Robin Conley Riner*

ISLANDS OF SOVEREIGNTY: HAITIAN MIGRATION AND THE BORDERS OF EMPIRE *by Jeffrey S. Kahn*

BUILDING THE PRISON STATE: RACE AND THE POLITICS OF MASS INCARCERATION *by Heather Schoenfeld*

NAVIGATING CONFLICT: HOW YOUTH HANDLE TROUBLE IN A HIGH-POVERTY SCHOOL *by Calvin Morrill and Michael Musheno*

THE SIT-INS: PROTEST AND LEGAL CHANGE IN THE CIVIL RIGHTS ERA *by Christopher W. Schmidt*

WORKING LAW: COURTS, CORPORATIONS, AND SYMBOLIC CIVIL RIGHTS *by Lauren B. Edelman*

THE MYTH OF THE LITIGIOUS SOCIETY: WHY WE DON'T SUE *by David M. Engel*

POLICING IMMIGRANTS: LOCAL LAW ENFORCEMENT ON THE FRONT LINES *by Doris Marie Provine, Monica W. Varsanyi, Paul G. Lewis, and Scott H. Decker*

THE SEDUCTIONS OF QUANTIFICATION: MEASURING HUMAN RIGHTS, GENDER VIOLENCE, AND SEX TRAFFICKING *by Sally Engle Merry*

INVITATION TO LAW AND SOCIETY: AN INTRODUCTION TO THE STUDY OF REAL LAW, SECOND EDITION *by Kitty Calavita*

PULLED OVER: HOW POLICE STOPS DEFINE RACE AND CITIZENSHIP *by Charles R. Epp, Steven Maynard-Moody, and Donald Haider-Markel*

THE THREE AND A HALF MINUTE TRANSACTION: BOILERPLATE AND THE LIMITS OF CONTRACT DESIGN *by Mitu Gulati and Robert E. Scott*

THIS IS NOT CIVIL RIGHTS: DISCOVERING RIGHTS TALK IN 1939 AMERICA *by George I. Lovell*

Additional series titles follow index

UNION BY LAW

Filipino American Labor Activists, Rights Radicalism, and Racial Capitalism

Michael W. McCann
with George I. Lovell

The University of Chicago Press
Chicago and London

The University of Chicago Press, Chicago 60637
The University of Chicago Press, Ltd., London

Published 2020
Printed in the United States of America

29 28 27 26 25 24 23 22 21 20   1 2 3 4 5

ISBN-13: 978-0-226-67987-7 (cloth)
ISBN-13: 978-0-226-67990-7 (paper)
ISBN-13: 978-0-226-68007-1 (e-book)
DOI: https://doi.org/10.7208/chicago/9780226680071.001.0001

Library of Congress Cataloging-in-Publication Data

Names: McCann, Michael W., 1952– author. | Lovell, George I., author.
Title: Union by law : Filipino American labor activists, rights radicalism, and racial capitalism / Michael W. McCann with George I. Lovell.
Other titles: Chicago series in law and society.
Description: Chicago : University of Chicago Press, 2020. | Series: Chicago series in law and society | Includes bibliographical references and index.
Identifiers: LCCN 2019035335 | ISBN 9780226679877 (cloth) | ISBN 9780226679907 (paperback) | ISBN 9780226680071 (ebook)
Subjects: LCSH: Filipino Americans—Political activity. | Salmon canning industry—Labor unions. | Labor unions—United States.
Classification: LCC HD6515.S2 M33 2020 | DDC 331.88/11664942—dc23
LC record available at https://lccn.loc.gov/2019035335

♾ This paper meets the requirements of ANSI/NISO Z39.48-1992 (Permanence of Paper).

We dedicate this book to the legacy of Silme Domingo and Gene Viernes, whose struggles for social justice have so inspired us and many others.

From the history of the enslaved, we might make our way back toward the question of rights.—WALTER JOHNSON (2018)

Contents

Abbreviations

ACPFB	American Committee for the Protection of the Foreign Born
ACWA	Alaska Cannery Workers Association
ACWU	Alaska Cannery Workers Union
AFCSIU	Alaska Fish, Cannery, Seafarers International Union
AFCW	Alaska Fish Cannery Workers Union
AFL	American Federation of Labor
AFSC	American Friends Service Committee
AFU	Alaska Fishermen's Union
ASI	Alaska Salmon Industry
AWOC	Agricultural Workers Organizing Committee
BIA	Bureau of Internal Affairs
BSCP	Brotherhood of Sleeping Car Porters
CAWIU	Cannery and Agricultural Workers Industrial Union
CCA	Central Contractors Association
CIA	Central Intelligence Agency
CILS	Children of Immigrants Longitudinal Study
CIO	Congress of Industrial Organizations
CJDV	Committee for Justice for Domingo and Viernes
COAC	Court Order Advisory Committee
CPFR	Committee for the Protection of Filipino Rights
CPP	Communist Party of the Philippines
CSI	Canned Salmon Industry
CWFLU	Cannery Workers and Farm Laborers Union
DOJ	Department of Justice
EEOC	Equal Employment Opportunity Commission

FBI	Federal Bureau of Investigation
FCC	Federal Communications Commission
FEPC	Fair Employment Practices Committee
FLA	Filipino Labor Association
FLAG	Free Legal Assistance Group
FLU	Filipino Labor Union
FLPA	Filipino Labor Protective Association
FOIA	Freedom of Information Act
FTA	Food, Tobacco, Agricultural, and Allied Workers
HUAC	House Un-American Activities Committee
IBU	Inlandboatmen's Union
IFAWA	International Fishermen and Allied Workers of America
ILA	International Longshoremen's Association
ILWU	International Longshoremen's and Warehousemen's Union (changed in 1997 to International Longshore and Warehouse Union)
INA	Immigration and Nationality Act
INS	Immigration and Naturalization Services
IWW	International Workers of the World (Wobblies)
JCWA	Japanese Cannery Workers Association
KDP	Union of Democratic Filipinos (Katipunan ng Demokratikong Pilipino)
KMU	Kilusang Mayo Uno, or May First Labor Movement
LELO	(Northwest) Labor and Employment Law Office (later changed to Legacy of Equality, Leadership, and Organizing)
LSNR	League of Struggle for Negro Rights
MFP	Maritime Federation of the Pacific
NAACP	National Association for the Advancement of Colored People
NEFCO	New England Fish Company
NFWA	National Farm Workers Association
NIRA	National Industrial Recovery Act
NIS	Naval Investigative Service
NLRA	National Labor Relations Act
NLRB	National Labor Relations Board
NPA	New People's Army
NRA	National Recovery Administration
PATCO	Professional Air Traffic Controllers Organization
PCCS	Philippine Commonwealth Council of Seattle
RFC	Rank and File Committee
SACB	Subversive Activities Control Board

SCRLHP	Seattle Civil Rights and Labor History Project
STFU	Southern Tenant Farmers Union
SWU	Seafood Workers Union
TFDP	Task Force Detainees of the Philippines
UCAPAWA	United Cannery, Agricultural, Packing, and Allied Workers of America
UCWA	United Construction Workers Association
UFW	United Farm Workers
USAFFE	US Armed Forces in the Far East
UW	University of Washington
UWSC	University of Washington Special Collections
WLB	War Labor Board

Preface

This book chronicles the struggles of Filipino American labor activists *for* rights-based social justice and *against* racism, predatory capitalism, and imperialism throughout much of the twentieth century. Our analysis of this history highlights law's constitutive role in authorizing and administering the violent subjugation of racialized low-wage workers as well as in facilitating their relentless efforts to elude, challenge, and transform the hierarchical social relations intrinsic to racial capitalist orders.

The research for this book began in 1997, when local political engagement and affiliation with the Harry Bridges Center for Labor Studies at the University of Washington connected one of us (McCann) to some of the key activists and their stories that eventually became the core of our analytical historical narrative. The original vision for a book materialized very quickly, but, for a host of reasons, the empirical research was halted after just over a year. A dozen years later, around 2010, McCann decided to resume the research and asked Dr. George Lovell to join as coauthor. We quickly shared ideas about the overall theorization, outlined the architecture of the book, submitted applications for grant funding, and set about conducting the massive research enterprise. The book took almost another decade to complete, in large part because both of us were active in other separate research projects and, especially, diverted by major administrative roles on our university campus. As a result of Lovell's serial conscription for university administrative leadership, Michael ended up writing the majority of the book's words, although George wrote the original draft for one chapter, contributed directly to two other chapters, and provided ideas and commentary on every part of the book. The intellectual collaboration between us authors remained profoundly formative throughout the process of the project's development. In the end, though, George felt that claiming equal coauthorship was inappropriate, so we agreed to the present listing of authors.

Most of the research and early writing thus took place while Barack Obama served as the first African American (or mixed race) president of the United States. The fabulous soundtrack from *Hamilton* ("Immigrants—we get the job done") blared loudly while many words were written. We imagined from the start that our historical narrative would serve in part as a critical reflection on the palpable manifestations of repressive politics, policies, and law in the American racial capitalist empire over the previous century, both before and following the midcentury global "racial break." The now familiar forces of neoliberal marketization and exclusionary neoconservative punitiveness were rapidly ascending during the period covered in our book's final chapters, thus leading us to theorize about legal rights mobilization amidst the new forms of "repressive law" that had developed in our historically hierarchical legal system.

However, even we were surprised by the intensity of white backlash against Obama and the ascendance of Donald Trump as candidate and then elected president. Most of the book manuscript was actually written while news of Trump's racist odes to white supremacy, criminalizing rhetoric about immigrants, indulgence toward rapacious capitalism, overt misogyny, reckless reconfiguring of America's role in the world, and generally erratic, lawless behavior increasingly dominated the digitally mediated public space. Contrary to the hopes of liberals but consistent with our expectations, American courts have deferred to many of Trump's basic designs, including upholding his "Muslim travel ban" once the executive order was cleansed of explicit reference to Muslims. Racial innocence has continued to thrive in official law! We believe that Mr. Trump's presidency lamentably highlights the relevance of this book, not least because our analysis makes his actions—and those of cronies like Paul Manafort, who has a cameo role in our story—seem less unusual and more comprehensible in America's history of racial capitalism. The concurrent rise of President Rodrigo Duterte, another ruthless, murderous strongman president in the Philippines, likewise offers eerie parallels (as well as differences) to Ferdinand Marcos, whose era of rule plays a critical part in our chronicle.

At the same time, we also did not foresee the reinvigoration of appeals to democratic socialism, substantial income redistribution, a Green New Deal, criminal justice reform, universal health care, racial reparations, and other progressive agendas in American national politics. Those developments also seem to make this book, which charts the rise of immigrant-based, multiracial socialist activism in America over several generations, relevant to contemporary readers. We do not make direct references to the recent clashes of these contrasting contemporary political currents within the main text of the book, but they shadow virtually every page of the written historical study.

A book that gestates for over twenty years accumulates an enormous number of debts to colleagues, supporters, and friends. For one thing, we benefitted from the diligent work of numerous graduate research assistants who labored scouring archives, web sources, and secondary literature. The list included James Chamberlain, Filiz Kahraman, Milli Lake, Tania Melo, and Kirstine Taylor. Their interest in the project from the start was inspiring as well as instrumentally helpful. In addition, Emma Rodman provided superb editing work and thoughtful commentary on several early chapters as the book developed. Other PhD students who provided valuable commentary include Erin Adam, Chelsea Moore, Walid Salem, and Hind Ahmed Zaki. Doug Baker, who began but never completed an extremely insightful and helpful dissertation on legal tactics of the first generation of Filipino cannery workers, was an early collaborator (in the late 1990s) whose research proved influential to the final manuscript. Undergraduate Jacqueline Wu also performed valuable research work for us as well.

A number of colleagues at the University of Washington were invaluable contributors to our empirical research. Labor archivists Conor Casey, Crystal Rodgers, and other associates in the Labor Archives of Washington (LAW) Special Collections were extremely helpful at many points in the research; we are very lucky to have them among us at UW. Professor James Gregory was important and helpful in dozens of ways, including his inspired work directing the remarkable online Seattle Civil Rights and Labor History Project, which provided us invaluable baseline knowledge of many historical developments. Moreover, the scholarship by Project codirector Trevor Griffey on the extraordinary activist leader Tyree Scott and the Black Power movements that followed profoundly shaped our understanding of the context of radical politics in Seattle from the late 1960s through the 1990s. Griffey's FOIA-accessed records detailing FBI surveillance of leftist Filipino labor activists also were highly informative. Andrew Hedden, associate director of the Harry Bridges Center for Labor Studies, was a great source of insights regarding the positioning of Seattle in the Philippine colonial legacy and US capitalist empire generally. Dorothy Cordova graciously cooperated in providing us access to archives at the Filipino American National History Museum, including many original photographs that appear in this book. Archivists at the Museum of History & Industry in Seattle (Adam Lyon and Kathleen Knies) as well as the American Friends Service Committee (Donald Davis) were extremely helpful in supplying other photos. Steven Dunne performed much labor and technical magic in making old photographs viewable in print.

The Mellon Foundation-funded Sawyer Seminar on "Capitalism and Comparative Racialization" at the University of Washington in 2017–18 proved to be a timely theoretical resource for the project. The ongoing seminar, its local members and invited visitors, provided considerable enlightenment that benefitted us greatly. Most directly important, codirectors and participants Megan Ming Francis, Moon-Ho Jung, Chandan Reddy, and, especially, Chip Turner, along with invited participant Mario Barnes, generously organized a book scrub to comment on a manuscript draft in October 2018; their input was highly instructive on a variety of counts that helped to improve the book. Vincente Rafael also was active in the seminar and very influential at many phases of book development.

Other UW colleagues likewise provided useful input and ideas at various points. These included political science colleagues Rachel Cichowski, Jamie Mayerfeld, Christopher Parker, and Becca Thorpe and sociolegal colleagues Katherine Beckett, Angelina Godoy, Steven Herbert, Stephen Meyers, Arzoo Osanloo, and Carolyn Pinedo Turnovsky. Conversations with Naomi Murakawa, both while she was a UW colleague and beyond, greatly contributed to refinement in core ideas about how legal proceduralism legitimates repressive law in the postwar era and serves to reinforce racial innocence. Joel Migdal, a brilliant scholar, intellectual colleague, mentoring partner, and good friend, offered wisdom from the earliest days of book development. Gail Nomura's scholarship on early Filipino struggles in the metropole was enormously helpful, as was the work of Rick Bonus and Roneva Keel.

We can only begin to list the dozens of professional colleagues beyond the UW campus who provided input and directly or indirectly influenced the ideas in the book. We include in particular Catherine (KT) Albiston, Clara Altman, Celeste Arrington, Bernadette Atuahene, Rick Baldoz, Scott Barclay, Elizabeth Beaumont, Anne Bloom, Susan Carle, Lynette Chua, Renee Cramer, Michael Dawson, Richard Delgado, Jeffrey Dudas, Lauren Edelman, David Engel, Chuck Epp, Sean Farhang, Malcolm Feeley, Catherine Fisk,

Mary Gallagher, Jon Goldberg-Hiller, Laura Gomez, Jennifer Gordon, Jon Gould, Cheryl Harris, Lane Hirabayashi, Liora Israel, Robin Kelley, Anna Kirkland, Dilek Kurban, Jules Lobel, Anna-Maria Marshall, Mark Massoud, Charles Mills, Tamir Moustafa, Frank Munger, Bob Nelson, Laura Beth Nielsen, Jerome Pelisse, Aziz Rana, Julie Ringelheim, Cesar Rodriguez-Garavito, Gerry Rosenberg, Richard Rothstein, Carroll Seron, Susan Silbey, Helena Silverstein, Jonathan Simon, Eve Darian Smith, Rogers Smith, Susan Sterett, Dara Strolovitch, Robin Stryker, Sidney Tarrow, Christopher Tomlins, Jean-Christian Vinel, and Emily Zackin. Many other scholars contributed ideas at a host of conference panels and invited talks at institutions around the world; we are sorry that we cannot list them all.

We note specific contributions by several scholars. Our close friend and long-time intellectual colleague William Haltom offered vivid memories about his high school classmate Silme Domingo, adding further details about the life of the charismatic, transformative individual whose assassination haunts the second half of our book. Professor Stephen Wasby volunteered important correctives and suggestions early on about our analysis of the *Wards Cove* case. Scott Cummings provided extensive, detailed, extremely helpful commentary on a draft of the book manuscript. Stuart Scheingold passed away just as the book research was restarting, but his enduring intellectual influence on both authors and on the book will be abundantly evident to readers familiar with his work. Austin Sarat also has contributed greatly to our development as sociolegal scholars over many years, and his indirect impact on this book should not be underestimated. Sally Engle Merry's scholarship, and especially her landmark book *Colonizing Hawaii*, provided a model that informed our very different but, we hope, complementary book; her careful reading of our manuscript draft was enormously helpful and made our volume much better. We note a similar debt to Paul Frymer. His fabulous book on US territorial and political expansion ends where ours begins, and his work on civil rights and unions shaped some of our core questions and arguments. Our book is better for his influence; he also contributed a supportive and helpful review of our manuscript.

We appreciated abundant financial support along the way. A University of Washington Royalty Research Grant supported the initial explorations of the history and interview-based research in 1998. A substantial National Science Foundation grant (#SES-1060698) was critical to supporting the labor-intensive archival research for several years. The Harry Bridges Center for Labor Studies provided a pivotal Washington State Labor Research Grant as well as additional research funds over half a dozen years to us both while serving as consecutive center directors. McCann benefitted greatly from a stimulating sabbatical year at the Program in Law and Public Affairs at Princeton, which created time for writing as well as early conceptual development from program colleagues, especially from Kim Lane Scheppele. The Simpson Center for Humanities at the University of Washington provided course release and vibrant intellectual exchange for McCann while a fellow as well as support for the Sawyer Seminar on comparative racial capitalism. And the Mellon Foundation was the primary funder of that latter seminar for well over a year, an ongoing intellectual engagement that shaped the book in fundamental ways. We appreciate the permission of *Law & Social Inquiry* to draw heavily on an earlier published article for chapter 6.

We must acknowledge our greatest debts to activists in the ACWA, CJDV, KDP, ILWU Local 37, IBU Region 37, and other affiliated groups chronicled in the book. These inspiring people talked to us, endured questions they often found limited in relevance, pointed us to other interviewees and sources of information, granted permission for access to files and materials, and much more. We benefitted from many ongoing collaborative relationships with them concerning contemporary political and community activities, which in turn provided grounds for making sense of their histories, aspirations, and actions. But these engagements also sensitized us to the distances that separated our experiences, especially with those from decades before. We tried to understand and integrate their input into the book, but we are very aware of our inadequacies in doing justice to their stories and legacy. We are particularly indebted to Cindy Domingo, who signaled her trust in our capacity to tell this story through her ceaseless assistance with the research and efforts to connect us with many of the other participants in the story. Among those others who assisted us so generously were David Della, Nemesio Domingo Jr., Rich Gurtiza, Terri Mast, Bruce Occena, Tyree Scott, Emily Van Bronkhorst, and Michael Woo, who graciously provided us interviews and more. Abraham Arditi, Michael Fox, and Mike Withey provided very helpful accounts of their work as lawyers, and Withey provided invaluable transcripts for the civil murder trial discussed in chapter 5. Ligaya Domingo, daughter to Silme Domingo and Terri Mast and herself a labor activist, kindly shared her outstanding PhD dissertation on the Rank and File Movement in the Alaska Cannery Workers Union, providing us details and insights that fundamentally influenced our somewhat different, law-focused interpretive account. Longtime Philippine socialist activist, former legislator, and international scholar

Walden Bello helped us to understand changing currents of politics in the Philippines and its relationship to US imperialism. Journalist Tom Churchill was very helpful early on, and journalist/activist Ron Chew was supportive directly in a number of ways and indirectly through his terrific book. Finally, we never met Silme Domingo and Gene Viernes in person, but our research has led us to spend a great time getting to know and dwell on their extraordinary and inspirational legacy; we dedicate this book to them.

This is the third book with the University of Chicago Press for McCann and the second for Lovell. One reason we returned to UCP was its long-time, highly distinguished editor, John Tryneski. John responded to our initial book proposal by issuing a contract and working with us in the early phases. However, the slow development of the book cost us John's sage collaboration when he retired. Fortunately, Chuck Myers took over and worked with us as we completed a book manuscript, endured revisions, and finally produced the work. Both editors served us extremely well, as did the entire staff at UCP. Copyeditor Steve LaRue did a great job improving our prose and correcting or identifying many errors in the original manuscript. Derek Gottlieb constructed a detailed and useful index.

Finally, we thank each other. We each wish that our contributions to the final manuscript could have been more equal, as that would have produced a better book and also would have been more fun in the process. We remain good friends, nevertheless, and that is reason for much gratitude.

Notes on Terminology

Throughout, we tend to use the terms *Filipino* and *Filipino American* interchangeably to refer to people who are of Philippine descent but reside in America. Both terms identify people who were originally immigrants as well as those who were American born. These labeling practices are consistent with those employed by historical and cultural scholars working on closely related topics (L. Domingo 2010, 12; see also Baldoz 2011; Chew 2012; Fujita-Rony 2003; Ngai 2004; and Rafael 2000) as well as by the activists who are the subject of our study. We specifically chose to use the term *Filipino Americans* in our book title to avoid misrepresentation about the topic. Moreover, we often tend to use the first, simpler term (*Filipino*) when referring to cannery worker activists, as the term *Filipino cannery workers* is widely deployed in ordinary language practices of labor activists, scholars, and archivists. This is especially the case for Filipinos residing in the United States before 1946 as "colonial nationals" (Ngai 2004, xx; Fujita-Rony 2003, xviii), but the construction is commonplace for and among those activists in later generations as well. By contrast, we tend most often to use the latter term when referring to Filipino/a Americans generally, especially after World War II, when naturalized citizenship was widely granted. We also use mostly the masculine construction of *Filipino* because nearly all of the migrant workers and labor activists in our study were male. We use the term *Filipina* in the few instances when we refer to females alone. However, we do not use the contemporary term *Filipino/a* when referring to the general immigrant population, as that usage predated ordinary practice during the historical periods of our study (Fujita-

Rony 2003, xviii). We do not use the currently familiar construction Filipinx to overcome gender binaries for the same reason.

We also use the term *migrants* in two related ways. One meaning signals those persons who migrated from the Philippines or other nations to the United States. Many but not all migrants became immigrants who settled in America, and not all of the latter were naturalized as citizens. Another meaning of *migrant* refers to the migratory circuits of seasonal work that Asian American laborers traveled *within* the United States, mostly around the West Coast of North America but also more broadly around the Pacific Rim, including Hawaii and the Philippines. The two meanings are often concurrent and interrelated in many usages. We also recognize that many contemporary migrant workers are elite "astronauts" who hold multiple passports, travel the world comfortably, and benefit from the privileges of "flexible citizenship" (Ong 2006). But the focus of our study is low-wage migrant workers.

INTRODUCTION

> The salmon industry as described by this record takes us back to a kind of overt and institutionalized discrimination we have not dealt with in years: a total residential and work environment organized on principles of racial stratification and segregation, which, as Justice Stevens points out, resembles a plantation economy. . . . This industry long has been characterized by a taste for discrimination of the old-fashioned sort: a preference for hiring nonwhites to fill its lowest level positions, on the condition that they stay there. The majority's legal rulings essentially *immunize* these practices from attack under a Title VII disparate impact analysis. . . . One wonders whether the majority still believes that race discrimination—or, more accurately, race discrimination against nonwhites—is a problem in our society, or even *remembers* that it ever was.—JUSTICE HARRY BLACKMUN, dissenting in *Wards Cove Packing Co. v. Atonio*, 1989 (italics added for emphasis)

Justice Harry Blackmun's strident dissenting opinion (quoted above) underscored the deep divisions among the US Supreme Court Justices in *Wards Cove v. Atonio* (1989), a class action civil rights case initiated by Filipino American and Native plaintiffs against an Alaska salmon cannery during the mid-1970s. A five-justice majority led by Justice Byron R. White rejected the claims by workers of color regarding pervasive invidious racial discrimination in the cannery and, in the process, issued a landmark ruling that significantly increased the obstacles for all plaintiffs seeking judicial remedies for institutionalized racism and sexism. Blackmun and his fellow dissenters charged the White majority with ignoring both key factual evidence presented by the plaintiffs and important legal precedents that had made the 1964 Civil Rights Act a potent resource for aggrieved nonwhite and female workers (Belton 2014; McCann 1994). The most provocative claim by Blackmun, however, turned on his speculation that the majority of justices failed to *remember*—or, perhaps, willfully ignored—not just legal precedents but a long, dark, continuing history of legally enforced racial and class domination in America. This allegation of legal forgetting and "immunization"[1] against challenge evokes the classic argument of scholar Robert Cover about the fundamental ways that official law kills off challenges to status quo legal hierarchies and systematically diverts attention from its violence, thus erasing both legal rights claims and their authoritative rejection (Cover 1984; Charles W. Mills 2017). Indeed, a later chapter (chap. 6) will elaborate on how Justice White's majority opinion relied on fanciful hypothetical scenarios, legal abstractions, elevation of procedural over substantive justice, and racial stereotypes to discount the material facts of institutionalized practice that long had exploited minority workers.

That erasure has been compounded by mainstream legal scholars who routinely, if unwittingly, validate as binding law the majority ruling that systematically privileged white business interests without acknowledging the many decades of abuse that led racialized working-class plaintiffs to file the lawsuit in the first place (Brigham 1991). The Supreme Court's emphatic authorization of racial and class hierarchy at work as well as its embrace of neoliberal economic rationalization was so routine that it generated only modest critical commentary in the mainstream mass media and, then, in scholarly publications (Lovell, McCann, and Taylor 2016). Meanwhile, scholars who routinely characterize litigation by social movements as a "hollow hope" have further normalized the outcome as an episode of misdirected energies by litigants, thus discouraging efforts to explore seriously the activists' goals and strategic actions (Rosenberg 1991, 2009). In the process, a history of struggles for egalitarian rights and global justice by minority and female workers over the previous two decades, and more generally for over hundreds of years, has been nearly expunged by the conventions of official legal knowledge. A willful posture of "racial innocence," as James Baldwin (1963; see also Charles W. Mills 2017; Murakawa and Beckett 2010; Pierce 2012; Taylor 2015) labeled white America's endemic cultural "crime," infused the highest law in the land.

The study that follows is the first effort to situate the infamous *Wards Cove* case in the broader social and legal history of racialized workers' struggles for social justice that culminated in the lawsuit. Organized as a chronological narrative that spans most of the twentieth century, the account begins with the bloody US invasion of the Philippines and the extension of oppressive colonial rule at the dawn of the twentieth century. The chronicle then follows the migration of proletarianized[2] Filipino workers to the US metropole where they worked seasonally as wage laborers in West Coast agricultural fields and the Alaskan salmon canneries, formed a series of unions to represent their interests, and struggled persistently for class, race, and gender-based social justice throughout the Cold War political contexts of national security state development and global empire building.

Official American law was repressive in three senses—first, in upholding systematic exploitation of Filipino workers' productive labor and marginal racial status over many decades; second, in repressing the labor activists' relentless political campaigns challenging capitalism, racism, and imperialism; and third, in the *Wards Cove* opinion continuing a long tradition of erasing those interrelated histories. As such, our analytical narrative is very much intended to be an act of *recovery*—a reclamation of a long legacy of racial capitalist domination over Filipinos and other low-wage or unpaid migrant workers; of noble aspirational struggles for human rights by the workers over several generations; and of the many ways that law was mobilized both to enforce and to challenge race, class, and gender hierarchy at work.

While organized in chronological terms, the historical account that we offer is shaped by an ambitious and complex set of interrelated premises and themes. We begin below by outlining our core substantive themes and then the analytical framework that informs the narrative.

The Core Thematic Threads of the Historical Narrative

The Contradictory Power of Law

Our narrative social history of Filipino migrant workers focuses analysis on the complex character and role of *law*. This should not be surprising, given the book's title and our already stated aim of providing a long history of struggles for rights and social justice leading up to a landmark Supreme Court case. But our project takes legal analysis in unconventional directions. In short, our interpretive history underlines in particular the profoundly contradictory role of law in mediating contentious power relations between proletarianized Filipino migrant workers and the imperial racial capitalist order.

On the one hand, we document that the great majority of Filipinos were subjugated by the American legal order from the very moment in 1898 when the United States invaded the Philippine islands. Soon after the military conquest that left a half million or more Filipinos dead, the US imposed a constitutional scheme that secured rule by local oligarchs and institutionalized obstacles that worked to thwart democratizing forces over the following century. Moreover, US-sponsored land reform legislation forced large numbers of former subsistence farmers and peasants into exploitative, low-wage labor in mass agricultural production for commodity export in global commercial markets. Those Filipinos who subsequently traveled to the US West Coast in search of work, economic opportunity, and citizenship—the promises of the American legal culture taught in US colonial schools—found themselves in proletarian conditions that paralleled the colonized homeland. Most importantly, they discovered that their status as conscripted colonial national subjects accorded them few basic rights and opportunities for legally secured freedom, relegating them to a marginal position shared with other low-wage, racialized workers in the metropole. Moreover, Filipino agricultural and salmon cannery workers were routinely subjected to racial violence by white citizens as well as the exploitative commodified work conditions of plantation capitalism insulated from the restraints of liberal legal governance. Their vulnerability and powerlessness were exacerbated by the everyday reality or threat of criminalization, deportation, and dispossession imposed by legal officials.

Carlos Bulosan, the renowned literary chronicler of the Filipino experience, captured in memorable terms the brutal, precarious reality of Filipinos in both the "external" and "internal" American colonies. Early in his most famous book, *America Is in the Heart*, he repeatedly compared his young life in the colonial Philippines—"my father fighting for his inherited land, my mother selling bagoong to the impoverished peasants"[3]—with his later "swift and dangerous life in America" (Bulosan 1973, 56–57). "I know deep in my heart that I am an exile in America," wrote Bulosan in the early 1940s. "I feel like a criminal running away from a crime I did not commit. And this crime is that I am a Filipino in America" (San Juan Jr. 1995, 173). Bulosan vividly documented an America where a large and diverse underclass suffered from severe racial and class domination enforced, directly and indirectly, by official law:

> America is not a land of one race or one class of men. We are all Americans that have toiled and suffered and known oppression and defeat, from the first Indian that offered peace to the last Filipino peapickers. . . . America is also the nameless foreigner, the homeless refugee, the hungry boy begging for a job and the black body dangling from a tree. (Bulosan 1973, xxiv)

Filipino colonial subjects slowly, unevenly began to gain formal standing as citizens, thus winning rights to claim and exercise rights in the American metropole by the late 1940s. The change in status reflected in large part shifts in domestic US political alliances as well as the exigencies of American strategic international economic and military policy between the world wars. But the grant of citizenship status to Filipinos did not mean the end of legally sanctioned marginalization of subaltern Filipinos at and beyond work. Overt racism and institutionalized racial discrimination continued as foundational forces in American society. In particular, the organization of seasonal agricultural and salmon cannery work for Filipino migrant laborers remained segregated and exploitative along racial as well as class lines. These workplace relationships and practices that treated workers as disposable commodities continued through the 1970s, when young labor activists filed their civil rights suits leading to the *Wards Cove* ruling. Moreover, two generations of left-oriented Filipino union activists were harassed, surveilled, and subjected to violence by corporate, state, and state-supported social actors for challenging traditional race, class, and gender hierarchies in domestic workplaces as well as US imperial policies abroad. In short, the Filipino labor activists at the center of our story experienced American law over most of the century as an integral element in a tangled web of systematic domination.

On the other hand, legal doctrines, institutions, and processes as well as general legal ideals of civil and human rights proved enticing and episodically empowering assets for Filipino workers. In the first generation, Filipinos were forced to negotiate with and through law when they could not elude its repressive force. They learned the political arts of "pragmatic resistance"—how to endure, evade, and even challenge criminal prosecution, deportation for violations of immigration law, restrictions on property ownership, prohibitions on racial intermixing in social and personal life, exclusion from political participation, and exploitation at work (Chua 2014; McCann and March 1996). Eventually, as our historical narrative demonstrates, the workers learned how to creatively invoke the promises of legal rights and to muster scarce resources in struggles to moderate the repressive, illiberal features of the US socio-legal order. This understanding was again central to Bulosan's often-cited aspirational embrace of "America." The writer repeatedly trumpeted the unrealized dreams and promises of equal rights to freedom, social and economic security, and democratic political participation for all persons that many derived from foundational American legal texts. "America is in the hearts of men that died for freedom; it is also in the eyes of men that are building a new world" (Bulosan 1973, xxiii–xxiv).

Most important for our story, the cannery workers developed sophistication in mobilizing New Deal–era labor law to facilitate their organizing efforts, forming a union that survived for many decades, across a series of changes in name and affiliation, as an important resource for empowerment. The union organizations developed by cannery workers were notable not just for their democratic, antiracist, anti-imperial, and overtly socialist agendas but also for their highly legalistic internal processes and commitments to workers' rights. This included a high level of activity around workers' grievance arbitration and litigation, routine demands for democratic accountability within the union, and high-profile, often successful constitutional and statutory challenges waged in US courts against various injustices. Through their struggles the activists developed an "oppositional" legal consciousness (Mansbridge and Morris 2001) committed to a capacious, transformative vision of egalitarian rights that promised social justice and democratic empowerment to all persons.

The union mobilized law against new forms of state repression in the 1950s when many of the leftist leaders, including Bulosan, became targets of McCarthy-era purges. Undaunted, union leaders and activists responded with a variety of defiant actions, creative legal challenges, and novel articulations of rights claims. Activist workers were aided by prominent Left civil liberties attorneys, some of them allied with the International Longshoremen's and Warehousemen's Union (ILWU).[4] The workers themselves took pride in their own legal knowledge. For example, the ILWU Local 37 *1952 Yearbook*, edited by Carlos Bulosan during a late-life stint as union employee, powerfully challenged how workers were "forced by restrictive law" into unjust subordinate positions even as they expressed their own commitments to aspirational legal ideals of "human rights and liberties" that merged "the fundamental principles of our union and the continuation of the democratic spirit in America" (ILWU Local 37, 1952, 1). The *Yearbook* clearly evidences that Bulosan's familiar appeal to "America" was far more radical than reverential, as he and his fellow activists persistently strategized "to rearticulate the liberal discourse of civil rights toward a socialist direction" (San Juan Jr. 1995, 12).

The contingencies of World War II and continued democratic rights advocacy brought a mix of increased integration for many patriotic Filipino Americans inclined toward assimilation and new forms of persecution for Filipino cannery workers allied with leftist unions, creating tensions among the immigrants that continued for the next half century. The legacy of radical rights struggle was reborn in the early 1970s with a new generation of young Filipino Americans who worked in the same canneries as their fathers had, and often along with them. These young militants mobilized newly enacted civil rights law as a resource for challenging racially segregated job opportunities and exploitative work conditions in the canneries. The activists creatively used lawsuits filed under Title VII of the 1964 Civil Rights Act—two of which won at trial and produced favorable damages awards—to generate support from rank-and-file workers for ousting and replacing the corrupt, undemocratic union leadership that assumed power in the aftermath of Cold War state purges. Many of the activists were also members of the KDP (Katipunan ng Demokratikong Pilipino [Union of Democratic Filipinos]), a grassroots leftist organization that allied with radical social movements in the Philippines to challenge US imperialism and to end support for authoritarian rulers around the globe, including especially President Ferdinand Marcos. For many of them, as for their muse Bulosan, demanding democratic rights was a critical part of truly "revolutionary" socialist praxis (Toribio 1998). The historical legacy of initiating legal action to catalyze and leverage democratic socialist organizing proved invaluable in subsequent years. After two young leaders, Silme Domingo and Gene Viernes, were murdered in the Seattle union office in 1981, surviving activists generated widespread national and international support to win retributive justice. Suspecting that the murders were part of a broader conspiracy, the activists raised money to finance a civil lawsuit against Ferdinand Marcos, eventually demonstrating in federal court the details of a plot involving local thugs, the corrupt union boss, Marcos, and complicit US officials.

The activists' different campaigns culminated in a remarkable historical convergence of three important events in 1989: (1) Marcos fell from power in 1986 and died three years later; (2) the long developing civil trial exposed the nefarious domestic operations of both US and Philippine intelligence agencies supporting Marcos that were implicated in the murders of the two young Filipino American activists; and (3) the US Supreme Court issued the devastating ruling in the third civil rights lawsuit filed against the canneries. In *Wards Cove Packing Co. v. Atonio* (1989), the court disregarded the evidence that workers of color had presented to demonstrate racial disparities—including segregated job assignments, promotion opportunities, sleeping quarters, and mess halls—and announced new evidentiary standards that made it nearly impossible for workers of color to prove invidious discrimination at the canneries. As noted in our opening lines, the ruling erased precedents of principle along with historical social facts, and it reconstructed official law in ways that virtually killed the potential for future collective worker challenges to institutional racism and sexism in the workplace. The activists quickly began to mobilize as part of a new national coalition to pass legislation reversing the judicial retrenchment. However, the resulting 1991 Civil Rights Act fell short of reviving key elements of the disparate impact doctrine essential to class actions challenging systemic discrimination at work. The last decades of the century underlined the mix of legally imposed tragedy and periodic triumph that marked the entire history of Filipino labor activist radical egalitarian struggles for civil rights, democratic reform, and social justice.

The ambiguous preposition—*by*—connecting *union* with *law* in this book's title intentionally suggests the contradictory character of law. Perhaps most important, the identities, status, and standing of Filipino workers were constructed in important ways *by* the official legal system. The dominant order divided between white American capitalist privilege and racialized low-wage, largely nonwhite, subaltern laborers—and their various titles as colonial nationals, immigrants, migrant workers, criminals, communists, subversives, citizens, and the like—has been constructed and enforced, as Ian Haney-López has aptly put it, "by law" (Haney-López 1997; Gomez 2012). At the same time, the Filipino activists organized themselves by, or through, invoking and exploiting the contradictory logics of liberal law to *defend* themselves. They developed organizational forms (e.g., union constitution, collective bargaining, 501(c)(3) status, etc.) in accordance with law, mobilized legal claims and resources to advance their interests, and struggled to change many laws in the process. But they also knew that their aspirations as defiant subaltern *radicals* were often beyond, outside of—so "by" as in "besides" or "apart from"—and opposed to the narrowly individualistic legal principles privileging market relations and racial hierarchy over democratic principles that were generally enforced by US legal officials. One of the most distinctive features of the labor activists was their appeal to the socioeconomic promises of universal human rights to challenge narrow liberal constructions of rights and undemocratic capitalist traditions that have defined US politics and law from the earliest days. In other words, the activists were routinely subjected to the constraints of official law, framed their aspirational claims by pushing the boundaries of authorized liberal law, and yet also imagined and acted on radical possibilities of rights and justice well outside of the borders of official American law. Filipino labor activism was thoroughly constituted, at many levels, by law.

The Multiple Dimensions of Historical Union

Another key substantive theme is expressed by our book title's evocative reference to legal *union*, or more accurately, a tangle of very different types of interrelated unions. The first, broadest, but still conventional referent is to our study of legally constituted unions at the nation-state level. This includes attention to the evolving American constitutional state committed to "a more perfect union" of its people as well the constitutional order that structured governance of the Philippines from the colonial era through its development as a semi-independent client state during the twentieth century. Our narrative underlines in particular how shifting currents in the American legal system structured the political constraints and opportunities experienced by Filipino workers in the racial capitalist metropole, which were reshaped in turn by the workers' collective struggles, both successful and unsuccessful.

A closely related dimension of such attention concerns the tenuous international union forged *between* US and Philippine polities throughout the twentieth century, from the periods of reluctant but repressive US colonial rule to its role as imperial patron propping up the Philippine client state in the global capitalist order. That imposition of imperial power was, again, crafted in large part through law—by constitutional legal principles institutionalized by US rulers, by contractual and commercial relations forged among public and private actors, and by a long line of legislation and treaties that structured the evolution into an interdependent bond between the two political economies. "The U.S. did what empires do: expanded the jurisdiction of the state to draw different territories, peoples, and cultures within its reach and then developed legal and political mechanisms for managing difference within its sovereign borders" (Altman 2013, 544). This hierarchical international relationship dramatically shaped Philippine political, social, and cultural history until the present, but it also substantially inflected the particular character and practices of American state development from settler nation to imperial global power (Frymer 2017; Kramer 2006). Relations with the Philippines, after all, were critical to development of American military and commercial power in the Pacific from World War I to the present. Moreover, decades of

US collaboration with Philippine elites to quash democratic rebels generated experimentation with many practices—secret surveillance and information gathering, use of rumors and lies to divide the opposition, guerilla jungle warfare, classic torture techniques—that became central to US repression of domestic subversives (including Filipino labor activists) during the Cold War and foreign enemies in hot wars abroad in Korea, Vietnam, Central America, Iraq, and Afghanistan (see McCoy 2009). In sum, our attention to these complex unions between the United States and the Philippines is critical to our account about the development of the contemporary American global empire.

By contrast, the most specific and obvious referent of legal union in our narrative is the labor associations representing cannery workers that evolved from the late 1920s through numerous changes in organizational form and affiliation and eventually becoming ILWU Local 37 in the 1950s. Our historical narrative explores the political development of these many union organizations amid the context of changing national laws and legal practices regulating labor organizing, workplace relations, and civil rights. We underline that the labor unions from the start were very much civil rights organizations that both conferred legal standing to noncitizen migrant workers in the first generation and provided organizational, financial, and solidaristic resources to support their continuing struggles for substantive rights causes, political transformation, and material empowerment through the contemporary period.

Moreover, the Filipino cannery workers' union on which we focus from the start struggled to form political alliances with other Asian, Native Alaskan, African American, Mexican, and white workers—including minority ethnic and, eventually in the second generation, white women (Ruiz 1987)—who also labored in low-wage, physically demanding jobs. The potential challenges posed by these multiracial, class-based unions greatly amplified the anxieties experienced by corporate employers and white Americans generally. Labor union organizing efforts forged connections of other sorts as well. Indeed, the migrant workers at the center of our story were engaged in a complex, ever expanding series of alliances with many other types of political actors, from the archipelago of Filipino American communities that developed across the West Coast to a host of political alliances with left-oriented activist groups, political advocacy organizations, and lawyers, including in the Philippines. The KDP, or Union of Democratic Filipinos, was a transpacific radical organization that proved especially influential on cannery activists in the 1970s and 1980s. Our narrative will demonstrate how rights-based activism was a catalyst and a medium for a complex array of progressive, class-based, multi-racial, multi-issue, and anti-imperial transnational political networks—which harbingered what in later decades would be labeled "social movement unionism" (Engeman 2015: Rosenblum 2017; Turner and Hurd 2001)—in both the first and, especially, second generations of union activity.

Finally, we are especially interested in documenting and analyzing the aspirational visions, what we call the oppositional legal rights consciousness, that animated and united the leaders of the Filipino-led unions, union dissidents, and their political allies. This oppositional consciousness evolved during years of resistance against Spanish and then US colonial domination and eventually matured into a coherent social movement ideology through persistent struggles against manifold injustices in the racial capitalist order of the American metropole and the rule of strong-arm oligarchs in the homeland archipelago. The vision uniting the coalitions of activists at the heart of our narrative, we show, was fundamentally antiracist, anticapitalist, and anti-imperialist. Stated more affirmatively, the activists were united by commitments to racial inclusiveness, a democratically accountable socialist political economy, and a global order grounded in respect for human rights, including socioeconomic rights, of all persons. The union activists' pervasive faith in rights principles at once aimed for strategic "resonance" within dominant legal traditions and "radical" egalitarian transformation of the American and Philippine social orders (Ferree 2003).

Law and Legal Mobilization in the Racial Capitalist Order

Legal Mobilization Theory

This book chronicles the long history of select persons, institutional relations, and political struggles leading up to a single, narrowly divided but highly significant 1989 Supreme Court ruling on workplace civil rights. Yet our study also builds on and aims to develop in new ways a rich tradition of sociolegal analysis regarding how law works to shape political contestation practices within ostensibly liberal constitutional regimes. That framework is conventionally known among scholars as "legal mobilization" theory (McCann 1994; Scheingold 1974; Lovell 2012; Cichowski 2007). In our concluding chapter we will develop at greater length the many generalizable analytical implications of our historical empirical study for academic legal mobilization analysis. We present in this introductory chapter just a basic, commonsense summary of conceptual premises that we put to work in the construction of the historical narrative.

The classic definition of legal mobilization was provided long ago by Frances Kahn Zemans (1983, 700): "The law is. . . . mobilized when a desire or want is translated into a demand as an assertion of rights" or other legal entitlement. Legal mobilization analysts tend to focus on how people think and behave when they make claims of legal entitlement and status, especially when claiming rights leads to disputes with other parties. One related topic of interest for some scholars is why people sometimes do and at other times do not act when their perceived rights are violated (Engel 2016; Merry 2003). At one level the approach envisions law as a strategic resource available for instrumental "use" by social actors to advance their interests and causes (Nader 1984–1985). Zemans characterizes legal mobilization as a form of "democratic participation." At the same time, later versions of the theory portray law as a constitutive force that structures first the institutional and ideological context of instrumental action and second the intersubjective cognitive maps of "legal consciousness" through which people imagine, aspire, calculate, and make sense of that institutional context in which they are embedded (Ewick and Silbey 1998; Lovell 2012; A.-M. Marshall 2016; McCann 1994). Thus, Zemans (1983, 697) writes, "perceptions of desires, wants, and interests are themselves strongly influenced by the nature and content of legal norms and evolving social definitions of the circumstances in which the law is appropriately invoked." From this perspective people are at once legal subjects constructed and restrained by law and to some limited degree also situated agents who contest and reshape legal meaning in practical interaction.

Much sociolegal research focuses on legal mobilization by individuals, but other scholars focus on mobilization by groups or movements to effect broad social change, what Scheingold (1974) called the "politics of rights." This book fits the latter group-based approach. Virtually all scholars in this tradition follow Scheingold in underlining that litigation alone rarely achieves substantial social change and that legal mobilization need not even involve filing lawsuits, much less going to court. Rather, most scholars recognize that rights advocacy takes place in many sites and through many forms of action across state and society. Rights-based social movement advocacy commonly engages conventional and social media advocacy, demonstrations, protests, electoral campaigns, and other political maneuvers both with and without litigation in the mix.

The constructivist analytical framework adopted by most scholars of group-based legal mobilization recognizes that legal norms, practices, and discourses are—like all language practices (Pitkin 1972)—relatively indeterminate, polyvalent, malleable, and contestable. Law by its very nature is manifest in social conventions that are variously constructed and disputed over time in different terrains of society, state, and beyond. In some times and places, the possibilities of creative legal construction and contestation by ordinary individuals and subaltern groups are relatively open. Generally, though, official law enforced by nation-states is highly constrained by the inherited structures and ongoing actions of dominant social, economic, and political actors. In most historical moments, legal representatives of those groups with the greatest social, economic, and political power severely delimit the range of acceptable constructions and enforcement of legal meanings generally to sustain the status quo and dismiss or "kill" off the rival claims and visions of other groups (Cover 1984). In Marc Galanter's (1974) famous terms, the "haves" tend to come out ahead in routine legal interaction and mobilization practice. The variable degrees of openness to and constraints on contestation define the dynamically paradoxical character of law's hegemonic power in practice (McCann 2014b).

But official law does not kill off rivals only symbolically or epistemically. Rather, our version of legal mobilization underlines that law's words authorize physical coercion and violence by both state and social actors (Cover 1986). Law "plays a critical cultural role in defining meanings and relationships, but it does so in the context of state power and violence," argues Sally Engle Merry (2000, 17); "the power of law to transform sociocultural systems is two-sided: it depends both on the direct imposition of sanctions, and on the production of cultural meanings in an authoritative arena." While legal meaning construction permits a wide range of discursive possibilities among contending groups, the exercise of law's violence to enforce official meanings tends to reduce significantly the repertoire of defiant actions realistically available to those aspiring to challenge or change official law. This capacity to exercise institutionalized power in the form of physical coercion and material incentives or penalties is manifest in both domestic national and international spheres and in our story through forms of both colonial and postcolonial rule.

The recognition of the unequal power relations in which legal conventions are contested and selectively enforced has led most legal mobilization theorists to emphasize analysis of the contingent features of social and political contexts in which legal disputing occurs. While the focus of legal mobilization theory on disputing underlines agency and instrumental contestation among actors, attention to structural factors of institutional and ideological power (McCann 2007, 2013) is considered essential to how we understand and assess how law works or matters. We follow earlier work in emphasizing that the configurations of power relations affecting legal mobilization by marginalized or subaltern groups, who are our focus, differ according to two types of factors.

One set of factors is often referred to as components of shifting opportunity structures, which refers to the relative vulnerability or stability of the overall hierarchical power structure. The key factor is the degree to which inherited structural arrangements are open or closed to challenge and change. Commonplace factors that increase vulnerability of dominant groups and their hold on official law include relative economic volatility or crisis, international military and diplomatic instability or war, rapid internal changes in population demographics or cultural trends, and emergencies of all types. When status quo hierarchical arrangements are especially vulnerable, dominant groups may find that their interests converge with those of traditionally less powerful groups and causes, thus leading the former to concede basic changes in legal arrangements (Bell 1980). But vulnerability and instability can also induce greater repression as well as openings for challenge. We will see both dynamics in the context of Filipino workers' struggles between the two World Wars and during the early and late Cold War periods.

The other key variables that affect possibilities for effective legal mobilization from below are often categorized as the unequally distributed organizational resources available to disputants. In our historical narrative, this includes especially Filipino-led unions and other union allies, solidaristic political advocacy coalitions, financial support, political elite support, and committed legal counsel (Epp 1998; McCann 1994). In the following study we will variously identify how such factors in the context of contestation by Filipino cannery workers and other subaltern groups matter greatly.

Law in Racial Capitalist Regimes: A Patchwork of Liberal and Illiberal Forms

Our study builds on but also complicates the tradition of legal mobilization analysis. Simply put, we reprise the focus on instrumental rights claiming by social movement activists aspiring to close the "gaps" between liberal egalitarian legal principles and those practices or policies that promote or permit hierarchical social relations (Gould and Barclay 2012; Scheingold 1974). We go further, however, in underlining how the contradictory logic at the heart of liberal legality itself works both to institutionalize social arrangements and to construct variably subjects in ways that sustain radically asymmetrical social power relationships. Specifically, our analysis concentrates on the historical development of American law as inextricably, continuously, if variably constitutive—both producer and product—of hierarchical institutional and ideological structures that we, following others, call *racial capitalism* (Kelley 2017; Melamed 2011; Robinson 2000). This line of analysis recognizes that law in liberal capitalist orders from the start was committed above all to securing protection for unequally owned private property, exchange-based contractual relationships, and commodified differentiation of value regarding both human and nonhuman resources (E. P. Thompson 1975; Goldwin and Schambra 1982; Melamed 2011). The "protection of different and unequal faculties of acquiring property" is the "first object of government," James Madison ([1787] 1961, 79) intoned in "Federalist Paper #10." As the young Karl Marx contended, the egoistic, acquisitive spirit institutionalized by rights to unequal property ownership routinely trumps the promises of formal legal equality, rendering the latter an illusory "political lion's skin" incapable of advancing human emancipation, empowerment, or what many later have referred to as "social justice." The political citizen is "an imaginary member of an illusory sovereignty," so legal equality is "the *sophistry* of the political state itself" (Marx 1844; see also Balbus 1977; McCann 1989).

In the classic scheme of Marx, the key terms of differentiation undermining formal equality were *classes*: on the one hand, the capitalists, who own the social means of production and appropriate its surplus; on the other hand, the propertyless, who are exploited but legally free citizen workers who sell their commodified labor power to survive. Less clearly recognized in the Marxist scheme but equally important to our analysis is the differential valuation of wageless, dependent, unfree noncitizens and surplus populations—slaves, indentured servants, imported migrants, women in the reproductive sphere, children, and others—whose "expropriated" labor has been essential to the continuing processes of accumulation (Fraser 2016).[5] Overall, in this framework, capitalism is viewed as driven by violent processes of relentlessly expansive development that inherently produce increasingly complex, hierarchically differentiated relations of domination. And this violence of capitalism is authorized and enforced, both directly (by the state) and indirectly (through property rights), by official law.

We posit further that these inequalities of class power relations within capitalist societies have been integrally interrelated, or *intersectional*, with racial and gendered hierarchies from the start through the contemporary period (Crenshaw 1989, 1991). Contrary to Marx, we recognize that such racial and gendered constructions of difference among subjects historically preceded capitalism but developed their own independent dynamics as ideological and institutional forces shaping capitalist power relations (Kelley 2017; Robinson 2000). After all, property ownership initially was reserved for white males, so legally institutionalized property sustained white control while "whiteness" became a social signifier of privilege (C. Harris 1993; Williams 1992). There was, quite simply, no capitalism historically before or apart from racial and gendered differentiation (W. Johnson 2018). On the one hand, the inherited conventions of racial and gender differentiation provided crucial markers for designating devalued populations subjected to *both* unfree, wageless, dependent labor and exploited low-wage labor status as second-class citizens in the critical processes of capital accumulation (Fraser 2016). On the other hand, racialized subjection of unfree, dependent laborers also has served as a "hidden condition of possibility for the freedom of those" (white or whitened male) workers whom capital exploits, thus driving a structural wedge between subjectively entitled white wage-earning citizens and racialized (and gendered) noncitizens or second-class citizens (Fraser 2016, 166). These power dynamics of differential value again have been clearly constituted, directly and indirectly, by official law and legally authorized social practices. As Gomez (2012, 47–48) has put it, "law and race construct each other in an ongoing, dialectic process that ultimately reproduces and transforms racial (and class, gender) inequality." We will see these relationships play out again and again in our historical narrative.

While capitalist regimes traditionally have invoked universalistic liberal legal language regarding political membership, from the very start most liberal legal regimes, including the United States, in practice explicitly excluded various subject groups from full, equal rights standing and social status according to constructed ascriptive characteristics (Smith 1997; Haney-López 1997). The following pages will illustrate these historical practices with regard to many racialized groups, including African Americans and several waves of Asian and Mexican migrant workers, among others. The official American ideology espoused by ruling white males stipulated that such devalued, "othered" subjects are undeserving of rights status—either de jure or de facto—because they lack the capacities for the disciplined self-governance required of propertied, rights-bearing citizens, including exploited white wage laborers. Racial and gender hierarchies in particular have been rationalized by a host of stigmatizing markers designating intellectual, physical, moral, or cultural inferiority. Racialized outsiders, including the first generation of Filipino migrant workers, have been commonly marked as inherently deviant, criminal, violent, predatory, and dangerous. We thus invoke Nikhil Singh's (2005, 223) understanding of such racialization processes as "historic repertoires and cultural and signifying systems that stigmatize and depreciate one form of humanity for the purposes of another's health, development, safety, profit, or pleasure."

We note further that racialized (and gendered) subaltern persons who have supplied much of the expropriated wageless and exploited low-wage labor on which capitalist development depends have typically been subjected to "repressive" rather than "liberal" forms of legal control (Nonet and Selznick 2001). Repressive law is inherently yet variably more violent and punitive than liberal legality, which emphasizes due process, equal protection, and restrained force in regulating members of civil society. If liberal law tends to normalize and legitimate its enforcement of unequal productive power through the tropes of contract, market exchange, and freedom among rightful citizens, repressive law administers "order management" among both semifree wage laborers and unfree, disposable, internally and externally colonized populations necessary to capitalist production. Repressive law thus is more overtly transparent about its targeted subjects, violently coercive character, and institutional role in enforcing hierarchies of differential value among persons. In the United States, slavery was the archetypical institutional manifestation of repressive law governance practices in early phases of capital accumulation (W. Johnson 2018; Dayan 2013; Rana 2010; Williams 1994). But legally authorized forms of authoritarian control and repression of low-wage as well as wageless, disposable, and surplus workers have been the norm throughout the history of capitalist development.[6] Overall, racial capitalist regimes thus have been organized around a patchwork of liberal, repressive, and hybrid legal forms varying in different institutional sites and in enforcement among differently constructed subjects. The following narrative history of Filipino laborers will document in particular how the practices of repressive law persisted but took different institutional manifestations, combining in different hybrid forms, in the American racial capitalist order before and after World War II.

Our recognition of these different forms of law thus aims to disrupt commonplace assumptions about the ubiquity of liberal legalism and stability of citizenship status. Like Rogers Smith (1997; see also Ong 2006), we view national citizen standing or status complexly on a continuum from noncitizen to full citizen but with many intervening tiers of status, each susceptible to different forms of legal treatment and access to rights protections in social practice. Furthermore, our recognition of the competing but interrelated or hybrid forms of repressive law and liberal law in some ways parallels and builds on the important argument about the dual, interacting "racial institutional orders"—labelled "white supremacist" and "egalitarian transformative"—in American history developed subsequently by Smith and Desmond King (King and Smith 2005). In particular, their recognition of the fundamental shift in the balance of power between racial orders before and after World War II is echoed in our account. One significant difference, however, is that our approach focuses on forms and practices of *law* that blur lines between state and society more than on partisan alignments among political elites. Equally important, whereas King and Smith treat economic factors of class differentiation as secondary and alignments of political coalitions around race as central, our approach underlines the interrelationship between *both* class and racial differentiation as social forces mutually constituting the changing historical contours of American law, legal practice, and rights contestation. In our framework, the violence of repressive law is intrinsic to capitalism, authorizing "private" imposition of harsh discipline in varying degrees on free wage earners generally, while more brutal, debilitating forms of order management are deployed to control racially differentiated, devalued, and disposable semifree and unfree laborers in and beyond segmented sites of production and reproduction (Fraser 2016). Both class and race-specific (and gendered) domination have been broadly authorized by legal rules and principles grounded in propertied hierarchy.

Moreover, we disaggregate King and Smith's conception of a single egalitarian transformative order into two different if related equality-based traditions: a *liberal* egalitarian tradition and a *radical* egalitarian tradition. The predominant mode to which King and Smith refer is the "formal equality" of liberal state law. Such liberal equality principles, which ruled political relations among the dominant white citizenry in earlier periods, were mobilized to challenge the most extreme forms of (male) white-supremacist racial domination before World War II. Most important, slavery and involuntary servitude were legally abolished by the Thirteenth Amendment, except as punishment for criminal conviction, which figures prominently for the legacy of continuing repressive law. Fourteenth Amendment guarantees of "equal protection" and Fifteenth Amendment prohibitions on racial discrimination in voting processes similarly advanced formal legal equality for many persons, although they posed only limited restraints on Jim Crow–era practices of racial segregation, discrimination, and labor exploitation, including for imported colonial workers.

These formally egalitarian principles then became the basis of the reconstructed legal order and broader antiracist, "racially liberal" social reform engineering projects in the post–World War II era. Such further advances for liberal equality in the civil rights era were undeniably "transformative," as King and Smith put it. Overt racism and sexism, what Justice Blackmun called "old fashioned" discrimination, receded in public life, and some segments of low-income white, racial minority, and female populations—including some Filipino Americans—rose into professional occupations, the ownership classes, political leadership, and cultural stature during the racial liberal era. At the same time, however, the fusion of universalistic formal equality principles with liberal ideological norms privileging individualism, contractual freedom, and equal opportunity generally worked to naturalize and normalize the intersectional race and class hierarchies of social power inherited from earlier periods of the capitalist accumulation process (Melamed 2011, 2015). The promises of citizen rights to race and gender-neutral, formally equal treatment thus remained severely compromised by unequal socioeconomic conditions that persisted in the racially liberal and neoliberal eras (McCann 1989). In fact, inequalities of wealth, political power, and class hierarchy actually grew over the decades after the 1960s (Hacker and Pierson 2010; Piketty 2014). Racialization practices in this period did become less rigidly grounded in phenotype (e.g., skin color) and more loosely tied to norm deviation, but the continuing effect of formal equality was to legitimate hierarchical relations to make structural inequality *seem* to be fair (Melamed 2011). This was the context in which the "racial innocence" exhibited by Supreme Court justices in the *Wards Cove* case ascended in American legal culture even as white-supremacist advocacy networks, politicians, and business elites continued and even escalated their campaigns for sustained domination.

We further underline how racial and class hierarchies were reinforced by newly reconstructed institutional forms of violent legal control during the postwar eras of racial liberalism and neoliberalism. This includes especially the ways that repressive law practices inherited from the white-supremacist era—in criminal/penal/police control, suppression of subversive political challenges, national security state regulation of borders and noncitizen residents, and especially authoritarian managerial control of "private" production processes where both exploited citizen workers and dependent noncitizens labor or languish—were reorganized and expanded into bureaucratically administered, ostensibly race-neutral, procedurally legalistic but de facto racially and class targeted protocols of control. While facially neutral and "color-blind," all of these institutionalized sectors of administrative-state violence have remained haunted by ghosts of earlier materialized forms and practices of racial and class domination (Dayan 2013). Multiple manifestations of bureaucratically reorganized, rule-bound repressive law will be on display in our historical narrative of second-generation Filipino laborers.

By contrast, we further distinguish principles of antiracist formal liberal equality from a third tradition of radical egalitarian legal traditions that aspire to transform citizenship equality ideals into an "alchemical" force challenging many material manifestations of racial, class, and gender hierarchy (Williams 1992; Bell 1987; Guinier and Torres 2014). Such materialized antiracist logics have been advocated in various forms by Left (mostly labor-, race-, and gender-based) social justice movements since the origins of the republic, including by the Filipino labor activists at the center of our study. Although such aspirational egalitarian movements have mobilized limited support and have only occasionally altered in substantial ways the prevailing official hybrid order of liberal and repressive law, they have left important imprints reshaping the legal administrative state and modifying the racial capitalist order in different eras.

In a final contrast to liberal legalist frameworks, our approach also underlines that processes of racial capitalist differentiation in value are geopolitical in character, thus highlighting our attention to "empire" (Fraser 2016). Because capitalist accumulation is inherently expansive, economic development thrives on continuous expropriation of natural and human resources beyond national borders, international trade, transnational production supply chains, globalized markets, and supranational financialization as well as extensive organizational management by international legal agreements and military investments that are necessary to facilitate the multistate global system. The result has been an ongoing process of fundamentally differentiated racial and class valuation and status at two levels, both institutionalized by law. On the one hand, individual states are increasingly impelled to police their borders to intensify separation between legal citizens and noncitizens, advancing conceptions of membership that promote nationalism and impede transnational alliance among exploited classes. Noncitizen transnational migrants who are conscripted to cross global borders to supply expropriated labor are especially subject to processes of racialized differentiation, marginalization, and criminalization. As such, the intrinsic "illegality" of migrant laborers is a spatialized socio-legal condition because "deportability" is a critical implication of illegal, semicriminalized status and repressive control of disposable workers (De Genova 2004). The various grades of relative citizen status again vary between the poles of full citizenship and noncitizenship, rightful (but socially unequal) freedom and rightsless unfreedom. This is an important dimension of our study of Filipino worker history and a key site of increased repressive legal administration and contestation generally in contemporary national politics.

On the other hand, the global capitalist system assumes an "imperialist geography of 'core' and 'periphery'" valuation, dividing "metropolitan citizens versus colonial subjects, freeman versus slaves," northern Europeans versus natives, whites versus nonwhites, and Global North versus South, among others (Fraser 2016). "Capitalism does not simply incorporate racial domination as an incidental part of its operations," Chen notes, "but from its origins systematically begins producing and reproducing 'race' as global surplus humanity" (Chen 2013, 6). These ongoing distinctions, we shall see, continued from before the settler era through US colonial rule in the Philippines and through subsequent imperial phases of global capitalist development. This point makes sense of why the democratic socialist project of Filipino labor activists persistently linked domestic antiracist, anticapitalist egalitarian struggles for migrant workers in the metropole to struggles in the Philippines and anti-imperialism around the globe. In our final chapter, we will briefly draw evocative generalizable comparisons between the workings of repressive law within racial capitalist orders and law in postcolonial and authoritarian state contexts, thus challenging familiar distinctions between liberal and illiberal law as well as contexts of North and South.

In sum, we thus fully acknowledge that the conceptual scheme of rival racial orders formulated by King and Smith (2005) is useful for historical analysis of racial coalition politics. However, we think that the more complex, intersectional, geopolitical racial capitalist structural framework better serves our analytical focus on the dynamics of hegemonic legal governance and Filipino workers' antiracist, rights-based struggles on that legal terrain over the twentieth century (W. Johnson 2018; Melamed 2011).

The following study of Filipino American workers—who initially were colonial subjects, legally categorized as noncitizen nationals, exploited as proletarian laborers, informally but brutally criminalized, and eventually granted US citizenship but recriminalized for political activity in the metropole—will document the various ways that such a patchwork of repressive and liberal law practices has both enforced and yet provided modest openings for contesting economic and racial exploitation at different moments. Our historical narrative will identify different forms of both legal rule and concomitant legal contestation through changing phases of racial capitalism, highlighting in particular the above-noted shifts from explicitly white-supremacist legal repression of racialized populations before World War II to varieties of liberalism after the war that reorganized the forms of repressive law in new, formally antiracist ways (Melamed 2011).[7] The important interrelationship between developments within American borders and wider global economic, political, legal, and military entanglements will be granted continuous if, admittedly, secondary attention. Specifically, fundamental shifts in the status and power of imported workers within the metropole will be tracked by parallel changes in the economic and political status of the Philippines as it developed from dependent colony to semi-independent client state in the global capitalist order.

We recognize that heteronormative patriarchal constructions of unequal gender and sexual status also traditionally have permeated official law and social organization in racial-capitalist orders, thus sustaining and at times shaping the terms of contestation over economic, social, and political marginalization (Pateman 1988).[8] We note in particular that the conscription of Filipino workers dramatically magnified the traditional capitalist division and distance between waged production by males (in the metropole) and nonwage female reproductive labor (largely left behind in the colonial islands). Gender and sexuality thus figure into our story at various points, not least because the first generation of mostly male Filipino bachelors was feared by anxious white Americans as sexual predators threatening patriarchal control and racial purity. Nevertheless, we have chosen to limit our attention to those dimensions of gender and sexuality while emphasizing the intersection of capitalist and racial hierarchies (Gomez 2012; C. Harris 1993; Leong 2013).

Expanding the Contours of Case Study

Our goal of mapping the changing racial-capitalist institutional and ideological context in which Filipino labor activists struggled has led us to expand dramatically the empirical scope of sociolegal analysis. Most empirical "case studies" of legal mobilization focus on bounded manifestations of legal contestation usually confined to a restricted range of discrete policy issues, disputing actors, time period(s), and geographic location(s). Ethnographic and qualitative methods as well as aspirations for generating generalizable comparative theory tend to reinforce these conventional boundaries. Our study, by contrast, examines a plethora of rights mobilization episodes (Adam 2017; Merry 2000), entailing

- a *wide range of contested national and local legal rules, policies, and practices*, including immigration and citizenship law, civil rights law, labor law, contract law, property law, and personal injury law, among others;
- contestation within a *wide variety of geographic locations and legal jurisdictions*, including multiple sites up and down the North American West Coast as well as in the Philippines and in transnational relationships between the United States and the Philippines; and
- the *changing terms of contestation at different times* over the course of the twentieth century, as the United States evolved from an expanding white-settler society to global commercial and military empire.

This temporarily and spatially multisited approach reflects our interest in the dynamic historical experience of Filipinos forced to migrate across wide global circuits to find work in the first generation. The narrative trajectory increasingly focuses on the Seattle-Alaska circuit, but relationships of interdependence around the Pacific Rim remain salient even after the 1960s. At a theoretical level, the expanded field of empirical study also demonstrates how broadly and continuously law constituted the Filipino experience, how "law is all over" (Sarat 1990), at nearly every place and time in the development of the racial capitalist order. This is precisely the value of the racial capitalist analytical framework: to emphasize the continuities as well as changing forms of legally authorized domination inherent in historical processes of capital accumulation.

The fact that law so heavily regulated the lives of the racialized, migratory proletariat might seem to qualify our marginalized subjects, like the welfare poor studied by Sarat, as a "least likely case" for findings of persistent group-based legal mobilization. Quite the contrary is true, though. Our study suggests that it was precisely the more developed character of the administrative state in the American West that makes sense of why Filipinos were far more legalistic, even litigious, than Chinese and Japanese migrant workers before them in the less developed "wild west." The aggressive violence authorized by repressive law put more pressure on the third wave of Asian migrant workers to learn the arts of legal evasion, legal defense, and eventually offensive legal rights mobilization.

Finally, like most legal mobilization studies, our multisited historical study aims to contribute to generalizable assessments about how law actually matters for subaltern populations and especially how legal contestation does or does not contribute to advancing social justice and democratic transformation. Like many previous studies (Lovell and McCann 2005; McCann 1994; see also Albiston 2010; Barclay, Jones, Marshall 2011), we show that law overwhelmingly serves racial, class, and gender hierarchies, but it is not *just* an instrumental expression of the most powerful groups in society (E. P. Thompson 1975). Contestation by subaltern groups is incessant if often relatively invisible, and sometimes those groups actually prevail in courts, legislatures, and other sites of legally constituted social practices. "Law," Samuel Johnson once claimed, "supplies the weak with adventitious strength," although we again underline addition of the important qualifier *sometimes* (Zemans 1983, 694).

Nevertheless, we recognize that winning specific battles often produces limited positive change in hierarchical structures of power either in the larger society or in the lives of "ordinary" people and especially among racialized and gendered low-wage workers. Again, one reason is that the overall legal edifice is a product of unequal social power aggregated over history, yielding legal forms that both reproduce hierarchies and insulate them from fundamental challenge. Discrete legal "wins" may sometimes benefit subaltern groups in both direct and indirect ways (McCann 1994, 1996)—our analysis demonstrates both—but they rarely change the fundamental terms of the hegemonic order, whatever their aims. Our multisited historical study thus helps to demonstrate how law is only relatively, or perhaps barely, autonomous from interrelated racial, class, and gendered hierarchies (Balbus 1977).

It follows that our approach, focusing on manifold episodes of struggle by one small group of workers, renders no simple, clearly defined measure of relative "impacts" from legal mobilization efforts either individually or in the aggregate. Our account is replete with evidence of small material gains, occasional symbolic triumphs, and a great deal of tragedy, defining a complex legacy that defies simple terms of measurement even though we do offer lots of judgments about effects and implications of rights contestation at various moments. Our more fundamental aim is less to measure outcomes than to make sensible the *aspirations* for realizing novel rights visions, democratic change, and social justice that animated the subjects in our story. Our subjects aimed for revolutionary change, but we see no reason to treat them as deluded or naive. Much like radical African Americans, Filipino labor activists were animated by what historian Robin Kelley (2002) calls "freedom dreams." Documenting and critically analyzing the record of their ongoing, protracted struggles on legal terrain is, we think, our primary contribution.

Data Sources and Methodology

The bulk of this book, we already have noted, is organized as a chronological social history. The historical narrative integrates a great deal of qualitative research that we have conducted over a twenty-year period with support from a variety of grants, including especially a multiyear National Science Foundation grant. Three types of original data form the core of our scholarly contribution.

The first is an expansive array of archival records, amounting to many hundreds of boxes, most of which were available to us in the Labor Archives of Washington (LAW), which is part of the Special Collections of the University of Washington Libraries. The largest collection provides a record of the cannery workers and their unions over the course of the twentieth century; other collections donated by over a score of specific individuals in the first and second generations of Filipino immigrants or allied activists add dramatically to this rich set of resources. We also have found useful records in the archival collections of the Filipino American National Historical Society and the Wing Luke Museum of the Asian Pacific American Experience, both in Seattle.

Most of the archival investigation has been conducted by trained graduate and undergraduate students in the Department of Political Science and Comparative Law and Society Studies Center at University of Washington who worked under our supervision and with the support of a professional labor archivist. Moreover, we have benefitted greatly by the Seattle Civil Rights and Labor History Project (SCRLHP) led over the last twenty years by our colleague Professor James Gregory, an eminent historian and affiliate of the Harry Bridges Center for Labor Studies, and his students, especially cofounder and project coordinator Trevor Griffey. This web-based collection features a wide range of documents, photographs, interviews, and oral histories selected from University of Washington Special Collections or initiated by project affiliates along with a number of student essays on various historical themes. This invaluable resource has been the starting point for many phases of our study.

A second, very important source of original data has been generated by personal interviews with many key actors in our narrative. To supplement the many oral histories and interviews on the SCRLHP website as well as in LAW, we have conducted personal interviews with roughly twenty activists and attorneys from the period of the 1970s forward. More than a dozen of the interviews were first conducted in the late 1990s. Among the most important of these were interviews with the extraordinary (and now deceased) African American activist Tyree Scott, who pioneered dynamic legal mobilization campaigns for black workers in the building trades around the nation in the early 1970s, mentored the young Filipino activists, and founded with them the (Northwest) Labor and Employment Law Office (LELO), the Seattle-based, worker-led, public interest law firm that represented cannery, construction, and farm workers for several decades. We have stayed in contact with these and other activists interviewed in that initial research and acknowledged in the preface. Another dozen or so more interviews, some repeats with previous interviewees but most with additional figures, were conducted from 2012 to 2018.

For the third type of data, we draw on primary popular cultural texts from Filipino history to provide both empirical evidence and theoretical understanding. This includes, above all, ample reference to Carlos Bulosan's previously cited novel *America Is in the Heart* and other related writings, including his poems. The semiautobiographical novel is clearly fictional, but it is grounded in Bulosan's actual experiences—as an educated but persistently poor migrant, as an exploited and often unemployed worker, and then as a radical labor activist—as well as the experiences that he witnessed of fellow Filipinos. Bulosan's writings are important not just as dramatic accounts of select events but also as a revealing window into the experiences, understandings, and aspirations of first-generation Filipino migrant workers. He was praised by fellow Filipinos who "for the first time are depicted as human beings" (Mejia-Giudici 2003). Moreover, Bulosan's writings provided something of a historical lens, or "legend," through which progressive Filipino American activists and scholars in the second generation, beginning in the late 1960s, came to make sense of their legacy and to forge their defiant political commitments (Gurtiza 2015; San Juan Jr. 1972; Pante and Nery 2016).

Our mixing of such quasi-fictional accounts with scholarly empirical accounts is hardly novel, and other historians have inspired and instructed us about this convention (San Juan Jr. 1995). Moreover, we also give attention to other cultural texts, including especially the dramatic mock trial of Ferdinand Marcos constructed by young KDP activists, Filipino folklore, poems, and songs that were meaningful for the actors in our study as well as various films, documentaries, and printed narratives about their history. Between the time we started and completed this book, four very rich nonacademic books were published and a documentary film was released by people close to the activists or who were activists themselves in time periods we address (Churchill 1995; Chew 2012; Withey 2018; Domingo, Occena, and Cruz 2017). We wish we had completed our version earlier, but these books have inspired as well as informed us; we heartily recommend them to readers interested in insider personal accounts. Our project is very different in its academic approach and aims, but our work is better for engagement with these other texts.

Finally, of course, our empirical research has drawn on a wide array of secondary scholarly studies of the Filipino experience, labor unions, labor law and civil rights law, US colonial rule in the Philippines, and much more, including sociolegal and critical race theory. As our references attest, we draw heavily on noted historians—including especially Rick Baldoz, Mae Ngai, Alfred McCoy, Chris Friday, and E. San Juan Jr.—along with superb essays posted on the SCRLHP website by students at the University of Washington to construct the history of the first generation of Filipino migrant workers. Ligaya Domingo's PhD dissertation on the Alaska Cannery Workers Association (2010) and Trevor Griffey's dissertation on Tyree Scott and LELO (2011) were important resources documenting the 1970s activists when we resumed research for this book. Finally, we integrate a great deal of sociolegal theory into the construction of and meditation on our analytical narrative. Those sources are listed in our long bibliography.

Our hope is that drawing from these widely varied sources provides a well substantiated and richly textured history of socio-legal engagement by multiple generations of Filipino workers in the Alaska salmon canneries and beyond. We frankly recognize, however, that all of this research over many years has not unearthed a great deal of new historical information. Other scholars (some noted above) have told much of our story in small or partial bits, most of it in publications or outlets more familiar to historians than to sociolegal scholars. We do add some new factual details from various original sources, but that is not what we consider our primary contribution. Rather, it is the integration of mostly available data into a historical story about law and rights-based struggles for social justice that we claim as our most original and important achievement.

Book Organization, Style, and Epistemological Standpoint

The historical narrative that unfolds in the remainder of the book covers a span of the entire twentieth century. Part 1 begins with the American invasion of the Philippines in 1898 and the establishment of colonial rule by the United States over the island archipelago (prologue). We then focus attention on the first generation of Filipino workers who migrated as colonial subjects to the American metropole for seasonal work and fought on multiple fronts for basic citizenship rights (chap. 1), and then struggled for workplace justice through union organizing, from the 1930s (chap. 2) through the initial Cold War era of the late 1940s and 1950s (chap. 3). A key part of this story is the workers' development of skills in mobilizing law to escape or limit state repression and their eventual mobilization of law to empower union organizations for political leverage in the workplace and broader public spheres of the "internal colony."

Part 2 recounts the story of the second-generation Filipino-led workers in ILWU Local 37 during the late Cold War era. The prologue to part 2 outlines political developments during the 1960s within and between the Philippines and the United States, which remain important background for the three following chapters. Chapter 4 focuses on the young reform activists who, in the 1970s, aimed to revitalize the progressive democratic aspirations of the earlier generation by mobilizing civil rights claims in federal court, developing new political alliances to reform the union, and organizing with others around the Pacific Rim to depose Philippine president Ferdinand Marcos. The legal and political mobilization campaigns in the 1980s to redress the murders of two young radical union leaders, culminating in a triumphant civil lawsuit, are the focus of chapter 5. Chapter 6 documents the fate of the third antidiscrimination lawsuit, *Wards Cove v. Atonio*, in 1989 and assesses it as the culmination of the tragic historical quest for egalitarian civil rights and social justice. The changing character of macropolitics, including US-Philippines relations, will remain important to the context and content throughout the chronicle. To some extent, we repeat, this entire book can be viewed as a social history of the struggles of Filipino workers within and against American racial capitalist empire that the *Wards Cove* majority willfully ignored and erased from the official legal record.

We have labored to limit expansive intellectual theorization in the narrative account of chapters 1 through 6, choosing to put the big ideas to work in the interpretation of the history rather than making them a topic of direct, expansive attention. Extended academic theorizing about law, power, legal contestation, and the like will remain mostly episodic until the concluding chapter, in which we aim to map out the larger, generalizable analytical implications of our study for scholars who may be interested (conclusion). A primary aim of that theoretical project, we have noted, is to disrupt the conventional assumptions about the unitary character of liberal legalism and to explore the implications of identifying concurrent liberal, repressive, and hybrid forms of law for legal mobilization politics, especially by workers in racial capitalist orders. Our hope is that this backgrounding of theory in the historical narrative will make the rich, revealing story of the Filipino worker legacy more accessible to readers of all types.

The modest segmentation of attention to analytical theory and storytelling exposes some tensions in the epistemological foundation of this project, we admit. On the one hand, the historical narrative endeavors to be highly attentive to the stories, accounts, and normative perspectives of our primary subjects, the activist Filipino workers and their allies. Our efforts to represent the world views, aspirations, strategic calculations, and personal connections—all elements of what we call an oppositional legal consciousness—animating actors over many years express what we often call an "ethnographic leaning" in our historical narrative and analytical arguments. Like many legal mobilization studies, our angle of vision is grounded in the standpoint of activists whose endeavors we recount, relying heavily on their own accounts. This commitment inherently privileges their roles, voices, and critical positions against those of their adversaries in local, national, and international politics. The historical recovery of Filipino labor activist subjectivities thus will have a distinctly normative ring to it, as we write in a voice expressing their defiant, often radical aspirations and strategic gambits. In these regards, our methodology is substantially indebted to the tradition of Critical Race Theory (CRT) in the American academy. In constructing a narrative relying heavily on racially subaltern activists' voices, experiences, and aspirational struggles, we draw on and parallel the "legal storytelling" conventions of providing alternative, oppositional narratives by nonwhite, historically subjugated persons central to the CRT project (Bell 1987; Delgado 1989, 2003; Williams 1992). We specifically link our focus on radical egalitarian rights struggles to what Guinier and Torres (2014) label "demosprudence."

On the other hand, we the authors are not simply reporting in objective terms the aspirations, understandings, and practices of our subjects. We have constructed the story from our own standpoints as privileged white male affluent university professors interested in theory-driven research on law, politics, and power, with particular attention to race and class dynamics in American history. Our primary intervention is in analyzing the practices and understandings of Filipino rights activists within the legally constituted relations of racial capitalism.[9] In many ways, this intervention again reflects our engagement with contemporary trends in CRT to "materialize" racial narratives by empirical study, and, in particular, to interrogate the intricately interrelated intersectional dimensions of racial, class, and gender differentiation mediated and contested through law (Barnes 2016; Crenshaw 1989; Delgado 2014a, 2014b; Obasogie 2013; Oh 2005; San Juan Jr. 2005). Our approach thus does not claim to be a politically or intellectually neutral rendering; rather, it is anchored in commitments to scholarly conventions that temper normative predispositions, privilege analytical rigor, and invite critical interrogation by others in many scholarly communities (Barnes 2016). And these commitments to critical understanding and analytical conventions shape how we tell the story, what we choose to include and exclude, and what we judge to be most significant. While direct, explicit attention to our guiding questions, ideas, and concepts is most developed in the opening and concluding chapters, the analytical project is manifest on every page, although we hope in mostly unobtrusive ways. We know that this endeavor makes the book as much our theory-driven narrative about how law works as the activists' own stories about their history.

To some extent, this selective recounting is inevitable, because the archival data, secondary scholarship, and activists whom we interviewed are copious, diverse, and often in implicit or explicit disagreement about what our chosen subjects were trying to do, did, and accomplished. At times we acknowledge these differences both within and between generational cohorts, often offering our views about the relative merits of differing accounts. In any case, our assessments about which version to emphasize have been guided by different, competing standards: first, by what is most credible in view of the multiple sources of data, and second, by what seems most germane to our selective analytical account about law, power, and political struggle. We also point out in endnotes topics, evidence, or interpretations that we chose to omit or treat briefly in the interest of analytical coherence as well as narrative clarity and economy.

In our view, such strains among different positions of partiality are unavoidable. But these tensions also can be potentially productive. To some extent, our study reflects an ongoing engagement between ourselves and our various historical subjects and especially those with whom we have interacted personally while they are alive. The best we can do is to try to be honest about our explanatory interventions and selection biases, laboring to make the tensions among interpretive standpoints enhance the project. We hope that by underlining the encounter among different perspectives, we increase sensitivity to the complexity of events, relationships, and workings of power. As such, we maintain that identification with our subjects itself is as much an analytical enterprise as a normative commitment. Indeed, we call attention to these inevitable tensions in order to encourage more critical engagement with the challenges of developing significant analytical insights from complex historical empirical study. And whatever our differences with our historical subjects, we share a general commitment to providing a critical understanding about how law works in racial capitalist America and imagining alternative possibilities for a more just, egalitarian, democratic social order.

PART I

American Capitalist Expansion, Colonialism, and Empire

PROLOGUE TO PART I

The American Colonial Project in the Philippines

Law is merely the expression of the will of the strongest for the time being, and therefore laws have no fixity, but shift from generation to generation.—BROOKS ADAMS (1895, 165)

You, who say the Declaration (of Independence) applies to all men . . . how dare you deny its application to the American Indian? And if you deny it to the Indian at home, how dare you grant it to the Malay abroad? . . . There are people in the world who do not understand any form of government . . . (and) must be governed.—ALBERT J. BEVERIDGE (1900)

The problem of the twentieth century is the problem of the color-line—the relation of the darker to the lighter races of men in Asia and Africa, in America and the islands of the sea.—W. E. B. DU BOIS ([1903] 2007, 7)

During the twilight years of the nineteenth century, the United States embarked on a new epoch of imperial expansion overseas extending as far as the islands of the Philippines. America's novel experiment in colonial rule over populated islands in the Pacific and Caribbean built on the rubble of brutal governance by the Spanish monarchy. Spain's control of the Philippines began over three hundred years earlier after explorer Ferdinand Magellan chanced upon the islands while circumnavigating the globe in his quest for profitable spices in the Indies. Over the next few centuries, Manila became a harbored haven for Spanish galleon trade ships as well as a source of land, minerals, and forced labor. Spain put down a political anchor with land grants to Spanish settlers who formed the oligarchy of mestizo families that ruled into the twentieth century. The island archipelago also offered the Europeans a fertile terrain for moralistic projects of conversion to Christianity and, later, other disciplining forces of modern civilization. Spain ruled the Philippines and its other island colonies in the Pacific and Caribbean, it is commonly portrayed, by both "the sword and the cross" (Truxillo 2001). Much of the vast empire was lost to multiple wars of independence early in the nineteenth century, but Spanish monarchists who regained power in the 1860s renewed the national commitment to control over the islands in a vain effort to restore a semblance of an imagined glorious past. The Philippines and Puerto Rico both were important subjects of this mission, yet Spanish rulers viewed Cuba, with its tropical beauty and sugar plantations, as its most important remaining gem.

The Cuban jewel was snatched from Spain's grasp by century's end, however. After Spanish rulers failed to make good on promised concessions following their defeat of a sustained provincial revolt in Cuba decades earlier, an independence movement mobilized in the 1890s under the leadership of Jose Marti. The Cuban Revolutionary Party was established, and in 1895 it initiated a formidable struggle for *Cuba libre*. Spain's military responded with a concerted and cruel campaign to quash the rebels. Among the most ruthless of its tactics was General Valeriano Weyler's "reconcentration policy," begun in early 1896, that relocated Cuban civilians in detention centers under military control, resulting in the deaths of an estimated four hundred thousand people due to disease, squalid housing, and scarce or contaminated food (O'Toole 1984). While Spain offered the remaining rebels some modest concessions to restore order, the European state commenced with "waging a total war against revolutionaries who made a reasonable claim that their opponents were committing systematic acts of lawlessness" (Weiner 2006, 54).

A host of American leaders expressed anguish about the bloody clash over independence in Cuba; many US elites voiced support for the revolutionaries against the colonial tyrants. The motivations for such support varied widely, from general backing of anticolonial independence movements to antipapist contempt for Spain to concern about implications for US commercial interests. But other leaders, including President McKinley, were wary about US involvement. Eventually, the explosion that sunk the battleship USS *Maine*, increasing revelations about humanitarian crisis, and pressure from sensationalist "yellow" journalists such as Hearst and Pulitzer galvanized American resolve to enter into war against Spain and, ostensibly, to free Cuba. "Remember the *Maine*, to Hell with Spain" became the animating cry for the Spanish-American war. The war was relatively short and lopsided. United States military action began in April of 1898, the two sides declared war against one another in late April, Roosevelt joined the Rough Riders cavalry unit and rode up San Juan and Kettle Hills in July, the City of Santiago soon surrendered, and Spain signed an armistice in August 1898. The United States quickly ended forever Spain's rule over Cuba.

Meanwhile, Filipino nationalists also initiated a revolt against longstanding Spanish rule over the Philippine islands. Filipino dissidents had been mobilizing over the previous quarter of a century, inspired by increased exposure to modern European Enlightenment ideas and culture. Jose Rizal formed La Liga Filipina and mobilized other liberal *illustrados* challenging Spain's authority. In 1895 Andres Bonifacio organized the Katipunan, a brotherhood of Filipino nationalists dedicated to independence. Katipunan collaborator Emilio Aguinaldo led Philippine rebel forces to a number of victories over the Spanish in 1896 as Rizal awaited execution. Once the United States initiated war with Spain over Cuba, the Philippines formally allied with the United States. Theodore Roosevelt, then assistant secretary of the navy and not quite yet a Rough Rider but eager for war, ordered a fleet led by Commodore Dewey to the Spanish Philippines as the battle in Cuba commenced. Early on May 1, 1898, Dewey piloted into Manila Bay and, in roughly seven hours, destroyed the archaic Spanish Armada.

In June ninety-eight Philippine leaders signed a Declaration of Independence modeled on the American prototype and unfurled a Filipino flag; the proclamation was promulgated in August. Following other defeats, Spain sued for peace, and the United States acquired multiple islands in the Pacific and the Caribbean through the Treaty of Paris on December 10, 1898. Aguinaldo, expecting that the US alliance would bring Filipinos the promised self-rule, was declared president of the First Philippine (Malolos) Republic in January 1899. To the surprise of Filipino nationalists, however, the United States denied recognition to the new government of the self-proclaimed independent state. The Philippines declared war on the US forces in the islands just two days before the US Senate ratified the Treaty of Paris. The Philippine-American War, dismissed as a mere "insurrection" and "splendid little war" by American officials, ground on for several years before it was declared over by President Roosevelt on July 4, 1902. Independence Day in the United States signaled imperial conquest and the repudiation of Philippine national independence along with the deaths of a great many soldiers and civilians.

The new era of American empire commenced with a grant of formal but limited independence to Cuba plus agreement to establish a US military base at Guantanamo Bay, the US purchase of the Philippines for $20 million, and annexation of Puerto Rico, Guam, and later the independent state of Hawaii and parts of Samoa.

Empire Old and New: Capitalist Expansion and Racial Hierarchy

The Settler Frontier Legacy of Racial Capitalism

At the time of Dewey's military triumph in Manila Bay, no grand American strategy had developed for annexation of the Philippines. President William McKinley barely knew where to locate the Philippines on a map, so as the popular legend had it, he appealed on bended knees to God for guidance about how to handle the situation. McKinley quickly determined that the United States should take control of the Philippines in order to make its denizens into Christians and introduce the rule of law, if by largely barbarous and lawless means. The moralistic justifications for the policy of "benevolent assimilation" barely masked the interests of sugar importers and other corporate interests who long had urged expansion (Lynch 2009). Robust debate among American elites was fully displayed as the US Senate considered approving the treaty in February of 1899, and divisions quickly escalated about what to do with the archipelago. Understanding these exchanges of divergent views requires some attention to the larger historical context of American national expansion.

Over nearly three previous centuries, American colonists had developed and enacted their own version of the imperial commitment to race-based territorial expansion and control inherited from Great Britain (Robinson 1983). The settler experience from early on was animated by an ideology that fused values of economic independence, republican freedom as self-rule, and white entitlement (Rana 2010). The project of expanding control of land required both settlers, who would turn land into commodified property, and laborers, whose work would turn propertied capital into profit. On the one hand, white northern Europeans were viewed as coparticipants in American expansion;

open immigration and naturalization laws invited them to participate as property-owning settlers in the colony and then young nation (Frymer 2017).

On the other hand, laborers from early on included indentured servants (Irish, Slavs, Jews, and others) from Europe but increasingly featured non-northern Europeans who were conscripted and entitled neither to own land nor to naturalization. Continuing many centuries of European-initiated Atlantic slave trade, as many as twelve million slaves were imported from Africa to the new world in the eighteenth century; many tens of thousands died in route, and three-quarters of a million slaves landed in what became the United States during this period. The distinction between settler and laborer established divisions of class and citizenship grounded in constructions of racial, ethnic, religious, and gender difference, thus continuing European traditions in the preindependence era (Rana 2010; Robinson 1983). These unfree, dependent laboring classes, and especially dark-skinned slaves, became explicitly identified by whites as inherently distinct, inferior, and incapable of self-governance in line with the emerging "settler supremacy" principle.

During the seventeenth and eighteenth centuries, as African slaves gradually replaced indentured English servants on plantations, Europeans newly freed from indenture gained access to land or privileged employment, social standing, and opportunities for prosperity along with landed elites (Rana 2010, 47). Routine hereditary succession of blacks born to slave parents of African lineage similarly solidified the racialization of chattel slavery, especially but not exclusively in the South. New hybrid forms of repressive, punitive legal control were developed specifically to sustain white governance over slaves (Tushnet 1981). After the British acquisition of Canada in 1763, the privileged status of white settlers who remained British subjects became threatened, providing additional impetus to equate property ownership and citizen freedom with white European lineage and the laboring classes as religiously, ethnically, and especially racially different, undisciplined, and inferior Others. European immigrants in urban areas, fearing loss of their artisan status and modes of work, increasingly found reason to invest in constructed racial distinctions to insulate themselves from servitude as the lowest of wage laborers, indentured status, and of course as owned slaves. "Free labor" came to connote white-male contractual independence of workers while "free soil" conferred status as owners as opposed to "unfree" dependent labor that was both racialized in absolute terms of difference as "nonwhite" and gendered as female in patriarchal domestic confines (Foner [1970] 1995; Fraser 2016;

Nakano Glenn 2002). Hence emerged the development in early colonial North America of a "two-track" legal logic of property rights and political citizenship. "Anglo settlers enjoyed core liberties and common law protection, while indigenous (and imported dark skinned laboring) subjects were governed by whatever means the Crown viewed as necessary to maintaining authority" (Rana 2010, 47). In other words, white citizens could claim rights to what was later heralded as liberal law, and racialized and gendered Others were largely rightsless, restricted to slave or low-wage labor, and subject to more arbitrary, violent, repressive control authorized by state law. Racial hierarchy and violent oppression were constitutive of the American capitalist polity from the very start (Goldberg 2002; Charles W. Mills 2008; Robinson 1983; Smith 1997; Winant 2001).

These developments built on British class and racial traditions, but institutionalized slavery throughout the South deepened the racialization of class distinctions that denied legal status to nonwhites in the young American republic. This development can be traced in no small part to the fact that the United States constitutional government was constructed on a compromise providing protection for the institution of slavery and a substantial electoral advantage to slaveholding states (Davis 2006). The result was that the country was dominated by Southern interests from the American Revolution until the Civil War, and white supremacy was normalized as a premise of American civil religion and routine institutional practice for many. At the same time, slave labor and the great profits it generated, especially through cotton production, was the fuel for industrial capitalist development along the eastern corridor. The Atlantic slave trade long before had catalyzed Western capitalism; banks capitalized the slave trade, insurance companies underwrote it, and profits were channeled into northern businesses, including shipbuilding (Williams 1994). The slave trade had created world trade, Karl Marx argued, "and world trade is the necessary condition for large scale machine industry" ([1846] 1982, 101–2). Westward expansion opened opportunities for growth of slave-based economic development for many in and beyond the South. Hence the observation by Du Bois that "Black workers of America bent at the bottom of a growing pyramid of commerce and industry, and . . . became the cause of new political demands and alignments, of new dreams of power and visions of empire" ([1935] 1998, 5). In this regard, the material interests of whites and ideological construction of those interests in westward movement developed in tandem. Westward expansion thus was central to the continued growth of settler ideology inextricably connecting republican freedom, property ownership, and deeply entrenched racial, class, and gender hierarchies.

Rather than "conquering" local subjects for labor and resource extraction, in ways typical of European colonial projects, the Anglo-American settler project of westward movement across the mainland generally aimed to avoid interaction with rival populations until white landowners amassed majorities or land became scarce and hence more valuable (Frymer 2017). Settler-based empire building thus proceeded initially by claiming territories on empty land or on land emptied by removing and/or killing indigenous peoples, who were viewed as uncivilized nonsettlers and incapable of property ownership or self-governance (Frymer 2017; Rana 2010). Replacing those *on* the land with those whites who would *own* the land required sustained, systematic violence. Settlers in the American West who were allocated land were largely charged with providing their own security and urged to eschew conflicts with other peoples, but settler expansion always entailed a state-building project that required organized military force to take and then defend new territories from indigenous peoples and other nations viewed as threats (Frymer 2017). Following the Northwest Ordinance of 1787, it was assumed that annexed territories in the West were subject to the Constitution and eventually would be incorporated as official states. The expansionist impulse materialized by the 1840s into the ideology of "manifest destiny," which underlined the exceptional character of American white people and their institutions, their redemptive mission of remaking the West in their image, and the fated destiny of completing this project (Merk 1995).

The promise of westward expansion thus facilitated capitalist economic development, promised bountiful opportunities for white northern Europeans, and morally justified continued violent subjugation of nonwhites (Rogin [1975] 1991). The imperial logic propelled murderous removal of Natives, the war against the "mongrel race" of Mexicans, and similar projects validating what the young Ralph Waldo Emerson referred to as "The Genius and National Character of the Anglo-Saxon Race" (Rana 2010, 165–66). To be sure, there was disagreement among white elites about various meanings and implications of manifest destiny as well as the racial boundaries of qualification for citizenship rights status (Frymer 2017). Many whites opposed territorial expansion largely out of fear about incorporating nonwhite populations and compromising racial purity. But the premise that western expansion was to be carried out by self-governing, property-owning settlers of Protestant northern European lineage was a widely shared, bipartisan premise in the emergent dominant culture. As such, the idea of appropriating and governing large swaths of land heavily populated by (nonslave) non-Anglos was relatively unnecessary and unappealing to Americans before the late nineteenth century (Frymer 2017).

Postbellum America: Between Old and New

The experience with frontier freedom and promises of manifest destiny that impelled and justified the white-settler republic faced important challenges as the twentieth century approached, however. Frontier enlargement had always been more difficult, uneven, and perilous than national mythology envisioned. For one thing, antebellum American expansionism had been led largely by the aggressive designs of Southern slave owners who wanted to extend the "peculiar institution" across the continent, including beyond the mainland. The divisive push to annex Texas and to take the territories gained by the Mexican War was led by Southerners. As these campaigns for expansion were stymied and openness to continued political compromises waned, the struggles between the South and North to control the political economy of the western mainland territories escalated inevitably into the bloody, destructive Civil War. After the Civil War, Reconstruction designs gave way to Southern efforts to consolidate by legal and extralegal means new terms of racial hierarchy, exacerbating a wide variety of racial and class tensions in the South and the entire nation (Du Bois [1935] 1998, 187). This included clashes among Southerners increasingly dependent on Chinese "coolie" laborers, which complicated dualistic legal classifications of race, class, and national status and prepared the way for later Chinese exclusionary legislation in 1882 (Jung 2006). Northern Republican efforts to effect meaningful Reconstruction by "waving the bloody shirt" further fed old tensions, and underlined the desperate need for national causes that could overcome regional animosity and regenerate national unity.

Moreover, in the West, always a battleground, white expansionists faced the increasing resolve and capacity of Indians to resist conquest and removal. As tribal elimination became less feasible, a new phase of colonial control requiring negotiation with Native tribes over division of land commenced in the decades after the Civil War. The capture of the feared Apache Geronimo in 1886 and the massacre at Wounded Knee in 1890 are often marked together as the moment in which the US campaign for conquest of the frontier western lands ended (Frymer 2017, 264). The Dawes Act of 1887 represented a classic expression of imperial law. To use Robert Cover's language, the act refused to recognize the nomos of sovereign Indian culture, banishing it from the juridical universe of white law, while advancing native assimilation into propertied society, propelling both capitalist interests and the state-building project (Cover 1983; Weiner 2006, 49). All the while, the promise of westward expansion available to free white settlers faced a geographic constraint: the simple fact of finite remaining territory in the West bounded by the Pacific Ocean was symbolically significant. The frontier was "closing."

Equally important were the forces of industrialization, corporatization, and urbanization—what historian Alan Trachtenberg summarized as the capitalist "incorporation of America"—that fundamentally changed lives for many Americans (Trachtenberg [1982] 2007; Lustig 1986). With the rise of large capitalist enterprises, new forms of unequal wealth and hierarchical organization compounded traditional inequalities of landed wealth. Energized by policies of the Republican-controlled Congress after the Civil War, the US economy grew toward becoming the largest in the world by the end of the nineteenth century. Key government policies contributed to the centralization of banking, protective tariffs for developing industries, large subsidies and loans to railroads, the creation of land-grant agricultural colleges, and labor laws that permitted employers to hire imported, foreign-born, low-wage laborers, threatening white workers and robbing opportunities for black workers (LaFeber [1963] 1998, 6–7). A new financial class developed as the United States began to replace London as the commercial center of the world. And a new, educated, white middle class led the way to professionalizing public and private organizations aiming to construct hierarchical, bureaucratic "order" amid rapidly changing circumstances within American domestic life (Wiebe 1967). At the turn of the century, the American state was constituted by a patchwork of centralized managerial executive bodies developed by Progressives and the old patronage-based urban party machines and regional interests (Abinales 2003; Skowronek 1982).

For many ordinary white Americans, the dream of agrarian landownership and self-governance increasingly gave way to the harsh discipline, unsafe conditions, and low wages of exploitative contract work in capitalist enterprises. As immigration of Europeans escalated and cities grew rapidly, pressures increased on the growing working class to secure stable employment amid the periodic deep dips into economic depression, especially in 1893. This in turn added incentives for white workers to protect their entitled status relative to blacks as well as to Mexican and newly arrived Asian workers (Jung 2006), who were viewed similarly as threats to both racial purity and jobs. "Whiteness was a way in which workers responded to a fear of dependency on wage labor and to the necessities of capitalist work discipline" (Roediger 1991, 131). At the same time the boundaries of entitled citizenship began to expand to include more groups of once racialized Europeans—Irish, Italians, Polish, Catholics, and Jews—who proved themselves worthy by hard work, discipline, English-language acquisition, and racial antipathy toward nonwhites, thus "whitening" their status and increasing their opportunities as workers or owners to prosper amid American racial hierarchies (Roediger 2005; Ong 2006). The rise of the Populist movement and diverse labor movements expressed in disruptive terms aspirations supporting political action to gain some control in a rapidly changing, anxious world succumbing to predatory corporate capitalism. All in all, tensions along lines of class, race, ethnicity, and gender escalated in the late nineteenth century while the dreams of agrarian westward expansion dimmed as a symbolic and material safety valve that might relieve pressures.

Some key policy leaders—most notably William Henry Seward, secretary of state under two Republican presidents in the 1860s—began to enact measures for expanding the American economic and political empire beyond the mainland in the postbellum years. A major treaty in 1876, signed by Seward's friend Hamilton Fish, accelerated Hawaii's transformation into a plantation economy dependent on the United States, opening the way for removal of Queen Liliuokalani and US annexation in the 1890s. Many Southerners continued to view Cuba and the Dominican Republic as potential sites for replanting seeds of growth for slavery. Slaveholders and opponents of slavery alike supported the American Colonization Society, which since the early nineteenth century had helped establish a private colony in Liberia to be populated by free African Americans. Overall, however, the postbellum era was defined by struggles to reorder the mainland political economy more than to expand beyond it, delaying but not denying dreams of developing overseas empire (Wertz 2008).

The New Frontier: Dreams of Overseas Empire Materialized

The Progressive Era hastened the fundamental restructuring of American society and the national state. But along with the pursuit of revitalizing transformation *within* American society was an increasing inclination to expand new frontiers *outward*, beyond the continental United States, that might revive American spirit and open economic opportunities (Frymer 2017, 268–75). The acceleration of momentum toward American expansion overseas was largely driven by material interests—by the desires to cultivate new markets, increase trade, and propel corporate capitalist development (LaFeber [1963] 1998; Kolko 1963; Shklar 1998). It is relevant that Admiral Dewey's conquest in Manila Bay unlocked the potential for acquiring the third largest sugarcane supplier in the world along with ports on a valuable trade route to Asia. But inherited ideological principles had to be adapted to make those aspirations meaningful, sensible, and politically palatable. And those powerful ideas were amply supplied by both professional historians and amateur historians who became professional politicians in the late nineteenth century. These ideas combined aspirations for capitalist transformation with established norms of racial and religious superiority, the latter providing both an additional motive and moralizing mask for dominant group interests. The United States inherited from Britain not only the role of commercial leader in the world but also the task of bearing the "white man's burden." At century's end, Progressive Era elites thus embarked on a new, more aggressive and international form of imperialism that extended American white-male dominion over newly racialized populations (Frymer 2017; Kramer 2006).

Perhaps no intellectual was more important than historian Frederick Jackson Turner, whose classic essay in 1893 focused attention on "The Significance of the Frontier in American History" for the development of American character.

> Since the days when the fleet of Columbus sailed into the waters of the New World, America has been another name for opportunity, and the people of the United States have taken their tone from the incessant expansion which has not only been open but has even been forced upon them. ([1893] 1921, 37)

But "now . . . the frontier has gone, and with its going has closed the first period of American history," he wrote (38). Turner's requiem was not limited to nostalgia about the lost capacity for continual national rebirth. Turner added that "he would be a rash prophet who should assert that the expansive character of American life has now entirely ceased. Movement has been its dominant fact, and the American energy will continually demand a wider field for its exercise" (37-8). The United States thus once again must make a constitutional "adjustment" as the federal government dealt with new territorial acquisitions. The United States was "obliged to reconsider questions of the rights of man and traditional American ideals of liberty and democracy, in view of the task of government of other races politically inexperienced and undeveloped" (315).

Reverend Josiah Strong, founder of the Social Gospel movement, anticipated by a few years Turner's analysis about the West as the foundation of American character and world empire. His most influential work, *Our Country: Its Possible Future and Its Present Crisis* (1885), linked national expansion abroad directly to Anglo-Saxon superiority, promise of empire, and disdain for foreigners.

> God, with infinite wisdom and skill, is training the Anglo-Saxon race for an hour sure to come in the world's future. . . . If I read not amiss, this powerful race will move down upon Mexico, down upon Central and South America, out upon the islands of the sea, over upon Africa and beyond. (Strong 1885, 213)

This thesis gained influence just as new defenses of white privilege—social Darwinism, social scientific racism, eugenics, and what Weiner (2006) calls "juridical racism"—ascended among intellectuals as well as in everyday American social relations and politics both in the segregated Jim Crow South and throughout the nation.

Many political leaders at century's end seized on these ideas. The young Woodrow Wilson embraced the idea of historical development. In 1893 he wrote that "the history of the United States . . . is a history of developments. . . . It is this transformation that constitutes our history" (W. Wilson 1893, 495–96). With the continent now occupied and "no frontiers . . . to satisfy the feet of the young men,'' the nation must turn to "new frontiers in the Indies and Far Pacific" (W. Wilson 1903:296). But the most important enactment of these ideas was by a group of four men who masterminded overseas adventurism in the Philippines from the Metropolitan Club in Washington: the historian and naval strategist Captain Alfred Thayer Mahan; his friend, the historian Brooks Adams; the cultured senator Henry Cabot Lodge; and Lodge's friend and confidante, the belligerent Secretary of the Navy and later president, Theodore Roosevelt (Karnow 1989).

Mahan wrote widely about the relationship between naval capacity and empire, arguing that the United States needed a strong, modern navy on the two great oceans to protect its commercial and political interests around the world. He focused on the need to conquer other lands abroad while avoiding invasion of alien foreign populations. As Mahan put it in 1900, "Asiatic domination . . . found no serious difficulty of acceptance, so far as concerned the annexation of the Philippines—the widest sweep, in space, of our national extension" (8–9; Miller 1982, 94). Roosevelt mostly agreed with this strategic logic, but his enthusiastic support for intervention in Cuba and the Philippines—he once said "I should welcome almost any war, for I think this country needs one"—was based also on his belief that his generation of young men needed to test their mettle in battle.[1] Roosevelt argued even more affirmatively in terms of American inherited obligation, linking conquest of the Philippines in the new overseas frontier to the legacy of Indian conquest in the old frontier. As he put it in challenging critics of imperialism, if the United States was "morally bound to abandon the Philippines, we were also morally bound to abandon Arizona to the Apaches" (quoted in Williams 1980, 825). Equating Filipino rebel leader Aguinaldo with defiant Lakota Sioux warrior Sitting Bull, he surmised that "as peace, order and prosperity followed our expansion over the land of the Indians, so they will follow us in the Philippines" (quoted in Vidal 1986). Language likening American governors to "fathers" and "saviors" of Filipino "savages" and "children" frequented the discourse of expansionist supporters, recalling the terms of conquest over Indians and familial rule over slaves in the previous years. White men ruled, in Wilson's words, "children . . . in these great matters of government and justice" (Rogin [1975] 1991, 313). This was the essence of what Vincente Rafael (2000) has called "white love" displayed by colonial rulers.[2]

Supporting the executive leadership group, Senator Alfred Beveridge offered an explicit racial defense of American expansion in a 1900 speech to the Senate defending Philippine conquest. "The Philippines are ours forever, territory belonging to the United States. . . . We will not renounce our part in the mission of our race, trustee, under God, of the civilization of the world." He proceeded in a fit of missionary zeal:

> God has not been preparing the English-speaking and Teutonic peoples for a thousand years for nothing but vain and idle self-contemplation and self-admiration. This is the divine mission of America, and it holds for us all the profit, all the glory, all the happiness possible to man. We are trustees of the world's progress, guardians of its righteous peace. (Beveridge 1900)

Both the motives and implications of the imperial project in the Philippines were widely contested, to be sure. Opposition arose from many different quarters. Samuel Clemens, better known by his pen name Mark Twain, declared that "we do not intend to free, but to subjugate the people of the Philippines. We have gone there to conquer, not to redeem." In a revealing letter, Twain observed that "there must be two Americas: one that sets the captive free, and one that takes a once-captive's new freedom away from him, and picks a quarrel with him with nothing to found it on; then kills him to get his land" (Clemens 1901). Clemens became vice president of the Anti-Imperialist League in 1900. "I am an anti-imperialist. I am opposed to having the eagle put its talons on any other land" (1900). Other intellectuals such as William James, W. E. B. Du Bois, and E. L. Godkin as well as politicians Benjamin Harrison, Grover Cleveland, and William Jennings Bryan identified with the League's cause. Some opponents of empire protested on moral grounds, while others, like Andrew Carnegie and Senator George Frisbie Hoar, objected that the expansionist drive defied basic constitutional principles. Other opponents worried that Filipinos would enter the United States and undermine racial purity. Many labor leaders voiced concerns that Filipinos would take jobs and drive down wages.

The protests in the end fell short. The Treaty of Paris was ratified by a Senate vote of 57–27 in 1899. But the divisions over annexation, between those who supported US rule over "lesser" races and those most concerned about undermining racial purity, should not obscure the consensus among white leaders about sustaining male Anglo-Saxon superiority in the process of capitalist development.

Race War: Brutal Conquest, Divided Loyalties

The war of conquest waged by the United States in the Philippines was notable for, in Edmund Wilson's memorable words, its patriotic gore ([1962] 1994).[3] There were, essentially, two phases of conflict in the Philippine-American War. The first phase, which was centered in Luzon and lasted from February to November of 1899, was defined by General Aguinaldo's futile efforts to wage a conventional modern war against the much better trained and armed American troops. The second phase was defined by the Filipino nationalists' shift to guerilla-style warfare, which reflected fragmentation and weakening of the initial forces as much as creative strategy. The battles of Filipino nationalists were paralleled by those of the Tulisanes, Babaylanes, and other peasant groups in rural areas, including the island of Negros, against planter elites and other mestizos who allied with US occupiers. This phase commenced in November of 1899 and lasted through the capture of Aguinaldo in 1901 and into the spring of 1902, by which time much of the organized Filipino resistance had dissipated.

Lawless Repression or Repressive Law?

The American military's effort to implement McKinley's policy of benevolent assimilation was hardly benign, and it became increasingly brutal and ruthless as the conflict wore on. Secretary of War Elihu Root alternately tried both to explain failure to suppress the rebels and to deny that the war and carnage were continuing, insisting that the nationalist movement was a marginal insurrection and not a war for independence that, as many Filipinos claimed, emulated the American invaders' own original resistance against the British metropole (Miller 1982). Following McKinley's presidential reelection victory in late 1900, General Arthur MacArthur circulated a proclamation that enlarged the scope of American violence. Specifically, the decree selectively reinterpreted General Orders No. 100, the Civil War–era regulations determining fair treatment of civilians and prisoners of war in the territories. Because the Filipino independence fighters were not recognized as an army of an actual state and relied on "uncivilized" tactics of guerilla warfare, the rules of conventional war were not binding, MacArthur reasoned. MacArthur's (1901, 7) decree specified that the US Army would protect only those Filipinos who showed "strict obedience" to US authorities; noncombatants who in any way, however indirect, aided rebels would be treated as combatants. By threatening to expel, transfer, imprison, or fine civilians who did not act in full allegiance to the United States, the message of intimidation dramatically expanded the number of Filipinos who would become "easy victims to be plundered and murdered" as "war traitors against the United States" (MacArthur 1901, 8). Guerilla fighters who were captured, moreover, would not be entitled to the privileges of war and could be treated as murderous criminals subject to execution (Kramer 2006, 136–37). Under this logic, the US forces engaged in a host of routine actions—arbitrary relocation of vast populations to detention camps, torture by the "water cure" and "rope cure," arbitrary individual and mass execution—during the official war and for years after

(McCoy 2009; Einolf 2016). All in all, the US occupying forces repeated many of the same brutal practices that Americans found repugnant when enacted by the Spanish in Cuba.

In one sense the form and extent of US brutality, like that of Spain previously, was *lawless*, if conventional liberal principles of due process and humanitarian restraint as well as established conventions of war are the standard. But by the logic of proimperialist historian Brooks Adams—that law was determined simply by the capricious will of the stronger—the United States was enacting the type of law that was appropriate to the situation. This claim parallels Schmitt's famous dictum that "sovereign is he who decides on the exception" to law's rule (Schmitt 2005, 5; Agamben 2005). The sovereign, in creating the law, exercises complete discretion in determining where and for whom law is and is not binding. And it is in this regard that the racialization of Filipinos and their struggles as "uncivilized" or "savage" and incapable of self-rule as rights-bearing persons was pivotal. Much as in the campaigns to quell slave rebellions and wars against Indians on the mainland, American commanders could rationalize that savages did not deserve liberal legal restraint, that a more repressive, violent, discretionary mode of control was warranted (Rogin [1975] 1991). In this sense, the brutal subjugation of the Philippines was more routine than exceptional in the development of the American racial capitalist state.

As we noted before, not all white Americans were comfortable with the war, much less its destructive excesses. But racist logics propelled extreme violence at all levels. Scholars have provided extensive evidence revealing how white troops identified Filipinos with Indians and blacks on the mainland, justifying in dismissive terms the quest for subjugation, cruelty, and even extermination. Soldiers wrote in letters repeatedly about the thrill of chasing and killing "niggers" and "savages" as observers commented regularly on the reenactments of earlier generational racial campaigns on the American frontier (Kramer 2006, 87–158; Miller 1982). The racial project of new empire building was not a simple transferal of past white constructions to a new context, to be sure. Rather, it was, as Paul Kramer has demonstrated, dynamic, contingent, complex, and rife with contradictions (Kramer 2006). That said, familiar forms of racialization generally justified the extreme viciousness and revenge aimed at the imagined enemy Others. By placing Filipino resistance outside the bounds of recognized civilized warfare, William Pomeroy (1970, 88) notes, "the American military authorities in effect and in practice gave sanction to barbarous methods." As another scholar (Fast 1973, 74) argues, the US campaign "degenerated into a grisly slaughter of non-combatants."

One of the most infamous episodes of indiscriminate killing emanated from the orders of General Jacob H. Smith in late October 1901 to avenge a surprise guerilla attack killing more than fifty men in US Company C at Balangiga on the island of Samar. "I want no prisoners," Smith declared. "I wish you to kill and burn, the more you kill and burn the better it will please me." Make the island a "howling wilderness," he exhorted. The commander ordered "all persons killed who are capable of bearing arms in actual hostilities against the United States," which included any person over the age of ten (Akiboh 2015; Miller 1982). Most soldiers reportedly interpreted the command to mean that "everybody in Samar was an *insurrecto*" (Kramer 2006, 144–45). Smith later explained that because the Filipino rebels were "worse than fighting Indians," the tactics that he had learned while battling "savages" in the American West were reasonable (Francisco 1973). In any case, over the next year the US army pursued a scorched-earth policy in Samar. Nearly the entire island population, tens of thousands of persons, was wiped out (Akiboh 2015). Not to be outdone, Major General J. Franklin Bell also set up concentration camps in Batangas for all Filipinos suspected of alliance with the insurgents. Everyone "should either be an active friend or classified as an enemy." By the time Bell was finished, at least one hundred thousand people had been killed or died at Batangas from his radical policies (Francisco 1973).

Such military atrocities could easily find justification in the words of leading elites in the metropole who rejected the option of negotiating with the Philippine state and aiming to make the islands into a protectorate, as was done in the Caribbean. Consider again Beveridge:

> They [natives of the Philippines] are a barbarous race, modified by three centuries of contact with a decadent race. The Filipino is the South Sea Malay, put through a process of three hundred years of superstition in religion, dishonesty in dealing, disorder in habits of industry, and cruelty, caprice, and corruption in government. It is barely possible that 1,000 men in all the archipelago are capable of self-government in the Anglo-Saxon sense. (1900)

Roosevelt characterized Filipinos as "Chinese half breeds" and assessed the bloody conquest as "the most glorious war in our nation's history" (Dumindin

2006). This American racialization of Filipinos worked to steel the resolve of the rebels. Filipinos were very deliberate in framing their claims for independence in terms of the ideals voiced by white Americans fighting against British colonial rule over a century earlier. Indeed, Aguinaldo in 1898 explicitly derided the palpable contradiction between the professed ideals of establishing in the Philippines "an independent republic . . . conceived in liberty, with a government like our own, of the people, by the people and for the people" and the cynical commitment of American officials to assure that the Philippines would *not* be "a separate and self-governing nation" (Delmendo 2004, 127–28). If, as Filipinos had much reason to believe, their fate was to be that of the Indians or black slaves in America, then fighting to the death for their independence was far more redemptive, if not realistic, than submission or cooperation (Kramer 2006). For Filipinos a "politics of rights" that appealed to American elites' proclaimed values of universal equal protection and freedom proved initially to be a futile cause that met with violent subjugation (Scheingold 1974; E. P. Thompson 1975).

Overall McKinley's policy of benevolent assimilation produced US casualties of 4,234 soldiers killed and about three thousand wounded. Scholarly estimates of casualties among Filipinos vary widely. Stanley Karnow (1989, 194), who described the war as "among the cruelest conflicts in the annals of Western imperialism," counted twenty thousand deaths of soldiers and two hundred thousand civilian deaths, while other scholars estimate up to six hundred thousand or more total deaths. Historian Luzviminda Francisco (1973) has estimated that one million is probably a low estimate for the period from 1899 to 1913. She and others (Pomeroy 1970; San Juan Jr. 2009) note that General Bell, a credible witness, in a 1901 *New York Times* interview estimated that six hundred thousand people died in Luzon alone as a result of war or war-inflicted disease (Francisco 1973). Gore Vidal (1981) and others have labeled the encounter "genocide," whether calculated by intent or bloody impact (see San Juan Jr. 2009). Hence, the common refrain that the US war in the Philippines was "the first Vietnam."

The Racial Complexities of Empire

The debates among American imperialists and anti-imperialists regarding the Philippines to a large extent grew out of the experiences of westward expansion and the challenges of Reconstruction on the mainland. At the core of the debate was a key question: in short, were whites capable of incorporating

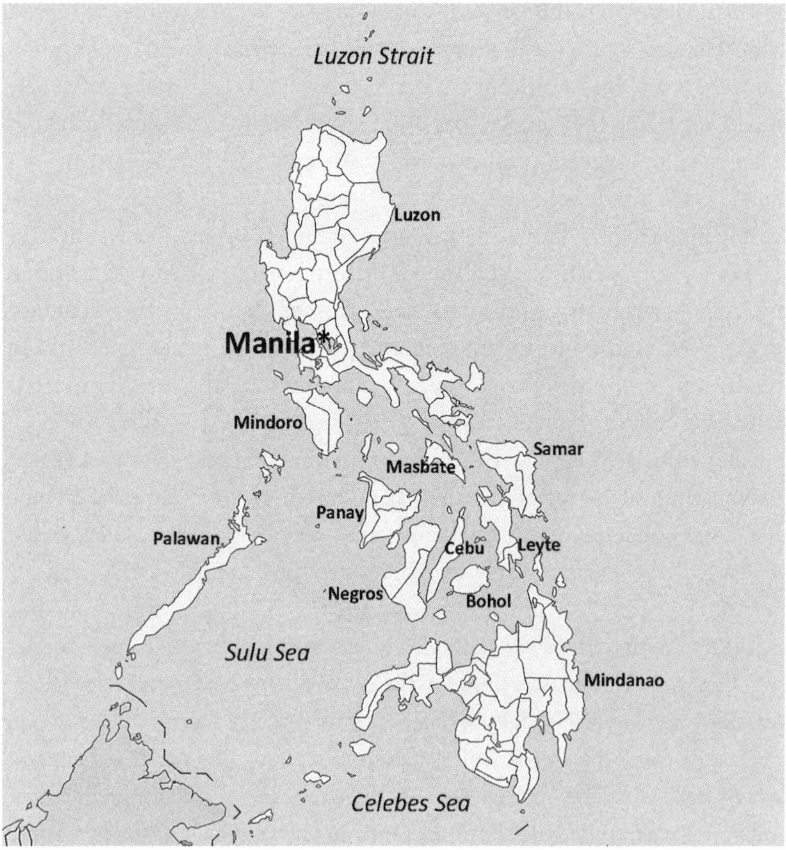

Fig. 1 Map of the Philippines. Public domain.

on near-equal terms nonwhite populations essential to capital accumulation, or were nonwhites irredeemably backward, undisciplined, and uncivilizable, therefore threatening the integrity of white civility? The racial politics of US colonial rule were complex in a variety of ways and none more striking than those regarding African Americans. Not surprisingly, many African American leaders saw the parallels between racial repression of black laborers on the mainland and dark-skinned Filipinos abroad and thus were highly critical of the imperial project. Among the most prominent opponents in the Anti-Imperialist League was W. E. B. Du Bois. His opposition was consistent with his plea for the unity of "Negro and Filipino, Indian and Porto Rican, Cuban and Hawaiian" in struggling for "an America that knows no color line in the freedom of its opportunities" (Du Bois [1900] 1996, 53). While initially hopeful that expansion of US territory might increase racial equality, he turned against annexation of the Philippines as the bloody war of racial subjugation ground on. Du Bois's concept of "double consciousness" was particularly salient regarding the complexities of imperial ventures. The core insight at stake was the inherent conflict between African American identity as exploited black people seeking human liberation from whites while still participating in the white-ruled society as (second-class) citizens. The war against the Philippines specifically confronted African Americans with the question of whether they should support the dark-skinned victims of white conquest on the grounds of transcendent universal principles of humanity or fight in the war and try to elevate their status and interests as rights-bearing citizens within the dominant white society.

This challenge was very real for many African Americans. While a host of black public leaders condemned the war, many others editorialized back home that it was not "a race war" and that patriotic service by black soldiers would be rewarded. More concretely, roughly seven thousand African Americans were deployed in the Spanish-American and then Philippine wars from four segregated regiments of the Buffalo Soldiers, who had earlier been deployed to fight against Native Americans in the far West. The black soldiers were especially valued by US leaders because they were viewed as more immune to tropical diseases than were whites (Dumindin 2006). The racialized context was fraught with deep paradoxes. Consider the scene as black soldiers disembarked after arriving in the Philippines on July 31, 1899. A white bystander reportedly yelled, "What are you coons doing here?" to which came the reply, "We have come to take up the White Man's Burden" (Silbey 2007, 107).

As the war worsened, Filipino rebels appealed to black soldiers to refrain from being used by white masters to oppress other people of color and even to join the Filipino nationalist army of Aguinaldo. At least twenty US soldiers, six of them black, did defect. The most famous of them was Private David Fagen of the 24th Infantry, who joined the rebels, became known as "Insurecto Captain" and even "General Fagen," and fought US troops on many occasions. White Americans labeled Fagen a traitor who deserved the death of a "mad dog," and a bounty of $600 was put on his head. One Tagalog hunter claimed to have killed Fagen, but the claim was never verified. Later sightings of Fagen were reported, and his fate was never fully confirmed (Robinson and Shubert 1975; Dumindin 2006; San Juan Jr. 2009). While pilloried as a subversive traitor by mainstream American society and many black people, he was viewed by others as a hero of conscience akin to rebel slave Nat Turner. Fagen thus represented the complexities of race in the imperial war (San Juan Jr. 2009; also Balce 2006). Should he be loyal to his nation, which subjected blacks to slavery and then to segregated, second-class status? Or should he be loyal to others also of dark skin even though they were foreigners with whom there were no other meaningful bonds? Or should he be loyal to the abstract universal principles that his nation espoused yet brazenly contradicted by domestic practice and lawless imperial war abroad? The paradoxes of race in the age of empire would play out repeatedly for Filipino migrants, other Asian Americans, Mexicans, and African Americans over the following century.

The Constitution of US Governance in the Philippines

Colonial Status under the US Constitution: The Insular Cases

Given the earlier aversion to classical modes of colonial rule, governance of the newly acquired colony in the Philippines—an archipelago of 7,100 islands populated by dark skinned, non-European inhabitants who lived twice as far from the mainland as Hawaii—posed a major challenge for Americans. President McKinley had proclaimed that the United States came "not as invaders or conquerors, but as friends," with the

> earnest wish and paramount aim of the military administration to win the confidence, respect, and affection of the inhabitants of the Philippines by assuring them in every possible way that full measure of individual rights and liberties which is the heritage of free peoples, and by proving to them that the mission of the United States is one of benevolent assimilation substituting the mild sway of justice and right for arbitrary rule. (McKinley 1898)

This lofty aspiration was, again, understood through the lens of deeply embedded racial beliefs that shaped the purview of governing elites. Generally, what Weiner (2006, 52) called "Teutonic constitutionalist" understandings dominated the perceptions of American leaders. In short, where Anglo-Saxons as a people possess "a special genius for law and state-building . . . , dark-skinned peoples . . . [are] incapable of legality and congenitally criminal." The risk of colonial governance thus was the impossibility of teaching natives to govern themselves and concomitant ineligibility of the Philippines for future statehood, possibly leading to an endless white man's burden of ruling over territories permanently unequal in status (Ngai 2004, 98; Smith 1997, 429–33).

This latter understanding was enacted in the bowdlerized version of McKinley's proclamation that General Elwell Otis, US military commander and governor-general in the Philippines, sent to Emilio Aguinaldo. The copy excised mentions of US "sovereignty," "supremacy," and "future domination" from the original text. General Otis later explained that the Tagalogs might use such terms as legal leverage to their advantage. "The ignorant classes had been taught to believe that certain words such as 'sovereignty,' 'protection,' and so forth had peculiar meanings disastrous to their welfare and significant of future political domination, like that from which they had been recently freed" (Miller 1982, 52). In short, the United States must carefully tailor the rhetorical cloak embellishing imperial control and capitalist interests. Conversely, many advocates of active annexation and colonial rule believed that the Hispanicized elites in the Philippines, many of them already active in mass sugar cane production and commercial trade, over time would learn to perform a governing role over the less civilized island "savages"— the Ilongots, Igorots, and Ifugaos in the mountainous north and Muslim Moros in the southern islands—with the proper tutelage of white Americans establishing a ruling racial class favorable to American ideals and interests alike.

As often is the case, the debate among political elites found its way to the US Supreme Court. In *Downes v. Bidwell* (1901), Mr. Samuel Downes, an importer of goods from the US insular territory of Puerto Rico, brought a case against the customs collector of New York. Downes's key claim was that he paid a very high tariff on imported oranges that was required by the Organic Act of 1900 (aka the Foraker Act) with which the US government established the civil government of Puerto Rico. Downes argued that because Puerto Rico was a part of the United States and the Uniformity Clause (art. I, § 8) of the US Constitution holds that all duties be "uniform throughout," the high duty was an unlawful exercise of the collector's power. The key question that arose was whether Puerto Rico and other insular territories, including the Philippines, were part of the United States and whether their laws were subject to the constraints of the US Constitution. Similarly, were the people in insular territories entitled to the same basic constitutional rights as American citizens?

On the one hand, traditionalists[4] on the court deferred to Congress' plenary power to acquire new territories, but they argued that the US Constitution applied to all acquired territories and their subjects. The Constitution "follows the flag," contended Justice Harlan. Otherwise, US power abroad would be legally unrestrained and potentially despotic. On the other hand, proimperial modernists in the majority argued that strict adherence to the constitution would limit necessary US discretionary options and flexibility as an emerging geopolitical power. In this position, territories acquired from Spain belonged to but were not part of the United States (Ngai 2004, 99). The court held that the Constitution did not "follow the flag." On December 2, 1901, the US Supreme Court in *Pepke v. United States* clarified that the insular decisions applied to the Philippines as well. The decisions represented a major modification in American law away from expansion of US territorial controls aiming for subsequent admission as states and toward a principle premised in indeterminate unequal political status for select territories, paralleling the status of Indians as "domestic dependent nations." Developing ideas of sovereignty, which underline capacities for self-governance, thus justified the logic of inequality enforced by law (Altman 2013, 548, 552).

Extrajudicial and consequentialist considerations clearly played an influential role in these cases. In particular, both sides tended to agree that the residents of the territories, and especially Filipinos, were racially inferior and incapable of governing themselves (Weiner 2006, 70–77). The understanding was expressed clearly in Justice White's majority opinion:

> Citizens of the US discover an unknown island, peopled with an uncivilized race, yet rich in soil, and valuable to the US for commercial and strategic reasons. Clearly, by the law of nations, the right to ratify such acquisition and thus to acquire the territory would pertain to the government of the US. Can it be denied that such right could not be practically exercised if the result would be . . . the immediate bestowal of citizenship on those absolutely unfit to receive it? (*Downes v. Bidwell*, 182 U.S. 244, 292, 1901)

Following the logic of American empire, Justice White underlined the close interrelationship between motivations of capitalist profit and paternalistic racial hierarchy at the heart of US law and politics.[5] The discourse of benevolent assimilation embedded material and military interest in a moral mission of modern uplift and civilizing protection. As Ngai (2004, 99) recounts, "Americans believed that their imperialist venture was noble in purpose, unlike Old World colonialism." And in this regard, the civilized nation's denial of stature to the people of the islands recalled the earlier efforts to construct the West as an imagined empty space devoid of civilized, self-governing natives and available to white commercial advantage.

Moreover, the US Supreme Court affirmed the peculiar union by law that connected the Philippine peoples as virtually rightsless subjects of the United States. As the islands were "denationalized," so were its peoples denied constitutional protections as US citizens. Instead, a new legal category of "US nationals" was created specifically for Filipinos. As we shall see in examining the later experiences of Filipino migrants to the mainland metropole, nationals were denied status as full-fledged rights-bearing individuals under the Constitution and subjected to discretionary, often arbitrary and brutal forms of American law. Filipinos were allowed "free" movement to provide low-wage labor within the territorial jurisdiction of the United States, but no legal rights status was accorded to that activity. Any such claim of right to movement was later dispelled, with the restrictive quotas placed on Filipinos by the Tydings-McDuffie Act in 1934.

The Constitution of Colonial Governance

Unlike in the Caribbean, and despite continued resistance from many Filipinos appealing to the legacy of American demands for independent self-rule against colonial control, the United States proclaimed and quickly exercised complete sovereign power over the Philippines. The official rhetoric of legitimating goals espoused by Americans, constructed under pressure from US anti-imperialists, was about promoting uplift and civilization, constitutional order and basic rights for self-governed citizens. The United States claimed "to provide for the maintenance of law and order, and for the establishment of good government and for the performance of international obligations" (A. L. F. T. Castañeda 2009a, 62).[6] To some degree, the experience of white leaders in establishing and administering reservations for Native Americans provided models for tutelary governance. But the "unincorporated" status of the Philippine colony required new, hybrid organizational forms that at once built on the inherited Spanish colonial institutions and differed from both western frontier management and the "informal imperial" rule in the Caribbean. One reason is that whereas Congress funded the Native American reservation system, the Philippines had to be self-financed, which in turn required state-like institutional mechanisms for legislating and collecting taxes (Go 2003, 9).

The shift from military to civilian colonial governing processes began with a series of commissioned studies to assemble data necessary to insular administration. The First Philippine Commission's work was largely descriptive, yet it was shaped by racial assumptions. It included an ethnographic survey of the different islands, some of these by the Bureau of Non-Christian Tribes, which in many ways followed protocols established earlier in administration over Native Americans in the metropole. In 1900 William Howard Taft was chosen by President McKinley to direct the second Philippine Commission (the Taft Commission), which was delegated legislative and executive powers of government. Through a variety of authorizing documents, the War Department and the US Congress crafted an Insular Government of the Philippine Islands that vaguely mirrored its American counterpart in institutional design but invested the bulk of governing power in the executive branch, especially the American-held office of the governor-general, and the upper legislative branch, dominated by Hispanicized elites form Manila and Luzon generally (Anastacio 2016). Large swathes of Filipinos, especially the non-Hispanicized, mostly Muslim populations (the "Moros") of the Sulu archipelago, Mindanao, and Palawan, were relegated to the lower legislative branch, which had little authority. With representation only in the lower legislative branch, local government authority was constrained by the capricious governance of the Philippine Commission, which alternated between military and civilian modes of rule. In short, there were essentially two representative governments in the Philippine state, both constituted by the hierarchical terms of constructed racial difference. As Anna Castañeda (2009b, 369) puts it, "dividing the branches of the central government . . . transmuted racial conflicts into legal contests, casting them as separation of powers disputes among the executive and legislative branches."

Proliferating legalization was critical to the new forms of governance. Between 1900 and 1902, around five hundred new laws were passed, and a legal code and judicial system were created. Hispanicized Filipino elites filled the lower justice of the peace positions, and Americans were accorded most judicial appointments, although the courts lacked necessary personnel because there were few Spanish-speaking American judges. Courts also lacked the authority to overturn executive and legislative failures to implement the Philippine Organic Act of 1902, the basic law for the Insular Government. The power of judicial review was inferred from the US Constitution, but that document was not and could not be the supreme law of the land in the Philippines because of the rulings in the *Insular Cases* (A. L. F. T. Castañeda 2009b, 372–73). As a result, political branches were more heavily invested with powers than were courts in early colonial government. Because the American-controlled governor-general had more power than the Filipino-dominated legislature, there thus were few checks on the governor-general's office. The Philippine

Supreme Court began to assert its independence from the executive branch in 1920, but even then it did not scrutinize executive and legislative actions very closely. Still, the courts symbolized adherence to rule of law while protecting centralized colonial government control and providing routine tutelage in the practices of constitutional governance.

The rhetoric of American commitment to "civilizing" Filipinos may have been an exercise in "myopic arrogance" and paternal domination, but it was not entirely insincere (May 1980). Indeed, the Americans attempted to implement some elements of civilized, Progressive Era governance in the Philippines. The new colonial state sponsored New England–style town meeting protocols, commenced building roads and communication infrastructure, and established health and hygiene programs (Go 2003). From the start, however, as we noted already, the Philippines were viewed by the American governors largely in terms of different populations requiring different strategies and timetables for control (Abinales 2003). American tutelage in the arts of governance was directed mostly at the Hispanicized political elite in Luzon who had cooperated with Americans and shown potential for self-rule friendly to US political and commercial interests.

Americanized schools proliferated to educate the masses in liberal capitalist values, while the *pensionados* program for sponsoring advanced administrative education among loyal *americanistas* in the US mainland was initiated. Formal legal training continued the Spanish colonial project for local elites just as many bureaucratic institutions of the colonial government built on the model initiated by the Spanish. The division of Filipinos into classes and functional roles not only reflected differently defined subject capacities but made sustained organizational resistance difficult. By working through local political elites, Americans were assured that many of the most volatile labor and agrarian movements in subsequent years would direct their campaigns against Filipino political oligarchs and *hacendero* plantation owners rather than US colonialists (Go and Foster 2003, 284). Literary giant Carlos Bulosan recognized the role of law and lawyers in this process. "The sons of the professional classes studied law and went to the provinces, victimizing their own people and enriching themselves at the expense of the nation," he wrote in *America Is in the Heart* (Bulosan 1973). "In a few years these lawyers were elected to the national government, and . . . took part in the merciless exploitation of the peasantry and a new class of dispossessed peasants who were working in the factories or on the vast haciendas" (1973, 84).

Despite odes to liberal constitutionalism, imperial rule thus thwarted popular sovereignty and the ideals of "liberty, equality, and fraternity" for the bulk of Filipinos, many of whom continued to fight as rebels (Rafael 2009). Even peaceful modes of expression critical of American occupiers and their Filipino elite allies were forbidden. In November 1901, the Philippine Commission enacted a sedition law that declared unlawful any speech, printing, publication, or circulation of material that encouraged Filipinos to fight against the American colonial rule in the Philippines. This law imposed the death penalty or long imprisonment on many Filipino nationalist leaders (Teodoro 1999, 158).

Agrarian land reform was another key element of the disciplinary project that was critical for tutelage of loyal subjects, although it was quickly compromised by the contradictory logics of colonial rule. Spanish rulers had made Catholic friars the primary landlords who presided over peasant tenant farmers even though sugar plantation owners already had begun the process of dispossessing peasants, converting them into a proletarian labor force, and commodifying land for commercial production. United States–led colonial government land reform laws purportedly aimed to redistribute commercial lowlands for cultivation by individual Filipino property owners, repudiating the Spanish past and catalyzing a modern capitalist future. The homestead policy replayed a familiar legacy of US frontier development, gesturing toward liberal universalist ideals and symbolizing the rectitude of America's revivified civilizing mission. "Modeling Philippine law on US laws turned the colony into the metaphorical and legal equivalent of a frontier," as Theresa Ventura (2016, 467) suggests.

As Ventura demonstrates, however, the idealistic project of yeoman homesteading yielded to more powerful forces. The Bureau of Public Lands rejected the overwhelming number of homestead applications on technical grounds, generating widespread noncooperation by tenants and peasant land claimants. White colonial rulers interpreted the plan's failure as demonstrating the incapacity of Filipinos to self-govern. Filipino tenants and claimants were labeled as unscrupulous or prisoners of "old customs," and rational actions of resistance were deemed criminal. Meanwhile, wealthy mestizo landowning families organized to buy and convert the land into mass plantation production for commercial export of sugar, rice, coconuts, and other tropical agricultural products. The plantation model thrived on commodifying public land into private property and turning the mass of previous tenants into low-wage commodified workers laboring in segregated, hierarchical conditions. Predatory capitalist practices embedded in local partisan political alliances undercut ideals of propertied independence for many and increased the fundamental social inequalities in the colony (Ventura 2016, 477). The plantation-based model of commercial progress quickly became further institutionalized in the Philippines as well as in the colony of Hawaii (Merry 2000).

These organizational projects of plantation capitalism were supported by development of sophisticated new tools for policing and punishing still relatively rightsless, racialized proletarian subjects, many of whom organized into gangs (*tulisanes*) that battled planter elites (Keel 2018a). The civilizing process, argues Vincent Rafael (1993, 195), was "predicated on white supremacy enforced through practices of discipline and maintained by a network of surveillance." As in the Reconstruction era on the US mainland, the Philippine Commission in 1902 enacted vagrancy laws that criminalized any persons with "no apparent means of subsistence, who has the physical ability to work" (cited in Keel 2018a, 12). The commission also passed the Brigandage Act, which defined armed bands of three or more persons as criminals, denying the aspirational political aims of peasant group resistance and producing a "new kind of subject—one which violated the law but was subsumed within it" (Keel 2018a, 12). Together, these laws enabled the colonial government to guarantee the cheap labor force necessary for large-scale export-based commercial agriculture.

Also important in this regard was the modernized Manila Metropolitan Police and the paramilitary Philippine Constabulary (PC), established in August of 1901, under the general supervision of the civil governor-general of the Philippines for the purpose of fighting insurgents and maintaining order and law in the various provinces of the Philippine Islands. With around 180 officers commissioned by the end of 1901, the constabulary assisted the US military in suppressing the remaining revolutionaries, including the capture of Aguinaldo in 1901 and the execution of one of the remaining rebel leaders, Macario Sakay, in 1906. Governor-General Taft maintained the police forces after the war to combat the residual nationalist insurgents and to quell the increasingly restive working-class and peasant populations around Manila. Historian Alfred McCoy has shown in great detail how aggressive police forces fused new, technically sophisticated modes of information technology with military intelligence to create a novel surveillance state largely removed from constitutional restriction. The wide array of extralegal tactics combining coercion, persuasion, and deception—clandestine infiltration, psychological warfare, disinformation, media manipulation, rule by scandal mongering, bribery, assassination, multiple forms of torture, and other covert techniques—developed initially to subjugate Filipinos established templates for imperial adventures elsewhere over the next century (McCoy 2009). Pressed by American missionaries, the colonial regime also launched a war on drugs focused on prohibiting the smuggling and smoking of opium (Foster 2003). Similarly, a new complex of prisons, including the Iwahig Penal Colony on the remote Palawan Island, was created to join punishment, discipline, and capitalist labor routines in a Progressive Era effort to force Filipinos to become "free" (Salman 2009).

In contrast to the disciplinary project in the Hispanicized northern islands, the generally non-Hispanicized, non-Christian, Muslim Moros in the southern islands were considered to be fundamentally "barbarous, semi-civilized, and semi-savage" (Amoroso 2003,125). Often likened to Indians in the American western frontier, the Moros were viewed as incapable of self-governance and were subjected largely to military rule; even more coercive "direct control and supervision" were imposed on them than in the north. This began with a protracted war between US forces and the Moros that lasted until 1912, a war that surpassed the brutality of the theaters in the north and that was more focused on killing directly with weaponry than imprisonment. An estimated 13 percent of the archipelago's population was slayed before surrender (Boudrou 2003, 262). The massacre at Bud Dajo in 1906 wiped out all but six of the nearly one thousand Moro rebels, provoking terrible press at home, including Mark Twain's acerbic "Comments on the Moro Massacre": "Death List is Now 900 . . . I was never so enthusiastically proud of the flag 'til now!" (Clemens 1906).

Establishing the rule of colonial law in the southern islands of the Moros was a challenging enterprise (Abinales 2003; McKenna 1998). The Moros had continued to practice their diverse, localized Muslim customs and variants of sharia law during the long period of Spanish colonial rule. The US colonial government initially adopted a similar policy of legal hybridity in the southern Philippines parallel to that of British Malaya (Hussin 2016) and including a 1899 treaty with the Sultan of Sulu promising that the United States would "not interfere in Sulu religion, law and commerce." (Holbrook 2009, 11). The United States entered into comparable, if more informal, agreements with other parts of Moroland. In 1905, however, the United States abrogated those treaties and imposed uniform secular law that preempted Muslim customary law (*adat*).

Nevertheless, many colonial civil courts continued to recognize local laws and customs governing personal relationships and disputes. Ironically, this legal and cultural independence helped for a period to insulate much of Mindanao from transformation into plantation-based commercial agriculture. Scholars debate whether sharia was fully recognized or merely tolerated, but legal hybridity grew through regular practice (Merry 1998; Hussin 2016; Sezgin 2013).

Americans eventually expanded that colonization program by encouraging multinational agricultural corporations and Filipino Christians to take over the land and, thus, political control in Mindanao. While Mindanao's population was about 90 percent Moro Muslim at the start of US colonial rule, almost 75 percent of the inhabitants were Filipino Christians by the end of the twentieth century. When the Philippines became a commonwealth in 1935 on the way to independence, the new constitution protected religious freedom but did not recognize Moro identity or sharia law. The second-class minority status of Moros under uniform law was a routine source of contestation and rebellion for the next century. "The long term result was their marginality, dissatisfaction, and ultimately, among many, the rejection of the Philippine nation-state" (Amoroso 2003, 143). The local media frequently compared the "conquest and colonization" that turned the Moros into a separate, marginalized nation on their traditional lands to the experiences of dispossessed Native Americans who violently resisted American rule in the West (Macabenta 2015; Magdalena 2017). In sum, the Philippine-American union by law was a divisive, contested, illiberal experiment heavily dependent on strong-arm military repression.

Philippine In/dependence: Client Statism in the American Empire

Woodrow Wilson, in accepting the Democratic nomination for the presidency in 1912, portrayed Americans as "trustees" of the Philippines, arguing that colonial rulers had to "make whatever arrangement of government will be most serviceable to their freedom and development" (Wertz 2008, 114). Wilson did not issue a call for independence so much as echo the established rhetoric of American benevolence and lawful governance in the Philippines masking racial capitalist designs. The first legislative victory for anti-imperialists came in 1916 when the Jones Act created the Philippine Senate to replace the Philippine Commission with an elected legislature and promised eventual self-government for an independent Philippine nation-state. Wilson reluctantly signed the act, although he would not publicly call for granting Philippine independence until after Republicans won the presidential election by large margins in 1920. Eventually the 1934 Tydings-McDuffie Act established a process through which the Philippines would become a formally independent nation-state after another decade, although the actual transformation was delayed until after World War II. While legally independent, the Philippines remained locked into military and economic client-state interdependence with the United States throughout the Cold War era.

The legal and political imprint of America's colonial governance through racially constructed repressive law would endure for many decades. The centralized constitutional order imposed by the US colonial administration provided the legal path for continued strong-arm rule and episodic martial law by entrenched elite oligarchs in the Philippines (B. Anderson 1988). The Moros in the south sustained their campaigns of armed resistance for the rest of the twentieth century, winning recognition of separate Muslim personal law authority in 1977 and formalizing the hybrid legal system. At the same time, American experiments with policing the periphery of the empire, largely unconstrained by the constitution and courts, accelerated the growth of a technologically sophisticated national security surveillance state in the metropole and provided protocols of Cold War repression at home and hot conflicts abroad, most notably Vietnam, and continuing into the adventures in Afghanistan, Iraq, and beyond (McCoy 2009; McCoy and Scarano 2009). In the remainder of this book we will demonstrate many of the ways that proletarianized Filipinos who were conscripted for work in the West Coast agricultural fields of the metropole as well as in Alaskan salmon canneries would be subjected to and also resist through legal and extralegal means the harsh police power of plantation capitalism throughout the century. The US experiment in the Philippines forged an overseas colonial empire that became "part and parcel of new intra-imperial and inter-imperial dynamics" in a globalizing world (Go 2003: 22; Rodriguez 2006).

1

Filipino Migration to the Metropole

Racism, Resistance, and Rights

Capitalists depended on workers, just as free men needed Indians and slaves. But the persistence of free labor ideology and the influx of immigrants buried that dependence, shifting a class opposition into an ethnic one that pitted Americans against aliens.—MICHAEL ROGIN (1987, 237)

I feel like a criminal running away from a crime I did not commit. And the crime is that I am a Filipino in America.—CARLOS BULOSAN (1973, vii)

Their judges lynch us; their police hunt us;
Their armies and navies and airmen terrorize us;
Their thugs and stoolies and murderers kill us;
They take away bread from our children;
They ravage our women;
They deny life to our elders.
But I say we have the truth
On our side, we have the future with us;
We have history in our hands, our belligerent hands.
—CARLOS BULOSAN, "I Want the Wide American Earth" (1950 [UWSC])

Filipino Migration to the Metropole

The American colonial venture into the Philippines opened the way for the transpacific migration by Filipinos to the metropole that many anti-imperialists and nativists had feared. Indeed, the expansion of American overseas empire accelerated circulation by both Filipino colonial subjects and American citizens across the commercial transit lanes between the two increasingly interconnected lands. Filipino migration to North America actually had begun far earlier, in the sixteenth century, when Philippine-built Spanish galleons crossed the Pacific Ocean during Spanish colonial rule (Cordova 1983, 1). The first, barely noticed waves of Filipino servants, stowaway refugees, and mariners landed at New Orleans, Vancouver Island, and Hawaii from 1763 until the end of Spanish rule in the Philippines. Records show that the first Filipino to live in Washington Territory worked at a Port Blakely sawmill, on Bainbridge Island, in 1883 (Nonato 2016).

Significant rates of transpacific migration did not commence, however, until after the Insular Cases rulings in 1901 established that Filipino colonial subjects could travel freely to the US metropole. In instrumental terms, Native Filipinos were both pushed and pulled into this "third Asiatic invasion" of the American metropole (Baldoz 2011). They were *pushed* by the increasing displacement of landownership to elites that proletarianized peasants into commodified wage laborers, disruption in traditional community life, the brutal violence of US colonial rule, and related costly conflicts produced by armed resistance. Filipinos were *pulled* by the growing demand for cheap labor and promises of opportunity in the American metropole, especially in the western states. Carlos Bulosan captured both dimensions: "the younger generation, influenced by false American ideals and modes of living . . . [and] those who could no longer tolerate existing conditions adventured into the new land, for the opening of the United States to them was one of the gratifying provisions of the peace treaty that culminated the Spanish American War" (Bulosan 1973, 5).

An important minority of the Pinoy[1] migrants hoped to build on the educational foundation that they received in American colonial schools and to use advanced university training to propel them into leading roles in the nation-building program in the Philippines. The pursuit of American education directly followed from the colonial *pensionados* program in which the government sponsored mostly privileged, English-speaking mestizo students to study in the United States (Teodoro 1999). While the Philippine government eventually developed a comprehensive domestic education system to the university level, the colonial hierarchy meant that the ideal institutionalized instruction was in the United States. The fact that many of the first generation Filipinos pursued the path of higher education is one of the many ways that Filipino migration was different from that of other Asians, Mexicans, and even European migrants. A fair number of those students returned to the Philippines to take positions in government by the start of World War I. A modest number of Filipinos also followed President McKinley's entreaty to join the US Navy, thus adding a new episode in the long history of American conscription of largely rightsless subjects to fight the country's wars (Klinkner and Smith 1999).

The overwhelming bulk of male migrants, however, were conscripted into low-wage, labor-intensive jobs. Increased militancy and a rash of strikes by Japanese sugar plantation laborers in Hawaii prompted the Sugar Planters Association to recruit Filipino workers, who were viewed as hardworking and docile, to the Hawaiian Islands. An estimated twenty-four thousand arrived between 1907 and 1919, and the numbers rose to forty-eight thousand in the 1920s. Demand for imported Filipino labor increased during World War I and, after a short postwar recession, boomed in the 1920s: fourteen thousand Filipinos migrated from Hawaii to the West Coast and another nearly thirty-eight thousand traveled directly from the Philippines (Baldoz 2004). Both the national US and territorial governments discouraged Filipino migration, but congressionally legislated immigration restrictions prompted West Coast commercial farmers to turn to Filipinos and Mexicans to replace Japanese laborers (Ngai 2004, 101). Farm operators reported that they preferred Filipino workers over native whites because of their dexterity, hard work, subservience, and willingness to put up with poor lodging and working conditions. By 1930, sixty-four thousand Filipinos worked in the oppressive Hawaiian plantations while another forty-five thousand worked on the mainland, ten times the number in the 1920 census. Most of the latter worked on the West Coast, including over thirty thousand in California and nearly four thousand in Washington. Well over 90 percent of the proletarian Filipino migrants in this early period were male, most of them young and single. Many of them circulated back and forth between the metropole and the colonial homeland to sustain families and communities, but the strains of isolation on individuals and collectives were palpable (Cordova 1983, 17).

Most of these laborers came from agricultural families in the Ilocos region of the northern Philippines. Historian Dorothy Fujita-Rony (2003) links the migratory inclinations of Ilocano/as to traditional work patterns of small landowners and peasants, conventions of dividing inheritances equally among sons, and the regional overpopulation that forced Ilocanos to seek work in other regions of the Philippines first and then migrate to the United States as opportunities arose. The economic attraction for many was sufficient to override the prospects of education and advancement within the Philippines, again reflecting the colonial hierarchy between the two lands. Migration to America also was propelled by American propaganda about boundless prospects for landownership and employment as well as the concerted campaign of "Americanization" through public education. As Filipino collaborator H. Pardo de Tavera outlined the Americanization project, "the study and propagation of the English language in the Philippines is justifiable, so that we will internalize the American spirit, and though this, we can acquire the aspirations, political traditions and its unique culture in the hope that, in the end, our safety and redemption will become full and complete" (quoted in Teodoro 1999, 160). Active recruiting efforts by Asian labor contractors who already had relocated to the United States also enticed workers and encouraged migration.

Filipino literary chronicler Carlos Bulosan, who came to the West Coast in 1930 from a poor but shrewd sharecropping farm family, captured the promises of America in his many writings. The title of his book embraced the ideal of America that was "in the heart." His poem "I Want the Wide American Earth" (1950 [UWSC]) similarly expressed the promise of America as a land of hope, opportunity, and freedom. It begins and ends with dreams of finding love and truth in an idyllic land:

> Before the brave, before the proud builders and workers
> I say I want the wide American earth,
> Its beautiful rivers and long valleys and fertile plains,
> Its numberless hamlets and expanding towns and towering cities,
> Its limitless frontiers, its probing intelligence,
> For all the free.
> . . . .
> I want the wide American earth for my people,
> I want my beautiful land,
> I want it with my rippling strength and tenderness
> Of love and light and truth
> For all the free

The distinction drawn here between Filipino elites seeking education and the proletarianized laborers from peasant farming backgrounds conscripted for employment can be quite misleading, though. Two-thirds of Filipino university students in the United States were not *pensianados*, so they had to find work to help pay for their education, which means that they split their time between low-wage jobs—whether in the cities, such as Los Angeles and Seattle, or in rural areas—and time at school (Nonato 2016). Many could not sustain the divided time commitment or cover the costs of schooling, especially during periods of economic depression, so they became destitute and stuck as laborers. "We did not earn much money during the summer times. . . . I did not know any other job, except to go to the cannery. So I didn't make enough money to continue the whole year of my schooling," recalled a cannery union leader about his youth (quoted in Fresco 1999). Others came from the start with the simple hope of earning a livelihood for a short time, then returning with enough money to purchase land in the homeland or pay for family members' education (De Vera 1994).

The bulk of the work available to Filipinos was in rural regions—in the Hawaiian sugar plantations (as *sakadas*); in the agricultural fields of fruit and vegetable production in central California, Oregon, and Washington; and in the Alaskan salmon canneries (the *Alaskeros*). Most of the work for wage laborers was seasonal, which compelled the migratory patterns up and down the coast from south to north, including to Alaska, and then through cities, which provided layovers during the routine treks. Some worked in urban restaurants and hotels—as busboys, bellboys, dishwashers, janitors, or doormen—as well as domestic service on private estates. Filipinos tended to find only the lowest-paying unskilled jobs in all these sectors, many of them previously held by earlier waves of Chinese and Japanese workers before the restrictive, exclusionary immigration laws targeting Asians. By 1921, Filipino workers outnumbered the other two Asian groups on the metropole.

Filipinos initially tended to congregate in urban "China Towns," where they were relatively welcome or at least tolerated by other Asians, as opposed to their emphatic exclusion as "undesirables" in white sections of cities. Chinese and Japanese Americans owned the majority of small businesses in these enclaves, but some Filipino-run businesses, restaurants, bars, and retail merchandise shops sprang up to serve the migratory populations. These areas also included brothels, fraternal club halls, billiard parlors, and gambling joints that developed a bad reputation among middle-class whites but that transient Filipinos and other Asians found vital centers of community life and social support (Nonato 2016).[2] Boxing and cockfighting were other important social activities in the mostly male migratory community. Families bound by bloodlines continued to be important but became geographically separated and strained, so localized constructed kinship networks of ethnic solidarity among *manongs* (Ilocano term of respect for older brothers or respected male leaders) in Manilatowns became increasingly important for the mostly migratory male workers.

Seattle was an especially prominent hub in the seasonal labor circuits within the empire (Fujita-Rony 2003, 118). The University of Washington enrolled many Filipino students, and Seattle's Chinatown at the southern edge of downtown (in the 1970s becoming known as the International District) was a vital crossroads of Filipino life. Seattle was, as we shall see in the next chapter, especially important for *Alaskeros* who traveled to the Alaskan salmon canneries in the summer months. Again, most Filipino migrants were male, producing a largely Pinoy "bachelor society." The Jenkins family, a mixed-race family of Filipino, African American, and Mexican origin, was the first Filipino household to settle in Seattle, around 1908, but the presence of a Filipina mother was atypical (Large 2016). African Americans also frequented the Chinatown area; the Black and Tan Club was a favorite Seattle nightclub that, after World War I, derived its name from serving black, white, Asian, and Filipino people alike.[3] More generally, Seattle itself developed into a dynamic city through the process of expanding transpacific empire and colonial rule. Seattle's port became a critical site for shipping military supplies to and receiving agricultural products from the Philippines on return trips. Seattle still bears, in the twenty-first century, the palpable markers of that formative imperial era: streets, bridges, and parks are named to honor both colonial rule, including Volunteer Park and Fort Lawton, and resistant colonized subjects, such as the Dr. Jose P. Rizal Bridge and Park (Hedden 2013).

It would be difficult to overstate the degree to which Filipino migrant experiences in the American metropole, both in Hawaii and on the West Coast of the mainland emphasized here, contradicted what they had been led to expect by official propaganda and ordinary talk about freedom and opportunity. "I was so disappointed to come to this country because I found it was not so easy as we were led to believe when we were in the Philippines," Vincent "Vic" Bacho explained in an interview. He had come for an education at the University of Washington, but like many others he was forced to migrate up and down the coast to find work in the fields, ending up in Sacramento, California. "We were not considered as human beings like white people here" he reflected (Hinnershitz 2013, 136). Again, Bulosan's writings powerfully captured the disjuncture between the aspirational ideals of America that Filipinos learned in colonial schools and felt in their hearts on the one hand

and the violent reality of intersectional racial and class oppression that they experienced once they arrived on the other. "Western people are brought up to regard Orientals or colored peoples as inferior. . . . I was completely disillusioned when I came to know this American attitude" (Bulosan 1943, xiii). But most early migrants also proved amazingly resilient, resistant, and even committed to social transformation. The bulk of their struggles initially were simply defensive gambits for survival, but over time the newly arrived migrants labored to increase their personal freedom and collective political power. Many of their aspirational struggles were defined in terms of realizing basic rights and included mobilizing around rights causes that challenged the legal status quo in the United States. We shall see in the remainder of this book that their "politics of rights" took many forms in many institutional sites and over many decades.

The Legal and Social Foundations of Racialized Class Oppression

Filipino migration brought to the metropole the brutal material realities of the colonial venture that previously had seemed remote, inconsequential, or benign to most white Americans. "The arrival of Filipino immigrants in the imperial metropole rendered visible the colonialism that Americans had tried to make invisible through myths of historical accident and benevolence," summarizes Mae Ngai (2004, 97). However, the "invasion" of the American West by many thousands of migrant Filipinos mostly worked to intensify the deep fears of racial contamination voiced by opponents of the colonial venture in previous years.

It is important in this regard to underline the broader historical dimensions of the racial capitalist context into which Filipino migrants were recruited. Following the Civil War, the bulk of African Americans "liberated" from slavery in the South embraced the promise of "forty acres and a mule" as compensation for unpaid slave labor and the means to build new lives as independent family farmers. A small percentage of former slaves did manage to acquire property, and others took jobs as low-wage laborers, especially in the sugar plantations. However, the collapse of Southern currency ruptured the economy, giving white owners ample reasons to resist land redistribution and instead to force many black families into new forms of wageless labor for white property owners (Blackmon 2008). The bedrock of the new quasi-slave system was annually contracted sharecropping organized around the crop lien system of credit, which drove many black farmers into perpetual debt and vulnerability to the servitude of peonage. Laws criminalizing theft of farm animals and unemployment as a form of "vagrancy" forced many poor black persons into prisons, which "leased" convicts to agricultural and commercial interests, while chain gangs were enlisted for public projects necessary to market infrastructure development. Along with legally enforced political disenfranchisement, these institutional mechanisms provided the cheap, disposable, brutally exploited labor force that supported the Southern agricultural economy during the Jim Crow era. As one scholar has summarized, "the evidence indicates that the law, not the market, was the chief oppressor of blacks in the Jim Crow period" (Roback 1984, 1192).[4]

In the Western agricultural and extraction industries, capitalist accumulation and commercial development similarly required a large supply of cheap, expendable, mostly seasonal laborers. Starting in the late nineteenth century, economic demand led to the proliferation of low-wage jobs that were primarily filled by successive waves of conscripted Chinese, Japanese, and Mexican workers who gradually formed a transnational, migratory, proletarian class of racially marked inferior, rightsless "aliens" ineligible for naturalization as immigrant citizens. These workers, who often were recruited by contractors, labored under extremely difficult conditions, were paid very low wages and were often not paid as promised, were relegated to segregated social spaces, and were subjected to harsh, violent forms of repressive social and legal control. In the wake of slave abolition, Du Bois ([1935] 1998, 632) observed, "a new industrial slavery of black and brown and yellow workers of Africa and Asia" was beginning. Filipinos who began to travel to the US metropole in the 1920s made up the third wave of Asians that joined this racialized proletarian workforce.

The majority of white, rights-bearing citizens in the West thus faced an immediate challenge concerning how they could live among the expanding racialized laboring classes that were both needed for capitalist material development and reviled as inherently inferior, undisciplined, uncivilizable, unassimilable, and threatening foreigners at many levels. The result, in short, was that Filipinos were consigned to the segregated "colony" of nonwhite, rightsless, brutally exploited laborers long subjugated *within* the western region of the metropole (Hayes 2017). Ngai (2004) has labeled this model of conscripted labor supply "imported colonialism," as it differed from both the classic European colonial exploitation of labor in foreign lands and domestic slavery in the US South, although it paralleled in some aspects racialized labor relations of the Jim Crow South. And in both regions, racism played a key role in undermining efforts to challenge the class foundations that oppressed poor whites and nonwhites alike. The result was that Filipino migrant workers found themselves thrust into a host of ongoing political conflicts—with white-capitalist employers, white workers, the broader white society, and other racialized ethnic groups of workers as well as among themselves—while endeavoring to cope with the harsh, bewildering new predicament.

Official Legal Foundations of Racial Exclusion

The domestic social environment of colonial rule over Filipinos in the metropole was shaped and facilitated in large part by official law. Indeed, a complex, volatile web of rules and practices constituted the repressive law system that constrained newly arrived migrants. At least four domains of law (Baldoz 2004) institutionalized this web: (1) federal immigration law regulating who could cross national boundaries and enter into U.S. territory, (2) federal naturalization law and judicial judgments that regulated who could be accorded citizen status, (3) a variety of national and mostly state laws that regulated how migrant workers were distributed among different sectors of the segregated labor market and social space, and (4) the discretionary judgments of officials about when and how to apply legal coercion to control the allegedly dangerous alien forces. This complex, mutable tangle of laws thus engendered a new stage of American state building that drew on and yet refashioned racial and class categories, boundaries, and hierarchies developed in the earlier eras of settler expansion, Southern Reconstruction, and overseas colonial ventures. Together, the social and legal forces that developed to address the "Filipino problem" added new dimensions to what Omi and Winant (1994) call the contested "racial formations" constructing group identity and sustaining white propertied domination over the terms of societal participation in the early twentieth century.

These racial formations were clearly evident in ever-changing laws regarding the fundamentals of citizenship. A series of exclusionary federal statutes and policies restricted both immigration and naturalization for nonwhites. In 1790 the first American naturalization law restricted citizenship to "free white persons" but was expanded after the Civil War to include "persons of African nativity" (Baldoz 2011, 72). The Chinese Exclusion Act in 1882 and the Scott Act of 1888 introduced a new era of racially constructed federal policy regarding immigration and naturalization. These acts clearly signaled commitments to restricting entry of immigrant populations from

Asia, including first the Chinese and then the Japanese, who were viewed as unqualified for membership in the national community of rights-bearing citizens. Congress authorized the new Bureau of Immigration and Naturalization in a 1906 act to administer more systematically the policing actions of naturalization courts in managing the plural populations and protecting the privileges of whites (Ngai 2003).

During the 1880s, Ngai has written, the number of excludable classes expanded to include

> [The] mentally retarded, contract laborers, persons with "dangerous and loathsome contagious disease," paupers, polygamists, and the "feeble-minded" and "insane," as well as Chinese laborers. The litany of excludable classes articulated concern over the admission of real and potential public charges as well as late nineteenth-century beliefs, derived from Social Darwinism and criminal anthropology, that the national body had to be protected from the contaminants of social degeneracy. (Ngai 2003: 73)

These restrictions were based on deeply rooted assumptions that Asians generally were "unassimilable." These governing premises were upheld as legally permissible by important Supreme Court cases (Ancheta 2006). The 1889 case of *Chae Chan Ping v. United States* was the first of what came to be known as the Chinese Exclusion Cases. The plaintiff was a Chinese citizen who moved to San Francisco in 1875 under the terms of the Burlingame Treaty, left in 1887 to visit his homeland, and then was forbidden reentry the next year under the terms of the 1888 Scott Act. The Supreme Court unanimously upheld a lower court ruling affirming the authority of exclusionary legislation to override an earlier treaty, in the process expressing deference to broad legislative and executive discretion in matters of immigration policy and enforcement. If absolute sovereignty was necessary to prevent foreign invasion by armies during wartime, the justices implied, why not also to restrict invasions by foreign migrants in peacetime (Ngai 2003, 71)?

It is worth noting that many of the justices who ruled in this case also ruled later in *Plessy v. Ferguson* (1896), which affirmed the constitutionality of Jim Crow segregation, as well as on federal Indian law (*Lone Wolf v. Hitchcock* [1903]) and the Insular Cases—all cases affirming the plenary authority of law constructing the racial republic (Saito 2003). This was long before the reconstructive rulings on constitutional law in *Brown v. Board of Education* and the 1960s civil rights and immigration legislation. The facts of the *Chae Chan Ping* case are also notable, for denying reentry to migrants who leave the United States temporarily would become a routine means of excluding political undesirables and disciplining those who stayed with the prospects of deportation. Congress followed up by passing additional Chinese exclusionary acts in 1892, 1902, and 1904.[5]

The Supreme Court expanded the terms of its initial ruling in subsequent cases to uphold these new legislative acts, including in *Fong Yue Ting v. United States* (1893), *Lem Moon Sing v. United States* (1895), and *United States v. Ju Toy* (1905). Justice David Brewer's dissent against the plurality ruling in *Fong Yue Ting* was important for its protest against broadly exclusionary legal authority. He argued that the penalties authorized by the Geary Act of 1892 were wrongly directed at persons lawfully residing in the United States and who thus deserved due process of law and constitutional guarantees. Brewer queried more generally that, while the sovereign power of the state was "directed only against the obnoxious Chinese" in that case, "who shall say it will not be exercised tomorrow against other classes and other people? If the guaranties of these amendments can be thus ignored in order to get rid of this distasteful class, what security have others that a like disregard of its provisions may not be resorted to?" (149 U.S. 698, 744). These concerns proved prescient as white nativist anti-immigrant sentiment and anticommunist Red Scares escalated over coming decades.

Arguably the high (or low) point of later developments in "white immigration policy" (De Genova 2004, 63) was the Immigration Act of 1924, also known as the Johnson-Reed Act. That act limited the annual number of immigrants who could be admitted from any country to 2 percent of the population from that country already living in the United States according to the 1890 census. While primarily aimed at restricting southern and eastern European along with African immigrants, it also completely banned Asians and Arabs. One important implication of the act was to create a new class of nonwhite people within the nation titled "illegal aliens," who were a social reality and yet were "impossible subjects" under law (Ngai 2004). The administration of immigration and deportation laws built on and entrenched further longstanding norms distinguishing between deserving and undeserving persons largely defined by reference to criminality, sexual deviance, and racial inferiority generally. Indeed, actual or attempted entry by unwanted persons itself was defined as criminal; persons identified as racially deviant in white society were criminalized in law simply by the fact of alien status and thus deprived of basic constitutional rights including due process and habeas corpus.

Such a racialized discourse shaped the exercise of broad administrative discretion by state officials, especially the newly authorized border patrol, and offered a legal rationale for resurgent nativist social interests (Ngai 2003). Immigration bans and active deportation became staple practices of population control and rallying cries of ascendant white nationalists for decades right up to the present day.

To the consternation of many white Americans, Filipino migrants were formally exempted from the reach of these legislated exclusionary prohibitions on entry to United States territory by the Supreme Court's ruling in the Insular Cases. These legal constructions deemed that Filipinos in the colonial era were formally neither US citizens nor aliens. Filipinos were designated instead as "nationals," as colonial subjects bound by loyalty to American sovereign authority but allowed to travel within and among the territorial borders of the United States. This novel and highly uncertain status posed a host of questions about the construction of Filipino identity within law. Most generally, how did they fit among the racial categories embedded in evolving statutory law? Were they of the "yellow race," or "Mongolians" like the Chinese and Japanese, or a distinct Malay race (Baldoz 2011; Ngai 2004)? Finally, Filipinos were clearly "separate and unequal," but what rights, if any, could such "wards of the state" claim (Bonus 2000, 38)?

The uncertainties of legal status and the broad discretion accorded to legal officials meant that determinations of Filipino entitlements in a host of contexts were highly variable, even arbitrary. For example, colonial nationals were formally denied rights to naturalization, but we shall see that the question of naturalization for Filipinos was hotly disputed and variably determined for some qualifying Filipinos in different institutional sites of the American state. As relative freedom of movement made Filipino nationals more visible, moreover, white citizens and officials became increasingly alarmed and ratcheted up legal constraints, policing, and social barriers to contain the allegedly unruly colonial subjects.[6] Specifically, Filipinos in many western states were denied basic rights to political participation, property ownership, marriage freedom, due process in criminal matters, and enforceable contracts with employers. "Equal protection" under the Fourteenth Amendment, guaranteed to noncitizens by *Yick Wo v. Hopkins* (1886), was circumvented in the ways invented for African Americans. First, constitutional protection limited only "state action," not "private" discrimination. Second, the Supreme Court had ruled that "separate" treatment was not "unequal," thus allowing many types of differentiated policies and practices for devalued foreigners (Ngai 2004, 6). Third, the Thirteenth Amendment prohibited "slavery . . . (and) involuntary servitude, except as punishment for a crime," constitutionalizing the practice of criminalization to mark relatively unfree, rightsless persons. Hence, while formally unique in legal status, Filipinos were to a large extent subjected to the same marginalized, exclusionary treatment as other Asian low-wage workers in the West and as black people in the South. Indeed, Filipinos arguably faced greater difficulties, because they could not claim the formal citizenship that African Americans gained after the Civil War, and they had no independent nation-state speaking for them, as had been the case for Japanese and Chinese migrants (De Witt 1979).

After passing the 1924 legislation excluding immigration by other groups, nativist activists redirected their attention to restrictions on Filipinos. In 1928, California Republican congressman Richard Welch introduced a bill that reclassified Filipinos as "aliens," thus banning further Filipino immigration. The bill failed, however, so nativists shifted their strategy to supporting the movement for Philippine independence. As with the coalition that opposed Philippine annexation several decades earlier, nativists formed an uneasy alliance with Filipino nationalists, in the colony and in the metropole, who had long fought for the goal of establishing a separate Philippine state and sovereign self-rule. Escalating nativist sentiments feeding widespread hostility toward Filipinos eventually led to passage of the Tydings-McDuffie Act in 1934, which committed to eventual independence for the Philippines as a "foreign country," imposed extremely strict immigration quotas on Filipinos, and changed the latter's status in the metropole to that of "aliens" (Ngai 2003, 120). The exceptional status as nationals, as wards of the state, no longer was binding from that date forward. But the marginalization of Filipinos as undeserving, foreign, racially inferior laborers continued as they transitioned from being "colonial subjects" to undesirable, illegal, rightsless aliens (Ngai 2003, 97). And this complex history of fundamentally racialized but shifting classifications of Filipinos—as also for black, Native American, Chinese, Japanese, Mexican, and other nonwhite people in the laboring class—played a fundamental role in constituting the evolving legal terms and variable social reality of citizenship in white-dominated America (Ngai 2004).

Official Promotion of Racism in American Society

As with US colonial rule in the Philippines, the racialized terms of legally defined membership status declared by the state both licensed and promoted, naturalized and normalized, rampant racism in social practice. Indeed, the racialized profiles of colonial subjects in the islands produced by the Third Philippine Commission's demographic studies were quickly reproduced by public officials for domestic audiences in the American metropole. Prominent among these institutions of imperial racial construction in the colonial era were popular public expositions and fairs.[7] Such expositions, President McKinley (who was assassinated at the 1901 Pan-American Exposition in Buffalo) proclaimed, are "timekeepers of progress" (Rydell 1984, 4). Historian Robert Rydell (1983, 1984) has demonstrated that these expositions and a host of spin-off fairs served, largely by design of America's political and corporate elites, to justify American racial exploitation of Filipinos at home as well as imperial rule abroad. The fairs were quite literally panoramas of American racial stereotypes masquerading as a mix of scientifically confirmed facts, propaganda extolling the benevolence of American imperial expansion, and popular circus-like entertainment.

The Louisiana Purchase Exposition in 1904, held in St. Louis, offered arguably the most important celebration of racial capitalist empire. Its largest exhibit was a Philippine village on a forty-seven-acre site that became temporary home to some 1,100 imported Filipinos. Initiated by the Philippine Commission, organized by the Philippine Exposition Board, and funded by a congressional appropriation of $1.5 million, its official goal was "giving to the people of the United States a more intimate knowledge of the resources and possibilities of the Philippine Islands" (Philippines Exposition Board 1904, 7). Departments of "Publicity" and "Exploitation" were formed and then merged to mobilize local press attention and stimulate attendance. School teachers were encouraged to attend and issued six hundred tickets a week.

The organizers decided that they could not represent all of the seventy or more Filipino groups identified by the commission, so they included representatives from three general groupings: "the least civilized in the Negritos and Igorots; the semi-civilized in the Bagobs and the Moros; and the civilized and cultured in the Visayans, as well as the constabulary and scout organizations" (Philippines Exposition Board 1904, 7). This division allowed white viewers to rank both foreign and domestic nonwhite peoples on a hierarchical scale of progress and civilization, thereby reinforcing popular understandings about the linkages between national expansion and racial group status. The most popular exhibit showed off many "specimens" of Igorot life—eating utensils, clothing, and especially simple arms and weapons of warfare. The Igorots were forced to dance and sing their native rituals while wearing skimpy loincloths daily in front of audiences, reducing their traditional, sacred customs to mere stage performances. They were portrayed as "dog-eating," "head hunting" savages and unruly children, much as were Native Americans. As the organizers wrote in their official report, "the world had already been informed of the dog-eating tastes of the Igorot and to this fact may be attributed no small part of the income of the Philippine Exposition" (Philippines Exposition Board 1904, 39). The Negritos were displayed as an aboriginal race of dwarves "dressed up like plantation nigger(s)," at least until they objected and donned their own native clothing (Baldoz 2011, 39). Newspaper coverage often used the term *monkeys* to characterize them. The contrast between these "wild tribes" and the educated, elite Philippine Constabulary underlined the Social Darwinian logic of hierarchical racial categorization and US refusal to grant autonomous self-governance to the majority of Filipinos. The alleged racial division between the Negrito and other Filipinos was constructed to maintain divisions central to the exclusivity of whiteness: most tribes could aspire to being white, but the Negrito, like black Americans, never could, while Igorots and Native Americans were condemned to liminal semicivilized status.

The successful 1904 exposition in St. Louis was followed by similar events elsewhere, including prominently in Portland (1905) and Seattle (1909). Portland's Lewis and Clark Centennial and American Pacific Exposition and Oriental Fair in 1905 more emphatically underlined the teleology of US imperial expansion as a mix of racial rule, civilizing uplift, and capitalist triumph. "This Exposition logically follows the great Exposition which commemorated the Louisiana Purchase," Vice President Charles Fairbanks explained on opening day, invoking Thomas Jefferson's vision of an expanding America. Fairbanks predicted "the future has much in store for you. Yonder is Hawaii, acquired for strategic purposes and demanded in the interest of expanding commerce. Lying in the waters of the Orient are the Philippines which fell to us by the inexorable logic of a humane and righteous war. We must not underrate the commercial opportunities which invite us to the Orient" (quote from Rydell 1984). The "Trail" scheme of the fair placed Filipinos alongside exhibits of Native Americans and Japanese, all using highly choreographed stereotypical representations offered through a hierarchical "white racial frame" (Trafford 2015). Both Native Americans and the Igorot were portrayed as wild, primitive, and warlike. If Native Americans were the vanishing past, then Filipinos, divided between the civilizable and noncivilizable, portended the future of imperial rule. The Philippine Village plan in Portland failed to win

Fig. 2 Governor-General James Smith, General Ira Nadeau, and other officials with Igorrote villagers and chief, Igorrote Village, Alaska-Yukon-Pacific Exposition, Seattle, Washington, 1909. Frank H. Nowell photographer. University of Washington Libraries, Special Collections, UW 28329z.

federal financial support, but local funders finally succeeded in producing the exhibit after delay and attracting great attention.

Seattle's Alaska Yukon Pacific Exposition in 1909 reproduced many of the themes. Constructed by the Olmstead brothers (as in Portland), directed by St. Louis Fair commissioner Henry E. Dosch, and troubled during construction by labor conflicts, the exposition was built on the grounds where the University of Washington now stands. The zoo-like Philippine Village was located where the William H. Foege Genome Sciences Building was completed in 2006.[8] As in early exhibits, Filipinos were portrayed as primitive people prone to spear throwing, endless fighting, skimpy clothing, head hunting, and dog eating. The July 11, 1909, *Seattle Times* ran a headline proven to draw crowds: "Igorrotes to Have Dog Feast." The university also followed practices elsewhere by inviting known anthropologists to present talks and undertake studies to confirm with scientific authority the inferior status of Filipinos highlighted in the circus-like shows.

In the years before World War I, white Americans thus were thoroughly primed by debates over empire, news about the savagery of stubborn rebels, and propaganda efforts such as those manifest in the expositions to assume that most Filipino migrants were inherently inferior and wild, potentially dangerous, uncivilizable, and unassimilable.

Dangerous Bodies: Sexual, Health, and Labor Contamination

The stereotypes produced in the expositions did not fit well the actual Filipino migrants who arrived in coming years, however. Most Filipino migrants to the metropole were Ilocanos rather than Igorots or Negritos. Indeed, the brown-skinned migrant laborers from agricultural peasant families shared much more in common with the mestizo elites catapulted by the *pensionados* program into American universities. They were mostly Christians, were educated in American schools, spoke English, dressed in Western clothing, and were familiar with American history, law, and popular culture (Ngai 2004, 109). They thus did not fit in appearance or cultural habits the stigmatizing "Oriental" stereotypes previously applied to Chinese and Japanese immigrants, while their agricultural work heritage distinguished them from stereotypes of Native Americans. American whites generally feared, scorned, and rejected Filipino migrants as inherently un-American, foreign, and unassimilable, to be sure, but attributions of undesirability had to draw on other racist conventions that constructed American identity. Already embedded in a racially segregated post-Reconstruction society, "white Americans could deny the 'American-ness' of Filipinos by ascribing to them attributions that derived from racial representations of African Americans, especially those that depicted black men as sexually aggressive," Mae Ngai astutely summarizes (2004,110; Balce 2006). In this way, Filipinos could be portrayed as wild, dangerous, backward, and undisciplined despite their adoption of familiar American traits. To some extent, they became identified with the familiar lack of discipline attributed to black people in the Jim Crow era. It thus is clear that delineations of racial difference were "the child of racism, not the father" (Coates 2015,7). Black, brown, red, and yellow were less descriptions of skin color than signifiers condemning some people to the bottom, as objects of exploitation for profit and yet pariahs immutably unfit for civil society.

The concentration of mostly young, single, physically lean, and seemingly "exotic" Filipino men in the third Asian wave created a great deal of sexual anxiety among white Americans that compounded growing racism (Tapia 2006). Especially important sites of this sexual tension were the taxi dance halls that popped up in West Coast towns. These clubs, where Filipino male patrons could pay ten cents for a dance, usually with lower-income white immigrant women, were important locales of boundary transgression and even resistance in white patriarchal society. For one thing, dancing was an important outlet for migrant "stoop workers" who labored all day in machine-like repetition of tasks picking lettuce or other agricultural work. The chance to move freely, exercise the entire body, and feel the music was liberating, offering moments defying and transcending the discipline of hard work (Parrenas 1998). Moreover, the opportunity to interact with white women itself was a form of resistance to the racial and sexual segregation imposed on Filipino men, who were usually single, "womanless," and segregated from whites (Ngai 2004, 111).

It is hardly surprising that white Americans were alarmed by the contravention of race, sexual, and class boundaries at the taxi halls. Many whites viewed Filipino men, who often dressed sharply and displayed charming manners, as sexually undisciplined and predatory "little brown monkeys" taking advantage of uneducated, working-class white women with few prospects among middle-class white men (Baldoz 2011). The facts that Filipino men were mostly single and that Filipina women were, after 1934, prohibited from entry further fed assumptions about the likely unchecked sexual drive of the male brown bodies. Yet others viewed Filipinos as the *victims* of female "white trash" whose promiscuity undermined the moral will and discipline of working-class men, thus underlining the latter's weak, childlike, undeveloped character. Hence, whether to protect white female purity or to enforce male migrant workers' discipline, white citizens became increasingly concerned about social and sexual contact between Filipinos and white women. As one member of the Fruit Grower's Supply Company management, an employer of many Filipino farmworkers, put it, "it is natural that most Americans hate to see a Filipino associate with a white woman, whether she be good, bad, or indifferent" (quoted in Parrenas 1998, 116).

Judge D. W. Rohrback in Monterrey County, California, gave an interview in 1930 referring to "little brown men attired like 'Solomon in all his glory' strutting like peacocks and endeavoring to attract the eyes of young American and Mexican girls." Unlike Negroes, who "usually understood how to act" among white women, he continued, "these Filipinos feel they have the perfect right to mingle with white people and even to intermarry and feel resentful if they are denied that right" (Baldoz 2011, 122). Elsewhere, he expressed worry about the Filipino who "won't keep his place." "The worst part of his being here is his mixing with young white girls from 13 to 17, buying them silk underwear . . . keeping them out till all hours of the night. And some of these girls are carrying a Filipino's baby around inside them" (quoted in Tashiro 2015, 37). Judge Rohrback successfully urged the local county Chamber of Commerce to pass a resolution excluding Filipinos from many areas. Starting in the late 1920s, whites imposed bans quarantining Filipino male workers to restricted spaces up and down the West Coast. "Positively No Filipinos [often with 'or Dogs'] Allowed" became familiar on banners implementing racially motivated practices of segregated social control (Tiongson Jr., Gutierrez, and Gutierrez 2006).

Starting in the late 1920s, as their population grew on the West Coast of the metropole, Filipinos increasingly were subjected to prohibitions specifically on interracial mixing and marriage. Laws criminalizing interracial marriage between white and black people had thrived throughout the American colonies since the seventeenth century and continued as policies in US states and territories until deemed unconstitutional in 1967 (Novkov 2008a, 2008b). Such laws defined a cornerstone of racialized and gendered legal order in America (Pascoe 2009). Prohibitions on Asian marriage to whites began to spread around California in the 1870s. By 1880, the state passed a law adding "Mongolians" to the list of racial groups ("Negroes," "mullatos") excluded from intermarriage with whites. Later amendments to this law would retroactively invalidate as "illegal and void" marriages between whites and "Mongolians" that had taken place before the passage of the law (Baldoz 2011, 89; Volpp 1999–2000). By the time that large numbers of Filipinos populated the metropole, many western states already had antimiscegenation statutes barring marriage between Asians and whites. As we shall review in later pages, the application of these statutes to Filipinos was much disputed, and some campaigns to prevent prohibitions on racial intermarrying were successful, as in Washington State. But the development of bans on interracial marriage, on movement and habitation, on property ownership, on political participation, and much more contributed to a dense web of race and class-based repressive law quarantining Filipinos by the 1930s.

The impetus to racial subjugation and exclusion grew from other concerns about the proliferation of foreign brown bodies amid white society. If the bachelor society of Filipino workers, which lacked the disciplining forces of bourgeois heterosexual family obligations, nurtured white fears of predatory behavior of men toward women, it also ironically enabled depictions as "feminized males"—small, thin, weak, ostentatious, even dandyish, thus potentially homoerotic and homosexual (Ngai 2004,113). Again, these fears of queered Filipinos were ironic given official legal restrictions on heterosexual racial intermarrying and on entry of Filipina women and wives to the metropole beginning in the late 1920s. Allegations of poor hygiene and disease—including meningitis and tuberculosis—as well as illicit drug use were also routinely voiced and rumored by whites regarding nonwhites. Indeed, Filipinos were purported to pose a public health risk (Volpp 1999–2000, 806; Baldoz 2011, 117–18). The Filipino, Judge Rohrback of Monterrey County testified, "through his unsanitary living habits is a disease carrier." The judge charged that the "Oriental" is "a spreader of meningitis germs among the products he handles, causing innocent persons to suffer through their consumption" (De Tagle 1930).

In all the ways enumerated above, Filipinos who were valued for the cheap labor performed by their disciplined bodies were at the same time feared as undisciplined and dangerous in body, mind, and habit. But even their disciplined bodies posed threats to many, specifically to the labor power of privileged white workers who often alleged that Asian workers took white jobs. San Francisco Municipal Court Judge Sylvain Lazarus thus protested about multiple interrelated evils: "It is a dreadful thing when these Filipinos, scarcely more than savages, come to San Francisco, work for practically nothing, and obtain the society of these [white] girls. Because they work for nothing, decent white boys cannot get jobs" (cited in De Vera 1994, 3). A letter by a veteran organizer of the AFL (American Federation of Labor), W. J. Henry, to the Seattle Central Labor Council claimed that Filipinos were "swarming" into the Northwest and crowding out white workers from the agricultural, lumber, and maritime sectors. The "intruders" were not only taking white workers' jobs, but they were a "narcotic menace" who posed a negative influence on young white people and were "marrying white girls" (*Seattle Star* 1929).

Contrary to such allegations, though, proletarian Filipinos did not actually threaten white jobs. Rather, Filipinos primarily competed with Mexicans and other Asians for low-wage agricultural jobs in the racially segregated labor market that whites generally would not accept. The deeper rift with white workers emanated instead from Filipino demands for equal wages with whites (Ngai 2004). As we will see in the next chapter, Filipinos began organizing in the late 1920s to advance their interests and rights as workers. They increasingly demanded equivalent wages not just as a matter of equity but also to diffuse hostility from whites who complained that cheap migrant labor drove down the wages of white workers in better jobs. Such increased Filipino labor militancy for better wages provoked animus among white farmers and workers alike, including those in Jim Crow AFL craft-based unions, regarding the entitlements of foreign, un-American, racially inferior workers. These same white resentments barred Filipinos, and Asians generally, from public employment, welfare benefits, and ownership rights to private property. And such repressive practices only increased as the Great Depression overtook the nation in the 1930s.

All in all, the intersectional fears of racial inferiority, predatory sexuality, and intraclass labor competition marked Filipinos as a danger requiring forceful control. White racial anxieties produced laws authorizing repressive regulation and segregation of Filipinos (and other ethnic laborers), which in turn reinforced the racist understandings and practices of dominant groups.

Escalating Social Violence

By the mid-1920s, a complex mix of anti-immigration proponents converged into a well-organized, politically potent force on the West Coast as evidenced by the passage of the 1924 Immigration Act and eventually the Tydings-McDuffie Act in 1934. Nativist opposition, which elected officials often exploited, was not restricted to the national legislative arena, however. As fears and resentment toward migrant Filipino nationals grew, white citizens increasingly acted out their racial hostility in violent ways, paralleling in graphic terms the ugly repression of previous Asian immigrants in the West and African Americans in the South.[9] Brutal assaults on individuals became more frequent, while mob attacks on Filipinos by white groups began to make and respond to news headlines. In the late 1920s, over twenty high-profile incidents of documented racial violence against Filipinos were reported in western states alone (Okada 2012; Baldoz 2011, 90).

The first large-scale vigilante incident was in the Toppenish district of the Yakima Indian Reservation, Washington, in 1927. Filipinos had been lured to the Yakima Valley to provide low-wage labor in local agricultural production, mostly harvesting crops of hops, cherries, potatoes, apples, and asparagus. Hundreds of Native Americans from the Pacific Northwest and Filipinos from Seattle joined the over thirty thousand workers enlisted for September harvests. The work often lasted no more than a week and paid $2–3 per day (Fujita-Rony 2003, 108–10). In November of 1927, incendiary newspaper coverage reporting inappropriate contact between Filipino men and white women as well as the threat of low-wage labor competition by migrant workers sparked vigilante action by whites. Over two days, mobs of white men descended on the town of Toppenish and assaulted Filipino laborers. Homes were destroyed, and migrants were apprehended, beaten, ordered to leave, and physically placed on trains by vigilantes. Any Filipinos who refused to leave were admonished that "they would be hung if found in the valley after dark" (cited in Baldoz 2011, 136). Local sheriffs ultimately halted and dispersed the mobs of heavily armed rioters and took the remaining Filipinos to jail for protection—an understandable but symbolically resonant initiative. Similar vigilante actions by large white mobs and lesser assaults against Filipino laborers were repeated a year later in nearby Cashmere, Washington, and became commonplace around the valley in subsequent years.[10]

Fig. 3 Map of the Western American metropole with sign warning "Filipinos Keep Out." From the *Filipino Forum*, January 15, 1929, next to an article reprinted from the *Seattle Star* warning that "Filipinos are swarming into the Northwest" and crowding out white workers. Article by Mark Mabanag, SCRLH. Image in UW Suzzallo Microforms and Newspaper Collection. Permission by James Gregory.

Violent vigilante actions soon exploded in California, where more than thirty thousand Filipino laborers were working by 1930. The initial signs of anti-Filipino sentiment emanated from a New Year's Eve barroom fight in Stockton, which the local paper portrayed as a "race war." This took place after years of concerted propaganda by the California Joint Immigration Committee—which was led by *Sacramento Bee* publisher V. S. McClatchy and included the Native Sons of the Golden West, the Jim Crow oriented AFL, and Congressman Ricard J. Welch and Senator Hiram W. Johnson—opposing the "Third Asiatic Invasion" of California (De Witt 1979; Baldoz 2011). Incidents of harassment became routine, but with the onslaught of the Great Depression, hostilities escalated in scale and number. In late October 1929, a large-scale anti-Filipino riot took place in Exeter, a small farming town in the San Joaquin Valley. The riots grew out of anger about farmers' use of Filipino labor to harvest figs and grapes. It was set off when, after days of harassment for commingling with white women, a Filipino laborer angrily knifed a white tormentor. A furious mob of three hundred, led by the local police chief, burned down the barn of a farmer who employed the Filipinos and then moved on to order all Filipinos in the labor camp to vacate the area. Newspaper coverage in surrounding communities aggravated hostilities with racist diatribes about the predatory sexual and labor threats of Filipinos.

It was in this context that Judge D. W. Rohrback launched his previously noted verbal assaults on Filipinos at taxi dance halls in a series of speeches and interviews in the media. A follow-up story in the Watsonville *Evening Pajaronian* ignited white mobs in the streets and five days of rioting in Watsonville. The events replayed the Exeter riots on a larger scale, involving an estimated seven hundred white protestors who forced dozens of Filipinos to find safety in a city council room and culminating in a murder when young Filipino worker Fermin Tobrera was shot through the heart with machine guy spray. For the most part, local police attempted to protect the Filipinos and used martial law enforcement to scatter mobs and stabilize the area in the following days. The murder sparked a surprising negative public reaction among many whites and calls for a coalition of police and citizens to restore law and order. Meanwhile, Filipino leaders protested Judge Rohrback's racist rants and assailed local politicians and business people for their role in stirring up anti-Filipino fervor. News about the riots traveled to the Philippines and led to protests in solidarity. Fermin Tobera's body was sent to Manila, where he quickly became a martyr symbolizing the Filipinos' struggle against an imperial oppressor and for national independence and equality (De Witt 1979).

Overall, though, Filipino leaders in the US metropole were deeply divided in their strategic political response. Most elected white leaders and the police enforced order but refused to prosecute for the murder, and hostility from the local white community continued to simmer. Local white townspeople vilified large agricultural corporations for their practices of hiring Filipino workers, while the AFL joined in to protest that megafarms, like sugar plantation owners in the Philippines, were undermining labor standards for white workers (Ngai 2004, 117). Racist stereotyping of Filipinos continued to saturate local news media and popular culture (De Witt 1979). In subsequent years, violence spread to Stockton, San Francisco, San Jose, Gilroy, Salinas, and other California communities. Much of the time, Filipinos were accused of instigating or causing the violence, adding a new chapter to the long American tradition of justifying brutal oppression by demonizing the racialized victims (Rogin [1975] 1991, 1987). Capital accumulation is a violent process, and Filipinos joined the many groups of racialized laborers who bore the brunt of oppression.

Violence against Filipino workers escalated and became more systematic and organized as they began to organize into unions during the 1930s. For example, the Associated Farmers in California worked closely with the State Bureau of Criminal Identification to create an elaborate espionage system following one thousand "dangerous radicals" and to orchestrate a "propaganda machine" to persecute union militants in the Cannery and Agricultural Workers' Industrial Union (CAWIU) who allegedly allied with communists. The well-financed industrial employers, with state assistance, surveilled workers constantly and forced them to live in guarded quarters with "no trespass" signs and bordered by barbed wire fences and moats. It was an era described by two contemporaneous journalists in the *Nation* as "organized terrorism" and "Fascism from above" (Klein and McWilliams 1934):

> The great company farm factories are watched by armed special deputies and machine-gun equipment has been installed in several establishments. Living in company camps, the workers are made to realize that they can be summarily evicted. The existence in the locality of a sturdy "stockade" is a visible warning of possible concentration. The threat of deportation is constantly used. . . . With state officials working under their direction to help ferret out, fingerprint, and incarcerate trouble-makers the organized big growers have sought to establish a network of "controls" throughout the state.

Constructed labor camps sprang up to corral intransigent workers. Such establishments were referred to as "a stockade, a cattle corral or a prison, and to its inhabitants as slaves or prisoners." Packing employers reportedly told the workers that the stockade was built "to hold strikers, but of course we won't put white men in it, just Filipinos" (Klein and McWilliams 1934). We shall see that fears of communist labor organizers would continue to fuel repression of Filipino rights claimants for the next several decades.

Criminals All: Bulosan's Incisive Imagery

Carlos Bulosan's fiction, and especially the semiautobiographical *America Is in the Heart* (1973), provides numerous vivid portrayals of the racist verbal assaults, routine acts of discrimination, individual physical attacks, mob violence, lynchings, and systematic repression endured by Filipino migrants in the late 1920s through the 1930s. Part 2 of the book focuses on the discrimination and violence that the author and other Filipinos initially experienced in the metropole. Many of the scenes that his prose describes are worth quoting, but we cite just one. Chapter 19 begins "It was now the year of the great hatred; the lives of Filipinos were cheaper than those of dogs" (1973, 143). Allos, the narrator (Bulosan), notes that he was beaten several times when he applied for jobs. At first, he innocently blamed or "responsibilized" other Filipinos who behaved badly and nurtured white prejudice, harbingering that this naive view would eventually grow into a more informed and politically astute "historical attitude." Allos then traveled by freight train to a small desert town where he was told that "local whites were hunting Filipinos by night with shotguns." His wariness increased with reports that a local labor organizer had been found dead in a ditch, so he adopted a low profile as a worker during harvest season. Bulosan's narrator then reports that a Filipino man came to town with his wife and was refused the opportunity to buy milk for his small child at a local restaurant. The proprietor knocked the man down and shouted loudly, repeating an incident like that described just a few pages earlier, "You goddamn brown monkeys have your nerve, marrying our women. Now get out of town." The narrator observes that "years of degradation came in to the Filipino's face. All the fears of his life were here—in the white hand against his face." The Filipino father retorted, only to end up bludgeoned unconscious by a horde of white men (1973, 144–45).

Allos follows this harrowing account with a spirited recounting of an escape journey to a large farm near Bakersfield. After noting that Filipinos were housed separately from Japanese workers to "forestall any possible alliance" among Asian workers, he reports hearing rumors that a nearby Filipino labor camp had been burned. "My fellow workers could not explain it to me. I understood it to be a racial issue, because everywhere I went I saw white men attacking Filipinos. It was but natural for me to hate and fear the white man." When, in the next lines, white men attacked the camp where Allos was staying, he and his friend Jose began to "run"—a desperate gambit that summarizes the individual Filipino experience chronicled in much of part 2 of *America Is in the Heart*. We learn that Allos successfully jumped on to a moving freight train, but Jose slipped and fell as railroad detectives chased them. "I thought he was dead. One foot was cut off cleanly, but half of the other was still hanging." In short, Jose lost his capacity even to run and evade, a critical expression of agency for strangers in a strange, hostile land. After a sympathetic old man drove them to the hospital, Carlos (Allos) "began to wonder at the paradox of America." Reflecting on the murderous railroad detectives and the white Americans who provided "refuge and tolerance," he asks, "Why was America so kind and yet so cruel?" (147).

This passage, and in fact the whole book, explains Bulosan's incisive words that to be a Filipino is to "feel like a criminal running away from a crime I did not commit." Bulosan's mature judgment, from what historian Carey McWilliams calls the "down under" or "bottom up view," was *not* that Filipinos typically performed acts that qualified them as criminals, as official accounts of US criminal law might suggest (Bulosan 1973, xx). Rather, "the crime is that I am a Filipino in America." Filipinos were criminalized for their racially constructed and class-based subject status—dark skinned, foreign, undisciplined, sexually predatory, unclean, unskilled, poor, homeless noncitizens—and then linked to imagined and sometimes real actions rather than the other way around.[11] Baldoz cites records of police officers in Seattle who confirmed the point about the intrinsic danger of Filipinos. "The Filipino is bad; by nature he is a criminal. . . . In addition, they intermingle with white girls," claimed one. Another officer added that "Filipinos are 'our great menace' and are 'all criminally minded'" (Baldoz 2004, 123). In short, Filipinos were routinely blamed for who they were and for events in which they were most often victims rather than perpetrators. As such, they were wholly deprived of possible status as rights-bearing individuals in the community of white property owners and accorded an exceptional status as undeserving of anything better than the arbitrary, violent, repressive law inherited from the traditions of slavery and Indian wars on the frontier. The designation as "nationals" marked their exceptional status and presumption of immutable criminality, justifying the exercise of illiberal state violence against them. As such, they were excluded from the liberal community of rights-bearing citizens but were very much subjected to the extreme violence of official law.

The experience of racial oppression toward "Filipino peapickers" was, Bulosan suggests, like that of the "first Indian that offered peace in Manhattan" and "the nameless foreigner, the hungry boy begging for a job and the black body dangling from a tree." This is the essence of how race and class hierarchies thrive in the white American legal imagination, the author implies, especially through the tropes of criminalization. After all, the Thirteenth Amendment allowed the extreme punishment of "slavery or involuntary servitude" for those defined as the equivalent of rightsless criminals. In short, to be a Filipino was to be a criminal in many senses and thus to become a laboring commodity subject to extreme, arbitrary, but pervasive violence and subjugation by the dominant white propertied population. Indeed, they were condemned to a status of rightslessness, arguably below that of a legal criminal, because they lacked due process and habeas corpus legal protections. Such sustained, symbolically redolent violence by white state officials and social groups against Filipinos continued a legacy of terrorism in the United States drawn from the historical playbook of white repression against African Americans, Native Americans, and other people of color.[12] And that is just how Bulosan (1973, 119) puts it: "I was in flight again, away from an unknown terror that seemed to follow me everywhere." And it was through this "criminalization of everyday life" that American law manifest its most pervasive and palpable constitutive power in the lives of Filipino migrant workers (Merry 1998). Their aspirations to become rights-bearing subjects were, as Ngai (2004) put it, "impossible."

Aspirations of the Heart: Equality, Freedom, and Rights Politics

Filipinos Labor Activists' Quest for Rights

As Stephanie Hinnershitz (2013, 133) summarizes, "Filipinos who migrated and settled along the West Coast realized that their racial background overruled their rights to protection from harm and discrimination in America." As already noted, however, many Filipino migrants continued to believe in the promise of equality, freedom, and rights that had lured them to America even if those promises were not fulfilled in practice. The ideal of equal rights was, to recall Carlos Bulosan, the America "in the heart" for those who migrated from the colonized island to the metropole.[13] As such, many Filipinos developed what Du Bois called a double consciousness or even what Cornel West calls a triple consciousness—as racialized Asian foreigners, as colonial subjects, and as Americans—at once denied basic rights yet aspiring to become respected, rights-bearing members of the American community (West 1982; see also Ancheta 2006; Hinnershitz 2013, 133). Bulosan's chronicle provides a window into the pervasive investment in demanding the promises of rights despite the experienced fact of routine denial. Indeed, Bulosan's semifictional characters repeatedly turn the promises of rights for all persons into a critique of the status quo and an agenda of collective transformative action. In this regard, *America Is in the Heart* is a narrative of intellectual and political awakening—and specifically the development of a critical, committed "radical egalitarian" rights consciousness by Allos and his comrades—that reflects in profound ways on the early experiences of Filipino migrant workers (Merry 1990; McCann 1994; Lovell 2012).

Bulosan's chronicle identifies that the first stage of awakening was disillusionment with the ideals of American promise and recognition of the naked struggles for domination that characterized American racialized capitalist culture. Alfredo thus exhorts, "Open your eyes. . . . This is a country of survival of the fittest" (Bulosan 1973, 170). In a brutal world defined by greed, fear, resentment, and exploitation, alternative experiences of justice, fairness, love, and equal rights were elusive for Filipinos. Bulosan's tale underlines that the migrants first had to find ways to survive in the harsh new conditions, which meant learning basic skills of evading and dodging violence when they could not elicit kindness or conciliate members of the dominant white society with docile demeanor and simple hard work. Hence, Bulosan's dominant motif is of everyday resistance by the migrants—that of astute vigilance and readiness to "run" from ever-present dangers. Part 2 of *America Is in the Heart* is a fast-paced log of constant motion, both traveling to find short-term work and escaping from angry mobs of citizens, police, detectives, and other enforcers of hierarchy. At the same time, both words and actions expressed undaunted defiance. Filipino men continued illicit practices of cavorting and cohabiting with white women, of pursuing work where they could find it, and of chasing their dreams of a good life in America.

As the story progresses, though, disillusionment increasingly gives way to more refined critical sensitivity about the gap between the promises and practiced denials of basic rights to Filipinos. Early in part 4, Allos hears a conversation at a Communist Party meeting about the contradictions of America that crystallizes his developing defiant rights consciousness:

> "How come we Filipinos in California can't buy or lease real estate?" a man asked.
> "Why are we denied civil service jobs?" asked another.
> "Why can't we marry women of the Caucasian race? And why are we not allowed to marry in this state?"
> "Why can't we practice law?"
> "Why are we denied the right of becoming naturalized American citizens?"
> "Why are we discriminated against in relief agencies?"
> "Why are we denied better housing conditions?"
> "Why can't we stop the police from handling us like criminals?"
> "Why are we denied recreational facilities in public parks and other such places?"
>
> (Bulosan 1973, 268–69)

And from that moment of questioning directly the hypocrisy of the dominant society, Allos/Carlos decides to become an activist and writer committed not just to documenting the contradictions of American dreams but also encouraging action to turn the promises of equal rights against the practical reality of hierarchical relationships and brutal experiences. In short, many Filipinos not only challenged white claims about their criminal status but they did so from an aspirational normative standpoint as equally deserving rights-bearing "citizens."

The process of adjustment to life in American society by most Filipinos thus was not a predetermined, easy, orderly, or natural outcome willingly granted by white-capitalist society, as is often suggested in standard accounts about immigrants. Filipinos survived and then began to thrive through persistent political and legal struggles for general status as rights-bearing citizens and for specific rights claims. At first, many of their demands for rights were reactive and defensive, often following experiences of brutality. For example, Bulosan relates an episode of detectives breaking into a Filipino man's apartment and taking him to jail for cohabiting with a white divorcee. "You can't do this to me. . . . I know my rights. I haven't committed any crime" (Bulosan 1973, 136). As a result of that humiliating experience, the man went on to become an international lawyer fighting "against injustice and intolerance." Individual stories like that one permeate the quasi-autobiographical novel.

Or consider a well-documented historical event. The leading Filipino newspaper in California responded to the harassment and mob actions at Exeter in 1929 by insisting that Filipino workers were guaranteed the same rights as white American laborers. The Los Angeles–based weekly, *Ang Bantay*, editorialized that white-Filipino violence could only be relaxed through ending the double standard of justice, housing, and jobs that marginalized Filipinos. This was a bold statement, one that was not immediately followed by many other Filipino newspapers, which were intimidated into endorsing acceptance of second-class status (De Witt 1979, 295). The exact balance of defiant rights claiming and resignation is difficult to assess, but it is worth recalling Judge Rohrback's inflammatory statement that unlike Negroes who "usually know how to act . . . these Filipinos feel they have the perfect *right* to mingle with white people and even to intermarry and feel resentful if they are denied that right" (Baldoz 2011, 122).

The Development of Community Support Networks

A concerted politics of rights among Filipinos was greatly enhanced by the development of support networks (Epp 1998; McCann 1994) that represented and advocated for rights causes. Over time a host of newspapers like *Ang Bantay* became important players taking up the cause of advocating equal rights for Filipinos. Especially important was the *Filipino Forum*, a Seattle-based "mouthpiece of enlightened Filipino opinion," founded, published, and edited by Victorio Velasco, a prominent community leader who had become a labor activist while working in the Alaskan canneries (M. S. Brown 2007; Mabanag 2005). Starting in 1928, the newsletter routinely called for Philippine independence and assailed discrimination against Filipinos in all spheres of American social life—housing, education, jobs, voting, and more.

The case for independence was framed in terms of ideological consistency, of closing the hypocritical gap between American deals and practice. An editorial in early 1929 thus cited Judge Williams, of San Francisco, proclaiming that "Filipinos became subjects of the United States without their volition." Hence, "so long . . . as the Islands remain under the American flag, we are obligated . . . to accord the Filipinos the same right and privileges that we apply or extend to the inhabitants of any other territory of the United States." A following editorial affirmed support for the new Katipunan's work to win Philippine independence as well as equal rights of Filipinos in America: "We believe in race equality . . . demand just treatment everywhere, and oppose discrimination on account of color, and insist on equal protection of the laws." Citing a host of atrocities against Filipinos, from Washington State to California, the editors assailed the unconcern of whites and the Filipino government alike. "Its indifference is criminally accountable as is the propaganda that has impelled American citizens to shoot down Filipinos" (*The Philippine Review* 1931). Other newspapers, like the *Philippine Advocate*, also were important. For example, the newspaper provided a forum for an influential essay by University of Washington graduate and later cannery workers' union president Trinidad Rojo, who protested against US exclusionary practices and for inclusionary policies (Rojo 1935). Up and down the West Coast, other Philippine newspapers chronicled ongoing deprivations as well as defenses of basic rights, although they often divided and competed ideologically. Such newspapers were widely read because they reported "News from the Homeland" and included many columns written in the native language of Tagalog.

A variety of community organizations provided material aid and education as well as generated a sense of Philippine identity and pride in diasporic communities. Some organizations, such as the Balagtas Society, which promoted the Tagalog language, pursued explicitly nationalist identity-building goals. Fraternal lodges—including the Caballeros de Dimas-Alang (CDA), the Legionnarios del Trabayo, and the Gran Oriente Filipino—not only provided social services such as burials, but they infused Philippine nationalism and rights consciousness into a wide range of community activities. The Dimas-Alang, which was founded as part of the resistance movement against Spain and moved overseas in the early 1920s, in particular aimed to keep alive the egalitarian dreams of the Katipuneran revolutionaries and supported inclusionary rights-based political causes. Such fraternal groups thrived in part because white lodges excluded Filipinos and other people of color and also because some of them provided spaces for involvement by the limited female Filipina population. The Filipino Community was a formal umbrella organization in Seattle that took up the cause of Filipino representation and solidarity (Nonato 2016).

Religion was also an important part of Filipino American community life with both Catholic and Protestant (often Methodist) members. "Religion and church life have always been an integral part of the Filipino American experience" (Cordova 1983, 167). The YMCA was a critical support network for Filipino and Japanese students in Seattle and other cities (Hinnershitz 2015). The Filipino Catholic Club was an especially vibrant center in many communities. Religious ties, along with regional and ethnic differences, were as much a source of division as solidarity in defining political positions during and following the colonial experience, however. These fissures between "neighborhood" and "community" often limited the commitments to rights and political agendas of Filipinos in America (Nonato 2016). Rizal Day, one of the most important community events celebrated every December 30 in most Filipino communities, long has been exemplary of the tensions that divided colonial subjects and later generations of Filipino American citizens. Initiated to celebrate the heroic rebellion against Spanish imperialists, the day provided a focus for unifying Philippine nationalism but generally was organized by business and community elites and hence tended to mute or exclude voices that were anti-American, anticapitalist, or politically radical. In such a context, celebrating the rights of Filipinos was often left to vague and safe platitudes (Guyotte and Posadas 1995; Fujita-Rony 2003, 162).

It also is important to recognize that Filipinos could count on some support and protection from the official criminal justice system. We noted above that police often broke up mobs and provided some security as well as rough justice for Filipinos. For example, in early January 1931, a dozen "American young men" forced their way into a house rented by Filipinos near Kent, Washington, badly beat up several of the workers, and stole their most valuable possessions. The justice of the peace in Seattle filed charges against ten of the attackers, and Judge B. Wright sentenced them to six months suspended sentence in the county jail. He explained to them that "your attack on these men was uncivilized and un-American. This is a country in which everyone has a right to labor" (*Philippine Review* 1931). Again, this example illustrates that the promise of equality of American law was not entirely a sham and that noncitizen migrant workers had some reason to hope that rights could be won over time (E. P. Thompson 1975).

The most important support structures and associational resources for robust egalitarian rights activism, however, developed in the 1930s around labor unions, radical political associations, progressive lawyers, and interrelated networks of Left activists grounded in the Philippines, the US West Coast, and internationally. These ventures are the subject of the following two chapters.

A Politics of Rights: Three Episodes of Struggle

We complete this chapter with brief accounts of several quite different modes of struggle for rights by Filipinos, each different in form, in the hostile metropole of American empire. The first case study focuses on litigation, mostly by individual plaintiffs. The second features a mix of strategic political actions circumventing and subverting official law along with litigation aiming to challenge the laws. The third mixes litigation and grassroots political mobilization to challenge repressive legislation that restricted individual rights. As we shall see, these cases involved both individual actions and collective struggles; each legacy also resulted in different types of direct and indirect effects on the lives of Filipinos in the colonial era. Not the least of the effects was to compel American officials at least to recognize and respond publicly to Filipino challenges regarding unjust laws. As Francesca Polletta (2000, 388) argues regarding the African American civil rights struggles, "the legal rituals of formal hearings . . . made public the mechanics of white supremacy and forced white officials to acknowledge and justify them." Our primary interest, however, is less in the relative success of specific rights claims than in the varied, creative aspirational struggles themselves as expressions of agency by a poor, exploited subject population and as precedents for action that became part of the Filipino political legacy and identity.

Immigration, Citizenship, and Naturalization: Pressing for a Military Service Exception

One critical legal challenge concerned the potential for naturalization of Filipinos who migrated to the United States. This issue tested and exposed the fundamental tension explored in previous pages among competing principles of US citizenship—between a universalistic position grounded in belief in common national values on the one hand and the dominant view privileging ethnocultural membership in a common white European heritage on the other (Calavita 2005; Smith 1997; Sohoni and Vafa 2010). While Filipino colonial nationals were clearly categorized as noncitizens of the United States and ineligible for naturalization by the Insular Cases, some of them sought to create exceptions for those who were discharged honorably from service in the American military (Baldoz 2011, 74–86). In 1908, a Washington State district court had ruled that a Japanese born claimant, Buntaro Kumagai, was not entitled to naturalization after military service because an 1862 congressional statute limited the privilege to US-born "white people" and, after the Civil War, to African Americans; Japanese born persons were both aliens and nonwhite, and thus not eligible.[14] In this and several other cases, US federal courts implicitly affirmed the authority of Congress to regulate unilaterally the naturalization of aliens on racially or ethnically based grounds. It was not clear, though, whether this decision applied to Filipinos, who at the time were legally defined as *not* aliens but were treated by white society as a foreign menace and as undeserving by race. Some Filipinos found hope in Section 30 of the 1906 naturalization law allowing residents of the US territories who were neither aliens nor citizens to obtain citizenship (Ancheta 2006, 97). Did the act of 1906, which aimed to create uniform rules for naturalization and led to the establishment of the Bureau of Immigration and Naturalization, alter the prevailing racial basis of citizenship?

The first case that pressed for naturalization of Filipino servicemen was *In re Alverto* (1912). The district court in Pennsylvania cited the *Kumagai* ruling in denying Filipino claimants naturalization after US military service both on the basis of "racial qualifications" and the fact that Filipinos were not aliens, a requirement for naturalization. Subsequently, at the outset of World War I, in which the numbers of Filipino service men rose to six thousand, Congress passed the act of June 30, 1914, granting citizenship for aliens who were honorably discharged after serving four years in the military. This again opened the question of whether Filipinos, who were neither aliens nor citizens, could earn citizenship through disciplined military service.

With mixed results, Filipino retirees from service filed multiple lawsuits to win their citizenship. A district court ruling in New York (*In re Rallos* [1917]) generally affirmed the restrictive position in *In re Alverto*. By contrast, in the case of *In re Mallari* (1916), Massachusetts district court judge Morton used the record of legislative hearings to determine congressional intent. The judge argued that Congress intended to expand naturalization rights to those born in Puerto Rico and the Philippines who completed US military service, although the plaintiff Mallari was ruled ineligible for procedural reasons. The District Court of Northern California issued a similar ruling for a Filipino claimant in *In re Bautista* (1917), affirming congressional intent to expand "the admission to citizenship of all persons not citizens who owed permanent allegiance to the United States," although other terms of qualification were added. Naval service met such qualifying criteria (245 F. 765, 771). Clearly, persistent rights mobilization exploiting contradictions in white racial constructions was creating new legal paths to citizenship in some venues and expanding the political questions at stake. At the same time, none of the court rulings challenged in general terms the constitutional status of congressionally established ethnoracial qualifications for naturalization (Sohoni and Vafa 2010).

The questions raised by the earlier cases were answered in part by affirmative congressional legislation a few years later. In the act of May 9, 1918, Congress clarified that "Filipinos" and "Porto Ricans," along with aliens, who honorably served in the US military were eligible for naturalization. Another act a year later expanded eligibility to any person of foreign birth who served in the US military. The motivation for the legislation owed greatly to the pressures of wartime service recruitment and the ideological appeal of warrior-citizen ideals. In addition, the vague congressional language left room for conflicting interpretations (Salyer 2004). Indeed, in subsequent years, a trio of cases, led by *Toyota v. United States* in 1925, affirmed the inclusion of Filipinos and Puerto Ricans along with whites and African Americans in naturalization eligibility, but the rulings sustained the position that other Asians were excluded (Sohoni and Vafa 2010).[15] These decisions had several effects. They arguably clarified and minimized while sustaining contradictions in race-based precedents for naturalization. Indeed, Filipino claimants in the service thus found incentives to demonstrate their unique ethnic status along with their disciplined loyalty to unifying American ideals. Beyond formal law, these rulings emphasizing ethnic difference arguably undermined incentives for multi-Asian political and legal alliance, compounding the fragmenting ethnic and racial divisions in workplace organization and societal racial politics (Baldoz 2011).

This confusion about how ethnicity and race figured into naturalization was modified yet further years later after the Tydings-McDuffie Act. The act of June 24, 1935, stipulated that any alien military veterans who served honorably over specified years of World War I then were eligible for naturalized citizenship. But the criteria of naturalization eligibility again were restricted to categories that excluded members of Asian groups outside of Filipinos. During World War II, as we shall see, Chinese exclusion was repealed, and the 1952 Immigration and Nationality Act eliminated all racial categories from naturalization exclusion. This latter change owed largely to the complexities of Cold War racial politics (Dudziak 2000; Parker 2009), but persistent Filipino legal mobilization had provided additional pressures and precedents for policy reform. Moreover, it is clear that the later struggles for rights not only benefitted Filipinos relative to other Asian groups but also helped to expose and question the arbitrary and contradictory racial politics of citizenship law generally in the United States, in turn supporting inclusion of other Asians. "These judicial decisions . . . had a significant impact on the evolution of American national identity" (Sohoni and Vafa 2010, 148–49). We shall see that this is just an early example of how Filipino workers' rights mobilization efforts figured into the erratic legal development of the twentieth-century American racial capitalist regime.

Landownership and Leasing: The Long Struggle over Property Rights

A second terrain of protracted contestation concerned property rights of Filipinos in the western states.[16] Consistent with government policies promoting westward expansion in the previous century, the Washington Territory passed its first alien land laws in 1864. These laws authorized and encouraged aliens to own land *as if* they were citizens. The goal was to attract white residents who might farm the land in order to displace Natives from their traditional terrains and promote economic development (Grant 2008). The policy worked; the white population grew rapidly, although the eastern part of the state proved too arid for profitable farming. This in turn prompted a combination of private and federal government investment in irrigation following statehood in 1889. Before long, the Yakima Valley became known as the "Fruit Bowl of the Nation" for the abundant apples, cherries, pears, grapes, and other fruits grown in the area.

Some of the best terrain for fruit and vegetable crops was on the Yakima Indian Reservation. The US federal government encouraged Native Americans to cultivate the land and increase their revenues by leasing it at low cost to farmers. From the start, the majority of lessees were white. Japanese immigrants early in the century were prohibited by law from owning land, but they were initially permitted to lease or contract hundreds of acres from the Indians for farming. However, Washington State followed California in passing two new alien land laws, in 1921 and 1923, that prohibited leasing, renting, and sharecropping by aliens who had not declared their intentions to become US citizens. Application of the law to the "unassimilable" Japanese aliens, who were ineligible for naturalization, was upheld by the US Supreme Court in *Terrace v. Thompson* (1923). State law technically was not binding on reservation lands, but the standard policy was one of comity, so the Yakima Indian Agency for the most part refrained from issuing new leases to Japanese persons looking to settle after 1923. The laws prohibiting aliens from landownership and leasing thus extended to Asians the same white racist policies regarding property rights previously directed at Native Americans (Grant 2008). Property rights remained a privilege of whiteness, and whiteness conferred a host of privileges that were sustained and enjoyed as a form of property (C. Harris 1993).

As hostility from white workers and then Depression pressures restricted access to farm labor jobs for migrant Asian workers, some Filipinos, like the Japanese before them, began to lease lands from the Indians for truck farming. It is relevant to recognize that Filipinos were largely motivated by aims to secure independent control as small-scale agricultural producers—somewhat akin to their experience as peasants, sharecroppers, or independent landowning farmers in their homeland—and to create a bulwark against subjection to status as permanently proletarianized workers in mass agricultural production for white-capitalist elites. Their aspiration for landownership or control thus was less one of bourgeois assimilation than economic resistance, paralleling an earlier generation of white anticorporate Populist farmers and concurrent black farmers in the post–World War I South seeking to escape the bonds of tenancy and, as we shall see, drawn to affiliation with communists (Kelley 2015).

The creative leasing arrangements with Native tribes inevitably raised the question of whether the alien land laws also applied to Filipinos, who technically were not aliens. From 1926 to 1932, the national Office of Indian Affairs equivocated when asked for rulings, implicitly allowing the Yakima Reservation superintendents discretion to defer to the state laws and discriminate against Filipinos. Filipinos in turn followed the Japanese model of negotiating labor contracts as farm "employees" of Indian owners or white intermediaries that functioned like leases, although the Filipinos generally remained independent farmers in practice. These creative legal tactics generally survived challenge not least because a great deal of land remained unleased and thus uncultivated. Filipinos obtained yet other leases by marrying Native or white women who could legally lease as well as by sharing secured tracts with other Filipinos. In this way, the population of Filipino settlers grew in the Yakima Valley during the late 1920s. In fact, a Filipino Farmers' Marketing Cooperative was formed in 1935 to coordinate the sales and delivery of their produce. But these developments also provoked escalating backlash by white farmers and workers against the "barbaric black natives" (Normura 1986–1987, 103). The violent vigilante episodes in Wapato and around the valley mentioned in previous pages were motivated in large part by Filipino gambits with strategic land leasing as well as endeavors as wage laborers.

Washington state officials responded to nativist pressures with efforts to take control of the situation. In 1935, Yakima Reservation superintendent C. R. Whitlock initiated a ban on the creative labor agreements by noncitizen Asians. The Secretary of the Interior overruled such action because of the financial harm to Indians and unsettling international implications. The state governor then responded by ordering the attorney general to sue five Filipinos who subleased reservation land, alleging a violation of the alien land laws; all five pled guilty. Despite a 1937 opinion by a Yakima County deputy prosecuting attorney that Filipinos were not aliens, the state legislature went on to amend the 1921 alien land law to define aliens as "all persons who are non-citizens" and who were "ineligible" for citizenship by naturalization. The 1937 alien land law criminalized all alien contracted corporations, and the state shut down the Filipino Marketing Cooperative. In the same year, the same state investigator who previously prosecuted the five Filipino lessees arrested another dozen Filipinos for perjury regarding their violation of the new alien land law amendments through faux labor agreements.

This aggressive action by state prosecutors led Roy Baldoz and other local activists to form a social justice advocacy organization, the Filipino Community of Yakima Valley, one of many such groups that Filipinos would organize to defend their rights during the twentieth century. They hired attorney Charles F. Bolin. Widely recognized as a local baseball star and cowboy as well as gifted lawyer, Bolin lived in what was purportedly the finest home on the Yakima Indian Reservation. He fought the perjury charges in multiple stages of proceedings and on numerous grounds, but Judge Arthur McGuire ruled that Filipinos were aliens under the state law and that state law in this instance could apply to the Indian reservations. Two defendants were found guilty as charged at trial and, then, the rest pleaded guilty and received jail sentences of six months. The Filipinos and their attorney nevertheless persisted, eventually winning release after repeated appeals.

This battle for land rights in the courts generated a large-scale mobilization effort within the Filipino community, one that again harbingered similar efforts in later years. The Filipino Community of Yakima Valley appealed to labor unions and community groups, to the US president and congressional leaders, and to officials in the Philippines as well as to individual local community members. After hearing from many sectors, the Commissioner of Indian Affairs responded that a legal ruling from a high court was necessary to settle the matter. This in turn prompted the Filipino Community group to join the case initiated by a Filipino in Seattle, Pio De Cano, then on appeal to the State Supreme Court. A Philippine native born in 1894, De Cano migrated to the United States in 1911 and in 1914 became a resident of Seattle. He began working in the Alaskan salmon canneries in 1916, initially as a laborer, then as foreman, and eventually as a prosperous labor contractor. De Cano had positioned himself as a major community leader by the time of his legal dispute (Fujita-Rony 2003, 100, 133). The dispute arose from the fact that despite never having served in the US military and thus remaining ineligible for naturalization, De Cano shrewdly filed a declaration of intent to naturalize in order to qualify for purchasing a tract of land in Seattle. After the purchase, a King County prosecutor charged De Cano with violating the state alien land law. His case raised a variety of issues, including whether Filipinos should be counted as "aliens," the relationship between De Cano's eligibility for naturalized citizenship and his declared intention to naturalize, and the constitutionality of the land act amendments (Baldoz 2011, 109).

On April 18, 1940, De Cano triumphed when a King County Superior Court issued a declaratory judgment that the 1937 alien land act amendments were unconstitutional. While symbolically significant, the initial court victory did not translate directly into a change in state policy or practices. State officials appealed to the Washington State Supreme Court and held firm to their position on the status of Filipinos under the land act, granting them no more leases. The Filipino Community of Yakima Valley at that point, before the Supreme Court ruled, changed their tactics for advancing their rights. Following the advice of the Philippine Resident Commissioner, they formulated and passed a resolution in 1940 proposing that three thousand acres of Yakima land be leased to Filipinos and sent the proposal to a variety of high-level government agencies. The Filipino Community presented their case directly to the Yakima Tribal Council in 1941 with strong support from key Native American leaders who aimed to promote competition against the monopolistic efforts of the white grange groups and testified that Filipinos were hardworking, reliable tenants. In short, Filipinos brilliantly exploited an opportunity created by the plural legal systems that governed racially differentiated populations in the western states.

Concurrently, the Washington State Supreme Court ruled on the De Cano case. The Court's en banc ruling in February 1941 denied standing to the Seattle Filipino Community Clubhouse because the corporate body had not suffered a direct injury, but standing was affirmed for De Cano. The court then dismissed De Cano's declaration of intent to naturalize as lacking feasibility due to the ineligibility of Filipinos with no military service for citizenship: "citizenship by naturalization is limited to the white race with the exception of Aliens of African nativity and persons of African descent" (at 614). More important, though, the court ruled that the amendment "relating to the rights and disabilities with respect to land" was not sufficiently broad to warrant inclusion in an act regarding "non-citizens . . . ineligible to citizenship by naturalization," such as Filipinos (at 614). In short, the amendment was unconstitutional, so the issue of De Cano's declared intent was moot (Baldoz 2011, 11). As if to underline once more the lack of respect for judicial institutions, however, the attorney general persisted in his resistance, and the state legislature attempted to pass another new law again restricting Filipinos. This time, however, the bill failed to win the required votes. Fortified by the support from multiple state courts and the Tribal Council, Filipinos persevered in demanding their rights to leases in 1941.

As often is the case in long-term struggles, events beyond the local actors' control transformed the larger context, in this case benefitting the Filipinos. In the language of social movement scholars, the opportunity structure (McAdam 1996) for rights claiming by Filipinos opened up in positive ways, forging a new "interest convergence" (Bell 1980) between the dominant white population and former colonial subjects. In short, we shall see how World War II radically altered the white public views of Filipinos, both elevating them above the Japanese "enemy race" and highlighting the needs for Filipino farmers' contributions to expanded wartime food production. The commissioner relented in 1942, granting the Indians authority to lease to Filipinos but in conditional terms related to wartime exigencies.

This was a major legal victory for Filipinos. Gail Nomura's pithy conclusion is apt: "Ironically, a world war had to be fought before Filipinos as allies in arms were granted legal rights to lease land" (Nomura 1986–1987, 113; see also Klinkner and Smith 1999). But the advance came at the price of increasing state surveillance of Filipinos and government capacity to compel military enlistment by denying deferrals. Moreover, this progress did not offset two decades of restrictions on developing economic power as independent farmers along with pervasive labor market discrimination, racial barriers on citizenship, and denials of marriage freedom that substantially undercut the social position of Filipinos. The net result was that large numbers of Filipinos relinquished dreams of control over small-scale production and were driven into wage labor within expanding military and large-scale capitalist industrial production. Nevertheless, the small victories of struggles for rights to land leases figured prominently in the historical memory of Filipino workers who would continue to fight for inclusion and political transformation in the following decades.

Challenging Antimiscegenation Laws: A Tale of Filipinos in Two States

We noted earlier that the fears of white Americans about Filipino male hypersexuality drove campaigns to pass antimiscegenation laws up and down the West Coast. Such efforts to protect white women and racial purity reinforced white male patriarchal privilege (Gillmer 2012; Baldoz 2011) while denying Filipinos basic rights of association, sexual intimacy, marriage contracts, reproductive capacity, and kinship units that could facilitate personal support and capital accumulation over time. As Novkov (2008b, 16) has argued, antimiscegenation law constituted a key site "for the creation, articulation, rationalization, and ultimately reflection of the supremacist state, through its attention to the meaning of racial boundaries."[17] Not surprisingly, Filipinos challenged such laws and advocated for their rights through litigation as well as collective political action. We briefly recount actions in the quite different political contexts of California and Washington State.

During the tumultuous era of Chinese exclusion during the 1870s, the California legislature imposed statutory prohibitions on marriage between whites and Asians. In 1880, the category of "Mongolians" was added to the list of races ineligible to marry whites, and in 1905, the state civil code made the ban retroactive to include marriages between Mongolians and whites before 1880. Once again, uncertainty arose regarding the status of Filipinos, although the issue was more about racial classification than legal status as colonial nationals. The question became important because Filipinos, unlike Chinese and Japanese, commonly and openly flouted the marriage bans, thus compelling state officials to ratchet up enforcement actions. As legal historian Rachel Moran (Moran 2003, 36–37) has summarized, the Filipino response to miscegenation laws was generally "not compliance, but defiance." In California, which by the mid-1920s had the largest Filipino population on the West Coast, the Joint Immigration Committee assailed Filipinos as the source of a major "sex problem." Representative V. S. McClatchy argued that Filipinos were the "worst form of Orientals" because of the "criminal nature in which we find them engaged . . . in the delinquency of young girls" (Ngai 2004, 117).

Filipinos aggressively challenged the applicability of the statutory ban on racial intermarriage. The issue was addressed repeatedly in Filipino newspapers such as the *Three Stars*. Filipino labor activist Pablo Manlapit in particular issued impassioned pleas to his compatriots. "It is now a high time for every Malayan-blooded Filipino to come to the front and help defend his nationality that is being gravely insulted," he wrote in an editorial (quoted in Esguerra 2013, 102). In supporting a legal challenge by Filipino Gavino C. Visco and fiancée Ruth M. Salas to denial of a marriage license, Manlapit contended that the case had "a far reaching effect involving marriage relationship, immigration, and all other questions where that of race is a discriminating factor" (Esguerra 2013, 102). The plaintiff's general strategy in *Visco v. Los Angeles County* (1931) was not one of Filipinos claiming "whiteness" but rather that they were biologically and culturally Malayan, not Mongolian or Oriental, and that their colonial past Westernized them in ways different from groups targeted by bans on racial intermarrying. "We are Malayans," explained a 1930 article in the *Filipino Nation*. "We . . . protest because we are . . . a distinct race" (Esguerra 2013, 104; Foster 1932; Volpp 1999–2000).

There was some legal precedent for the general position that Filipinos were Malays. For example, in 1920, Filipino military veteran Leonardo Antony and his Mexican American fiancée Luciana Brovencio successfully appealed a Los Angeles County marriage bureau disqualification for marriage on the basis of race. An assistant county counsel responded by ordering the issuance of the license, ruling broadly that Filipinos who were Malays (as opposed to Negritos and Chinese) were exempted from the state antimiscegenation statute (Baldoz 2011, 91). Visco and Salas also won their case but largely because Salas was ruled to be a mix of Mexican and Indian blood rather than white; the victory thus had little significance for the larger cause. More often Filipinos lost their claims. For example, a Southern California court in 1925 ruled against a Filipino who defended his murder of a man caught in bed with his wife as a traditional honor killing. The court rejected the defense because the marriage between Timothy Yatko and a white woman was not legal under the statute banning mixed marriages. Judge Carlos S. Hardy, in *California v. Yatko* (1925), agreed with the prosecution that "the dominant race of the country has a perfect right to exclude other races from equal rights with its own people. . . . The Filipino is a Malay and . . . the Malay is a Mongolian. Hence . . . intermarriage between a Filipino and a Caucasian would be void" (Fabros 1995).

Filipino activist groups such as the Filipino Civic League and Filipino labor organizations along with community newspapers protested the spurious reasoning of Judge Hardy and insisted that the state statute banning intermarriage should not apply to Filipinos. Some white groups also disagreed with the judge's logic and joined in the protest, but nativist forces, including state attorney general U. S. Webb, continued to press their position. As the numbers of Filipinos defiantly applying for marriage licenses with white women increased, advocates of racial purity took action to strengthen their position as legal precedent. Judge J. A. Smith restated the earlier *Yatko* logic in *Robinson v. Lampton, County Clerk of Los Angeles County* (1930), ruling that ordinary popular perceptions provided a better standard than scientific expertise in legal matters of racial classification; by this standard, a Filipino was deemed to be of the yellow or Mongolian race. Despite escalating protests from the Filipino community press, the Los Angeles County Clerk Lampton began to deny more licenses to Filipinos applying to marry white women (Volpp 1999–2000, 819). The courts ruled similarly in a variety of other cases, including applications for annulments, continuing to reject scientific classifications and upholding the principles that Filipinos were included in the marriage ban on Mongolians. These cases reveal two critical points. First, the justifications for white supremacy were constantly in flux and often wholly arbitrary, resisting science or other grounds that conflicted with the interests of the dominant population. Second, the repeated denial of marriage licenses illustrates the considerable role of low-level bureaucrats in enforcing racial ideology through everyday legal decisions and constituting racialized social norms generally (Pascoe 2009).

The most important of these cases that came before the superior court was *Roldan v. Los Angeles County* (1933; Volpp 1999–2000, 821). Salvador Roldan was an Ilocano mestizo with some Spanish blood who sought to marry English-born Marjorie Rogers. In 1931, the Los Angeles County Clerk once again denied them a license. Roldan won the support of Pablo Manalpit and Gladys Towles Root, a flamboyant attorney who had defended Visco and made a name for herself creatively defending other Filipinos. Root viewed the Roldan challenge as a pivotal legal precedent. "We believe that the importance of this question as presented in the Roldan case to-wit, whether a Filipino is to be classed as a Mongolian and denied the right to marry a person of the opposite sex who belongs to the white race, has never been fully understood or appreciated," she wrote in a letter to Manalpit. "It is the test case of maximum importance not only to all Filipinos in the United States but in the Island as well" (quoted in Esguerra 2013, 111–12). Root adopted a different strategy from that in the Visco case. She argued, first, that Filipinos are not ethnologically, historically, or legally Mongolian and, second, that the prevailing scientific judgment at the time the miscegenation statute was legislated distinguished Malayan (brown) from Mongolian (yellow). The counsel for Los Angeles County countered that scientific opinion actually had been divided in the earlier time, and that Filipinos were Mongolian in the "generic" sense. Judge Gates ruled simply and clearly that neither one of the couple applying for marriage was "Mongolian," Negro, nor Mulatto, so the he ordered that the license be approved.

A divided California appellate court ruled against the state on appeal, upholding the superior court position that there was no intent of the legislature to include Malays in the amended statute covering Mongolians. The appellate ruling endorsed the traditional, "common sense," nonscientific classification of five basic races (white, black, yellow, red, brown), and held that Roldan's Malayan status distinguished him from Mongolians. The victory for the individuals thus once again narrowed only slightly the explicitly racist reach of official law. Meanwhile, a campaign of nativists was building support for a bill introduced by State Senator Herbert Jones to include "Malays" in an amended antimiscegenation statute. Several months later, the state senate passed the bill unanimously, with the only voice of opposition coming from a Los Angeles County representative in a district with a large Filipino population. The new law and then the 1934 Tydings-McDuffie Act shortly thereafter, which dramatically reduced Filipino immigration, greatly alleviated white fears about Filipino sexuality. Not until 1948, however, in *Perez v. Sharp*, did California become the only state after Reconstruction to declare its antimiscegenation laws unconstitutional, and even then the legislature did not remove the unconstitutional law from the Civil Code for another decade (Volpp 1999–2000, 823–25).

The struggles by Filipinos in Washington State, by contrast, focused on *preventing* the passage of legislation banning interracial marriage.[18] Mixed marriage had long been feared in the "white utopia" of Washington. The legislature of the Washington territory in 1855 had made it illegal for whites to marry either black people or Indians, and all previous interracial marriages were declared void. That legislation was repealed during the Reconstruction era, but white society continued to apply social pressure to discourage racially mixed marriages, and the legislature for decades attempted repeatedly to reinstate criminal penalties for interracial marriage (Gillmer 2012). The first major struggle over banning Filipino marriages to whites did not commence until 1935. In February, the King County auditor, Earl Milliken, acted with no clear authorization to deny a request for a marriage license by a Filipino man and a white woman. Days later, House Bill No. 301, modeled on earlier legislative initiatives, was introduced by prosecuting attorney Warren Magnuson and endorsed by leading politicians. The bill prohibited marriages between "white persons" and "Negroes, Orientals, Malays and persons of Eastern European extraction" (S. Johnson 2005; Strandjord 2009). After a good deal of public furor, the bill eventually was tabled in the House Committee on Public Morals. A similar bill, adding penalties for statutory violation, was proposed in the state senate two years later in 1937. Its fate was the same, as the bill stalled and then died in the Senate Rules Committee. Three features of these failed efforts deserve notice.

First, the two bills' broad agenda for separating multiple groups solely based on racial classification failed because they generated a broad-based, multiracial, labor-based coalition of dynamic, effective opposition centered to a large extent in Seattle. African American organizations were the most numerous and important leaders. The Colored Citizens' Committee in Opposition to the Anti-Intermarriage Bill formed in 1935, choosing influential political leader and journalist Horace Cayton Sr.—the son of a Mississippi slave and a white plantation owner's daughter—as its spokesperson (S. Johnson 2005; Taylor 1994). The committee organized its effort around winning commitments from the South End Progressive Club, the local NAACP, and the Urban League. Black churches, including the First African Methodist Episcopal Church, and the YMCA joined the cause in lobbying Olympia and leading protest rallies and meetings. Despite a smaller population, the Filipino Community of Seattle and the Filipino-led Cannery Workers' and Farmers' Labor Union Local 18257 also became critical contributors to the coalition both in Seattle grassroots politics and in lobbying efforts in the state capitol of Olympia. Community newspapers for black people, most notably the *Northwest Enterprise*, and for Filipinos, especially the *Philippine Advocate*, regularly reported on the issue and offered strong positions opposing the bills (Viado 1937). The *Japanese American Courier* also covered and questioned the marriage ban, but in rather more temperate terms. Other labor groups and communist organizations, including the communist League of Struggle for Negro Rights (LSNR) and the Communist Party, made important contributions to the cause. This coalition mirrored precisely the diverse array of aspiring American outsiders whom Carlos Bulosan portrayed as the transformative heart of America's destiny. The coalition was as diverse in its many political tactics and institutional sites of contention—legislative lobbying, street protests, newspaper editorials, threats of litigation, etc.—as in its constituent base. And this multiracial, labor-based coalition challenging bans on racial intermarrying provided a foundation and model for liberal, inclusionary, egalitarian oppositional politics for decades to come. "The 1935 and 1937 campaigns laid the groundwork for future multi-ethnic collaboration on subsequent civil rights and progressive issues" (S. Johnson 2005).

Second, these oppositional campaigns enacted a general strategy of invoking mainstream American legal symbols, rights traditions, and moral values to expose and challenge hypocritical practices by dominant white groups. The framing of news coverage and opposition focused especially on the issue of "exploitation and discrimination" that violated the nation's Constitution and exposed the "false ideals" of American law and rights traditions (Strandjord 2009; S. Johnson 2005). One Filipino who lobbied the legislature was quoted in a news article as saying that the bill was "unconstitutional in the sense that it deprives either party of their rights in the pursuit of happiness" (*Philippine-American Chronicle* 1935a, 1935b). A 1937 article in the *Philippine Advocate* questioned whether "this is the America that Franklin and Jefferson dreamed of" (quoted in Strandjord 2009). An editorial in the *Philippine-American Chronicle* similarly underlined that the antimiscegenation bill was "Un-American" and antithetical to "the spirit of 1776." The writer then shifted to melodramatic rhetoric, noting that, paralleling Bulosan, "It has been deeply rooted in the hearts of every people of the world that this country is the melting pot. The fire that keeps the pot melting is now smoldering into ashes of insignificance, because of laws that are being made in this country which [are] a direct violation of individual freedom" (*Philippine-American Chronicle* 1935c).

Finally, it is relevant that these struggles for rights made Washington State something of an anomaly—the only state in the West, and one of the few in the nation, that did not legally ban interracial marriage in the twentieth century. This legal legacy is one of the reasons why Filipinos and other people of color were drawn to the area, relocating to a more hospitable place for settlement and families. Even so, the deep currents of antipathy to Filipinos, Japanese, Chinese, African Americans, and Native Americans continued to impose social pressures discouraging interracial marriage in Washington as well as in other states (Gillmer 2012).

Conclusion: The Genesis of Novel Rights Claims

The initial experiences of most Filipinos in the US metropole mirrored their subjugated condition under colonial rule in their island home. Racism, class oppression, and economic depression imposed precarious, violent, often desperate conditions on most of the newcomers to the American West. In fact, given that migrant workers left behind the familial support and communal sanctuary enjoyed in their native lands, their situation in the metropole arguably was even worse. However familiar they were with American occupiers, migrant workers found themselves to be at once unwelcome strangers in a hostile land and needed as cheap labor for profitable capitalist development. As Bulosan put it, the insecure, rightsless situation of proletarianized Filipinos was like that of perennially suspected criminals, distant cousins to black people in the "authoritarian enclaves" of Jim Crow America to whom they were routinely likened in the racialized white American imaginary (Mickey 2015). Nevertheless, most Filipinos worked hard, persevered, and labored to prove that they deserved respect and basic rights.[19] "Deterritorialized in this way, members of this 'internal colony' fought to affirm their human rights and dignity," eminent historian E. San Juan Jr. (1995, 5) has summarized. By claiming human rights, they rejected the dehumanizing brands placed on them and demanded rights equal to citizens and more (C. Johnson 2017). For the majority, these efforts entailed little open defiance and protest against widespread white exploitation, as rebelliousness might invite even greater, more violent repression. But many Filipinos did engage in everyday acts of resistance as well as sustained political campaigns and legal claims seeking to improve their position in the hierarchical status quo and to alter that order itself.

The propensity of Filipinos, even as colonial subjects, to embrace rights as aspirational resources for radical egalitarian struggle in some ways should be unsurprising. After all, they had been introduced to American history, language, customs, and values in colonial schools. The fact that "America" initially was far away and romantically portrayed by others, moreover, rendered its norms highly abstract, subject to imaginary projection, and a dream of sorts. A community of equal-rights-bearing individuals thus was more "a figment of the imagination" than "real" to them before arrival, and thus it remained a discrete object of desire (Scheingold 1974). Carlos Bulosan (1973, xiii) acknowledged how the amorphous kinship with America nurtured an abstract investment in equal rights among Filipinos once they arrived: "Adhering to American ideals, living American lives, these are contributory to our feeling of equality." Filipinos' political quests for rights recognition thus aimed to deploy such familiar egalitarian ideals as resources to contest the racist constructions of difference and to challenge the (il)liberal forms of legal subjugation that branded them as inherently criminal. Their struggles for independence against American colonial rule at home and repressive rule in the metropole shared this common, mutually confirming aspiration. A commitment to legal rights permeated the discourse of Filipino labor activists from the start. For example, Ernesto Mangaoang, later union business agent and leader for cannery workers, wrote to the *Oregonian* in 1931 protesting the efforts of "white and Indian pickers . . . to get their jobs." The letter outlined in simple language the pervasive racist characterizations of Filipinos as a "menace" to white economic and social welfare. The just course for all involved, he wrote, is that the United States should grant the Filipinos their "equal rights or independence. . . . As long as she insists that the Filipinos remain under the American flag, we don't want to surrender our right to live in this country through such an arrangement" (Mangaoang 1931).

In this sense, Filipinos arguably aimed not to "close the gap" between liberal promise and illiberal practices so much as to demand entry into the closed liberal community of rights-bearing subjects, individually and collectively. Most colonial national subjects wanted the same rights and legal status that white citizens enjoyed; they wanted to "make rights real." The early struggles for rights, in the western states as well as at home, thus could reasonably be interpreted simply as gambits for acceptance, or assimilation, on equal terms into capitalist America. In this process, Filipinos' struggles for rights contributed to the slow, uneven liberalization and democratization of the American capitalist racial state and society (Mickey 2015).

But passages accompanying the quote from Bulosan also point toward the distinct heritage and experience of Filipinos that shaped their uneasy, complex relationship to American traditions of rights. "Western people are brought up to regard Orientals or colored peoples as inferior, but the mockery of it all is that Filipinos are taught to regard Americans as our equals," he wrote (Bulosan 1973, xiii). We underline in this regard that it was the dominant white society and racial state that initiated and imposed the terms of adversarial, group-based "identity politics" recounted in this chapter. Rights guaranteeing some measure of individual autonomy historically had been restricted to white, mostly male property owners (Charles W. Mills 2008). As such, the material experiences of Filipinos left little room for delusion about how the ideals themselves were flawed and fantastic. Filipinos were hardly duped by what Scheingold (1974) calls the "myth of rights." "The terrible truth in America shatters the Filipinos' dream of fraternity. I was completely disillusioned when I came to know this American attitude. If I had not been born in a lyrical world, grown up with honest people and studied about American institutions and racial equality in the Philippines I should never have minded so much the horrible impact of white chauvinism" (Bulosan 1973, xiii). This mention of Filipinos' dreams of "fraternity" in a "lyrical world" further suggests that Filipinos tended to embrace "equal rights" from a nonwhite, class-based subject position grounded less in individualistic perspectives and more in collectivist aspirations.

Bulosan's *America Is in the Heart* again is evocative in this regard. Early in the novel, Allos recalls that when he was a young boy, his brother Macario read to him from the Old Testament the "story of a man named Moses who delivered his persecuted people to safety in another land" (Bulosan 1973, 45). Allos asks if there is a man like that in his country. "Yes. . . . His name is Jose Rizal" (46), invoking the mestizo revolutionary hero of Philippine independence. Even at this early point in his intellectual and political awakening, the young Carlos announced that like the martyred radical Rizal, "I would like to fight for you, our parents, my brothers and sister" (46). In this scene, we see the fusion of multiple cultural influences on the collective rights imagination and legal consciousness of Filipino dissidents—the story of tribal Jewish exodus from persecution in the Old Testament Bible, the ideals of independent national self-determination associated with the Enlightenment-influenced Rizal, the traditions of opposition to Spanish and American colonial rule, and the localized communal norms and familial bonds that had sustained traditional peasant struggles against mestizo landlords. Some analysts have seen in these ideals a distinct residue of the redemptive folk understandings grounded in Christian *Pasyón*, which historian Raymond Ileto (1979) argued loomed large in the oral traditions that had informed Filipino resistance against Spanish colonialism. The potency of Rizal's appeal rested on his ability to summon populist visions of revolutionary communities "held together by an ethos of mutual caring, the sharing of obligations (damayan) and the exchange of pity (awa)" (Rafael 1997, 275). Other scholars (Scalise 2009) have analyzed these cultural understandings as a sort of subversive "hidden transcript" in the Philippine tradition of resistance.

We agree even more with scholars who underline instead the Pinoys' "third world consciousness," which was born of "experiential knowledge of colonial oppression and a sense of identity with an oppressed group" (Evangelista 1982, 47–48). As such, Bulosan should be regarded as "a third world writer" in the tradition of "revolutionary realism" constructing a history of subaltern praxis that he observed and shared with other Filipinos who traveled to America in his time. To recall Bulosan's proud poem:

> we have the truth
> On our side, we have the future with us;
> We have history in our hands, our belligerent hands

We find it significant that all of the resonances noted above are precapitalist or noncapitalist, suggesting that freedom and equality were understood in terms independent of and even antagonistic toward capitalist exchange relations and class exploitation. The poem extols an ideal of freedom where "Friendship is our bread, love our air . . . each a neighbor to the other, boundless in freedom" (Bulosan 1950 [UWSC]). Moreover, we have noted that Bulosan's book is filled with accounts of additional influences that many Filipino workers absorbed in their West Coast travels. Starting in the 1930s, this included especially those of Wobblies, radical labor union activists, intellectuals associated with the Popular Front, progressive lawyers, and the Communist Party. In his essay "My Education," Bulosan wrote

> I knew that I was living in the collective era. . . . I read Marxist literature. . . . Socialist thinking was spreading among the workers, professionals and intellectuals. Labor demanded immediate political action. For the first time a collective faith seemed to have appeared. To most of us it was a revelation—and a new morning in America.(Bulosan 1995. 129)

These influences are tracked in coming chapters as we probe both the dynamic discursive terms propelling political struggles and the developing support structures that enabled Filipino mobilization, or praxis, around rights.

Our attention to Filipinos' distinctive political discourse and growing oppositional rights consciousness matters, we argue, because the select groups of activists highlighted in this study clearly sought not just to be accepted as formally equal members of white-dominated American society. They did not want to "become white," because that would endorse the exploitative terms of capitalism. They instead wanted to change that world according to novel visions of rights, justice, and freedom that grew out of the grounded experiences of an exploited, racialized, subaltern laboring class (Apostolidis 2009; Polletta 2000). Specifically, while they fought for conventionally individualized "negative" civil rights protecting security and autonomy along with political rights to civic participation, they also advocated a host of "positive," group-based socioeconomic rights to material empowerment in a multicultural nation (T. H. Marshall 1950). "Because Filipinos linked their civil rights demands to a more abstract notion of what it meant to be an American rather than citizenship alone," Hinnershitz argues, "'civil rights' spoke more to the guarantee of basic protection and freedoms in the pursuit of happiness than specific political rights" (Hinnershitz 2013, 135). Indeed, we shall see in coming pages that Filipino workers' persistent demands for rights recognition directly fed into—rather than diverted from, as many critical legal scholars might expect—a legacy of class-based struggles for fundamental change in capitalist economic as well as racial relations (Fraser 2000; W. Brown 1995, chap. 5). Simply put, Bulosan and his comrades labored to reconstruct liberal civil rights discourse in a more "socialist direction" (San Juan Jr. 1995, 12).

All in all, the Filipino aspirational struggles were undeniably shaped by US legal traditions but in ways that, at least for some, came to represent defiant and potentially transformative challenges to the hierarchical foundations of empire. The rights the activists claimed arguably were both old and new, familiar and disruptive, sincere and strategically subversive, "resonant" and "radical" (Ferree 2003). Filipino activists struggled to make these ambitious rights claims increasingly real over coming decades, aided in part by the changing legal opportunities opened by President Franklin Roosevelt's New Deal agenda and the international context of the Second World War.

2

A Cannery Workers' Union by Law

The Formative Years

> The workers submit[ted] to abuses which virtually made them economic serfs or slaves.—TRINIDAD ROJO (1947, 5 [UWSC])

> We learned to fight back . . . [and] organized ourselves into unions. . . . We wanted to organize to combat white people who were beating us up and to raise the wages of our people and to get the public to sympathize with us. It took us three years to make people believe. . . . I spent lots of evenings speaking between King Street and Seventh Avenue (in Seattle). There were oceans of Filipinos gathered in Chinatown . . . once as many as 20,000 Filipinos. . . . It was like a *fiesta*.—PONCE TORRES (interview in Schenk 1975, 9)

> Labor unionism has its roots in labor's grievances. Soon or late the realization comes that gods and governments help those who help themselves.—LAUREN WILDE CASADAY (1938, 338)

Struggles waged by Filipinos over basic civil rights in legislatures, the courts, and civil society produced many small protections and advances for justice during the late 1920s and 1930s. But these early legal campaigns did not thwart, and may even have exacerbated, the overall marginalization and repression of Filipinos on the West Coast. A loose coalition of white nativist groups, patriotic organizations, midwestern agricultural business interests, and racially exclusionary AFL locals converged to repel the Filipino "invasion." We have already recounted many of the legal gambits and acts of social violence that propelled this ongoing campaign to restrict and remove the cursed Filipinos along with other Asians. These campaigns eventually led to the 1934 Tydings-McDuffie Act, which granted Philippine independence and imposed dramatic quota restrictions on further Filipino immigration to the metropole. Filipinos were reclassified generically as Asian aliens, rendering them even more rightsless than before, because they could no longer travel freely within the empire.

The legislation did not resolve the many "problems" posed for whites by Filipinos already living in the United States, however (Baldoz 2011, chap. 5). Nativist forces thus escalated campaigns for sending all Filipinos back to their soon to be formally independent homeland. Amid the growing social and legal repression as well as the economic Depression reviewed in the previous chapter, US officials passed the Filipino Repatriation Act of 1935, which aimed to convince Filipinos to leave the US metropole voluntarily in return for financial and logistical support, including "free transportation" to Manila (Daniels 2004, 71). Because Filipinos were prevented from returning to the United States by strict immigration quotas, repatriation thus constituted a thinly veiled program of de facto deportation. The effort to remove Filipinos, like Mexicans, in the 1930s was essentially what is called today a form of "ethnic cleansing" (K. R. Johnson 2005, 6). Some Filipinos supported repatriation. For example, a *Philippine-American Chronicle* editorial by a Manila publisher, Manuel Insigne, was in favor of return: "The condition of Filipinos in the United States is intolerable. They are not paid white man's wages. They come to the United States to find opportunity and instead find oppression" (Insigne 1934). But most Pinoys in the United States declined the opportunity. Despite sustained efforts from many quarters to coerce departures, repatriation was slow and attracted only small numbers of Filipinos—157 by the end of 1936 and only a total of 2,064 by the last sailing in 1941, few of them from the racialized, low-wage laboring class (Ngai 2004, 122; Baldoz 2011, 192).

One reason for hope among Filipinos about remaining in the United States was that the persistent campaigns for civil rights and citizen status became closely comingled with increasing labor militancy by agricultural and Alaska salmon cannery workers during the mid-1930s. This labor militancy and rapidly escalating unionization among Filipinos was facilitated by four factors. The first was the exploitative, precarious character of commodified work, employment relations, and living conditions that heavily burdened the migrant laboring class. "The canned salmon industry epitomized the extractive process so common to the American West—the provision, through the transformation of nature's bounty into commercial products, of wealth for a relative few and toil for the comparatively many," historian Chris Friday (1994, 5–6) has summarized. The exploitation of workers increased as competition for jobs intensified during the Depression years. A large number of Filipinos did not passively tolerate the oppression at work or in the broader society but instead organized to change the structural context of their subordination.

Second, however marginalized and repressed socially and politically, the growing Filipino migrant labor force had become an "indispensable" pillar to the US political economy on the West Coast just at the Philippines had become an essential base for the American commercial and military empire. For example, between 1880 and 1937, the canned salmon industry in Alaska, which was dependent on migrant Asian labor, produced more value than the sum of all minerals mined in the territory in the same period (Friday 1994, 2). In short, Filipinos were unwelcome and scorned but still needed as low-wage workers by the dominant society. This dependence of Americans on Filipinos and their native country grew steadily until World War II, when it intensified rapidly to the benefit of the latter's relative social and political power.

Third, the West Coast and especially the Pacific Northwest context featured a variety of conditions that proved hospitable to militant, radical Left immigrant labor activism (Gregory 2004). The vibrant currents of syndicalism and socialist commitment influenced many Left Coast labor activists, including the Filipino agricultural and cannery workers, who mingled with the International Workers of the World (IWW, the Wobblies) and were attracted to communist invectives against capitalism, racism, and imperialism (Dubofsky 1966). Indeed, West Coast communists made their greatest inroads in industries with a high percentage of immigrant workers. We shall see how the early break of Filipino cannery workers from the exclusionary, craft-based AFL, affiliation with the more progressive Congress of Industrial Organizations (CIO), growing ties to the International Longshoremen's and Warehousemen's Union (ILWU) led by socialist Harry Bridges, and defiant resistance to Cold War red-baiting all contributed to and exemplified this leftist militancy. In short, as the salmon canneries were a quintessential western extractive industry, so did the cannery workers' union that developed in the 1930s display the radical substantive commitments and internally democratic organizational principles that distinguished much West Coast labor politics from that of the East Coast (Kimeldorf 1988).

Finally, developments in national law and legislative policy during the New Deal era provided institutional resources for Asian workers to mobilize around workers' rights, to unionize, and to develop collective leverage focused on work-related and other social issues. Filipino trade unionists began to mobilize politically in the late 1920s and formed the first unions in the early 1930s, in the process becoming "important figures in the Pacific Coast labor movement" (Ngai 2004, 125). This and the following chapter will track and analyze the difficult, volatile formation of union power in the periods before and after World War II, focusing especially on Filipino-led salmon cannery workers. Our focus on unionization will not leave behind attention to legal rights mobilization, as the labor unions themselves were very much civil rights organizations constructed by and through law in a host of fundamental ways.

"It Is Just Like They Were Slaves:" Work in the Alaska Salmon Canneries

The Changing Forms of Salmon Production in the North Pacific Ocean

Salmon have long thrived in the rivers and coastal waters of the Pacific Northwest from California to Alaska. For many hundreds of years before the nineteenth century, the economy and culture of coastal indigenous peoples—especially the Tlingits and Haidas—in southeastern Alaska were heavily dependent on the Pacific salmon (Colt 2000; Cooley 1963; Daley and James 2004). Salmon spawn in freshwater streams, and their offspring migrate to the open sea where they mature. Both humans and nonhumans (bears, eagles) routinely snare the fish on their annual summer runs back to spawning grounds. The fish were highly accessible to Alaskan Indians relying on simple tools (spears, nets, baskets) and technologies (weirs, or dams) for direct in-stream fishing; the caught salmon were conveniently stored after open-air drying or smoking. Because of the capacious river systems in Alaska, thousands of Natives as far as a thousand miles from the ocean could make salmon a staple part of their diet (Colt 2000). Salmon fishing was, moreover, a glorious social ritual as well as a material subsistence activity. In addition, the relative ease of securing salmon for sustenance during summer months facilitated much time for alternative Native activities, such as customary spiritual ceremonies, storytelling, craft and arts production, armed defense, and the like.

Aboriginal claims to salmon resources were organized around a sophisticated, well-established scheme of clan-based property relations. Tlingit property "encompassed all of their subsistence practices including salmon streams, hunting grounds, berry patches, and sealing rocks" (Oberg 1973, 55). Fishing in a stream owned by another native clan required an invitation (Cooley 1963, 20). The location and size of Native settlements usually reflected the proximate quantity and runs of salmon. Redistribution of surplus food secured by fishing or hunting to others was an important source of honor and prestige for individual clan leaders (Daley and James 2004, 47–50).

Indigenous peoples remained in control of salmon fishing until the sale of Alaska by Russia to the United States in 1867. Russian capitalist fur traders during the early nineteenth century had exploited the resources of southeastern Alaska, but their preoccupation with profitable trapping of sea otters diverted them from extensive interest in the salmon. Other groups of white settlers from North America poured in with the Klondike gold rush around 1900. The non-Native population grew within a few years by five times, to nearly nine thousand, while the Native population was cut in half, mostly due to diseases introduced by the pioneers (Colt 2000). Eventually, these white settlers took much of the land and access to salmon from the Natives, turning the fish into mass-produced commodities for commercial sale and many of the indigenous peoples into colonized proletarian low-wage workers. Eventually, capitalist mass production and predatory market competition led to a dramatic reduction in the basic resource of available fish for natives and whites alike (Cooley 1963).

Salmon fishing and canning by white settlers started around 1852 on the Sacramento River in California, 1866 on the Columbia River, 1874 around Puget Sound, and 1878 in Alaska.[1] Most denizens of the region know that there are five species of salmon—sockeye, coho, pink, chum, and chinook (or "king"). The sockeye and chinook from the start were considered the premium varieties, but all were used in the commercial canning industry. Catching the fish was not the primary problem for white industrialists seeking to produce profits; preserving and packaging the fish was the challenge for the developing industry. The core imperative was that canning must be located close to the point of capture to ensure efficiency and freshness. Placement of canneries evolved as industry leaders grew more sophisticated in tracking the migration patterns of salmon. Increasingly, Alaska became the center of salmon canning, with 118 canneries operating there by 1917. In that year alone,

Alaska canneries "packed more than half of the world's supply of salmon, nearly six million cases valued at $46 million" (Viernes 2012, 122). American involvement in major wars, from the Civil War through World War II, generated escalating demand for canned salmon for over a century. Cannery owners over time learned the value of mergers for increasing efficiency and profits; the National Canners Association was founded to facilitate coordination, including monitoring cannery sanitation, in 1907.

Cannery Workers and Their Work

The first Alaska canneries relied primarily on indigenous peoples for the difficult, low-wage factory work cleaning, packing, and canning the fish. Asian migrants entered the cannery workforce in three waves beginning in the late 1880s, each wave virtually halted by subsequent episodes of exclusionary legislation. In 1894, Alaska canneries employed 1,027 Chinese, 810 white, and 505 Native workers. The number of Chinese workers rose to 5,376 of 13,822 workers in 1902 but fell dramatically because of restrictive immigration statutes. The high point of Japanese workers, the second wave, was 3,256 a decade later. The first Filipino *Alaskeros* showed up in the canneries around 1911 and increased during the 1920s to a high of 4,210 workers by 1930, roughly three times the number of Japanese workers in Alaska at that time (Rojo 1947, 1 [UWSC]; Friday 1994, 2–3, 121). "In these early days about ninety-five percent of the Pilipinos on the west coast went to Alaska. They had no jobs, no families and no place to go," reported Trinidad Rojo, the cannery workers' union president during the 1940s and self-appointed historian (Masson and Guimary 1981b, 2). Mexican workers had preceded the Filipinos in the canneries, numbering 1,866 in 1919 and an estimated seven thousand overall during the period of the First World War, but that fell to twenty-four by 1935 (Rojo 1947 [UWSC]; Masson and Guimary 1981b, 1–2). Some black workers were also hired by contractors. In 1921, there were 108 black workers in the canneries, and that figure nearly tripled during World War II.

Work and working conditions for laborers in the "plantation model" of cannery organization, which "had more in common with nineteenth century colonial practices than modern industrial relations" (Ngai 2004, 138), were extremely trying. The processing of salmon required disciplined crews of workers who performed rapidly, precisely, and in highly concentrated time periods, generally from early June through September. Given that the salmon fishing season in some sites lasted just a month, cannery factory line workers

Fig. 4 "Iron Chink" cleaning machine in operation with Asian worker at the Pacific American Cannery, Fairham, Washington, ca. 1911–1913. University of Washington Libraries, Special Collections, UW 39788.

often labored up to eighteen hours a day, from 3 am to 10 pm or later. Workers first had to sort the fish by species into separate bins. The fish slicers and cleaners then performed the most onerous labor, wading through wet, slimy, slippery fish offal and bathed in blood. The slicing and packing of fish was done by hand in the early years, but Filipinos arrived in the 1920s to work with an "Iron Chink," the racist, dehumanizing name for the butchering machine that automated work performed originally by Chinese men on the production line.[2] The machine chopped off the heads, tails, and fins; eggs were "pulled" from the fish by hand, often by female workers. A conveyor belt then transported the fish to "slimers" who cleaned and fed the fish into another machine that sliced it into standardized chunks. Yet another group of workers, called "fill feeders," pushed the salmon into other machines that filled the cans with fish, salted it, and steamed the salmon in stacked containers. Although increasingly mechanized, a great deal of physical labor was required. From the start, the work was dangerous as well as exhausting, and mechanization did not halt the high incidence of bodily harm; fingers, hands, and arms were often maimed or severed by the process, and illness from unsanitary conditions was common. While the Iron Chink reduced available jobs for Chinese butchers initially, the efficiency it added facilitated rapid growth of the industry and thus aggregate growth of jobs and profits (Viernes 2012, 124).

The Labor Contractor System

The recruitment, compensation, and living conditions attending this demanding and dangerous work compounded the hardship. One primary mechanism of abuse was the contract labor system that had developed among the earlier Chinese "compradors" and operated throughout the system. Contractors performed as institutional intermediaries that provided "stability to an unordered and chaotic labor market" (Masson and Guimary 1981a, 377). The system, above all, provided a stable reserve of cheap, flexible, short-term labor to employers who rarely understood the foreign workers' language or culture. At the same time, the system also initially benefitted immigrant workers in many ways, especially in providing assistance to workers in immigration cases, offering laborers a measure of collective security and influence in the labor market, and preserving ethnic solidarity for Chinese. Many labor contractors worked through the Chinese Six Companies, a network of benevolent organizations that fought anti-Chinese legislation and provided legal representation against deportation actions from 1880 to 1920 (Qin 2009). As new waves of Japanese, Filipino, and Mexican workers replaced Chinese laborers, Chinese contractors continued to dominate the system. By the 1920s, salmon cannery labor contracting thus had evolved into an ethnically fragmented, casualized system paralleling early twentieth-century California agricultural labor contracting. Fierce competition among contractors and related ethnic rivalries came to mark both the agricultural and fish canning labor markets (Baker 1997, chap. 2).

Labor contractors ruthlessly exploited the conscripted workers even as they assisted them. Under the system, third-party labor contractors negotiated with employers to provide a work crew that would pack an arranged number of cases during the canning season. The contractor was responsible for operating and supervising the entire canning process, and he was paid a price for each case of packed salmon, usually with a guaranteed minimum. Contractors recruited the work crew, arranged transportation and living quarters for the workers, negotiated their wages, and paid them at the end of the season. As such, employers avoided most responsibilities for worker welfare and treatment.[3] The extreme competition among contractors provided powerful incentives for them to cut costs, thus minimizing concerns about worker pay, work conditions, and living circumstances. As historian Fred Cordova summarized, "the less contractors doled out to their crews for food, clothing, transportation and other cannery needs, the more profit contractors made" (cited in Dade 2009). Trinidad Rojo confirmed this judgment: "If the contractor realized that his bid was too low . . . he resolved to make profit anyway by chiseling on the wages, comfort and food of the workers" (Rojo 1947, 3 [UWSC]). For example, workers were routinely stuffed into extremely cramped quarters on ships taking them to and from Alaska, sometimes doubling the berth capacity for which contractors had paid. As Ponce Torres recounted, contractors "made deals with the ship's captain. . . . For instance the boat accommodated 500 workers and the deal was that there was supposed to be only 250 in the boat. The transportation money for the other 250 was shared with the captain" (Schenk 1975, 8; Rojo 1952 [UWSC]).

Wages offered in the early years were very low, around $150 for a three-month short season to $250 for a longer season. The actual distributed wage was nearly always far below the promised wage, however, because the predatory contractors employed a wide range of tactics to "steal" back the money promised to workers. The contractors generally issued credit or tokens to workers to buy basic supplies—food, clothing, toiletries, tobacco, liquor, etc.—around work sites at prices inflated well above reasonable market rates. Because canneries were in remote areas with no local stores or only merchants that refused to sell to Asian migrant workers, the latter had little choice but to pay exorbitant rates for necessities. The most extreme version of these swindles was by a white contractor in San Francisco, the Young and Mayer Company, fronted by a men's "furnisher and outfitter" store, who required young Filipinos to buy expensive suits and related clothing at radically inflated prices to qualify for jobs in the cannery (Masson and Guimary 1981a, 388; Rojo 1947, 5 [UWSC]). As labor leader and historian Trinidad Rojo later wrote,

> The contracting system deteriorated to murky depths in San Francisco, where a contractor required his workers to buy suits costing from $40.00 to $75.00 before they were given a chance to go to Alaska. If a worker bought a suit costing $40.00 he was given a green card, which meant a hope to go to Alaska. If he bought one costing $75.00, he was given a blue card, which

> meant a positive certainty of going to a cannery. Investigation revealed that the suits were bought from a New York wholesaler at $12.00 each. (Rojo 1952, 14 [UWSC])

This long-standing enterprise was eventually convicted for violation of California peonage laws, but most contractors evaded legal regulation.

Even more profitable for the corrupt contractors and costly to the workers were the gambling enterprises, employing experienced hustlers and grifters, that the contractors organized on ships and in the cannery living quarters. Gambling was a highly tempting diversion from the laborers' hard work over long hours amid few other indulgences. As a result, workers often incurred considerable debt while in Alaska and were forced to borrow against future wages at high interest rates; very commonly, workers left Alaska and returned to Seattle, Portland, or San Francisco broke or in debt. Many labor contractors favored workers known for gambling, took bribes from workers in exchange for jobs in Alaska, and sold subcontracted foreman positions with designated supervisory roles. In 1933, workers filed 555 complaints after receiving less than $15 for an entire season after the charges deducted by contractors (Viernes 2012, 130; Casaday 1938, 237–38).

Some contractors also engaged in sexual exploitation of the *Alaskeros*, a government investigation in the 1930s revealed (Hinnershitz 2013, 141). As some interviewees reported, employees who were viewed as predatory "perverts" used candy, cigarettes, marijuana, and other treats bought at the foremen's local shops to entice lower level employees, including especially university students, into sexual associations (Rojo 1952 [UWSC]). The victimized recipient of the enticements then became a dependent sex slave who benefitted the others in the relationship; the foremen could expand his product sales while the manipulative employee gained a sex partner. The government investigation reported that this ongoing exploitation was driven by the financial gain of the rapacious contractors rather than by the apparent sexual identity and inclinations of the exploited workers (Fujita-Rony 2003, 102; NIRA Hearing 1934 [UWSC]).

Chinese and Japanese workers and their foreman were generally hostile to the new waves of Mexican and Filipino laborers who arrived after World War I because they created competition for the better jobs. Hence, the newer workers were restricted to the least desirable and worst-paid jobs in the canneries. Not only did whites forbid Filipinos to compete for better, nonlabor jobs in the racialized "dual labor market" system, but also the low-wage cannery labor force was ethnically segregated on a hierarchical basis. "The Filipino was the bottom dog; he occupied the lowest rung on the ladder," journalist and attorney Carey McWilliams once summarized (Bulosan 1973, xx–xxi). Filipinos often referred to one another as "virtual slaves" of the contract system (Dade 2009). As one Filipino *Alaskero*, Antonio Rodrigo, recounted years later, "conditions in Alaska at that time was so awful. That is just like they were slaves. . . . They go there and get money from the contractor so they can go to Alaska and work. And, then, they come back, they are broke" (quoted in Cordova 1983, 65). Trinidad Rojo wrote similarly that the workers submitted "to abuses which virtually made them economic serfs or slaves" (Rojo 1947, 5 [UWSC]). They typically were issued "yellow dog" contracts forbidding union membership, which they had to take or leave, or work with no contract at all just to find jobs. If workers asked for a contract, the reply was "Don't you trust me?," the classical ruse for exploitation among familiars (5). Government investigators for the code hearings referred to the institutional work relationships as akin to "indentured servitude" (Hinnershitz 2013, 139).

Life outside of work was organized around racial hierarchy as well. Work life in the canneries required a certain amount of spatially proximate interaction among Asian migrant workers and local aboriginal laborers as well as with the white settlers who occupied the more privileged occupations. Racial mixing in social and sexual interaction as well as interracial solidarity among workers thus posed a potential threat to white domination and work discipline in the cannery communities. One mechanism to regulate such possibilities was assignment of differential housing, food consumption, and leisure arrangements on the basis of race as well as class. White elites tended to live in ample, single-family homes, while white workers lived in modest bungalows and cottages. By contrast, Filipino laborers, like other Asians before them, resided in separate "overcrowded and unsanitary" bunkhouses, while aboriginal laborers were pushed to the periphery in separate camps or villages. The living quarters for Filipinos were insubstantial, and food in separate mess halls was substandard, unsavory, and limited in nutrition. The result of this quasi-legal residential segregation was to reinforce preexisting racialized identities and hierarchies in the newly diverse geographic setting (Mawani 2010).

Not surprisingly, Filipino *Alaskeros* were routinely oppressed by pervasive racism in community life around the canneries just as they were in the

US metropole. Filipino college journalism students who worked at the canneries in the summers provided especially vivid portrayals of such discrimination. In July of 1929, the student-edited *Chomley Spectator* in particular railed against racist charges that Filipinos were dirty, uncivilized carriers of meningitis and other diseases to justify segregation in all aspects of cannery community life (Hinnershitz 2013, 137–38). Another article protested the confinement ordered for all Filipino workers after some young Native American women disappeared. The women were soon found, but the moral panic was used to justify strict prohibitions on Filipino males' contact with women, including at the regular cannery dances. Filipinos responded in characteristic ways by decrying the violations of their basic rights. In a July 29, 1929, editorial labeled "Natural Rights in Danger," the *Chomley Spectator*'s editors Emeterio C. Cruz and Jose Blando defiantly assailed segregationist policies at the Chomley cannery, arguing that rights outlined in the US Constitution were "natural rights" available to all persons regardless of ethnicity or race.

> In constitutional interpretation we have, the freedom to live, the freedom to speak and the freedom to pursue his [*sic*] happiness and be happy. These are rights inalienable because they are inherent and emanating from man himself. . . . We consider the [segregation] order as the most daring and restrictive attempt to ever lay on the way of man's enjoyment of his natural rights. It is a wholesale denial of rights unequaled yet.

As the composition of the ethnic workforce changed in the 1920s, Chinese and Japanese contractors increasingly needed Filipino foremen to recruit and oversee Filipino workers. The most ambitious of these Filipino foremen soon advanced to the more lucrative positions as labor contractors. One of the earlier Filipino labor contractors was Pio De Cano, whose lawsuit over property rights in a Seattle court we discussed in the previous chapter. De Cano began as a laborer in Alaska in 1916. The Chinese contractor who hired him promoted him to foreman, and De Cano initiated his own enterprise as a contractor by 1927. He was sending up to one thousand men to Alaska each season in the mid-1930s (Masson and Guimary 1981a). One of De Cano's innovations was to recruit *barcada* Filipinos from his Philippine hometown in Ilocos Sur in an effort to secure loyalty that might check the workers' own entrepreneurial ambitions; he made his brother, Herman, a foreman, and often helped with workers' travel costs and other matters of resettlement to gain trust (Fujita-Rony 2003, 133). De Cano worked hard to be an "uncle" not only to these workers but also to the Filipino community. In the process, he became wealthy, donated funds as patron to community organizations and schools, and established himself as an influential leader of considerable prestige.

De Cano was a controversial figure, however. Like most labor contractors, he was frequently criticized and widely resented for gaining his wealth by exploiting cannery workers, especially as he undertook efforts to impede unionization in the 1930s. Trinidad Rojo (1947, 3 [UWSC]) explained the irony: "If he exploited workers sufficiently and became wealthy, he was acclaimed a success, a 'big shot' by his contemporaries and the community." And this is how the contractor system worked from the start: contractors built on ethnically based, clientelistic relationships of paternal obligation and social assistance to sustain their commodified exploitation of the migrant workers. By 1932, more than eight major Filipino contractor firms worked out of Seattle and hired a total of 2,333 laborers in the canneries (Viernes 2012, 129; Casaday 1938).

Fig. 5 Manong cannery workers, 1928. Courtesy Filipino American Historical Society Museum.

Filipino Workers' Grievances

Filipino workers initially were forced to adapt to the labor recruitment and management system created by the Chinese and continued by the Japanese contractors. "As competition for contracts among Chinese, Filipinos, Japanese, Jews, etc. became keener, the contractors became more resourceful and vicious," Trinidad Rojo (1952) summarized in retrospect. In this regard, Filipino migrants were subjects of three different legal orders—in their informal ethnic communal life of traditional norms and moral obligations, in the official US public realm of racial exclusion and white domination, and at work in the class-based, clientelistic legal order of male subservience to Asian labor contractors (Baker 1997, 10). Even so, cannery work on balance benefitted many Filipinos, supporting those students pursuing an education and providing some limited opportunities for mobility denied in the rest of the white-dominated economy. But Filipinos also were not content to be passive, powerless subjects. Many factors in the exploitative environment—the grip of corrupt labor contractors; the trying, insecure conditions of work in the canneries and agricultural fields; the increasing pressures of the economic Depression that eliminated jobs and slashed wages; and pervasive racial oppression—provided incentives for workers to organize into unions. "As we grew older in the cannery," Ponce Torres reported in an interview, "we learn[ed] that we are being abused and improvement should be done" (quoted in Friday 1994, 135).

Filipinos displayed an inclination and capacity for labor militancy early on. During 1919, the Filipino Labor Union (FLU), led by Pablo Manlapit, organized among sugar plantation workers in Hawaii. Despite the divide and conquer efforts of employers, the FLU initiated a strike of 8,300 Filipino and Japanese laborers in 1920 and then another strike in 1924 that resulted in the deaths of sixteen workers and four policemen (Fujita-Rony 2003, 172; Cordova 1983, 74). Labor militancy and strikes continued in Hawaii through the 1930s. Asian workers who traveled to the metropole brought with them these experiences of struggles against white capitalists in the homeland Philippines and Hawaii, and this militant labor consciousness and solidarity migrated with low-wage workers to the fields and canneries up and down the West Coast from California to Alaska. "Because most of these people worked as unskilled laborers, the same sets of people moved among various work sites, thus promoting a common consciousness about the need for unionization," historian Dorothy Fujita-Rony has summarized (2003, 172).

Ethnic fragmentation among workers, both among Asians generally and among Filipinos from different regions in the homeland, inhibited successful organizing to challenge the contractors' control, however. Labor activists Virgil Duyungan and Ponce Torres tried to organize the workers as early as 1925, but they failed. The California-based Cannery and Agricultural Workers Industrial Union (CAWIU) mobilized Mexican, Filipino, and European American workers to form a multiethnic struggle for solidarity, but it did not organize workers in the Alaska salmon canneries. The CAWIU collapsed in 1934. This atrophy reflected in part the fact that the large unemployed workforce during the Depression created additional pressures on those competing for the increasingly unskilled jobs in the mechanized canneries (Masson and Guimary 1981b, 9).

Nevertheless, the even more exploitative work that laborers endured in the agricultural fields, the increasing militancy of California farmworkers, and antipathy to the labor-contracting system fed steadily into aspirations for unionizing at the canneries. Chris Mensalves, who was active in fighting racial discrimination and then organized fieldworkers in California and Washington, in particular proved influential in working with militant Filipinos in Alaska. The prospect of a worker-controlled union was so great that Filipino labor contractors and foreman created the Filipino Labor Association (FLA) in 1930 to target Japanese growers, but the organization did not represent cannery workers, and it failed to offer agricultural workers sufficient benefits to justify joining (Friday 1994, 136; Cordova 1983, 75). The situation was changed markedly by the introduction of Franklin Roosevelt's New Deal, which provided cannery workers legal opportunities, incentives, and resources for collective action.

The New Deal: A Rights (Semi)Revolution for (Some) Workers

The New Deal era is widely viewed as a pivotal moment in US History. Scholars of American political development have underlined how a mix of liberal voluntarist ideology, concentrated corporate power, and fragmented national government before the 1930s impeded development of labor policy protecting workers while simultaneously privileging capitalist property rights (Forbath 1991; Hattam 1993; Fisk 1994). The promise of due process and equal protection conferred by basic citizenship rights in the public sphere under the US Constitution provided few checks on employer discretionary authority over work in those years. Political scientist Karen Orren has argued that organization of workplace power before this period was essentially "feudal" in character, guided by common-law principles of master-servant relations that granted employers plenary control over hours, wages, and workplace conditions (Orren 1991; Atleson 1983). This regime was sustained by a mix of powerful business influence and the "deference" of congressional leaders to judicially enforced principles of private contractual "freedom" (Lovell 2012).

After many disruptive strikes and protests by workers during World War I, President Wilson authorized the War Labor Board (WLB) to recognize the "right to organize in trade unions and to bargain collectively through chosen representatives" (National Labor Relations Board, n.d.). But the board had no enforcement powers, depriving most workers of legal resources to make their rights real. Following the war, major strikes in steel, coal, and rail industries were brutally suppressed; union memberships fell dramatically. The one notable exception was the railroad industry. The Railway Labor Act of 1926 provided a framework for collective bargaining that minimized strikes and lockouts on the railways crucial to national market infrastructure. This arrangement arguably paved the way for national labor policy in later years. Moreover, in the last year of the Hoover administration, Congress passed the Norris-LaGuardia Act, which curbed the authority of the courts to issue injunctions or restraining orders against strikes. In short, Congress declared an official policy of the United States to allow at least some workers to join unions and to bargain collectively.

Franklin Roosevelt's New Deal—passed amid radical market instability, economic collapse, and deep Depression—advanced a variety of policies aiming to empower workers. The National Industrial Recovery Act (NIRA), which created the National Recovery Administration (NRA), was passed in 1933. Its charge was to eliminate "cut throat competition" among employers and to organize industry, labor, and government in a cooperative effort to create codes of "fair practices" for workers and set prices. In an effort to reduce the "destructive" aspects of competition and to aid workers by setting minimum wages and maximum weekly hours, Section 7-a of NIRA provided workers with rights to organize and bargain collectively (Dubofsky 1994, 112). In August 1933, Roosevelt created the National Labor Board to implement union representation elections, mediate labor disputes, and address violations of NIRA codes. Generally, the NLB lacked enforcement power and the NRA was declared unconstitutional by the Supreme Court for violating the limitations of the commerce clause in 1935 (*Schecter Poultry v. United States*, 1935). Union organizing proliferated nevertheless.

The National Labor Relations Act (NLRA)—better known as the Wagner Act for its legislative sponsor, New York senator Robert F. Wagner—followed in 1935. The act expanded democracy at two levels (Frymer 2008). First, increased labor militancy, growing public support for an increased federal administrative role, and FDR's dogged court-packing gambit compelled the Supreme Court to relax its long-standing limitations on government regulation of private corporate power. Second, the New Deal–era legislation injected some measure of democracy directly into industrial workplace relations by recognizing and ostensibly enforcing workers' rights to organize into unions for collective representation of their interests in negotiations with employers over working conditions, wages, benefits, and the like.

Scholars disagree widely on the actual effects of New Deal–era labor law and the mix of new regulations and rights extended on behalf of workers. Contemporary liberals tend to romanticize the legacy, conservatives vilify it, and progressive leftists have been profoundly mixed. The Wagner Act as enacted by Congress, critical legal scholar Karl Klare boldly proclaimed, was "perhaps the most radical piece of legislation ever enacted by the United States Congress" and represented "an almost unbelievable capitulation by the government" to unprecedented working-class pressure (Klare 1978, 265–66). However, Klare found that the original promise of the Wagner Act was never realized, in part because of hostile court rulings. Another scholar thus similarly summarizes that the legal regime initiated by the NLRA in retrospect "seems marginal, . . . ineffectual, or downright repressive" (Fisk 1994).[4] The fact that the NLRA provided a "bare legal framework" that facilitated procedures of private ordering and conferred no substantive rights is hardly disputable as a bottom line for most critics (Stone 1981, 1513). Overall, we suggest that the Wagner Act did open far-reaching democratizing possibilities for collective action by workers, but those openings were soon narrowed by war, restrictive legislation, and judicial deradicalization (Lovell 2012; Tomlins 1985a).

Whatever the long-term effects, the most relevant critical concern for this study is the immediate implications for low-wage minority workers in the 1930s. Generally, we underline that the advances for organized labor did *not* extend to most workers of color. This is important, as African Americans were especially hurt by the Depression, with half of the black people in Southern cities unemployed, economic prospects for rural black people in agricultural production undermined, and their fates in northern cities only marginally better. The Agricultural Adjustment Administration offered white landowners cash for leaving their fields uncultivated, to which many farmers assented but which was a loss for abandoned African American sharecroppers and tenants. White landowners had little incentive to share their government subsidies with those racialized dark-skinned laborers who actually worked the land. Southern legislators similarly excluded agricultural and domestic workers—including Mexicans and Asian Americans as well as African Americans—from core relief programs, including the minimum wage, Social Security, unemployment insurance, and workers' compensation (Katznelson 2006).

The Wagner Act similarly focused on benefitting industrial workers and excluded agricultural and domestic workers, denying organizing rights to two-thirds of African American workers. This is doubly true because legalization of closed-shop practices enabled white unions to exclude black and other nonwhite people, a practice that was widespread among AFL locals in the Jim Crow era. Closed union shops thus became "white shops." The Wagner Act also omitted what later became known as racially inclusionary civil rights protections. African American organizations, including the NAACP and the Urban League, lobbied hard for adding civil rights provisions and a "duty of fair representation," or antidiscrimination obligation, to the new labor law (Frymer 2008, 29; Lee 2014). However, these groups exercised little influence in national politics, so their interests and ideas were excluded while Southern Democrats and the AFL prevailed. Southern congressmen, in defending their region's racist policies, "altered the full range of the New Deal's policies and accomplishments," putting it into a "southern cage," forcing a "Faustian" pact with liberals that benefitted white workers (Katznelson 2006, 9, 16).) The AFL, moreover, actually expressed great hostility to the NLRB's national authority over workplace representation in part because of the latter's potential threats to challenge the racial economic order, a tension that fed into the growing AFL rift with the industrial-based CIO after 1935. Southern power in Congress grew during the 1940s, enabling passage of the Taft-Hartley Act, which directly thwarted the power of labor unions, prohibited closed shops, limited state authority in socioeconomic matters, and authorized repression of Left union activists. Finally, the NLRB in general carried out its mandate of noncommitment to civil rights for workers of color that had been encoded in the original statutory authority (Frymer 2008). As Katznelson (2006) has summarized, the New Deal legacy of labor law deserves to be remembered as a time "when affirmative action was white."

The New Deal administrative state thus was ambiguous. It was a weak, fragmented "state of procedures" with little authority to intervene. It was also a "crusading state" capable of forceful action lacking in democratic oversight. While providing a statutory framework for a metaphorical "workplace Constitution," the "state action" requirement of the Fourteenth Amendment precluded a constitutional foundation for employees' rights in private workplaces, opening the way to curtailment and inversion in subsequent decades (Lee 2014). Even so, the New Deal era, Katznelson argues, nurtured a strong faith among many marginalized people that they belonged and that they were members of the community of rights-bearing individuals. The New Deal produced "whole openings for social change that were grasped by an incipient, soon powerful, movement for equal rights for blacks" and other racial minorities, a transformation advanced by litigation before high court judges appointed by President Roosevelt and then Truman (Katznelson 2006, 486).

Indeed, union organization among African American and other minority workers was not entirely blocked. By the time the Wagner Act was passed, between fifty and one hundred thousand nonwhite workers belonged to trade unions (Frymer 2008, 55). Mine workers, steelworkers, and autoworkers were among the most unionized. A particularly important group bolstered by New Deal reforms was railway workers. The 1926 Railway Labor Act was amended in 1934 to outlaw company unions and to provide a certification process for union elections while reinforcing earlier provisions, including protecting porters' rights to organize into unions and bargain collectively, requiring mediation and then arbitration for labor disputes, and securing their right to strike and to initiate lawsuits against railways for alleged violations. This official action enabled the overwhelmingly African American constituency of workers in the struggling Brotherhood of Sleeping Car Porters (BSCP), led by socialist visionary A. Philip Randolph, to gain viability. In 1935, Randolph, as inaugural president of the National Negro Conference, had courted the new CIO and proposed an ambitious resolution demanding that the AFL oust any unions that discriminated against racial minorities (Bynum 2010, 154–55). The AFL rejected the proposal, but in 1937 it succumbed to Randolph's tactics and NLRB pressures to charter the BSCP as the first of its unions representing African American workers. The union quickly managed to force the tenaciously antiunion Pullman Car Company to the bargaining table with union representatives. Both achievements were national civil rights milestones. Randolph built on that success to become a leading advocate and organizer of black workers nationwide. In 1941, Randolph successfully used the threat of a March on Washington and support from various Popular Front allies as well as FDR confidantes to force the administration to ban discrimination by defense contractors and to establish the Fair Employment Practices Committee (FEPC) to enforce that order. Milton Webster, the BSCP's first vice president, played a key role in making the FEPC a modestly effective tool in combatting employment discrimination. That said, the FEPC was a wartime concession, was accorded little authority or resources, and was opposed by powerful interests of white labor and industry.

Other groups of black and minority workers managed to unionize anew as well. In particular, the Wagner Act facilitated some degree of unionization in the South, where it had been fought bitterly, and these organizing efforts did empower some African Americans. As Robert Korstad (2003) has chronicled, black tobacco workers—supported by national labor legislation as well as political alliances with the Communist Party, the CIO, and various Popular Front groups in the 1930s—organized into a powerful union that joined civil rights and workers' rights by the early 1940s. They affiliated as Local 22 with the United Cannery, Agricultural, Packing and Affiliated Workers of America (UCAPAWA), a union that also was critical to the history of Filipino cannery workers (Korstad 2003; see also Kelley 2015). Local 22 took the lead of a defiant labor-based civil rights movement that challenged the long-standing class, race, and gender-based system of white supremacy. In 1944, the union negotiated a historic contract that won higher wages and established both seniority principles and worker-driven grievance procedures. The left-leaning leadership generated and sustained a vibrant union culture that connected workplace and community. Local 22 represented one of many episodes of labor politics that joined socialist inspirations and civil rights, a period in which "industrial jurisprudence" proved transformative, rather than a "legalistic barrier to militancy," amid a legacy of racial capitalist hierarchy. "In the context of their times, it offered their only conceivable route to power" (Korstad 2003, 224). While eventually crushed by reactionary Cold War forces, the model of civil rights unionism provided an influential legacy for nonwhite worker politics in the 1960s and 1970s (Kelley 2015).

The struggles of Filipino migrant workers on the West Coast are less well known, but their experience resembles more the BSCP and UCAPAWA Local 22 than the fate of most workers of color in the New Deal era. Eventual cannery union president and historian Trinidad Rojo summarized the importance of the New Deal legal legacy: "The election of President Roosevelt gave strength to the [Filipino] labor movement. The workers and the Roosevelt administration through the N.R.A. and the Wagner Act resolved to get rid of the abuses" imposed by the labor contract system (Rojo 1947, 6 [UWSC]). Union cofounder Ponce Torres (1952, 11) confirmed the point, stating that the formation of the union "was the culmination of a series of brutal assaults on the rights of workers to organize. . . . This was done throughout the presidency of Franklin D. Roosevelt by fighting for the passage of pro-labor legislations [*sic*] and for the rendering of court decisions favoring labor." The most immediate and direct effect on Filipino workers resulted from the investigation and hearings on fair practices conducted by the NRA in California during 1934, which bolstered efforts to eradicate the "involuntary servitude" of cannery work (Hinnershitz 2013, 139; NIRA Hearing 1934 [UWSC]). The hearings provided incentives for the canneries to centralize policy through the Alaska Salmon Industry, Inc., as well as opportunities for the fledgling cannery workers' union to negotiate codes of fair workplace practices and collective bargaining processes. As Charles Romney (2016, 39) has argued regarding California dried fruit cannery workers, "legal procedure shaped NLRB structure and framed worker agency" in salmon cannery union building. What the New Deal–era Tydings-McDuffie Act took away from Filipinos in terms of citizenship rights, labor legislation and legal processes thus contributed anew as possibilities of empowering rights for workers and unions. And these contradictory currents of rights construction, we shall suggest, proved formative to the radical aspirations of the union that developed by law.

The Birth of a Union by Law: The Early, Factionalized Cannery Workers and Farm Laborers Union

Beginnings

In late 1932, a group of seven Filipino students and nonstudent workers began to meet regularly in Seattle—home base for Alaskan cannery contractors and workers alike—to discuss ways that they could "fight race discrimination," alter the awful work conditions in the canneries, and get rid of the labor contractors (*Filipino Labor Journal* 1932 [UW Special Collections]). "Well there are four of us that decided together how we can improve the Filipino conditions and the differences in canneries in Alaska. As we go along, we contacted a few more to become some leaders of the organization," wrote Tony Rodrigo (Cordova 1983, 73). It is notable that associations among Filipino students who worked during summers at the canneries to fund their education at the University of Washington provided bonds of solidarity that diluted differences of ethnic and regional origin. "When we started the organizational work, we looked upon each other as brothers. To me, it did not matter what island they came from or what dialect they spoke" (73). In any case, they concluded that "the only solution to the problem is to be organized" in an "independent union" (Friday 1994: 135–36). In June 1933, the leaders convened a meeting of the FLA to deliberate about affiliation with the AFL. After an affirmative vote by members, the AFL granted a charter to the Cannery Workers and Farm Laborers Union (CWFLU) Local 18257. Longtime activist Virgil Duyungan became the union's inaugural, and quickly controversial, president. Other officers included: M. Espivitu, vice president; Tony Rodrigo, treasurer; Joe Mislang, secretary; Ramon, publicity director; and Ernesto Mangaoang and Ponce Torres, trustees. John Ayamo, a Filipino attorney in Seattle, agreed to represent the union in all legal disputes and future contracts with employers. He was a

Fig. 6 Union pioneers Virgil Duyungan, Tony Rodrigo, C. Mislang, and M. Espivitu in 1933. Courtesy Filipino American National Historical Society.

classic "union lawyer," at once a vital player yet often at odds with the union's elected leadership (Casaday 1938, 361).

The Seattle union local got off to a slow start. In 1934, the leaders Duyungan and Ayamo testified before the NRA hearings in California about the abominable work conditions, and they began efforts to organize fieldworkers in Washington State and cannery workers in Alaska. Employers and labor contractors hired thugs to harass the union organizers. The union leaders excoriated labor contractors of all nationalities in private memos, but the organizers of the new union initially sidestepped direct mention of Filipino contractors as they protested the labor contractor system in the hearings perhaps because Pio De Cano submitted a petition signed by many Filipinos supporting the contract system. As a result, the message to the NRA was muddled (Friday 1994, 140). At the same time, it is clear that the "contract work culture evolved into a union work culture" shaped by ethnic, racial, and ideological affiliations (5). Despite its motto of "Unity Is Strength" for the Filipino-first union, factionalism dominated the early period. The CWFLU faced competition by rival unions, including the militant, communist-fronted Fishermen's and Cannery Worker's Industrial Union and the AFL-based Japanese Cannery Workers Association (JCWA), represented by Seattle lawyer and influential Nisei community leader Clarence Arai. The CWFLU itself was also divided internally between moderates and radical leftists as well as by homeland regional differences among Ilocanos, Viscayans, and Tagalogs. As a result, the new union made only limited gains in organizing either agricultural or cannery workers.

President Duyungan, after testifying before NRA hearings, did manage to negotiate with employers and NRA officials a new "Code of Fair Competition for the Canned Salmon Industry" that specified a minimum wage for workers, authorized the right of employees to bargain collectively, and banned the labor contract arrangement. The hearings provided a "necessary opportunity for self-assertion," feeding the unionizing momentum, historian Casaday (1938, 353) concluded. In short, select official legal actions during the period also provided support for unionization. John Arnold, a middle-level bureaucrat at the NRA, worked hard to eradicate the contract system, but the new code only modified the system, although it arguably weakened industry ties and won increasing support for a more cooperative union alternative (Friday 1994, 143–44). Still, the subsequent union bargaining for the 1934 season only ratified the terms of the code, and the labor contract system continued largely as before, with contractors recruiting workers and paying their union dues

Fig. 7 Cannery worker Labor Day float with Margaret Ray Duyungan, wife of President Virgil Duyungan, in the early 1930s. Courtesy Filipino American National Historical Society.

to CWFLU. Duyungan nevertheless quickly found a clever way to exploit the new system. The union collected dues and fees for many hundreds of workers from different ethnic groups but excluded them from union membership while terminating membership for others at the end of the season, thus enabling the leaders to amass funds without having to pay monthly per capita membership fees to the national AFL office (Stotts-Johnson 2009; Masson and Guimary 1981b,: 13). Duyungan promised to use the funds to build a year-round union, a goal that won a mix of support and criticism from workers.

Accusations of fund mismanagement soon divided the union, driving dissidents—led by lawyer Ayamo, contractor De Cano, Leo Raduta, and Vicente Navea—to break away and found a competing union, the Filipino Labor Protective Association (FLPA) (Stotts-Johnson 2009; Masson and Guimary 1981b: 13). In April of 1935, the new Maritime Federation of the Pacific (MFP), led by International Longshoremen's Association (ILA) president Harry Bridges, attempted unsuccessfully to reunite the two unions of predominantly Filipino cannery workers.[5] In a curious twist, the CWFLU took money from employers to cross the ILA picket line in the ground-shaking strike of 1934 at West Coast ports, in the process misleading workers that their extra fees supplying the funds covered their union membership. Duyungan also was criticized for plotting with ILA strike leaders and contributing large amounts of funds to the ILA strike fund. While workers labored in the canneries, moreover, Duyungan and other officials raised salaries and bought cars for themselves, fueling further resentment (Dade 2009). Soon thereafter, the FLPA filed charges alleging CWFLU leadership misuse of funds, the Seattle Central Labor Council launched its own investigation, and the AFL threatened to suspend the union charter if it did not pay its full per capita tax. The judge dismissed the legal charges initiated by FLPA for insufficient evidence, but the trial revealed that the union was broke.

Subsequently, in the summer of 1935, Duyungan pleaded guilty to defrauding the Emergency Relief Administration of a small amount, landing him in jail for six months (Masson and Guimary 1981b). Duyungan was reelected president when he was freed from jail, but his much publicized corrupt practices had greatly eroded support from the thinning ranks of union members. He thus initiated a creative strategy to recruit Japanese workers and then black cannery workers ("The Colored Organization") into the union to expand the membership and to demonstrate his leadership skills. When the cannery employers urged an alliance between the FLPA and CWFLU to consolidate the bargaining agent in 1936, the two unions overcame disagreement regarding the latter's corrupt practices and united around the common goal of replacing the labor contractors' grip with union control. Through this troubled, tense period, the CWFLU managed internal factionalism, negotiated wage increases, mollified remaining Chinese workers, and grew in size to a multiethnic, multiracial union of three thousand members. Before the canning season that year, "from ten to fifteen thousand Filipinos struck" along the waterfront where steamers were readying to transport cannery workers. The result was that the companies were forced to sign a contract improving working conditions. As Ponce Torres recalled, "by giving us, raising us good wages, better conditions . . . we all come to agreement that there was no speed up, there was no cheating in the overtime and also the food should be improved. . . . It was all improved during that season" (cited in Fujita-Rony 2003, 187; Cordova 1983, 80). In the same period, Ernesto Mangaoang, a skilled and militant activist, ascended as the lead organizer of agricultural workers in the Pacific Northwest, although the union still had made few efforts to organize resident Filipino and other cannery workers in Alaska.

In fall of 1936, Virgil Duyungan again won election, defeating the FLPA faction by vowing to eliminate, finally, the labor contractors and their exploitative system from the salmon canneries. During the previous year, Duyungan also had led a much publicized popular campaign against the illegal gambling halls in Seattle and the canneries, which were robbing workers of their wages. The union also undertook a very influential public relations endeavor to provide financial support to the important newspaper the *Philippine-American Chronicle* in exchange for a regular column that served as a mouthpiece for union causes (Stotts-Johnson 2009; Friday 1994, 145).

Then, on a December night in 1936, a violent tragedy ripped the union. Virgil Duyungan and union secretary Aurelio Simon dined with Placido Patron at the Gyokko Ken Café in Seattle's Chinatown at Patron's request. Patron left the table around 9 p.m., returned with a gun, and shot to death both of his "guests," although the dying Duyungan managed to return fire and kill his murderer. Patron was the nephew of a Japanese labor contractor, so the leading interpretation by historians—including Trinidad Rojo (1952 [UWSC])—is that he acted as a hit man on behalf of the contractors or perhaps as an angered relative (Dade 2009). Before he died, Patron reportedly defended his action because the labor leaders "had been trying to cut in on his hiring-hall business and he wouldn't let them" (quoted in Fresco 1999). Many others at the time, including Duyungan's wife, speculated instead that it was angry union adversaries who plotted the murder. In a later interview, she recounted repeated threats from union rivals and contractors against Duyungan, which is why he obtained a license to carry a gun in 1936.[6] Years later Trinidad Rojo reported that Duyungan's last words to Ponce Torres were "Ponce, be careful," harbingering another consequential murder of union leaders forty-five years later (Rojo 1952 [UWSC]).

Regeneration through Violence: The Union Expands

Whatever the murderer's motive, and however controversial Duyungan's performance as leader had been, the deadly deed ended up solidifying and energizing the fractionalized union. As often with emerging political organizations, murderous violence against the founders proved to be regenerative, as the two slain leaders quickly became martyrs for the union effort. Instantly, the routine hostile coverage of Duyungan's crooked ways in the local press subsided and news coverage focused instead on thousands of people who marched in a memorial procession through Seattle. "It was the biggest funeral parade ever given to Filipinos in the United States" (Rojo 1947 [UWSC]). A Memorial Fund Committee was established, and an investigation into the murder was initiated by the union. The San Francisco Cannery Union, Local 5, contributed $1,000 to the memorial fund. A representative for the CWFLU was quoted in the progressive Washington Commonwealth Federation's newspaper, the *Sunday News*, as saying "Our brothers faced death for us. . . . For their sakes, we must pick up the reins where they left off and eradicate the evil that killed them" (Dade 2009). Cannery unionization was widely celebrated in the press for advancing workers' welfare, and commitment to eradicating the labor contractors from the salmon canning industry became a rallying cry. The union demanded a hiring hall and got it in the spring of 1937, consolidating control over worker hiring.

Union solidarity was short lived, however. The new president, Casimiro Abella, from the FLPA, proved less adept than Duyungan at managing the ethnic factions dividing workers. This provided an opportunity for Norwegian American business agent Conrad Espe, a militant unionist from the MFP, to broker peace and work on organizing agricultural workers while pushing the union to the Left with the goal of joining ally ILWU in eventually affiliating with the newly formed progressive CIO. Espe was supported by the growing majority of young, radical Ilocanos and university student activists who had ascended to leadership roles, thus exacerbating educational cleavages along with ethnic and regional splits in the union.

Amid these internal developments arose a major external political and legal challenge. In February 1937, AFL organizer Leo Flynn and Seattle Labor Council secretary C. W. Doyle, both allies of the more conservative Teamsters, maneuvered to charter three new ethnically defined unions—one each for Filipinos, Japanese, and Chinese—under AFL control as the Alaska Cannery Workers Union (ACWU) Local 20454. While vowing to counter its racist reputation, the new ethnically based unions chartered by the AFL seemed to many a continuation of the factional past. These rivals emerged at the same time that the CWFLU and the Canned Salmon Industry (CSI) were negotiating a new contract that raised wages by up to 40 percent over the previous year, established a closed shop, banned the labor contractors, and recognized the CWFLU as the unitary bargaining agent for Alaska cannery workers. The ACWU immediately established a picket line, which Teamsters honored, while 1,200 CWFLU workers and their powerful allies in the ILWU defiantly trampled the line and continued to work. The latter delegation formed the largest group in the May Day parade that year. The CWFLU then went to the Seattle Superior Court and on May 4 secured a temporary restraining order instructing the AFL unions to halt picketing and related efforts to undermine the CWFLU (Masson and Guimary 1981b, 20). The CWFLU also worked to challenge the AFL separate ethnic-based union model by rebuilding around a vision of a single, multiethnic union of Japanese, Chinese, Koreans, Hawaiians, blacks, and whites along with Filipinos. Union leadership remained primarily in the hands of Filipinos, but they yielded seats to representatives of other groups in a good faith commitment to their recovered "one big union" vision.

On the one hand, by early 1937, the CWFLU had managed to take huge steps forward toward fulfilling the founders' aspirations. The union claimed several thousand members, it was recognized as sole bargaining agent for most cannery workers in Alaska, and it was accepted by the Seattle Central Labor Council and the increasingly potent MFP. With a growing treasury, the union commenced with organizing agricultural workers in Washington and Oregon (Masson and Guimary 1981b, 21). The union unquestionably provided new opportunities for economic mobility to Filipinos who were denied access in other domains of the economy. On the other hand, tensions grew between militant leftists—led by Conrad Espe and University of Washington student Ireneo Cabatit—increasingly linked to the Bridges-led ILWU and the smaller group of moderates—including President Casimiro Abella—who leaned toward the AFL. Moreover, escalating military conflict between Japan and China ramped up nationalism that increased divisions among Asian ethnic workers (Friday 1994, 164–66). The first period of "dual unionism," where two unions or union factions claimed rights to represent the same workers, was in 1937–1938. While dual unionism was often heralded by Wobblies and leftists as necessary to push moderate unions in more aggressive, radical directions, the cannery unions experienced the opposite. The radicals dominated the winning union, while it was moderates allied with the AFL that posed challenges. As we will see, similar divisions continued through World War II.

These tensions were exacerbated by aggressive competition between the AFL and the CIO to organize cannery and agricultural workers up and down the coast. In July 1937, the MFP, in which CWLFU was a member, left the AFL for the CIO after the AFL turned over its warehousing dominion to the teamsters. Around the same time, a jurisdictional dispute over workers in a small Alaska cannery coincided with the CWFLU decision to cease paying fees to the national AFL, so the AFL temporarily canceled the CWFLU membership. The AFL then secured from the Seattle Superior Court an order freezing CWFLU funds. After it was revealed that the CWFLU concealed upward of $15,000 from the auditors, the CWFLU negotiated a compromise payment to the AFL in exchange for dropping criminal charges (Masson and Guimary 1981b). Once again, factional disputes played out in the mainstream legal system.

In an October union referendum vote, after many workers had left for agricultural harvests, the membership of CWFLU voted 1117 to 124 (9 to 1) to leave the AFL and to become Local 7 of the CIO-affiliated UCAPAWA. Along with the new Local 5 in San Francisco and Local 226 in Portland, these three unions represented six thousand workers and became among the most militant and influential forces in UCAPAWA. These locals provided up to half of UCAPAWA income; their "per capita dues were used to organize Negroes, whites, Mexicans, and other agricultural workers in various parts of the country," Trinidad Rojo (1952, 15 [UWSC]) later recalled. Many of the moderates complained that the referendum did not include most workers, especially the Japanese, so they left the union in an attempt to reaffiliate 18257 with the AFL and break up UCAPAWA, a move supported by the CSI (Friday 1994, 167). These divide and conquer efforts were fueled by red-baiting against Conrad Espe and other allegedly communist leaders. The AFL colluded with the FBI and immigration officials to harass Local 7 members, leading to some arrests. Local 7-CIO filed several rounds of complaints with the National Labor Relations Board (NLRB) charging both the AFL and the canning industry with unfair labor practices and then applied for a consent audit that affirmed the union's representation of cannery workers (Viernes 2012, 136). Leaders in the CIO worked to overcome divisions among Filipinos by appealing to fraternal organizations and the memory of slain leaders Duyungan and Simon (Friday 1994, 169). In April 1938, Local 7 won the consent audit handily.

The NLRB then set a new date for elections in early May. The industry and AFL, with support from the Seattle mayor and police, continued to harass Local 7 members. Amid many physical skirmishes, Local 7 won the vote, 1560 to 1307 (with over five hundred neutral votes). The AFL refused to accept the outcome, but Local 7 prevailed with MFP support and began dispatching workers weeks later. By 1938, following NLRB legal procedures and with critical support from both government and the ILWU, the multiracial CIO affiliate Local 7 was recognized as the sole bargaining agent for the cannery industry. On June 15, 1938, the MFP convention in San Francisco seated Local 7 of Seattle and Local 5 of San Francisco as coastwise affiliates and Local 226 of Portland as an independent local. As Chris Friday summarizes, "once Chinese, Japanese, and Filipinos recognized their common circumstance, they proved indispensable allies to one another in determining what should replace contracting." The 1938 victory "for an ethnically inclusive union was momentous" (Friday 1994, 149, 172). Dual unionism was overcome, for a time.

Expanding Legal Capacity

Our narrative of this complex history of factional disputes within and among unions representing Asian workers illustrates how legal wrangling and litigation in various courts and before the NLRB dramatically shaped the character of the evolving salmon cannery workers' union. Indeed, litigation and grievance claims increasingly infused and constituted virtually every aspect of ongoing activity by salmon cannery workers and their representatives. In the process, a small group of loosely allied attorneys developed skills and alliances with the union for ongoing representation.

The merger of the Seattle-based, Filipino-led salmon cannery workers with California locals in UCAPAWA added further to these legal capacities and inclinations. For example, the San Francisco local ACWU grew very directly out of ongoing legal mobilization activity. One important experience that contributed to collective union commitment was the long legal battle against Young and Mayer, the exploitative San Francisco contracting firm (Baker 1997, 11–13).[7] In the 1920s, cannery workers disembarking in California were authorized to file claims with the Deputy Labor Commissions for underpayment. The workers sometimes pooled funds and hired San Francisco attorneys to press their claims. Historian Lauren Casaday found evidence of many group claims filed by lawyers representing groups of cannery workers in the 1920s. These early efforts were notable acts of collective legal mobilization, but California law, the NRA Code, and the labor commissioners offered limited resources for "alien" workers challenging the entrenched contractors who had many allies in government and forces of intimidation at their disposal (Casaday 1938, 233). At the close of the 1933 cannery season, though, cannery workers' complaints against Young and Mayer—charging contractors with bribery, blacklisting, intimidation, and violence—proliferated to over six hundred. Initially, the deputy in the Labor Commissioner's office "sabotaged" the claims, and a biased trial judge rebuffed the claimants. However, the abundant evidence supplied by the complaints and a long list of witnesses enabled attorney Arthur L. Johnson to successfully prosecute Young and Mayer in superior court on a felony charge of criminal conspiracy (Casaday 1938, 241) followed by a settlement of civil claims for damages. The reliance on grievance processes in the ACWU exploded after 1934; one analyst estimated that *each* of the 1,500 cannery workers may have participated in two or more legal grievances during the last half of the 1930s (Baker 1997, 13–14). This routine mobilization around legal grievances, rights claims, and demands for justice was formative for the increasingly militant union workers in the early ACWU that just a few years later joined CWFLU in the CIO-based UCAPAWA (Baker 1997, 14; Casaday 1938, 353–54).

The CIO affiliation also connected the Seattle-based cannery workers with the robust legal support network and practices that had developed to aid farmworkers and dried fruit cannery workers in California (Romney 2016, 10–14). The vegetable and fruit packing industry in California generally preferred the business union model of AFL representation for workers. However, Mexican and Asian seasonal workers often inclined toward the newer, more left-leaning and democratic CIO unions, including the ILWU and UCAPAWA. In the late 1930s, the AFL and the industry escalated efforts to head off CIO affiliations, often blacklisting and harassing workers who advocated for change. The CIO unions regularly filed claims for unfair labor practices with the mostly responsive NLRB regional offices, establishing close working relations between CIO attorneys and board attorneys as part of their organizing efforts. The industry protested that workers were exempt from NLRB jurisdiction both because food packing did not involve interstate commerce and because the work was "agricultural" rather than "industrial." In most instances, local NLRB officials conducted careful, evidence-based, legalistic hearings that rebuffed industry claims and supported their jurisdictional authority to halt and remedy unfair labor practices. The AFL then used its influence in Washington DC to stall or alter national office rulings on recommendations from the local offices along with litigation in federal courts. However, the Ninth Circuit Court several times rejected industry appeals and affirmed NLRB jurisdiction to enable CIO organizing, including two important 1938 rulings that drew on Supreme Court jurisprudence concerning the reach of Wagner Act authority.[8] These legal battles often protracted disputes and imposed delays in workers' struggles for rights, but they facilitated the overall advance of progressive union forces (Romney 2016).

UCAPAWA and other CIO unions made only limited gains in wresting food-packing workers' representation from the AFL in subsequent years. But these early legal battles established the UCAPAWA tendency to eschew strike-based organizing tactics and instead focus on vigorous engagement with New Deal industrial regulatory agencies and courts. Moreover, the affiliation of salmon cannery workers with California UCAPAWA locals provided alliance with networks of effective "repeat player" attorneys—such as Luisa Morena, Carey McWilliams, Manuel Ruiz, Ben Margolis—and other civil rights activists who in the late 1930s were amply experienced in fighting against racism and for rights of workers (Vargas 2007). Alliance with the powerful MFP and especially the ILWU and its extensive legal network was important as well and would become even more critical in the post–World War II era. This connected the cannery workers with many skilled, committed, Left lawyers, including communist attorney John Caughlan. One of the little appreciated implications of the cannery worker affiliation with the CIO thus was, as political scientist Doug Baker (1997, chap. 4) put it, the dramatic enhancement of a "resource vital to survival: access to the radical strategy to revive a legal activism network, reminiscent of the 19th century Chinese" contractor era. As Baker (1997, 2) summarizes, "throughout the 1930s, 40s and 50s legal advocacy on behalf of the salmon canning union movement remained energetic and effective."

Internal Consolidation, Formalization, Legalization

Leftist Irineo R. Cabatit served as president amid the continuing turmoil that attended reaffiliation as UCAPAWA Local 7. In 1939, Trinidad Rojo was elected to the first of several nonconsecutive terms. Rojo quickly discovered that previous leaders had been inattentive or corrupt in their fiscal management of the union, which was nearly bankrupt and more than $10,000 in debt. "Now that we had beaten our external enemies, we had to conquer our internal problems." Rojo thus made his two year term a period of "internal consolidation and many reforms" to increase fiscal integrity, transparency, and sustainability (Rojo 1947, 5 [UWSC]). His own documented account of organizational achievements included payment of past debts, institutionalization of cheaper and more efficient dispatching methods, reduction of officer and staff salaries as well as numbers, formalization of permanent membership cards and records to reduce corrupt tampering, more frequent and accurate reporting of union transactions, reorganization of leadership to fit the union constitution and bylaws, credit authorization restricted to the treasurer-secretary departments, formalization of staff office working hours, implementation of standardized grievance procedures along the lines of the ACWU, and more. "The overwhelming majority of the constructive rules which have guided the Union were drafted in 1939–40," he later summarized (Rojo 1947, 11 [UWSC]). In short, just as the union was constructed through mobilization of workers' rights supported by national New Deal law, so did the union under Rojo increase its internal administrative legalization and formal democratization (Edelman 2016). Local 7 became a union very much constituted by law.

Moreover, Rojo several times moved the union office location in downtown Seattle, which increasingly was the urban hub for the industry and where it would remain for decades to come. These actions recognized that the union hall was the center of union life, the locus of the union power to dispatch workers. The commitment to upgrading the office location and space also was emblematic of Rojo's pledge to increasing the organizational rationality of the union. Rojo himself took pride in making the union more "business like," a commitment that expressed his disdain for many of his leftist colleagues and compromised the memory of his achievements for many who identified with the union's radical aspirational struggles. As he wrote in his own history of Local 7,

> Left wing extremists in our Union may be allergic to a business like administration which is practiced by capitalism. But as stated elsewhere Donald Henderson, International President of the FTA who was reportedly a communist, used to say, "A union is a business just like any others. If it does not balance its budget, sooner or later, it shall hit the rocks." It is a capitalistic aphorism from the lips of a realistic and brilliant alleged communist. (Rojo 1947, 11 [UWSC])[9]

Between 1938 and 1942, union leaders also struggled to replace contract-era practices and relationships among rank and file workers (Friday 1994, chap. 6). The first challenge was to institutionalize a new system for worker recruitment. Members were supplied "books" that were stamped each time they paid their dues; dues payment put members in line for the first dispatched jobs. Members often loaned or sold their books to other workers, however, creating a perpetual problem of union control and demands for worker allegiance. The new dispatch system was committed to establishing "a fair race quota" (Rojo n.d., 30), but it also continued to be dogged by the ethnic factions and favoritism on which the old system was built. Dispatchers were routinely torn between fidelity to union principles of ethnically neutral seniority, ethnic group loyalties, and personal gain (bribes). Imposing discipline on the workers also posed another continuing challenge. Workers commonly fought with each other and gambled, both violations of union rules that merited fines or expulsion. The biggest obstacles to reform of union principles were the foremen, who were wedded to old contract system practices and still derived power from management of crews and roles as ethnic representatives. Union leaders countered by removing foremen from dispatching processes, implementing stricter screening policies, and imposing fines for insubordination. The union also created new bureaucratic positions—including timekeepers, coordinating committees, department heads, and delegates—to wrest control from the foremen.

The imposition of discipline and internal reorganization not surprisingly alienated many workers, again exacerbating long-standing ethnic tensions and loyalties. Union efforts to win allegiance from workers focused on constantly improving wages and work conditions. Trinidad Rojo thus boasted that the union under his leadership negotiated, against industry protests, a 33 percent wage increase and new rates of overtime pay as well as the right to appoint all foremen, killing off more vestiges of the exploitative contract labor system. One creative strategy for raising wages was to change the three-tier job classification system from the contracting era, reducing it to two tiers by folding semiskilled into the skilled category. That accomplished little in fact, however, as increased mechanization sped up work and wage increases barely kept up with living costs (Friday 1994, 180). The unions did make greater progress in pushing for better sanitation at work, and living conditions were improved. By late 1930s, "the worst problems associated with wages, hours, and conditions had been resolved," historian Chris Friday (1994, 180–81) summarizes, although the union's claims taking credit for improvement were inflated. As a result, a "fragile alliance" among multiple ethnic groups of workers and the commitment to union internal reform were sustained until World War II forced more dramatic changes.

The Proliferating Power of the "Civil Rights Union"

The cannery workers' union evolved into a formidable social force during its first decade. Above all, the union developed as an organizational advocate for advancing Filipinos' rights both at work and more broadly in American society. Indeed, the "indispensable" roles of Filipino laborers in the American economy were at the heart of their demands for rights as both workers and deserving citizens. The union was involved in nearly every struggle over civil rights by Filipinos in the Pacific Northwest during the 1930s and years beyond, including those reviewed in the previous chapter. The CWFL and then Local 7 fought for years against restrictions on Filipino landownership and leasing, including joining a resolution challenging Yakima officials who confiscated property from Filipinos and issuing a petition in 1937 demanding a veto of House Bill No. 663, which aimed to restrict permanently Filipinos from owning or leasing land. They also supported workers denied rights to employment in shipyards and other workplaces because they were deemed aliens, joined in long-standing battles against antimiscegenation laws, helped organize farmworkers in order to defend their rights, and mobilized to ameliorate or protest many incidents of violence and intimidation (Fujita-Rony 2003, 175). All, in all, as Hìnnershitz (2013, 132) summarizes, "Filipino workers used the CWFLU as a vehicle for labor as well as basic rights and protections as American subjects and economic contributors to the United States."

In this regard, the cannery workers' activism exemplified what Robert Korstad (2003) labeled *civil rights unionism*, much like UCAPAWA Local 22 and the BSCP led by A. Philip Randolph in the same era. Some of their struggles for rights were waged in American courtrooms, but the campaigns for rights took place all over (Sarat 1990), in virtually every sphere of society, through a host of advocacy tactics. Indeed, the core project of cannery workers was a radical demand for egalitarian rights of citizen entitlement and democratic practice within all aspects of social life, including at work. Unions conferred collective legal standing to migrant workers of uncertain status as individuals along with organizational resources to support collective rights campaigns. To recognize the union as a support network (McCann 1994; Epp 1998) of rights politics, as social scientists often do, hardly begins to appreciate how much the union and its legal engagements were mutually constitutive forces.

Union solidarity built on bonds forged among leaders who were students at the University of Washington and the oppositional work culture nurtured by the contracting system. But it is important also to recognize the degree to which the union, its members and leaders, established a powerful foothold in Filipino community life. By challenging the labor contractors, the union exposed and altered power hierarchies in and around the community in several ways. First, the union significantly empowered Filipino workers by eliminating their dependent relationship on Chinese and Japanese contractors who exploited them in the early years. Second, the union expanded Filipino social as well as workplace power relative to rival Japanese, Chinese, and white workers' unions that developed in the period. Third, in supplanting the influential, often prestigious Filipino contractors like Pio De Cano, union activists increasingly became authoritative leaders within the Filipino community in Seattle. The union in particular became an important organizational site for the emergence and experience of university-educated community leaders, developing into "an alternate base for power within the community and a public arena for men of diverse class orientations and interests" (Fujita-Rony 2013, 192). Prominent union members came to share educational and social status with business interests and former contractors, again altering the balance of power within the community. This new influence to some degree democratized the community, joining egalitarian commitments as civil rights activists with capacities to build solidarity among the many factions of Filipinos divided along lines of ethnicity and regional background, educational levels, religious faith, ideology, and sites of work.

Union leaders such as Chris Mensalves and Ponce Torres led the way in these early campaigns for Filipino unity. The former had migrated to the United States for advanced education and a career as a lawyer, but he ended up working on farms in California during the 1930s, where he became a labor activist and developed affinity with communists. As Gene Viernes summarized in "Daring to Dream," his 1978 valedictory article about Mensalvas,

> In America, Filipinos could not practice law or medicine . . . own land . . . marry whites. Disenchanted with the "American Dream," Chris returned to the fields. Chris brought with him a new belief, a new dream acquired . . . [from] the International Workers of the World (IWW). . . . He joined with other Filipinos and formed the Committee for the Protection of Filipino Rights. . . . One right the committee targeted was the right for Filipinos to organize.

Mensalvas was elected secretary in the Filipino Labor Union and, as an opponent of AFL racial exclusion and ethnic balkanization, led the FLU to join the Cannery Workers and Farm Laborers Union (CWLFU) in forming UCAPAWA-CIO. In these years, Mensalvas became a friend and ally to Carlos Bulosan, with whom he cofounded the proletarian magazine *New Tide* in 1934 (Denning 1998, 222) as well as the CPFR in 1939. Mensalvas became the model for the character Jose in *America Is in the Heart*, the aforementioned laborer whose foot was severed while escaping white detectives. The CPFR launched a campaign to generate twenty-thousand signatures supporting a bill for Filipino naturalization sponsored by radical New York congressman Vito Marcantonio, who represented the American Labor Party. Using the knowledge that he had acquired from interactions with the IWW and working in conjunction with the CPFR, Mensalvas began organizing in the fields of California and then moved back and forth to Portland and Seattle. Atop lettuce crates he gave speeches on the need for organization, preaching the principle "With unity comes strength" (Mabalon 2013, 227).

Ponce Torres was animated by the same commitment to worker solidarity, which he cast often in terms of a male brotherhood. He was, historian Chris Friday reports, viewed as "crazy" for advocating a union in Seattle's Chinatown, the home of the contractors' offices in the late 1920s. He replied, "We are but [a] laboring family that would belong to one class, that [we] are brothers rather than . . . Visayans or Ilocanos or Tagalogs or Pangasinan(s) or any sectionalist feeling. That [is] . . . the hardest part for us to do, to make ourselves realize that we are one Filipino race" (Friday 1994, 125). In short, the common subjection along intersectional lines of race and class solidified the union cause, moderating the ethnic and regional divisions and shaping the developing political rights consciousness of the union activists.

As noted previously, the union increased its influence early on by establishing a complementary relationship with an important newspaper, the *Philippine-American Chronicle*, and leading popular causes such as campaigning against gambling halls and drug use in Seattle. The union also worked hard to win support from a broad array of Filipino fraternal and ethnic associations. In 1938, this included the Narvacan Club, the Bauangenian Club, the Pangasinan Association of the Pacific Northwest, the Vigan Club, and the Santa Maria Association, among others, in Seattle (Fujita-Rony 2003, 190). Union leaders played key roles in the important Caballeros de Dimas-Alang, the organization inspired by Jose Rizal honoring the "brotherhood of workers" that became a pillar of Filipino communities on the West Coast. Union activists became key organizers of important community events, such as the annual Rizal Day, beauty contest spectacles, and dances (Fujita-Rony 2003). The students who built the union, including Trinidad Rojo, also were members of the Filipino Students' Christian Movement (Hinnershitz 2013), a key organization that linked race, religion, and class struggle for young Filipinos. At the same time, the union increased its stature by offering support to actions by Filipino workers in the homeland. In all these regards, the union provided something of a "mutual aid organization" to people in need. While its influence was democratizing in many regards, though, it is worth noting that the exclusively male union brotherhood also tended to reinforce traditional gender hierarchies and devaluation of women's reproductive labor within the Filipino community (Fujita-Rony 2003), although commitments to gender equity would grow over subsequent decades.

In some ways, the union thus served as a consolidating, even conservative force in the community, nurturing internal solidarity and collective identity, fortifying the important local havens in a hostile, often heartless world. But, of course, the union was also very much a *radicalizing* political force among many Filipinos as well. From the beginning, many leaders of the union were profoundly influenced by the Wobblies, socialists, and communists who thrived on the West Coast, especially around the waterfront and in the rural extraction and agricultural industries. The workers' ideological inclinations were shaped and expressed by regular alliances with radical groups, unions, and individuals. Communist-affiliated unions on the West Coast such as the Trade Union Unity League and the CAIWU actively recruited Filipino laborers and cultivated left-wing commitments (Baldoz 2014). Similarly, the CPFR initiated by Mensalves, Bulosan, and other leftists was inspired by the Committee for the Protection of the Foreign Born, an important Popular Front organization. The alliance with the ILA and then the ILWU, led by Harry Bridges, bolstered leftist inclinations and identities. As we noted in the previous chapter, Carlos Bulosan's writings provide ample evidence regarding leftist, including communist, alliances in Filipino union politics. Indeed, the moment of Allos's political awakening to critical consciousness about deprivations of rights recounted in our previous chapter took place after attending a local meeting of the Communist Party around the time of the affiliation of Local 7 with the CIO. "The meeting was only a sampling of ideas—although I found out later that it was the beginning of a statewide campaign for the recognition of Filipino rights and privileges" (Bulosan 1973, 269).

The union and the community were undeniably divided between Left radicals and moderates, a division that would grow over time. But this split was softened by the fact that many radical activists also were flexible, pragmatic, and grounded in the historical, material, lived experience of Filipinos as an oppressed people. As Bulosan (1973, 269) wrote, "it was comforting to know that these men [communists] were stirred by the social strangulation of our people. But it was our plan to listen to the community, not to propose a program of action." The hallmark of radical leaders such as Duyungan, Espe, and Mensalvas—like that of ally Harry Bridges, who provided inspiration and support—was their political skill in managing factions, strategizing for concrete incremental campaigns, and negotiating for leverage and just improvements for the workers. They were committed to democratic community building among all Filipinos as well as advancing the union, reformist rights campaigns, and transformation of the American racial capitalist order.

The activists similarly balanced different types of demands for rights, recognizing the intersectional dimensions of racial and class injustice they endured. On the one hand, Filipino activists routinely and humbly requested simple inclusion and assimilation; as P. V. Algas put it, "we only ask the gaining of rights which she accords her citizens" (quoted in Hinnershitz 2013, 144). In this modality most frequently directed publicly to the dominant white society, the focus usually was in challenging racial exclusion and hierarchy, mirroring civil rights discourse of African Americans, Mexican Americans, and Asian Americans that was ascendant in that era. On the other hand, they also demanded radical social transformation, most often focusing their challenges on capitalism and imperialism, and on the promise of economic rights (Goluboff 2007). One motivation was that class-based appeals proved effective to muting ethnic divisions among Filipinos and with Chinese and Japanese. This discourse arguably was most common in internal dialogue among activists, at least in the early years; it was strategically less public so as not to alienate white supporters, undermine relations with business interests, and invite state repression. As the Trinidad Rojo quote above testified, communist activists knew the value of acting like business agents and adapting to capitalist social relations even while organizing to challenge and change that socioeconomic order. In sum, claims of rights to both ethnic inclusion and class-based economic justice proved to be essential for efforts to nurture solidarity among Asians (Friday 1994, 171). They believed that "labor rights are civil rights" (Vargas 2007).

Again, Carlos Bulosan provides an intriguing window into this developing praxis of egalitarian rights radicalism. His writings illustrate repeatedly how Left worker activists reconstructed familiar claims for equal rights from hypocritical rhetoric into a clarion call for fundamental change. This understanding is captured directly by Bulosan's repeated invocations of the struggle for fundamental change in the core organizing principles of America. "We in America understand the many imperfections of democracy and the malignant disease corroding its very heart." The core imperfection was that the promise of rights remained tethered to white supremacy, predatory exchange relations, capitalist hierarchy, that is, to social and economic inequality. "It is a great wrong that anyone in America, whether he be brown or white, should be illiterate or hungry or miserable" (Bulosan 1973, 212). The term *hungry* (or *hunger*) is repeated many dozens of times in *America Is in the Heart* for a reason: it describes a discrete human condition of subaltern peoples and becomes a metaphor for pervasive material want and aspirations to reduce

Fig. 8 Cannery Crew, Wards Cove Packaging Co., Ketchikan, Alaska, 1940. University of Washington Libraries, Special Collections, UW 39789.

economic inequality. The centrality of the idea in Bulosan's writings is probably why FDR late in the New Deal era commissioned him to write "Freedom from Want" as one of the "Four Freedoms in America." The statement is simple, subtle, and only slightly "deceptive" about its radical defense of redistribution according to needs as well as abilities, of the freedom to produce and to use the fruits of labor, and of basic rights as workers and consumers as well as citizens. Bulosan's words clearly echo Karl Marx's maxim "from each according to his ability, to each according to his needs" (Marx [1875] 1978, 531).

> You usually see us working or waiting for work, and you think you know us, but our outward guise is more deceptive than our history. . . . Our march toward security and peace is the march of freedom—the freedom that we should like to become a living part of. It is the dignity of the individual to live in a society of free men, where the spirit of understanding and belief exists; of understanding that all men are equal; that all men, whatever their color, race, religion or estate, should be given equal opportunity to serve themselves and each other according to their needs and abilities. But we are not really free unless we use what we produce. So long as the fruit of

> our labor is denied us, so long will want manifest itself in a world of slaves. It is only when we have plenty to eat—plenty of everything—that we begin to understand what freedom means. To us, freedom is not an intangible thing. When we have enough to eat, then we are healthy enough to enjoy what we eat. Then we have the time and ability to read and think and discuss things. Then we are not merely living but also becoming a creative part of life. It is only then that we become a growing part of democracy. . . . But sometimes we wonder if we are really a part of America. We recognize the main springs of American democracy in our right to form unions and bargain through them collectively, our opportunity to sell our products at reasonable prices, and the privilege of our children to attend schools where they learn the truth about the world in which they live. . . . We are the living dream of dead men. We the living spirit of free men. (Bulosan 1995, 131–33)

Transforming the promises of equality into a community of free persons, required, as Bulosan's contemporaries such as labor activists A. Philip Randolph and Harry Bridges advocated, at the least socialist reorganization of production, national redistribution of wealth, expanded state social services, and democratic governance. "That is why in this war we are bringing into the light our real aims and purposes. We are united in the effort to make an America in which the common man can find happiness. We are engaged in the gigantic task of building a new America. Whatever we are doing, we are all working toward a democratic society. . . . The old world will die so that a new world will be born with less sacrifice and agony on the living" (Bulosan 1995, 214). From the late 1920s, a democratic, multiracial civil rights union became for many Filipinos the primary expression and organizational resource of that radical egalitarian aspirational project.

3

Rights Radicalism amid "Restrictive" Law

The War Years

War was declared. Many of us were called to the service. Those left behind contributed to the war effort. . . . Everyone did his share. It is a difficult job to fight a war. We finally won. Many sacrifices were made. Trade unions suffered a setback. . . . During the organizational period men were clubbed and beaten on the picket lines. They were hungry, and their families suffered with them. Leaders were framed and murdered. The history of the union was written in blood.—ERNESTO MANGAOANG[1]

We are forced by restrictive laws, dangerous moves by certain branches of the government, the vicious lies of the capitalist press and yellow journalism, the warmongering of big business, the race-hating hysteria of reactionary organizations and groups . . . [and] by the living spirit of the great American heritage—the uncompromising stand to defend human rights and liberties in time of war or peace—to expose in our pages the maniacal machinations to undermine the American people's greatest and most sacred gift from the revolutionary fathers: that this nation was founded on the proposition that all men are created equal, that they are endowed by their Creator with certain inalienable rights, that among these are life, liberty and the pursuit of happiness.—CARLOS BULOSAN[2]

The complex, volatile episodes of union development during the Depression era were followed by instability and even deeper conflicts, both within the union and between militant union activists and the larger racial capitalist order, during the 1940s and 1950s. World War II brought contradictory consequences. On the one hand, the war enabled Filipino migrants to demonstrate that they deserved US citizenship through military service, while the soon to be sovereign Philippines nation-state was pulled even closer to the United States as a commercial partner and military ally against a common Japanese enemy. The overall status of Filipinos and the Philippines rose among white Americans just as that of Japan and Japanese Americans plummeted, leading to mass incarceration of the latter in concentration camps around the West Coast. One result was that citizenship rights were granted for some but not most Filipinos, who were still considered nationals or aliens, in the metropole. On the other hand, UCAPAWA Local 7 lost half of its members to the military and to better-paying defense industry jobs, while the pressures of wartime patriotism exacerbated tensions between moderates and leftists in the union leadership.

The effects of the subsequent Cold War years were more uniformly repressive and divisive. United States control of the Philippines for military and commercial ends escalated and took new forms. In the metropole, anticommunist legislation, government red-baiting campaigns, and media pressure harassed left-leaning union leaders, which led to hardships and imposed punitive or disciplinary pressures of many types. Filipino militants already familiar with local modes of repression in the 1920s and 1930s were subjected to dramatically escalating federal government surveillance and persecution during the second Red Scare in the late 1940s and 1950s (Baldoz 2014). In short, Filipino workers' foreign "brown" bodies that had been racially "blackened" in the colonial era metropole now were highlighted in "red"—merging into a kaleidoscope of imagery that radically magnified white citizens' anxieties in the racial capitalist empire. Citizenship rights were conferred on a small number of Filipinos but denied or withdrawn for those labor leaders accused of subversive activity or affiliation and labeled as "threats to national security." The Cold War–era legal regime created new categories of "restrictive" law that authorized highly discretionary, even arbitrary state violence against alleged political dissidents and their organizations, including Filipino cannery activists and their union. Once again, these Left activists were deprived of full liberal rights status, but they were hardly "outside" of law; they were very much subjected to harsh, punitive harassment by official law. Amid the patriotic purges of alleged communists, conflicts between union moderates and Left leadership factions deepened. Somewhat surprisingly, the Left leadership cadres in the union survived and even triumphed at nearly every point not least because of their strong standing in the Filipino community and alliance with the powerful International Longshoremen's and Warehousemen's Union (ILWU) and its revered leader Harry Bridges.[3]

Throughout the period, union activists struggled both against and through official US law, leading to numerous high-profile legal disputes, trials, and appellate court rulings. As political historian Doug Baker put it in his granular study of the cannery union culture, "contests for control of the cannery movement were played out in hundreds of internal trials. Factional battles spilled into the courts and dockets of several federal agencies" (Baker 1997). Despite ideological and personal cleavages among leadership factions, however, union activists remained steadfast in their invocations of American legal principles and deployment of rights discourse to advance their causes. Indeed, the growing harshness of US state repression, through both law and lawlessness, only solidified and intensified Filipino activist appeals to basic constitutional rights and liberties, often reframed as "human rights." Hence, one of the most important, perhaps surprising, features of the struggle was that self-identified socialists and communists articulated their struggles in the vernacular of basic rights and embraced the ideals and legal constructions of the "revolutionary fathers." As the lines from the union's *1952 Yearbook* cited in the second epigraph to this chapter proclaim, union activists were unified in ceaselessly invoking "the living spirit of the great American heritage—the uncompromising stand to defend human rights and liberties."

This chapter offers a sketch of this complex period that balances attention to internal union politics, the broader political context of official reaction, and the many ways that law worked as a constitutive force in both spheres. Our chosen chapter title, like our book title, is intentionally evocative. In our telling, Filipino cannery union activists were at once defiant toward repressive US law, wary about the promises of justice that official legal institutions might provide, and yet inspired by their own radical constructions of empowering possibilities grounded in egalitarian, democratic principles of legal rights. After documenting a series of struggles on the contested terrain of law in this chapter, we will directly address the curious character of persistent legal rights mobilization by committed socialist and even avowedly communist union activists at the high point of Cold War tensions in the United States.

The Second World War: Reconfiguring the Color Line Again

World War II created a variety of opportunities for Filipinos and incentives for white America to redraw the color line embedded in formal citizenship, naturalization, and immigration policies in the United States. The 1934 Tydings-McDuffie Act established a plan for transition of the Philippines to formal independence in 1946, but little changed in the skewed paternalistic relationship between US imperial authority and the Philippine Commonwealth during the interim probationary years. Two key provisions of the 1934 act sustained the hierarchical position of the United States (Baldoz 2011, 194). For one thing, all Filipinos were required to maintain their allegiance to the United States until independence. Second, the US president was authorized by the act to conscript Philippine people and resources for military action. Additional statutory acts and a patchwork of inconsistent legal policies and practices further complicated the uncertain status of Filipinos during and beyond the war years.

For example, the Neutrality Act of 1939, which amended the Immigration Act of 1924, banned all US citizens from traveling to combat zones. Claiming that they had been defined as aliens rather than citizens, fifty-three Filipino seamen on a ship to Great Britain sued in District Court to challenge as unlawful their firing by the US Customs Service. In 1940, the trial judge ignored the contradictions in standing legal constructions of Filipinos and ruled that the US government could conduct foreign affairs as it saw fit (Baldoz 2011, 200–201). "There is no merit in the contention that the inclusion of Filipinos within the definition of 'citizenship' is against public policy because the conduct of foreign relations is committed by the Constitution to the executive and legislative branches of the government, and the propriety of what is done is not a subject for judicial inquiry," Judge Hulbert wrote. The claimants were offered an opportunity to submit a "proper pleading" within ten days, but the judge ultimately found a "failure to state a cause of action" (*Suspine v. Compania* 1941, at 272–73).

In previous pages (chap. 2) we discussed how honorable military service had provided one possible, if highly uncertain, legal path to naturalized citizenship for some Filipinos after World War I. The Nationality Act of 1940 confirmed this path, authorizing a right to naturalization for "white persons, persons of African nativity or descent, and descendants of races indigenous to the Western Hemisphere" as well as for "Filipinos having the honorable service in the United States Army, Navy, Marine Corps, or Coast Guard" outlined in the act (§§ 303, 324); amendments in 1942 relaxed the usual residency requirements for Filipino military veterans. Following the Smith Act in authorizing the state to exclude anyone who was determined to engage in criminal "subversive" activity, the act also stipulated that full allegiance to the

United States was required for citizenship (§ 317). World War II thus increased the opportunities and incentives for Filipinos to serve in the US armed forces as a path to winning US citizenship. "Fighting for democracy" through military service thus was linked to struggles for equal rights and democratic inclusion for Filipinos as it was for African Americans (Parker 2009). Like African American civil rights activists, Filipino labor spokespersons, including Trinidad Rojo and Carlos Bulosan, publicly linked the fight against global fascism abroad to demands for ending racial exclusion and class subjugation within the United States (Keith 2013, 50).

Many Filipinos took jobs in defense plants and joined the military to show their patriotism even though they were discriminated against at work and in military organizations. Executive Order 8802 barring discrimination in the military and defense industry technically covered Filipinos, but the Fair Employment Practices Committee (FEPC) had little enforcement power (Baldoz 2011: 278; Klinkner and Smith 1999). As the United States entered the war, several thousand Filipinos were conscripted into the US Armed Forces in the Far East (USAFFE), a military force that combined multiple units in the Philippines and proved critical to victory against the Japanese in the Pacific. These soldiers joined nearly two hundred thousand Filipino enlistees in the Philippines under US command (Ancheta 2006). Many of these soldiers met and married Filipinas in the Philippines during their service. The 1945 War Brides Act allowed entry of these spouses and children of the members of the US Armed Forces while a 1946 act allowed for heterosexual fiancées and fiancés to enter (Mabalon n.d.).

Japanese occupation of the Philippines restricted US naturalization of Filipino immigrants during the war, however, and in 1945 procedures were revoked until 1946. Facing increasing pressures from Soviet accusations of hypocrisy for racially exclusionary immigration policies in the early Cold War (Dudziak 2000), Congress passed the Luce-Celler Act declaring Filipinos and (East) Indians eligible for naturalization even while substantially restricting immigration from India and the newly independent Philippines. This was the moment of what Derrick Bell (1980) called maximum "interest convergence" between dominant white society and the subaltern population of laboring dark people. Four thousand Filipino veterans were granted citizenship and were ostensibly made eligible for veteran's benefits before the termination date at the end of 1946. In 1942, General MacArthur had promised "equal pay and allowances" as incentives to the more than two hundred thousand Filipino soldiers who fought under US command, but the legislation was never passed in Congress. In 1946, two Rescission Acts reclassified USAFFE service as "inactive," dramatically reducing the benefits promised to veterans who fought in the Philippine units and closing off further military naturalization; only two hundred million dollars was appropriated for disability and death pensions. Once again, official US policy demonstrated that military service mattered less under law than did the dominant white group's exclusionary constructions of race and nationality. Following the argument that the veterans had been US nationals or aliens rather than citizens during the war, President Truman reasoned in supporting the Rescission Acts of 1946 that the United States was bound only by discretionary "moral obligation" rather than a higher order of legal rights entitlement. Immigration officials then used the reclassification as a justification to deny naturalization to Filipino veteran applicants. Waves of lawsuits, including unsuccessful appeals to the US Supreme Court, were filed to challenge once more the racialized denials of citizenship and benefits to Filipino veterans. But the courts continued to follow the logic of the Insular Cases that "Congress has complete and ultimate rule over U.S. Territories." With the general failure of litigation efforts, only a small number of veterans were able to obtain citizenship through the federal courts in subsequent decades (Cabotaje 1999). Surviving veterans were not finally made eligible for citizenship until the Immigration Act of 1990, half a century after they first had been promised eligibility (Ancheta 2006, 98).

The year 1946 was important for migration of Filipino workers to the United States in another sense. In the spring of that year, over six thousand Filipinas/os were hired by employers to alleviate a substantial postwar labor shortage and, as scabs, to impede an incipient labor strike on privately owned Hawaiian plantations. Led by the ILWU, which already had about twenty-six thousand members, including many Filipino immigrants, the newly arrived *sakadas* surprisingly joined rather than undercut the Great Sugar Strike of 1946. The seventy-nine-day strike was stunningly successful in winning union recognition, higher wages, rights of free speech, pensions, homeownership rights, and major steps toward reducing the racist, paternalistic system that had governed the sugar plantations for a century. Historians have estimated that the strike benefitted up to one hundred thousand people who lived and worked on the plantations, one fifth of Hawaii's population, including tens of thousands of Filipino immigrant workers and their families (San Buenaventura 1996; ILWU Local 142 1996). The labor influx in 1946, shortly before the Philippines was granted independence, marked the last significant movement of Filipino workers into the United States until immigration laws were reformed in 1965 (Mabalon n.d.).

Union Tensions amid Transitions into the Cold War

UCAPAWA Local 7 in the War Years

Following Trinidad Rojo's initial campaign to formalize internal organizational processes, Vincent Navea won election as president of Local 7 in 1940. A former union business agent and committed official, Navea had never labored in the canneries. Moreover, he had been employed by a company linked to the labor contractors before the union era. As such, he became identified as a company man, an exemplar of business unionism. Rojo, who had been a cannery worker and farmworker, was closer to the rank and file and was more effective in administration, so he was elected president once again in late 1942. He formed an alliance with the influential progressive Prudencio Mori. Consistent with the past, two factions developed between these men and their allies. Navea ally and former president Irineo Cabatit bent rules to make it into the 1943 election but lost to Rojo. Navea then filed a petition to the War Labor Board (WLB) claiming that he, as the American Legion head of the Rizal Post, deserved recognition as the head of the sole bargaining agent for cannery workers to the Alaska industry (Ellison 2005). This action challenged the established relationship of the Local 7 union to the cannery employers, which had consolidated into the Alaska Salmon Industry organization early in the war. Navea's tactic was unsuccessful, and he was charged by the union leadership with antiunion scheming and promoting dual unionism. The 1944 rank-and-file vote expressed a closer membership vote (38 to 32) than that by the nearly unanimous executive board, which punished Navea with a ten-year suspension from union involvement (Ellison 2005).

During this period, UCAPAWA union locals lost over one thousand—more than one half—of its Filipino members, including many militant leftists, to war service and defense industry work. Many workers were exempted from the draft because canned salmon was important to the military campaign, but patriotic loyalty to the Philippines nation under assault from Japan, promises of citizenship for military service, and the lure of higher-paying defense jobs motivated workers to leave the canneries. "When the war broke out, the competition for Filipinos was keen. Everyone wished there were one or two

Fig. 9 Cannery leader contract negotiations, including Filipino leaders Ernesto Mangaoang (*far left*), Vicente Navea (*center seated*), and Ireneo Cabatit (*standing middle*). Courtesy Filipino American National History Society.

million Filipinos here," wrote Rojo (in Cordova 1983, 23). Many Filipinos also hoped that international pressures following the war might compel expansion of civil rights protections in the United States. Local 7 bought $6,000 of war bonds in 1942 and still was able to ship eleven million cases of canned salmon to the armed forces (Rojo 1952 [UWSC]). Trinidad Rojo was elected for a third term in 1943–1944.

The shrinking membership prompted Local 7 leaders to expand the union's organizing efforts. As the cannery companies increasingly moved administrative operations to Seattle, Local 7 took control of dispatching workers to Alaska, including the predominantly Chinese workforce organized by Local 5 in San Francisco and Local 226 in Portland. Japanese workers in Seattle continued to fight for position in the union, but Japan's invasion of Pearl Harbor and Manila ended their effort. Canneries halted hiring Japanese altogether, and then the latter were forced en masse into concentration camps. The union did reach out in support of Japanese American farm families, but that effort was limited in commitment and effect (Ellison 2005). With the Chinese marginalized and the Japanese removed, Filipinos seized opportunities to take more positions as foremen, delegates, and other leadership roles as well as factory line workers (Friday 1994, 186–89). By 1942, Filipinos dominated cannery work and the cannery workers' union; the shaky coalition among Asian ethnic groups collapsed. Tellingly, Local 5 and Local 226 merged with Local 7 in 1943. Local 226 was allowed to keep its union hall in Portland in order to sustain community ties and to initiate organizing efforts among asparagus workers in the fields near Stockton, California (Ellison 2005). But Local 7 became the most militant Filipino union in the United States, one that offered summer employment for thousands of men and grew as an influential social center of the Filipino community in Seattle. By the mid-1940s, four thousand Filipino cannery workers made up around 80 percent of the union membership. Perhaps as many as one out of ten Filipinos employed in the West Coast labor force were members of the union (De Vera 1994). Trinidad Rojo left the union leadership in 1944 to pursue a PhD in labor economics at Stanford (Rojo 1947 [UWSC]).

The Food, Tobacco, Agricultural, and Allied Workers and Early Internal Struggles

The relative success in building union power hardly meant that Filipino cannery workers marched in lockstep. Rather, the factionalism of earlier periods continued. In particular, the early Cold War years of the middle to late 1940s brought a new phase of intense conflict between socialist and communist-leaning union militants and union moderates as well as state officials. Another Local 7 change in affiliation during 1947 harbingered things to come. The Arkansas-based Southern Tenant Farmers Union (STFU), founded in 1934, had affiliated with UCAPAWA during the war years. However, a power struggle developed between UCAPAWA and the STFU over organizing strategies for farmworkers, union governance, and the growing communist influence in the CIO. The STFU left the union in 1939 as a result (Ruiz 1987, 44). In 1944, UCAPAWA shifted its focus from agricultural workers to industrial food processers, cannery workers, and fishermen, who could organize for collective bargaining rights under the Wagner Act, and became the Food, Tobacco, Agricultural, and Allied Workers (FTA) (Ruiz 1987). This is but one of the many ways that national labor law and tensions around communist leadership together shaped the trajectory of Local 7.

Even before the war ended, the Alaska Salmon Industry fought to check the power of the varied fishing and cannery unions, several times refusing WLB mandates for wage increases (Baunach 2013). Nevertheless, Local 7 of the FTA scored some early successes immediately after the war. Most notable was a joint strike with the International Fishermen and Allied Workers of America (IFAWA) Local 47, a communist-led local that represented resident Alaska Native cannery workers, including many female workers, in Bristol Bay. The strike began on April 20, 1946, with pickets halting the loading of cannery equipment and a parallel longshore strike in Alaska. After a week, the strike ended when employers granted a 10 percent wage increase and substantial pay for inactive standby times for Local 7 members; the IFAWA scored wage increases, an eight-hour day, and a closed shop. The campaign was a "remarkable example of CIO civil rights unionism and working-class unity between two disparate groups—Alaska Natives and Filipino migrants—who shared common experiences with American empire and exploitation by capital," notes historian Leo Baunach (2013). The two unions subsequently failed to consummate a proposed merger, although they allied again in negotiating with the Alaska Salmon Industry (ASI) in 1949.

Prudencio Mori was president of Local 7 in these immediate postwar years, but he was replaced amid the growing internal split between conservatives and militant leftists. One factor in this division was the wartime departure of many former leftist leaders, including the tough-minded business agent Conrad Espe, who took a post with FTA International. A concurrent development was the growing influence of the Caballeros de Dimas-Alang, the Tagalog-based fraternal organization that during the war emerged as a powerful, conservative, actively anticommunist and industry-friendly leadership group in the union. That conservative faction found itself on the defensive when, in the year after the war's end, twelve hundred Alaskeros were stranded as their ship, the SS *Santa Cruz*, ran aground, and they eventually returned to find their belongings ransacked and valuables pilfered. Leftists Leo Lorenzo, Mario Hermosa, and Chris Mensalvas formed a "Rank and File Committee" to voice complaints to the union leaders (Viernes 2012). In a February 1946 union meeting in Seattle, a leftist member of the Rank and File Committee who later became secretary, Matias Lagunilla, questioned Vice President Max Gonzales about the *Santa Cruz* incident and a host of charges alleging lax leadership. Among the accusations of corruption in the exchange it was revealed that the delegation had consented to payment of $13,000 in debts without consulting the membership. A diehard anticommunist, Gonzales became furious, grabbed his concealed pistol, and fired at Lagunilla (M. S. Brown 2012; Ellison

2005). The wild shot hit no one, but Lagunilla filed legal charges against Gonzales nonetheless.

President Mori and other officers refused to discipline Gonzales, however, citing his exemplary service record in the union and the need for collective solidarity. While the Rank and File Committee claimed to represent a broad base of workers, there is little empirical evidence to support that claim, and the leftists did poorly in the delegate election during the fall of 1946 (Marquardt 1992, 39). Meanwhile, FTA International president Donald Henderson had traveled to Seattle in March and vigorously rebuked the executive council for failing to condemn the outrageous assault by Gonzales. The board defied the demand by Henderson, a known communist who supported Local 7 leftists, for expulsion of Gonzales and continued to stand by him. Gonzales remained an active member and pressed for Local 7 to separate from the left-led FTA International and to form a new union with the same conservative leadership. Mori eventually expelled Gonzales and, in late June of 1947, wrote a report accusing board members Victorio Velasco, Cornelio Briones, and Vincente Pilien of multiple violations. The left-leaning FTA International appointed a new board and recalled moderate Trinidad Rojo again as president, Mori as secretary, and Ernesto Mangaoang as business agent (Viernes 2012). The executive council continued to be a highly educated group; most had BA or MA degrees, many in political science, from the University of Washington (Rojo 1947 [UWSC]). The leftists consistently were leaders among the activists with the highest levels of university education in the union.

Several weeks later, Gonzales, Velasco, and Briones wrote to Local 7 rank-and-file members to call for a revocation of the union's charter and then filed a lawsuit seeking to override their suspension (*State ex rel. Cannery etc. v. Sup. Ct*, 1948). The trial led to a finding of contempt by Local 7 Left leadership (Rojo, Mori, Mangaoang, Navarro, et al.), for alleged improper use of the union's burial fund, freezing union finances, and crippling its negotiating leverage with the cannery industry (Ellison 2005). Matias Lagunilla was sentenced to county jail, and others were fined fifty dollars each for failing to turn over records. The punishment for contempt was challenged by union attorneys John Caughlan and Barry Hatten and was eventually overruled for exceeding the aims of a civil injunction.[4] Meanwhile, in September 1947, Gonzales and Briones filed a petition with the National Labor Relations Board (NLRB) to create the independent Seafood Workers Union (SWU) to represent cannery workers. Frustrated by the slow response of the NLRB, Gonzales resorted to rabid red-baiting, taking advantage of growing anticommunist fervor in the government. "The Communist International, Communist puppets, Communist sympathizers . . . took control of Local Seven. . . . Don't be deceived. . . . The Seafood Workers Union . . . believes in American democracy, not in Russian democrazy" (quoted in M. S. Brown 2012, 114). Nevertheless, the NLRB refused the SWU's petition, finding that, because Gonzales was a cannery foreman, the SWU was an illegal company union (Rojo 1947 [UWSC]). Briones, Velasco, and other conservatives were, as the Local 7 News (September 1947, 1) reported, "swamped in (the) election" that same month. The leftist leadership faction proclaimed itself the "honest union slate" and thus prevailed once again, in part because of the Rank and File Committee's bottom-up mobilization but mostly because the intervention of the FTA International union leadership and the NLRB (Marquardt 1992).

A host of historical events—the death of President Roosevelt, the ascendance of the more ardently anticommunist President Truman, the civil war in China, the antisubversion provisions of the recently passed Taft-Hartley Act, the House Un-American Activities Commission hearings in Hollywood and beyond, the Alger Hiss trial, the Canwell Committee purge of faculty members at the University of Washington in Seattle—all encouraged the red-baiting tactics of SWU and other rivals. The Taft-Hartley Act, also known as the Labor Management Relations Act of 1947, especially increased pressures on leftists in the union during ensuing years. That act, passed over the veto of President Truman, amended the NLRA by enumerating a series of unfair labor practices by unions, including jurisdictional strikes, wildcat strikes, solidarity strikes, secondary boycotts, secondary and mass picketing, closed shops, and financial donations by unions to federal political campaigns. Amendments to the act notably allowed states to outlaw union security clauses by passing right-to-work laws. In short, the act eliminated many of the most important tactical sources of union power developed under previous legislation (Tomlins 1985b, 242–316). The act also required union leaders to submit affidavits to the US Department of Labor declaring that they were not members of the Communist Party and did not support overthrow of the US government by illegal means. Taft-Hartley thus provided many of the most important legal resources supporting new levels of government harassment and deportation of union officials suspected of communist allegiance.

In such a context, it become common practice for disgruntled members of the politically divided Filipino community to report alleged communists to government officials (Rojo n.d.). As International Longshoremen's and Warehousemen's Union (ILWU) president Harry Bridges complained, "All you have to do is establish by testimony of CIO labor fakers that a union is 'dominated by Communists,' declare it is against public policy to permit such a union to have bargaining rights and—zingo!" (Bridges 1952). Taft-Hartley was the centerpiece of the repressive law regime that grew during the Cold War era.

Re-enter Chris Mensalvas, Exit the CIO, Join the ILWU

"Dual unionism flourished for the next two years," activist and historian Gene Viernes summarized decades later (1978). Fissures related to communist allegiances also figured into deepening divisions within Local 7 leadership during the late 1940s between the moderate progressives such as Trinidad Rojo and militant leftists allied with Chris Mensalvas. Mensalvas had moved to Portland years earlier, and after his wife died in 1944, he became business agent for Local 226 and then publicity director in Seattle in 1947, but he left again for Stockton and unsuccessful efforts to organize asparagus workers. As noted previously, he was one of the leaders of the Rank and File Committee who had challenged moderate, allegedly corrupt Local 7 leaders in 1946–1947. President Rojo complained, without clear evidence, that Mensalvas was a feckless, ideologically blinded leader who had helped to orchestrate strikes in California that were ineffective and extremely expensive. For many years, Rojo also bitterly rebuked Mensalvas's alleged abandonment of organizing farmworkers, his financial mismanagement of the union, and the integrity of his friend and ally Carlos Bulosan. The condemnation was typical for the business-minded Rojo, but the acerbic venom directed toward Mensalvas and Bulosan by Rojo's later writings seems to reflect a toxic mix of personal and ideological antipathy (Rojo n.d. [UWSC]). The fact that Mensalvas won the Local 7 presidency in 1949, a position he held for the next decade, no doubt exacerbated the disdain exhibited by Rojo.

In August 1949, shortly after the election for union president, US immigration officials led by District Director John P. Boyd raided Local 7 and arrested Mensalvas, business agent Ernesto Mangaoang, and other officials accused of communist ties. They were charged under the Immigration and Nationality Act with membership in the Communist Party, a crime punishable by imprisonment and deportation. The FBI had been collecting information on the leaders for years (Baldoz 2014; Griffey 2018a, 2018b), some of which almost certainly was supplied by the SWU, which had joined the Alaska Fish, Cannery, Seafarers International Union (AFCSIU), an AFL local that John Ayamo had led since the first phase of dual unionism in 1938 (M. S. Brown 2012). The merger then produced the Alaska Fish Cannery Workers union (AFCW), with Ayamo as president and Briones as the business agent. The NLRB responded to an AFCW petition by authorizing an election in April 1949, just after the raids. One reason that the NLRB originally denied representation to Local 7 and called for a new election was that the union had not filed the required affidavits disavowing communist ties required by the Taft Hartley Act. Local 7 subsequently filed the necessary papers and again won the election for representation, but before long the FTA International was ousted from the CIO in a broadly based purge of unions with leaders who were alleged to be Communist Party members.

The Navea faction of leaders in Local 7 then formed a union of anticommunist moderates, Local 77, affiliated with the increasingly "red free" CIO. Local 7 responded by leaving the besieged FTA and affiliating as Local 7-C with the ILWU, a move opposed by the self-identified "liberal" Rojo but one that had seemed destined for years. In the summer of 1950, the union won yet another NLRB-authorized election for representation, beating out Local 77 and other competitors. A strong presence among members in the union hall and in the Filipino community as well as an alliance with the powerful ILWU again provided Local 7-C's Left leaders a firm foundation of power (Ellison 2005). After signing a four-year union shop contract with the canning industry in 1951, the union adopted a new designation, Local 37 ILWU, which it would keep for decades to come.

Deportation Campaigns: Resurgent Repressive Law

The McCarran Acts Turn the Screws on Leftists

The raid to harass business agent Ernesto Mangaoang and other alleged communists in 1949 was the first of many over subsequent years. It began with the delivery of letters and subpoenas to hundreds of Local 7 leaders in Seattle and Portland, most of them Filipino nationals, requesting appearance for questioning or documenting submission at Immigration and Naturalization Services (INS) offices. At the time, union officials believed that the primary motivation was to disrupt and discourage Local 7 from efforts to organize cannery workers in southeastern Alaska. Union members gathered to support the union's lead negotiator and to post bail. Mangaoang was out in a few days. When Chris Mensalvas, Ponce Torres, Casimiro Bueno Absolor, and, later, Joe Prudencio were subsequently arrested, the union rallied and posted bail, charging government complicity as "the hidden card up the sleeve of the employers" in their effort to intimidate if not subdue the union's organizing efforts (De Vera 1994, 7).

These dramas unfolded amid the national government prosecution of Julius and Ethel Rosenberg for Soviet espionage and new congressional legislation aiming to quell worker militancy by reclassifying it as subversive activity. In September of 1950, Congress passed the McCarran Internal Security Act of 1950, which required members of Communist organizations to register with the United States Attorney General and established the Subversive Activities Control Board (SACB) to investigate persons suspected of engaging in seditious activities or otherwise promoting the establishment of a "totalitarian dictatorship," either fascist or communist. Those persons who were determined to be in violation of the act could lose their citizenship for five years and be deported. The attorney general and local officers were granted wide latitude, with no obligation to provide incriminating evidence about informers, to investigate, arrest, and detain aliens suspected of dangerous allegiances. FBI records reveal a complex web of surveillance activities and routine pressuring of former fellow travelers as well as organizational rivals to provide names of those Local 7 activists suspected of collaborating with communists (Alquizola and Hirabayashi 2012; Baldoz 2014; Griffey 2018a, 2018b.). The act also authorized preparation for and establishment of concentration camps for purposes of internal security (De Vera 1994).

Local 7 activists quickly protested. Secretary Mattias Lagunilla, who headed the Local 7 Defense Committee, wrote shortly thereafter decrying the new laws for aiming to discourage union organizing efforts and advocacy for workers:

> Due to the war preparations and the intervention of the U.S. imperialists in the internal affairs of other nations, our Union has become the target of union-busting agencies of the government and the enemies of organized labor. Nine officers and members of our Union are facing deportation because of their militant stand against the move to destroy organized labor, intimidation of progressive foreign born labor leaders, and the hysteria to abrogate the civil rights of the United States Constitution. But our members are solidly behind our Union policies, and will fight to the last man for the detention of our leader and members as guaranteed by the Human Rights section of the Constitution of the United Nations. (ILWU Local 37, 1952, 6).

Weeks after the McCarran Act went into effect, Ernie Mangaoang, out on bail for his previous arrest, was again apprehended in his home in the middle of the night. The arresting officers had no warrant, and the charges were different from the previous time. Mangaoang was the first of many arrested for "past" membership in the Communist Party, which was newly constructed as a crime under the McCarran Act. Once again, Mensalvas and dozens of others in Seattle and Portland were arrested. Union members read the legal actions as renewed efforts of intimidation and harassment aiming to deter union organizing in Alaska canneries and beyond. Bail was posted quickly, for some by the religiously based Committee for Defense of the Foreign Born and for Mensalvas by the ILWU International. Mangaoang languished for seventy days in solitary confinement ostensibly because of legal technicalities related to the warrantless arrest. A month after the passage of the McCarran Act, the Department of Justice (DOJ) outlined plans to deport well over three thousand noncitizens under the act. In the next several months, a total of ten Local 7/37 leaders, including Ponce Torres and Joe Prudencio, were detained and charged with crimes that could lead to deportation. The broad discretion granted by the McCarran Act enabled immigration authorities to wield repressive state violence as they saw fit. Union rivals, mostly in the AFL, seized the opportunity to testify against Local 7/37 leaders, often offering half-truths to protect themselves but providing sufficient reason for DOJ prosecution and deportation (De Vera 1994, 10). The litany of government actions and decertification efforts provide strong evidence of collaboration between union rivals and the WLB, the INS, the DOJ, and other state security agencies.

The union defense committee accelerated its campaign defending persecuted comrades. Delegates at the ninth biennial ILWU convention in 1951, representing over eighty thousand members, unanimously affirmed a resolution demanding a congressional investigation of the INS harassment of Local 7 leaders (ILWU Ninth Biennial Convention 1951). The ILWU resolution focused on the corrupt logic of government attacks on unions while "handing out lush contracts and pay-offs to their friends" in industry. Resolution number 13 demanded "immediate repeal" of the McCarran Act:

> A legal strait-jacket has been tailored to fit the American people and to bind them with restraints of their liberty—the McCarran Act. Measures which all Americans thought were outlawed by the Bill of Rights . . . dismissed as the products of diseased minds when introduced in Congress in past decades, have now been rolled up into one compact law of repression and

> given the approval of Congress. . . . The Act provides for the jailing and possible deportation not only of aliens but of all foreign-born citizens, including those who come to this country as babes in arms. Leaders in ILWU have been singled out for attack under this law for the "crime" of battling to raise the wages of Alaska cannery workers from $30 to $250 per month. (ILWU Ninth Biennial Convention 1951, 2)

Union leaders published appeals for public support of efforts to resist the government's union-busting efforts. Letters of solidarity—from leaders in multiple West Coast unions, the National Negro Labor Council, the Finnish-American Association, the American Committee for the Protection of the Foreign-Born—poured into the union and were published in a wide array of newspapers (ILWU Local 37, 1952, 25). A letter from ILWU regional director Bill Gettings is typical of the appeals: "The attempted deportation of Ernesto Mangaoang is a serious threat to our union and our democratic rights. This writer is convinced that if Ernesto Mangaoang was not an honest official of the real democratic unions of this nation he would not be threatened with deportation" (ILWU Local 37, 1952, 25). The union committee meanwhile focused many of its efforts on raising money to finance the defense efforts. At the same time, though, some in the Filipino community and in the union derided communists and fellow travelers, continued to actively red-bait Mangaoang and others, and advocated their deportation. Once again, government repression split Filipino workers into conflicting factions fed by fear, ideology, rival regional loyalties back home, and personal antagonism.

In late June 1952, as legal defenses and appeals for Local 7 members proceeded in multiple courts, Congress again altered the legal context by passing the McCarran-Walter Act, more formally known as the omnibus 1952 Immigration and Nationality Act, over the veto of President Truman. The bill's primary sponsor, Walter McCarran, a conservative Catholic and ardent Cold Warrior, characterized immigration policy as a matter of "internal security" (the title of the 1950 act) and a vital resource in the struggle against Communism (Ngai 2004, 237). The act supplanted the Immigration Act of 1917 as the core national immigration law, but its aim was more to consolidate and fortify than substantially alter the existing mosaic of inherited laws.

First, the act abolished racial restrictions on immigration and naturalization going back to the Naturalization Act of 1790, reflecting sensitivity to Cold War pressures of antidiscrimination and recent human rights conventions. The color-blind policy ended Japanese and Korean exclusion, as had earlier repeals of exclusion for Filipinos, Chinese, and Indians. Importantly, the act declared that those persons born in designated Asian lands but who were permanent residents of the United States were eligible for citizenship (Ancheta 2006; De Vera 1994; Ngai 2004). Second, the Act preserved nonquota immigration from countries in Northern Europe while imposing strict quotas on Caribbean, and mostly black, inhabitants as well as those from the "Asia Pacific Triangle." While bowing to the exigencies of Cold War geopolitical symbolism, the United States still excluded Asians and could only admit those few who were deemed "desirable." Third, the act expanded and hardened further the strict terms of exclusion from naturalization along lines of desirability. The criteria included educational and skill levels along with familial ties to de jure American citizens. Moreover, the attorney general was granted broad authority to deny naturalization or to deport naturalized citizens for activities "prejudicial to the public interest," including for affiliations and actions not grounds for deportation when they were committed. Once-naturalized citizens could be deported for past membership in groups deemed to be subversive and for refusing to testify about known subversive activity, among other acts of disloyalty (Ngai 2004, 239). Accused persons were granted expanded due process rights, however. One important implication for cannery workers suspected of militancy was they could be denied reentry into the United States when attempting to return from work in Alaska.

Seattle immigration district director John P. Boyd immediately seized on the new legislative mandate to crack down on "undesirables," especially those in the cannery workers' union. As historian Alfred McCoy (2009, 2017) has demonstrated, many of the surveillance, intelligence, interrogation, rumor mongering, and harassment practices of the US police state in this period had been developed during the American colonial occupation of the Philippines fifty years earlier. The salmon canning industry chose to cooperate with the government in weeding out subversives. By September 1952, thirteen Local 37 members were placed on the deportation list under the two McCarran Acts; one hundred and twenty persons overall, including thirty Filipinos, had been arrested and charged with subversive affiliations or activities. The ILWU International and Local 37 initiated lawsuits demanding that federal courts issue injunctions against enforcement of the exclusionary screenings and undertook broad letter-writing campaigns and petition drives (De Vera 1994, 12). A Seattle federal court quickly ruled against the union, upholding the INS political persecution while attorneys John Caughlan and Siegfreid Hesse pursued appeals. The union meanwhile fought the dual battle of protecting the

UNION BACKS CAUGHLAN: Leaders of the Cannery Workers' & Farm Laborers' Union (FTA-CIO) turn over $312.75 to the Caughlan Defense Committee collected from members working in Bristol Bay. Standing (l. to r.) Pablo Sorio, Pauline Paet, Pete Quitoriano and Balbinc Tacazon. Seated: Hazel Wolf, Committee secretary; Attorney John Caughlan and Ernesto Mangaoang, chairman of the union's Defense Committee.

Fig. 10 "CWFLU Backs Attorney John Caughlan." From *New World*, August 19, 1948. University of Washington Libraries Microforms. Image use courtesy Seattle Civil Rights and Labor History Project.

rights of its members and the organization while vowing reluctant, symbolic cooperation with the government laws imposing repressive order. As historian Mary Dudziak (2000, 11) has put it, "civil rights activists had to walk a fine line, making it clear that their reform efforts were meant to fill out the contours of American democracy, and not to challenge or undermine it."

Attorney John Caughlan was an important activist throughout this period and deserves special attention. A native of Missouri, he earned a degree at

Harvard Law School in 1935 and moved to Seattle soon afterward. There he joined the locally well-connected Communist Party, began representing Communist Party members, and became known as a "commie lawyer" (Burnett 2009). Caughlan played important roles in working with black Communist Party members to promote multiracial coalitions for social justice, including the Seattle Civic Unity Committee, the Seattle chapter of the Civil Rights Congress, and the Washington Pension Union, the latter two closely affiliated with the Popular Front. He handled legal affairs for the Cannery Workers Local 7/37 from the late 1930s through the 1950s. In the 1940s and 1950s, he and his partner C.T. "Barry" Hatten represented labor unions, union activists, the Communist Party, and a host of foreign-born individuals accused of subversive action and facing deportation under the Smith Act, the McCarran Act, and the McCarran-Walter Act. Caughlan represented witnesses on committee hearings investigating "Un-American Activities" in Washington State, including the Canwell Committee purge of faculty members at University of Washington and the national House Un-American Activities Committee (HUAC). Caughlan himself was charged with perjury for testimony denying that he was a member of the Communist Party and then acquitted in 1948, but he was charged again in 1954. Caughlan was continuously involved with ILWU Local 37 in these years and then again in the 1970s and 1980s, as later chapters of this book will document (Caughlan 2009). And Caughlan and Hatten were just two of many lawyers working out of Popular Front organizations on issues related to rights of workers, and especially workers of color, in Seattle at the time, providing representation paralleling and loosely coordinated with the International Labor Defense for civil rights and labor radicals on the East Coast.

The Mangaoang Case in the Courts: Resisting Persistent Prosecution

Local 7/37 business agent Ernie Mangaoang's legal battles challenging multiple arrests and orders of deportation for allegedly subversive action or affiliation dragged out over nearly four years.[5] These episodes are worthy of attention as a window into the larger travail of repressive law in the United States during this period.

Mangaoang was released after the first arrest on August 2, 1949, on a $5,000 cash bond. When rearrested on November 17 of the same year, District Director Boyd ordered an increase in the bond to $10,000. District Court Judge John Clyde Bowen on November 28 affirmed petitioner Mangaoang's claim that the attorney general had abused his discretion in requiring a higher bail bond without reasonable justification and thus violated basic due process rights (*Ex Parte Mangaoang* 932). The relentless District Director Boyd immediately arrested Mangaoang for a third time, and then, while the business agent was out on bail, for a fourth time in October 1950 along with forty-seven others under the (McCarran) Internal Security Act of 1950. Boyd conducted a deportation hearing for the Local 37 business agent soon thereafter. Mangaoang's attorneys were not notified, so he was denied representation by counsel and the capacity to cross-examine witnesses who testified against him. The District Court this time denied Mangaoang's petition for habeas corpus, but the Ninth District Court of Appeals reversed and remanded that ruling on December 27, 1950. The court recognized that "aliens" are not granted the same due process rights as are citizens, but state discretion still must meet a standard of "reasonableness."

> In the classical habeas corpus proceeding the petitioner is held upon a warrant of commitment issued by a tribunal after a hearing. . . . It is highly important to notice that the instant proceedings do not have the background in which the basis for the detention must be shown. The Director (under advice of the Attorney General) upon his own motion and upon his own undisclosed reasons decided the discretionary point at issue. . . . At once it is apparent that the rule requiring petitioner to go forward with his proof in these circumstances throws an impossible burden upon him for he cannot well negate every possible combination of circumstances which might have convinced the Director that he is not a safe risk to be bailed. . . . In all of the referred to evidence there is not a word as to any specific fact taken into account in the decision that petitioner . . . is not entitled to bail. (*Mangaoang v. Boyd* 1950)

Mangaoang again posted bond and was released January 12, 1951, after eighty-three days in King County Jail. Yet another deportation order was issued on August 10, 1951. An appeal to the Board of Immigration Appeals (BIA) was denied in December, and the District Court again denied another habeas petition to overturn the deportation order. The legal skirmish, which was a continuation of challenges to repeated harassment by the INS, again ended up in the US Court of Appeals for the Ninth Circuit. The court once more reversed and remanded the District Court ruling on June 17, 1953. The appellate court judges underlined that the warrant of deportation alleged that appellant Mangaoang entered the United States as an "alien" and became a member of the Communist Party, which rendered him deportable under the 1950 Act. Attorneys Caughlan and Hatten, themselves subject to McCarthy-era harassment and charges of communist affiliation, argued that the 1950 act did not correctly apply to Mangaoang. They insisted that the appellant had been born in 1902 and entered the continental United States for permanent residence in 1926 as a Filipino "national," not as an alien. Moreover, it was during the years 1938–1939, before transition to alien status with Philippine Independence in 1946, that his affiliations with the Communist Party were alleged. While the District Court rejected that distinction, the Court of Appeals found it convincing. "We think it was not sufficient to prove that the appellant was an alien at the time of his arrest and that he was a member of the Communist Party at some prior date on which he was not shown to have been an alien" (*Mangaoang v. Boyd* 1953). The court also dwelled on the commonplace meaning of terms regarding "entering" the United States.

The case went to the US Supreme Court, which denied the writ of certiorari and let stand the supportive ruling by the Ninth Circuit (*Boyd v. Mangaoang* 1953). None of these rulings found that the McCarran-Walter Act violated the US Constitution, however. As a result, INS inspector Boyd pledged an appeal and ratcheted up interrogations and incarceration of cannery workers returning from Alaska. In subsequent months, two thousand Filipinos returning to Seattle were interrogated, and "more than a hundred were jailed, and eventually, over a dozen singled out for exclusion" (De Vera 1994, 15). But the US Supreme Court seized on two pending cases to go further toward reining in the INS. In June 1954, the court ruled in favor of Max Gonzales, who had been ordered deported for his assault charge (against Lagunilla) in 1941 and a second degree burglary in 1950. In *Barber v. Gonzales* (1954), a narrow court majority restated the logic of the Ninth Circuit in Mangaoang's case and again for Gonzales: Filipinos who committed crimes of "moral turpitude" before 1946 were not subject to deportation under the Internal Security Act of 1950. Gonzales "entered" the United States in 1930 as a national and did not become an alien until after 1946, so he was not deportable under the Immigration Act of 1917.

A final case involved a habeas petition for Alejandro Raca Alcantra, a Filipino who came to the United States as a national in 1928 but was denied entry on return to Seattle from cannery work in Alaska in 1953 under the Immigration and Nationality Act of 1952. On May 10, 1955, the Ninth Circuit reversed and remanded a Board of Immigration Appeals denial of his petition, narrowing the statutory reach of the 1952 act to prevailing interpretations of the Immigration Act of 1917 regarding "excludable classes of aliens." In short, the courts ruled that the McCarran-Walter Act did not expand authorization of the INS to deport Filipino cannery workers who originally entered the United States before 1946. The court somewhat surprisingly framed the ruling in terms of potential harmful economic impact on the fishing and canning industry, which employed thousands of Filipino "aliens" who traveled back and forth between Alaska and the West Coast US metropole (*U.S. ex rel. Alcantra v. Boyd* 1955).

The *Alcantra* decision for the most part signaled the end of the repression of Filipino cannery workers through deportation. The INS terminated its screening program and dropped its remaining cases, enabling cannery workers to travel to and from Alaska for work (De Vera 1994, 16). In the end, no leftist Filipino cannery workers were successfully deported during the McCarthy era. The concentration camps that had been prepared for holding alleged alien subversives were left empty. Hazel Wolf, secretary to attorney John Caughlan, social justice activist, and herself subject to fifteen years of INS deportation harassment for membership in the Communist Party, assessed the era of legal contestation over expulsion in these terms a year before she died in 2000: "In summation, we lost most of the battles, but won the war in all of these cases" (Kowalski 2000).[6]

Overall, investigations of alleged subversive activity directly affected as many as fifteen thousand people. But historian Ellen Schrecker (1996–1997, 416) counted only 253 actual deportations of suspected alien subversives. The relative success of the Filipinos' stalwart legal defense and the migrants' economic contributions as wage laborers perhaps explains why Filipino cannery workers' struggles won little national attention and are rarely mentioned in history and case law books. But such a story of "success" minimizes the huge personal costs in money, time, and insecurity for those accused of violations. It does not include recognition of those persons whom the INS expelled under other pretexts or the many who exiled themselves to escape harassment or the many thousands who lost jobs. The story of success also minimizes the chilling effect on political speech, organization, and advocacy of novel rights claims and visions (De Vera 1994, 16). This history is a classic demonstration of how the personal, social, and political impact of even "successful" litigation is complicated to assess.

At a more general level, the anticommunist campaign arguably should not be measured just by the numbers of alleged subversives who were deported or jailed or even the individual lives broken by state persecution. Arguably the larger effect of anticommunism was ideological in that it demonized communists and reinforced commonsense assumptions that Americans espousing leftist commitments or affiliated with Left associations were outside the law and were in fact illegal. It is important to note that being a communist was not technically illegal. Most deportation charges were based on civil contempt and perjury violations, not criminal offenses. "As a result, the charges that the cold war defendants faced . . . often bore little relation to the presumed offense for which they were on trial," notes Schrecker (1994, 26–28). But the symbolism of charges and trials was to make dissidents into criminals, to delegitimize and mute their critical voices, visions, and aspirations. Schrecker (1994, 27) underlines the point:

> Perhaps no single weapon in the federal arsenal was as powerful in the government's construction of the anti-Communist consensus as the criminal justice system. By putting Communists on trial, the Truman administration shaped the American public's view of domestic communism. It transformed party members from political dissidents into criminals—with all the implications that such associations inspired in a nation of law-abiding citizens.

For Asian Americans, especially Filipinos, a critical effect was to reconstruct and reinforce images of their inherent criminality and un-American status. As Bulosan might put it, those valuable workers on the cusp of winning citizenship, many of whom served honorably in the US military or Allied forces, were made into criminals and threats to "national security" once again for their political commitments and racialized status. The federal surveillance and red-baiting harassment of Filipino militants in the 1950s was a continuation of the long-term campaign to discipline and subjugate Filipino labor activism in the United States (Baldoz 2014).

A Defiantly Leftist Civil Rights Union by Law

The *1952 Yearbook* of ILWU Local 37

The preceding narrative about Local 37 activists' struggles with the repressive efforts of the American state to crush dissent and multiracial Left activism in the Cold War years, not to mention the decades before that, evidences the many ways in which the union and the lives of its members were *constituted by law*—by legal norms and rules, legal practices and protocols, legal disputes and aspirations, legal ideas, ideals, and images. While subjected to the harsh manifestations of repressive law, the activists also were defiant agents actively contesting, reconstructing, and enacting law in more egalitarian directions. We have seen that this was the case in routine internal union organizational activity as much as in relationships with employers and the imperial US state.

Equally revealing are the extant records of how cannery activists were selectively using and deploying legal knowledge as political rhetoric, as protest and propaganda. Fortunately, along with other sources cited so far, a single written text survives that provides a wide, wondrous window into the thinking, aspirations, and strategic gambits of union activists. That landmark text is the *1952 Yearbook, Local 37, International Longshoremen's and Warehousemen's Union*. Union president Chris Mensalvas recruited his longtime friend, the activist writer Carlos Bulosan—then in poor health and probably an alcoholic, a half dozen years after publication of *America is in the Heart* and a few years before his death—to edit, organize, and write substantial chunks of the *Yearbook*. Bulosan's editorial hand surely was influential, but over a dozen union activists independently authored essays, and many short contributions by other union members or allies filled out the text, which provides a rich record of struggles filtered through a well-defined, largely consistent lens of ideologically mediated experience. A full exegesis of the *Yearbook* would require a chapter in itself, but we offer a selective review to illustrate our larger point about the intersubjective oppositional legal consciousness that had developed among left-leaning Filipino cannery activists in the 1950s.[7]

The opening editorial by Bulosan introduces and amplifies the core themes, rhetoric, and tone that follow in the *Yearbook*. As the second epigraph to this chapter demonstrates, the *Yearbook*'s opening statement offers an incessant critique of official American state action, which often is portrayed as arbitrary and repressive force. Bulosan begins by protesting the "restrictive laws, dangerous moves by certain branches of the government, the vicious lies of the capitalist press and yellow journalism, the warmongering of big business, the race-hating hysteria of reactionary organizations and groups, and the unconcealed coordination of all these forces to destroy progressive trade union movement" (ILWU Local 37, 1952, 1). But the very next paragraph testifies to the virtues of the democratically animated union, its kinship with

Fig. 11 *1952 Yearbook Cannery Workers ILWU Local 37* cover. University of Washington Libraries, Special Collections, UW 39791.

the "common goals" of good Americans, and their members' uncompromising faith in inherited American ideals of equal rights for all and democracy. These left-oriented union activists sincerely, we think, proclaimed that they "believe in the fundamental principles of our union and are a continuation of the democratic spirit in America" grounded in "the proposition that all men are created equal, that they are endowed by their Creator with certain inalienable rights, that among these are life, liberty and the pursuit of happiness" (1). No doubt these lines are rhetorically strategic, but that does not mean that they were not sincere and heartfelt, even animating, in fidelity to the activists' uniquely constructed meanings of those principles.

The essays in the *Yearbook* covered many topics, but none so frequently and so passionately as the government deportation campaigns that we have briefly reviewed. These articles repeatedly make clear that the deportation efforts were aimed at impeding union organizing activity by the multiracial workers' rights activists. The first essay following the opening editorial is an anonymous tribute, probably by Bulosan, to the "18 Years of Persecution" suffered by alleged[8] communist Harry Bridges, the immigrant from Australia subjected to repressive state persecution for over twenty years, including multiple deportation and perjury trials, which high courts repeatedly found "unlawful" (Afrasiabi 2017). Several selections from judicial opinions in such rulings then are cited in text boxes, including this from Justice Frank Murphy in 1945: "Seldom if ever in the history of this nation has there been such a concerted and relentless crusade to deport an individual because he dared to exercise the freedom that belongs to him as a human being and is guaranteed to him by the Constitution" (ILWU Local 37, 1952, 2). The time line of Bridges's legal ordeal is followed by a short message from Bridges himself about the defiant case that they together must make before the American people (ILWU Local 37, 1952, 2). The message concludes with the Wobblies' motto that Bridges made famous through the ILWU: An Injury to One Is an Injury to All. That motto powerfully evokes what union activists understood by the solidaristic aspirations for equality and justice. That Bridges and the Asian cannery workers found common cause and understanding is hardly surprising. The essay preceded by only a year the Supreme Court's decision overruling Bridges's last deportation order and by three years his subsequent victory in civil court on charges of fraud and perjury (Afrasiabi 2017).

That page is followed by other articles and editorials confirming the key themes:

- A short message from ILWU secretary-treasurer Louis Goldblatt links the battles of Ernesto Mangaoang directly to that of Harry Bridges. Goldblatt notes that "both are militants; both refuse to be intimidated; and both are in the American tradition of fighting for the rights of the majority" (3).
- An instructional message in a box entitled "Know Your Rights" outlining the entitlements that "foreign born" workers can claim and protocols they should follow if they are screened, harassed, or arrested by INS authorities.
- A page of supporting testimony, including the previously mentioned message from ILWU northwest director Bill Gettings, and a defiant

Fig. 12 Carlos Bulosan at his desk and typewriter, ca. 1950s. University of Washington Libraries, Special Collections, UW 513.

essay, "Taking the Offensive," against "anti-labor and anti-civil rights legislations," by Local 37 president Chris Mensalvas.

- Essays by Mattias Lagunilla and Trinidad Rojo on the history of Local 37 as well as by Ernesto Mangaoang and then Ponce Torres on the legal battles over deportation.
- A short essay characterizing the McCarran-Walter Act as "An American Nuremberg Law" precedes a page featuring short bios of four militant union activists, the text of Articles 23–25 on workers' rights in the *Universal Declaration of Human Rights*, and the text of the "Four Freedoms" sponsored by FDR (16).
- Pictures of union leaders and an article celebrating Jack Hall, the prominent union leader in Hawaii, and an essay by lawyer C. T. (Barry) Hatten on "The Deportability and Immunity of Filipinos in the United

States." Hatten concluded with an aspirational statement no more or less optimistic than that of the rank and file: "We will keep up the good fight, and we will win a great victory for the civil rights and freedom of all people" (20).[9]

- An open letter by Bulosan, "To Whom It May Concern," outlining his commitments in the *Yearbook*. These include that the "union is a progressive organization of honest workers who are demanding higher wages and better living conditions, preservation of our civil rights and liberties as guaranteed by the Constitution of the United States, and a chance to live free in a world of peace" (21).
- An article by Abner Green, of the ACPFB, on deportation of foreign-born Americans, focusing on the *Harisiades* case that confirmed that "past membership in the Communist Party" was a deportable offense. "All minorities—racial, national, and political—are scapegoats of the drive to war" (22).
- A reproduction of the ILWU Local 37 official "constitutional" charter (23) and testimonies from a dozen prominent leaders in diverse unions on behalf of Mangaoang (25).
- "Our Proud Record" (26), culminating in the union fight for *rights* to a job, to a decent wage, to a decent living standard, to medical care, to adequate care in sickness and old age, and to live in freedom. The essay endorses that "the whole structure of our policy follows the 'Economic Bill of Rights' of Franklin Delano Roosevelt." And once more the Wobblies'/ILWU motto "An Injury to One Is an Injury to All!"
- An article decrying state "terrorism" exercised against workers in the US-dependent Philippine client state (27). This essay elaborates on many passages in the *Yearbook* that express strong internationalist commitments and alliances with the communist-led Huk guerilla movement and other radicals in the Philippines, providing additional reasons for repression by US government officials.[10]
- "Stand Up for Freedom," by Lloyd L. Brown, invokes the struggles for civil rights by American Negroes as parallel and inspirational to Filipino migrant struggles. "No Americans have been more concerned about laws than our people, the Negro people. No Americans have had to be more concerned. That's because we always have had to fight for our rights under laws that are supposed to apply to all citizens; and because we've had to fight laws made against us" (28).

- An article excoriating Wall Street's influence that "chains" the Philippines, underlining the economic dimensions of imperial repression (29).
- Two essays assailing the "attack" on unions by colluding ship owners and government officials—"Negro-baiting and red-baiting go hand in hand with lawsuits by dingbats" (30)— and a spirited essay in "Defense of Trade Union Rights" by Louis Saillant, general secretary of the World Federation of Unions (31).[11]
- "Greetings from Members of Local 37" introduces the final several pages (34–44) listing union members from the many fisheries and canneries in whose name the *Yearbook* speaks.

The *1952 Yearbook* as Defiant Egalitarian Ideology

The specter of McCarthy-era legislative restrictions, deportation efforts, and court battles dominates the *Yearbook*. It is clear that the law was "all over" in the lives of cannery workers at this time (Sarat 1990), largely in daunting, repressive ways. The fact that Filipino activists embraced traditional rights discourse, legal symbols, and legal strategies to defend their interests further reflected the deeply hegemonic institutional and ideological forces at work. However, Local 37 activists arguably were less constrained than other subaltern groups struggling for justice through rights mobilization in that era. Historians routinely argue that Cold War politics and the pressures of McCarthyism substantially "confined civil rights talk to a narrow sphere" for many subaltern activists, including activists of color and workers, in this period (Darian-Smith 2012, 499.) In particular, Goluboff (2007) has demonstrated, the NAACP-led civil rights movement "lost" the promise of economic rights during this time as rights claims were narrowed to appeals for public desegregation that served as symbolic concessions to Cold War pressures (Bell 1980). The bold egalitarian claims and rhetoric of Local 37 activists stand in contrast to these understandably attenuated agendas of other movements. Indeed, the *Yearbook* essays staked out the contours of a defiant political posture and distinctive vision of fundamental social transformation that transcended the constraints of the specific historical context. We thus pose two related puzzles. First, how could cannery activists sustain their commitments to Left radicalism, even to communism, while also fully embracing the principles of rights enshrined in core founding traditions of the United States, especially amid persistent state harassment? Second, how and why did they think that rights mobilization could contribute substantially to wide-ranging democratic changes in hierarchical economic and race relations?

In earlier pages we have traced the legacy of relentless legal mobilization activity by Filipino labor activists and speculated about the multiple traditions and influences that infused meaning and strategic appeal into their developing rights-claiming practices. We have found much value in scholarly arguments about the creative, rebellious "third world consciousness" that Filipinos developed from experiences of oppression under Spanish and US colonial rule and then as diasporic migrant workers in the metropole of the expanding racial capitalist empire. By the 1950s, we argue, the core meanings and discursive strategies of their novel rights claiming (Polletta 2000) crystalized as political ideology at once more clearly delineated, sharp edged, and firm. The influence of the young Karl Marx, already provocatively evoked throughout Carlos Bulosan's earlier literary writings, in particular found more direct expression in the *Yearbook*. Simply put, Local 37 activists consistently turned the liberal principle of rights-based equality governing the formal public realm of citizens into an agenda for transformation of all those forms of highly unequal power and exploitative exchange relations protected by private property rights in white-dominated civil society: ownership of production, workplace governance, distribution of wealth, security of housing and health, political leverage within the state, global capitalist expansion, war profiteering, and racism everywhere. The activists displayed an understanding that racial exclusion and labor exploitation were distinct but interconnected—intersectional, we often say today—features of the racial capitalist order. Merging the promise of equal rights as citizens with workers' rights facilitated their powerful egalitarian challenge to capitalism, racism, and imperialism in a familiar American vernacular. And this is why battles over full citizenship status mattered so much: citizenship rights were less an end in themselves so much as the foundational principle as well as intrinsic resource of organizational and institutional power for fundamental transformation of America, of the demand to realize its egalitarian promises. Dreams of a society that guaranteed "life, liberty, and the pursuit of happiness" were refracted through commitments to a republic governed by and for workers (or "the people") generally, overcoming the marginalization of racialized laboring classes on which racial capitalist subversion of democracy had been built.

At the same time, the Left activists' appropriations of liberal rights for transformative ends were admittedly vague and remain difficult to define in specific terms. There can be little doubt that the activists challenged both racism *and* commoditized market relations. Much like Bulosan's literary writings (e.g., see 1995, 181–82), critiques of egoistic exchange relations, rapacious self-interest, greed, and lustful domination in the racial capitalist order radiate throughout the *Yearbook*. But did equality at work require an end of wage labor? Did economic equality require socialization of productive ownership or at least selectively of public infrastructure and utilities? What were the implications for distribution of wealth? We have few clear, consistent indicators on such matters of aspiration. The rhetoric of Local 37 activists pointed in evocative directions, but the activists were neither political theorists nor policy specialists, so the answers to these questions are elusive but also somewhat irrelevant. They were not enacting a holistic architectonic vision of the good society so much as expressing a developing if inchoate aspirational vision of egalitarian, communitarian possibilities.

It is also important to underline that Local 37 activists were not violent revolutionaries; they were, instead, at once radical visionaries and realistic, incremental *reformers*. "Left-progressives, despite all persecutions and name-callings, are still fighting to see that the best traditions of the American people are preserved," wrote Chris Mensalvas (ILWU Local 37, 1952, 5) in his bold article "Taking the Offensive." As previous pages have demonstrated, the workers mostly advocated for rights through peaceful, nonviolent tactics of "mass democratic action for more and more democracy" (5), including protests and strikes, media campaigns, legislative lobbying, union bargaining, arbitration processes, and of course litigation. Local 37 activists did not aspire to equality and freedom on a blank canvas; their specific appropriations of legal ideals and American tropes reflected to some degree the violently enforced constraints of hierarchical power.

The Filipino activists' visions of Left transformation matured in the era of the Popular Front, in which the Communist Party allied with socialists and even liberals. As a result, just what the "Communist" label signaled is less clear, even elusive. In our view, Filipino leftists, including those tilting toward communism, are better understood as committed to what might best be labeled "democratic socialism" and a "workers' state" than the centralized brutal Soviet state about which little was clearly known in the period. Their practical aim was to push the New Deal social programs and principles of the Four Freedoms far further, against the revanchism of racist, hypercapitalist,

Fig. 13 Carlos Bulosan and Chris Mensalvas with union workers, ca. 1950s. University of Washington Libraries, Special Collections, UW 36415.

and "fascist" forces in America. Their lists of immediate goals—"higher and higher wages; union hiring hall; genuine Health & Welfare Plan; Job Pensions; Shorter Hours of Work; and Paid Vacations" (5)—clearly built on realistic programs often celebrated but unrealized then (and now) for most working people and especially for low-wage migrant laborers of color. Their struggles also were thoroughly internationalist in scope; they identified with "the great offensive of people everywhere—in Europe, in Asia, in America, in Africa. Everywhere the working peoples all over the world are fighting back" (5). Filipino American activists supported not just those who struggled against racial capitalist empire in the metropole but also struggles in the Philippines and other anticolonial, anti-imperialist movements that were percolating around the globe at the time. In all these regards, the rights-based aspirations of Filipino labor activists paralleled and drew on the aspirations of black prolabor socialists—such as A. Philip Randolph and W. E .B. Du Bois—as well as a wide array of Left unionists—such as Harry Bridges and Popular Front polemicists so prominent on the West Coast. In the classic American tradition, they were pragmatic radicals—ambitious, even utopian, in their egalitarian aspirational ideals but realistic in their incremental actions.[12]

Aftermath: Leftists Retreat, Conservatives Rush In

The legal victories in the deportation cases were celebrated heartily within and beyond ILWU Local 37. Long-respected business agent Mangaoang momentarily emerged as a hero linked to martyred former leaders Duyungan and Simon who sacrificed for the union. For a time, as the *Yearbook* suggests, Local 37 seemed to be revitalized, unified, and empowered by the episodes of defiant contestation over rights and democratic commitment.

But the mien of militant solidarity displayed in the *Yearbook* obscured the growing disgruntlement of the union's moderate liberal members (Ellison 2005). Former president Trinidad Rojo, still a trustee, bitterly criticized those leaders who proudly displayed their communist allegiances for drawing government wrath and depleting the union financially, emotionally, and organizationally with legal battles. "Common sense dictated that when the President of the U.S. is a rabid Red Baiter . . . a labor leader performs a disservice to the Union by using the local as a grand stand to proclaim his personal ideology which most of the members do not subscribe to," Rojo (n.d.) wrote years later. It is worth noting that he did not publicly criticize the animating visions of his comrades so much as their imprudent public visibility to state officials and poor administrative discipline. Rojo continued to berate viciously President Mensalvas and his friend Bulosan in particular. Specifically, Rojo accused Mensalvas of misusing union funds in violation of procedures designated in union bylaws. Rojo sent a resolution requesting that the ILWU International investigate Local 37's leadership practices and financial books, aiming to decertify the union. He and Feliciana Blanco then filed a lawsuit in King County Superior Court in an effort "to pressure the International to take over the affairs of the local union" (Rojo 1952, 11). The discovery phase for the lawsuit revealed, among other things, that Mensalvas had taken union funds and "loaned" them to the impoverished, ailing Bulosan. The executive board, led by Mensalvas and Lagunilla, protested to the International that the allegations were "false, unfounded and dishonest" (Mensalvas et al. 1954).

Mangaoang disagreed with the dismissal of the resolution by his colleagues, arguing that the union should be committed to legal transparency. He distributed a contentious leaflet outlining his position and raising issues about a cover-up. This in turn alienated Mangaoang among the leftist leaders and catalyzed a series of bitter, highly personalized conflicts in 1954 with incendiary allegations about indolence and drunkenness mixed in with those regarding financial mismanagement. Mensalvas then pulled a power play, omitting Mangaoang's name from the list of nominees as the next union election approached. A union trial committee was formed to adjudicate the growing list of charges in the heated conflict. In January 1955, Mangaoang was found guilty on charges of contempt and making unfounded allegations against union brothers. Mensalvas and Bulosan were largely vindicated, signaling the triumph of their leadership bloc once again (ILWU Local 37 Trial Committee 1955). Mangaoang had already resigned from the union months earlier, however; he spent the rest of his life working different jobs around the Pacific Northwest until his death from cancer at age 66, in 1968.

Other tensions bubbled up in the union. For one thing, attorney John Caughlan issued notice that he would not release the $5,000 returned for Mensalvas's bail until the attorneys were paid $7,227.58 by the union for their legal services. The union already faced a deficit of $15,000, so the executive council dodged the demand and proceeded for the next several years to borrow from union burial funds and to mortgage the union hall building in order to pay their other bills. Caughlan persisted, as he had in the deportation cases for which he remained uncompensated, and he finally prevailed in a King County Superior Court jury trial and then on appeal by the union to the State Supreme Court in 1958. The courts ruled that the case was a simple contract dispute in which records clearly demonstrated that the union executive committee repeatedly authorized compensation for Caughlan's legal defense of Mensalvas, Mangaoang, and others (*Caughlan v. International Longshoremen's and Warehousemen's Union, Local 37-C*, 1958).

Records from the union for subsequent years, from the late 1950s and 1960s, are limited, inconsistent, and unrevealing (Ellison 2005). We do know that Chris Mensalvas was harassed by INS officials in 1959 on his return to Seattle after attending a labor conference among socialists in Canada and that he decided to relocate to Hawaii, where he remained until returning to live in Seattle during the 1970s. With Mensalvas gone, the Left faction undermined by allegations of corruption, and the union fiscally broke, more conservative and less politically aggressive leaders seized the opportunity to take over. Gene Navarro, previously considered a moderate while a business agent, consolidated power in the combined roles of president and business agent and pushed the union rightward for two decades into the mid-1970s. The union focused on survival more than political transformation in the coming decades, as many Filipino union members began to assimilate more fully and easily amid the postwar American economic boom and increased opportunities to indulge in domestic family life. There is evidence of growing involvement of the union in the increasingly Americanized Filipino community but also of less active member political engagement within or through the union (Ellison 2005). Meanwhile, the salmon canning industry experienced a steady decline after a peak in 1936, as wasteful overfishing practices, deteriorating fish habitats, and dams reduced supply, while fresh seafood and other food products became available for changing consumer tastes (Harrison 2011).

All in all, the Left leadership of Local 37 survived McCarthy-era persecution in the short term but ended up divided, deflated, and debilitated. The long-standing dreams of a multiracial workers' coalition committed to democratic socialism withered, much like for other Left labor groups and coalitions that were vanquished around the nation (Kurashige 2010; Schrecker 1998; Cherny, Issel, and Taylor 2004). Chris Mensalvas would not again have a role in a union committed to a Left, democratic, rights-based, social justice agenda until he offered inspiration and counsel as a *manong* to a younger generation of Local 37 cannery worker activists in the 1970s. Carlos Bulosan, who died in 1956, similarly faded from view until he was revived as a literary hero and political inspiration among college-educated Asian Americans developing their political consciousness during the Vietnam War and civil rights era. Many activists in the new generation would allege that Navarro and his successor Constantine "Tony" Baruso—whom moderate leader Rojo labeled "extremists on the right" (Rojo 1952, 12)—had restored a clientelistic *compadre* system, reintroduced bribes into the cannery worker dispatch process, recruited gangs to run gambling rackets that drained workers' wages, and failed to aggressively represent the workers' interests. The young militants would cultivate radical civil rights movement allies in the US metropole as well as protest Cold War expansion of American imperialism that supported strong-arm autocrats around the Pacific Rim, including Ferdinand Marcos in the Philippine client state. In many ways, the factional battles between young university-educated leftists and conservative, arguably corrupt leaders that marked the union's past would be replayed in the 1970s. And once again, animating ideals, instrumental tactics, and institutional forces in the American legal tradition would prominently shape the terms and outcomes of those struggles in varied and complicated ways. We take up these themes in part 2.

PART II

Challenging Empire: Transpacific Rights Radicalism

PROLOGUE TO PART II

The Cold War Era

Global Empire, the Rise of Marcos, and Civil Rights

The modern world must remember that in this age when the ends of the world are being brought so near together the millions of black men in Africa, America, and the Islands of the Sea, not to speak of the brown and yellow myriads elsewhere, are bound to have a great influence upon the world in the future. . . . Let the nations of the world . . . take courage, strive ceaselessly, and fight bravely, that they may prove to the world their incontestable right to be counted among the great brotherhood of mankind.—W. E. B. DU BOIS, "To the Nations of the World" (1900)

Liberal anti-racisms have both disconnected race from material conditions and linked anti-racism to the expansion of U.S.-led global capitalism. Whereas in the 1940s political economic critiques of racism made race appear as an index for the inequalities of capitalist modernity, after the racial break official anti-racisms have not only suppressed this reference but also lent anti-racist codes to the pursuit of new forms of capitalist development.—JODI MELAMED (2011, 10)

All the system's got to be changed . . . and it's got to be socialism because if you stick to private enterprise, there is always misappropriation, some will be wealthy, and too many people will be without.—PHILIP VERA CRUZ (cited in Toribio 1998,157–58)

From the start, the American colonial experiment in the Philippines had been driven by the imperial imperatives of capitalist expansion, strategic military proliferation, missionary idealism regarding the diffusion of civilizing democratic government, and racist paternalism (Bello 1998). However, World War II brought dramatic changes to the character and reach of American empire and hence to the relationship between former colonizer and colonized. For one thing, the Commonwealth of the Philippines finally gained formal independence on July 4, 1946, exactly forty-four years after President Roosevelt declared American military triumph over the First Philippine Republic and, because of the wartime Japanese occupation, a year later than authorized by the 1934 Tydings-McDuffie Act. In a formal ceremony, the American flag was lowered in Manila while the red, white, and blue Filipino national flag was raised; both the American and Philippine national anthems were played. The ceremony harbingered the interdependent relationship between the former colony and its colonial ruler that persisted for the remainder of the century. Indeed, the joint military campaign against Japan forged an enduring if hierarchical and shaky political alliance between the nations. Subsequently, the Cold War further intensified the continued relationship of the United States with the Philippine client state as a military and commercial outpost over many decades (Karnow 1989).

For most Americans, the liberation of the Philippines from Japanese occupation erased the repressive colonial past from the American imagination and restored the old contradictory narrative of benign guardianship even as the exploitative relationship persisted (Ngai 2004, 125). This perception was bolstered by the fact that the Second World War prompted the United States to deliver on promises of naturalized citizenship to Filipinos within the metropole, largely in return for their military service. A variety of enactments during and after World War II further benefited Asian immigrants in special situations. For a host of reasons outlined below, the United States passed legislation to admit immigrants who came as the spouses of US military and civilian personnel (War Brides Act of 1945), who had been displaced by wars, or who suffered actual or threatened persecution by mutual enemies. While citizenship was delayed and even denied for some, the legal and social status for most Filipinos in the metropole improved during the 1950s and 1960s relative to previous decades. Even so, the socioeconomic situation of most Filipinos remained peripheral to the "model minority" stereotype attributed by privileged white society to other Asians (David 2016). The experiences of Filipinos in the United States changed in important ways in part because America had changed, but the colonial legacy still loomed large.

In the remainder of this prologue we will elaborate on how the Cold War, continued US influence in the Philippines, the American civil rights movement, and liberal US immigration reform together shaped the context of political struggles waged by a second generation of Filipino labor activists connected to ILWU Local 37 in the American Pacific Northwest during the latter half of the century.

The Postwar Philippines: A Postcolonial Client State

The Philippines: Devastation, Economic Stagnation, and Political Corruption

Philippine independence was undermined from the start by the harsh experience and devastating effects of World War II. Military destruction and savage Japanese occupation left the Philippine socioeconomic infrastructure eviscerated. An estimated 80 percent of the economy and large parts of Manila were destroyed; upward of one million (of seventeen million) Filipinos lost their lives. Moreover, deep, long-standing political conflicts among Philippine group interests were exacerbated by charges of collaboration with the Japanese during the war and complaints about the unreliable dependence on US aid, thus impeding broad consensus on plans for rebuilding. Long-standing tensions between small-scale peasant farmers, low-wage workers, allied landed interests, and the new corporate capitalist elite similarly resurfaced, often violently, and continued for many decades. The Huk guerilla forces, which effectively took up arms against Japanese invaders, turned again to domestic clashes with large landowners in the postwar years. The later Huk rebellion was identified with communist insurgence, feeding into Cold War fears of local elites and US patrons alike (Karnow 1989).

The fate of the Philippine economy was highly dependent on United States policy and actions. The United States could have reconstructed Philippine society along more democratic, egalitarian, and independent terms akin to its investments in Europe. Such was not the case, however, as the United States was far more committed to advancing its own interests, prioritizing "order and stability" over populist and democratic demands that were even mildly noncapitalist (Harvey 2003, 59; Weekley 2006). In particular, the US institutionalized a powerful military presence in the Philippines after the war. Following the Military Bases Agreement in 1947, the Philippines became a fundamental site of US security plans in the western Pacific. The agreement granted the United States rights to discretionary use of twenty-three military bases, including Clark Field and Subic Bay, rent free for a period of ninety-nine years. While US authorities were initially granted full jurisdiction over the installations, the relationship was contested and renegotiated repeatedly in the following decades, especially during the Vietnam War, and then continuing through the contentious rule of autocrat Ferdinand Marcos and into the twenty-first century (Gregor 1984).

The prewar Philippine political elite for the most part remained in control and even more dependent on US economic power (Karnow 1989). Indeed, large landowners and corporate interests allied with the US elites strongly supported free trade relationships, codified by various legal treaties, between the two nations. The 1946 Bell Trade Act in particular outlined policies—including preferential tariffs on US products imported to the Philippines, a stable currency exchange rate, and a "parity clause" guaranteeing US parties rights to natural resources equal to those of Philippine citizens—regulating the terms of trade between the two nations. Many Filipinos viewed the act as a forfeiture of Philippine national sovereignty that offered few benefits to working people, but US aid for war damages authorized by the Philippine Rehabilitation Act of 1946 was contingent on acceptance, and sugar exporters welcomed the legislated deal (Shalom 1980). Newly elected President Manuel Roxas and his Liberal Party allies in both houses of Congress approved the Bell Trade Act through a variety of parliamentary maneuvers, including removing members in the opposition alleged to have won seats by fraud and terror as well as by ample distribution of pork barrel funding to achieve the needed three-quarters vote. The Democratic Alliance, a left-leaning coalition that included the Huk guerillas and was supported by the overwhelming majority of farmworkers, offered the only organized opposition to the parity clause. An amendment addressing the parity issue was approved in September 1946 followed by a typically deferential Supreme Court rejection of challenges and then a national plebiscite in March 1947. The outcome, many critics alleged, "was very much in the classical pattern of neocolonialism" leveraged by US economic power (Shalom 1980, 517). The parity agreement was modified in 1955 by subsequent US legislation.

As a result, imported American manufactured goods poured into the Philippines, creating a gross trade deficit that sapped foreign aid and undermined use of revenues for national economic development. In response, the Roxas government established a Central Bank that, with Congress, imposed controls, depreciated the peso, and tried to spur manufacturing. But continued reliance on loans from abroad and reparations payments from Japan, much of which was directed to private profit and corruption rather than needed land reform and industrial development, added to the large trade deficit and debt. Poor management and corrupt profiteering became worse in the 1960s and 1970s under President Ferdinand Marcos, who expanded public-sector enterprises and monopolies benefitting friends, feeding crony capitalism and an economic crisis that peaked in the deep recession of 1981 (Balisacan and Hill 2003). By the late 1970s, the Philippines lacked palpable, sustainable development in basic industries and capacities to serve the material needs and well-being of its citizenry.

The Rise of Marcos: The Multiple Dimensions of US Influence

Most political scientists attribute the overall economic malaise and failed state leadership in the Philippines to political dynamics enabled by the constitutional system that Americans imposed in the colonial era. On the one hand, American colonial rule had succeeded in decoupling the Catholic Church from politics, institutionalizing elections, creating ample constitutional powers for presidents, stimulating formation of political parties, and protecting private property as a foundation for liberty. Importantly, the 1916 Jones Law authorized a bicameral legislature elected by an expanded male electorate. By 1920, the United States gave up direct control of the government even though it retained great economic and political influence as patron to the client state. At a superficial level, the Philippine political system was a "mirror image" of the American system (Karnow 1989; Bello 1998).

On the other hand, however, Americans also left a state system riddled with major institutional flaws. Most important, the inherited constitutional scheme permitted and even encouraged rule by a powerful if fragmented oligarchy of municipal, regional, and national family-based "bosses" who used state resources to consolidate their undemocratic, often extralegal dominion. Scholars disagree about the degree to which the strongman bosses emanated from preexisting local, quasi-feudal social hierarchies (Migdal 1988) and then grabbed state power or arose with the state and then built new forms of local patronage-based control through the state (Sidel 1999); evidence of both patterns is abundant. In any case, building on the American colonizers' distrust of the popular forces and investment in privileged elites, the oligarchs' strong grip impeded the organized articulation and influence of mass interests, especially by small farmers, workers, and Muslims in the south. "The dominance of the newly created national oligarchy was so well entrenched that challenges from below—motivated by deep social injustices—faced monumental odds," David Wurfel (1988, 11) summarizes.

The Americans' initial vanquishing of nationalist forces seeking independence similarly hampered development of a strong grassroots commitment to nation, while the corrupt, predatory, vertically organized oligarchical system impeded the development of an economic middle class. In addition, unlike European colonial ventures, Americans did not go far in building the infrastructure of a strong, well-coordinated, professionally staffed, and legally trained administrative state. Indeed, many in the emerging legal profession occupied positions as "double agents" for the oligarchs, mostly serving the rulers even as they also moderated and occasionally opposed them (Dezalay and Garth 2010). Relatedly, Philippine courts, including the Supreme Court, developed a tradition of extreme deference to the oligarchical elite. As Benedict Anderson summarized in his classic account of "cacique democracy," "it was above all the political innovations of the Americans that created a solid, visible national oligarchy" (B. Anderson 1988, 11; see also McCoy 1995; San Juan 2005; White 2014).

The rapid consolidation of centralized autocratic power by President Ferdinand Marcos was, arguably, both an aberration and the "apotheosis" of this legacy of rule by strong, rival oligarchical bosses (Unjieng 2009). Indeed, with the exception of six Democratic Alliance candidates elected but then expelled in 1948, most national elected officials from 1946 through Ferdinand Marcos's iron grip in the 1970s came from families wielding considerable influence over local elections in their respective provinces (Unjieng 2009, 43). Marcos was born in 1917 in Ilocos Norte province in Luzon. In the late 1930s, he was charged with murdering a rival of his father and sentenced to death, but young Ferdinand creatively argued for and won acquittal on appeal. He gained a reputation in the 1950s as an ambitious attorney prone to false boasts about his wartime military heroism and athletic achievements. Ferdinand married Imelda Romualdez in 1954. Mr. Marcos became the leader of the Liberal Party in the House of Representatives by 1957, and he quickly set his eyes on a seat in the Senate. Distrusted by many, his trademark strategic shrewdness was already on display. By 1963, he became President of the Senate and of the Liberal Party but then switched to the Nacionalista Party where he would win presidential nomination. Marcos won election as president in 1965 by 670,000 votes and was reelected in 1969 (Celoza 1997).

The rise of Marcos was fueled by his virulent anticommunism; he endorsed the US campaign in the Vietnam War, urged Philippine involvement in the war, and repeatedly drummed up popular support by linking his regime with the battle against Asian communism. Marcos proved to be an ideal ruler for the ambivalent American model of imperialism; he was a deferential surrogate for American power while maintaining a semblance of national independence (Bonner 1987). For two decades, he thus won the continued support of US leaders. Marcos also promised a "New Society," and he did take some measures to use reparations and loans to build infrastructure. Despite the improvements, however, Marcos's administration suffered from the chronic ills of runaway inflation, increasing national debt and trade deficits, growing unemployment, and rampant corruption. He doubled the government budget and greatly increased the number of state employees, but economic mismanagement resulted from deference to the oligarchs, many of them his cronies. All this provided incentives for the rapid rise in vocal popular dissent. Beginning in 1970, student activism committed to a "people's war" led to periodic riots protesting the Marcos regime, which retaliated by killing several persons and injuring many others. Armed communist insurgency by the New People's Army (NPA) and the Communist Party of the Philippines escalated in the next two years, while rumors of a military coup began to circulate. Like President Nixon in the United States, Marcos used fears of violent disorder and communist infiltration to justify "law and order" politics, but on a harsher scale. Considerable evidence exists confirming that Marcos staged events, like a 1971 grenade bombing, to escalate dread of lawlessness blamed on radicals.

Marcos then issued Proclamation No. 1081, effectively installing martial law in the Philippines and imposing military rule in the country. He extended his rule beyond the constitutional two-term limit, immediately adjourned the National Congress, shut down most of the mass media, suspended civil liberties, banned all political parties, and in the next year jailed rival Senator Benigno ("Ninoy") Aquino Jr. Workers were explicitly targeted by the regime: strikes were outlawed, wages were cut by nearly 40 percent, and many top labor leaders were arrested. Marcos not only removed legislative checks but he outmaneuvered the judiciary, which displayed its traditional deference (Robles 2016). As political scientist C. Neal Tate recounts, "Thus by the end of 1974 the Philippine judiciary was no longer in a position to provide any serious check on the martial law regime. Until the end of the crisis regime, the

Supreme Court rendered not a single decision that posed even a mild threat to Marcos' rule" (Tate 1993, 327; see also Haynie 1998). By 1977, the Marcos regime quadrupled its military capacity and arrested over sixty thousand persons for political reasons, winning continued support by US presidents Carter and Reagan. Historian Alfred McCoy (2009, 403) estimated that the Philippine Constabulatory under Marcos, between 1975 and 1985, was responsible for a "pyramid of terror" that included 3,257 extrajudicial killings, 35,000 tortured, and 70,000 incarcerated.

Resistance to Marcos by radicals, including the NPA and Muslims in the south, and liberals persevered. Liberal legal reform groups such as FLAG (Free Legal Assistance Group) and the TFDP (Task Force Detainees of the Philippines) fought for civil rights and justice. More than any other NGO, Clarke argues, the TFDP "undermined the Marcos dictatorship" because it was able to crystallize "Church concern for human rights" (Clarke 1998, 187). "People Power" and legal rights mobilization worked together to advance resistance and spark political change. A key moment occurred when in 1983 opposition leader Ninoy Aquino returned from exile but was assassinated at the Manila airport. Amid growing protest, Ferdinand and Imelda Marcos fled the country in 1986. Corazon Aquino, Ninoy's widow and prominent figure in the People Power Revolution, won a snap election for the presidency in 1986. She was sworn in by two existing justices of the Supreme Court, Claudio Teehankee and Abad Santos, who had started out deferring to Marcos but, in classic nimble reversal for legal professionals, moved into opposition as court dissenters.

In the Metropole: Cold War Domestic Politics

The Escalation of American Economic and Military Power

By contrast with the Philippines, the United States emerged triumphant, economically and militarily, from the Second World War. With its primary allies and rivals alike devastated and its own economy revitalized, "America in 1945 bestrode the world as a colossus" (Sargent 2013, 397). The United States continued to expand its empire as an economic and political global hegemon. In subsequent years, the United States grew into the leader of a market-based international capitalist economic order committed to rebuilding allies in Europe and former enemy Japan while opposed to the planned economies of its Cold War ideological adversaries, the Soviet Union and World War II ally China. The United States and other advanced countries in the Organisation for Economic Co-operation and Development (OECD) experienced two decades of rapid but steady Keynesian-managed economic growth attended by robust unions representing industrial workers, increased social welfare programs, and a growing, mostly white middle class along with declining but still substantial rates of poverty. At the same time, this economic growth depended on imperial projects of multinational plundering of resources in the Global South, global production supply chains relying on expropriated and exploited labor, favorably leveraged multinational trade agreements, new conventions of international law, foreign policies aiming to nurture friendly democratic alliances around the world, and military ventures to secure the geopolitical context of expanding capital accumulation and political control. The imperial project foundered at many points, including prominently with wars in Korea and Vietnam. Those experiments exposed the flaws of relying on despotic elite heirs of colonialism to execute democratizing missions, underlined the limits of military power, imposed huge financial and human costs, and produced deep political conflicts at home and in the world that would reshape subsequent US foreign policy commitments. As we noted above, the United States sustained its client relationship to the Philippines, but that relationship was uneasy, as perpetual domestic conflict in the former colony, changing US imperial designs in foreign policy, and domestic conflict in the metropole festered. United States support for the Marcos regime in the 1970s illustrated the shifting American inclination to choose allies based on their commitments to anticommunism and authoritarian order rather than ostensible democratic principles (Bello 1998).

World War, Cold War, and the Civil Rights Racial Break

The resurgence of the American industrial economy converged with post–World War II and Cold War ideological politics to produce a major transformation, what has been called a "racial break" (Winant 2004), in the racial capitalist order of the United States and around the globe. World War II dramatically exposed and politicized the violence of white supremacy, enabling antiracist activists to make connections between the terror of Nazi genocide and racist hierarchies throughout the world, thus "demonstrating affinities between European fascism, racial segregation, and colonial rule" (Melamed 2011, 5). The war experience encouraged many returning veterans to view the Jim Crow American South and other colonial homelands in relation to broader global patterns of racial hierarchy and repression (Parker

2009). Moreover, postwar demands for industrial workers sparked large-scale migration from the rural South to the North both in the US metropole and globally, relocating populations that eventually would find affinity with race-based social movements promoting inclusion in the metropoles as well as independence in colonies (Gregory 2005). Equally important, the Cold War ideological clash between the ostensibly "free" United States and the "egalitarian" Soviet Union elevated the issue of racial apartheid and injustice. Soviet propaganda called attention to histories of violent racial subjugation by white supremacists during slavery and Jim Crow to question American claims about equal opportunity and promises of alliances as equals with people of color in the Global South (Dudziak 2000; Borstelman 2001). Prominent African American activists echoed charges about US hypocrisy and took their challenges regarding continued racial hierarchy to the United Nations (C. Anderson 2003). As a result, pressures mounted for elites to address and overcome at least the appearances of the long-standing racial divide in order to secure America's hegemonic stature as leader of the postcolonial global capitalist order. To a large extent, therefore, the interests of white elites and those of long oppressed African Americans "converged" around agendas of legal reform and official rights recalculation (Bell 1980).

This context thus created a favorable opening for revitalization of the long civil rights struggle by black Americans (McAdam 1982). The heady mix of insurgent actions—including nonviolent marches, sit-ins, and other forms of direct action—combined with conventional political modes of strategic litigation, legislative lobbying, and elite alliances to turn political opportunity into legal change. The provocation of white violence against nonviolent black protestors in particular proved powerful, especially once graphically reproduced on national television and in print media (Garrow 1978). Many scholars have viewed this history as the paradigmatic example of multidimensional, bottom-up, rights-based legal mobilization politics (Scheingold 1974; see McCann 1994). Its outcomes were forever associated with public school desegregation initiated by *Brown v. Board of Education* (1954) and passage of landmark civil rights legislation, including the 1964 Civil Rights Act banning racial discrimination in private workplaces and the 1965 Voting Rights Act, although the impact and reverberations of the movement extended far more widely.

Title VII of the 1964 Civil Rights Act was especially important, as it created a second regime of regulatory support for workers and in particular for minority and female workers who benefitted little from the earlier regulatory regime of the New Deal (MacLean 2006). Whereas New Deal labor law tended to support collective rights of mostly white industrial workers, however, civil rights legislation often has been criticized for encouraging *individual* rights claiming that actually undermines *collective* political action (Lichtenstein 2002, chap. 5). Indeed, one important and ironic implication was that minority and female workers could sue unions as well as employers for discriminatory practices, thus compounding tensions over racial and gender politics among workers that long divided the labor movement (Frymer 2008; Lee 2014). At the same time, though, class action litigation facilitated a fair amount of group-based legal mobilization, including by union workers, around Title VII claims during the 1970s and 1980s (McCann 1994; MacLean 2006). Such collective civil rights mobilization provides a central story line in the remainder of this book.

The critical point here, though, is to note the ascendance of the broader ethos of *racial liberal* ideology in the postwar era (Charles W. Mills 2008, 2017; Melamed 2011; Dawson and Francis 2016). On the one hand, the formal equality guaranteed by racially liberal laws and policies was explicitly antiracist and went a long way toward challenging inherited traditions of overt white-supremacist domination and racially repressive rule both in the United States and around the world (King and Smith 2005). The Old Jim Crow in the US South was in part dismantled, and racially organized colonial governments gave way to new political alignments and institutional arrangements, including liberal constitutions. On the other hand, racial liberalism abandoned the earlier "promises" of much civil rights advocacy—in the United States by the early NAACP and black socialist leaders such as A. Philip Randolph and W. E. B. Du Bois, among others, and around the world—that challenged the class bases of racial hierarchy and linked demands for racial recognition to demands for material redistribution remedying centuries of economic oppression (Goluboff 2007; Fraser 2000, 2016).

The touchstone of the racial liberal framework followed the hugely important work of sociologist Gunnar Myrdal (1944) that defined racism as a matter of prejudice, moral failure, and flawed psychology. Discrimination was thus viewed as individualized, irrational, and aberrational residue of the past rather than systematically embedded in organizational structures, relational practices, and market dynamics (Frymer 2008; Murakawa 2014). Such a focus on explicit, intentional discrimination did provide a foundation for challenging some long-standing barriers impeding entry of racial minorities to educational institutions, employment, housing purchase, bank loans, and the like. But absent direct commitment to affirmative redistribution of unequal wealth, control of capital, and political power, egalitarian legal advances fell well short of structurally transformative change for the bulk of marginalized persons. Moreover, as liberal antiracism severed the link between racial hierarchy and material conditions, so did official antiracism serve to bolster US claims as the hegemonic leader of the global capitalist order (Melamed 2011, 11). "If America should follow its own deepest convictions, its well-being at home would be increased directly. At the same time America's prestige and power abroad would rise immensely," Myrdal (1944, 1022) preached; "The century old dream of American patriots, that America could give the entire world its own freedoms and its own faith, would become true. . . . America saving itself becomes savior of the world."

Beyond Racial Liberalism: New Left Freedom Dreams and Antiracist Struggles

These limited promises and imperial designs of racial liberalism did not go unheeded or unchallenged by Left social justice activists in the 1960s and 1970s. Indeed, the more radically egalitarian, materialist orientations of earlier activists in the long civil rights struggle were rearticulated by new voices to challenge the nexus of capitalism, racism, patriarchy, and imperialist expansion (Melamed 2011). In the United States, a variety of parallel if mostly unaligned postliberal civil rights movements formed and found new organizational modes of expression: Black Power, black feminism and other feminisms of color, American Indian sovereignty, Chicano nationalism, Asian American civil rights, gay and lesbian liberation, and the New Left generally, among others. Many of the new activists located their origins, discovering and recovering their group histories, in the practices of racial, ethnic, gender, and sexual communities. These new radical collectives connected with many allies from veterans of the Old Left, including socialists and communists, trade union activists of color, survivors from the Southern civil rights movement, and migrants from beyond the metropole. The new activism tended to be "prefigurative" (Boggs 1977) in practice and to congregate around local communities and neighborhoods as well as on or near university campuses. The focus on "cultural" contestation variably highlighted and diverted from a focus on redistribution of economic power. Increasingly, most such activists expanded their support for anticolonial movements abroad as well as challenges to American support for dictators, like Ferdinand Marcos, and related imperial ventures (Young 2006).

The Black Panthers, who numbered around two thousand at their peak in 1968, in many ways were representative of and influential on the new materialist antiracist activism. A prominent wing of the larger Black Power movement, their program called for an end to police brutality, full employment for African Americans, and redistribution of land, housing, and other economic recourses for all. While openly socialist and nationalist, the Panthers advocated greater local control and initiated free breakfast programs, free health clinics, and other community ventures for self-determination and "freedom." The Panthers also drew severe repression from the FBI and other law enforcement agencies culminating in the murder of Panther members Fred Hampton and Mark Clark (Singh 2005).

The political manifestations of materialized antiracist activism on the West Coast were not confined to urban centers. During the same period in which both civil rights and radical post–civil rights activist challenges to racial capitalism were on the rise, California farmworkers initiated a dramatic strike that catalyzed a nationwide boycott against grape growers in Delano, California. The strike began in 1965 with the Agricultural Workers Organizing Committee (AWOC), an AFL-CIO affiliated union of mostly Filipino American workers led by former International Workers of the World (IWW) member Philip Vera Cruz, longtime ILWU activist Larry Itliong, and other Filipino labor veterans. As one of the opening epigraphs to this chapter evidences, Vera Cruz carried on the insistent radical socialist tradition of Filipino labor activists.

AWOC leaders asked the National Farm Workers Association (NFWA), led by Mexican American activists Dolores Huerta and Cesar Chavez, to join in a solidarity strike. The NFWA response was complicated by the fact that it represented a diverse workforce of mostly Mexican but also Chicano, Puerto Rican, and African American farmworkers, but the union committed to solidarity once employers violently retaliated against AWOC. Over five years, the Delano grape workers' nonviolent strike became the longest in farmworker history, one that changed the power relationship between agricultural capital and farmworkers in California and that trained a new generation of activists. After the strike generated more violent retaliation from growers, the NFWA and AWOC merged into the United Farm Workers (UFW) Organizing Committee, which was supported by the AFL-CIO. The new UFW expanded its efforts into a massive national boycott against retailers of California fruit products that enlisted community support from unions, civil rights activists, and religious and student organizations around the nation. The Black Panthers were one of the first groups to endorse the boycott, and the prodigious effort mobilized a new generation of both female and male leaders to fight for workers' social justice. In 1970, the largest grape grower agreed to a contract, and more contracts followed. In the midst of the civil rights era, a multiracial and multigender coalition of exploited, low-wage workers—led jointly by Filipino American and Mexican American leaders—achieved a major milestone in material antiracist struggle (Sharma, Jones, and Cheng 2016; Scharlin and Villanueva 2000). This alliance shook white American elites, who generally tolerated homeland nationalism among legions of diasporic imported workers but feared class- and race-based radicalism among those crossing national borders into the metropole (Ngai 2004, 171).[1]

Many of the radical post–civil rights Left groups expressed skepticism not just about racial liberalism but also about the promises of reliance on litigation and legal reform that were central to the liberal civil rights agenda. That said, engagement with official law continued on many levels. For one thing, the Panthers and other groups effectively politicized and publicized "defensive" trials challenging police brutality and other manifestations of repressive law (Danelski 1971). The UFW relied heavily on coordinating creative lawyers and strategic litigation as key elements of their organizing and bargaining activities (Gordon 2006). Left liberal minority and feminist groups, Ralph Nader's consumer-based public interest movement, environmentalists, and other movements continued to rely heavily on litigation to protect public goods jeopardized by the violence of capitalist accumulation (McCann 1986). Moreover, many activists labored to reconstruct civil rights principles to fit the situations and new aspirational demands of marginalized claimants. In particular, a new generation of radical lawyers arose to join veteran civil rights attorneys in exploring and expanding new possibilities and promises of legal mobilization among workers. Among these projects were efforts by unions, feminist organizations, and other rights-based groups to advance broad, impact-oriented challenges to institutional racism and sexism in workplaces as well as generate support for expanding the social welfare obligations of the liberal state. One such movement made notable gains by organizing female workers around the nation to challenge institutionalized gender-based wage inequity by invoking the newly developed logic of "disparate impact" in antidiscrimination law und Title VII of the 1964 Civil Rights Act (McCann 1994). Other activists focused on mobilizing the impact standard to challenge institutional racial discrimination at work, including among unions (Lee 2014; Frymer 2008). Important episodes in this new politics of radical civil rights will be the focus in the remaining pages of this book.

Immigration Reform and the New Imported Colonial Workforce

Cold War civil rights politics were paralleled by and interconnected with dramatic changes more generally in US immigration policy. As always, immigration policies and practices were rooted to a large extent in the need for imported labor to support capitalist accumulation, especially in the agricultural sector but also beyond, increasingly in more skilled sectors. But the symbolic geopolitics of the Cold War era pushed reform again in a racially liberal, universalist direction that implied at least moderately greater appreciation for the benefits of immigrant workers' contributions to capitalist development.

The Bracero Program

Understanding the immigration reform efforts in the mid-1960s requires accounting for policies and practices in previous decades. We noted earlier that World War II accelerated the demand for low-wage, flexible labor, which involved drawing women out of domestic social reproduction as well as importing new waves of migrant workers, the latter mostly in the agricultural sector. Military service enlisted over one million African Americans, half a million Mexican Americans, and a combined one hundred fifty thousand Japanese American, Chinese American, Filipino American, Puerto Rican, and Native American residents—many of them longtime contributors to the low-wage labor force. As such, American business interests looked to new waves of Mexican migrants as replacements. After all, during the twentieth century, Mexicans more than any other group had supplied the flexible, disposable imported colonial labor in the agricultural sector outside of the US South (Ngai 2004). The geographic proximity of Mexicans made them a particularly attractive and elastic resource for American capital. Like Asians before them, their work status was situated between free and slave; their foreignness distanced them from the free-labor status of even second-class racialized citizens, and yet they were semifree contractors who enjoyed limited capacity for movement and thus could manipulate market power, although under the constrained conditions of subjugated transnational labor "necessity" (Ngai 2004, 138; De Genova 2004, 2010).

Unlike for imported Filipino colonial national workers, moreover, there were few pretenses to civilizing uplift or benign assimilation for Mexicans, whom white Americans had conquered and whose land was expropriated in the nineteenth century (Frymer 2017). This meant that Mexican workers had little moral or legal leverage to challenge the highly repressive, often violent disciplinary control exercised by employers on the large commercial farms. The exclusions of agricultural workers from New Deal regulatory reforms proved especially disempowering for imported migrant Mexican workers as opposed to Asians and Filipinos and many African Americans. Again, the plantation model of workplace organization and relations continued with little legal or organized challenge in West Coast agricultural production until the 1960s (Ngai 2004; Calavita 1992).

The bracero program formally institutionalized the conscription, or expropriation, of Mexican migrant workers from 1942 to 1964. Euphemistically labeled a "guest worker" program that would convert illegal workers into legal braceros, the United States fashioned a bilateral agreement with Mexico in 1942 that broke with its long-standing law and practice of avoiding contracts with another nation for labor power (Ngai 2004, 138; Calavita 1992). The aim was for the US government to document many of the contracted workers, guaranteeing them many types of legal protections—including assurances they would be paid for their work and living resources, including housing, food, and transportation—while regulating their flows across the border to meet capitalist needs. In actual practice, US employers preferred undocumented workers who came through the "revolving door" with fewer legal protections and less leverage for wages. As many as half of the nearly five million Mexican workers admitted during the program's duration were undocumented and thus subject to arbitrary deportation and intimidation by the border patrol as "illegals." Eventually, the government ceded contracting authority to the growers, which further reduced regulatory protections and wages (Calavita 1992). Mexican workers were further undercut by AFL hostility and the Migrant Labor Agreement barring of braceros from participation in strikes. That said, bracero workers organized to represent their interests more successfully in the Pacific Northwest (Gamboa 1990), far from the Mexican "back door" borderland, than in the American Southwest (Calavita 1992).

Ultimately, whatever its design, the bracero program could not overcome its historically contradictory goals of meeting western growers' demand for imported workers with a regulated supply of contract laborers who were ensured better working and living conditions than they received as illegal aliens

(De Genova 2004). The tensions in design were exacerbated by the bureaucratic division of program authority among the Immigration and Naturalization Services (INS) in the Department of Justice, the Department of Labor, the State Department, and Congress (Calavita 1992). Critics blamed the program for depressing farmworkers' wages generally, reducing work opportunities for both black and white Americans, institutionalizing harsh treatment of imported colonial workers, and, especially, increasing rather than reducing the flow of undocumented workers. In 1954–1955, a panic developed about the open-door practices that led to expulsion of nearly three million workers in Operation Wetback (Ngai 2004, 165). Overall, the bracero program harbingered the problems of reconciling conflicting racial capitalist imperatives within the increasingly legalistic and bureaucratic national security state. One implication was the rapid unionization and militancy of farmworkers that followed program termination in the 1960s as exemplified by the dramatic Delano grape strike episode recounted previously.

Immigration Reform: The 1965 Hart-Celler Act

Before 1965, there were no specified *restrictions* on the quantity of Mexicans who could cross borders to provide labor. But the demands of Cold War politics and the reduction of demand for laborers created by mechanization of agricultural production led to the end of the bracero experiment in 1964 and a major reconfiguration of US immigration law in 1965. The Hart-Celler Act of 1965, which superseded the 1924 Johnson-Reed Act and entailed amendments to the Immigration and Nationalities Act of 1952, represented a high point of ostensibly liberal egalitarian legislation. It reversed the explicitly racialized exclusions of Asian migration legislated since 1882, and it abolished the draconian system of national origins quotas long privileging Northern Europe, establishing a new, more egalitarian system. Each country in the Eastern Hemisphere received an annual quota of twenty thousand visas up to a maximum of 170,000 for the hemisphere. The Western Hemisphere was accorded the same system in 1976. Then in 1978 the hemispheric maximums were abandoned and a worldwide ceiling of 290,000 annual immigrants was established. In effect, the 1965 bill authorized large-scale importation of workers from the Global South, and especially from Asia, into the United States and offered them the promise of naturalized citizenship (Ngai 2004).

It is significant, though, that for the first time, the quantity of Mexican workers who could legally enter and reside in the United States was restricted. That in turn accelerated the number of undocumented Mexican workers deemed illegal within US borders along with the practices of heavy, often arbitrary and repressive policing of migrants generally. Liberalized immigration law went hand in hand with increasingly repressive legal practice. Moreover, the Hart-Celler Act reduced barriers to entry and naturalization but was silent on matters of political economy, racialized differentiation in value, and the "social question" of material inequality that attended citizenship. And finally, while racial liberalism and liberal multiculturalist ideology ascended, political radicalism, especially if linked to communism, was—as during the McCarthy era—constructed as repugnant to neoliberals and repressed, often violently. An old legacy discriminating between good, compliant immigrants and bad, politically defiant immigrants—familiar among Jews, Irish, and Asians in earlier eras—was replayed again. This is true, we shall see, of divisions imposed on the Filipino American population as well in the post–World War II era.

Implications for New Filipino Migration

All of the previously mentioned developments shaped subsequent migration patterns for Filipinos and growth of Filipino American communities in the United States. The 1945 War Brides Act enabled about sixteen thousand Filipinas to enter the metropole in the years after World War II. About twice that many total Filipina/os overall entered the United States between the war and 1965. In abolishing racist national origins quotas, the 1965 Immigration Act permitted selective entry primarily on the basis of desirable occupational qualifications (e.g., productive "merit") or family reunification. In the two decades after the legislation, about 40 percent of "legal" immigration to the United States emanated from Asia (Espiritu and Wolf 1999). The Philippines represented the largest influx, making up nearly a quarter of the total Asian immigration. The number of Filipina/os who emigrated to the United States between 1981 and 1985—around 221,000—was fourteen times greater than the sixteen thousand immigrants in 1961–1965. Filipino immigrants represented the second largest group of immigrants in the United States after Mexicans during the later decades of the twentieth century, numbering 1.5 million by 1990, one half of them in California (Espiritu and Wolf 1999).

This pattern reproduced to some degree the transnational migratory circuits of conscripted global labor developed earlier in the century. At an instrumental level, migration was fueled by legally constructed opportunities, by economic betterment promised by American media, by desires to reconnect with family and friends in the United States, and by the 1974 Marcos government overseas employment program. But the political push from the brutal repression of the Marcos regime was also hugely significant as well. An estimated three hundred thousand Filipinos emigrated from the Philippines to the United States during the Marcos era, many of them to escape the regime's repressive practices and failed economic policies.

The profiles of immigrants from the former colony in the metropole changed, however. For one thing, the immigration of war brides and women generally enabled development of heterosexual nuclear families, and family reunification after 1965 added to this. These changes subjected Filipino males to new disciplinary pressures, which privatized incentives, encouraged assimilation, and discouraged collectivist radical politics. But this integration of heteronormative patriarchal family dynamics also normalized and increased acceptance of Filipinos into white American society. The profiles of Asian "sojourner" gave way to new waves of "settlers" who filed for citizenship papers and represented a large share of newly naturalized persons in the 1970s and 1980s. "They began a spiral of chain migration: the numerous spouses, children, and parents who entered in the unlimited class of 'immediate relative' in turn sponsored their 'immediate relatives,' and so on. . . . These factors caused total immigration from Asia to skyrocket" (Ueda 1994, 67).

The new Asian immigrants, including Filipinos, also were more widely distributed between professional and working-class skills and occupational eligibility. In particular, medical professional personnel made up a larger percentage of immigrants. By the late 1980s, the Philippines was the largest supplier of health professionals to the United States, sending nearly twenty-five thousand nurses between 1965 and 1985. That said, strict licensing procedures and racial discrimination diverted many medical professionals to jobs as nurses and laboratory assistants far below their skill levels. A second stream of immigrants claiming family connection grew to a much larger proportion of overall immigrant number in the 1980s, thus continuing the flow of unskilled and semiskilled labor from the period before 1965. One result was to further splinter the Filipino American community along lines of income and class (Espiritu and Wolf 1999).

Children of Immigrants Longitudinal Study (CILS) surveys during the 1990s found that many Filipinos in the San Diego area, then with the third largest Filipino immigrant population, were indicative of the broader Filipino American experience. Overall, most Filipinos in the United States were college educated, but Filipina women reached higher educational levels, higher occupations, and higher earnings than Filipino males, who were more likely to be US born. In 1992, nearly 90 percent of Filipino respondents in the CILS survey sample ethnically self-identified as being Filipino; 50 percent chose the hyphenated Filipino-American identifying label, while 31 percent choose the label Filipino and only 5 percent chose American. Immigrant identification as Filipino actually grew in subsequent years as did consciousness about experiences with racial and ethnic discrimination. At the same time, over half of respondents were positive about the promises of equal opportunity in America. In short, the ambiguities and paradoxes of the colonial experience—at once a part of and yet apart from America, both equal and unequal—continued to be manifest among those Filipinos who resided in the metropole (Espiritu and Wolf 1999).

We conclude this section by noting two ironic developments in the "pervasive culture of migration" among Filipinos during the late twentieth century. For one thing, in 1973, the Marcos regime reached out to Filipinos overseas, especially in North America, with attractive incentive packages to encourage temporary return visits to a commodified, sanitized version of the homeland as consuming "tourists." The balikbayan plan, as Vincente Rafael (1997, 270) astutely analyzes, preyed on sentimental attachments to home and family "rather than loyalty to the nation-state." Philippine residents often discerned a characteristic "shameless" flaunting of the superior American way of life by the tourists, which in turn incited local humiliation and envy. The privileged balikbayans thus not only seemed "to corroborate the terms of colonial hegemony; they also mirror(ed) the 'failure' of nationalism to retain and control the excess known as overseas Filipinos" (Raphael 1997, 272).

Second, in roughly the same period, as international demand for skilled and semiskilled workers grew, large numbers of Filipino/as submitted to conscription in contracted work—mostly as rightsless, noncitizen, temporary employees—in the Middle East, Asia, and Europe. The Marcos regime actually developed a prominent policy program to encourage and facilitate this outward migration of transnational, largely exploited labor. The flow of overseas contract workers (OCWs) numbered a few thousand a year in the 1970s and then accelerated dramatically in subsequent decades. The total number passed one million by 2006 and nearly doubled a decade later (Asis 2017). As female migrants engaged in caring labor and domestic work began to surpass the numbers of men in the 1990s, new laws and policies were aimed at protection of contracted workers (Parrenas 2000).

Despite the relatively powerless, exploitative conditions of work for many in the diaspora, President Corazon Aquino recognized OCWs as "national heroes" (Rafael 1997, 274). At least two related reasons make sense of this curious characterization.[2] First, the exportation of workers relieved to some extent the pressures of joblessness in the weak economy at home, which provoked the same type of national embarrassment and shame as did the visits by balikbayans. Second, exported workers came to provide a large, steady flow of remittances, which became the country's economic "lifeline" and a major source of growth in GNP by the 2000s. By 1995, remittances were estimated to be $6 billion and grew more than fourfold by 2016 (Asis 2017; Zong and Batalova 2018).

Resurgent Racial Capitalism: Neoliberal Countermobilization

The changing cultural and legal currents of the racial liberal era along with dynamics of global market expansion provided new impetus for restructuring racial capitalist governance within the United States. At an instrumental level, countermobilization efforts developed among corporate interests and white elites endeavoring to "reclaim" government and roll back commitments to egalitarian change that were blamed for undermining employer freedom and profits (MacLean 2006). Scholars often point to a 1971 memo by future Supreme Court Justice Lewis Powell as the signal moment, if not a blueprint, for widespread political coordination and strategic action by business organizations to take back the "American economic system . . . under broad attack" (see Hacker and Pierson 2010). The memo was followed by increased synchronization among the greatly expanded Chamber of Commerce and National Federation of Independent Business along with the formidable new Business Roundtable.

That common corporate agenda has since been identified with "neoliberalism," which overlapped with but was not identical to the religious New Right. This ethos used stagflation in the 1970s to chart and to justify departures from Keynesianism, downsizing of the welfare state, rolling back business regulation, accelerating capital investment abroad, growing economic and political influence of the finance sector, and increased class unity of corporate capitalist elites around a global agenda. Similarly, the liberal ideology of "free labor," embodied in the ethos of "right to work," was used to undermine labor unions and militate further against political capacities to improve the bargaining power of wage earners generally (Lee 2014). The Roundtable was followed by a succession of new political think tanks and right-wing, public interest law firms. These included the Heritage, Charles Koch, Scaife, Lynde, and Olin foundations as well as the Pacific Legal Foundation, the Cato Institute, the Federalist Society, and the Chamber of Commerce National Litigation Center—all fertile advocacy centers and training grounds for conservative legal activists who would staff the administrative state and courts for decades to come (Stefancic and Delgado 1996; Teles 2008; Hollis-Brusky 2015). As we shall see in coming pages, neoliberal advocates in the Reagan administration enacted a systematic plan to contain civil rights law through nonenforcement and then judicial retrenchment, just as had an earlier generation of reactionary, corporate-influenced legal officials narrowed and trimmed the Wagner Act. In the shadows of these elite movements, grassroots white-supremacist movements also grew in rural and suburban authoritarian enclaves around America (Belew 2018).

As racial liberalism was melded with neoliberal deference to markets and privatization in the Reagan administration during the 1980s, the obstacles to redistributive remediation for historical racial and gender injustices proliferated. Moreover, as we shall see in subsequent chapters, the explicit racial agendas and institutional mechanisms of the white-supremacist era—targeting African Americans, three generations of Asian Americans, Mexican Americans, and Native Americans in particular—were reorganized into new, facially neutral, ostensibly antiracist, systematically coordinated bureaucratic forms of coercion to reinforce racial class hierarchy in the late-century era of deindustrialized, financialized capitalism (Melamed 2011). At least three general manifestations of repressive legal government, inherited from the earlier era and bolstered in the post–civil rights era, of racial capitalism are worth noting: (1) the penal-industrial complex of intensified policing, mass incarceration, expanded surveillance, and financial penalties aimed primarily at subjugation of the racialized, resource-poor surplus population; (2) the expanded national security complex that policed borders, controlled legal membership, and enforced new repressive legal violence toward racialized "illegal" immigrant workers as well as those criminalized as political subversives; and (3) the enlarged discretion of employers generally to control and exploit both citizen and noncitizen wage workers enabled by evisceration of labor and employment laws; civil rights laws; federal agency capacity, authority, or integrity;[3] and key elements of the social welfare state. The first two manifestations were realized by a mix of both direct public legal administration and contracted nongovernmental corporate implementation. The third sphere of resurgent repressive governance was indirectly authorized through enhanced property-rights protection for profit-driven business owning and managerial classes, so it is often overlooked in analysis of illiberal, even authoritarian legal practice (Orren 1995). While highly bureaucratic in form and typically governed by extensive procedural rules that are facially color blind and gender neutral, all of these reconstructed managerial institutions continued to target primarily, and most violently, racialized and gendered low-wage workers, the poor, undocumented immigrants, felons, and others viewed as disposable or surplus populations, negating the purported benefits from racially liberal civil rights and immigration laws (Melamed 2011; Murakawa 2014). All in all, the expansion of formal rights in the racially liberal era reaffirmed the insubstantial, even elusive promises of abstract, formal legal equality among citizens (Fraser 2016).

The Political Economy of Seattle and the Pacific Northwest

Much of our narrative in the coming pages focuses on political struggles centered in Seattle during the 1970s through the 1990s. The Seattle context that both second-generation Filipinos and new Filipino immigrants experienced in the postwar years in many ways mirrored the trends in the larger American political economy, culture, and law. The city emerged from the war years as a thriving outpost of US imperial development and transformation. Before the 1970s, historian Andrew Hedden (2018, 3) writes, "the city and its surrounding region were paradigmatic examples of Keynesian economic policies, organized labor strength, as well as the generalized prosperity they appeared to generate, central characteristics of the three-decade reign of political liberalism historians have framed as the 'New Deal Order.'" The Emerald City became a shining symbol of middle-class white progressivism and modernity showcased for the nation in the 1962 World's Fair. Represented by prominent democratic senators Warren Magnuson and Henry "Scoop" Jackson and economically anchored by aerospace pioneer Boeing's federal contracts, Seattle was at once a beneficiary of the Cold War military-industrial complex and an exemplar of the globally expanding American empire.

Postwar stability and prosperity in Seattle became deeply unsettled in the 1970s, however. Boeing went nearly bankrupt in the early 1970s, shedding sixty thousand high-paying skilled jobs; unemployment rose markedly, especially in the city's heavily black populated Central area; and economically squeezed white workers migrated to the Republican Party. During the Boeing bust, the militant ILWU initiated a strike of 130 days at the modernizing Seattle Port, long a key site of global commercial empire. The strike drew intervention from the Nixon administration and was interrupted repeatedly by the exigencies of shipping goods for the Vietnam War. As the industrial sector waned and struggled, new high tech, international finance, and service sectors began to expand. In short, joblessness, poverty, and shrinking prospects for many working-class people, especially racial minorities and women, greatly increased as the wealth of a small segment of mostly white corporate moguls, managers, and professional people escalated. The growing class divisions were mirrored in changing Seattle politics as the new business and professional leadership elite committed to neoliberal paths of development increasingly clashed with antiwar, civil rights, and New Left urban grassroots activists (Hedden 2018).

As in an earlier part of the century, the University of Washington (UW) was an important site of radicalization and protest politics. At the UW, coalitions of students in Afro-American Studies, Asian American Studies, and the Center for Chicano Studies during the late 1960s pressed for creating an integrated American Ethnic Studies program and a host of related curricular and institutional changes, among other issues. The UW Black Student Union (BSU), founded by later Filipino labor activist ally Larry Gossett, took up the banner of Black Power. Some members of the BSU connected with the small but dynamic chapter of the Black Panthers that arose in 1968, one of the longest active chapters, until 1978 (Schaefer 2005). The Seattle chapter of the Black Panther Party combined antiracist, anticapitalist, and anti-imperial campaigns in ways that were a lightning rod for other groups. Allies included the Union of Democratic Filipinos (Katipunan ng Demokratikong Pilipino [KDP]), which in the 1970s developed a formidable profile protesting against the Marcos regime in the Philippines and for democratic socialism in the United States. That radical association will figure prominently in coming pages.

The continued presence or return of radical *manongs* from the earlier period also proved important. Communists and leftists like B. J. Mangaoang—who had been married to Local 37 radical activist Ernesto, was a Communist Party leader, ran for many political offices, and held a job at UW—remained highly visible activists. The return to Seattle in the 1970s by former Local 37 activist and communist leader Chris Mensalvas was especially important to the young Filipino activists whom we chronicle in coming pages. Indeed, Philip Vera Cruz often publicly celebrated Mensalvas, along with Ernesto Mangaoang, as "the most outstanding Filipino organizer in this country through the 1940s and 50s," and insisted that "people should know more about them." (Scharlin and Villanueva 2000, 17). Through both the new multicultural university curricula and living testimonies of the *manongs*, moreover, the writings of Carlos Bulosan, who had died in 1956, experienced a rebirth among many young Filipino Americans. *America Is in the Heart* became a classic. As activist John Foz reported, "I can't remember when I first read the book—it may have been when I was a student . . . but Bulosan's book was definitely a 'must-read' for anyone seeking their identity as a Filipino American." Indeed, "it was very impactful. As far as Filipino American literature in the 1970s, there is no other book that can compare" (quoted in Chew 2014).

It is relevant that nearly eight thousand Filipino Americans lived in the Puget Sound area in 1970. By 1990 Filipinos represented the largest Asian population in Washington State, estimated at around thirty thousand (Mejia-Giudici 1998). As in the national immigrant population, this demographic influx represented a small number of professionals and a much larger share of low-wage laborers in the marginal economy. Again, many Filipino Americans were inclined toward assimilation. As a hub of integration, the former Philippine Commonwealth Council of Seattle (PCCS) changed its name to the Filipino Community of Seattle, and in the 2000s upgraded its former home in the Empire Bowling Alley (Mejia-Giudici 1998). But the transitional period also included a fair number of exiles and political refugees aiming to build support for opposition to the increasingly repressive Marcos regime in the 1970s. Many of these exiled immigrants were important, Mark Thompson argues, "not only because they were active at a time when domestic opponents were largely silent but also because they cultivated crucial American support." This influx of radicalized Filipino immigrants who joined second-generation scions of past labor radicalism will be important in the narrative that follows (M. Thompson 1995, 68–70). Again, the KDP was one cell of such activism.

Overall, the Filipino American population in Seattle became increasingly splintered between those who arrived before and after 1965, those in different occupations and class strata, those from different provinces in the homeland, those closely or loosely tied to the Philippines, and those in different political ideological camps. One structurally formative force was spatial dispersion, as the newer Filipino communities became cut off from the Manilatown neighborhoods of the *manongs* and earlier support networks. Seattle's Manilatown became ridden by corruption and gangs during the 1970s, while the broader Chinatown became increasingly gentrified and developed in the 1980s, shrinking the old neighborhood inside as new Filipino Americans, most now in nuclear families, moved outward to cultivate a broader Filipino community. As the "newer families entered with no connection to the *manongs*, they were less politically sympathetic to movements by the migrant workers living in the Filipino quarters of Chinatown and Manilatown" (Nonato 2016, 21). These tensions also will be manifest in the coming pages.

Additional Developments

We note four other developments of particular significance for the rest of our historical narrative. One is that the former territory of Alaska, with a "colonial economy" whose natural resources were significantly depleted by the time it became a federally managed US territory in 1912, gained increased strategic military significance in the Cold War and was authorized to become the forty-ninth state in 1959. The former territory of Hawaii, where thousands of Filipinos had labored in sugar plantations, became the fiftieth state in the same year. Second, Alaska cannery employers in the late 1960s initiated efforts to recruit white college students and white women as well as Native Americans for summer work. These actions repeated the historical pattern of continually hiring new waves of differently situated workers to replace or neutralize disgruntled employees, dividing workers along lines of ethnicity, race, gender, and class so as to undercut union organizing and solidarity. The number of Filipino Americans employed in the canneries dropped from a high of nearly six thousand to no more than five hundred in 1977 (Chew 2012, 144–45). Third, and related, while successful Alaska state management significantly rebuilt salmon fishery capacity, the Alaska salmon canning industry declined precipitously in the second half of the century under the pressures of local salmon depletion because of many years of overfishing, competition from global salmon farming, new shipping technologies for flash-frozen "fresh" salmon, and changing consumer tastes in the global market (Sisk 2005). A fourth and final related development was that amid a declining workforce and reorganized industry, ILWU Local 37 reaffiliated as Region 37 with the Inland Boatmen's Union (IBU) in 1987, continuing as a small but progressive force representing Alaska seafood processing workers.

4

LELO, ACWA, and the Politics of Civil Rights Mobilization

We had figured out some sophisticated approaches of dealing with the law, so we would not just demonstrate, but we would also file lawsuits and make up causes of action and whatever. That's what [lawyer Michael] Fox was best at. We'd go in and say can we file a lawsuit on the basis of this, and he'd make up some cause of action . . . and we would file it. And pretty soon we're sitting up in the courthouse like we had some legitimate claim to be there. It was really creative, and effective.—TYREE SCOTT[1]

Tyree Scott would say, poor people should be able to treat their lawyers like rich people treat their lawyers: they tell them what to do. All these movement lawyers always try to tell the poor folks what to do. What may be the best legal strategy may not be the best movement strategy. And if you're trying to build a movement, you say "fuck the law, we're trying to build something here." And we did not defer to lawyers at all at any time. . . . That's the genesis of . . . LELO.—MICHAEL SIMMONS (quoted in Griffey 2011, 412)

The original plan [of ACWA] was organizing the cases similar to the civil rights case that opened up the construction industry in Seattle. And our hope was that the strategies there would also work in the canneries.—NEMESIO DOMINGO (2003)

This was not radical—it was just democratic politics.—MICHAEL FOX[2]

The Rebirth of Rights Radicalism

The legacy of left-progressive politics and rights activism among cannery workers affiliated with ILWU Local 37 languished for nearly two decades in post–World War II America until the early 1970s. The resurgence of progressive labor activism was initiated by a multiracial group of young workers with strong ties to Seattle's Filipino American community. Their interest in the canneries reflected not just their firsthand experiences working in Alaska canneries but also their realization of the important place of Alaska salmon canneries in the Seattle Asian American community. For generations, traveling to Alaska for the late summer canning season was a rite of passage for a succession of migrant Asian populations on the West Coast. Most of the new reform leaders were second-generation Asian American immigrants who grew up hearing that their fathers had worked in the canneries, and they eventually began working in canneries themselves as teenagers and college students in the late 1960s and early 1970s.

One key figure in this young group of workers was Silme Domingo, a native of Texas raised in Ballard, a white working-class section of northern Seattle, although in his teen and college years he was drawn to the racially diverse inner-city neighborhoods of Beacon Hill and the International District. His father, Nemesio Domingo Sr., migrated to the metropole from Ilocos Sur Province in 1929. Nemesio Sr. worked in the canneries for half a dozen years until World War II, and, like many other Filipino male migrants, joined the US Navy. He was stationed in the Philippines in the aftermath of the defeated Japanese occupation. Silme's older brother, Nemesio Jr., and sister, Lynn, also worked in Alaska and became active in the broader reform campaign. Other key participants—including Michael Woo, John Foz, David Della, and especially Gene Viernes—similarly followed their fathers in working at various Alaska canneries.

Most in this new generation of young workers who entered the canneries around 1970 were startled by what they found. The turn of the century plantation model of mass production based on an exploited labor force seemed archaic and barbaric to young workers enmeshed in the rapidly changing social world in the lower forty-eight states. The most palpable feature of workplace organization was the continuation of rigidly racial segregation in the workforce. "Basically, white fishermen catch all the fish, Asians and Alaskan Natives do the actual handling and canning of the fish while white-dominated management supervises the entire operation," summarized two young Asian workers who conducted a systematic study of the cannery operations (ACWA Report 1973, 5 [UWSC]). The production-line work handling the fish—including sorting, butchering, sliming, sluicing, egg pulling, and lye washing—remained extremely arduous and tedious, often driving workers for up to eighteen hours a day in peak season. The wet, slippery, and unsanitary working conditions were as dangerous as in earlier days; injuries and illnesses were common. The Iron Chink still drove work routines of mechanized Asian labor and inflicted physical harm, including severed limbs, sometimes after workers dozed off on the production line because of long hours. Moreover, "Asian and minority workers have always received the lowest pay, while white employees have received greater wages. The difference is sometimes several thousand dollars" (ACWA Report 1973, 5 [UWSC]). In sum, conditions were "separate and unequal" (C. Domingo 2001). On top of all this, the employment of Asian males was falling in the canneries because of both overall industry decline and the increasing recruitment of white and female college students for summer work. And this fact of job scarcity significantly deterred Filipino workers, especially in the older generation, from challenging the widespread discriminatory policies and practices. "To the Asian, it has been a question of survival versus the factors of discrimination and hardship in the Alaskan salmon canning industry" (ACWA Report 1973, 9 [UWSC]).

Workers at these lower levels still were denied opportunities for mobility into middle-level production, machinist, and managerial jobs, which were reserved exclusively for whites. One reason is that the cannery managers retained discretion about whom to hire or reject regardless of whom the union dispatched. Hiring decisions were based on subjective, informal, unspecified, and variable criteria. Different channels for recruitment were used for different jobs, and nepotism among whites in hiring for nonproducing supervisory and administrative jobs was routine. Indeed, company records and communications earmarked different jobs by the race or ethnicity of the workers who were hired to perform them. As we shall see, a record of obedient compliance was as important as job experience in the hiring of cannery line workers, and blacklisting those who challenged exploitative practices and claimed their rights to fair treatment was commonplace. Moreover, low-wage workers still lived in corporate-supplied quarters that remained racially segregated, cramped, and poorly insulated against the harsh Alaskan weather. Washing and dining facilities were similarly segregated, often designated by different color-coded buildings marking the location of the inferior and often unsanitary facilities for minority workers. The quality and range of food served to whites was far superior to that served to Asian and Native workers.

When the young, second-generation workers began in the canneries during the late 1960s, they quickly realized that the union long representing the cannery workers had become corrupt and unresponsive. In earlier chapters we documented that ILWU Local 37 had been a powerful political voice for migrant laborers, both at work and in the community, from the New Deal period through the early 1950s. Indeed, we have shown that the union had succeeded for a while in replacing an abusive labor-contracting system with a transparent, accountable dispatching process. However, the anti-red campaigns led by the FBI in the Cold War era of the mid-1950s diverted and then purged the union's more radical, democratically committed leadership. As Nemesio Domingo Jr. put it, "Just like in the rest of the labor movement, McCarthyism and Anti-Communist hysteria, uh, basically drove much of the progressive leadership and members out of positions within the union" (N. Domingo Jr. 2003, 15–17). In the 1960s, the union was taken over by more politically conservative leaders who were closely aligned with the industry's interests and the US government's foreign policy goals. Those new leaders reintroduced the types of corrupt practices that the earlier democratic union activists had fought to eliminate. The leadership used their control over the dispatch process to collect bribes from workers and enriched themselves through affiliations with gang-run gambling operations at the canneries. "For that reason, issues such as discrimination just were not on the front burner of the union because of the leadership at that time" (N. Domingo 2003).

Meanwhile, the basic contract governing employment had not been revisited and revised for decades before the 1970s. The union was habitually unresponsive to complaints from its members about dangerous, violent working conditions and contract violations by employers. "There is very little union democracy and it is also very unaggressive" (ACWA Report 1973, 37 [UWSC]). When workers did voice grievances, the union preferred to side with the employers and to blacklist troublemakers who disrupted things.[3] Unlike when "the union was good" in the 1930s, "the leadership has come to be an extension of the companies and has not provided the working members with any democratic system for the workers to be heard" (ACWA Report 1973, 40 [UWSC]). Meanwhile, the separate Alaska Fishermen's Union (AFU) represented all the workers who transported fish and maintained the canneries. The AFU worked closely with the salmon industry to control the supervisory and higher-paying positions reserved for whites. Observers estimated less than 5 percent of total membership in the AFU was of nonwhite minority origin.

The younger generation of workers who entered the canneries in the 1970s often reported that they learned of the corruption in the dispatch process when their fathers had to pay bribes to the "uncles" in order for them to get a spot on a crew in Alaska. As one interviewee told us,

> In 1967 my dad took me down there, and uh, he had to talk to one of the uncles. I remember he would go into this old cannery office, and he went in and talked to him alone, you know. Now I realize that probably some money changed hands, and next thing you know I was on a list to be dispatched.[4]

Similarly, in 1972 David Della journeyed to Alaska to work in the Wards Cove Packing Company plant after his father payed $100 to the Local 37 dispatcher to secure the job for his underage son (C. Domingo 2001, 43). Sometimes the bribes involved cash, other times "a couple of cartons of cigarettes . . . some discussion, and a handshake" (N. Domingo Jr. 2003).

Second-generation activists were like their fathers in one key regard: they took seriously the aspirational ideals of American culture taught in formal education.

> We were raised in American schools. We were taught about Abraham Lincoln. We were taught about justice. We were taught about all this stuff. . . . We grew up with all the things that everyone else grew up with: American values of justice, and democracy, and equal representation. I guess the difference is, that we believed it.[5]

As we shall see, though, the young activists also reconstructed the meanings of those values much as had the *manongs*. Moreover, this new generation of cannery workers, who had grown up as US citizens in working-class families and many of whom entertained hopes of college education and professional careers, proved less willing than their fathers to tolerate the harsh, arbitrarily enforced working conditions in the racially segregated canneries.

> It was a different environment. I'd been in the city all my life, and you know, I learned first-hand about the disparities between the cannery worker crew that came out of the ILWU, and this other group of [white]

> workers. . . . I'm talking about the beach gang, the nephews and the sons, you know, and friends of all of the cannery management. But it was just like summer camp versus forced labor camp. And it was very clear that the wages and the benefits and everything were very different. And that was just something that stuck in my mind.[6]

The young Asian workers repeatedly observed that the "particular work conditions hadn't changed since my father had gone to the canneries." The difference is that the "old normal" in the canneries looked even more unjust and unacceptable to a younger, civil rights era generation. "We grumbled about . . . the unequal living facilities . . . [and] about the food we were eating too."[7] Some of the young workers who questioned the status quo were identified by the companies as troublemakers and prevented from returning in subsequent seasons.

The differences between the generations are very important to understanding the 1970s activists, although they also can be overstated. For example, both generations of Filipino seasonal cannery workers were split between those working to support education leading to better jobs and those fated to remain in seasonal low-wage work splitting time between agricultural and cannery labor. Nemesio Domingo discussed this in an interview: "Ironically, [many of] the very first Filipino cannery workers, they were called *pensionados*. Those folks actually came to this country, educated, to be college students. But once they graduated, they were not welcomed in this society. So they wound up in the agriculture fields of California . . . and the canneries" (N. Domingo Jr. 2003). In both generations, the more educated cannery workers created community newspapers and brought an intellectual dimension to labor organizing. "Labor organizing was an important intellectual outlet" for Filipinos in both eras. Still only a "minority" in the later generation "were college students, looking at this [summer cannery work] as a kind of stepping stone" to better-paying professional jobs down the road. The continuities in these features of the organized workers helps make sense of the deep communicative connections between those Filipino activists struggling for justice in and beyond work over many decades (N. Domingo Jr. 2003).

It is highly relevant that many of the young workers in both generations were influenced by the radical politics of their era—West Coast socialist labor radicalism in the 1930s–1950s for the older generation, and the countercultural New Left multiracial politics of the 1960s for the later generation. While radical, reform-minded workers of the previous generation had formed a militant labor union as their organizational voice, the new generation of the 1970s was influenced by different organizing models and political strategies. Nearly all of the more than two dozen activists whom we interviewed cited participation in the campus antiwar agitation of the late 1960s as a formative, politicizing experience. "I think a lot of it just came from growing up in the '60s and kind of being anti-establishment, if you will," Terri Mast told us. "For me it was more the anti-war movement. But my father was always a union person, so that wasn't something that was foreign to me."[8]

Many of the budding worker activists were active in student organizations. For example, Silme Domingo was engaged in the Asian Student Coalition at the University of Washington, where he became involved in a variety of civil rights, antidiscrimination, and antiwar political activities before graduating with honors. Inspired by the African American civil rights movement and later black radicalism, the Asian American movement labored to recover the "hidden history" of Asian immigrants and their contributions to the United States, leading to development of Ethnic Studies programs at UW and other West Coast universities.

In 1971, Domingo and others started the short-lived *Kapisanan* newspaper, which soon developed into *Asian Family Affair*. Domingo became editor in 1973. In 1974, he met Filipino American activist Russell Valparaiso, a member of the L.A. Yellow Brotherhood. Silme also began to develop contacts among community organizers in the International District, home to many activist Asian communities in Seattle. There he met "Uncle Bob" Santos, the progressive director of the International Improvement Association. Silme's first large-scale direct action was protests in Seattle against construction of the King Dome, which led to the destruction of many low-income housing units in International District neighborhoods (Chew 2012).

It was about this time that Chris Mensalvas, former president of Local 37 and harassed communist during the 1950s, met and became a mentor to the young Seattle activists. Retired and living at the edge of the International District, he recounted for the young Filipinos the racial persecution and class exploitation experienced by the first generation of migrant workers, their disenchantment with the American Dream, his affiliations with the International Workers of the World (IWW), his leadership with Carlos Bulosan in the Committee for the Protection of Filipino Rights, and the struggles of the evolving cannery workers' union. "I really got politicized by being around Chris. He and his friends. How incredible it was to go hang out with them on a weekend and they'd be drinking wine and telling stories . . . and talking politics, talking about the daily events and things that were going on," Terri Mast later recounted (Taylor 2007, 219). Mensalvas regularly gave lectures in ethnic studies classes at UW, May Day events, and community gatherings. He counseled the young activists as they began their own political organizing gambits (Viernes 1978). Chris was unabashed in celebrating the socialist legacy in which he had participated.

The crisis in the Philippines that began with declaration of martial law by Ferdinand Marcos led the 1970s generation of activists to a renewed interest in politics in the Philippines and the longer history of US colonial rule and imperial power. Some of the young Seattle-based activists quickly allied with the newly formed KDP (Katipunan ng Demokratikong Pilipino, or Union of Democratic Filipinos), a Marxist-aligned group that formed in the Santa Cruz mountains in 1973. Inspired by third world revolutions and Left social movements in the United States, the KDP identified with the Communist Party of the Philippines and the New People's Army (NPA) against president Ferdinand Marcos and US imperial support for his regime. The KDP, like Mensalvas, also played a key role in revitalizing the radical socialist legacy of labor activism by Carlos Bulosan. Among the KDP's founders were US born leftist Filipino Americans, including Bruce Occena and Melinda Paras.[9] The group eventually formed ten chapters around the United States to cultivate opposition to Marcos and force a shift in US imperial policies supporting Marcos as a bulwark against communism. In 1973, Silme Domingo and Angel Doniego were recruited by Dale Borgeson, a Swedish American KDP leader from California. Soon thereafter a KDP chapter was formed in Seattle, and before long it became one of the largest and most diverse in the nation. The KDP also included radical activists from the Philippines who traveled regularly to the United States, and young American activists reciprocated with journeys to the Philippines. Adopting an increasingly internationalist orientation, Domingo and his cohort expanded their activism in the Filipino community. He became involved with the Filipino Community of Seattle and helped found Filipinos for Action and Reform, which focused on immigrant rights issues and education about conditions in the Philippines under Marcos. Domingo also played a role later in organizing Philippine Annual National Day Celebrations as well as hosting the Filipino People's Far West Convention in Seattle.

All of these engagements and experiences contributed to the unique activism that developed to challenge conditions in the canneries and Local 37 during the 1970s. For one thing, the young group of workers was more demographically diverse. While male Filipino Americans were still most prominent, the young activists included women, Chinese Americans, African Americans, and Native Americans from the Alaska region. Equally important, the models of politics and modes of political activism that they knew best were stylistically quite different from the union politics of the *manongs*, including the socialists as well as the later liberal leaders, who still were abundant in the union and a social force in the Filipino community around the Puget Sound area. The official leaders of Local 37 in the 1970s were resistant to challenging the industry, and some older *manong* workers were concerned about jeopardizing their jobs. "Don't rock the boat," the latter repeatedly intoned in cautioning the younger workers. These complex generational relationships at once created tensions, posed challenges, and opened opportunities for the rights-based reform politics that followed over the decade of the 1970s. In classic terms of legal mobilization analysis, they defined both a complex but mostly favorable opportunity structure and the potential for tapping organizational resources necessary to effective legal and political action (see McCann 1994).

Among the most important but subtle relationships between early and later cannery activists were the constructed subjectivities as radical rights advocates. Earlier chapters of this book traced the developing novel rights consciousness in the first generation that alchemically transformed liberal principles of equal citizenship into challenges to intersectional racial and class hierarchies in capitalist orders (Williams 1992). As we shall see, those commitments continued to animate the second-generation activists, but they were reconstructed through the prism of late civil rights African American and Asian American radicalism challenging institutionalized racism, class rule, and global imperialism. The strategic political manifestations of these expansive, overtly socialist rights claims are addressed in the remainder of this chapter, while closer examination of their provocative but problematic translation into official legal claims before US federal courts is the subject of chapter 6.

Race, Class, and Rights Politics at Work

The younger generation of cannery workers in the 1970s was poised to act on the inspiration of the Left democratic *manong* forbears in challenging racial and class injustice at work. But what would they do? We shall show that they developed a very complex, subtle, multidimensional political strategy. The decisions to file complaints at the Equal Employment Opportunity Commission

(EEOC) and then a series of class action lawsuits under Title VII of the 1964 Civil Rights Act were the initial steps of that broader strategy. We begin with the genesis of that creative politics of rights.

Tyree Scott and the Template for Creative Legal Mobilization Politics

The ambitious model of reform politics developed by the young cannery worker reformers was greatly influenced by the dynamic crusades of Tyree Scott in the late 1960s. Scott was an African American from Texas who fought as a marine in Vietnam and moved to Seattle in 1966 to find that he, like his father, was excluded from work as an electrician in the racially segregated building trades.[10] Disenchanted with the limited achievements of the civil rights movement and attracted to the more revolutionary socialist politics and aggressive tactics of the Black Panthers, the young Scott embarked on a creative, explosive campaign that fused conventional legal challenges with disruptive grassroots protests, strikes, and work stoppages.[11] Scott first demonstrated his leadership skills in 1969 when he formed a new organization, the Central Contractors Association (CCA), and led local black contractors in a fight to gain lucrative federal construction contracts.

In 1966, the Washington State Board Against Discrimination found evidence of rampant discrimination in the building trades. Few nonwhite applicants were being admitted to apprenticeship programs, and those admitted were often harassed and prevented from advancing. The Seattle Building Trades were still overwhelmingly dominated by white workers. Scott thus worked through CCA to develop a sustained, creative array of direct actions protesting such discrimination around the Puget Sound. Scott made headlines leading a series of high-profile, direct-action, civil-disobedience campaigns that temporarily shut down construction projects at the University of Washington (where he ran a bulldozer into a pit), Medgar Evers Pool at Garfield High School, and King County Courthouse among many others. The CCA's most dramatic protest enlisted one hundred demonstrators to stop air traffic by walking on to the flight apron at SeaTac Airport. Largely based on this grassroots action by CCA, the Department of Justice filed a lawsuit against five prominent white-dominated trade unions. In June of 1970, Federal District Court Judge William Lindberg ruled that the Seattle building trades violated Title VII of the 1964 Civil Rights Act and ordered an affirmative action plan to be implemented by a multiparty Court Order Advisory Committee (COAC). It

Fig. 14 Tyree Scott (*pointing*) and Larry Gossett (*far left*) outside the Federal Courthouse during a United Construction Workers Association rally, June 15, 1972. *Seattle Post-Intelligencer* Collection, 2000.107.216.06.03. Courtesy MOHAI.

was one of the most sweeping and effective early Title VII decrees ordered by a US court (Gould 1974, 1977: 378; Melo 2018; Griffey 2011: 340).

These actions generated substantial disruption in the Puget Sound area and division within the CCA. Scott ended up leaving the CCA to found the United Construction Workers Association (UCWA) at the invitation of the Seattle branch of the American Friends Service Committee (AFSC). Scott was quite wary of lawyers and skeptical about the power of court orders to transform workplaces, except when they were combined with robust, on the ground organizing. He thus recruited workers and potential workers into the UCWA to monitor enforcement of Judge Lindberg's order. Scott continually challenged the COAC for dragging its feet in implementation of the affirmative action program ordered by the court. Faced with a lack of sufficient progress, Scott led UCWA members back to the streets in 1972, again paralyzing numerous construction sites in Seattle. In July 1972, Judge Lindberg added UCWA as a party with double representation on the COAC, giving Scott and his colleagues more formal power to monitor and pressure for implementation in the apprenticeship programs.

These activities in turn provided Scott considerable notoriety on the national scene of antidiscrimination activists. In particular, Professor William B. Gould, a visiting professor of labor law at Harvard and much later chairman of the National Labor Relations Board (NLRB), invited Scott to a conference on employment discrimination in 1971 where Scott also met William Brown III, the director of the EEOC. A serendipitous summit followed. As Scott said in an interview,

> We got stuck in the airport together for like three hours or something. And on the way to the airport and in the airport we had this long conversation. . . . He [Brown] had heard what I had to say about our work, and he thought it was a really good idea, the way that we were approaching this whole thing. And what had happened was the EEOC had just been mandated to do this kind of thing in lawsuits instigating justice. They didn't know, they didn't have any systematic way of going in to enforce complaints, and so . . . he was saying, how can we work together? "I'd like to know how we can complement each other's work." And we were elated with the idea of being able to get the government to conspire with us, if you will.[12]

What Scott only vaguely gleaned from Brown was the larger strategy aggressively developed by progressives within the EEOC of the Nixon Justice Department. Brown, a liberal African American, and other reformers realized that the EEOC had been granted grossly inadequate resources and authority to take direct administrative action on complaints and attack problems of employment discrimination. Their alternative was to develop an aggressive outreach program to mobilize private litigants to file Title VII lawsuits. As Quinn

Mulroy has documented, early decisions by the EEOC—to make its charge process amenable to private litigant initiatives, to issue broad interpretations of Title VII law, and to provide direct support for development of a civil rights bar that could take on cases—expanded the potential for private litigation efforts challenging employment discrimination (Mulroy 2018; see Farhang 2010; Melo 2018). This strategy institutionalized a hybrid "private-public attack on discrimination" as a viable enforcement strategy. Indeed, based on the chance meeting, Scott ended up contracting with the EEOC to undertake a massive organizing campaign coordinated with workplace discrimination lawsuits around the United States. The logic was to use the lawsuits as a resource to mobilize workers, local lawyers, and other progressive groups in alliance with federal government supporters in the EEOC. Before long, the "Seattle Plan" became a nationally recognized model for race-based affirmative action in and beyond the construction industry. Tyree Scott summarized it this way:

> We went to the South to do this EEOC contract. And the idea of the EEOC contract . . . was to educate workers about Title VII. But what we actually did was we organized . . . [, w]e got the names of all the workers who had filed complaints with the EEOC . . . [, w]e got local lawyers together in every one of these towns. In every one of these towns, there was a couple three young black lawyers fresh out of law school. And the black preacher, and the black undertaker, sometimes they're the same people. . . . And we would go and find who the workers at the plant were who had filed complaints against the EEOC or who had filed discrimination complaints with the human rights department of wherever in the cities. Sometimes they had nothing in place. But we'd find who was who from the workers. . . . So we would connect these lawyers up, with the EEOC folks, so they had support, because they didn't know nothing about stuff. And then we'd put them together with these workers. And so, at the end of the year, we had more than two dozen lawsuits filed in those six or seven cities. . . . We were having a ball.[13]

At the same time that the EEOC provided paid contracts for Scott's skillful organizing efforts, the UCWA was finding success raising money to support its various causes. Along with funding from the AFSC, liberal foundations and public interest groups donated substantial amounts to support the legal campaign.[14]

This explosion of legal mobilization politics combining grassroots organizing, public protest, EEOC complaints, Title VII lawsuits, and fundraising marked Tyree Scott as an extraordinary activist for the civil rights of minority workers. He made EEOC complaints, litigation, and monitoring of court orders important components in his organizing and activism in the late 1960s and early 1970s because he brilliantly discerned the favorable opportunity structure and mobilized to take advantage of it.[15] As he explained in an interview years later, he was developing these strategies in an unusually supportive, if short-lived, legal climate. Those years followed soon after the passage of the 1964 Civil Rights Act, the appointments of many liberal federal judges, a momentarily progressive EEOC that was willing to work creatively with activists, and a still volatile Cold War climate pressuring American elites to honor the official ideology of legal equality. As Scott summarized, the "law was good then, so we were winning."[16] Yet even as he developed a supportive network of government regulators, judges, and attorneys, Scott remained quite wary of law, judges, and lawyers, both private and those claiming to work in the public interest.

Scott thus insisted that formal legal action had to be supplemented by other activities designed to ensure implementation. Filing EEOC complaints alone did little. "The log jam of the EEOC and the local state human rights commission is a joke. So you file a complaint and it's a formality, it never sees the light of day," he told us in 1998. "We had decided that we wouldn't let the Justice Department just do it, come in and do the law and take the initiative from us. Because that's what was happening" in lots of cases.[17] Scott was politically savvy, and he understood that Republicans continued to support some civil rights lawsuits after President Nixon's victory in 1972 because doing so served political goals by weakening unions and splitting the Democratic coalition. "It was John Mitchell's Justice Department, so you can imagine how sympathetic John Mitchell was to Black workers. . . . They saw that as a way to weaken the trade union movement within" (see Frymer 2008).[18] Scott developed strategies that took advantage of opportunities and allies in official law when they appeared, and then built on them as long as they contributed to egalitarian change within workplaces *and*, at least potentially, in unions. But he never relied on law or litigation alone, and he never gave up on direct action as the primary component of his campaigns. Scott, who always talked of law as a site of contested power, often distinguished between "normal" lawyers and more "creative" lawyers who were more politically oriented and willing to bend and use legal standards to advance equality and serve substantive justice. Bill Gould and Bill Brown were, for Scott, "creative," as was Judge Lindberg.

The Northwest LELO Develops

Another especially creative activist was Michael Fox, a Seattle lawyer who teamed up with Scott on several civil rights lawsuits. Fox followed his undergraduate career at Cornell with law school at the University of Virginia, worked for a while as a legal services attorney for the rural poor, and then moved to eastern Washington State to work with the fourth largest migrant farmworker population in the nation. Fox won a major lawsuit in 1971 that protected the rights of farmworkers to organize (*Garza v. Patnode*), was arrested with Chicano activist and United Farm Workers organizer Lupe Gamboa for trespassing in a labor camp, and succeeded notably in overturning their conviction in a 1973 decision that affirmed the right of workers to meet with union representatives (*State v Fox*). While working to build the legal foundation of Wagner Act organizing rights for nonwhite farmworkers in Washington, Fox met Tyree Scott when the latter was arrested for obstructing operations at the airport. Scott and Fox quickly developed a close working relationship born of a common strategic view about how to integrate lawsuits, Alinsky-style grassroots organizing, and disruptive protests to challenge continuing workplace inequalities.[19] As Scott said in an interview,

> We had figured out some sophisticated approaches of dealing with the law, so we would not just demonstrate, but we would also file lawsuits and make up causes of action and whatever. That's what Fox was best at. We'd go in and say can we file a lawsuit on the basis of this, and he'd make up some cause of action . . . and we would file it. And pretty soon we're sitting up in the courthouse like we had some legitimate claim to be there. It was really creative, and effective.[20]

Michael Fox later reflected that "this was not radical—it was just democratic politics."[21] In the early 1970s, Scott's organizational reach began to extend well beyond Seattle as he used funding from the AFSC and contract funding from the EEOC to develop rights campaigns in the American South and Southwest, including Shreveport, Tulsa, and Waco (Griffey 2011; Melo 2018).

As Scott expanded his activism beyond Seattle to the South, he needed to develop a broader and more stable funding base for his activities, especially after the reelection of President Nixon in 1972 threatened a reduction of federal grant money for social justice causes. It was the need for a larger financial base that led Scott and Fox to develop a new model for an activist law firm, resulting in the creation of the Northwest Labor and Employment Law Office, or LELO, in late 1973. Scott's innovation was to establish his own law office that could initiate Title VII lawsuits rather than contracting with outside public interest attorneys at private firms or separate organizations. Creating LELO meant that legal fees collected through the Title VII suits could then be used directly to fund broader organizing campaigns rather than paying independent attorneys or their organizations (Griffey 2011, 55–60). It also gave the political activists considerably more control over the lawyers with whom they worked. The UCWA

> saw Title VII of the 1964 Civil Rights Act as an important tool that, combined with organizing, could win justice for workers of color in the struggle against employment discrimination. But the UCWA had learned some important lessons about working with lawyers. . . . The lawyers didn't want to lose control of "their" cases. So it became clear to the UCWA leadership that we needed our own lawyers. (Scott 1989 [UWSC])

Michael Simmons, a black activist who had been hired by the AFSC to work on campaigns with Scott, later explained in more colorful terms expressed in an epigraph to this chapter. "Tyree Scott would say, poor people should be able to treat their lawyers like rich people treat their lawyers: they tell them what to do. . . . If you're trying to build a movement, you say 'fuck the law, we're trying to build something here.' . . . That's the genesis of what became LELO" (quoted in Griffey 2011, 412). The original proposal that was used for fundraising explicitly distinguished the LELO model from government-funded legal services programs and nongovernmental "public interest" lawyers. The proposal warned, "Lawyers attracted to this sort of work sometimes have a more pronounced disposition to serve 'the law' by changing or expanding it than serving the client" (quoted in Griffey 2011, 413). The goal of the new model was to carefully select creative, politically oriented lawyers and employ them directly so that movement goals would be guiding the lawyers rather than the other way around.

The formation of LELO also tied Scott directly to the cannery worker activists. The original proposal was for LELO to provide services not just to UCWA campaigns but also to parallel campaigns of the United Farm Workers and the new independent organization of young cannery activists patterned after UCWA, named the Alaska Cannery Workers Association (ACWA). The three organizations all participated in start-up fundraising for LELO, which was quite successful, including large grants from the Catholic Church's Campaign for Human Development and the Methodist Commission on Race and Religion (Griffey 2011, 414).

Scott continued over the next three decades to be a major advocate for low-cost housing, multiracial progressive organizing, anti-imperialism, and causes of international human rights for workers. In all of this, Scott was both an ardent advocate of workers and a controversial civil rights challenger to white-controlled unions, embedding him in processes that created deep tensions between civil rights legal mobilization and white-dominated segments of the US labor movement (Frymer 2008). It is notable that Scott undertook his campaign with a clear-eyed recognition that his approach threatened some unions and with an understanding of the political cynicism displayed by the Nixon administration in facilitating such antiunion efforts. Scott's decision to go after some unions was not haphazard but instead reflected his deep belief that it was better to build new, community-based labor organizations than to mute opposition against established unions that were racist and politically reactionary.

The ACWA Is Born around a Legal Strategy

The campaigns led by Scott generated a great deal of attention in the Puget Sound area and provided a spark for organizing a multiracial alliance of progressive workers' groups. Scott thus soon became an ally of the young activists in ACWA who were trying to advance reforms in the canneries. He used his financial resources to provide some early help in their campaigns and, as just noted, integrated their organization into the plans for LELO. The strategies that the cannery workers developed quite clearly mimicked Scott's understanding of the need to mobilize legal resources when the law is "good" but also his understanding of the limits of law and his awareness of the need for ongoing organizing work to supplement any legal advances. As Nemesio Domingo put it, the "original plan" of ACWA "was organizing the cases similar to the civil rights case that opened up the construction industry in Seattle. And our hope was that the strategies there would also work in the canneries" (N. Domingo Jr. 2003).

The ACWA Builds on the UCWA Model

The key person who initially helped link Scott with the cannery workers was Michael Woo, one of a handful of Asian American activists who participated in the movement led by Scott, which mostly included older African Americans who had done military service in the Vietnam War. Woo later recounted the way Scott's campaign became a model for other activist campaigns in Seattle and helped to facilitate a variety of coalitions across racial lines.

> Things began to pick up, and certainly the quick action that brought the US Justice Department in that case just gave so much visibility and so much immediate credibility and success to the UCWA as an organization that was able to go out and actually . . . translate their work into concrete jobs and put their people to work. This is the construction workers' thing. So that all the communities were able to rally around . . . . And so, you know, my community, the Asian community, didn't walk away and continued to participate as supporters around the question of implementing the court's goal, the court's orders. So there was a lot of success there. I think that that was one concrete thing that helped bring the community together.[22]

The UCWA initially helped Woo find employment in the desegregating building trades, but he later remembered that he had to work with the UCWA to fight continued unequal treatment and wage theft.

> Even though it was a city contract, and they were supposedly getting paid timely and prevailing wages and all that, I wasn't getting my check. And so, um, most nonunion workers don't have any recourse, right, they just kind of hang there as long as they can hang. But fortunately, I got referred by this organization, so I went back and talked to them [UCWA], and they said "hey, that absolutely isn't right." And low and behold I had an organization on my behalf talking to the contractor, and before I knew it, I was getting paid again, and then I could put milk on my table. So I really had learned a good lesson in the value of organizational support. . . . And I became a very strong supporter of all of the United Construction Worker activities. . . . I really started opening my eyes. It made me more curious, and just by the association with other people in the community, you know, it really became a whole social thing.[23]

Woo was also connected to the campaign in the canneries because he worked in Alaska during summers while he was in high school in the late 1960s. Woo's father had labored in the canneries in the 1930s, when the workforce was still heavily dependent on Chinese immigrants. His father eventually became a nightclub owner in Seattle's International District and knew many key figures in the local Filipino community, including the leaders of the cannery workers union. In typical fashion, he paid a bribe that allowed Michael to work in the Uganik Bay cannery. It was there that Michael Woo met Silme Domingo, Nemesio Domingo Jr., and other key members of the reform movement that eventually led to the rights-based reform activism that produced three Title VII lawsuits, including one against Wards Cove Packing Company.

The Domingo brothers and Woo had already become known as "trouble makers" for their expressions of discontent about the terrible work conditions at the canneries. Nemesio told a story about how, at the end of one good season, the foreman gathered the workers to thank them. Then, one of the Filipinos "started saying something about the food . . . and everybody started saying something about, you know, what they felt was not fair. . . . I joined in too, and so did my brother [Silme]. And, somehow out of that whole session my brother and I were kind of identified as the ring leaders for dissenters."[24] As Woo recounted for us, "Not only did we try to work hard and try to play hard because we were young men, but we were vocal. We were vocal in the fact that things weren't just quite right. It was unusual that we would be willing to say that. And, the old cannery foreman . . . would actually try to quiet us down, saying 'Don't make waves, you know, this is just how it is.'"[25]

After the summer of 1971, Silme and Nemesio Jr. received letters firing and blacklisting the young workers from future employment. Their father, Nemesio Sr., appealed to the company on their behalf, but to no avail. Even union boss Gene Navarro made a display of anger about it. But "the cannery management just simply walked out and said, uh, they're still not coming back to the canneries. So I was really ticked off about this."[26] They then talked to Ricardo (Dick) Farinas, an investigator at the EEOC since 1969 and the first Filipino American in that position. Farinas was establishing the EEOC field office in Seattle. He had worked in the canneries during the early 1950s while at student at the University of Washington, and he was supportive of efforts to investigate racial discrimination in Alaska. Farinas was key in moving the complaints of the young workers into the legal arena. Before long, he filed complaints against several canneries, including on behalf of a young Filipino American from Seattle, Kevin Ebat, who complained about radical inequalities in housing for whites and Filipinos at New England Fish Company (NEFCO) canneries. From 1972 to 1978, Farinas traveled around Alaska developing his own EEOC report and sending evidence to Washington, DC.

However, consistent with the EEOC model, dismantling the workplace discrimination required private class action lawsuits to supplement action by the "toothless tiger" agency (Melo 2018).

A plan developed to send Silme and Michael Woo on an undercover trip to Alaska in the summer of 1973 to observe conditions, gather information, take pictures, and assess prospects for organizing workers to file lawsuits at four canneries. Farinas advised the two young activists about how to collect information that might be used later in civil rights claims. Traveling to the canneries to record observations and make contacts was difficult and risky, as many canneries were located in remote areas of Alaska accessible only by sea plane. Moreover, the cannery owners, wary of outside inquiry into their working conditions, very strictly limited access to the workplace. In order to gain entry, Domingo and Woo used a counterfeit cover letter identifying themselves as University of Washington Business Administration students on a summer project researching the salmon canning industry. A report filed by Domingo and Woo upon returning explained the trip: "The basis of this trip was to observe firsthand the employment of minority individuals in the Alaska Salmon Canning Industry. Of immediate concern were Asian cannery workers, of which the majority were Filipino. . . . A true picture of the problems and their nature cannot realistically be visualized unless documented in a constructive fashion" (ACWA Report 1973, 2 [UWSC]). The UCWA paid $10,000 from an EEOC contract fund to sponsor the trip and granted paid release time to Woo, a UCWA staff member, for the project. "With the EEOC contract, we were able to free up the money that we had raised for the Seattle project, because it didn't have strings attached, and use that for the cannery stuff in Alaska," Tyree Scott later confirmed.[27]

Domingo and Woo also investigated and reported on the capacities of some of the government-funded agencies that might be allies in the antidiscrimination campaign. The young self-appointed investigators determined that the Alaska State Human Rights Commission (ASHRC) was understaffed and poorly funded. Meetings with officials there "made it apparent that the agency was incapable of motivating action or making an impact upon the industry." The commission understood that there were problems of discrimination, but the agency was "unable and inactive in respect to Asian cannery workers" (ACWA Report 1973, 3 [UWSC]). They also determined that Alaska Legal Services could do little because of "inability to organize and mobilize minority canning workers and a lack of resources" (4). "But if legal action was taken by other parties who are directly affected by the salmon industry, there is a possibility that Alaska Legal Services would intervene" (4). Domingo and Woo did convince the ASHRC to send an investigator involved in EEOC matters, Jim Beltran, to assist them and provide cover for the mission. The trio visited four canneries in the following order: NEFCO-Fidalgo and Wards Cove Packing Company, both in Ketchikan; Excursion Inlet Packing Company, by far the worst-offending cannery; and the Uganik Bay cannery on Kodiak Island. Dick Farinas also joined them to observe conditions at Wards Cove.

Woo later recalled that, in addition to documenting conditions through photographs and observation, he and Domingo spent a good deal of time getting to know workers. They needed to find potential plaintiffs for future lawsuits, and they also knew that they would have to organize workers as on the ground observers in order to facilitate any settlements. Cannery officials around Alaska were uneasy and suspicious about their activity, however, and their cover was blown at Excursion Inlet. On arrival, a "check-up phone call was made concerning our presence and credentials," they wrote later (21). The vice president of Columbia Wards, a lawyer for the association of Pacific Fisheries, and Alaska state representative Willard Bowman were flown in for a meeting with Domingo and Woo. As Woo recounted the episode,

> It was like 10:30 at night . . . and they just confronted us with that information. And the guy from the state (Beltran) was just—he knew what we were up to, but he was busted, and he had nothing to say in our support. And we were actually afraid for our lives. It was just not a good scene. There were a lot of accusations thrown around. . . . What they had said they were going to do was that they were going to call every cannery superintendent and tell them not to let us on the property. So, they had taken our little sleeping bag and little knapsack and thrown it out on the dock . . . out there in the cold. We just sat out there all night till the mail plane came in the next day, and we just got on there and left.[28]

The report that the two activists later filed is striking in two regards. One is the sophistication of the young activist workers' understandings about the legal dimensions of job segregation. The report outlines at length the facts of racially segregated hiring practices, reserving less laborious but better paid positions for whites and the most torturous, low-paying work for nonwhites. It documents in detail the poor, unsanitary work, living, and eating conditions for the latter. The report frames the situation relentlessly in terms of "discrimination." Their understanding went far beyond "intentional" discrimination to structural discrimination and institutional racism, the types of claims that fit the "pattern and practice" logic of structural discrimination as well as disparate impact theory upheld as a cause of action by the US Supreme Court only two years earlier in *Griggs v. Duke Power Co.* (1971). When they later founded an organization to bring these lawsuits, the document used in fundraising appeals reflected this broad understanding: "many of the problems, despite the conflicting arguments, have evolved from one source, which is discrimination. It is discrimination in the economic sense, but also the moral sense" (ACWA Proposal 1973, 1 [UWSC]).

Equally striking is their realization that they had to take matters into their own hands because they could not rely on the EEOC. Forty-three complaints had been filed against the Alaska canning industry, and all were still pending. "Because of the EEOC's weakness, ineffectiveness, and understaffing, EEOC has been able to do very little in this area" (ACWA Report 1973, 30 [UWSC]). The EEOC was unwilling, unable, "afraid," "weak," and "powerless," they complained. Their comments on the EEOC also indicate their understanding that workers would not automatically join with them in a struggle against the canneries. "Like the average Asian worker, the EEOC has assumed that the industry is too powerful to fight" (ACWA Report 1973, 30 [UWSC]). And that represented a "big difference" relative to the cases pressed by Tyree Scott. The African American workers in the UCWA "were able to entice the government to intervene. . . . The federal government sent a task force of assistant attorney generals to Seattle . . . and that case won very quickly." Whether the reason was the remote Alaska context, the Asian and Native identities of workers, or the changing currents of national politics and federal law, the EEOC did not rush in to support them (N. Domingo Jr. 2003).

Domingo and Woo also went on the trip with the understanding that ILWU Local 37, the union representing the workers, would not support any lawsuits against the companies. Thus, the young activists had very limited available options. Before they left Excursion Inlet, they talked at length with Willard Bowman, the Alaska State Representative who was consultant for the Alaska salmon canning industry. He admitted that the industry knew about the discrimination, but it was not willing to invest in correcting it: "as of now, nothing impels the industry to create changes." "The ultimate question of our discussion was: how can the industry be motivated or forced to respond to the problems in Alaska? We contended that the only real motivating alternative would be through court action with possibly a class action Title VII suit. With a smile, consultant Bowman agreed" (ACWA Report 1973, 29 [UWSC]).

Enter Gene Viernes

Several other very important developments occurred in the Alaska canneries during the summer of 1973. First, while visiting one of the canneries, Silme and Michael met Gene Viernes, who would quickly become a key leader in the reform campaign. The serious and scholarly Viernes was from Wapato, in the rural Yakima Valley of Washington. His father, Felix, was a Filipino American from Pangasinan Province who came to the United States in the 1920s and married a woman of Irish descent. One of ten children, Gene started work in the canneries at age fourteen, learning early about how bribery, corruption, and abuse ruled cannery work life. Gene graduated in 1969 from Wapato High, where he was a wiry wrestler. He worked in the canneries to pay for courses at community college and then Central Washington State College, majoring in history and ethnic studies. Viernes was close to EEOC official Dick Farinas, who was a good friend with Gene's father (Chew 2012, 12). Gene, who developed into a key intellectual force within the reform movement, had become a quiet rebel leader for the "Wapato boys" in the canneries. Gene, like Silme and Nemesio Domingo, had a difficult time accepting the working conditions.

Figs. 15 and 16 Silme Domingo (*left*) and Gene Viernes (*right*) in Tukwila, WA, 1981. University of Washington Libraries, Special Collections, UW 39786, UW 39787.

He practiced everyday forms of pragmatic resistance by stealing fruit, sneaking into the Whites Only mess hall, and in 1972 leading a successful hunger strike protesting unsanitary food in the mess hall for Filipino workers (Chew 2012, 20–1).

It was Gene who first told Silme and Michael that the cannery managers had suspected their ruse in the summer of 1973. He also gave them a letter detailing various incidents that compounded systemic discrimination, including refusals of medical treatment for older workers, unsafe machinery, unsanitary work conditions, inadequate safety equipment, insufficient housing, and poor food. He continued to take detailed notes and revealing photos, adding to the evidentiary record for the eventual legal actions. At the end of the 1973 season, Gene Viernes was notified that he was being terminated, a blacklisted target like the Domingo brothers. Silme and David Della, another activist cannery worker from Seattle, traveled to Wapato to meet with Viernes and recruit him for their campaign. Viernes, who was researching the early history of Filipino immigrants in central Washington, agreed to go to Seattle to meet with other activists.

Following the completion of the report about the exploratory excursion to Alaska, the young activists formalized the developing progressive workers' group as the ACWA. On October 12, 1973, they established a constitution and incorporated as a 501(c) tax exempt, nonprofit organization in order to be able to raise foundation money and donations for their campaign. The organization was modeled directly after Tyree Scott's UCWA and was completely independent of ILWU Local 37. Sam Cabansag was named chairman, but he was soon replaced by Nemesio Domingo Jr.; Lester Kuramoto was vice chair and secretary; Clark Kido was treasurer; Woo, Domingo, lawyer Michael Fox, and Tyree Scott were listed as advisors. All three officers were plaintiffs in the developing lawsuits. The stated goals of the ACWA in their constitution and early fundraising appeals were very simple: "to better the terms and conditions of employment for all non-whites" (ACWA Proposal 1973). Their tactics in many respects followed Scott's successful model. "The association is attempting to do this by challenging each of the problems mentioned earlier through the use of class action lawsuits . . . and the organized efforts of workers initiating, directing, and monitoring the lawsuits, as well as developing specific strategies, other than legal actions, against industry employers and unions" (ACWA Report 1973: 40 [UWSC]).

One of the organization's primary challenges was to continue to raise money on behalf of the workers' legal and political campaigns. "I think I spent the next 2 years living out of a suitcase, living out of airports, raising money for these cases," reported Nemesio Domingo. "The strategy was to win one case, then use the court award to sue the second case and sue the third case in order rather than try to pursue them simultaneously" (2003). The strategy did not initially work out as well or as quickly as in the construction trades cases. Eventually, though, the ACWA did generate financial support from Scott's UCWA, the United Methodist Church, the Presbyterian Church, and the Catholic Church.

While the ACWA early on planned Title VII suits against the canneries, both the founding documents and later recollections of key participants make it clear that the litigation activity was, from the very beginning, closely connected to broader community organizing efforts and goals. "The main goal of the ACWA is to eliminate the injustices that Minority workers must suffer, through a strong workers advocate group and the use of Title VII . . . of the 1964 Civil Rights Act" (ACWA 1974, 2 [UWSC]). The ACWA Incorporation Papers (1973 [UWSC]) show that the activists, like Tyree Scott, understood that law was a contested resource, and mobilizing law through litigation had limited transformative power unless combined with broader, sustained grassroots organizing. The proposal referred to the campaigns of the UCWA and the related scholarship by William Gould on how the UCWA lawsuits became a vehicle for political organizing that eventually elicited support from federal regulatory agencies and Judge Lindberg. The report noted both the promise and limitations of litigation. "Recent court victories have demonstrated a potential for holding employers accountable regarding employment of minorities and women. However, many of these victories become headlines only to lie dormant while the affected class fails to take advantage of them." The proposal thus outlined a "comprehensive" approach that combined pursuit of legal victories with diverse efforts to mobilize the community for broader political action through "the formation of a worker association to enforce court decisions and generate community support" (ACWA Proposal 1974 [UWSC]). Thus, the lawsuits were conceived not as an end in themselves but rather as a vehicle for broader organizing work.[29]

The appeal for support to the workers and community through the lawsuits was complicated, however. On the one hand, the civil rights lawsuits drew explicit connections to the progressive past of Filipinos on the West Coast of the metropole. Nemesio Domingo acknowledged in a later interview (2004) that the Title VII cases recalled earlier widely celebrated legal actions for basic rights of Filipinos—Pio De Cano's lawsuits challenging property ownership restrictions, the challenges by Ponce Torres, Ernie Mangaoang, and others to deportation and travel restrictions in the McCarthy era, and so forth. "So there are actually some cases that, that really resembled civil rights." On the other hand, "the suits themselves were very controversial in the community, because this is the first idea of making a legal struggle [with]in the community . . . The cannery cases were heralded by young Filipinos as civil rights issues, but I don't think that kind of paradigm really caught on in the larger Filipino community at the time." One key reason is the familiar "stereotype" that "Filipinos didn't cause trouble . . . that we were good-hearted workers because we didn't cause trouble."[30] This historical antipathy to "trouble making" was compounded further by the charge that the ACWA was trying to divide the union or create a second union, recalling the episodes of dual unionism that split the earlier generation and the charge by the canneries that segregation was the fault of the union dispatch system itself (N. Domingo 2003). In sum, the ACWA strategy to build support for the civil rights lawsuits was not an easy pitch to many in the older generation.

That said, there were few other options for the reformers. David Della, a member of the core group of activists who formed the ACWA, later recalled that the new organization was necessary to fill a void created by the ineffectiveness of existing community organizations. He noted that "the union was probably ideally in the best position to deal with that stuff," but union leaders were wholly unwilling to take part in efforts to challenge the companies. Moreover, "there was no community organization in the position to organize in the community around it." As a result, the ACWA was designed to focus on "both sides of the spectrum," that is, both legal and community organizing work. One indicator of the importance of these twin goals is that the ACWA also structured the lawsuits in a way that would facilitate community organizing. For example, the class of plaintiffs was consciously developed to span generations.

> It would span not only those who were working in the cannery but take into consideration the previous generations of people who had experienced discrimination in the canneries. So, the idea was to not only have a legal component, which was the centerpiece of it, but have a community organizing piece to span the generations and to get the kind of community support we needed to move the lawsuits forward. . . . It was important to . . . get people feeling like this was a movement that affected all of us, affected all of our families. And it really helped in terms of serving not only the plaintiffs

> who were part of the class action lawsuit. It also was important in bringing the kind of political support in the community we needed.[31]

In 1974, the ACWA leased an office space at in the Seattle International District that quickly became a lively crossroads and busy meeting center for a variety of progressive groups working on labor and racial discrimination issues (Chew 2012, 22). The ACWA also began to develop a staff, including Julia Laranang, whose father was a Filipino cannery worker, and Terri Mast, a young white woman who had worked as a cook in an Alaskan cannery and later became Silme Domingo's spouse. Both had also been Volunteers in Service to America (VISTA) members (Chew 2012, 22–23). As we noted earlier, the ACWA (1973–1974) all the while collaborated with Tyree Scott in the UCWA and the United Farm Workers (UFW) to develop LELO, the progressive workers' organization that directed the key legal actions.

The Lawsuits Are Filed

The activists thus found themselves in a situation that strongly favored litigation. On the one hand, few credible alternative strategies existed. The EEOC had proved incapable of effective civil rights enforcement. Local 37 leaders were viewed as corrupt and unresponsive and were collaborating with employers to keep the activists away from the workplace, making it impossible for them to engage directly in additional organizing or outreach work in Alaska. Moreover, many cannery workers were intimidated by corporate control of dwindling jobs and were thus not inclined to join a reform campaign without assurance that it would be effective. On the other hand, US federal courts recently had been ruling in favor of minority workers in a variety of challenges to segregated employment policies and practices, and judges had established procedural and evidentiary standards that made it much easier to pursue civil rights remedies in employment than before. We postpone until chapter 6 our detailed analysis of the activists' constructed legal narrative that bridged their progressive, egalitarian nomos to new opportunities created by the Supreme Court's reading of Title VII in *Griggs v. Duke Power Co.* (1971). The key point in this chapter addressing the political activities of that campaign is that the reformers found support from both the EEOC and the UCWA that helped them undertake fact-finding in support of their claims, and they also had secured funding for their legal campaign and an organized legal support structure through LELO.

In late 1973, Silme Domingo, Nemesio Domingo Jr., and several dozen Asian American and Native American workers filed a class action lawsuit against NEFCO, charging discrimination in violation of Title VII of the 1964 Civil Rights Act. A few months later, with funding from ACWA, Michael Woo and ACWA director Sam Cabansag went to central California to meet with both young and old workers in an effort to identify plaintiffs. They learned that sixty-five members of Local 37 had staged a wildcat strike at the Wards Cove cannery and filed a petition for redress of grievances with the management. Woo and Cabansag found much interest among workers in taking additional legal action, but they also heard once again reservations from wary *manongs* who feared they might lose work in the canneries. They also met with Philip Vera Cruz, the legendary Filipino activist who had helped Cesar Chavez organize the 1965 grape strike in Delano, the momentous event that led to the formation of the UFW (Chew 2012, 22). In the spring of 1974, two more lawsuits were filed, one against NEFCO-Fidalgo in Ketchikan and another against Wards Cove Packing, Columbia Wards Fisheries, and Bumble Bee Seafoods. All three lawsuits against the canneries challenged segregated hiring and promotion practices, segregated housing facilities, unsafe work and living conditions, and inequitable wages for jobs performed by minorities and women. "They framed their grievances around equity, fairness, and civil rights" (quoted in L. Domingo 2011, 1).

The lead attorney for the federal lawsuits was Abraham (Rami) Arditi. Rami Arditi grew up in New York, earned his law degree at Yale, and moved to Seattle in 1972, where he started his career at Seattle Legal Services. He was hired by Tyree Scott's collaborator, attorney Michael Fox, to join and eventually lead the LELO legal team in court. Arditi clearly supported the reformers' causes, but he was, by his own terms, a plaintiffs' attorney and did not consider himself as a political activist in the ways that Fox did. "All I can say is we as lawyers do our part and non-lawyers are doing their part."[32] Even so, in multiple forums he later heaped praise on colleagues in LELO and the ACWA as well as the worker plaintiffs. Moreover, he was fiercely committed to the causes of challenging institutional racism in corporate organizations. "We were a bit naive about what we were up against and what could be accomplished and how easily. . . . I don't think there was anything we did that was easy in any way, shape or form."[33] Arditi developed and argued the early lawsuits with Fox, but Rami was largely alone and notably underresourced as the lawsuits proceeded through multiple levels of the judiciary.

The legal processes were slow and played out over many years, with one case winding through appeals courts for nearly two decades. Two of the legal actions under Title VII were very successful. *Domingo v. New English Fish Co.* prevailed at trial, and an appellate ruling by the Ninth Circuit Court affirmed the finding of employer liability and expanded greatly the award for damages to nearly $6 million. *Carpenter v. NEFCO-Fidalgo* also won at trial, and companies agreed to settlements that included substantial damages and enforceable commitments to undertake reforms at the canneries. Much of the damages award was directed to workers from the older generation who had toiled in the canneries for a long time without chance of advancement. "We didn't take on the employers for ourselves. We did it for our fathers and uncles that had toiled in the canneries for decades. All we wanted was justice for them," Nemesio Domingo stated (2000, 45 [UWSC]). But the settlements also provided significant financial help to the young workers. Michael Woo later summarized the impact of the lawsuits:

> People who were in the affected class, including myself, were able to get a financial monetary settlement out of it. Which took me out of renting to being able to put a down payment on a house. . . . That's my legacy, from all that is this place, a roof over my head.[34]

Woo also noted that participation in the lawsuits had been a politicizing event for him:

> You know, that was really the first thing that I had done that even resembled anything political. But, you know, it got me starting to read books, we started attending rallies, and Seattle in the '70s, as you know [. . .] I just had an article in here from the '95 *Times* that was talking about the whole movement at that time that was going on.[35]

The third lawsuit, *Atonio v. Wards Cove Packing Co.*, will be the subject of chapter 6.

Rights Near and Far: Defeating Marcos, Democratizing the Union

Inspired by the radical post–civil rights movement, aided in limited terms and then abandoned by the EEOC, guided directly by Tyree Scott, and alienated by the unresponsive, arguably corrupt union leadership, the young activists' legal campaign initially sidestepped mobilizing directly within or through

ILWU Local 37. However, the litigation ended up providing the young activists leverage for engaging the union rather than motivation to bypass it. As David Della told one interviewer, “there was no way in which we were going to sustain our efforts in the lawsuits without having the union aboard” (quoted in Chew 2012, 28). Indeed, the impact and effectiveness of the lawsuits cannot be understood without also considering two further substantive agendas that the same activists were pursuing while the civil rights suits were slowly advancing through the legal process: an attempt to build multiracial community and international support for the struggle against Ferdinand Marcos in the Philippines and a struggle to reform the union from within. Those agendas were in some respects independent of the lawsuits; they were pursued through different organizations and involved building different sorts of coalitions and alliances. However, as we show, the other two campaigns were also in many important ways intertwined with and bolstered by the lawsuits.

Challenging Marcos and Martial Law: The KDP Connection

We noted previously that several of the key ACWA activists began to work closely with the radical, openly Marxist political organization KDP soon after President Marcos declared martial law in 1972. The focus on the Philippines sparked by affiliation with the KDP was significant because it broadened the ACWA activists' reform vision by exposing them to new types of radical ideas and new examples of historic struggles against colonial oppression and imperial domination. National KDP leaders were quite intellectually oriented, and KDP activists spent considerable energy on analysis of Left political thought, often influenced by the long tradition of radical ideas and protest politics in the Philippines. The KDP made the highest priority for “third world people” very clear. “Imperialism in, particular U.S. imperialism, is the main enemy of the people of the whole world. As such it creates the conditions to unite the vast majority of mankind in one struggle against a common enemy” (M. S. O. Castenada 2009, 67–68). From the start, KDP allies within the ACWA thus joined their struggles for workplace justice to the global struggle against Marcos and other US-supported autocrats. In this way, the ACWA-KDP alliance replicated what Bruce Occena called the “dual line program” of the earlier generation *manongs*—fighting against racism and for socialism within the United States and against antidemocratic imperialism in the Philippines (Cruz, Domingo, and Occena 2017: 86; see also Toribio 1998, 5).[36]

The growing collaboration between ACWA and KDP activists also converged on a key principle of Tyree Scott's political agenda. One of Scott's trademark mantras was "No Separate Peace," which became the title of a radical newspaper published by UCWA and edited by Silme Domingo, Douglas Chin, Larry Gossett, Elaine Ko, and others around May Day, 1975. The purpose of the paper was to serve and clarify the global terms of struggle by the growing multiracial, multisexual revolutionary movement in Seattle. "The task of the paper, then, is to encourage all those who want to build principled unity among all the diverse communities in our area, to point out that, ultimately, *there is one struggle and one enemy*, for there shall be NO SEPARATE PEACE" (Chin et al. 1975, 2).[37] The first edition of the paper illustrated the need for international solidarity in concrete, immediate terms. It featured the transcript of a speech by Scott to "Third World students" at the University of Washington after two Chicano faculty leaders were fired for defiant protests regarding university policy. Scott, who several years before returned home radicalized by military service in Vietnam, used the history of Black Buffalo Soldiers as a metaphor to underline the dilemma of how racial groups are manipulated into divisions against one another by "U.S. imperialism." "If we can't transcend the fact that we're Black and Brown or Red or Yellow, and start looking at who our common enemy is," Scott said, then struggles for overcoming the injustices endemic to racial capitalism are bound to fail (Scott 1975, 4–5). In short, multiracial unity in local struggles for justice required a big-picture focus on global struggles against capitalist empire building. Scott did not mention, and probably knew nothing about, Black Buffalo Solider David Fagen's defection from US forces to join the Philippine anticolonial resistance seventy-five years early (see prologue to pt. 1, pp. 54). But Scott's message about black/Asian/white/Native alliance both paralleled that legacy (San Juan Jr. 2009) and amplified the KDP's call for global solidarity against US imperialism.

The affiliation with the KDP further reinforced for ACWA activists Scott's ambivalence about official US law and wariness regarding reliance on lawyers and litigation as resources for justice. For example, the KDP organized workshops that used Marxist-Leninist and New Left readings to teach activists from local chapters to avoid the lure of law and lawyers' ideological constructs when using legal resources as components of their campaigns. Moreover, they, and especially Bruce Occena, strongly urged the ACWA leaders to reintegrate into Local 37 and to fight for change from within the union after the lawsuits were filed.[38] The KDP also exposed the activists to an alternative model of a national organization with branch offices in multiple communities. The KDP leaders, knowing that their campaign would upset both Marcos and his patrons in the US intelligence community, carefully structured the organization to make it difficult to infiltrate and monitor (M. S.-O. Castaneda 2009).

Anti-Marcos activism also led the activists to engage more broadly with the Seattle Filipino community and its institutions. As part of the struggle against Marcos, ACWA activists and allies worked to transform Seattle's Filipino Community Center into a more political organization and made an unsuccessful effort to win elective office at the center (L. Domingo 2010, chap. 3). They also appealed to many opponents of Marcos among the younger generation of American-raised Filipinos who had experienced the 1960s counterculture and more recent immigrants who had experienced brutal life in the Philippines under Marcos (Chew 2012, 31–32). The anti-Marcos activism and community outreach efforts also seem to have broadened the radical rights consciousness of the activists.

Among the novel outreach efforts to the local community was the public staging, in 1977 at the Langston Hughes Cultural Center, of a mock trial charging codefendants Marcos and the US government on international human rights violations for mass arrest and incarceration without due process, torture and inhumane treatment of prisoners, trampling of civil liberties, corruption, misuse of funds, and economic exploitation. Marcos's own published words were recited to expose his regime's empty rationalizations and masking of brutal truths. John Caughlan, the socialist attorney long affiliated with the ILWU as well as part of a US team headed by former US Attorney General Ramsey Clark to investigate alleged Philippine state injustice, spoke to "confirm the credibility of the prosecution," describing in detail the physical and psychological scars of tortured victims. In the end, one news account reported, "the overwhelming verdict of the audience was 'Guilty!'" (Laranang 1977). The event combined the activists' interest in dramatic performance with aspirational ideas about law, legal process, and substantive rights that drew on but challenged mainstream US legal traditions. In particular, the open embrace of human rights discourse to challenge Marcos's martial law mask for overt repression expressed the worker activists' radical substantive agenda. As we shall see in the next chapter, the mock trial eerily harbingered an actual civil trial of Marcos for murderous human rights violations that the defiant activists waged in federal court a decade later.

At the same time, the KDP activists' opposition to Marcos was controversial within the broader Filipino community. Many of the older generation of Filipinos, including prominent community leaders in Seattle, supported Marcos because of mutual connections to Ilocos Norte Province in the Philippines. Meanwhile, the young activists in the KDP were seen by some Filipinos as radical extremists and trouble makers, and not without cause. KDP members self-identified as Marxists, and they were steeped in New Left and anticolonial writings. Another crosscutting alignment was that key people on both sides of the Marcos divide were members of a fraternal lodge known as the Caballeros de Dimas-Alang. The political commitments of the young activists put them at odds with their fathers; this included pitting Nemesio Jr. and Silme against Nemesio Domingo Sr., who was at first discomfited by the strident activism of his children but who nevertheless ended up offering crucial support at key moments.

The Internal Drive for a Democratic Union Movement

The ACWA activists' campaign to transform the union representing the cannery workers progressed from the mid-1970s through the early 1980s while the civil rights lawsuits were slowly working their way through the courts and covert KDP activism intensified. And it is at this point that the ACWA's creative departure from the UCWA model of reform pioneered by Tyree Scott became most palpable. In short, while Tyree Scott regularly filed lawsuits targeting unions that excluded workers of color, the cannery workers consciously chose *not* to take legal action directly against ILWU Local 37 despite the union's passivity toward, and even complicity in, the rampant racial discrimination at the canneries. The reason is simple and fundamental: challenging the union would have interfered with the broader political goals of the young cannery activists that went beyond the antidiscrimination suits. Earlier pages have documented that the union was a long-revered cultural center of the Filipino community in the Puget Sound area, and direct challenges to the union would have alienated many *manongs* still working in the canneries, important cultural leaders, and others whose support, or at least tolerance, was necessary to effect broader political change.[39]

The union's esteemed stature in the community required the activists to advance their broader goals by working increasingly from *within* to transform the union into a more effective resource for workers and the community. However, the aspiring reformers faced a number of formidable obstacles raised by hostile employers, scornful union bosses, and wary fellow workers. This in turn required a variety of creative political maneuvers, including masterful manipulation of internal union procedures and rules as well as external judicial support to gain leverage over the union's operations. The biggest initial challenge was for the aspiring reformers to regain access to the cannery workplaces and union processes as venues for organizing. As already noted, the Domingo brothers, Gene Viernes, and many of the other activists had all been blacklisted by the companies before the lawsuits were filed, and many had also been expelled from the union. This further complicated reform efforts, as many other workers were given good reason to believe that they, too, would be blacklisted if they collaborated with the reformers. Domingo and Woo had been able do organizing work undercover in 1973, but the actual filing of the lawsuits gave the reformers notoriety that made future undercover work impossible. Moreover, the employers were undertaking a variety of strategies to divide and conquer the reform movement. Perhaps most important was increasing hiring of young white college students, many of them family friends of the middle- and upper-level management, to take the seasonal summer jobs. This provided the equivalent of a scab labor force that undermined both the union dispatch system and the Filipino-led reform movement that filed lawsuits and challenged union leaders. For the activists, all these factors increased the urgency of taking over the union and increasing workplace power in the hiring hall.

At the same time, groundwork for the lawsuits importantly supported the internal union reform efforts. During their undercover fact-finding trip at the very beginning of the process, Domingo and Woo were already working as much on outreach and connecting with workers as they were on taking photographs to build an evidentiary record for trial. In their report, Domingo and Woo reported on their engagements with workers at the canneries and efforts to estimate their likelihood of taking part in broader struggles: "Many individuals voiced interest in possible action against the company to improve their conditions. While there were those who were concerned about jeopardizing their future employment, there were those who didn't care if they never went back to that 'hell hole.'" (ACWA Report 1973, 16 [UWSC]). They also noted that "before departing from Wards Cove, we were assured that the potential for organizing at that specific cannery was quite positive. It was of great significance that we met many Asian brothers . . . who were willing to commit themselves for change in the Alaskan Salmon Canning Industry" (20).

The very idea of democratizing the union thus developed concurrently with the lawsuits. In fact, members of the ACWA reform movement ran for elective union office beginning as early as 1974, the year of the civil rights case filings. Of course, many steps in these complicated and overlapping campaigns were not planned in advance. The strategy, focus, and forms of action evolved over time, as the reformers responded to changing conditions and unforeseen events and as they tried to take advantage of unanticipated openings and new ideas.

One potential opening was created in 1975 when union president Gene Navarro died and was replaced by Tony Baruso. However, Baruso also refused to dispatch the Domingo brothers for the 1976 season. In response, their father, Nemesio Sr., returned to work in the canneries for the first time since 1942 in an effort to convince Baruso to allow Nemesio Jr. and Silme to work under the watchful eye of their father (L. Domingo 2010, 84). Nemesio Sr. was a respected community leader and made a personal appeal to Baruso, who reportedly replied that the two would return "over my dead body" (quoted in Stamets 1982, 46). Despite the continued opposition of Baruso and the companies, the reformers craftily maneuvered their reentry into the union and return to the workplace for the 1977 season by using the Title VII lawsuits. Specifically, the attorneys working with the ACWA won a court order for the reinstatement of the ACWA members, claiming that the exclusion by employers and union bosses alike was itself a form of retaliation for challenging discriminatory conditions at the union (L. Domingo 2010, 84).[40] Thus, once more, the litigation campaign intersected crucially with and leveraged the reform campaign within the union.[41]

The campaign within the union was also intertwined with the anti-Marcos campaign. Bruce Occena, the KDP leader based in San Francisco, visited the Seattle KDP chapter as an outside reviewer of chapter outreach strategies. He urged the Domingos to find a way to cultivate allies within the union in order to have substantial impact on the local community (L. Domingo 2010, 83).[42] The efforts of the ACWA to organize workers so as to ensure compliance with court orders and reform the union were linked to their efforts to rally the Seattle Filipino community to oppose Marcos. Terri Mast later recalled,

> A number of us belonged to the KDP and made that perfectly clear in our union work. We'd sell the KDP newspaper at union meetings or outside, or during dispatch. . . . That was part of the work we did was to politicize

> Filipino workers about what was really going on in the Philippines and give them access to our newspaper and our politics on what was going on there. So that, we were always very up front with that.[43]

Unsurprisingly, the anti-Marcos stance of the activists led to further clashes within the union, particularly with Baruso, as well as with the broader community. Baruso was from the same Ilocos Norte Province as Marcos and reportedly had visited the Marcos palace in the Philippines on multiple occasions.

> We'd have fights with Baruso on it, on the floor. It was real clear in the union, that we did not agree on that issue. . . . Oh, he'd yell at us at meetings, and he'd just yell and go off, and red-bait us . . . tell us to get that goddamn paper out of there. . . . He and Silme would get into it big. But, the other thing, though, within the membership, you know, people were used to having debate and struggle over social issues, or political issues. So it wasn't something new. . . . But then it was a little closer home, because it was the Philippines, so all of them had something to say about it or knew something.[44]

One key component of that strategy to build cross-generational support for reform was to draw attention to the long history of struggle by Filipino Americans in the United States, emphasizing the continuity between the current reform campaign and earlier efforts to protect workers' rights and reform the union. The plan to engage with the cannery workers' traditions was earnest, and it deepened the activists' understanding of the place of law and aspirations for rights in political struggles. Gene Viernes worked particularly hard at recovering the region's history. For example, he was the first to introduce many others to the writings of Carlos Bulosan (Chew 2014). Moreover, in 1977, he published a fifteen-thousand-word, seven-part article series on the history of Local 37 and the cannery industry in the *International Examiner* (republished in Chew 2012). The *Examiner* was a leading newspaper for the Asian American community that had been taken over by Ron Chew, a close personal friend of Viernes and an ally of the other ACWA activists. Viernes's account was careful and scholarly, but it was also constructed with immediate political goals in mind. As labor historian Steve Marquardt has pointed out, most of this history was dutiful reporting of events, names, organizational developments, and dates. The exception was the lively account of events in 1946–1947 when angry workers formed a Rank and File Committee to challenge corrupt and complacent leadership. What Viernes left out, or at least downplayed, Marquardt rightly observes, was the role of the International Union's decisive intervention on behalf of the radicals. Nevertheless, the point of Viernes's historical narrative was clear: to provide a legitimating historical legacy for intraunion conflict and a "militant tradition of the labor movement" that served the young reformers' ambitious but divisive campaign. The essays were as much "an emotional reclamation of a personal past" as a strategic gambit to build on historical bonds to and among an ethnic community (Marquardt 1992, 3).

The Rank and File Committee Is Born

The reformers made a variety of symbolic moves to highlight these historical connections (L. Domingo 2010). Most obviously, in 1975 they adopted the name Rank and File Committee (RFC) for the reform caucus in the ACWA, recalling the union reform effort of the same name led by lionized union leader and later political mentor Chris Mensalvas in the 1940s. They also called their newsletter the *Alaskero News*, adopting the name given to the earliest migrant workers in the Alaska canneries. When the reformers announced the formation of the RFC, moreover, they listed "research and documentation" of "the history of the union" as the first of four "proposed solutions" to addressing the problems in Local 37. "[We] were able to build on things that had been created before," Mast recalled. "And a lot of that really was the CP [Communist Party] and I think a lot of people don't give credit to the early years and the work they did" (quoted in Taylor 2007, 219). They emphasized the need for Filipinos to study the past for the "roots" of their ethnic identity, "to explain who we are and how we became this way." And these acts of historical recovery were essential to developing a sense of agency as exploited subjects seeking to shape their destiny rather than just accepting a status as "the nigger in Alaska," as Michael Woo put it, or "being treated like a coolie," as Gene Viernes said of his father's experience. In Nemesio Domingo's words, "our determination to correct some wrongs became a struggle to correct the past" (N. Domingo Jr. 2003). Through his work in reconstructing the cannery worker history, Viernes increasingly joined Silme Domingo as coleader of the reform activists.

This recovery of history offered the young reformers many resources: a critical standpoint for challenging present problems, insights about possible courses of practical reform action grounded in experience, and especially legitimation of present actions as continuous with group traditions (Nietzsche [1874] 2010). The invocation of the past by the younger reformers was especially necessary to win trust from the older, wary *manongs* as well as to inspire younger workers in the canneries. Conversely, resurrected accounts of radical militants in the heroic first generation enabled the young activists to challenge conservative community leaders who supported the complacent union officers and preached deference, conformism, and political quietism as the recipe for Filipino integration into America. "Why did some of us become part of the organizing?" speculated Nemesio Domingo. "I think some of it was, uh, we felt a real connection to the history of many of our *manongs*. I think we were really moved by some of the stories we heard in terms of their struggles and what they tried to do. . . . We were really inspired" (N. Domingo Jr. 2003). In short, recovering radical unionism as the legacy of the first generation made the challenges to present leaders appear as "nothing radical, just a continuation" of tradition.[45]

By 1977, the young ACWA activists were back in Alaska at the canneries again, now having crafted a powerful rhetorical story supporting reform militancy and laid the groundwork for effective organization. They reconstituted the RFC, which originally formed as a caucus of the ACWA, then became a separate incorporated 501(c)(3) organization in order to facilitate separate fundraising for the union reform mission. The RFC members developed a strategy that focused on creative coalition building and serving the needs of workers. Early positive developments in some of the antidiscrimination suits helped to counter the existing leadership's efforts to discredit the reformers, but the very slow legal process meant that additional steps had to be taken to win over workers. The RFC tried to build support among the workers by doing the kind of service work that a normal union would already be doing for its represented workers. As David Della later recalled,

> Part of our strategy of influence is to reseize the union and to change the way that it operates. So there's a focus on the dispatch system, there's a focus on organizing the unorganized that had been lost. And then there was a focus on grievance, handling grievances and complaints. Shop steward training, you know, and getting people to actually advocate. And to move complaints from the floor into some sort of resolution with the industry through the union and all that kind of stuff.[46]

Equally important, the RFC activists formed a committee to draft a new union constitution and new bylaws that would increase responsiveness of the leaders and strengthen the grievance process binding leaders to reform for the workers. Explaining these efforts in a 1979 article in the *Alaskero News*, the reformers recalled, "they seem like such small changes—but they are in fact two giant first steps. They are the expression of renewed interest in the Union—a renewed interest in democracy" (quoted in L. Domingo 2010, 91).

The attention to the union's rules and procedures allowed the reformers to amplify demands for legal accountability of the union's leaders and to articulate new rights entitlements. The reformers, unlike the entrenched leadership, learned the rules and took them seriously as both ends and means of reform. They also called attention to the terms of their contract with the employers, which created legal rights and employee entitlements that were routinely ignored. Their campaign to train delegates and shop stewards was an effort to compel the union to take seriously the rightful grievances of workers and to correct contract violations by managers. The *Alaskero News* also routinely attacked the bribery-based dispatch system and advocated for reforms that would honor rights related to worker seniority. These strategies of advocating for ways to facilitate worker assertions of legal and contractual rights had deep roots for the activists. Long before his involvement with the ACWA, Gene Viernes' had instituted a shop steward training program in 1970 "to help workers understand their rights and press their grievances" (Stamets 1982, 47), which became the model for such new campaigns. In the pages of the *Alaskero News*, the reformers routinely used the language of rights in connection with a variety of reform topics.

Almost immediately on reentry into the union, the RFC members also focused their eyes on the 1978 leadership elections. Although the existing leadership of the union was corrupt, they were still required by union bylaws to hold biennial elections. This feature reflected Local 37's affiliation with the ILWU, which had strong commitments to allowing democratic rank-and-file control over union locals. However, the entrenched system of cronyism meant that established leaders in Local 37 rarely had been subject to serious challenges. The RFC members, inspired by the successful reform efforts in the late 1940s, tried to mount a credible challenge by constructing a campaign platform and endorsing a slate of recommended candidates for leadership positions. A pamphlet outlining their election slate explained that the RFC's goals were to make the union into a "fighting organization of the rank and file membership," to make the leadership "accountable" to members, and to make the union "a fair, honest and above board organization." Their ten-point plan for implementing reform included a variety of references to protecting rights granted through statutes, their contract, and the union's bylaws. These included a commitment to a forty-hour week, a seniority based dispatch, "stronger contract enforcement," and "stronger safety regulations." In line with their long-standing awareness of the need for practical, on the ground activism, the platform noted, "we recognize that it is not enough simply to state the issues; we must work to implement the program" (RFC Election Slate Pamphlet 1978).

The 1978 election pamphlet also gives some hints about the challenges facing the campaign. It noted the RFC's desire to "make the election an honest and fair one" and to have workers decide based on "the issues and not through favoritism with people voting for their friends, *Kababayan* or *Compadres*" (RFC Election Slate Pamphlet 1978 [UWSC]). The activists learned from their defeat in the 1974 election that the fact that the union was visibly corrupt and unresponsive to members would not automatically produce worker support for reform in union elections. The existing leadership's control over the dispatch process built loyalties among some members, and many union members cast votes based not on whether leaders ran a clean union but instead on factors such as whether the leaders had roots in their home provinces, could speak a similar dialect, or were linked by membership in fraternal organizations.[47] These traditional loyalties created dilemmas for the reform strategy, both organizationally and ideologically competing with the reformers' own crafted story of union history that linked fairness, procedural legalism, and democracy. For example, when Gene Viernes was a candidate for dispatcher in 1980, he wrote an article for the *Alaskero News* in which he reported that he had been approached by many workers who suggested that their own personal connections to Viernes would mean a victory for the latter who would then give them favorable treatment. Viernes tried to counter such expectations by emphasizing the sincerity of the RFC's egalitarian legal reform goals. Tellingly, however, he was careful not to denigrate expectations rooted in such connections:

> For those who honor me by calling me a compadre [one who is a friend who will remember them] or a *Kababayan* [one who is of the same blood or town], I respect them for carrying on such a tradition. Without those cultural traditions many of our fathers who came to America during the depression would have starved to death. For a union election, though, our

> Rank and File Committee feels there is no place for such practices. If you vote for us, and in particular myself, we want you to vote because you're confident we will do our job. (Viernes 1980 [UWSC])

Another feature of the campaign strategy, clearly specified in the 1978 election pamphlet, was the commitment to fighting for women's rights. That commitment was no doubt sincere, as it expressed the growing influence of strong young women in the ACWA and in the KDP. But it also reflected the way RFC members attempted to build a winning coalition by gaining the votes of many of the non-Filipino workers in Local 37. Over the previous several years, many women, including white women, had been hired into the sex-segregated position of "egg puller" as the companies began exporting salmon roe to Japan.[48] The reformers worked to win the support of these women workers as well as Native Alaskan workers who were less likely to be part of the personal loyalty networks that led other workers to support the existing leadership.[49]

The RFC decided not to run a candidate for president in the 1978 election largely to avoid the appearance of overreach. Instead, the top of the slate was the nominee for vice president, Nemesio Domingo Sr. The elder Domingo gave the RFC a credible flagship candidate with long-standing connections to the unions and cannery; he was a member of the Caballeros Dimas-Alang and a respected community leader. Also on the slate was Gene Viernes for secretary, Silme Domingo for dispatcher, and John Hatten, son of longtime Local 37 leftist attorney C. T. "Barry" Hatten, for one of three trustee positions. The RFC also ran several candidates for the executive board, including Sue Williams, Emma Catague, and, in a further gesture toward intergenerational coalition building, the sixty-nine-year-old Henry Ceridon.

The RFC scored some gains but was disappointed by the election results. While the RFC won the vice presidency and several seats on the board, they did not win the key secretary and dispatcher positions. Undeterred, the RFC immediately began to refocus efforts toward on the ground organizing in preparation for the next election in 1980. Their wins in 1978 facilitated increased involvement in the operations of the union. As a result, they were able in 1979 to lead a successful recall campaign against Ponce Torres, the secretary who had defeated Gene Viernes in the election, because of questions about money he had taken illegally as business expenses. After Torres's replacement died unexpectedly, the union's executive board (with the new RFC members) appointed the charismatic reform leader Silme Domingo as secretary in 1980. Meanwhile, the RFC continued to make progress in its efforts to train a cadre of shop stewards and to formalize a new system of written communication between the union and its delegates. These developments created a significant challenge to union president Tony Baruso, who had long believed that the reform campaigns, like the civil rights lawsuits, had little chance of succeeding. The shop steward program, together with Silme Domingo's new position, ensured that the RFC was well informed about the day-to-day activities of the union. That further threatened Baruso, because the RFC was in a better position to have the next union election, in 1980, conducted fairly (L. Domingo 2010, 92).

The RFC ran a similar slate in 1980. Nemesio Domingo Sr. and his son Silme Domingo ran for reelection as vice president and treasurer, and Gene Viernes ran for the key position of dispatcher. The RFC also again ran a slate of candidates for executive board and trustee positions, this time including Terri Mast and Lynn Domingo, the youngest Domingo sibling. However, they decided once again not to challenge directly Baruso's position as union president. The reform strategists saw themselves as making incremental changes as part of a longer-term struggle and hoped that winning the other positions would allow them to institutionalize further reforms that would strengthen their position against Baruso in 1982 (L. Domingo 2010, 93).[50] This strategy and the extensive organizing efforts finally paid off. The RFC swept the officer positions and gained control of eleven of the seventeen positions on the executive board. While Baruso remained president, winning the other positions meant that the RFC had amassed considerable institutional power.

The decade-long struggle to democratize the union and to advance the campaign for cannery workers' rights was viewed widely as a major triumph. The crucial test, however, would be the first dispatch of workers by new dispatcher Viernes, set for late summer of 1981. The RFC's control over the dispatcher position was a formidable threat to Baruso, whose power in the union and Filipino community rested on his ability to dictate who would go to Alaska and enter the workplace. A fair dispatch process also threatened Baruso's patrons and supporters. Those supporters included the Tulisan gang,[51] which profited from the gambling operations run in the canneries, and the cannery owners and bosses, who benefited from Baruso's unwillingness to stand up for his workers' interests and rights. More distantly, but ultimately quite consequentially, Baruso's allies included Philippine president Ferdinand Marcos himself. Marcos, whose intelligence agencies closely monitored political and social activism in Filipino communities in the United States, was increasingly alarmed by the activities of the KDP and the takeover of an

Fig. 17 ILWU Local 37 dispatch hall and office, Second Avenue and Main Street, Seattle. Taken from Rank and File Election Slate pamphlet, Summer, 1982. University of Washington Libraries, Special Collections, UW 39792. Courtesy University of Washington Libraries. Special permission by Cindy Domingo.

important community institution by KDP-affiliated activists. Winning officer positions also allowed the activists to make some more direct threats to Marcos's continued hold on power in the Philippines. Thus, even though the reformers had taken advantage of the internal union rules and election process to win control of key positions, very powerful and dangerous enemies were well situated to fight back against them.

Conclusion: The Rebirth of Radical Legal Mobilization Politics

The young reformers in the ACWA and RFC self-consciously reenacted modes of political struggle that were pioneered, in much more challenging circumstances, by the first generation of Filipino migrant workers. In each generation, both the union and the larger Filipino community were split between radical leaders and liberal assimilationists or political moderates. The radicals in each generation struggled against the multiple intersectional forms of hierarchy endemic to the racial capitalist empire. Moreover, the radical leaders in both generations were impelled by Marxist-socialist, antiracist, and decidedly anti-imperialist visions of political transformation. While Carlos

Bulosan's writings and Chris Mensalvas's leadership contributed to continuity in these visions, however, the immediate ideological influences on the two generations of activists subtly diverged in ways that 1970s activists tended to downplay. Specifically, the 1930s–1950s radicals were far more inspired by the class-based, socialist promises inspired by the Russian Revolution and early Soviet communist experience, while the 1970s were informed directly by black radicalism, Maoist communism, and global anti-imperial commitments, including but not limited to challenging US support for autocrat Ferdinand Marcos.

One of the most important continuities was that radicals and moderates alike in both generations framed their challenges to racial capitalism in terms of equality, freedom, justice, and, especially *rights*—mainstream political and legal ideals in the racial capitalist order. An obvious strategic advantage of using such familiar, normalized discourse was to win support from, or at least reduce overt dismissal by, political moderates in the union, the Filipino community, and the larger American establishment long hostile to Left radicalism. To interpret this discursive embrace of resonant conventions as evidence of hegemonic cooptation would not be wrong, but it can be quite misleading. After all, radicals in both eras reconstructed these familiar rights conventions through the lens of their oppositional socialist, antiracist, even revolutionary aspirations.[52] Most important, as noted in previous chapters and in a chapter to come (chap. 6), the activists followed the young Marx in embracing the liberal principle of equal citizenship in the public realm as a principle for transforming the organization and control of civil society, challenging especially the ruthless competition of alienating exchange relations, hierarchies of private wealth, rampant racism toward nonwhites, shrinking services of the welfare state, and imperial push of capitalist accumulation. As such, democratic equality was the key commitment for alchemical transformation of social hierarchies institutionalized by racial capitalism. In short, activists in both generations appropriated the discursive resources of rights long reserved for white property owners to challenge whiteness and/as propertied privilege (C. Harris 1993).

In the first generation, the struggle for "immigrants' rights" included freedom to own means of production, to marry, to vote and hold office, to organize into unions and bargain with employees, and to access due process legal protections in the metropole. In the second generation, demands for a broad array of race-, gender-, and sex-based civil rights as well as immigrants' rights became central to their political campaigns. But in both generations struggles over such specific rights were always understood as part of a larger struggle for democratic socialism in the United States, in the Philippines, and around the world.[53] Helen Toribio (1998, 176) summarizes the point well:

> When the KDP was founded it pledged to "take up the revolutionary banner of the first *Katipunan* organization" which fought against Spanish and American colonialism, and committed itself to "mobilizing the broadest number of Pilipino people in the United States to support and participate in struggle." In many respects the organization did what it set out to do. Its legacies are the ongoing contributions former KDP members have made and continue to make in civil rights organizations, institutions that address the rights of women, immigrants, minority workers, and gays and lesbians; unions; legislative bodies; schools from the grade level to institutions of higher learning; social service programs that prioritize the needs of the youth, elderly and the indigent; cultural programs. . . . The list goes on.

One practice very common in both generations was the invocation of demands for "human rights," signaling the allegiance to more globally derived egalitarian social rights traditions alien, and even potentially antagonistic, to the American empire.

The organizational forms and strategic modes of rights struggles in both generations also shared much in common. One noteworthy continuity was the consistent commitment to multiracial and multiethnic—including people of Asian, African, Mexican, and Native heritage routinely racialized by white people of northern European heritage—as well as cross-gender and sexual alliances and coalitions, although in many ways that latter effort was realized more fully in the 1970s and 1980s. Moreover, in both generations, changes in national law, especially New Deal legislation in the 1930s and civil rights law in the 1960s, reshaped the institutional opportunities and resources for democratic struggle. These struggles for radical egalitarian rights in both eras routinely combined litigation with union building, grassroots organization, direct-action protests, strikes, publicity campaigns, and to a lesser extent electoral politics. Indeed, litigation often, but not always, was the initial action that generated and continued to interact with other tactical gambits. As Michael Fox summarized, "litigation and discovery are great ways to organize."[54] At the same time, the activists, including their own lawyer allies, remained deeply wary about reliance on lawyers, judges, legal institutions, and legal processes to deliver justice. In both generations, it should be clear, activists were brilliant exemplars of strategically savvy legal rights mobilization. In all these ways, many dimensions of Filipino political union developed by, with, and against *law*—legal discourse, institutions, processes, and officials.

One final enduring relationship between the generations remains to be explored: the tragic violence that frequently ruptured and restricted egalitarian political struggle. We saw in the first generation a mix of political and legal defeats along with periodic advances, and we also clearly witnessed the painful effects of repressive violence, including the murders of reform leaders. The next two chapters will review in turn similar tragic themes of both material and epistemic violence that reshaped the second-generation activists' experience.

5

The Trials of Tragedy

Turning Anguish into Anger

The legal system and the rule of law are not infallible—they are tools for the wealthy and powerful to perpetuate their rule, but they can also be used for social change. Exposing the cover-ups of human rights violations can be a function of the civil justice system if used properly. Never give up.—MICHAEL WITHEY (2018, 242)

The thing I find completely amazing about this case is that the plaintiffs, the two families involved, with little to no financial backing really, took on not only Ferdinand and Imelda Marcos, and not only the Philippine government, but the United States government and the United States intelligence community.—JEFFREY ROBINSON (Maeda n.d.)

It's not easy to work with lawyers. . . . We were lucky to work with lawyers who had radical politics and were committed to working with us, on our agenda.—CINDY DOMINGO (2016)

Tragedy amid Triumph

Buoyed by the Rank and File Committee's recent electoral victories, Gene Viernes made his first ever trip to the Philippines in April 1981.[1] In addition to visiting with relatives in his native town, Viernes worked with KDP allies to arrange several visits with high-level leaders in the May 1 movement opposing Ferdinand Marcos, including Felixberto Olalia, Crispin Beltran, and

Ernesto Arellano of the militant KMU (Kilusang Mayo Uno), the largest trade federation in the Philippines. Viernes, using the alias John Fernandez, also brought with him a modest sum of $2,900 from a KDP account to support the opposition movement.

After the visits, Gene flew from the Philippines to Honolulu, Hawaii, site of the ILWU biennial international convention. Viernes, armed with detailed notes on what he had learned and seen regarding Marcos's oppression of trade unionists and violations of basic human rights, worked with other members of the Local 37 reform movement, including Silme Domingo, to draft a convention resolution targeting the Marcos regime (Churchill 1995; Withey 2018). The ILWU was a powerful player given its jurisdiction over the West Coast ports where most goods imported from the Philippines entered the United States. At the convention, Viernes made an impassioned plea for the ILWU to join the fight against the Marcos regime. The powerful longshore workers' union had a history of building international solidarity with other trade union movements and could credibly threaten to impede access to US ports for countries that violated human rights and worker rights. Silme Domingo's subsequent address directly linked previous ILWU opposition against repression in El Salvador and Chile to their appeal regarding Marcos in the Philippines. However, the ILWU convention was divided on the issue of Marcos largely because many Filipino members in ILWU affiliates, especially those in Hawaii, remained supporters of Marcos. Using their political and persuasive skills, Viernes and Domingo managed to win enough votes to pass a compromise resolution that called for an ILWU fact-finding team to visit the Philippines to investigate reports of abuses against workers and unions. Local 37 president Tony Baruso, a well-known advocate of Marcos, supported the resolution once passage was assured and unexpectedly volunteered to head the investigation (Withey 2018, 68–73).

As these events were taking place, the reformers saw signs of impending danger. Upon his return to the United States, Viernes told close friends that he was being followed and surveilled while he was in the Philippines. Both Domingo and Viernes also told of having their cars tailed and suspicions that their phones were tapped once they returned to Seattle. There were also harbingers of increased willingness to resort to violence among the opponents of the reform effort. Perhaps most salient, in March of 1981, Rudy Nazario, the former Local 37 dispatcher, was murdered outside of his Seattle home. Many suspected that the Tulisan gang was responsible.

Nevertheless, Gene proceeded with implementing his plan to clean up the dispatching process and to eliminate favoritism and bribes, in the process angering those who had benefitted from special treatment in the past. The first dispatch for the new season in the Alaska canneries took place on June 1, 1981. That afternoon, two men entered the Local 37 office and shot the two twenty-nine-year old reform leaders with a gun as they finished the day's work. Gene Viernes died immediately from two gunshots to the back. Silme Domingo took four shots to the midsection but was able to chase the gunmen out the door. As he lay wounded on the sidewalk, he gave a paramedic the names of two Tulisan gang members recognized as the gunmen. Silme died the next day.

This chapter tells the story of the subsequent legal and political mobilization in pursuit of justice for Domingo and Viernes. Three criminal trials, spread out over a decade, produced four first-degree murder convictions for perpetrators of the crime. A fourth trial, involving civil claims, helped to uncover important information about what had led to the murders, including elements of an international conspiracy targeting political activists in the United States. That trial resulted in an unprecedented federal court judgment for damages against a former foreign head of state. We also document the essential underlying story of how law was mobilized, at many levels and in many ways, for political influence in response to the murders.

The allies of the two slain ACWA activists immediately sensed that there was a broad political conspiracy behind the assassinations, and they pushed hard to convince local law enforcement officials to pursue a thorough investigation and response to the killings. Surviving friends of the two murdered activists—led by Silme's indefatigable sister, Cindy Domingo, and a legal team led by LELO attorney Mike Withey—formed a Committee for Justice for Domingo and Viernes (CJDV). Committed and courageous young women—along with Cindy Domingo, including Elaine Ko, Terri Mast, Emily Von Bronkhorst, Emma Catague, Julia Laranang, Velma Veloria, and others—had become prominent activists in the KDP/ACWA network during the 1970s, and we highlight how the murders of Silme and Gene pushed them to the forefront of leadership activity. Over a decade, the allies mounted a dynamic, multidimensional legal and political campaign to generate justice for their fallen comrades and, simultaneously, to support the broader causes that Domingo and Viernes had been fighting to advance. Our account of these events is a sometimes shocking story of economic exploitation, state repression of dissent, and state-assisted murder—all either lawless or expressions of illiberal repressive law—in support of imperial racial capitalist policy agendas. The

Fig. 18 Emma Catague, Elaine Ko, Terry Mast, Leni Marin, and Cindy Domingo in anguished protest at the funeral for Domingo and Viernes. From CJDV pamphlet, ca. 1981. University of Washington Libraries, Special Collections, UW 39793. Image courtesy Mike Withey and Wildblue Press.

story is dramatic but complicated, involving many other murders, numerous other criminal trials and legal actions, and a sustained and courageous struggle to oppose oppression and to ensure that the truth was revealed.

The Context: Seattle's Filipino Community and Beyond

The pivotal elements of our narrative once more turn on its very particular time and place: Seattle's Filipino community of the 1970s and early 1980s. Long an outpost supporting American colonial rule in the Philippines, we noted in previous pages, Seattle had become "the nexus of the Pacific Northwest's 'military-metropolitan-industrial complex'" and the city's economy was highly dependent on American projects of global capitalist expansion (Kingle 2008, 206). Seattle politics was torn by the 1980s conservative backlash against civil rights and antiwar activism of the 1960s and 1970s. While the Alaska Cannery Workers Association (ACWA) activists and KDP (Katipunan ng Demokratikong Pilipino [Union of Democratic Filipinos]) allies made numerous important advances in the 1970s, by 1981 they were facing a rising tide of political conservatism within the United States and imperial adventurism by the US government, both signaled and accelerated by the election of Ronald Reagan in 1980.[2] Just a month before the murders, ACWA activists helped to organize a May Day demonstration and militant march enlisting over ten thousand people to protest the Reagan administration's gutting of welfare programs, bashing of unions, imperialist support for foreign dictators, and broad conservative agenda.

As in many other cities during this period, Seattle's Filipinos were deeply divided in their political allegiances and specifically on the political situation in the Philippines. The divisions over Marcos were, as we saw in the last chapter, manifest within ILWU Local 37 as well as in the broader Filipino community. Key people on both sides of the Marcos rift, including Baruso and the young Domingo brothers in ACWA, were all members of the Caballeros de Dimas-Alang civic association. The political alignments of the young activists also put them at odds with members of the older generation whom they courted for support, including Nemesio Domingo Sr., the family patriarch who was at first embarrassed by the outspoken political activism of his children but who also at times offered crucial support.

Moreover, the murders of Domingo and Viernes resonated with the long history of violent political struggle by Filipinos against US military aggression and economic exploitation, including many earlier murders in Seattle's Filipino American community. One specific, well-known precedent that had haunted Domingo and Viernes was the previously discussed 1936 murder of union reform leaders Virgil Duyungan and Aurelio Simon, who were shot dead in a Seattle restaurant by a rival who himself died from Duyungan's return fire. Union leader Max Gonzalez attempted murder at a union meeting years later, in the 1950s, but his wild shot missed the target. More important, as we already noted, was the brutal murder of Rudy Nazario, who had preceded Gene Viernes as the elected dispatcher, as an apparent "connection" that news coverage highlighted (Guillen 1981). Murders continued after the assassination of Domingo and Viernes, including Teodorico Dominguez, also known as Boy Pilay, a Tulisan member who might have been a witness and even party to the conspiracy that executed Silme and Gene.

The history of violence within the Seattle's Filipino community along with the long-standing racialized stereotype of Filipinos as inherently dangerous criminals led, or at least enabled, local law enforcement in Seattle to cling to a relatively narrow account of the Domingo and Viernes murders. That emerging version, one that leaders in the CJDV called "the cover story," held that the two young activist leaders were killed because their union reform efforts threatened the profitable Alaskan gambling operations of the notorious Tulisan gang. That story also made some sense to a general public primed to expect criminal gang violence in and around the International District (i.e., Chinatown and Manilatown). The murders of Domingo and Viernes received considerable local media attention, including a parade of front-page stories in the *Seattle Times* and *Seattle Post-Intelligencer* over several months as the initial criminal trials played out. "Union Official Slain, Another Hurt: Hiring Dispute Probed" read one headline (Guillen and Birkland 1981); "Job Dispatching Hinted as Death Motive," read another (Gough 1981); "Union Reform: And Then Gunfire," read a third (Bailey 1981b).

Gang activity in Seattle had given rise to numerous sensational shooting stories in that era, including the broad daylight shootings of two people in front of the China Gate restaurant in 1977 and the 1983 Wah Mee massacre, in which 13 people were killed inside a gambling club. The immediate media coverage obscured that the killings of Domingo and Viernes were in some very important respects quite different from the other seemingly similar events, however. Far from involving rival criminal gang factions, the murders of ACWA activists featured one notorious gang wielding extreme violence against two "good guy" victims unaffiliated with any gangs—idealistic young reformers committed to civil and human rights, both outstanding students, who were well loved by the large group of followers who worked relentlessly to uncover the "real story" behind the killings. Nevertheless, the cover story became difficult to dislodge once Silme Domingo was reported to identify two members of Tulisan gang as the gunmen in the murders. "Dying Man's Clues Lead to Union Slaying Arrests," read the *Seattle Post-Intelligencer* headline (Bailey 1981a).

Surviving friends and family of Domingo and Viernes from the very start insisted that the official story of community gang violence was obscuring the more sinister political forces behind the murders. They and RFC activists understood that Silme and Gene had made local enemies through their democratic, progressive union reform activities. Yet they also continually pointed out that Silme and Gene's new positions of authority did not grant them full power to shut down Tulisan gambling operations in Alaska, so that alone was an insufficient motive. The activists instead believed from the beginning that their deeply intertwined involvement in the KDP and links to the Philippine movement opposing Marcos figured prominently in the murders. The *CJDV Newsletter* (1981a [UWSC]) quickly published its own story with the headline "Anti-Marcos Labor Activists Murdered: Marcos Linked to Seattle Slayings."

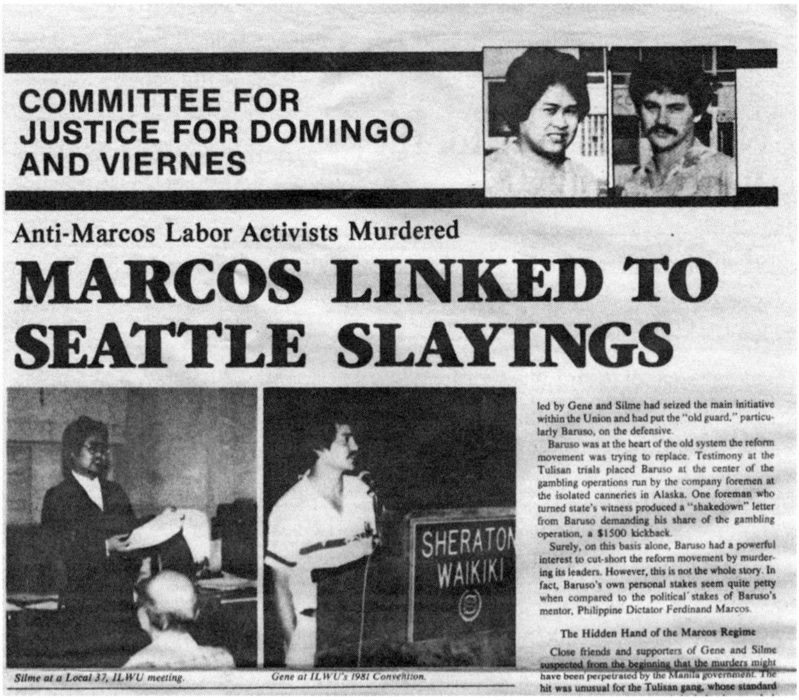

COMMITTEE FOR JUSTICE FOR DOMINGO AND VIERNES

Anti-Marcos Labor Activists Murdered

MARCOS LINKED TO SEATTLE SLAYINGS

Silme at a Local 37, ILWU meeting.

Gene at ILWU's 1981 Convention.

led by Gene and Silme had seized the main initiative within the Union and had put the "old guard," particularly Baruso, on the defensive.

Baruso was at the heart of the old system the reform movement was trying to replace. Testimony at the Tulisan trials placed Baruso at the center of the gambling operations run by the company foremen at the isolated canneries in Alaska. One foreman who turned state's witness produced a "shakedown" letter from Baruso demanding his share of the gambling operation, a $1500 kickback.

Surely, on this basis alone, Baruso had a powerful interest to cut-short the reform movement by murdering its leaders. However, this is not the whole story. In fact, Baruso's own personal stakes seem quite petty when compared to the political stakes of Baruso's mentor, Philippine Dictator Ferdinand Marcos.

The Hidden Hand of the Marcos Regime

Close friends and supporters of Gene and Silme suspected from the beginning that the murders might have been perpetrated by the Manila government. The hit was unusual for the Tulisan gang, whose standard

Fig. 19 *CJDV Newsletter* article linking Ferdinand Marcos to murders, ca. 1982. University of Washington Libraries, Special Collections, UW 39794. Special permission by Cindy Domingo.

To uncover that broader story, they worked hard over the next decade to mobilize law—legal claims, legal processes, legal counsel—in order to help produce the truth.

The CJDV was formed in the days after the murders. The original cochairs were Elaine Ko and Nemesio Domingo Jr., joined by Cindy Domingo, attorney Mike Withey, widow Terri Mast, and Dale Borgeson. Their first action was to circulate an appeal for Justice among influential leaders in Seattle, with Local 37 President Baruso ironically and strategically featured as the lead signatory. They also immediately developed plans to increase security in the dispatch office and for CJDV members, who began to wear bulletproof vests and to carry firearms (Withey 2018, 35). Their public launch was on June 22, attracting a group of over one hundred supporters and observers, including an invited guest, El Salvadoran labor leader Fernando Beltran. The event formally initiated their long quest for justice entailing (1) relentless political efforts to convince local law enforcement officials to dig more deeply into the case and (2) an independent effort to mobilize law by filing a federal wrongful death lawsuit and attempt to use the civil discovery process to uncover evidence of a broader conspiracy.

The first of these efforts was very frustrating. Local prosecutors steadfastly resisted demands to go much beyond proving the guilt of the gunmen and their gang and to target higher levels of the conspiracy even after considerable evidence emerged that union president Tony Baruso had been directly involved. CJDV leaders later reported that they suspected, with good reason, that local officials were facing political pressure from Washington, DC, to limit the reach of their investigation. This suspicion was bolstered by the fact that the FBI initiated a separate investigation parallel to that of the Seattle Police Department. The FBI team was led by a special agent who answered to a veteran of J. Edgar Hoover's aggressive harassment of antiwar, left-leaning, and black radicals in earlier decades. While the reasons for the FBI's interest in the case were unclear, the local law enforcement officials insisted that the activists' demands to uncover the "real story" were misguided attempts to valorize the reform efforts of martyred friends, an account reproduced by mainstream local media as well. The result was that the CJDV activists' lobbying could not compel a full government investigation of the murders. The second prong of their campaign, mobilization of private law through the civil suit and carefully orchestrated publicity, thus became essential to uncovering key evidence of a broader conspiracy behind the murders. The remainder of this chapter outlines the contested stories of the murders, subsequent legal mobilization activities, and trial outcomes.

The First Criminal Trial: Constructing the Events of June 1, 1981

In each of the criminal and civil trials, the basic facts around the shootings of Domingo and Viernes were established for the jury through testimony of eyewitnesses, doctors, and family members. On the afternoon of June 1, Frank Urpman, a twenty-two-year veteran of the Seattle fire department, was working at the station in Pioneer Square across the street from the headquarters of Local 37. After hearing great commotion, he ran across the street and encountered Silme Domingo in an alley, sitting and holding his stomach. Domingo was obviously badly wounded and had lost a great deal of blood, but he remained conscious and lucid during a four-minute encounter with Urpman. While a coworker checked vital signs, Domingo gave Urpman the names of two gunmen, taking the time to spell their last names as Urpman wrote them down: Jimmy Ramil and Ben Guloy.[3] As Domingo was lifted into an ambulance, Urpman heard that there was another victim inside the building. There he found Gene Viernes, unconscious and without a pulse. A Seattle police detective named Henry Gruber later established that Viernes was found on his back in a large pool a blood with bullet slugs near his leg as well as several in the wall.

Testimony by medical examiners and doctors revealed that Silme Domingo had been hit by four bullets to his chest and abdomen. Gene Viernes had taken two bullets to his chest, one of which had entered through his back and passed through his heart before exiting. Domingo was taken to nearby Harborview hospital, where he had several surgeries and twelve episodes of cardiac arrest before dying the following afternoon. In his final hours, Domingo experienced several brief periods of consciousness during visits with family members. Unable to speak because of a breathing tube, Domingo nevertheless communicated more information about the shootings. During one early morning visit with his mother, Ade, and his spouse, Terri Mast, Silme Domingo repeatedly pointed toward his right leg while making a pistol gesture with his hand. Asked if he was trying to tell them about who had shot him, Domingo indicated affirmatively and insistently. Friends and associates believed that Domingo was attempting to identify an associate of Ramil and Guloy known in the community as Boy Pilay, who walked with a pronounced limp from an earlier gunshot wound to his right leg.

Jimmy Bulosan Ramil and Pompeyo Benito Guloy Jr. were arrested and charged with first-degree murder on June 3, 1981. A key break in the case then came several weeks later, on June 28, when a local citizen found a .45 caliber MAC-10 automatic pistol in a trashcan in West Seattle's Lincoln Park. State officials identified it as the one used in the murders. They also made a shocking discovery: law enforcement records linked the serial number on the gun to its registered owner, Constantine (Tony) Baruso, the president of Local 37 and target of the RFC reform movement. Ballistics tests confirmed that it was the murder weapon. Baruso was questioned and then arrested on July 17, but he was released a few days later without being charged, as he claimed the gun had been stolen from him before the murders.

In the first criminal trial growing out of the case, Ramil and Guloy were tried together. The trial began on August 14, 1981, with King County Superior Court Judge Lloyd Bever presiding. A sentencing memorandum by the King County prosecutor who tried the case, Joanne Maida, detailed the local officials' account of the murders. Ramil and Guloy were members of the Tulisan gang. The Tulisans had been based originally in Stockton, California, and had largely gone underground in the 1970s after the China Gate shootings in Seattle. The gang had recently resurfaced in Seattle under the leadership of Fortunado "Tony" Dictado. Ramil was employed in a Chinatown gambling house as a dealer in a high stakes game called High-Q, and Guloy served as an armed guard. Ramil and Guloy also worked seasonally in Alaska, where—we noted earlier—gambling was one of the few diversions available for workers in the remote canneries and also a long-established way to separate laborers from their earnings. Testimony at trial established that Ramil and Guloy were enforcers who followed Dictado's orders and also that Dictado lived close to the park where the murder weapon was found.

Prosecutor Maida relentlessly pressed the theory that the motivation for the murders was the rage Ramil and Guloy had toward Gene Viernes because his new position as dispatcher for Local 37 positioned him to prevent their assignment to Alaskan worksites. Before the election, we noted earlier, Gene earnestly promised that, as dispatcher, he would strictly adhere to seniority rules for the dispatch and would not take any bribes or do any favors. He was committed to the RFC platform of "fighting to insure the Union is run fairly, honestly, and above-board in union affairs such as dispatching, finances, etc." (*Alaskero News* 1979 [UWSC]). Gene and Silme were murdered at the beginning of the 1981 dispatch as the Tulisan gang sought to test that campaign promise, Maida insisted.

Testimony revealed that Tony Dictado had approached Robert San Pablo, the foreman at the Peter Pan Cannery in Dillingham, Alaska, earlier that year. Dictado proposed a 50-50 split of the house commission, which had been more than $3,000 the year before. Dictado had promised protection for the operation and requested that San Pablo place Guloy and Ramil on his list of workers for assignment. However, when the dispatch arrived, Viernes refused to send Guloy and Ramil as well as other members of the Tulisan gang who lacked the requisite seniority. Viernes had several heated arguments with Dictado and other gang members in the days before the murders. In one that was witnessed by San Pablo, Dictado threatened to "get rid of" Viernes. The day before the murders, Jimmy Ramil told San Pablo that Dictado would kill Viernes the next day. Guloy and Ramil showed up at Local 37 on the morning of the murders to request dispatch, but were again refused. At trial, Robert San Pablo appeared as a witness for the prosecution, providing testimony regarding the threats made by Dictado and Ramil and producing extortion letters that he had received from Dictado and union president Tony Baruso.

Other trial witnesses gave testimony placing Ramil, Guloy, and other Tulisan members near the crime scene on the day of the murders. One witness testified that he had seen a distinctively painted Pontiac Firebird Trans Am that appeared to be casing the Local 37 headquarters earlier on the day of the murders. The Trans Am belonged to Tony Dictado, and witnesses identified Guloy, Ramil, and Dictado as seated in the car. Other witnesses identified Ramil, Guloy, and Boy Pilay as gathering on foot outside the union hall in the hour before the murders and Ramil and Guloy as running from the scene carrying a paper bag just before the wounded Silme Domingo staggered out of the hall. No witnesses claimed to have heard gunfire because a silencer was used on the weapon. Tony Dictado also appeared at the initial criminal trial as an alibi witness for Ramil and Guloy, alleging that both had been working in a Chinatown gambling house at the time of the shootings. However, Dictado was discredited effectively on cross-examination. Shortly after the first trial, Dictado was himself arrested and charged in the murders. The fact that he was represented by local celebrity attorney John Henry Browne fueled suspicions that he was backed by deep pockets.

Moreover, late in the trial, the defense presented a surprise witness, named LeVane Forsythe. Forsythe testified that he was outside the union hall at the time of the murders and had encountered the wounded Silme Domingo when he emerged from the building. Forsythe claimed that Domingo never offered information about who had shot him, contradicting the key testimony of the Seattle firefighter who reported that Silme had named Ramil and Guloy as the shooters. Mike Withey, the lead lawyer working with CJDV, recognized Forsythe's name as the person who gave sensational but ultimately discredited testimony in a legal dispute regarding the will of Howard Hughes, the eccentric, reclusive billionaire. Withey immediately alerted the prosecutor, who was then able to discredit Forsythe effectively by questioning his role in the bizarre Hughes case. Years after, while working on the civil suit, Withey proved that Forsythe had been a longtime informant for both the FBI and IRS (Miletich 2018). In the face of fierce legal obstruction from the FBI, Withey was later able to conduct a limited deposition of Forsythe's control agent in the FBI, who confirmed that, at the time of the 1981 trial, Forsythe was employed by both the FBI and IRS and was considered a reliable informant. The appearance of Forsythe convinced Withey that the FBI was running interference on the investigation into the murders from the very beginning. Withey also speculated that Forsythe's testimony was not a complete fabrication. He may actually have been near the scene of the murders, placed there by the FBI as an observer.[4]

In any case, Maida's tight narrative about gang violence and her strong closing argument convinced the jury who committed the murders, leading to a unanimous verdict. On September 28, both Ramil and Guloy were convicted of aggravated first-degree murder and later were sentenced to life in prison without possibility of parole. The Domingo family had asked the prosecutor not to request execution, even though the crime would have qualified as a capital offense. Tony Dictado was tried in a packed King County Superior Court in late April, 1982. He, too, was convicted and, on May 12, condemned to a life sentence. After the two criminal trials and three convictions, local prosecutors considered the case concerning the murders of Domingo and Viernes to be closed. Again, the long history of internecine rivalry and violence in the International District shaped the narrative of prosecutors and the mainstream media. Despite relentless pressure by members of the CJDV, the King County prosecutor's office refused to prosecute Tony Baruso, who owned the murder weapon and had participated in Dictado's extortion scheme targeting the cannery foreman. The prosecutors claimed that they did not have enough evidence to justify charges against Baruso even though there was reason to believe that Dictado would have offered evidence in a plea bargain incriminating Baruso in the murders. Instead, the US Attorney proposed giving Baruso immunity for testimony against Dictado. The bizarre move to let the influential Baruso walk in order to convict a lowly thug like Dictado made little prosecutorial sense and only increased suspicion among CJDV allies that US officials were orchestrating a cover-up (Withey 2018, 110).

Beyond the Courtroom: A Multipronged Campaign for Justice

The murders shocked the community of young activists who had worked with Viernes and Domingo. Many omens and signs, including the reports by Gene and Silme that they were being followed after returning from Hawaii, crystalized after the murders. There was much reason for fear and caution, but defiant friends and coworkers remained determined to carry on Gene and Silme's unfinished work. At the funeral service for Gene Viernes, David Della, a Rank and File Committee leader, called on the audience to let out a "floodgate of outrage and a pledge to redouble our efforts to complete the work that Gene and Silme started."[5] A few days after the murders, Della's theme was picked up and reconstructed when a large sign reading "Turn Anguish into Anger" appeared at a memorial march that drew more than five hundred participants (Churchill 1995, 122–23). The phrase remained a key slogan for the newly formed Committee for Justice for Domingo and Viernes.

In responding to the murders, friends and associates had to fight a complex war on multiple fronts. Given the many challenges, it is remarkable that a group of community activists in their late twenties and thirties, working primarily through local grassroots organizations, were able to press their cause relentlessly for nearly a decade on a national and international stage. Their relative success was the result of an unusual combination of tenacity and determination, tremendous networking skills, and a willingness to improvise and endlessly adapt tactics to fit opportunities. There was no single overall strategy but rather a dynamic, creative combination of litigation, direct action, conventional political lobbying, and carefully cultivated and sometimes hidden alliances with elite actors in government and media. Most strikingly, the activists were able to integrate their campaign to uncover the truth behind the murders with their efforts to advance the broader political causes championed by their martyred friends, particularly the goal of bringing down Marcos by disrupting his support from the US government and challenging

Fig. 20 CJDV-led march protesting the assassination of Silme Domingo and Gene Viernes. Photo by John Stamets. University of Washington Libraries, Special Collections, UW 39718.

US imperial policies more generally. What makes all this less surprising is recognition of the expansive movement building, coalition nurturing, and multidimensional political activism on which the activists cut their teeth during the previous decade. In short, they could build on a vast array of political experience, solidaristic alliances, and long-developing ideological commitments forged through struggles surrounding the ACWA civil rights lawsuits.

Consolidating Control within Local 37

One immediate challenge was to sustain the ongoing struggles over leadership within a union that was suddenly under scrutiny from a variety of hostile federal agencies and whose president was a suspect in the murder conspiracy. In the immediate aftermath of the murders, ACWA activists worked to ensure that the reform campaign continued within the union. "I would say that period we were in, after the murders, was a time of a resurgence of a democratic progressive union within Local 37," David Della later judged (in Gee 2014). Members of the Rank and File Committee, including Silme's older brother, Nemesio Jr., made a point of appearing for work at the Union Hall the day after the murders. Over the next several weeks, Silme's widow Terri Mast emerged as the key leader in the ongoing reform crusade. At a union meeting shortly after the murders, she angrily stood up to Tony Baruso when he made comments suggesting that he had been on the side of the reform movement. While her courage strengthened the position of the reform movement in the union, Baruso still maintained considerable support among some members of Seattle's Filipino community. More generally, the many simmering divisions that the murders helped bring to the surface complicated the task of organizing an effective community response to the murders in Seattle. For example, when one member suggested that the memorial for Silme be held at the Filipino Community Center, Silme's outraged mother Ade took a swing at him, complaining loudly in Tagalog and English that her family had been red-baited and run out of that ostensibly apolitical community organization (Churchill 1995, 123).

The long reform campaign within the union faced other difficult political dilemmas. The FBI announced shortly after the murders that it was initiating an investigation not into the murders themselves but into the internal finances of the union. Within weeks, more than twenty agents were on the case in Seattle questioning many union members in their homes and workplaces. This effort momentarily united the reformers with Baruso, as both sides wanted to resist what they saw as opportunistic government intervention into an internal union issue. Rank and File Committee members were also very sensitive to the 1950s history of FBI harassment and attempted deportation of union leaders with ties to leftist organizations. Yet even as union leaders spoke out publicly to oppose the FBI investigation, Terri Mast and attorney Mike Withey worked quietly with FBI investigators to focus the investigation on Baruso's questionable financial practices rather than ties between the reform movement and the KDP (*CJDV Newsletter* 1982b [UWSC]). Mast and Withey also worked with Lee Zavala, a sympathetic FBI agent who seemed inclined to believe the CJDV suspicions of a broader murder conspiracy. However, Zavala grew frustrated that the FBI refused to devote sufficient resources to the case and left the agency in early 1982 to work for a seafood company, providing the CJDV some important legal documents revealing corruption by Baruso as he left.[6]

The activists' suspicions regarding federal law enforcement grew sharper after Mast and Withey met with the local US Attorney and FBI head to urge that they investigate Baruso and bring a federal prosecution in the murders. The refusal of local and federal law enforcement to pursue the case against Baruso protected him from criminal conviction, but it could not protect him from the reform campaign within the union. Mast and other RFC members worked with Department of Labor (DOL) officials who launched an investigation into Baruso's routine skimming from the union treasury. The DOL investigation, along with an ILWU international office finding that Baruso engaged in union election fraud, led to a successful recall election campaign that removed Baruso from the presidency in late 1981. After new elections in 1982, the Rank and File Committee was in full control of the union under new president Terri Mast, widow of Silme Domingo. The reformers seized control just in time to lead negotiations over a new and much more favorable contract with the canneries in 1982. Terri Mast reflected on the situation decades later: "I think that the measure of good leadership is that they [Gene and Silme] trained other people. . . . They thought by killing Gene and Silme they were going to kill the movement. But we had built . . . a reform movement within the movement. And so they took them out, but they didn't stop the movement" (Gee 2014). Baruso was convicted in 1983 on federal criminal charges of embezzlement and wire fraud and eventually sentenced to three years in prison. However, the more transparent, democratic, and effective post-Baruso union soon began to struggle in the face of the collapsing canned salmon industry. In 1986, Local 37 had to move out of its Pioneer Square union hall because it could not afford necessary repairs to the collapsing building. A year later, the union local became part of the Inland Boatmen's Union and, with most canneries closing or converting to frozen fish operations, gradually ceased to be a central institutional force in the Filipino community.

Organizing the Legal Team and Its Larger Strategy

Gene and Silme's closest allies insisted from the start that Tony Baruso was directly involved in the murders, and they also believed that Baruso's motivations went beyond his gambling interests to his association with Ferdinand Marcos. Terri Mast and others in the reform movement thought it was very unlikely that the Tulisan would have carried out the murders without Baruso's knowledge and consent. While Baruso adopted an outwardly conciliatory stance toward the reform movement in the immediate aftermath of the murders, friends of Gene and Silme believed that posture masked darker, more insidious designs. When Baruso insisted on joining Mast and attorney Mike Withey on a propeller-plane trip to Alaska days after the murder to investigate a grievance against witness Robert San Pablo (and potentially involving Dictado and Pilay), the two CJDV activists wore bulletproof vests.

Within days of the murders, Mike Withey volunteered to assemble a legal team to build an evidentiary case exposing the suspected international conspiracy involving Baruso, Marcos, and collaborating US officials. The CJDV legal cohort included Jeffery Robinson, a young, African American associate of Withey and criminal trial expert; Jim Douglas, an activist attorney specializing in disabilities and labor law; and Liz Schott, a Yale Law graduate working in the Evergreen Legal Services. Also advising the legal team and the families was John Caughlan, the veteran radical lawyer in the Pacific Northwest who had worked on the landmark deportation cases in 1950s targeting Local 37 leaders who, like himself, were accused of being communists. Along the way, Withey enlisted a diverse group of investigators, including a mysterious but invaluable former military intelligence officer named "Bill" (Withey 2018, chap. 14) and young law clerks to work on the campaign.

The legal team did not participate directly in the initial criminal trial, but team members fed much evidence to the police and prosecutors and pressured persistently for taking seriously the larger conspiracy narrative involving Baruso, Marcos, and others. Withey assiduously pursued multiple lines of investigation that Seattle police failed, or refused, to undertake. One notable example was finding Boy Pilay, the Tulisan member identified at the murder scene and dispatched by Baruso to intimidate incriminating witness Robert San Pablo in Alaska. The CJDV team believed that an arrest of Pilay could produce testimony from a material witness sufficient to convince prosecutors to charge and convict Baruso. However, Pilay had disappeared before the criminal trials commenced, and the police devoted little effort to finding him. While near Washington, DC, in autumn 1982, Withey traced Pilay to a family residence in Chevy Chase, Maryland, but a Maryland State Police SWAT team clumsily bungled the arrest, and Pilay again escaped. Withey and his associates subsequently found Pilay hanging out with the Tulisans once again in Seattle. After several weeks of staking out likely clubs in the International District, Withey identified Pilay and called a police detective involved in the criminal case who used an existing warrant to make an arrest. After extensive interrogation, though, the prosecutor did not charge Pilay, and the police again let him go. Several weeks later, in late January 1983, Pilay was found dead in his car from gunshot wounds to the head. Withey's extraordinary efforts to nail the conspirators thus once more were thwarted by reluctant officials, further convincing CJDV members that a well-orchestrated cover-up remained in play. Withey's dogged shoe-leather investigating did turn up a Maryland friend of Pilay's, Noni Aquino, who confirmed suspicions about Baruso's role in the murders of Silme and Gene (Withey 2018, 193).

Overall, CJDV members were both gratified and frustrated by the successful prosecutions of Ramil, Guloy, and Dictado. Cindy Domingo is quoted in a published *CJDV Newsletter* (1981f [UWSC]) declaring that "this sentence is just, although it will not bring my brother back. This is just the beginning of our search for justice. . . . We have a long way to go, but we are determined to see this effort to the end, no matter how long it takes." As Terri Mast successfully mobilized union support for replacing Baruso as president, the CJDV team laid plans for initiating a lawsuit alleging a civil rights conspiracy and wrongful death action. Their early research revealed that they could sue a foreign government that conspired to commit a civil wrong (tort), including wrongful death, in US federal court under the Foreign Sovereign Immunities Act (FISA). They recruited established lawyers, including highly respected local attorneys Len Schroeter and Michael Ratner from the Center for Constitutional Rights, to build the case. Withey also had his team contact the lawyers for the estate of Karen Silkwood, the nuclear plant worker and union activist that a jury concluded had been murdered for her whistle blowing efforts (Rashke 2000). The lawyers and their investigators in the Silkwood case, including Father Bill Davis of the Christic Institute, offered extremely helpful advice about generating evidence as well as constructing the legal claims. In pushing to exact justice for violence by higher-level suspects, however, the activists continued to face resistance not just from local law enforcement officials who refused to pursue the case beyond the Tulisan gang but also from federal officials in several different agencies. During the civil trial, federal officials used a variety of legal maneuvers to block inquiry into whether US or Philippine intelligence agencies had knowledge of or involvement in the murders. As with the local prosecutors, federal officials claimed that the young activists and self-styled radicals were opportunistically trying to generate community outrage over the murders in order to advance a broader but unrelated anti-Marcos political agenda.

Mobilizing for Justice beyond the Courts

While Terri Mast, Silme's widow, was leading these fights *within* the union and the legal team was building its case, an overlapping group of activists was working on separate campaigns through the Committee for Justice. The CJDV, formed as a small group within weeks of the murders, eventually developed into a well-networked national movement. Silme Domingo's younger sister, Cindy Domingo, had been working as a KDP organizer in San Francisco at the time of the murders and moved back to Seattle to organize the political response to the murders. The organizing experience and networking skills she developed in her KDP position made her well suited to lead the new effort to push for justice in the aftermath of the crime.

The struggle that the CJDV waged against the official cover story was often fought out on legal terrain, but it was also irreducibly public, political, and widely aired in mass media. While local and federal officials may have felt that the activists were taking advantage of the shocking murders to advance their broader political agendas, the activists harbored deep distrust about the politicized motives of responding authorities. One example of the CJDV's uncompromising stance came in 1984, after Baruso was convicted for his abuse of union finances. When Baruso was sentenced to three years in prison, the CJDV called the prosecution a "diversion," and protested that the government was more interested in prosecuting union leaders for embezzlement than in investigating a related political murder with international implications. They also pointed out that the embezzlement investigation had uncovered further evidence of Baruso's link to the murders, including several large and unexplained bank deposits that Baruso had made just before and just after

Fig. 21 Elaine Ko outlines the CJDV theory of international murder conspiracy. Dean Wong photo, used by permission. Image courtesy Mike Withey and Wildblue Press.

the murders (*CJDV Newsletter* 1984 [UWSC]). The CJDV brought that same evidence to local prosecutors, but they were again rebuffed.

Because they recognized that law enforcement officials could not be counted on to press a case that was likely to embarrass US officials and perhaps even implicate the US government in murder, CJDV leaders had envisioned pursuit of the civil lawsuit from the very beginning. But while the lawsuit was important, the CJDV had few illusions about the efficacy or efficiency of civil litigation as a resource for advancing social justice causes. Many of the people who volunteered in early CJDV work had been involved in the ACWA's Title VII lawsuits against the canneries, which had proven very costly and were still grinding slowly through the legal process at the time of the murders, nearly a decade after being filed. In the murder case, the hurdles for a successful civil action were even higher. The costs of developing evidence to prove a broad international conspiracy could be enormous. And various legal immunities provided for foreign heads of state and US intelligence agencies would make it difficult to use the threat of liability to leverage concessions from defendants.

Despite these obstacles, Cindy Domingo and other CJDV leaders saw the civil suit as essential. Aside from any possibility of a financial settlement, the civil discovery process could give the CJDV activists the ability to access crucial records and build a larger case. In fact, the evidence they found through discovery, including otherwise private banking, telephone, and travel records, proved crucial in uncovering the broader conspiracy. But the CJDV activists also insistently viewed such legal action as just one element in a broader campaign that was undeniably political. Elaine Ko, one of the cofounders of the CJDV, provided a detailed analysis of the political stakes as part of a presentation that she prepared for allied groups. Ko explained that the campaign went beyond pressuring for criminal prosecutions, "because we understand the need to place these murders in their proper political context, that is in the economic and political conditions . . . we live in. The danger is to become passive receivers of the truth, hemmed into legal straightjackets. The legal cause is located in the context of the politics, but it is not the essence of things" (*CJDV Newsletter* 1984 [UWSC]). In the same presentation, Ko also emphasized the need to build a broader political movement that could give greater strength and protection:

> Do we dare continue our efforts to better the lives of working people knowing that at times we will come up eyeball to eyeball to powerful interests who have no second thought to repress? . . . Should we stop now for the safety of the next unknown victim? . . . There is one answer to this. Our protection is a political one. It is the broadest political shield that galvanizes working people throughout this city, a shield which must include ALL who can be part of it. In addition to working people, government and public officials, church members, and so on. This is emphatically what we have just done.

Ko's presentation emphasized that the murders were linked to broader political causes that could be advanced by careful efforts to uncover the truth, including struggles against racism and US imperialism, struggles to protect trade unionism, and fights to protect activists from government action in the name of "anticommunism." As the first epigraph to this chapter declares, even the experienced, successful LELO attorney Withey had few illusions about the limited but still important role of litigation in advancing social justice. Years later, he summarized his own learned wisdom by invoking the words of influential cause lawyer Vince Warren. "It takes activists, lawyers, and story-tellers to advance the causes of justice" (Withey 2016).[7]

The desire to build a broader political movement together with the need to raise money for their independent investigation into the murders drove Cindy Domingo and other leaders to develop the CJDV into a national movement. By September 1982, when the civil suit was filed, the CJDV's newsletter was listing offices in Seattle and Washington, DC, as well as contact numbers at offices of the Coalition against the Marcos Dictatorship (CAMD) in Oakland, Los Angeles, Chicago, New York, Honolulu, Toronto, and Vancouver. They also attracted high-profile media attention. In May 1982, *New York Times* columnist Tom Wicker (1982) wrote a column titled "A Manila Connection," presenting Withey's account of the Marcos link to the murders, arguing that the story's plausibility was bolstered by revelations about Marcos's harassment of US activists in a Senate Intelligence Committee investigation in 1979. Importantly, the growing national profile of the case did not cause the activists to lose sight of the ongoing local struggles. The Wicker column provided occasion for yet another round of CJDV and KDP letters to King County Prosecutor Norm Maleng protesting his ongoing refusal to prosecute Baruso and investigate his links to Marcos. A letter from Cindy Domingo and Elaine Ko was insistent about Baruso's role in a larger conspiracy (C. Domingo 1982–1983):

> You [Maleng] refuse to prosecute anyone other than the Tulisan gang or to admit that there is anything other than a dispute over union reform and gambling involved. And you imply that we are too "carried away" by our "political theory" that there are higher levels of the murder conspiracy, namely Philippine and U.S. intelligence agencies. However, we submit that a broader view of "the facts of the case" tends to verify our theory and demonstrate that your own theory is not only politically naive but conceptually inadequate to pursue the case to the next level of charging Baruso. If this were only a dispute over gambling versus union reform, why is there such resistance from federal authorities to charging Baruso? Why isn't he being charged with racketeering, interstate gambling, bribery, and embezzlement from his union? Certainly it is not for lack of evidence. . . . Why has the FBI investigation of Baruso been halted? What's behind the appearance of the mysterious LeVane Forsythe, the "professional witness" with ties to U.S. covert action activities, in the Ramil-Guloy trial? Why did the U.S Justice Department attempt unsuccessfully to get a protective order blocking Baruso's deposition in the civil suit filed in federal court?

A growing network of progressive organizations helped the committee with logistics and finances. Their Washington, DC, office was in a building housing the national Organization of Chinese Americans. Cindy Domingo and other CJDV representatives traveled frequently to Washington, DC, meeting with organizations such as the Institute for Policy Studies and the Christic Institute as well as with various congressional aides and national press figures. Some icons from the left side of the Democratic Party also gave the campaign some attention, including Ramsay Clark, John Conyers, and US Representative Ron Dellums, who spoke at CJDV events. The committee also obtained financial support from Trial Lawyers for Public Justice and various left-leaning philanthropists, foundations, and religious organizations. They also financed the case using Ade Domingo's and Barbara Viernes's family savings accounts, insurance money that family members had received after the murders, and money from the settlements growing out of the Title VII cases against the canneries.

As part of their outreach and political efforts, Cindy Domingo and the CJDV allied with simultaneous campaigns to investigate other possible state murders in the United States. One of their first outreach events was a Seattle teach-in on the Karen Silkwood case, featuring the two leaders of that national campaign, Kitty Tucker and Father Bill Davis. Another event featured Isabel Letelier, wife of Orlando, the Chilean opposition figure who was killed by a car bomb in Washington, DC, in 1976, a murder linked to Augusto Pinochet's intelligence apparatus in the United States. After Marcos fled the Philippines in 1986, Terri Mast wrote a moving letter requesting help from the new president, Corazon Aquino, whose husband had also been murdered in a shooting linked to Marcos. All of this work was built on a foundation of long-standing efforts to forge international solidarity with human rights struggles in the Philippines, allying not just with the KDP but with established radical, cross-national movements against imperialism in the developing world.

The Civil Trial: *Estate of Domingo and Viernes v. Marcos*

We turn now to the penultimate trial that developed to address the murders of Silme Domingo and Gene Viernes. The civil suit was filed on September 14, 1982, in the United States District Court for the Western District of Washington in downtown Seattle. The named plaintiffs included Terri Mast and Barbara Viernes, representing the estates of Silme and Gene. Also listed were David Della of Local 37 and Rene Cruz of the KDP, both asking for injunctive relief to stop Marcos's efforts to infiltrate their organizations. The named defendants included Ferdinand and Imelda Marcos, the government of the Philippines, US government officials including Secretary of State Alexander Haig and Secretary of State George Schultz, union president Tony Baruso, and other lower-level figures, including the Tulisan gang members who carried out the shootings. The case was presented in court alternately by attorneys Robinson and Withey.

The suit was filed the same week that Marcos was traveling in the United States on his first state visit in sixteen years. Marcos was ceremoniously served a requisite summons by CJDV ally Father Bill Davis at the National Press Club in mid-September 1982, the day after a formal dinner for Marcos hosted by President Reagan (Withey 2018, 136). Reagan officials Haig and Schultz were summoned soon thereafter. In a press conference announcing the lawsuit, and soon after in the CJDV's newsletter, the activists laid out their theory of the civil case. It was virtually the same case that they had outlined days after the murder, although it was far better evidenced in officially recognizable legal terms. The complaint alleged that Marcos had become alarmed when exiled opposition leaders began working with US allies in Filipino American communities and had launched a broad campaign to "surveil, harass and intimidate" opponents of Marcos in the United States including the KDP and other organizations in 1973 (Drogin 1986). The basic elements of this campaign—which CJDV activists had earlier labeled the "Philippine infiltration plan"[8]—had been discovered in 1979 by the Senate Foreign Relations committee, written by legal counsel Michael Glennon. The committee's findings had made national news when its classified report was leaked to syndicated national reporter Jack Anderson (J. Anderson 1979; Taubman 1979). The suit also alleged, speculatively, that Silme Domingo and Gene Viernes would certainly have come to Marcos's attention as KDP members who had just become officers of an ILWU local. That attention would have intensified after Viernes visited opposition leaders in the Philippines and then worked with Domingo to pass a resolution at the ILWU convention in Hawaii that directly threatened Marcos's economic interests. The complaint also alleged that US law enforcement and intelligence agencies had cooperated with the Marcos surveillance and harassment campaign, citing evidence revealed by the Senate committee, 1,300 pages of heavily redacted but revealing documents obtained by Freedom of Information Act (FOIA) requests, and Alexander Haig's recent pledge of FBI support for Marcos's infiltration efforts.

Tony Baruso, according to the lawsuit, was recruited as a key conspirator because he was perfectly positioned to help Marcos monitor and then eliminate Domingo and Viernes. The suit noted that Baruso had a long-standing personal relationship with Marcos. The union boss had visited several times with Marcos in Manila and had recently won an award from the Philippine government for his advocacy on behalf of the Marcos regime in the United States. As union president, he was able to track the activities of Viernes, Domingo, and other members of the Rank and File Committee with ties to the KDP. Baruso also had close, interdependent connections to the Tulisan gang that made it possible to carry out the murders. Finally, the separate conflict between the Tulisan gang and the union reform movement provided an obvious cover story that would limit the risk that an investigation would uncover the broader conspiracy.

While the complaint provided a plausible account of what might have caused the murders, developing the evidence to prove the direct involvement of Marcos or the US government was a formidable task. The uphill fight was made even more difficult on December 3, 1982, when the trial judge Donald Voorhees removed both Ferdinand and Imelda Marcos as defendants.[9] Marcos had claimed immunity under a provision of the Foreign Sovereign Immunities Act of 1976. The US Justice Department filed a brief supporting that position with a motion to dismiss. Subsequent rulings by Judge Voorhees removed other plaintiffs, including the Philippine government and General Fabian Ver, the head of Philippine intelligence (April 1983) and the US government and its agencies (November 1984).[10] Those rulings not only shielded Marcos and others from liability but also impeded the ability of the CJDV attorneys to discover documentary evidence and compel depositions from key figures. However, the plaintiffs' attorney, Withey, was able to have the Philippine government reinstated as a defendant in July 1984 in a ruling that was upheld by the Ninth Circuit the following February.[11]

The plaintiffs' attorneys adeptly used tools of discovery to target Baruso and other remaining defendants, developing evidence that Baruso had traveled to San Francisco and stayed in a hotel near the Philippine consulate immediately before and immediately after the murders. Building on the Labor Department investigation regarding embezzlement, the CJDV investigation also found unusual cash deposits into Baruso's accounts at the time of the murders. Withey was able to depose Baruso in January 1983 over the objections of the Justice Department. The defendants were still working to compel discovery from the Philippine government when Marcos, advised by the freewheeling young US Republican political consultant Paul Manafort (Vogel 2016),[12] called a quick election in November 1985, a year ahead of schedule. Amid escalating protests, a collapsing regime, and declining support from the Reagan administration, Marcos fled to Hawaii in February 1986, entering the United States. Whether Marcos realized that this move potentially undermined his claim of immunity from prosecution as a head of state is not clear.

Marcos's fall, in February 1986, and his decision to seek exile in the United States, provided a crucial break in the case. The reason is that US federal judges ruled that Marcos, who ironically became an "alien" in the US metropole, could be held liable for injury by lawsuits under the Alien Tort Statute (Davidson 2017). Withey moved quickly to reinstate Ferdinand and Imelda Marcos as defendants, and he traveled to Hawaii to take their videotaped depositions. Most significantly, Withey gained access to a large trove of papers and other records that Marcos had brought with him to Hawaii. Withey discovered records of some suspicious financial transfers to a Mabuhay Corporation in San Francisco, a shadowy enterprise under the control of San Francisco Physician Dr. Leonilo Malabed, who had gone to high school with Marcos and later described himself as "best friends" with Marcos.[13] The records in Hawaii revealed that Mabuhay operated as a slush fund supporting Marcos' efforts to infiltrate and harass opposition groups in the United States. Dr. Malabed coordinated closely with General Fabian Ver in the Philippines. The records also documented a $15,000 expenditure for a "special security project" on May 17, 1981, the same day that Baruso had inexplicably flown to San Francisco, staying one night at a hotel adjacent to the Philippine consulate. The $15,000 was also close to the amount of unexplained cash deposits that Baruso had made in the days before and after the murders. The record of that expenditure by Mubuhay was as close as Withey could expect to producing a smoking gun. The plaintiffs' lawyer moved immediately to depose Malabed in San Francisco, putting together the final crucial pieces of the case for Marcos's involvement.

The three-and-a-half-week trial finally began on November 20, 1989, a month and a half after Marcos died in Hawaii and over eight years after the murders of Domingo and Viernes. The opening argument offered by Richard Hibey, the attorney for the Marcos estate, helped to crystallize the stakes of the civil case for the friends and associates of Gene and Silme. Hibey told the jury that the case was "already solved," reaffirming the familiar, much publicized official story. After all, a thorough investigation by local law enforcement officials found that the murders were the result of a conflict between the union reformers and the Tulisan gang. The perpetrators were already in prison. He told the jurors that they would hear claims that Marcos had targeted important figures in the opposition, including in the United States. However, Hibey claimed that Silme Domingo and Gene Viernes had never been "visible leaders" in the Marcos opposition because they had "labored in a smaller vineyard."[14] In short, Silme and Gene were too insignificant to provoke the wrath that Marcos directed toward more weighty opponents.

The subsequent trial, and perhaps the entire long CJDV campaign, could be summarized as an effort to dispel Hibey's familiar account. Domingo and Viernes's friends and family were determined to demonstrate the importance of the work in which their fallen friends had been engaged and to expose the excesses of the Marcos regime. Ironically, the Marcos defense strategy made the civil trial into an ideal vehicle for advancing both of these agendas in a high-profile public setting. CJDV attorney Robinson's opening argument underlined that the Marcos regime routinely imprisoned, killed, or disappeared dissidents, usually with deference or even cooperation from the US government. "All of these techniques were used by the Marcos regime as business as usual to consolidate power and silence dissent," Robinson contended. He compared Silme and Gene to the fate of Benigno S. Aquino Jr., the antagonist of Marcos who was assassinated at the Manila International Airport as he returned from exile, and to Primitivo Mijares, the onetime insider who vanished in San Francisco after his book, *Conjugal Dictatorship* (1976), exposed Marcos's repressive excesses. "The common thread that will tie these people together" is the surveillance and murderous retribution carried out by Marcos intelligence operatives (*New York Times* 1989).

The initial stages of the civil trial largely followed the same script as the earlier criminal cases. Seattle firefighter Frank Urpman was again the first witness, followed by some of the same doctors and forensics experts who had testified in the first two criminal trials. But once the basic circumstances of the murders were laid out, the case diverged considerably, becoming a detailed exploration of the excesses of the Marcos regime. The witnesses in this new phase of the trial included Marcos opponents who had become high-level officials in the new Aquino government, opposition leaders from the United States, and academic experts on the conduct of intelligence operations by the US and other governments. In both dramaturgy and specific substantive claims, the "real" civil trial replayed the fictional "street theater" trial that the KDP staged in the late 1970s to convict Ferdinand Marcos of crimes against humanity and violations of human rights, all supported by US anticommunism, imperialism, and client-state protection.

The first of the witnesses was Raul Manglapus, who testified via a videotaped deposition from the Philippines. Manglapus became the Secretary of Foreign Affairs under Corozan Aquino in 1987, a position he had held previously under President Magsaysay in the 1950s. Manglapus had lost the presidential election to Marcos in 1965 and had also published several books and articles on the constitutional history of the Philippines. Manglapus painted Marcos as an aberrational figure in a country that had struggled to establish democracy in the aftermath of colonial domination and an authoritarian government authorized by an executive-centered, US imposed constitutional scheme. Manglapus had been a leader of the opposition to Marcos during the constitutional convention of 1972 that immediately preceded Marcos's declaration of martial law. Manglapus explained that Marcos quickly shut down democratic institutions such as the free press and independent judiciary, and he described how Marcos used his office to concentrate economic power toward a group of family and close friends.[15] Manglapus and his family escaped the Philippines in 1973, and he became a leader of the Free Philippines Movement, working with organizations such as Amnesty International to document Marcos's human rights violations. Manglapus also provided testimony about Marcos's interest in, and harassment of, opposition figures in the United States, including threats to family members who had remained in the Philippines.

The next witness, Steve Psinakis, provided dramatic testimony about the reach of violent Philippine intelligence agents in the United States. In 1969, Psinakis, a Greek business investor, married Presi Lopez, the daughter of Eugenio Lopez, patriarch of a prominent Philippine family that controlled major business and media interests, including electric companies, television networks, and the *Manila Chronicle*. Psinakis had returned with his family to Greece in the late 1960s but was drawn back into Philippine politics when Marcos began to target his wife's family as he consolidated his power under martial law. Psinakis explained that his father-in-law had been forced to relocate to the United States in exile but that three Lopez siblings remained in the Philippines, including Eugenio Jr., who was held as a political prisoner falsely accused of being involved in an assassination attempt against Marcos. In the 1970s, when Psinakis was living in San Francisco, his family was visited several times by Benjamin Romualdez, governor of Leyte province and younger brother of Imelda Marcos. Romualdez, Psinakis reported, used threats against Eugenio Jr. to blackmail the Lopez family into gradually signing over their economic interests in the Philippines to Marcos cronies. Romualdez also insisted that Psinakis and the Lopez family cease all participation in anti-Marcos activities in the United States. While the family reluctantly agreed to turn over their financial interests, Eugenio Jr. was not released as promised.

(Psinakis later helped to engineer his escape.) Psinakis reported a variety of additional machinations, including threats to his wife's immigration status, and various incidents of being followed in his car, including one where he was threatened with a gun. Psinakis also told the jury that Domingo and Viernes were important members of the Marcos opposition in the United States who would have been known to Philippine intelligence, particularly after the passage of the ILWU resolution supporting an investigation of Marcos's alleged human rights violations shortly before the murders.[16]

Another key witness providing firsthand information about Marcos's reach into the United States was Bonifacio Gillego, a government official who spent twenty years working in Philippine intelligence before being exiled under Marcos and joining the opposition. After Marcos's fall, Gillego was a member of a presidential commission looking into the Marcos regime's rule and was able to review many intelligence documents that Marcos had left behind. Gillego testified that he had been able to identify seventeen or eighteen officers working undercover in the United States during the martial law years and linked their operations to Dr. Malabed and the Mabuhay Corporation. Gillego said the documents also revealed that Marcos had viewed the KDP as a serious threat and that the organization had become a prime target for surveillance, infiltration, and harassment campaigns. Gillego was certain that the Philippine operatives would have been informed by their Seattle community asset, Tony Baruso, that two KDP members had become officers in the union and also that Viernes would have been surveilled during his trip to the Philippines to meet with KMU leaders.[17] The legal team also found evidence that Marcos had believed Gene carried $290,000 to the Philippines for support of KMU opposition, an erroneous amount one hundred times greater than the actual delivered fund. In short, there was reason to think that Marcos actually exaggerated, rather than minimized, the influence of Gene and the KDP in many regards (Withey 2018, 103). "We think that piece of misinformation was key to pinpointing Gene Viernes for murder," Cindy Domingo insisted, "because they wanted to stop the flow of money as well as his activities in building up solidarity between the US and Philippine labor movements" (Maeda n.d.).

Bringing the general account closer to home, Geline Avila testified as an influential, knowledgeable leader in the KDP and other anti-Marcos groups in the United States. Avila presented a chart showing many of the organizational links between different anti-Marcos groups and explained that Domingo and Viernes had both been important figures in the KDP. Silme

Domingo had been a member of the fifteen-member national council for the KDP and had served in several other positions. In short, Silme's bona fides as a radical opponent of Marcos ironically strengthened the plaintiffs' case. Avila also said that several people associated with the KDP had received direct threats that harm would come to their family members in the Philippines if they did not cease their anti-Marcos activities.[18]

Avila's testimony, together with the testimony of various exiled enemies who had been targeted by Marcos, provided the jury with a powerful counter-narrative to the claim by Marcos's attorney Hibey that Marcos would not have been bothered by "smaller orchard" operatives like Domingo and Viernes. Another set of expert witnesses served to place such personal testimony in context by providing a more general account of government intelligence operations and insider information about coordination between US client states and US intelligence operatives. This group included Ralph McGehee, a former CIA official involved in covert activities and counterintelligence in Asia, who explained to the jury how deniability was built into covert operations and provided hints about how to decode expenditures like "Special Security Projects." Also testifying was Richard Falk, the distinguished Princeton professor and human rights activist who spoke about the history of government harassment of American activists who opposed US-sponsored foreign regimes. The witnesses who provided this more general testimony about links between US and foreign intelligence were ostensibly brought into the trial because they supplied additional context to witnesses by providing direct information about Marcos's harassment of his enemies in the United States. They also allowed attorney Withey to build into the record a damaging picture of one defendant that he was never able to have reinstated in the case: the US government and its intelligence agencies. The veil over the long history of US repression and covert activities in the Philippines was lifted at least a bit, and it dramatically shifted the tenor of the trial.

Other highlights of the trial were the appearance of both Imelda and the late Ferdinand Marcos by videotaped deposition. Marcos defiantly identified himself as the duly elected president of the Philippines and denied claims that he had taken political prisoners or harassed trade unionists. He was more evasive on questions touching directly on the civil case, refusing, under the 5th Amendment of both the US and US-crafted Philippine constitutions, to answer questions about the Mabuhay Corporation or specific financial transfers to it. Imelda Marcos was similarly evasive, claiming that she was unable to recall what she had learned at the time about the murders of Domingo and Viernes and expressing only passing familiarity with Dr. Malabed. Tony Baruso also appeared, refusing, once again, to answer questions about his connections to the Tulisan gang. (Baruso had taken the 5th more than one hundred times during the criminal trials.) Baruso did acknowledge his trips to San Francisco, but he refused to answer questions about the purpose of the trip. He also denied having any relationship with Marcos and even denied being a strong supporter of Marcos's politics. This despite testimony by other witnesses that he had often bragged about his connection to Marcos and had proudly displayed a picture of himself with Marcos in his union office. In a move that could not have won him any points with the jury, Baruso also testified indirectly that Silme's mother, Ade Domingo, had been lying when she reported that Baruso had asked Silme to report on which cannery workers were KDP members. Ade Domingo had given some of the most moving and electrifying testimony at the trial, particularly regarding some unusual behavior by Baruso, a longtime acquaintance from mutual service at the Filipino Community Center of Seattle.

A final, particularly moving aspect of the trial was the testimony of numerous friends and family members of Silme and Gene. Many were called to contradict aspects of more hostile witnesses' testimony or to document further the importance of Gene and Silme's work for the KDP and the union. But the most powerful testimony, relevant to determining damages in a wrongful death case, involved statements regarding what the loss of two charismatic leaders had meant to the young friends and associates they had left behind. In addition to Ade Domingo, particularly effective testimony was provided by Cindy Domingo, Silme's spouse Terri Mast, and Barbara Viernes, Gene's sister. Cindy and Terri both told the jury about the impact of the murders on the two young daughters, for whom Silme had been a devoted and loving father. Together, this testimony established that the two murdered friends were charismatic, serious, humane, scholarly[19] leaders of tremendous promise and committed to democratic civil rights in the best American tradition, providing a clear rebuke to the defense argument that the two slain men were minor figures of insufficient stature to attract the attention of Marcos and General Ver.

Triumph amid Tragedy

On December 15, 1989, the six-person federal jury found Marcos liable for the murders and awarded $15.1 million in damages to the families of Domingo and

Viernes, far more than the CJDV attorneys had requested. A month later, trial judge Barbara Rothstein, who earlier had replaced Judge Voorhees, handed down an additional ruling of $8.1 million in joint liability for Tony Baruso and Leonilo Malabed. Marcos's assets in both the United States and the Philippines had been frozen in response to numerous other civil suits in both countries. The families eventually settled for a payment of close to $3 million. The award was a substantial amount of money, the largest jury verdict for personal injury in Washington state history. But it would be a mistake to assess the value of mounting the campaign for justice for Domingo and Viernes in terms of that financial reward. The civil case in particular was an essential vehicle for uncovering numerous unsavory aspects of Marcos's operations in the United States and clandestine US support for its repressive client state.[20] As Saul Landau, coauthor of *Assassination on Embassy Row*, admonished at a 1985 memorial for Domingo and Viernes in Seattle, "When you hear these two words—National Security—you know two things: a crime is being committed and it is being covered up" (*CJDV Newsletter* 1985 [UWSC]; Landau 1985). The initial allegations and the national media attention that they generated helped to create political conditions that made it increasingly difficult for the Reagan administration to continue to prop up their anticommunist ally in Manila. The civil trial also gave the friends of the victims the opportunity to establish a public record that their friends' political contributions extended further than the local union and the lawsuits against the canneries. Most generally, the conviction demonstrated that even the most repressive dictators could, at least sometimes, be required to make reparations to the families of those whom they harmed.

The fifth and final trial growing out of the murders was conducted a year and half after the jury's verdict in the civil case. Immediately after Judge Rothstein's 1989 ruling declaring that the evidence of Baruso's direct involvement in a broader conspiracy was "overwhelming," the King County prosecutor continued to tell reporters that there was insufficient evidence to bring criminal charges against Tony Baruso.[21] However, in the face of relentless pressure from Domingo's and Viernes' families and friends, the case was eventually reopened. Baruso was finally tried in February and March of 1991. He was convicted for Gene's (but not Silme's) murder and sentenced to life in prison without the opportunity for parole, the same sentence dealt to Dictado, Ramil, and Guloy. Baruso spent the remainder of his life in prison, eventually dying at Stafford Creek Corrections Center in 2008 at age 80.

In 2011, the names of Silme Domingo and Gene Viernes were added to

Fig. 22 Cindy Domingo, Terri Mast, and Mike Withey Litigation Victory Party, 1989. Dean Wong photo, used by permission. Image courtesy Mike Withey and Wildblue Press.

the Wall of Martyrs in Manila, a public monument to those who died in the struggle against the Marcos dictatorship. The two ACWA activists are the only Filipino Americans so honored.

Implications for Sociolegal Analysis

This chapter connects with several key themes developed throughout our larger narrative history. First, the events that transpired between the first and last trials, over nearly the entire decade of the 1980s, again represent unique episodes of ongoing *legal mobilization* politics by Filipino activists. The activists were fighting on the terrain of official legal institutions in both criminal and civil court, but they were engaged in a host of diverse organizing and advocacy efforts in many venues to advance multiple types of justice. "It took a sophisticated movement to win justice and challenge the Marcos regime. People thought we were crazy," Cindy Domingo summarized in a public event reflecting on the campaign. "We were able to do that because we had deep organizational ties, locally and around the country. We did not have much money, but we had lots of people power. . . . We had to be smart. Without us the prosecutors would never have been able to build the case" (C. Domingo

2016). In many ways, the 1980s activism by CJDV built on and continued the earlier ACWA efforts in the 1970s to use antidiscrimination lawsuits as resources to leverage their efforts to reform the union and to advance a socialist, antiracist, anti-imperialist political agenda.

The dogged efforts of CJDV to raise money for the trials and many larger struggles arguably were limited in success. However, the trials provided a forum for voicing the activists' many claims challenging workplace injustice and American imperialism that had been the primary projects of Domingo and Viernes. The extensive media coverage that the trials drew over time further amplified those messages for a national and international audience. In all these ways and more, this legacy represents a classic enactment of a strategically savvy and seriously radical politics of rights. The results of their effort were undeniably significant. The civil case brought by the CJDV resulted in a multi-million-dollar judgment against a former head of state, and the evidence uncovered in the suit generated national media attention that embarrassed the US agencies that had supported the Marcos dictatorship.

Second, the trials, and especially the civil trial for conspiracy to violate civil rights (wrongful death) and later criminal trials, underlined the interdependence between the local, national, and international dimensions of institutionalized race and class domination as well as political contestation. These linkages had been clearly recognized by Filipino migrant workers since the bloody US invasion of the Philippines and imposition of an authoritarian colonial constitutional government nearly a century earlier. The longstanding campaigns against predatory capitalism and racist repression at home and across the ocean have been outlined at length in earlier pages. This internationalist vision that animated the progressive union in the 1940s and 1950s was embraced once again by the young activists who aimed to resume the struggle in the 1970s. In this regard, the rights-based struggles of ACWA and CJDV activists followed and paralleled the efforts of African American civil rights leaders to internationalize their struggle, to link domestic civil rights to claims of economic justice against capitalism and demands for peace against the violence of colonial and imperial states in the early Cold War era (Dudziak 2000). These historical parallels in turn underline for us as scholars the analytical importance of integrating global and internationalist perspectives into empirical studies of domestic rights-based struggles. Viewing domestic legal struggles, whether concerning murder of activist workers or workplace discrimination, in purely local and national terms invites narrow parochialism, discourages comparative analysis, and occludes global interdependencies that are fundamental to the hierarchical power that rights movements and legal mobilization campaigns aim to challenge.

Finally, this chapter has underlined a substantive political theme at the heart of our larger story. In short, the American legal establishment denied and repressed for many years the narrative of international conspiracy voiced by the CJDV, evidenced fully by their lawyers, and eventually accepted by juries in several trials. This effort to kill off rival narratives of (in)justice, what Robert Cover once called *juridicide*, involved prosecutors, police, elected politicians at all levels, and the mass media in both the United States and the Philippines. There are many reasons to think that the efforts to silence the truth were encouraged at high levels of the US national security state, although the evidence is inconclusive. The next chapter, our final historical account, will similarly show how a majority of Supreme Court justices, backed by the Reagan administration and a coalition of powerful neoliberal business interests, willfully ignored precedents, social history, and contemporary social facts to kill off the ACWA's civil rights challenges to institutionalized racism at work in the canneries. One of the key aims of this book, like many legal mobilization studies, is to recover and promulgate such stories about democratic, rights-based aspirations that disrupt the silencing power of hegemonic narratives produced by official state practice and corporate-dominated mass culture, both enforced by legally authorized violence.

6

Wards Cove v. Atonio

The Execution of "Good" Civil Rights Law

You know the *Griggs* decision . . . The burden was on the employees to prove harm. You could allege a *prima facie* case of discrimination on the basis of statistics. And then once you did that, it was on the boss to prove that he wasn't (discriminating). So it was very easy, you know, to start this cause of action, to go into court, to set up a lawsuit. . . . We had more than two dozen lawsuits filed in six or seven cities. . . . We were having a ball. . . . The money came first from the lawsuits. And so when *the law was good* we were winning. . . . The *Wards Cove* case . . . was really the *death throes* to the '64 Civil Rights Act in terms of employment.—TYREE SCOTT[1]

I don't think any of us who were involved in the cannery cases ever expected to see them turn into quite the legal odyssey they became.—ABRAHAM ARDITI (1990)

There have been two constructions and two deconstructions of civil rights in our history. And *Wards Cove* was one of those watershed cases that clearly spells out the second deconstruction of civil rights.[2]—NEMESIO DOMINGO JR. (2003)

Introduction

The legal and political drama surrounding the tragic murders of Silme Domingo and Gene Viernes played out during the same period that the third of the antidiscrimination lawsuits initiated by ACWA in the mid-1970s wound its way through a labyrinth of federal court appeals. In this chapter we pick up the thread of that legal legacy and document its trajectory from local to national political significance culminating in another tragedy for the Filipino-led activists and for minority and female workers generally. Documenting the long history of this specific case has been one of the primary aims of this book.

Our analytical narrative is framed in terms of the contrasting statements in the opening quotes to this chapter. The first quote above is from Tyree Scott—the African American ex-Marine and workers' rights leader in Seattle whom we introduced in chapter 4 as a key player in the ACWA legal mobilization campaign. Scott recounted for us a period from 1970 through the mid-1980s when "the law was good" for workplace civil rights activists in locally based social movements (McCann 1994) around the nation. The good law he identified sprang from the expansive "disparate impact" standards developed by federal judges as they began to interpret Title VII in the 1964 Civil Rights Act. As Scott saw it, the court majority in *Griggs v. Duke Power Co.* (1971) and subsequent rulings provided critical resources for a wide array of transformative legal mobilization campaigns by minority and female workers in the United States for nearly two decades. Specifically, as we documented in chapter 4, the ACWA activists filed lawsuits challenging discrimination by the Alaska salmon canning industry in 1974 aiming to advance their multipronged political agenda though "novel" rights claims building on the newly authorized legal principles (Ferree 2003; Polletta 2000).

The activists won at trial and then secured favorable compensation for damages in two of the cases, but they lost at trial in the third case. After dragging on through multiple levels of clashing appeals rulings over fifteen years, a surprise intervention by the US Supreme Court produced the landmark ruling in *Wards Cove Packing Co. v. Atonio* (1989). That case was the most dramatic of a series of rulings in the late 1980s where the Supreme Court substantially narrowed disparate impact doctrine along with other civil rights resources in official law. The narrow court majority of five justices, led by Justice Byron White, introduced new evidentiary requirements that made it much more difficult for workers and activists to deploy antidiscrimination law as a resource for collective rights mobilization. While the White-led majority in *Wards Cove* downplayed any departure from precedent, experienced organizers such as Tyree Scott immediately recognized that the 5–4 ruling by the court signaled the "death throes" for the good law that, since the early 1970s, had empowered many worker organizations challenging institutionalized racism and sexism in efforts to advance workplace justice (McCann 1994). Eight years after the activists suffered the physical murders of two beloved leaders, their aspirations for advancing civil rights claims challenging institutionalized racism at work were killed, or, in Nemesio Domingo's words, "deconstructed" by the US Supreme Court. Recast in broader perspective, while US courts did deliver some measure of justice for Filipino labor activists in a series of related but arduous murder trials and two civil rights lawsuits, the highest court denied them justice in what became one of the most consequential workplace discrimination lawsuits of the era.

Tyree Scott's lament about the judicially inflicted death throes to civil rights law once again invites a reference to the systematic killing of normative rights visions invoked in legal scholar Robert Cover's brilliantly iconoclastic analytical framework. Challenging the later twentieth-century liberal infatuation with *progressive* liberal courts, Cover underlined the routine *jurispathic* role of courts in rejecting novel, minority community-based visions of rights that challenge the legally supported status quo order (Cover 1986; Lovell and McCann 2005). His analysis is illustrated well by the Supreme Court's destruction of promising civil rights law by abstract arguments that erased legal precedents, relevant social facts, and the plaintiffs' documented history of institutional racism in and beyond salmon canneries (Lovell, McCann, and Taylor 2016).

Finally, we use the cannery workers' story to draw attention to important dimensions of extensive extrajudicial political engagement by dominant groups that shaped the struggles to define civil rights in the era. The project of situating litigation campaigns in the context of concurrent political struggles outside the courtroom is central to the legal mobilization approach that has structured our analysis. Specifically, we locate the jurispathic ruling of a high court majority against ACWA plaintiffs amid the contingent forces of a well-orchestrated campaign by big business and related conservative interests that produced a palpable rightward shift among elected officials, judges, interest groups, and other powerful institutional actors in US politics starting in the 1970s and 1980s. In its broadest terms, the *Wards Cove* case contributed to and symbolized the pervasive power of neoliberal economic ideology that feigns innocence, or routinizes dominant group ignorance, regarding the continued institutionalization of racial, class, and gender hierarchy, thus fortifying the long-standing hegemonic rule of white-male capitalist privilege in the United States (Charles W. Mills 2017).[3]

Nomos as Praxis: Challenging Institutional Racism

In earlier chapters, we have traced the history of struggles, aspirations, strategic gambits, and political contests of Filipino American cannery workers over two generations. The key themes of Filipino workers' dissident oppositional consciousness were forged initially from aggregate resistance against Spanish colonial rule, US occupation and colonial rule, and the continued Philippine autocratic elite rule supported by American imperial state influence. This distinctively peasant-based, third world subaltern nomos was remade further by education in US colonial schools and encounters with uniquely American forms of dissidence on the mainland, including New Deal labor radicalism, the socialist-inspired Popular Front, literary populism, and, starting in the 1960s, radical civil rights, antiwar, and anti-imperialist activism. The influence of African American, Asian American, and Chicano identity politics as well as the allied communist movements in the Philippines and anti-imperial socialist politics of the KDP were especially significant for the ACWA reformers in the 1970s. Again, Tyree Scott was directly influential in transmuting the Filipino legacy of radical labor activism into a novel legal vision and political strategy in a new era. Through all of these developments, the key normative commitments found new expression, if in fragmented, volatile, and often half-articulated ways. The 1970s civil rights lawsuits are notable because they involved the formation of a specific oppositional narrative that bridged the activists' defiant nomos to newly opened possibilities for strategic legal challenges against the continued manifestations of race- and class-based injustice at work. In this sense, the activists' legal claims aimed once again to meld a *radical* agenda for democratic, antiracist, anti-imperialist socialism to the *resonant* terms of 1960s and 1970s antidiscrimination law (Ferree 2003).

In retrospect, it may be difficult to appreciate fully the promise that the radical labor activists found in the 1964 Civil Rights Act. Passed in the context of lunch counter sit-ins, Freedom Summer, the March on Washington for Jobs and Freedom in 1963, enduring Cold War pressures, and failures to overcome state action limits on efforts to institutionalize constitutional rights in the workplace (Lee 2014), Title VII of the Act was constructed to prohibit employment discrimination on the basis of race, color, religion, sex, or national origin. From the start, the terms of the legislation represented compromises between mostly white-male liberal and conservative legislators, the latter leveraged by sustained filibuster in the Senate. The compromises included a narrow definition of "employer" and exemptions for businesses of less than twenty-five people as well as vague or elusive guidelines regarding remedies for violations, including damage claims and, especially, affirmative action (Farhang 2010). The act passed after a late amendment added prohibition of sex discrimination, but it did not address rights of people with disabilities, nor did it include discrimination against LGBTQ persons.

Among the most important compromises was the authorized implementation mechanism. The act specified the EEOC as the new federal agency responsible for enforcement, which initially was granted adjudicatory and cease and desist authority. Civil rights activists strongly supported the initially proposed form of a New Deal–style, centralized, command and control federal regulatory body. Conservatives managed to remove most of the enforcement powers, however, so that EEOC authority for acting on grievances was limited to "informal methods of conference, conciliation, and persuasion" (§ 2000e-5(a)). In short, employer compliance was largely left to voluntary action. The only compulsory mechanism available to victims was private litigation, mostly by individual workers and their attorney(s), against employers. The one exception was that the Department of Justice (DOJ) could initiate lawsuits in response to findings of repeated "pattern and practice" discrimination. Overall, though, "the system of individual enforcement was the result of a conscious, explicit rejection of a system of administrative enforcement" (Farhang 2010, 110). The fact that ACWA activists in the 1970s at once called on and ridiculed the underresourced EEOC as a "joke" (chap. 4, p. 238), despite many committed individual administrators, thus seems unsurprising. At the same time, the reach of private enforcement was bolstered in 1966 by amendments to Rule 23 regarding "class actions" under the Federal Rules of Civil Procedure. The amendments sought to enable claimants for whom individual litigation was economically irrational to band together in group litigation against a common adversary aided by attorneys who could do well by doing good (Burbank and Farhang 2017a).

Equally important, though, the original act left wide open the meaning, scope, and terms of illegal, invidious "discrimination." The most obvious and widely agreed mode of prohibited discrimination involved employer actions that willfully, intentionally, and foreseeably caused harm to individual workers because of their race or sex/gender. The legacy of Myrdal's vision loomed large. Authors of the statute clearly aimed to prohibit palpable discriminatory employment actions such as termination and refusal to hire or to promote racial minorities and women, but the act was indeterminate about other terms regarding "conditions of employment," such as racial and sexual harassment. Discrimination that is evidenced by repeated "pattern or practice" seemed to qualify, but that generally also turned on the logic of demonstrated causation and intent. Intentional discrimination soon became the core of what evolved in the courts as the "disparate treatment" standard. The important implication of that framework is that such invidious discrimination—whether racial, gender, sexual, and later abled or age—was presumed to be anomalous and exceptional in an otherwise just, rational, meritocratic, market-based society. The policy logic thus fit comfortably with the "color-blind" ethos of formal equality and nondiscrimination that emerged in the racially liberal era of the 1970s and neoliberal era of the 1980s (Bonilla-Silva 1997; McCann 1989; Melamed 2011).

In the early 1970s, however, US courts tentatively ventured a second standard, what came to be called "disparate impact." The logic of this standard had developed decades earlier in some mid-Atlantic states (Carle 2011), but it was endorsed by some committed EEOC staffers and first articulated by a unanimous US Supreme Court interpretation of Title VII employment discrimination in *Griggs v. Duke Power Co.* (1971). Under this theory, plaintiffs are not required to prove an employer's discriminatory motive but may simply challenge a specific "facially neutral" employment practice or policy that has disproportionately unfavorable impact on racial minorities or women. Federal courts proceeded cautiously in enumerating and applying the principle over the following decade and then began to rein it back in (Belton 2014). Importantly, in *Washington v. Davis* (1976), the Supreme Court ruled against incorporating the disparate impact logic into constitutional equal-protection doctrine, once again impeding constitutional grounding for workplace democracy and a workers' "bill of rights" (Lee 2014).

The key point for our narrative is that the ACWA activists, who like Tyree Scott were represented by lawyers but were not themselves lawyers, saw great potential for invoking disparate impact to challenge the long-standing "plantation" conditions of racially segregated canneries. The activists viewed disparate impact not simply as a legal standard but as the foundation for a very different theory of structural discrimination that, when refracted through their radical historical nomos, opened up new dimensions of challenge to racial capitalist social organization. We outline in the following pages the key terms of the activists' vision challenging institutional racism that connected with and aimed to expand Title VII jurisprudence.

Law as Contested Terrain

It is worth underlining at the outset that, while Scott and the ACWA activists utilized Title VII litigation as part of their broader campaigns for social change, they always viewed American law and courts ambivalently at best. They understood the US legal system and American liberal ideology generally to be grounded in a fundamental tension between commitments to market rationality, private property, and systematic racial and gender hierarchy, on the one hand, and modestly egalitarian and democratic political values, on the other—with the former usually systematically trumping the latter abstractions (see W. Brown 2003). Moreover, we have seen how the activists understood the limitations of liberal democratic law that, even when most supportive, worked only selectively to soften racial capitalist violence, usually to stabilize exploitative relations and not to overcome them. Despite their wariness, the young activists followed earlier generations of Filipino radicals by embracing liberal democratic values as discursive resources for building more radical political challenges to racial capitalism that transcended liberalism. Like their muse Carlos Bulosan, the activists expressed a jurisgenerative language that blended familiar liberal odes to rights, equal opportunity, and political democracy with invocations of multiracial solidarity, anti-imperialism, and socialist transformation in the control of production and distribution. "They framed their grievances around equity, fairness, and civil rights," we noted earlier (L. Domingo 2010, 1), embracing democratic liberal principles as potentially useful if insufficient discursive resources for progressive political campaigns (Toribio 1998).

Consistent with their inherited leftist nomos, the young reformers viewed contests over the contradictory values and visions of social ordering embedded in law through the lens of fundamental conflicts among social *group* interests as well as fundamental principles. We cite in this regard provocative text from a letter that key leaders in LELO, including Tyree Scott and Cindy Domingo, wrote during a dispute with attorney Abraham Arditi over continuing civil rights litigation. "We recognize that we have a different view of law from yours, in part because you are a lawyer and your life's work has, in many ways, been spent trying to make the legal system be what it purports to be." That sentence clearly points to a decidedly critical understanding of law's proud promises and the darker reality of law's structural dynamics. The terms of this "realism" are stark: "We see the law as a set of rules that exists as a result of a tug of war, which is a constant between the class that rules and those democratic forces that are ruled. . . . At any given time a law, in our view, reflects the relative strengths and weaknesses of its opponents and proponents" (Northwest LELO 2000 [UWSC]).

Such an understanding not only displayed a defiant alternative nomos of the type that Robert Cover celebrated but also offered a politicized parallel to Cover's own theory of dialectical tensions between jurisgenesis and jurispathy. In both views, official law at any time reflects the outcome of continuous group contestation. And while the activists relentlessly fought against specific laws and legal constructions grounded in hierarchical social visions, they also waged their struggles to some extent through legally reconstructed norms, principles, and institutional processes. Although Cover emphasized the contest between official state law enforced by courts and the nomos of religious communities or social movements, however, the cannery activists urged a more complex view of social power and political organization that shaped law. In short, like many sociolegal scholars, the activists insisted that the official state law that courts enforce is shaped by dominant groups in civil society, by the haves over the have-nots, defined largely in terms of class, race, and gendered hierarchies. The result was that law tends to be ideologically biased toward the hierarchical, market-based commitments of white-male-governed capitalism. However, like Cover, the activists also recognized that courts do sometimes offer concessions by validating modest versions of alternative rights visions pressed by subaltern groups. While they understood that such moments are usually short lived and unlikely to reconfigure social hierarchy, they also saw value in pursuing even temporary openings that could help to advance intermediate goals, particularly given their limited alternatives. Disparate impact doctrine during the early 1970s provided such an opening for race- and gender-based claimants alike (McCann 1994). To quote again the letter by Northwest LELO leaders to their attorney concerning continuing litigation (2000 [UWSC]),

> We believe that this case has the potential to give us access to the courts, or it can deny that access. We won that right in the context of the Black liberation struggle; the Civil Rights Act did not fall from the sky, but during the Reagan period we lost certain gains. We have decided that the possibilities exist now for us to regain some of these rights. We do not believe that federal judges necessarily represent the solution to this problem of access. We do, however, intend to exercise our right to make our arguments in our courts and to criticize the institution when it is not responsive.

In chapter 4, we outlined at length how the activists prized creativity in framing contentious legal narratives over deference to legal texts, precedents, and jurispathic courts. As Nemesio Domingo, one of the founding ACWA activists, recounted,

> Tyree was saying we need to form our own law office because now we cannot depend on the good will of the government to pursue equal opportunity, particularly for workers. And so workers needed to be really in control. And one way to do that was to have their own law office.[4]

Scott later praised the LELO attorneys who allied with him in defying legal rigidity: "Lawyers generally say, there's no precedent for this, or we can't do that, or whatever. [Movement attorney Michael] Fox's thing was always, why not? And so, that's what would happen. I tell you, I give him a lot of the credit for not stifling the creativity of the ordinary workers who came with these ideas that weren't conventional." In short, the activists boldly undertook a mode of legal mobilization that pursued legal openings but was also self-consciously defiant toward existing workplace organization, official legal doctrine, and judges. "We were seen as the renegades, I'll tell you," Scott added.[5]

These points are crucial to understanding the ACWA legal narrative that bridged their transformative nomos to official antidiscrimination law. As they saw it, Title VII disparate impact standards that developed in the early 1970s provided an opportunity to leverage official law as a resource in their effort to advance equality and democracy against proprietarian racial privilege in advanced capitalist society. The ACWA activists fully agreed with civil rights visionary Alfred W. Blumrosen that "the 'disparate impact' concept adopted in *Griggs* paved the way for the massive improvement in the occupational position of minorities and women" (Blumrosen 1987, 3; Belton 2014). The "law was good," claimed Tyree Scott. But Scott's depiction of "good" law was more a politically strategic than a "moral" assessment amid an inherently unjust and hierarchical legal order. The activists did not "see the law as something that is morally right nor stagnant." After all, law was a historical product and producer of racial capitalist patriarchy. Good law thus was a momentary construction that could be mobilized as an episodic resource for progressively transformative purposes by those who "have our hands on history and . . . feel we have a right to shape it" (Northwest LELO 2000 [UWSC]). It follows that they did not count on courts or official law to deliver justice or to produce equality at work. From the start, we showed earlier, their creative legal narratives challenging institutionalized racism drew on what seemed to be settled legal principles at one historical moment but were embraced to support political organization and action that challenged and transcended extant legal doctrine and judicial remedy.[6] In the sections that follow, we outline some key dimensions of the strategic logic that bridged the activists' radical nomos to official disparate impact standards.

The Insistent Identification of Pervasive Institutionalized Racism

As we discuss later in this chapter, the ACWA activists did allege intentional discrimination in their initial lawsuits by invoking the disparate treatment standard to challenge blatant racism in and beyond the Alaska canneries. Indeed, it is difficult for many observers, including a Ninth Circuit panel that ruled on the appeal of *Domingo v. New England Fish Co.*, to see that routine practices in the canneries were facially neutral and did not involve knowing, willful discrimination under the disparate treatment standards of Title VII.[7] "We were confident we would prevail. There is no way we can lose, given the blatant discrimination," recalled attorney Michael Fox. "Geez . . . they (canneries) still referred to an 'Iron Chink.'"[8]

However, the ACWA reformers' jurisgenerative narrative portrayed much greater promise in disparate impact law because it could accommodate their understanding of racial discrimination as a historically inherited and pervasive *institutional* feature in workplace organization. As activist Andy Pascua succinctly put it, "There was institutionalized racism" in the salmon canneries (Chew 2012, 96). The activists did not see racial and class hierarchy as primarily aberrant expressions of irrational prejudice by individual employers in an otherwise fair society. They did not allege that the employers or managers were especially "bad," racist individual people, at least in the 1970s. They thus recognized the limits of disparate treatment claims with their focus on discrete and identifiable discriminatory choices by individual perpetrators. In the worker activists' view, the legacies of slavery, genocide against Native Americans, subordination of Asian immigrants, and Jim Crow still permeated the structural relations and routine practices of American life.[9] The young activists' understandings grew out of their careful attention to the historical roots of institutionalized racism in the canneries, where white men still dominated control of the workplace just as they had for over a century. Reform leader Gene Viernes had devoted enormous time to documenting that history of domination and resistance in the canneries over several decades (Chew 2012). Studying the historical reach of workplace racism and class division, Viernes at once deepened the young activists' understanding of the complex web of organizational forces that exploited minority workers and informed their renewed commitments to challenging current injustices.

KDP ally Bruce Occena later summarized the recurring problem that became apparent to many workers through efforts such as those of Viernes: "There's an unspoken rule. . . . Basically, the Filipinos are not allowed. This was the 1970s. My God! It was like a flashback" to white supremacy and crude capitalist rule early in the century (Chew 2012, 92). Moreover, one reason why the plaintiff class included Native Alaskans was to underline the history of white-settler displacement and colonization of indigenous peoples whose entire existence had depended on traditional salmon fishing just a century earlier. The activists' attention to history, discussed in chapter 4, shaped their claims of injury in the civil rights lawsuits, which included demands for back pay going to earlier generations of workers. The past was not dead; "it's not even past," as William Faulkner put it (1951, 73). In short, the historically grounded labor exploitation of Filipino and Native workers was present in the ongoing hierarchical racial segregation of work in the canneries. "We were part of a generation that started to raise questions about the company, about why it is like this, because many or our fathers and uncles before us, they just took the abuse because they had no choice," proclaimed David Della (cited in Chew 2012, 61).

In preparation for the lawsuits against the canneries, the activists carefully documented the many interrelated manifestations of racial and gender hierarchy in the canneries. During their covert investigation in Alaska, we noted earlier, Domingo and Woo had assembled employment statistics, photographs, and worker testimony illustrating the multipronged trampling of employee rights. The most general civil wrong was in the unequal access to different, racially segregated cannery jobs, from initial hiring to promotion. "The jobs in the cannery were very much segregated," Della contended. "The Filipinos were mainly in the fish part of the operation, which was continuously wet, with very long working hours. Upper mobility for us was getting out of the fish house and onto the boats. They made a lot more money there. We were never given the opportunity for those jobs. . . . Those jobs were reserved for the white people" (cited in C. Domingo 2013). In short, the industry "conflated race with skill"; skilled jobs were reserved for whites, and only unskilled jobs were available to nonwhites (Chew 2012, 20). Moreover, the conditions of work, housing, eating facilities, and health care access were also separate and unequal. As Della remembered: "I saw lots of things that were disturbing, things you wouldn't think happened, such as a segregated bunkhouse, segregated jobs . . . without any chance of promotion. Everything was segregated—your laundry, your mail, where you lived, the type of food you had. . . . We had to carry our own salted barrels of meat from the boat to our kitchen" (Chew 2012, 61). Discovery for the lawsuits documented the use of racial labels for different job categories in management files, "word of mouth" communications to different racial groups about job opportunities, widespread nepotism in hiring, and much more.

Again, the activists emphasized that these many institutionalized manifestations of racial, class, and gender inequality should not be understood primarily as the product of conscious choices by identifiable contemporary perpetrators or willful decisions to target individual workers. Rather, as inheritances of a long-developing racial capitalist past, the conditions were sanctified as normal, natural, and even inevitable by the employers and dominant white population. Hierarchical relations and practices were also fortified by a host of rationalizing ideological constructions that were embedded in state law, including ideas about private property, owner prerogatives, market competition, and meritocracy (McCann 1994; Nelson 1995). Employers routinely justified their adherence to established practices by claiming pressure to sustain profits, pointing to the paternal benefits of providing work to the migrant poor, and blaming voluntary contractual agreements made with the unions representing their workers. In response, the activists insisted that the core issue was more than just racial prejudice, even understood broadly. As Michael Woo told us, "The easiest way for people to understand it is to see this question of color . . . of race discrimination," especially after the African American civil rights movement. However, the activists came to "understand how much it is a class issue, a working people's issue, and the role discrimination plays in it."[10] Later, he added, "it was race and class together" that structured the cannery workplaces, pointing to a sophisticated argument about intersectional hierarchies, which was a familiar challenge for defining the complex subject position of Filipino labor activists (Crenshaw 1989). In short, the denials of basic rights articulated in the cannery lawsuits were neither simple in character nor aberrant in a society long organized to sustain racial, gender, and class hierarchy. The disparate impact logic of civil rights provided one modest, and momentary, resource that the activists could invoke in a broader struggle against those historical and structural dimensions of unequal power.

Evidencing Institutionalized Racism: Beyond Intent, Relaxing Causality

The activists' understanding of injustice at the canneries could be adapted to the distinctive evidentiary standards for disparate impact cases. First, and most important, plaintiffs advancing disparate impact claims did not need to demonstrate intentional harm, which entailed the often insurmountable burden of showing employers' discriminatory motivation or state of mind. The focus on intent often obscures largely irrelevant issues of organizational power (Brest 1976; Eisenberg 1977; Freeman 1998; Karst 1978), while disparate impact doctrine instead held the potential for recognizing institutionalized, structural manifestations of reproduced class, race, and gender hierarchy.

Second, the disparate impact standards allowed plaintiffs to build cases based on data that were accessible to plaintiffs and on other materials that were suitable for constructing narratives of structural discrimination. The most important foundation for making a prima facie case of unlawful discrimination was statistical measures of segregation in hiring, promotion, and wages, which are often made available from employers' own databases through the legal discovery process. As Tyree Scott noted in the first epigraph to this chapter, "You could allege a *prima facie* case of discrimination on the basis of statistics. . . . So it was very easy, you know, to start this cause of action, to go into court, to set up a lawsuit." Such measures are also well suited for linking disparities to practices rooted in past eras of more overtly hierarchical and exclusionary hiring, offering plaintiffs an opportunity to underline the inherited organizational character of unjust hierarchies. Further, as the efforts of the cannery workers show, evidentiary development, conventional discovery processes, and trials typically feature workers' own narratives that connect the many complex, interrelated dimensions of exclusion and subjugation in the workplace. The ACWA lawsuits each featured a host of plaintiffs and worker testimonies. Finally, as legal mobilization scholars have pointed out, gathering both statistical data and historical narratives as evidence of structural racism can facilitate consciousness-raising and direct organization among workers, helping to build protests, strikes, boycotts, and publicity campaigns that can influence judges and juries, legislators, and employers (see McCann 1994). We showed in chapter 4 how the three legal cases were used effectively in that regard.

A third feature of early disparate impact doctrine that the activists endeavored to exploit was that civil rights plaintiffs need not demonstrate direct, linear *causal* linkages between "specific employer policies or practices" and discriminatory outcomes. Where disparate outcomes were demonstrated statistically, plaintiffs could prevail by outlining a variety of indirect, interrelated features of workplace organization to supplement statistics. For example, the plaintiffs in the canneries pointed to a variety of previously enumerated secondary practices that each alone might not cause direct outcomes but which together make a holistic, process-based causal case for systemic discrimination in the "totality of circumstances."[11] In this regard, evidentiary records for disparate impact tended to be more empirically based but less narrowly or mechanically instrumental in their logic (see Rabin-Margoliath 2010). The ACWA activists pressed a view close to Charles Mills, who later argued that "racialized causality" should be understood to "include both straightforward racist motivation and more impersonal social-structural causation, which may be operative even if the cognizer in question is not racist" (Charles W. Mills 2017, 11). These doctrinal innovations reflected an understanding that institutional power is not often reducible to linear causality. Policies and arrangements that were "facially neutral" or well-intentioned adaptations to background market conditions could still violate civil rights in demonstrable ways. Again, institutionalized racism and class exploitation, rather than aberrant expressions of individual prejudice, were the focus (Freeman 1998; Bonilla-Silva 1997; Omi and Winant 1994).

Fourth, the early disparate impact doctrines established flexible, plaintiff-friendly burdens of proof in legal contests. Before the *Wards Cove* ruling, federal judges usually recognized that the burden of proof shifted to employers once minority and female workers made a prima facie case using evidence of statistical disparities. Employers then had to prove that the challenged practices were justified by "business necessity" (see *Dothard v. Rawlinson* [1977]). Judges before *Wards Cove* were not always consistent regarding what was needed to satisfy the business necessity standard, but the bar was often high, with courts discounting claims of profit maximization, questioning the calculus of supply and demand, and treating skeptically the classic "market defense" that businesses' practices are justified simply because "everyone else does it" (McCann 1994, chap. 7; Nelson 1995; Rabin-Margoliath 2010). The shift in burden of proof made it "easy," as Tyree Scott put it, for activists to pressure employers for reform without bearing all the costs of proving discrimination at trial. To quote Michael Woo again, "Back then, workers had the ability to just allege discrimination based on the whole prima facie evidence, right? That set the tone for all of the discovery and the charges and gave basis for it. A lot more opportunity, and interpretation was a lot broader."[12] Overall, the disparate impact doctrine allowed progressive plaintiffs to develop holistic, flexible, commonsense standards that assessed the "preponderance" of multiple indirect evidentiary claims for establishing "discriminatory animus," which in turn demanded high standards of business justification to avoid liability (*County of Washington, Oregon v. Gunther* [1982]).

Class Action and Political Organization

One of the most promising features of the disparate impact logic embraced by cannery activists was the amenability to collective mobilization through class action lawsuits. Indeed, the logic of class action was inextricable from disparate impact claiming practices for the labor activists challenging cannery organization. It is important to recognize that this linkage in legal principles was embraced by many groups of minority and female workers in the 1970s, what often has been labeled the "golden age" of class action doctrine (Mullenix 2014).

The focus on structural inequalities embedded in long-standing practices meant that violations were systematic, thus affecting groups of workers and not just individual "victims" of discrete discriminatory decisions. The opportunity for class actions was important in several ways. First, class action suits helped to overcome collective action and transactional cost problems by improving the incentives for workers and their attorneys to file disparate impact lawsuits (Cramton 1995; Hensler and Moller 2000; Burbank and Farhang 2017a). Moreover, as scholars have shown in other contexts (McCann 1994), the activists recognized that class action lawsuits can be useful beyond the courtroom as mechanisms for organizing workers, increasing union participation, and forging coalitions with other groups. As Tyree Scott put it, "The idea of the EEOC contract . . . was to educate workers about Title VII. But what we actually did in the process was . . . we organized."[13] The organizing began with the class of workers, but, as with the legacy of gender-based pay equity, it often extended well beyond to broad coalitions. Recalling David Della's statement cited earlier, the "idea was to develop a class action lawsuit . . . to not only have a legal component . . . but have a community organizing piece to span the generations and to get the kind of community support we needed to move the lawsuits forward."[14] In sum, disparate impact claims facilitated solidaristic group action advancing a collective nomos that overcame rather than perpetuated the individualizing logic of disparate treatment litigation and much American civil law (Scheingold 1974).[15]

Far from viewing the litigation and anticipated legal remedies as ends in themselves, we saw in chapter 4 that the activists from the beginning integrated Title VII class action mobilization into a much broader political organizing strategy for advancing a variety of goals grounded in their ambitious nomos and reaching well beyond the lawsuit (and beyond the borders of the United States). Those broader efforts were sometimes linked to their involvement in litigation, but they also persisted long after the Supreme Court's ruling led them to abandon the strategy of using Title VII litigation. The organizing for the lawsuits was both preparation for and catalyst to developing the Rank and File Committee, proposing reforms in union bylaws and procedural rules, and running a campaign to elect a slate of reform-minded union leaders. Quite unlike in other instances (Frymer 2008), civil rights litigation was viewed as a way to revitalize and democratize rather than undermine the union as a representative of the workers.

Throughout the 1970s and early 1980s, the activists continued to pursue these interrelated struggles and to cultivate alliances with local, national, and international activists battling at all levels of state and social power (Griffey 2011). These projects expressed the activists' jurisgenerative nomos of workplace equality, union power, and international socialist democratic change both in the United States and in the Philippines. And they demonstrated their nomic worldview that legal contests are inextricably group struggles between the "haves and have-nots" in society. Such political contests over hierarchical social power illustrate the collectivist dimensions of legal rights activism that legal mobilization scholars often highlight as possibilities of rights-based politics (see Nelson 1995).

Remedies: Institutional Injustice Requires Worker-Led Structural Reform

The ACWA activists' articulation of pervasive and historically based institutional racism led them to demand broad and multidimensional remedial reforms. We underline that while firmly committed to "affirmative action," they were not narrowly seeking quotas or any other discrete, technocratically defined, one-shot legal fixes for structural problems.[16] Abraham Arditi, the LELO counsel in the Title VII lawsuits, told us that they "did ask for goals and timetables as part of relief in the *NEFCO-Fidalgo* case. That was wholly unremarkable relief at the time."[17] But he underlined that these remedies were far "less rigid" than what the term *quotas* would connote. Moreover, the activists' primary remedial focus was on changes in job training opportunities, hiring processes, job ladder mobility, working and living conditions, and wage structure reform to remove race and gender bias.

> The objectives that we had for the cases were that we wanted to desegregate the housing in the canning industry . . . (and) to have bunkhouses that were like the white bunkhouses . . . that had more privacy for smaller groups of workers . . . and eating facilities that were more comparable to the white mess halls. And we wanted to have jobs that were higher pay . . . within the industry such as machinist, quality control, and even some of the management jobs. So, you know, those were our objectives. (N. Domingo Jr. 2003)

Most important, ACWA activists remained committed to direct participation by aggrieved workers in reform implementation processes. Like their mentor Tyree Scott (Griffey 2011) and gender-based wage-equity workers (McCann 1994), the activists appealed to judges to authorize direct worker involvement in creating and monitoring various processes of workplace transformation. Collective worker participation in ongoing remediation was as critical as in the initial processes of claims making.

Moreover, the activists did not think of their campaigns in terms of "desegregation" or even "integration" of the workplace. They valued increased individual opportunity for better work and wages, but they were focused on long-term collective political power in the workplace, through and in the union, in their local community, and in national and international politics. The scope of issues addressed by ACWA went far beyond the workplace to include immigration, health care, bilingual education, low-income housing, fair access to capital for home building and small business, and much more, including deposing the despotic Philippine president and advancing socialism at home and abroad (Chew 2012). As such, their aims better fit what Manning Marable has described as a "transformative" rather than merely integrationist nomos (Marable 1996). Again, this was "social movement unionism" at work.

The Jurisgenerative Project: Making Civil Rights Both Radical and Resonant

The previous observations call attention to a final point. Like Carlos Bulosan and earlier *manong* socialist leaders, the young reformers' movement narrative challenging institutionalized racism and capitalist exploitation was savvy in its conditional embrace of a liberal dialect of rights, justice, and democracy. "We wanted America to live up to its democratic ideals" (Chew 2012, 4). At the same time, though, the KDP activists in ACWA also self-identified as fellow travelers in the New Left, as antiracist socialists and anti-imperialists (Toribio 1998; also L. Domingo 2011, 1). The activists' aspirations were protean and ever evolving; they drew on a nomos grounded in an eclectic mix of inspirations and influences that inspired a wide range of social reform projects.

That said, they were persistent in their embrace of jurisgenerative inspiration from traditions of positive socioeconomic *human rights*. To quote Nemesio Domingo once more:

> We think that, if civil rights were based on a human rights construct, it [*sic*] would be stronger, and would be less prone to the kind of deconstruction that has happened in this country. . . . It would change the economic foundation of this country. . . . Every human being deserves adequate housing, adequate medical care, adequate education, jobs . . . [rights] that talk about the entire human being rather than a legal system that folks work in. (N. Domingo Jr. 2003)

Earlier chapters documented that an affinity for human rights language dated back at least to the earliest cannery worker unionizing efforts in the 1920s, solidified in the post–World War II era, and was reborn with the young ACWA reformers in the 1970s. As Scott explained, "Now is the time to push for a new human rights agenda for the US at home, one that encompasses what have been called civil rights, workers' rights, and women's rights, among others."[18] Clearly, their efforts in the class action lawsuits to pursue specific rights remedies for Title VII violations did not limit the workers' aspirational rights narratives to the terms of mainstream liberal civil rights law.

The Canneries on Trial: Initial Court Battles

When the ACWA activists initiated their lawsuits in the 1970s, the disparate impact logic had been an important component of civil rights discourse since the late nineteenth century, became a primary commitment of the EEOC starting in the late 1960s, was clearly endorsed by the Supreme Court in *Griggs v. Duke Power Co.* (401 U.S. 424 [1971]), and was utilized successfully in many cases for workers of color and women into the 1970s and 1980s (Belton 2014;

Blumrosen 1987; Carle 2011; Stryker 2001). By the early to mid-1980s, however, a new majority on the Supreme Court changed course in constructing both constitutional and statutory constructions of civil rights law. ACWA attorney Abraham Arditi later remembered the significant shift during the long period between the filing of the suit in 1974 and the Supreme Court's ruling in 1989: "In the beginning, I think we all had the feeling that we were swimming with the current. . . . Then there was the point when the current changed direction. We were swimming against the current even though we were swimming in the same direction as before" (quoted in Chew 2012, 19). In short, the once seemingly realistic appeal for resonance was later dismissed as unacceptably radical by jurispathic courts tacking from moderate racially liberal to neoliberal directions.

While the historical change in legal currents seems clear in retrospect, it is important to underline that class action–based disparate impact claims were quite viable and productive well into the 1980s. One powerful indicator of that viability is the successful outcomes of the other two ACWA lawsuits against the canneries, *Carpenter v. NEFCO Fidalgo Packing Company* and *Domingo v. New England Fish Company*. As late as 1984, federal trial judges in each case and one circuit court appellate panel affirmed the plaintiffs' allegations of employer liability. Damages were awarded in one case by the trial judge and another by settlement. Although the terms of the one settlement remain sealed, interviews with activists made it clear that numerous workers received substantial financial payouts and that the companies agreed to alter substantial features of their hiring practices. At the same time, the different approaches to the facts and doctrine taken by the two trial judges and the Ninth Circuit reveal how and how much civil rights doctrine was unsettled. Indeed, these three sets of affirmative rulings together provide a dramatic contrast to the rulings against the ACWA plaintiffs by the district court judge and, just a couple of years later, by the Supreme Court majority in the *Wards Cove* case. We review briefly the affirmative but little-known rulings as a preface to the dramatic doctrinal reversal in the third, much more famous and consequential case.

Pending and Partial Legal Success in District Court

The two successful ACWA lawsuits each were filed near the beginning of 1974, one in November 1973 and the other in spring 1974. The lawsuits initially were conceived as a single case against New England Fish Company, but early on they were split into two separate actions.[19] In both cases, the trial judge certified the class action and decided, in conventional terms, to divide the trial into two phases—the first phase to determine liability and, if the plaintiffs prevailed, a second phase to determine damages.

One complication in both the *Carpenter* and *Domingo* lawsuits deserves a preliminary note. In short, a concurrent dispute involved liability for the pending discrimination claims of Ocean Beauty Alaska, to which New England Fish Company (NEFCO) was selling the processing facilities at Egegik and Uganik Bay, Alaska, as part of a bankruptcy action. In 1980, the attorney for the claimants in *Carpenter* and *Domingo*, again Mr. Arditi, notified the trustee of NEFCO that the claimants would hold Ocean Beauty liable under the "successorship doctrine."[20] Ocean Beauty and its trustee NEFCO moved for summary judgment authorizing sale of the property free and clear of the pending civil rights lawsuits by ACWA plaintiffs. The bankruptcy court in 1982 certified the *Domingo* and *Carpenter* claimants as a defendant class ("Alaska Pacific Consortium") to determine the issue (*In re New England Fish Co.* 1982). The court then ruled for NEFCO, holding that the purchase may proceed free of any claims by the aggrieved workers' classes and that the latter have no interest in the assets of the estate. The primary effects of this legal sideshow by corporate repeat players in bankruptcy court were both to reduce potential damages in the cannery workers' antidiscrimination cases and, perhaps more important, to delay the progress of the two Title VII lawsuits. All this underlines an even more tragic irony: that the activists were making headway challenging racism and business power in an industry that was in financial decline because of long-term resource depletion and changes in technology and world markets.[21]

We give *Domingo v. New England Fish Co.* the greatest attention largely because it completed the two stages of trial and then was appealed to the Ninth Circuit Court by both parties. The New England Fish Company operated five salmon canneries and a fleet of tenders (supporting boats) in Alaska—at Uganik Bay, Egegik, Chatham, Pederson Point, and Waterfall. "The conditions and practices in the different canneries were very similar, for historical reasons. The union negotiated contracts union wide, not separately at each cannery," attorney Arditi confirmed.[22] Nemesio Domingo Jr. filed a charge with the EEOC on November 26, 1971. The EEOC investigated, found "reasonable cause" to believe that NEFCO engaged in discriminatory practices, issued the ACWA a right to sue, and in late 1974 reached a conciliation agreement with NEFCO. Domingo was not party to the agreement, which the workers considered unhelpful, so he filed a lawsuit on November 29, 1973, in the Western

District Court of Washington. Nemesio Domingo was joined by nine other named plaintiffs, including his brother Silme and six Alaska natives allowed to intervene.[23] The designated class was 780 self-identified "nonwhite" workers at the five canneries.

The local trial judge in the Western District reluctantly recused himself because one of his clerks had worked in cannery firm management. Gus J. Solomon, a senior judge from the Oregon District Court known for his strict sense of procedure as well as his commitment to civil liberties, took over the case and presided with an iron hand during the bench trial in November, 1976. Judge Solomon expedited procedures by requiring that all testimony be submitted in writing for the judge's scrutiny and railed against parties on both sides of the dispute for procedural errors. He certified the plaintiffs' class, however, and then ruled that they were not required to demonstrate "subjective intent" of discrimination; the case instead turned on "impact . . . of an allegedly discriminatory hiring practice or criterion." The "crux" of the evidence was statistical proof of percentage differences between the hired workforce and available workers, which, following the *Griggs* disparate impact logic, is equal to "direct evidence." In his 1977 ruling *Domingo v. New England Fish Co.* (1977), the judge found convincing the plaintiffs' statistical demonstration comparing the employer's racially segregated workforce with the available migrant labor pool. Significantly, he rejected NEFCO's reading of the recent important Supreme Court rulings in *Teamsters v. United States* and *Hazelwood School District v. United States* (1977) to challenge the plaintiffs' data. Comparisons between an employer's workforce and the labor pool should not follow "rigid" rules, he instructed, but should be "flexible," thus agreeing with the general rights-based narrative endorsed by the labor activists. By this holistic logic, Judge Solomon ruled that the seasonal migrant labor situation at the canneries differed significantly from the "fixed employment" context of cases that NEFCO cited in their defense.

Judge Solomon found it especially significant that eight departments of the best-paid employees were predominantly white and the only overwhelmingly nonwhite department was low-paid, cannery production-line work. Moreover, company records labeled work crews by race; time sheets included job titles such as "Fil.[ipino] Crew—1st Foreman," "Native Cannery Foreman," "White Bull Cook." The judge also found it significant that "transfers," which were the equivalents of promotion, only occurred across job titles held by whites. Hiring practices—use of separate hiring channels for different job categories, word-of-mouth recruitment, nepotism, vague and subjective hiring criteria—in particular created an institutional context ripe for invidious discrimination. Combining the statistical data demonstrating impact, the additional evidence of multiple discriminatory practices, and failure of the employer to rebut the plaintiffs' case or to provide adequate justifications, Solomon found NEFCO liable for prima facie discrimination in job hiring, job allocation, and housing, but not in the segregated mess halls.

The district court took several more years to assess the evidence for an award of damages. Judge Solomon's eventual 1981 ruling on relief greatly disappointed the plaintiffs, including Terri Mast, who substituted as administrator of the estate for the murdered Silme Domingo. Injunctive relief was precluded by the closure of NEFCO because of bankruptcy, individual damages were awarded to only eight of the 124 claimants, a lump sum of $55,000 was provided in back pay to compensate for poor housing, and the attorneys' fee award fell far short of normal expectations.[24] It is clear from both the ruling itself and accounts by participants that the judge's annoyance with the plaintiffs' procedural rule bending, often defiant or irregular tactics, and performative gambits led him to truncate the damages award. In short, the cannery workers won a huge victory on the claims of liability for institutional racism, but the small damages award was viewed as falling far short of compensatory justice and even as something of an insult. "Solomon acted almost like an agent for the industry by starving us to death financially and haranguing us and trying to humiliate us in court," Nemesio Domingo Jr. retorted. "Ironically, his name didn't reflect what that name has traditionally stood for," he added, turning his Catholic Filipino heritage into a sharp rhetorical sword (quoted in Chew 1984).

Carpenter v. NEFCO Fidalgo, which was filed in spring of 1974, a few months later than *Domingo*, worked out similarly on the issue of liability but better for the plaintiffs on determination of damages. The trial, which had been held up on the bankruptcy issues, began in 1981. Federal magistrate John Weinberg found for the defense, but the case was appealed to District Court Judge Barbara Rothstein, the same judge who years later would preside over the civil case against Ferdinand Marcos, Tony Baruso, and others regarding the murders of Domingo and Viernes. Judge Rothstein appointed a Special Master (see Schreiber and Weissbach 1998), which was a familiar way to handle such cases at that time. The appointed magistrate ruled broadly for the plaintiffs on employment practices, including a finding of disparate treatment in housing. The plaintiffs' subsequent appeal to Judge Rothstein produced a nearly total victory. In her opinion on May 28, 1982, Judge Rothstein appeared to rely heavily on Judge Solomon's reasoning about liability in the *Domingo* case, which assessed the claims almost entirely on the grounds of disparate impact. The statistical evidence showing disparities between the cannery workforce and the available labor pools again were found to be solid and compelling. Judge Rothstein went further, however, and made a special determination of disparate treatment in job allocation and job terminations under 42 U.S.C. Sec. 1981. As in the *Domingo* trial court case, NEFCO-Fidalgo lost also on the issue of discrimination in housing but prevailed on the segregated mess hall arrangements. After this judgment on liability, in 1985 the employer offered to settle the damages out of court, thus obviating the second phase of the trial. The settlement was confidential, but it entailed cash compensation to individual members of the class who suffered job and housing discrimination. The decision of NEFCO to settle in *Carpenter* may well have been influenced by the favorable appellate ruling of the Ninth Circuit Court in the *Domingo* case, to which we turn now.

The Ninth Circuit Rules More Generously

Both parties in the *Domingo* dispute were disappointed by Judge Solomon's ruling, so the defendants appealed the judgment on liability while the plaintiffs appealed the stingy damage awards. The plaintiffs, again with Terri Mast representing the estate of the slain Silme Domingo, were represented by Craig Tillery of Alaska Legal Services Corp. along with Abraham Arditi. Michael Dundy of Bogle Gates again represented the defendants-appellees and cross-appellants, NEFCO. The three-judge panel for the Ninth Circuit included Senior District Court Judge Thomas J. MacBride, who was designated for assignment from the Eastern District of California; Circuit Court Judge Betty Binns Fletcher; and Circuit Court Judge Herbert Choy, the son of Korean immigrants who worked in Hawaii's sugar plantations in the early twentieth century.

The court, in a per curiam ruling, affirmed the findings of liability but reversed and expanded the damage award. In short, the panel gave the ACWA worker plaintiffs virtually all that they requested. The standard that the judges used was the noteworthy surprise. "We hold that the plaintiffs established intentional discrimination; therefore, we need not decide the adequacy of the impact case" (*Domingo v. New England Fish Co.* 1984 at 20). They thus ruled that the comparative statistics were not determinative, although the facts added substantially to the case for liability. The court then upheld the district court finding that NEFCO had failed to provide adequate business justification for discriminatory practices; NEFCO was liable for housing discrimination and the inferior conditions of nonwhite housing; treating housing discrimination as a "wage differential" was sensible for determining relief; claims about discrimination in food were not justified; and the definition of the class at the starting date three hundred days before Domingo filed EEOC charges in 1971 held for the lawsuit. The circuit court opinion significantly reversed the trial court on multiple grounds, including the district court's conclusion that plaintiffs failed to prove intentional discrimination in housing; restrictions on communication, which violated both interpretation of Local Rule 23(g) and the First Amendment and which are not justified by alleged distortions of zealous advocates, especially by low-income plaintiffs with little access to counsel; class definition that ended at the date of trial, agreeing with plaintiff Domingo; denial of individual back pay claims because of communications violations, as that puts "an unrealistic burden on claimants," and ordered a remand of consideration for class relief; and the invocation of "many unnecessary and frivolous motions" as basis for "unusually low award" to cover attorneys' fees (1984 at 64, 78).

Aside from Judge Choy's staunch dissent on reversing the communications restrictions during the damages phase, the ruling completely vindicated the cannery workers' case. LELO issued a statement celebrating the "joyous and significant victory for minority workers in bringing equality and justice in the Alaska Salmon canning industry." After sadly acknowledging the sixth anniversary of the murders of original plaintiffs Silme Domingo and Gene Viernes, the press release announced the judgment on liability and the damages: $4,650,000 in total, of which $3,699,320 was set aside to cover job discrimination claims by class members and $690,000 was pegged to cover housing discrimination claims for nine hundred class members. An additional $1,000,000 was awarded to cover legal fees and costs. "This makes *Domingo v. NEFCO* the largest class action discrimination award in the Western Washington Federal Court District and one of the largest ever involving season and migrant minority workers." Moreover, the statement added that the legal action was motivated by outrage about exploitative conditions that "victimized our fathers and brothers before us" as well as the plaintiffs themselves, again underlining the historical, institutionalized character of the injustices at stake. The statement noted that the affected class included Alaska Native workers as well as black and Hispanic workers from five states. The ILWU Local 37 also issued a statement recognizing how Filipino workers "over the past fifty years have been the reliable, experienced workforce which built these companies . . . even at the expense of their dignity" and subjugation to "racial injustice" (Northwest LELO 1987 [UWSC]).

What remained both puzzling and revealing, however, is that the circuit court treated the charges of system-wide, institutional racism as a complex mix of facially discriminatory practices rather than a matter of facially neutral practices that produced disparate impact. As we shall see, both the trial court and, later, the Supreme Court instead made disparate impact the exclusive focus in the *Wards Cove* case, with strongly jurispathic implications.

Wards Cove in Court

Wards Cove Goes to Trial

Compared even to its more successful twins, the *Wards Cove* case represented "a long and complex history."[25] The lawsuit was filed in early 1974 and did not even go to trial until 1982. The lead plaintiff, Frank Atonio, was a Samoan American. Another named plaintiff was Gene Viernes, the ACWA leader who was slain in 1981 and later represented by his sister, Barbara Viernes, executor of his estate.[26] The defendants were Wards Cove Packing Co, Inc., Bumble Bee Seafoods, and Columbia Wards Fisheries. The first district judge, Walter McGovern, in the Western District of Washington, where the case was brought, agreed to a defense motion to dismiss the case against Wards Cove and Columbia Ward (which had been wrongly named in the original EEOC complaint), but on appeal the Ninth District reinstated the claim against Wards Cove ((703 F.2d 329 9th Cir. 1982).[27] On June 14, 1976, Judge McGovern certified a class of all nonwhite employees working at the canneries since March, 1971, which added up to about two thousand plaintiff class members (Fryer 2016, 71). After the plaintiffs' attorney, Arditi, wrote a letter suggesting that Judge McGovern was biased, the judge recused himself and assigned the case to Justin Lowe Quackenbush, US federal judge in the District Court for the Eastern District of Washington. Quackenbush was a former prosecuting attorney in Spokane County, an active Mason, and an appointee of President Jimmy Carter in 1980.

Judge Quackenbush faced a factual and legal case seemingly identical to those heard in *Domingo* and *Carpenter*. The workers again sought relief on their Title VII claims of both disparate treatment and disparate impact. But unlike district court judges in the other two trials, Judge Quackenbush decided that the case could not proceed as a "pattern and practice" case, thus rejecting all of the workers' claims after a bench trial. First, he rejected in summary fashion the workers' claims of disparate treatment and made disparate impact the sole focus, a ruling that was left intact throughout the later appellate process. The district court then ruled that the workers had failed to meet their burden of establishing a prima facie case of disparate impact in hiring or promotion. Importantly, Judge Quackenbush rejected the statistical comparison offered by the workers, arguing that the appropriate statistical comparison instead should be between the entire workforce of the company and the available labor supply for the geographical area. That comparison supported the company: the Alaskan region's workers were 90 percent white, while 48 percent of the cannery's workforce was nonwhite. Thus, Quackenbush concluded that the underrepresentation of minority workers in higher paying positions simply reflected the small number of minorities in the immediate region applying for those positions, discounting the historical migratory patterns of cannery workers. The judge further accepted the employers' argument that no nepotistic hiring preferences favored whites in upper-level jobs, while he declined to consider the impact of subjective hiring criteria that other judges had found significant. Finally, Judge Quackenbush ruled that he found no evidence that segregated housing and messing arrangements negatively impacted the minority workers.

All in all, Judge Quackenbush read both facts and case law in very different ways than did the trial judges in the other two cases and the Ninth Circuit on appeal in the *Domingo* case.

The Ninth Circuit Again Supports the Plaintiffs

The plaintiffs appealed Quackenbush's ruling on liability to the Ninth Circuit Court of Appeals, which divided on the question. An initial panel[28] upheld the district court's ruling supporting the employers' defense against pattern and practice discrimination (768 F.2d 1120, 1985), but that opinion was withdrawn because of deep disagreements within the circuit about subjective job hiring, allocation, and promotion criteria under the disparate impact test. A rehearing before the entire bench was granted (827 F.2d 439, 1987), and the en banc[29] court held that the disparate impact standard *could* be applied to subjective hiring criteria in order to demonstrate a prima facie case of discrimination (810 F.2d 1477, 1482, 9th Cir. 1987). The case was then returned to the original three-judge panel, which vacated the district court's ruling for the Wards Cove employers. The panel ruled that Judge Quackenbush's rejection of the workers' comparative statistics and application of precedents involving fixed labor forces was in error. Those comparative statistics, the panel determined, evidenced a much higher concentration of nonwhite employees in the cannery jobs than in the "at issue" jobs outside the canneries. As such, the circuit court panel determined, the comparative statistics demonstrated a prima facie case of discrimination in job hiring and promotion.

The panel thus ordered the case to be remanded to the district court to assess whether the employers could meet the burden of showing "business necessity" justifying practices that resulted in different proportions of nonwhites in cannery and noncannery jobs. The effect of this remand was that the company now bore the burden of proving that there was a lack of skilled minority workers, including in the migrant workforce, available for the higher-paid positions. Moreover, the circuit court panel ordered the district court to give more serious attention to allegations of nepotism; separate hiring channels, including especially word-of-mouth recruitment of white workers for better-paying jobs; subjective decision making; and whether segregated housing and messing produced disparate impacts on the workers (827 F.2d 445–49, 1987).

The lead attorney for the cannery workers, Abraham Arditi, was ecstatic and optimistic. "We won a smashing ruling in the Ninth Circuit *en banc* phase. It was written in a way that we felt we could not lose." Before the case could be reheard on remand to the trial court, however, the Supreme Court intervened. "We were very surprised that the Supreme Court took the case, given the statistical disparities . . . especially after the court in *Watson v. Ft. Worth* upheld the disparate impact standard."[30] This intervention was also frustrating at the time because it preempted a positive outcome on remand and the option for settlement.[31] In retrospect, we know that it also created an opportunity for the Supreme Court to eviscerate the disparate impact doctrine and perform what Cover labeled a profoundly jurispathic act.

A Supremely Jurispathic Exercise

In a 5–4 ruling,[32] the Supreme Court reversed the circuit court and instructed the trial court (and, in effect, all federal courts) to allow a much narrower range of statistical data as prima facie evidence and to demand higher burdens of proof for plaintiffs in disparate impact cases. The majority decisively rejected the legal claims and expansive rights theory of the ACWA activists. Together with other cases of the same era, the court substantially gutted the promise in *Griggs* that led many organizations for minority workers of color, female workers, and social justice causes to use Title VII as part of broader efforts to challenge structural discrimination in workplaces such as the canneries.

Our account in this section does not aim to offer a conventional legal analysis, nor does it pretend to be a more compelling reading of precedents or an objectively better interpretation of relevant statutory provisions than other scholarly analysts.[33] Rather, consistent with the general standpoint from which we have written this book, we offer a reading that respects the general aspirational democratic nomos of the plaintiffs and their progressive allies. We explore in particular questions about the rhetorical strategies the Supreme Court majority utilized as it shut down legal avenues for collective political mobilization challenging institutional racism. Our focus also is as much on highlighting what the justices left unsaid in *Wards Cove* as on what they did say. In particular, we note that the court majority said almost nothing about the actual conditions at the canneries that gave rise to the lawsuit, the many legal precedents that made the workers' challenges realistic, or the court's evisceration of prior case law. Crucially, the court's account created a distorted picture of what motivated the activists to file the lawsuit and of the factual and principled case they took to the court, which in turn discounts the impact that *Wards Cove* had generally on worker efforts to mobilize civil rights law. To appreciate such distortions, scholars need to look beyond the official version of law that emerges retroactively in appellate court decisions. Scholars can, we suggest, learn a great deal by taking seriously the legal vision of activists who identify and pursue what once seemed clear openings in the law even if those openings eventually were closed down by jurispathic judges (Goluboff 2007; Lee 2014). Taking the activists' alternative vision seriously reveals the promise of earlier doctrinal innovations and allows us to develop a better understanding of law's potential role in transformative change, the judicial rulings that narrowed that potential, and, in our final section, the limitations of Congress's alleged override of the court.

Eviscerating Disparate Impact

Under the *Griggs* framework, we noted earlier, plaintiffs could shift the burden of proof to employers by using statistical evidence of racial disparities to make a prima facie showing of discrimination. Employers could still defend themselves, but they had to prove that their employment practices were driven by business necessity. That often led to disputes between parties about what kinds of statistical comparisons the workers could use to establish a prima facie case. In *Wards Cove,* like the other two lawsuits, the plaintiffs presented statistics showing that nonwhite workers were concentrated almost exclusively in the lower-paying positions, while whites dominated the better-paying positions. The company responded that disparities across job classifications simply reflected a lack of relevant skills among minority workers. The trial court sided with the employer, ruling that the appropriate comparison was not across different jobs within *Wards Cove* but instead between the entire Wards Cove workforce and the available labor pool in the surrounding geographical area. On appeal, the Ninth Circuit panel, following instructions from the en banc panel, had applied standards that favored the workers' framing of claims (*Atonio v. Wards Cove Packing Co., Inc.* 1987).

The Supreme Court had begun treating statistical comparisons more skeptically in the years before the *Wards Cove* decision. These rulings together made it more difficult for plaintiffs to win disparate impact cases by establishing new guidelines that narrowed the use of statistical comparisons and altered standards for burden of proof in disparate impact cases. As Abraham Arditi, the plaintiffs' attorney, later said, the rulings in *International Brotherhood of the Teamsters v. United States* and *Hazelwood School District v. United States* "narrowed the criteria for demonstrating disparate impact with statistics," but many reasons remained to believe even in the late 1980s that "there was still lots of vitality and room for activity."[34] Indeed, the Ninth Circuit in appeals on the two other ACWA cases read those precedents to support the validity of comparative statistics demonstrating disparities in the canneries. Again, the per curiam ruling in *Domingo* insisted on "flexibility" in assessing such statistics in the context of a migrant workforce.

By contrast, the Supreme Court in *Wards Cove* majority confirmed that subjective criteria can be assessed for disparate impact, but the justices rejected both the trial and circuit courts' standard of comparing jobs in favor of yet another option that was even more indulgent toward employers. Declaring the plaintiffs' comparison "nonsensical" (*Wards Cove Packing Co. v. Atonio* 1989, 651), Justice Byron White's majority opinion declared that the appropriate comparison was between persons employed in each specific position and the pool of qualified, demonstrated *applicants* for those positions. The majority held that "if the percentage of selected applicants who are nonwhite is not significantly less than the percentage of qualified applicants who are nonwhite, the employer's selection mechanism probably does not operate with a disparate impact on minorities" (653). To make a prima facie case, plaintiffs had to show either that minority candidates applied for positions and were disproportionately rejected or prove that there were "barriers or practices deterring qualified non-whites from applying" (653). This position arguably might make some sense in a conventional urban factory setting. But, again, Justice White wholly ignored the century-long pattern of employer routine disqualification of the conscripted migratory Asian workforce and indigenous peoples in the remote, rural Alaska canneries from consideration for such jobs.[35]

The narrow majority in *Wards Cove* made a sharper break with the past in announcing a new standard on the relatively settled question of burden of proof. The majority ruled that a prima facie showing of discrimination using statistics no longer shifted the burden of proof to employers, claiming instead that the "burden of persuasion" remained always, from start to finish, with the plaintiffs. The majority further demanded that plaintiffs demonstrate a clear and direct causal connection—a narrow positivist standard—between documented racial disparities and specific employment practices. Taken together, the rulings on statistical comparisons, burdens of proof, and causation made it much more difficult—"impossible," the plaintiffs told us—for groups of workers to win Title VII cases by invoking their institutional racism narrative. The demand that workers disaggregate their complaints and prove intent and causation made it much tougher to challenge the cumulative effect of long-standing employer practices that shaped the market for labor. As Tyree Scott told us, "the Wards Cove case was one of the major retreats of the courts. . . . Basically what they did is they threw out all the tenets of *Griggs* and placed the burden on the workers."[36]

Ignoring Prior Case Law, Erasing Social Facts

As noted above, what the court majority did not explicitly say is important to understanding its impact. Crucial omissions in the majority opinion obscured the promise of earlier civil rights law and thus created an inaccurate picture of what led so many activists of the 1970s to use Title VII class action suits to challenge structural discrimination. In the process, "the Court reversed twenty years of disparate impact law" on a variety of key issues (Hart 2011, 267).

One set of omissions marked the court's treatment of prior disparate impact cases. Rather than defend the ruling as an effort to clarify doctrinal uncertainty or argue that the court was making a justified retreat from prior mistakes, White's majority opinion misleadingly positioned the court as defenders of a long-established status quo while obscuring the racial, gendered, and class foundations of that status quo. White barely mentioned the disparate impact precedents that inspired the plaintiffs to mobilize civil rights law in 1974. He presented some short general quotes from earlier, narrower rulings that were consistent with the court's new *conclusions*, but he could not cite any cases where any courts had adopted the newly restrictive *evidentiary standards*. The majority portrayed the case as an effort by cannery workers and renegade circuit court judges to push law in entirely new directions rather than as an effort by savvy activists to construct new but reasonable applications of the legal reasoning announced in *Griggs*. In particular, the court's majority ruling that plaintiffs bear the burden of persuasion from start to end and that an employer seeking to explain racial disparity with a business necessity need not have to demonstrate that the practice in question is "essential" or "indispensable" represented radical but unacknowledged departures from precedent (Hart 2011). Justice Stevens's dissent emphasized this issue, lamenting the "majority's facile treatment of settled law" (664) and stating that their "casual—almost summary—rejection of the statutory construction that developed in the wake of *Griggs* is most disturbing" (671–72). Stevens, voicing a view that aligned with the plaintiffs, added that the majority was "turning a blind eye to the meaning and purpose of Title VII" (663).

Even more striking than the court's failure to address directly disparate impact precedents, the majority opinion also paid almost no attention to the record of conditions in the canneries that the plaintiffs had developed to support their case. By ruling that the acknowledged disparities in the job force did not establish a prima facie case of disparate impact, the court majority could simply ignore the empirical evidence of historical conditions that persisted at the canneries and were at the heart of the multiple legal claims by the minority workers. The only information about the conditions in the canneries that made it into the US Reports were some dark hints in Justice Blackmun's short dissenting opinion. Blackmun referred to the "plantation economy" model of cannery production and protested sharply the majority's implicit sanctioning of "institutionalized discrimination." Blackmun lamented the majority's indifference to the plaintiffs' institutionalized racism narrative: "One wonders whether the majority still believes that race discrimination . . . is a problem in our society, or even remembers that it ever was" (662). The court majority instead justified its newly restrictive evidentiary rules by making speculative, abstract claims about hypothetical employers and imaginary lawsuits rather than serious, respectful consideration of the facts of the case.

The move away from the empirically demonstrated facts in Alaskan canneries toward abstract deduction and hypotheticals was crucial to the majority's justification of its new procedural rules regarding statistics and burden of proof.[37] Justice White's deductive argument rested on the claim that allowing workers to rely on statistical disparities within the workplace would inevitably lead employers to adopt rigid racial "quotas" in order to avoid the cost of defending their hiring practices in court. White expressed this claim about defensive quotas as a self-evident truth, not as a claim supported in the evidentiary record. Indeed, the stipulated "employers" were a hypothetical construct given that the real employers at Wards Cove had never responded to the threat of disparate impact lawsuits by adopting any type of quota. The topic of quotas was quite distant from the specific case that was before the court; as we noted earlier, the plaintiffs had not requested technocratic, one-time fixes like quotas as the requested remedy for alleged discrimination.

Of course, Supreme Court justices sometimes have reason to reach beyond the messy facts of cases to abstract principles in order to meet their institutional imperative of giving lower courts clear guidance on general and recurring legal questions. However, in this case, the majority's refusal to consider the copious, well-documented social facts underlying the case was not simply a stylistic quirk of formal legal reasoning unrelated to its conclusions. For one thing, the move toward abstraction allowed the justices in the majority to issue a much more sweeping ruling. The focus on deductive abstractions contrasts with the earlier *Hazelwood* case where the court also rejected a statistical comparison used by civil rights plaintiffs, not to mention the Ninth Circuit's rulings on the cannery workers' claims. In *Hazelwood*, the court's lead opinion focused on the claim, borrowed from the earlier *International Brotherhood of the Teamsters v. United States* (1977 at 340), that judges should take into account "all of the surrounding facts and circumstance" when they decided what types of statistical comparisons could be used in Title VII cases (312). This is precisely what Judge *Solomon* ruled in *Domingo*, and generally what the Ninth Circuit affirmed on appeal, just a handful of years earlier. In contrast, the *Wards Cove* majority's rejection of "nonsensical" statistical comparisons to the surrounding population was framed in more wholesale unempirical, universalistic terms that ignored specifics of context. As such, the majority largely ignored the circuit court's explanation of why the plaintiffs' unusual statistical comparison made sense given the unusual nature of the salmon canning industry, that is, the seasonal work in a very remote location and the use of third-party contractors and unions to supply the pool of workers for dispatch to the canneries. Indeed, the record of the case before the court showed precisely why demands for statistical comparisons to job applicants and for causal proof and disaggregation of employment practices would make it nearly impossible for many plaintiffs to secure legal remedies for structural discrimination even in a workplace with palpably segregated job assignment routines, bunkhouses, and mess halls.

The Supreme Court majority showed considerable neoliberal faith that the invisible hand of market forces of supply and demand could be trusted to produce fair allocations. One telling indication of that posture is the majority's demand for considerable deference to employers. "Courts are generally less competent than employers to restructure business practices. . . . Consequently, the judiciary should proceed with care before mandating that an employer must adopt a[n] alternative . . . hiring practice" (661). The majority's focus on the *skills* of job *applicants* was highlighted while discounting the ways that racially discriminatory structural conditions can shape labor markets. In particular, the justices devalued the workers' quite plausible argument that the visible, long-standing segregation across job categories and in recruitment processes rendered unrealistic minority worker options to apply for skilled positions as well as to develop relevant skills.[38] The court's newly rigid evidentiary rules made such social facts irrelevant, thus killing off efforts to document narratives of institutional racism in future Title VII cases. The ruling well illustrates Robert Cover's claim that abstractions used by jurispathic judges directly obscure and discount the normative foundations of alternative legal narratives.

The court also diverted attention away from how the ruling would affect collective efforts to challenge injustice using Title VII. Instead, Justice White frankly expressed the court's desire to protect the interests of employers, thus implying that property rights (of white owners) intrinsically trump employee rights (of workers of color). White complained that keeping the burden of proof on employers would mean that any company with statistical disparities within its workforce "could be haled into court and forced to engage in the expensive and time-consuming task of defending the 'business necessity' of the methods used to select the other members of his [*sic*] workforce" (652). White's hypothetical scenario caricatured the *Wards Cove* case as one in which greedy workers imposed costs on a benevolent employer by bringing a frivolous suit based only on incidental, irrelevant statistical patterns.[39] The justices' class bias and racialized constructions of the disputing parties were barely masked. This imaginary framing trivialized the evidenced case before the court in which the disparate impact claims based on statistical disparities were, from the beginning, combined with other well-documented factual claims, including disparate treatment claims growing out of rigid segregation of workplace facilities. It is worth underlining again that both trial courts and the Ninth Circuit appellate court found that many practices at the canneries were not facially neutral and thus were liable under the disparate treatment theory.

The vision that led the cannery workers to portray cannery conditions as unlawful discrimination was not simply based on a statistical pattern, we should remember, but on Gene Viernes's sophisticated historical analysis of the way the cannery industry had for most of the century preserved exploitative job segregation through a complicated set of industry-wide practices that determined what kinds of workers made themselves available for seasonal work (Chew 2012, 120–45). The problem for workers was not primarily that racist employers were rejecting skilled minority applicants but that the combination of industry-wide practices distorted the market, in particular by shaping the capacity and incentives for workers of color to develop relevant skills. Proving that any individual element of this long-evolving labor supply chain was motivated by overt discrimination and not any business necessity was nearly impossible given that any isolated element could be defended as a market-driven response to the remaining combination of factors (Nelson 1995). Hence Justice Blackmun's animated dissent in *Wards Cove*, protesting that the "majority's legal rulings essentially immunize these practices from attack" (at 662).

Justice White also had very little to say about what it would mean to shift the cost of proving violations onto workers in low-paying jobs. Tyree Scott identified this issue of burden shifting as fundamental. "If the burden of proof is on the workers, then you've in effect nullified the workers' ability to come into the courtrooms because the resources necessary are too great. And so, even when courts are sympathetic, you can't establish it because you don't have the resources to get to that point."[40] White's only comment on this issue was simply to assert that the new evidentiary standards were not unduly burdensome because "liberal civil discovery rules give plaintiffs broad access to employers' records in an effort to document their claims" (658). Such cavalier conjecture ignored not just a case record showing that imperfect

Fig. 23 Tyree Scott, 1990s. Courtesy American Friends Service Committee.

recordkeeping of highly discretionary decisions by employers, contractors, and the union created significant challenges for the cannery workers. It also dismissed the more general problem of high costs for low-wage blue-collar workers to hire attorneys to conduct discovery, in this case against an employer whose intransigence had already dragged out the case for fifteen years, in a classic class-based trench war of attrition (Galanter 1974).

At a more general level, we underline the form of jurispathic action at stake. For one thing, *Wards Cove* was "the most momentous and controversial" of several court rulings that produced a "civil rights massacre" during the late spring of 1989, as Robert Belton, NAACP litigator in the *Griggs* case, later wrote (Belton 2014, 282–90).[41] While *Wards Cove* "overturned almost eighteen years of judicial developments under the disparate impact theory," however, the ruling did not explicitly reject disparate impact or class action as inherited doctrines. Rather, the White majority reconstructed specific elements of the two doctrines in ways that privileged individualized standards, business prerogatives, and market myths over more expansive earlier judicial rulings regarding substantive civil wrongs and appropriate remedies. The court's legalistic maneuvers sustained general doctrinal traditions while quietly, indirectly sounding a "death knell" (Belton 2014, 282) to key substantive elements critical to progressive social movement rights mobilization for gender-based wage-equity advocates, African Americans, and other minority worker groups such as the ACWA.

Critical Responses: Anger Begets Reflection and Reaction

The Activists Respond: The Partisan Court Kills Minority Workers' Rights

Civil rights advocates (and many members of Congress) immediately saw through the majority justices' posturing and recognized the *Wards Cove* ruling as another significant Reagan-era neoliberal retreat that undermined emergent forms of collective rights politics challenging institutional racism and sexism in the workplace. Immediately after the court delivered its ruling, the LELO leadership called a press conference. Tyree Scott protested passionately the court's procedural tampering and substantive privileging of market rationality over liberal democratic principles and human rights. Scott recognized immediately the damage the case would do to efforts by workers to use Title VII as a weapon in struggles for workplace justice:

> The U.S. Supreme Court dealt a major blow to the struggle for human rights and democracy in the courts in this country when, by a 5 to 4 majority, they ruled against the workers and in favor of the employers in the fifteen-year-old *Wards Cove Packing Company v. Atonio* case. . . . Now the possibilities of most working people to go to court to prove discrimination suits are virtually nil. . . . In the case of class action lawsuits, it is extremely difficult, almost impossible, to gather specific information on each and every class member's individual situation to prove discrimination. In addition to the difficulty, it is extremely costly. Once again, [this is a] blow against democracy in the courts. . . . The Supreme Court's decision was a major defeat, but all of us who care about human rights in this country do not intend to let it rest there. (Scott 1989 [UWSC])

The cannery activists and their allies also understood the importance of the cases in the broader history of civil rights law. The case was, in Scott's words, the "death throes" of disparate impact as a political resource for minority and female workers' associations. And it was a historic setback for minority rights in the workplace. Years later, Nemesio Domingo recalled, "There have been two periods of construction and deconstruction of civil rights in our history. And *Wards Cove* was . . . clearly one of those watershed cases that clearly spells out the second deconstruction of civil rights in our history" (N. Domingo Jr. 2003). He added in another context, "As long as we see our struggle in the narrow confines of a civil rights framework, we will never have any permanent rights in this country" (quoted in C. Domingo 2001,46). In the long historical view, this critical perspective was hardly new. It recalls what labor activists and legal scholars have protested for decades about the evisceration of 1930s labor law and before that post–Civil War Reconstruction laws. Whenever workers have collectively mobilized to use labor law to expand their power, state violence protecting the discretionary freedom of capitalist employers under the cover of law has been the norm. The haves routinely, and effectively, strike back.

The Activists' Explanation: Exposing the Politics of Law

The activists involved in the case immediately linked the judicial shifts in doctrine that culminated in *Wards Cove* and related cases specifically to broader instrumental and ideological political struggles between minority workers and conservative, profit-driven business interests. Diane Narasaki, former executive director of LELO, noted, "When we first brought the case, we saw law as an ally. . . . But that changed with the appointment of a new set of conservative federal judges" (quoted in Zia 2000, 150). That same assessment was expressed by Tyree Scott in his press conference immediately after the ruling. Scott declared that the ruling "means that 'big business,' through the Reagan/Bush administrations' Supreme Court appointments, has reshaped the courts in support of management" (Scott 1989 [UWSC]).[42] Narasaki and Scott were not unique in pointing out that the US Supreme Court was hardly acting alone in its jurispathic retreat from the more expansive vision of civil rights law in earlier years. The justices and federal judges were players in a larger political campaign aiming to thwart civil rights and related struggles for substantive social justice politics in the workplace.

Several decades of scholarship have shown the activists' initial insights to be quite sound. We do not try to document the full scope of the surrounding political dynamics here, nor do we claim to prove causally that the justices in the majority were driven by broader political pressures. We instead focus on one part of that context to help explain that key symbolic weapon the Supreme Court majority deployed: the powerful counternarrative of "quotas." The invocation of "quotas" to contain workers' civil rights has a long, well-documented history in the twentieth-century United States. Sociolegal historian Anthony Chen (2006, 1238) has traced the invocation of the "Hitlerian rule of quotas" that "spell doom for the free market and meritocracy" back to Robert Moses and other opponents of New York's pioneering Fair Employment Laws in the 1940s and from there to a broader northern coalition of business leaders, conservative Republicans, and rural whites. In later decades, charges about the dangerous specter of quotas remained a staple of conservative challenges to fair employment laws that came from both southern Democrats and northern Republicans (Chen 2006).

The quotas counternarrative was a crucial weapon in the civil rights backlash that developed in the late 1970s and 1980s as multiple facets of long-developing opposition to civil rights advances coalesced into a formidable campaign. Most importantly, southern conservative whites began to realign with the Republican Party, creating the new Reagan coalition that linked a revitalized Christian evangelical movement with reenergized and newly ambitious big business interests connected through the US Chamber of Commerce and the Business Roundtable. The result was a powerful, albeit at times fractured, marriage of neoliberal free-market demands for less government regulation of business, socially conservative demands for more government intervention in private life, and backlash against the social changes that resulted from the civil rights revolution (Edsall and Edsall 1992; MacLean 2006). While it was at that time unpopular in the racially liberal era to oppose outright "civil rights" or "racial equality," opposition to quotas maintained broad appeal. Thus, complaints about quotas, real or imagined, became a powerful rallying cry connecting economic and social constituencies that wanted to contain advocacy for racial and gender justice. One sociological study of media reporting found that the specter of quotas had failed to neutralize claims of civil rights in the 1960s but "was much more effective in the late 1980s and 1990s, when quota rhetoric helped undercut affirmative action policies" (Stryker 2001, 13; see also Stryker, Scarpellino, and Holtzman 1999).[43]

The Reagan administration was both product and producer of the conservative countermobilization against civil rights. Administration leaders eagerly seized on the rhetoric of quotas to justify new efforts to roll back race and gender reforms in the workplace. Indeed, Reagan had made opposition to

EEOC initiatives in the Carter era a centerpiece of his electoral campaign. The presidential candidate argued that "equal opportunity should not be jeopardized by bureaucratic regulations and decisions which rely on quotas, ratios, and numerical requirements to exclude some individuals in favor of others, thereby rendering such regulations and decisions inherently discriminatory" (quoted in Devins 1993, 20). Not all of the Reagan administration's initiatives were successful. William Bradford Reynolds's attempt to restore racially exclusionary private colleges and urge a veto of the Voting Rights Act were too transparently exclusionary and thus backfired. By contrast, the more indirect, low-visibility bureaucratic maneuvering of Clarence Thomas at the EEOC seemed to be more effective. Instead of directly attacking civil rights, disparate impact, or the institutionalized racism narrative, he acted more quietly to refocus the agency's energies away from class action and disparate impact cases (which allegedly led to quotas) and into individual intentional discrimination lawsuits (Belz 1991, 184–91; Devins 1993). Charles Fried, who as solicitor general filed a brief in the *Wards Cove* case, also "was an enemy of disparate impact," Abe Arditi later told us.[44] Fried's own account confirms that claim. "I concentrated on what I cared about: taming *Griggs*, with its pressure toward quotas. . . . Our opportunity to tame *Griggs* came in *Wards Cove Packing Co. v. Atonio*" (Fried 1991, 119, 121).

More directly significant for the *judicial* evisceration of disparate impact, Reagan used new appointments to bring about a conservative shift in the federal courts. Indeed, Reagan appointed three new conservative justices (O'Connor, Scalia, and Kennedy) who anchored the five-judge majority that executed the *Wards Cove* ruling against the cannery workers. The broader animus against civil rights law that resonated throughout the domestic policy-making centers of the Reagan administration undoubtedly influenced judicial nominations and, over time, many more decisions. As Robert Belton (2014, 277) has put it, the Reagan administration's "assault on *Griggs*" began in the very early 1980s. LELO attorney Arditi later acknowledged that he had been aware of the change in judicial inclinations over the course of the *Wards Cove* litigation. "When we first started doing discrimination work it was much different from what it is today. . . . You could see a shift in the political winds as far as legal enforcement . . . in 1977. That's when I think the beginning of it was. That came with the election of Ronald Reagan. . . . And then, it really became different," he later told an interviewer. "I remember reading a headline in one of the Seattle papers. It must have been 1988. The headline was 'Supreme Court Backs Whites,' or something like that. . . . Conservative judges were worried about so-called quotas, going overboard in protecting the interest of minorities and women and what not" (quoted in Chew 2012, 57).

Again, quotas were not an important issue in the lower court proceedings in *Wards Cove*, and the word *quota* was never used by plaintiffs during oral arguments before the Supreme Court. Yet many of the amicus briefs filed in support of the employers made claims about the threat of quotas, including briefs from the Reagan administration, the Equal Employment Advisory Council, and the US Chamber of Commerce. As the *Wards Cove* plaintiffs saw it, "the quota issue was always a red herring, a rationalization for giving business what it wanted" (N. Domingo Jr. 2003). One of the LELO attorneys put it in even stronger terms: "There is a very deeply ingrained thing in this country about race and racism. . . . We see it in politics, in the Reagan/Bush era. . . . All those quota arguments. Those were . . . code words for race."[45] The cannery workers' characterization of law as, at any moment, a political contest between the haves and have nots once again was validated.

The 1991 Civil Rights Act: A Limited Legislative Override

The Supreme Court's 1989 rulings immediately provoked considerable alarm and political mobilization among both the local ACWA activists and national political and civil rights leaders. "As soon as the Supreme Court decision was handed down, Nemesio, Tyree, and I began strategizing about the legislation to reverse the decision and to restore workers' rights," recalled Diane Narasaki, who helped to shepherd the original cannery worker class action lawsuits (Zia 2000, 152). As the Seattle activists mobilized their allies to challenge the *Wards Cove* ruling, Democrats in Congress mounted their own effort. Senator Edward Kennedy and Representative Gus Hawkins introduced a bill for a Civil Rights Act of 1990, which sought to override the recent Supreme Court statutory decisions, including *Wards Cove*. Frank Atonio, the lead plaintiff in the Wards Cove lawsuit, testified in congressional hearings on behalf of new legislation. That bill passed both houses of Congress in 1990, but President Bush's veto prevented it from becoming law. The following year, after extensive negotiations over additional veto threats, the compromise Civil Rights Act of 1991 was successfully enacted. Today, that law is often characterized as a successful legislative override of the court (Barnes 2004; Eskridge 1991; Farhang 2010), including the ruling in *Wards Cove*. The reality is more complicated. Some provisions of the 1991 Civil Rights Act did restore civil rights law to where it had been before the Supreme Court's rulings of the late 1980s

(Selmi 2011; Spann 2010). Other sections took civil rights law in entirely new directions, including provisions enabling, for the first time, access to jury trials and punitive damages in Title VII cases.

The language targeting the *Wards Cove* ruling attracted considerable attention during the political maneuvering over the 1991 bill. The public conversation regarding those provisions was dominated, once again, by the quotas narrative. Indeed, President Bush singled out the language returning the burden of proof to employers in civil rights cases for making the proposal a "quota bill" that he would veto (Farhang 2010, 188; also: Devins 1993; Runkel 1994). Eventually, congressional leaders responded to Bush's threats with key compromises in the legislative language. The act dictated that nothing in its language should be construed to "require, encourage, or permit an employer to adopt hiring or promotion quotas on the basis of race, color, religion, sex or national origin, the use of quotas shall be deemed to be an unlawful employment practice." Republican representative Robert S. Walker claimed that President Bush "won a major victory in negotiations" by assuring that "there is absolutely no quota language in this bill." Democrats jeered. "Where did the quotas go? They swam upstream, as red herrings often do," declared Craig Washington, Democrat from Texas. Many observers attributed the Democrats' leverage in producing a final compromise bill to the prominent background events of Anita F. Hill's sexual allegations against Supreme Court nominee Clarence Thomas and the strong showing of former Ku Klux Klan member David Duke in the Louisiana primary for governor (*CQ Almanac* 1991).

The final version that Congress enacted did retain an important proviso shifting the burden of proof back to the employer in disparate impact cases, a fact that has led most commentators to conclude that the 1991 act overturned *Wards Cove* (Farhang 2010, 284n100). However, the gains made in the relatively clear burden of proof provisions were weakened by late changes in other associated stipulations. For one thing, the statute specified that a worker must demonstrate that each particular challenged employment practice caused a disparate impact, except unless the worker showed that elements of a company's decision-making process could not be separated for assessment. As a result, "a worker who challenged employment practices would have a tougher standard for pinpointing discriminatory practices" (*CQ Almanac* 1991). Equally important were changes in statutory provisions that defined "business necessity," changes that made it easier for employers to meet the burden of proof. In the original 1990 bill, the key guideline stated that the employer had to prove that a challenged business practice was "*essential* to effective job performance." That language expressed a higher legal standard than did the *Wards Cove* majority and aimed for a return to the *Griggs* standard. However, that robust language was changed during congressional deliberation in 1990 to the weaker standard of "bear(ing) a *significant relationship*" to business necessity. Before the law was finally enacted in 1991, Congress further amended the statutory language to the yet weaker standard of showing practices are "*consistent* with business necessity" (Devins 1993, 985–86). No less important, a political compromise over section 104 of the final act led to omitting any exact definition of business necessity itself, and thus it was left to increasingly conservative federal courts to construct meaning in light of rulings before *Wards Cove*, including those that narrowed *Griggs*.[46] The 1991 act also restricted the incentives for plaintiffs as well. It allowed compensatory and punitive damages for disparate treatment cases but not for disparate impact, leaving recovery under the latter only to already available equitable relief (Shoben 2004). The provision for punitive damages also made class certification more problematic, as entitlement to punitive damages tend to vary widely with each individual (Hart 2004).

Minority civil rights leaders and legal scholars were divided about the likely implications of the 1991 act for disparate impact litigation and in particular on the effect of the shifts in the specification of discriminatory practices and business necessity justifications (see, e.g., Runkel 1994). While many national civil rights groups celebrated passage of the law as a major step forward from judicial retrenchment, the ACWA activists and their allies in the Seattle community were much more skeptical. Tyree Scott told us that he saw the act as a "sellout," explaining that "what the civil rights leadership did is basically negotiate something that they saw was in their interests and saved face. But they didn't put back the most important thing. . . . I mean, yeah, the NAACP. That whole group in Washington that does the lobbying." He added an insight that seemed remarkably close to critical race theorist Derrick Bell's theory of interest convergence (Bell 1980). "When business needs them [civil rights lobby], they give them a voice, and when they don't need them, they shut them up."[47] At the least, it is difficult not to conclude that the compromise act rejected more than confirmed the substantively egalitarian narrative of the ACWA reformers in favor of legalistic proceduralism that protected business control.

A final, nearly invisible feature of the 1991 Civil Rights Act proved to be more directly devastating to efforts challenging conditions at the Wards Cove cannery. As the bill moved toward final passage, Senators Frank Murkowski and Ted Stevens of Alaska maneuvered to add a provision insulating the plaintiffs' case against the Wards Cove Company from any retroactive application of the new civil rights law. "Nothing in this Act shall apply to any disparate impact case for which a complaint was filed before March 1, 1975, and for which an initial decision was rendered after October 30, 1983." Murkowski and Stevens gained support from enough colleagues to make the "Wards Cove exemption" a condition for passage. The exemption was accidentally dropped from the text of the bill, but the Senate added it in a separate, last-minute amendment in a 73–22 roll-call vote (Hanson 1991). Senator Brock Adams, a Washington Democrat, denounced it as "an incredible piece of special interest litigation" (MacKenzie 1991). Other Democrats joined them in labeling the amendment "extortion," but a majority—including House Speaker Thomas S. Foley, from Washington State—were reconciled to preserving the larger act as a net advance for civil rights despite its extraordinary injustice to the original plaintiffs.

The surviving activists from ACWA did not submit quietly. They continued to press their case in court for another decade, to some degree against the counsel of LELO attorneys. They filed one final appeal of Judge Quackenbush's trial ruling to the Ninth Circuit, which was rejected in 2001 (275 F. 3d 797). Activists also channeled local outrage regarding the last-minute betrayal in the Senate into a broader political movement for civil rights reform. Forming "Justice for Wards Cove Cannery Workers," they mounted a national campaign to draw attention not just to the offending provision but also to the broader limits of the congressional complicity in the ongoing conservative evisceration of civil rights law. ACWA and LELO activists continued to use *Wards Cove* as a jurisgenerative vehicle for political mobilization. Nemesio Domingo Jr., Silme's surviving older brother, visited activist groups around the United States and routinely gave a talk titled the "Third Reconstruction" (2000) that focused on how recent changes in civil rights law betrayed the promise of civil rights legislation of the 1960s. Domingo and Garry Owens, a Seattle Black Panther leader who became involved in LELO, took the struggle of the Wards Cove workers as far as the United Nations Conference on Racism and Xenophobia in Durban, South Africa (C. Domingo 2013). The symbol on the cover of this book—a raised fist, recalling the Black Panthers, holding a fish—was created and displayed routinely in this campaign.

At the heart of their aspiration dwelled the desire to build law that facilitates subaltern workers' challenges to institutionalized racial and sexual inequality. "The only way we can have universal equality is if we recast the

Fig. 24 "Justice for Wards Cove" poster, 1994. University of Washington Libraries, Special Collections, UW 39790.

debate of civil rights in the framework of human rights," Domingo said, invoking the international standard embraced by two generations of Filipino labor activists. "The 1948 Universal Declaration of Human Rights does this. This is the standard that the U.S. needs to adopt! Then we will see justice for the Wards Cove workers" (quoted in C. Domingo 2001, 46). Memories of the collective mobilization against the canneries and bitterness over the outcome in Congress continue to inspire progressive visions of justice throughout the Seattle activist community. While the lawsuit finally ended in 2001, political activity around the *Wards Cove* case continued for many years. Seattle's US Representative Jim McDermott in subsequent years repeatedly pressed to repeal the exemption through a proposed "Justice for Wards Cove Workers Act," even though passage of that act would have been entirely symbolic (H.R. 4275 in the current 112th Congress). The legacy of Local 37—the murders of Silme and Gene, the dramatic wrongful death trial, the *Wards Cove* death throes—has been invoked endlessly in gatherings of social justice activists in the Puget Sound area well into the twenty-first century.

Conclusion: Historical Erasure and Racial Innocence

In retrospect, the animated reform movement seeking to reverse *Wards Cove* was far too little too late. It is now clear that the court's action was a watershed moment that appears highly emblematic in its dismissiveness about the historical reality of racialized class injustice at stake in the case. *Wards Cove* symbolized the period when official "good law" ended and the early Title VII cases that excited the cannery activists were overridden by forces that took official law in different directions (McCann 1994). Moreover, the political conditions of the 1960s racial liberalism that produced a bipartisan civil rights law rebuking, at least symbolically, racially segregated institutions gave way to the neoliberal "post-civil rights" context of "color-blind," race-neutral, process-focused law and proscriptions of affirmative action today (Bonilla-Silva 1997).

We thus restate our opening claim that the Supreme Court ruling in *Wards Cove* expressly represented the triumph of what James Baldwin (1963) famously labeled "racial innocence" and Charles W. Mills (2017) more recently portrayed as "racial ignorance." If that analysis seems harsh, we note that Justice White himself explicitly affirmed the presumption of white innocence. He protested that finding for the plaintiffs would result in employers being potentially liable "for the myriad of *innocent* causes that may lead to statistical imbalances in the composition of their workforces" (at 657).[48] Despite a well-documented history of racialized and racist workplace organization over the previous decades, the White majority simply willed itself into a posture of denying that white business interests might be liable for wrongful practices except in rare circumstances that required a very high, unrealistic standard of demonstrable evidence. White property owners prevailed by righteously drawing on whiteness as a basic property entitlement, as Cheryl Harris has insisted (1993). In short, employer rationality was the stipulated status quo, and racial injustice was assumed to be an aberration that must be proved by meeting unrealistic high bars of proof.

The dissenting justices pointed out clearly the willful historical denial and amnesia at stake. Justice Blackmun charged that the majority's reasoning "essentially immunize(s) . . . from attack" the range of long-established business practices that entrenched "racial stratification and segregation" (at 662). Justice Stevens protested that the majority was "turning a blind eye to the meaning and purposes of Title VII" (at 663). Blindness is another analogy that parallels the sensory failures of amnesia and innocence. And, perhaps most important was Blackmun's earlier noted rhetorical question about the majority's failure to "remember" the dark history of radical racial discrimination, segregation, and domination in America (at 662). The denial of history and of social facts we have documented in this book, the systematic forgetting of those elements undeniably sewn into social relations all around the Filipino workers and general American experience of racialized laboring underclass, is the essence of willful white fantasy and racial innocence. Such a denial is at the heart of the contemporary inherited ethos of neoliberal imaginary about the neutral workings of markets and the rationality of hierarchical propertied power. As Nemesio Domingo (2003) summarized with his claims about "the second civil rights deconstruction," *Wards Cove* was an early, powerful, and consequential sign and signifier constitutive of this destructive, self-serving, but all too familiar elite expression of official American law in the racial capitalist order.

Epilogue: The Continuing Legacy of Civil Rights Retrenchment

The *Wards Cove* case and related rulings symbolized the significant neoliberal turn against expansive civil rights jurisprudence, one that shaped how Left activists and their lawyers viewed the dramatically diminished possibilities for legal mobilization following the 1991 act. For example, we have written elsewhere that judicial rulings like *Wards Cove* symbolically "killed" the coalitions led by unions and feminist organizations mobilizing law to advance gender-based wage equity. "Whatever opportunities the federal courts opened for wage-equity litigation in the 1970s and early 1980s were thus largely closed by the end of the 1980s" (McCann 1994, 41). In the early 1990s, it was already clear that wage-equity lawyers, much like ACWA activists, were very disheartened by the actions of the courts and Congress and saw little future for legal mobilization challenging systemic, institutionalized workplace bias. The summary judgment by movement lawyers to whom we talked was that the *Wards Cove* "decision by the Court virtually eliminated disparate impact theory as a resource for pay equity claims" (McCann 1994, 40). Indeed, by 1991, activists were seriously exploring alternative political and legal pathways to social justice in the wake of the "watered down statute" and rightward-veering judges. Most progressives believed, as did LELO attorney Arditi, whom we interviewed in 2015, that the problem "was not the 1991 Civil Rights Act itself, but the Supreme Court justices who were hostile to disparate impact" and continued to rule in the spirit of the *Wards Cove* majority.[49]

Subsequent studies by leading sociolegal scholars have demonstrated that these early perceptions of radically reduced legal resources for private enforcement of civil rights were, if anything, insufficiently skeptical. The rigorous empirical study by Berrey, Nelson, and Nielsen (2017, 41) demonstrates that workplace discrimination filings in the United States increased during the 1990s to a high point in 1998 and then dropped significantly, as hopes about the 1991 act yielded to disappointing experiences and outcomes for plaintiffs. While annual rates of ten thousand to twenty thousand filings per year may seem significant, the proportions of parties claiming rights relative to those who experienced discrimination are telling. The landmark study estimates that only about 1 percent of those aggrieved by discrimination complained to the EEOC and 0.13 percent (thirteen in one thousand) sued (49). Plaintiffs "won" at trial in only 2 percent of those disputes, although around half settled early (61–62). Interviews with worker claimants documented the frustrations of delay, cost, and reprisal experienced by claimants.

More important for our analysis in this book are the findings about the *character* and substantive terms of employment discrimination litigation. Berrey, Nelson, and Nielsen found that 98 percent of all lawsuits involved claims of disparate treatment, while 4 percent were disparate impact claims; only 1 percent were certified as class actions. In short, the overwhelming pattern of workplace civil rights litigation after 1991 involved individual plaintiffs claiming intentional discrimination against powerful, well-resourced, repeat-player organizational defendants. These individualized actions were not a result of free choices by workers but rather reflected the official gutting of legal doctrine and processes for challenging what social science has demonstrated is widespread, systemic, institutionalized bias in workplace organization. "The processes by which the ascriptive hierarchies that the law is intended to disrupt (have been) reified and rearticulated through law in the workplace and in court," the authors concluded (Berrey, Nelson, and Nielsen 2017, 11; see also Nielsen, Nelson, and Lancaster 2010). Civil rights law has continued to "reinscribe" the radically inegalitarian logics of racial and patriarchal capitalism.

The theme of "retrenchment" and "counterrevolution" in civil rights law since the 1980s has been echoed repeatedly in much contemporary empirical scholarship on the topic. Many experts identify federal courts, and especially the US Supreme Court, as the primary agents of this assault. For one thing, the courts have continued to defer to employer defenses of unequal outcomes as responses to market principles of supply and demand despite the fact that "the market necessity argument" employed by courts "is empirically wrong" (Nelson 1995, 67; Nelson and Bridges 1999; Rabin-Margoliath 2010). Moreover, the provision for punitive damages in the 1991 Civil Rights Act available for disparate treatment claims unwittingly made class action certification by judges much more difficult, as punitive damages tend to vary among individuals (Berrey, Nelson, and Nielsen 2017, 14). At the same time, punitive damages were disallowed in disparate impact cases, greatly undercutting the economic incentives for potential plaintiffs and their attorneys. Other scholars underline how courts played a key role in civil rights retrenchment by narrowing standing for class certification and other procedural rules critical for plaintiff access to private enforcement action, especially by collective action of workers (Burbank and Farhang 2017a, 2017b; Staszak 2017; Selmi 2011; Shoben 2004, 598–99).

Even those scholars who attribute considerable significance to the role of the courts in rights retrenchment, however, recognize other players—Congress, executive agencies, big business, interest groups—for their important contributions (Staszak 2017). Conservative "repeat player" public interest law firms, corporate defense law firms, and business-friendly think tanks grew into powerful forces during the decades after the 1970s (Hollis-Brusky 2015; Southworth 2008; Teles 2008). Burbank and Farhang (2017) contend that retrenchment on civil rights became deeply partisan and conservative during the Reagan years, when efforts to use legislation, rule making, and executive administration to gut civil rights escalated in tandem with rightward-leaning federal judicial decisions. No less important were the ways that business organizations found to both co-opt compliance processes and reshape in turn judicial judgments about liability for discrimination.

Lauren Edelman's important book *Working Law* (2016) demonstrates these dynamics in expansive terms. On the one hand, employers "endogenized" civil rights by creating internal institutional mechanisms for addressing discrimination and "managerialized" the principles of compliance in the process, generating symbolic procedural fidelity to law while often short-circuiting substantive justice. On the other hand, employers successfully used these internal protocols as defenses against workers' claims of discrimination in court, managing to reduce liability while in turn reshaping legal obligations and expectations that the courts enforced. This analysis fits well with Anna-Maria Marshall's (2016) compelling empirical study regarding failures of legal rights mechanisms to challenge workplace sexual harassment. In sum, the political shift signaled by *Wards Cove* was a synecdoche for the larger forces narrowing workplace civil rights and, to recall again Justice Blackmun's term, "immunizing" employers against legal challenge over several decades beginning in the 1980s. The *Wards Cove* case was just one episode in this larger history of retrenchment, to be sure. But it was symbolically resonant in the most robust sense.

While we find the abundant empirical analysis of larger trends in employment rights disputing to be fully convincing, we note several interrelated omissions in the recent scholarship relevant to this analysis. For one thing, none of these studies provides much attention to the roles of labor unions (or their absence) in workplace civil rights politics. On the one hand, as our own studies have documented, many union locals and allied worker associations effectively mobilized civil rights law for minority and female workers in the decade and a half following the *Griggs* decision (McCann 1994; Lichtenstein 2002). The evisceration of civil rights legal resources by resurgent neoliberal probusiness forces and the decline of unions as political forces went hand in hand during the 1980s. On the other hand, increasingly hostile official law contributed greatly to that decline of union density and political power within workplaces and in the larger culture. As Paul Frymer (2008) has demonstrated, civil rights law itself undermined unions in a variety of ways, at once providing workers legal recourse for addressing grievances outside of unions and facilitating challenges to unions for complicity in discrimination. Victims of discrimination thus were provided incentives to challenge, directly and indirectly, those representative political organizations that could be most vital to empowerment, a development that Tyree Scott recognized was exploited by the Nixon and subsequent administrations. Unions that failed to mobilize female and minority workers share much of the blame, of course, as Tyree Scott underlined. And a host of other legislative and judicial actions have continued to cripple union organizational capacity to empower workers and protect workers' rights (Getman 2016; Lee 2014; Rosenfeld 2014; Hogler 2015). Overall, as Sophia Lee has demonstrated, the prospects for liberal democratic rights-based workplace law, whether constitutional or statutory, "all but vanished," leaving American workers stranded without basic substantive rights and organizational resources to challenge employer discrimination at work, while the conservative, antiunion "right to work" movement has been ascendant. Indeed, those workers most protected by legal principles at work today are "reverse discrimination litigants, workers unhappy with their union, and employers fighting unionization" (Lee 2014, 257–58).

More broadly, most studies demonstrate the important institutional constraints and implications of civil rights containment for racial minorities and women as demographic categories of workers in recent decades. But they offer little attention to *continued* group struggles by marginalized people (in and beyond unions) for more substantively egalitarian versions of civil rights and social justice during the same period. The persistent and episodic collective actions by workers and their allies almost disappear in most sociolegal accounts. This matters, as one theme of our long narrative historical account has been that egalitarian, even radical aspirational movements are not easily extinguished by political forces that undercut "good" law, either recently or in the distant past. Law in racial capitalist regimes from the start has privileged propertied interests over workers, whites over nonwhites, men over women, and other terms of intersectional hierarchy. But legal principles and resources nevertheless from the start have routinely been mobilized, and often reconstructed, by groups and movements creatively seeking to advance social justice. Of course, the ACWA activists in retrospective may seem like naive, marginal idealists to some academic observers. But their aspirations were grounded in a century of relentless rights-based struggles, and their achievements in mobilizing legal resources were as important as were their tragic setbacks. That political legacy, we noted earlier, lives on as a widely recognized inspirational story for many ongoing campaigns by low-wage workers on the West Coast of the United States and around the world (Polletta 2006).[50]

CONCLUSION

Theorizing Law and Legal Mobilization in Racial Capitalist Empire

> Different systems of justice are a centuries-old American tradition, indeed a foundational one. . . . We have built a colony in a nation. . . . In the Nation, there is law; in the Colony, there is only a concern with order. . . . In the Nation, you have rights; in the Colony, you have commands. In the Nation, you are innocent until proven guilty; in the Colony, you are born guilty.—CHRIS HAYES (2017, 24, 37–38, 73)

> The emancipation of man is the emancipation of labor and the emancipation of labor is the freeing of that basic majority of workers who are yellow, brown and black.—DU BOIS ([1935] 1998, 15–16)

> [We] need to embrace . . . legal pluralism and alternative conceptualizations of what constitutes law, justice and rights.—EVE DARIAN-SMITH (2013, 6)

We hope that readers of the previous pages find value in our historical rendering, its significance for understanding migrant workers' struggles for rights and justice in the United States, and specifically our interpretation of how the systematic racial innocence displayed by the Supreme Court's *Wards Cove* ruling eviscerated the transformative potential of workplace civil rights. But what of the broader generalizable significance of our narrative for analyzing law and/as power? What has this project contributed to critical inquiry about law, legal mobilization, and the prospects for egalitarian social change, especially by subaltern groups? What might a "third civil rights reconstruction" look like, and is it a promising aspiration? This final chapter reflects on the implications of the historical narrative for theorizing about law, hegemony, and contestation over legal entitlements generally and especially for those struggles by members of the laboring classes amid the long-developing racial capitalist order in America and beyond. We direct this chapter primarily to sociolegal scholars interested in these broad questions of theoretical analysis and empirical research design.

As we noted at the beginning, the ideas we outline here are not simply implications of or post hoc conclusions from an act of neutral history telling. Rather, most of the core questions, working assumptions, and analytical frameworks addressed in this chapter engaged us from the start of our historical inquiry. While our chapters of narrative history only lightly and episodically addressed analytical theory in explicit terms, our choices about how to present the narrative—what to include and exclude, how to weigh the significance of various data and insights, and how to comment on the story—all were formed by theory-building activities that preceded and were revised continuously as the research and writing commenced. In short, empirical research, storytelling, and theory building have been inextricably related, dialectical dimensions of the intellectual project.

We also acknowledge that our aim here is not to review, assess, or celebrate at length the tradition of sociolegal analysis regarding legal mobilization on which we rely. We cite only a small portion of the rich work by other scholars of legal mobilization, and we apologize for the exclusions; many important scholarly works are ignored or allotted limited attention in our discussion. Most of what follows instead aims to connect often ignored critical theoretical and historical scholarship to the legal mobilization legacy.[1] Our goal is less to rummage through the inherited archive of legal mobilization analysis than to challenge and reconstruct it by introducing ideas and focusing on themes that to date typically have not received the systematic attention that we believe they deserve. Like our historical Filipino cannery worker subjects, we invoke traditions of law—and especially sociolegal analysis—to disrupt, challenge, and change them. Our interventions in particular focus on more deeply theorizing law's complicity in sustaining hegemonic hierarchies, especially those of capitalist class relations and racial privilege, but also gender, sexuality, and other features of modern imperial order. If we are to analyze the possibilities, character, and implications of legal contestation, we need to recognize in theoretically expansive terms the ways that law constitutes the multifaceted architecture of power in modern society.

Legal Mobilization Theory

Legal mobilization scholarship emerged as an alternative to conventional, positivistic accounts of how, why, and to what effect individuals and groups claim legal entitlements and, in varying degrees, make demands on official legal actors and institutions. Those mainstream analyses typically assess litigation processes by confining them to demonstrable linear causal effects or "impacts" of judicial decisions on social and state actors (e.g., Rosenberg 1991; see also McCann 1994). Legal mobilization scholars instead have offered a sociolegal framework that conceptualizes law more complexly as indeterminate, pluralistic, contested cultural norms embedded in the organizational fabric of society and the state alike. In this approach, the language, logics, and threats of law that permeate people's understandings of social life and shared obligations are taken seriously, making legal practice and its effects inseparable from the symbols and rituals of legitimation that accompany legal pronouncements (Scheingold 1974; see also Brigham 1996). Contestation over legal entitlements, including formal litigation, thus routinely takes place in a variety of institutional settings that may or may not interact directly with courts.[2]

Legal mobilization scholars early on fashioned an analytical framework that focuses research on law as a practical discourse that structures social relations and shapes the aggregate knowledge, understandings, aspirations, and strategic gambits—often referred to as legal or rights "consciousness"—of legal "users" or rights claimants (Albiston 2010; Burstein 1991; Epp 1998; Lovell 2012; A.-M. Marshall 2016; McCann 1994; Nader 1984–1985; Paris 2010; Scheingold 1974). Analysts seek to balance how law constructs subjects and how subjects in turn struggle as constrained agents to deploy, reproduce, and sometimes reconstruct law in the process.[3] In this constructivist approach, formal pronouncements by authoritative decision makers such as judges matter as much through their indirect, "radiating" effects on individuals' routine identities, perceptions of legitimate entitlement, actionable risks, opportunities, possibilities, and strategic resources as through enforceable commands (Galanter 1983).[4] Much of such scholarship focuses on legal mobilization practices among individual subjects (Merry 1990), but a great deal of study, like this book, focuses on group or social movement struggles aiming for broader policy changes or structural transformations in institutionalized power relations. We became interested in the history of Filipino labor activists largely because of their palpable traditions of rights-based political and legal struggle with and against US labor, immigration, criminal, free speech, and antidiscrimination law over many decades. At many points, the Filipino-led cannery workers' mobilization of legal rights discourse and institutional strategies provided a revealing window into the changing currents of the larger American legal system and rights regime.

We have been inspired in this regard by taking seriously the ideas of legal scholar Robert Cover (1983), who rarely is invoked by legal mobilization analysts (Lovell, McCann, and Taylor 2015). Cover was highly interested in how legal meaning in any complex society is necessarily pluralistic, as people in different communities develop and enact competing visions of law and commitments to different precepts of legal governance. To understand how law is created and made meaningful, Cover (1983, 19) urged scholars to look beyond state institutions, and especially beyond judges, to "the multiplicity of the legal meanings created out of the exiled narratives and the divergent social bases for their use." Cover paralleled legal mobilization scholars in recognizing the unsettled cultural authority of official law and insisting on the value of bottom-up study of "the law evolved by social movements and communities" (Cover 1983, 68). He introduced the term *nomos* to describe the normative worlds of principles and commitments that shape and express group life in society. He coined the term *jurisgenesis* to describe the process by which various communities develop and express distinctive narratives of law out of their underlying nomos. Like most legal mobilization analysts in the constructivist tradition, Cover exhorted legal scholars to take these many rival community nomoi and their narratives as seriously as official law.

We thus adapted some of Cover's key concepts for our study of Filipino American labor activists and their aspirational constructions of a radical democratic nomos, although we also have expanded beyond his own applications in some fundamental ways. It is relevant in this regard to underline that while the subjects in our empirical study routinely mobilized law as a resource for increased security, empowerment, or justice, they were not elites by almost any measure. The first generation of migrant workers came to the US mainland in search of advanced education and jobs, but they were not recognized as citizens, and most remained poor, exploited, conscripted proletarians who were racially persecuted by official state legal institutions. The second generation of cannery workers were officially regarded as rights-bearing citizens and generally better assimilated, better off, and better educated than those in the first generation, but they were mostly working class or lower middle class and still subject to racial stereotypes, low status, wage labor exploitation, and political persecution in white-dominated capitalist society. In many ways, they were typical second-generation Asian immigrants pursuing the American dream, although their version of the dream was far more contentiously egalitarian, democratic, and socialist—in short, transformative—than for many around them. They were a group of extraordinary political activists animated by a distinct aspirational nomos, but they also were ordinary people whose radical politics to a large extent grew out of routine disputes and "freedom dreaming" (Kelley 2002) in many spaces of their everyday lives.

Expanding the Temporal and Spatial Scope of Jurisgenetic Praxis

While we share Cover's interest in exploring the normative content of alternative legal narratives, we are social scientists committed to addressing how, when, and to what effect individuals or groups mobilized those legal narratives for strategic action to defend or advance their radical nomos beyond courtroom battles. The remainder of this concluding, theoretical chapter aims to push attention to *social context* and *legal subject formation* further through engagement with critical social theory.

Most important, we follow classical legal mobilization scholarship in examining rights claiming and contestation as political practices *within* society as well as the state or suprastate institutions of governance. As noted previously, struggles over rights and justice may or may not include formal claims in court, much less proceed to trial and judgment, and, even less common, appellate court judgment; political advocacy often focuses as well, or instead, on other institutional sectors of the state and directly on adversaries, supporters, and broader publics in society (Scheingold 1974; Zemans 1983). Many legal mobilization scholars have worked to show how law-related movement activity fits into broader political struggles, including various forms of organizing for strategic rights advocacy by groups and movements in diverse forums of social interaction and state authority largely outside of courts (McCann 1994; see also Lovell 2012). Such activity includes both conventional and nonconventional extrainstitutional forms of "contentious politics" (Tilly and Tarrow 2006). Indeed, our study of cannery workers examined a history of contestation over law in many different social spaces—in workplaces, neighborhoods, community centers, and local, national, and international media—as well as, or along with, official adjudicatory and regulatory forums.

The focus on social context has led most legal mobilization scholars to accord special attention to questions of differential power. One focus typically has been the unequally allocated *organizational resources* that shape the terms of *instrumental* legal disputing processes. This includes financial resources, organizational clout, political alliances, legal counsel, and other features of "support networks" (Epp 1998) that affect the instrumental power of disputing parties. Another topic of attention is often categorized by macrohistorical dimensions of changing "political opportunity structures." This refers to exogenous institutional factors or incentives that limit or empower groups in actual or potential political contests. Doug McAdam has outlined four components of such contextual factors especially important to social movements: the relative openness or closure of the political system, the stability or instability of elite alignments, the presence or absence of elite allies, and the state's capacity or propensity for repression (McAdam 1996). Large-scale historical events such as war, economic crisis, global realignments among regimes, and fundamental discursive shifts in resonant ideas (Ferree 2003) can figure prominently in shaping political context as well. We also underline that opportunity structures are not purely objective phenomena but, rather, vary with the experience-based subjective perceptions of social actors (McCann 1994).

At the same time, our study of Filipino American labor activists required us to expand the scope of identified disputing activity subjected to sociolegal empirical analysis. Most legal mobilization studies are focused on discrete "episodes" involving limited players in limited geographic spaces and limited time periods on a limited number of issues (Adam 2017). These boundaries follow the much-respected logic of social science "case studies" (Ragin and Becker 1992). To some extent, our research also has focused on a limited group of actors, most associated with a very small labor union. But the empirical design of our study diverges in scope from most others in two fundamental ways.

The first elaboration of traditional legal mobilization theory attention to context has involved the *temporal* scope of empirical study. Our project has aimed to demonstrate that scholarly inquiries can benefit from looking backward in time to appreciate how communal nomoi and narratives develop over many years and across generations. Just as Engel and Munger (2003) took seriously the lifelong development of legal consciousness for many *individuals* with disabilities, so do we read Cover's analysis to invite investigations into the full genealogy of social *group* experience, frames of reference, aspirational visions, and vocabularies of motive (C. Wright Mills 1940), what we have labeled "oppositional collective legal (or rights) consciousness." Hence our effort in preceding pages to develop a "long history" entailing many, many episodes of Filipino worker struggles, tracing over nearly one hundred years the engagements of Filipinos with US law, first as local denizens subjected to colonial rule and then as multigenerational migrants to the mainland United States, culminating in the late-century civil murder trial of two activists and the *Wards Cove* struggle over civil rights. This chronicle aimed to make sense of how the activist workers developed the essential elements of their resistant subaltern subjectivity through a long history of arduous engagement on and beyond legal terrain. In short, we endeavored to identify how the radical nomos of cannery workers was forged through several generations of ongoing collective sociolegal praxis. Such an extended historical orientation also enabled us to trace the complex array of extralegal—ethnic, communal, religious, literary, ideological—ideas and norms that mixed with and reconstituted uniquely legal aspirations for substantive rights and social justice (Polletta 2000).

Our study of group nomos also has featured a second novel element: an expanded spatial scope of contestation over legal visions and ideas. The historical narrative in previous pages pushed well beyond the traditional geographic struggles of a domestic social movement or subnational community challenging dominant groups and the state. The range of developing contestation that we highlight has included transnational and transpacific circuits involving most prominently dominant power structures in the Philippines, the US territory and then state of Alaska, and much of the mainland US metropole. The campaigns by Filipino workers began in the homeland islands against two successive colonial powers but were waged in ever expanding geographic sites and eventually extended challenges broadly to American imperialism around the globe. Within the metropole, a defiant subaltern nomos developed primarily in West Coast sites of resource extraction where migrant workers traveled for seasonal work and some settled as home. We focused in particular on the workers who resided in Washington State, but we show that there were widespread flows of ideas and aspirations among the workers, both settled and migratory, and their allies up and down the coast as well as across the Pacific in the Philippine island homeland. As such, many of the legal struggles of the migrant workers, including the civil rights claims in *Wards*

Cove, addressed interrelated local, national, and transnational dimensions of political and economic power. In short, our multisited study has aimed both to compare different rights episodes and to underline the complex interconnections among diverse institutions, legal systems, and actors in globalizing processes (see Falzon 2016; Go 2003; Merry 2000).

Expanding the temporal and spatial scope makes clear the core themes of our overall analytical narrative in this book. In particular, our story illustrates the many ways and degrees to which law is "all over" (Sarat 1990)—a pervasive, powerful web of conventions that constitute the everyday experiences, practices, relationships, struggles, and aspirations of working people, including those excluded from full rights-bearing status, in multiple spaces of ordinary life. In response, Filipino workers expressed and enacted a distinct, deeply democratic, socialist, antiracist, and anti-imperial third world nomos, although one still contained by the hegemonic American legal tropes that they worked to reconstruct into transformative resources. This seems to be true for both the most militant activists and the union's radical lawyers, although the latter displayed greater degrees of specialized technical knowledge and professionally conditioned constraints. By the 1950s, the chaotic, long-developing union culture was thoroughly constructed, delimited but hardly duped, for better or worse, by and against law (E. P. Thompson 1975). That oppositional legal consciousness flagged until the 1970s, when the experienced context changed and radical rights politics was rejuvenated.

Bringing the Coercive State Back In

Our study has aimed further to overcome two related limitations or biases of the traditional legal mobilization approach. First, the commitment to decentering official law and focusing on rights claimants *in* society, which we continue, sometimes draws attention away from the active, undeniably imperious workings of state institutions. Many legal mobilization studies emphasize courts as the primary entry point into the state, thus underlining the reactive, adjudicatory, semineutral character of the state generally. The emphasis on political and legal "opportunity structures" in vulnerable or volatile state contexts underlines this emphasis on the state as passive, even impartial reactors to social pressure. Second, adherents to the legal mobilization approach often express a relatively optimistic or benign faith in the responsiveness of judicial institutions and the commitments of judges to citizens' claims for novel rights and legal justice. This book provides reason to question both tendencies (see also Brisbin 2002; Lovell and McCann 2005).

On the first issue, we are committed to "bringing the state back in" (Evans, Rueschemeyer, and Skocpol 1985) to serious study of the contexts in which legal mobilization transpires. Our account highlights how legal officials in various sectors of the state—including courts—routinely developed and enacted substantively consequential policy and political agendas. In our empirical study, for example, we highlighted how willful actions of state officials enforced the exploitative conditions experienced by Filipino workers, from elite decisions about repressive colonial policies imposed on the Philippines to a host of decisions about state positioning toward the legal status of Filipino colonial nationals, the brutal conditions of their work, and rejection of their defiant claims for citizen status and social justice. Our attention to repressive state force has given us reason to draw on another of Robert Cover's key arguments—about the inherent and endemic *violence* of official law. Cover emphasized the role of judicial authorities in selecting from among competing normative visions those claims that would prevail in official law and be enforced by state coercion. In his account, the state's "imperfect monopoly over the domain of violence" maintains judicial authority when judges seek to enforce established norms and narratives against the rival visions that inevitably develop among other communities (Cover 1983, 52). The primary work of judges is not embracing novel legal claims or declaring the best version of law, Cover argued, but rather the cold, bureaucratic role of sustaining effective state control and social order, of protecting inherited privilege against challenge (Cover 1983, 17; see also Shapiro 1986).

To do that, judges routinely deal death sentences to alternative visions of communal relations and justice that bubble up from below to challenge legal tradition. "Judges are people of violence. Because of the violence they command, judges characteristically do not create law, but kill it. Theirs is the *jurispathic* office. Confronting the luxuriant growth of a hundred legal traditions, they assert that this one is law and destroy or try to destroy the rest" (Cover 1983, 53). Cover distinguished, importantly, between two types of legal violence: the symbolic or *epistemic* violence that maims communally generated visions and meanings of rights or justice that challenge official law; and the lethal *material* violence, both threatened and deployed, that courts authorize state (and social) actors to use in enforcing official legal constructions against those who advocate alternative norms and ideas. Preceding pages have both documented those manifold dimensions of jurispathic violence and labored to recover the aspirations for justice that official law has attempted to erase, often at a cost of movement setbacks and great physical harm. Our study illustrates how the reliance on coercion to kill off rival nomoi is routine practice for most state actors, including the courts (Lovell 2012). A sober assessment, we have argued elsewhere, must conclude that US federal courts have been at best a moderately positive force for an inclusionary, democratic society (Lovell and McCann 2005). For example, we underlined that the majority Supreme Court ruling in the 1989 *Wards Cove* case was part of a proactive plan coordinated among politicians, executive appointees, and business elites trumpeting neoliberal designs to reign in various types of affirmative action seeking to remedy at least modestly the long history of racial and gender inequality and even to authorize a return to greater employer violent control over workers to expand profits.

Our historical chronicle illustrated further that cannery worker activists experienced law not just as legal mobilizers in overt disputes but as legal subjects who were aggressively regulated, hunted, hounded, imprisoned, deported, physically assaulted, and even killed, either directly or indirectly, by legal officials. Carlos Bulosan's image of first-generation Filipino migrants who were routinely, actively persecuted and prosecuted as presumptive criminals captures this point. In short, while the minority worker activists at times mobilized law in an effort to defend themselves and win justice, more often they were the stigmatized targets of state officials and social groups who used legally authorized violence to discipline, control, punish, and even terrorize the workers. The migrant laborers at times went looking for law's justice, but more often they were reacting to law's harsh, punitive, violent justice that was aggressively pursuing them. Legal mobilization by subaltern subjects in this sense is more often defensive or aversive rather than affirmative and reform oriented (Francis 2014).

In our story, state actors of all types—immigration officials, FBI, CIA, local police, and legislators as much as judges—authorized or exercised the violence that Cover identifies with the state, if in varying ways and for varying ends. Again, the long temporal history and expanded spatial context of our study helps to evidence the pervasiveness of official legal violence. Moreover, the focus on state monopoly of violence should not occlude that state actors often authorize or permit unofficial social actors to use violence to maintain social control (Henderson 1991). National officials often defer to state officials, and both defer to or collaborate with social organizations to use violence to enforce hierarchical social order. The long history of the American national policy authorizing and supporting white settlers to secure, or police, their land holdings with firearms and other instruments of violence is a classic example of this point (Frymer 2017). The willful noninterference of national legal officials and the complicity of state officials toward white mob violence and lynching, to which Filipinos as well as African Americans were subjected, is another classic example (Francis 2014; Kato 2012). And workplace organization is, ultimately, a site of imposed, often authoritarian discipline and brutal violence eschewing respect for basic rights and the welfare of employees promised, if rarely realized, in the "public" or political sphere (Orren 1991; Maltby 2010). In fact, we argued earlier that it was the more developed institutional capacities and rules of the administrative state in the American western regions that best explains why Filipinos engaged with law more than did earlier waves of Asian migrant workers. Following World War I, a more developed state relied on legalized agents to implement social control, and the workers used law in turn to challenge or moderate that force and even to expand group power.

Furthermore, a fundamental tenet of our approach is that dominant social groups and corporate organizations disproportionately steer the ongoing processes of legal contestation. As a result, official law reflects to a large degree the ideas, identities, imagination, and interests of the most powerful groups. Marc Galanter's (1974) general theory about why and how the "haves" routinely prevail over the "have nots" in civil disputing is especially relevant in this regard. In short, powerful organized actors not only control disproportionate financial and legal resources (lawyers) that advantage them instrumentally in mobilizing law but their representatives also are "repeat players" who strategically negotiate in specific disputes for long-run influence, over time shaping the rules, norms, and categories of official law defining entitlements and procedures for disputing generally. This systematic imbalance of aggregated hierarchical social power is manifest in legislative and administrative as well as judicial arenas of the state, not to mention within corporate economic and social organizations. Lauren Edelman's important scholarship on how business corporations and other large institutions create bureaucracies staffed by specialized technocrats enacting symbolic legal compliance and evading substantive enforcement of civil rights is a classic example of the larger point (Edelman 2016). Subaltern groups thus must endure and fight, defensively or offensively, on institutional terrain historically shaped in large part by dominant groups. In sum, we expand Cover's conception of jurispathic legal practices to include a broad array of actors, institutions, and sites in both the state and society. Our narrative has documented at length how cannery worker activists over two generations experienced the highly unequal structural bias of law's violent power in ways that clearly echo Galanter's understanding.

One implication is that our approach is deeply wary toward the romantic portrayals of lawyers, courts, judges, litigation, and even legal mobilization that are common among legal scholars and social scientists inspired by the civil rights revolution (Epp 1998; see also Rosenberg 1991; Scheingold 1974). Our vision of legal mobilization has never been grounded in such optimism. We recognize and value law as a site of contestation (E. P. Thompson 1975), and we appreciate lawyers and even judges who sometimes challenge various manifestations of legally authorized exploitation and injustice. But that appreciation makes us no less wary about the specific institutions or principles of law that have been shaped disproportionately by the most powerful groups in society. Indeed, we underline the complicity of law's work in sustaining structural inequality. We thus draw on the insights of critical legal theory, critical race theory, and postcolonial legal theory to complete contextual analysis of law and/as power.

At the same time, we depart from Cover's court-centered focus on official state law. Our legal mobilization approach instead grants greater attention to the important extrajudicial dimensions of official state law as well as to the broader context of social forces that constrain legal contestation. In particular, Cover's account of judges as jurispathic actors links them too simplistically to the policy agendas and interests of a unified bureaucratic state machine in the United States (see Post 2005). After all, modern constitutional states tend to be fragmented, poorly coordinated, internally divided, and unsteady over time (Migdal 2001). We thus direct attention to the complex, variable ways that American courts negotiate partisan and other divisions among state elites over how to advance those goals. Political scientists have developed a variety of analytical approaches for identifying and explaining the ways that judges at once influence and are influenced by other actors within an institutionally fragmented state (see Graber 1993, Clayton and Gillman 1999; Lovell 2003; Crowe 2012; Keck 2009). Our historical study clearly illustrated that judges and other political actors are at once important players in hegemonic policy processes and yet often significantly diverge on policy at various times, including about large issues such as empire building, constructions of race, and regulation of capitalism.

The Legal Constitution of Racial Capitalism

Capitalism, Inequality, and the Insubstantiality of Legal Equality

We have selectively invoked sociolegal scholarship to highlight *both* the institutionalized violence of state law and the constitutive power of legal narratives demonstrated by our thickly contextualized historical study. We turn now to analyzing that larger context more specifically in terms of "racial capitalism" (Dawson and Francis 2016; Fraser 2016; Kelley 2017; Melamed 2011; Robinson 1983) and its fundamental relationship to the workings of American law in historical perspective.

We are hardly unique in underlining the significance and character of capitalist forms of socioeconomic organization for understanding legal institutions, conventions, and practices. The framers of the American Constitution, we noted earlier, made quite clear that the "first object" of the new legal order was the "protection of the different and unequal faculties for acquiring property" (Madison [1787] 1961, 79; see also Nedelsky 1990). Private property was central to the varied visions of promise in America. "Property must be secured . . . or liberty cannot exist," insisted John Adams (2004, 386–87, 639). Indeed, Tocqueville (1969, 639) recognized early in the republic that "in no other country in the world is the love of property more alert than in the United States." The acquisitive imperative of legally protected property ensured accelerating capital accumulation and unequal wealth in the young American nation. Adams thus predicted that "as long as property exists, it will accumulate in Individuals and Families. . . . So sure as the Idea and existence of Property is admitted and established in Society, Accumulations of it will be made, the Snow ball will grow as it rolls" (Adams 2004, 511; see also Greenberg 1983; Horwitz 1977).

The young Karl Marx (1844), we noted in our introduction, incisively interrogated the contradictory relationship between property rights, the promise of legal equality for citizens, and differentiation of value among persons and resources intrinsic to capitalist accumulation. Marx stipulated that the legal equality of citizens in the public realm applies only to abstract representations of actual persons divorced from their diverse concrete social positions, needs, and interests. In other words, the logic of legal exchange depends on the reconstruction of qualitatively different, unequal subjects into uniform and impersonal citizens through the universal political equivalent of recognized rights (Balbus 1977; McCann 1989). Legal citizenship and the differentiation of value propelled by capitalist commodification thus clash, in the process rendering the former de facto insubstantial, even illusory.

> Where the political state has attained to its full development, man leads, not only in thought, in consciousness, but in reality, in life, a double existence. . . . He lives in the political community, where he regards himself as a communal being, and in civil society, where he acts simply as a private individual, treats other men as means, degrades himself to the role of a mere means, and becomes the mere plaything of alien powers. (Marx 1844)

Marx was initially most interested in the alienating, dehumanizing effects of market exchange relations that undermine communal bonds, but he shifted his concern to inequalities of power produced by capital accumulation but "masked" by formal citizen equality. The right to legal "equality," he later wrote, is "a right of inequality in its content, like every other right" (Marx [1875] 1978, 530; see McCann 1989, 235). The most fundamental social divide, of course, was the class division between propertied owners of production and exploited workers whose waged labor produces surplus value appropriated by the owners as profit. In this view, profits fuel capitalist accumulation as a dynamic, violent process of exploitative inequality and domination—much as John Adams had more benignly predicted. For Marx, though, the core fiction of legal equality both protects and obscures the source of these inequalities. Most important, citizen rights are depoliticizing in that they individualize subjects, impede group consciousness, and work to transform legal disputes into abstract, "unreal" terms that "mystify" the structural patterns of material inequality embedded in social life.[5] Hence, his famous claims that legal equality is "sophistry," analogized to a "political lion's skin" that shrouds and submits to the pervasive inequalities of power that constitute capitalist society, unable to advance human emancipation. As capitalist exchange relations permeate legal culture and institutions, promises of alternative egalitarian or collectivist visions thus are rendered relatively alien, illusory, and groundless (McCann 1989). "While rights may operate as an indisputable force of emancipation at one moment in history," Wendy Brown (1995, 98) has argued, "they may become at another time a regulatory discourse—a means of obstructing or co-opting more radical demands or simply the most hollow of empty promises."

In the Marxist framework, therefore, official state law has proved to be a critical force for sustaining class hierarchy: ideologically through the alluring fiction of legal equality; institutionally through protection of property rights, which owners invoke to control, discipline, and even violently repress workers; and instrumentally through capitalists' accumulation of social power to control state policy and the monopoly on coercion. That said, law's authoritative power typically has required at least some modest degree of "relative autonomy' from dominant capitalist interests and group preferences. Law structures class relations to the advantage of rulers, E. P. Thompson (1975, 264) has written, but "the law mediated these class relations through legal forms, which imposed again and again, inhibitions upon the actions of the rulers." Still, the material reality of formal legal rights protections in capitalist society generally has varied with the vastly different status, wealth, and organizational resources of actors—for example, with the amount and forms of property that are owned or controlled. To the extent that property ownership (i.e., capital) is still the foundation for meaningful, effective claims of all rights today, working-class people—and especially low-wage, poor, underemployed, and unemployed yet "free" citizen workers—in practice enjoy few or limited benefits from rights at or beyond work (Lee 2014; Maltby 2010). This insight has been supported by many decades of sociolegal research on legal disputing demonstrating the many reasons—unequal resources of time, money, and access to lawyers; legal knowledge; relational independence of adversaries; the advantages of "repeat player" status; and organizational leverage—why the (propertied) "haves come out ahead" (Galanter 1974). Overall, the substance of law itself at any point in time expresses the aggregation of outcomes from ongoing political and legal disputing processes dominated by various propertied interests.

The fundamental connection between rule of law, capitalist ownership, and class-based inequalities is so palpable as to deserve little further direct comment here. The insights of class analysis go directly to questions of both social context and the subject positions of actual or potential disputants in the legal mobilization framework. Our historical study of Filipino American migrant workers and our general approach to scholarship on legal contestation thus agree with Seron and Munger (1996, 197, 206): "Research without a structural concept of class impoverishes our understanding of law and inequality."

We do not dismiss legal realists who focus on gaps between legal principles and practices (Gould and Barclay 2012; Scheingold 1974), but it is the fundamental tensions inherent *within* liberal legal logics constituting capitalist orders and sustaining systematic class inequality that are our primary focus.

Racial Differentiation, Unfree Work, and Globalization

While the focus on capitalist relations and hierarchies is fundamental to our approach, we offer three important amendments to the classic Marxist analysis. First, Marx's focus on the plight of exploited wage laborers who sell their labor to survive provided scant attention to the wageless or very low-wage, dependent, unfree noncitizens and surplus populations—slaves, indentured servants, imported migrant "aliens," sharecroppers, women relegated to reproductive labor—whose "expropriated" labor has been essential to the violent processes of capital accumulation (Fraser 2016). If the promise of equal rights for working-class citizen laborers is relatively meager, the promise of rights for unfree, devalued noncitizens and the very poor in society is even more remote and illusory. Such populations not only are marked by material scarcity and political powerlessness but they often are subjected to the harshest types of disciplinary control and violence at work as well as in other dimensions of everyday social and domestic life. Moreover, lower-income, often disposable surplus populations are the most deficient both in de jure rights recognition and in the resources needed to challenge privileged repeat players and the legal system they have constructed over time (Galanter 1974; Merry 2003; Zemans 1983). In this regard, contemporary immigrant "day laborers" are to some degree both exceptional in their precarious marginalization and a synecdoche for the ranks of the low-wage, de facto expropriated laboring classes and surplus population who enjoy few de facto rights and experience routine oppression, some of it in direct encounters with the state and much more institutionalized in the private confines of economic and social subjugation (Apostolidis 2018). Understanding these unique experiences of devalued, unfree, noncitizen workers has been critical to our study of conscripted Filipino American migrant workers, especially in the first generation.

Second, we have emphasized throughout our book yet another critical dimension of official law's capacity to both value and devalue, to include and exclude, "who" qualifies for standing or status as legal rights-bearing and rights-claiming subjects. Official discourses of rights confer a limited, paradoxical, wealth-contingent promise of alienating freedom to citizen workers in capitalist society, but rights conventions have been historically grounded in *ascriptive* criteria that mark those persons as of lesser value, as undeserving of full rights or any rights at all, as consigned to low or no wages for their labor, and thus as at best semifree or unfree (Cacho 2012; McCann 2014a, 2014b). We underlined that capitalism and its evolved legal infrastructure in practice thus did not erase inherited ascriptive group identities and universalize membership, as Marx's analysis of destructive exchange relations predicted. Rather, capitalism institutionalized differential value grounded in race, ethnicity, religion, and gender, among other attributive criteria—which we generally identify with "racialization" (and gendering)—that intersected with and complicated class (Robinson 1983; see also Charles W. Mills 2008; Pateman 1988; Smith 1997). We again note that the dominant groups that controlled property and exercised sovereign power in Europe were white males committed to *racial* differentiation and coerced exclusion of nonwhites from rights-bearing status. "Capitalism emerged within a feudal order and flowered in the cultural soil of a Western civilization already infused with racialism," summarizes Robin Kelley (2017). The first European proletarians were "racial subjects" (Irish, Jews, Roma or Gypsies, Slavs, and others), victims of dispossession by enclosure, colonialism, and slavery within Europe (Kelley 2017). Capitalism everywhere has been racialized; hence, our use of the term *racial capitalism* (Melamed 2011).

One aim of our long historical narrative has been to analyze the US colonial experiment in the Philippines and Filipino migration as a window into the development of these racializing processes (Goldberg 2002). Our account outlined how, in the early United States, white northern European property-owning males continued to exercise sovereignty as privileged rights bearers. This tradition was deepened in the United States as white landowners tapped into the long-standing international slave trade and imported Africans for wageless, unfree slave labor and noncitizen status. Over its first century, moreover, the American national government promoted expansion of the empire through land policy committed to dominance by the white-settler majority, which grew steadily through materially subsidized northern European emigration (Frymer 2017; Rana 2012). Scattered populations of Native Americans were removed from the land, dispossessed from nature, and often exterminated by genocidal violence, while most lands populated by nonwhites were largely circumvented in westward expansion until substantial white majorities developed (Frymer 2017; Charles W. Mills 2017). Overall, males of northern European descent controlled the bulk of property, white workers were advantaged by that control relative to unfree others, and "whiteness" itself in practice defined the terms of settled expectation about property rights and citizen status (C. Harris 1993). The prerogative of the sovereign, after all, includes the capacity to name who is and is not included as citizens under official law, that is, those who are valued as rights-bearing subjects or devalued as the rightsless exceptions condemned to hierarchical control and violent treatment, including death (Agamben 2005).

Law, capitalism, and race thus have been mutually constitutive forces in the development of American political economy and culture (Gomez 2012; W. Johnson 2018; Robinson 1983; Weiner 2006).[6] As noted earlier, official law not only has deemed which subjects are entitled to rights in specific contexts but it has contributed to the creation of categories or labels—illegal, noncitizen, alien, slave, immigrant, colonial national, ward, Asian, worker, subversive, criminal, union member, and so on—that mark people for variable degrees of rights(less) status and subjugation in the hierarchical context of power relations (Haney-López 2006; see Gomez 2012; De Genova 2004; Kawar 2015; Merry 2000). Those dominant groups of white property owners who allied with the state became both the lead actors and the self-appointed exemplars of desirable character traits for adjudicating entry by other groups seeking inclusion in the community of rights-bearing citizens over time.[7] The premise that rights-bearing subjects must be disciplined, rational, and conventional to deserve rights provided a justifying, even motivating moral logic for dominant groups to deny rights to select categories of racialized, disposable populations because they were allegedly incapable of, or resistant to, demonstrating such responsible self-governance despite capitalist reliance on their arduous labor for profitable production. Alleged failures of responsibilizing discipline generally have tended to fall into three different categories—those branded as inherently undisciplined and prone to disorder and violence; those (including women) viewed as presently too undeveloped or weak in mind, will, or body to govern themselves but governable by disciplined white males; and those historically characterized as deficient in both regards but potentially civilizable by exposure to disciplinary socialization and incentives (Rogin 1987; Merry 2000; Kramer 2006). We have seen that Filipinos, in their colonized native land and in the metropole, were variably constructed and devalued in all of these ways as fit the varied, often contested interests or needs of different dominant groups.

The imagined liberal community of rights-bearing subjects (B. Anderson 1991) thus reconstructed the inherited precapitalist ideology of unequal status into individualized terms of recognized merit and moral character that naturalized and normalized hierarchies of lawful power and authority differentiating *between* relative insiders and outsiders as well as *among* insiders to the community (Shklar 1998; Smith 1997; Stychin 1998). The ideology of disciplined "merit" has been interpreted in different and shifting ways over time as the dominant white-male majority refashioned the markers that determined differential valuation, including especially the boundaries between deserving subjects entitled to rights and undeserving, expropriated others accorded few or no rights. Principles of liberal legal equality provided ideological support for these intersecting hierarchies of race and class (and gender) as well as grounds for outsiders to contest them (Smith 1997). In the process, the terms of whiteness expanded to include some new European immigrant groups, but the whiteness/property nexus remained a defining if indeterminate, malleable standard (Roediger 1991). The denial of full rights to large swaths of devalued people in the racialized (and gendered) laboring classes, many of them "criminalized"—the archetype of rights denial—thus has been routine, rather than aberrational, throughout American history (Cacho 2012; Merry 1998; Neocleous 2006).

As such, intersectional factors of race, class, and gender have structured the divides between the relatively free and unfree, citizen and noncitizen, unwaged and low waged, and, later, working class and middle class, poor and rich throughout history (Crenshaw 1989, 1991; Fraser 2016). The paradigmatic case of disqualification for full rights standing to racialized laborers was wageless slavery, itself an early component of capitalism, and then Jim Crow subordination for black people in America. But these distinctions have been extended in various degrees to other peoples of color, from Native Americans to Asian American and Mexican immigrants in the borderlands (Gomez 2012), as well as women performing reproductive labor, religious and ethnic minorities, the homeless, the poor, and others who populated the nonwage, low-wage, disposable, and surplus labor force in twentieth-century America (C. Johnson 2017). The practices of racialized subordination and control have remained similar over time, even if the institutional *forms* shifted with developments in the ever-changing stages of capitalist and administrative-state development.

Our historical study has illustrated how the dynamics of racial hierarchy mattered clearly and emphatically for Filipinos as the American racial capitalist empire expanded beyond western lands to exploit international markets and undertake global colonial experiments. From the first deliberations and debates over US colonial rule, Filipinos in the island homeland and those conscripted for work in the metropole were characterized by American leaders in overtly stigmatizing racial terms (Kramer 2006). Carlos Bulosan's earlier cited observation that Filipinos were treated as unwanted, uncivilized criminals in the American metropole again captured succinctly their constructed racial and class status as nearly rightsless, disposable subjects despite the Fourteenth Amendment promises of equal protection for all persons. The long history of overt, explicit white-supremacist rule over targeted racialized and gendered persons gave way to the racially liberal era after World War II, to be sure. Filipino American migrants were eventually accorded formal citizenship rights, but most Filipino migrant workers remained second-class, exploited citizens in the metropole with limited economic capacity, political power, and social status in daily life (Smith 1997). The rights of Filipinos to organize into unions and espouse leftist causes were, moreover, tested, diminished, even denied amid the escalating Cold War. Even as many Filipinos worked toward "whitening" (Roediger 2005) themselves and assimilated to some degree as disciplined[8] citizens and workers into American culture after World War II, racialized stigmas continued to diminish their status. Moreover, leftist political activists in the ACWA during the 1970s were again subjected to vilification as dangerous, un-American, criminal, and unworthy of citizen status. Our historical account underlined the paradox that those activists who arguably embraced most seriously and imaginatively the promises of equal rights for advancing social justice and democratic transformation were initially viewed as ineligible for even the minimal respect and protection that basic citizen rights ostensibly ensure. Our detailed analysis of the majority Supreme Court ruling in *Wards Cove* aimed to illustrate the enduring truth of that fact.

Our third, related amendment to Marx's class-focused analysis has been to underline the geopolitical dimensions of racial and class differentiation produced by imperial capitalist expansion. Global capitalist development continually requires interactions with foreign nonwhite people that clash with commitments to white racial insulation or dominance (Frymer 2017). This is a key part of our story regarding American global empire and its specific legacy of intervention in the Philippines. As the reach of US commercial plundering and military power spread around the globe, propelled by a great deal of violent force, racialized devaluation has been deeply implicated at two levels. One is that the increasing reliance on a transnational labor force has justified increased domestic policing of national borders to separate free and semifree citizens from noncitizens, feeding pressures for nationalism and undercutting possibilities of transnational alliance among racialized, exploited peoples (De Genova 2004; Ngai 2004). A second, related development is that global capitalism constitutes new geographic hierarchies of material wealth and valuation—between white and nonwhite, core and periphery, and Global North and South, among others (Fraser 2016). These larger global dimensions of racial capitalism may seem somewhat remote for some studies of legal mobilization within the US metropole, but few contemporary struggles over social justice anywhere in the world are not shaped by such interdependencies. We hope that our study of Filipino American labor activism illuminates some such types of global connections forged by racial capitalist empire.[9]

"Everybody Knows": Variable Forms of Racial Capitalist Law

The Variegated System of Liberal and Repressive Law

Our primary point so far has been that citizenship rights—the "right to have rights," as Hannah Arendt famously put it (1973, 296)—signal a possibility that varies widely among persons at three levels in the racial capitalist order:[10] first, in the de jure legal standing of membership accorded by official law and informal practice; second, in differential social status and subject construction; and third, in de facto access to key resources critical to effective rights claiming by individuals and groups as a limited check on powerful actors and dominant institutional forms in state and society. Again, those racialized persons held in bondage to slavery, however defiant and creative as political agents, defined a baseline of rightsless, noncitizen, unfree subject position.

The abolition of slavery and authorization of constitutional "equal protection" for all persons did not end the wide variation in capacities of differently situated subjects to claim rights. Rogers Smith's (1997) classic analysis in his majestic *Civic Ideals* is helpful for looking beyond simple duality in recognizing the variability of rights accorded to different persons. His analysis recognized four levels of legal status that had emerged by the early twentieth century and that seem still relevant today: (1) rightsless noncitizens denied entry or expelled from the national membership—such as exiles, deportees, or excluded immigrants—based on ascriptive traits or alleged ideological and behavioral danger; (2) uncertain or liminal rights standing, neither aliens nor citizens, and limited in resources as well as social status, such as Filipino nationals, undocumented imported colonial workers, and convicted felons; (3) second-class citizens formally entitled to rights but limited in capacities to exercise them and devalued in status, typically including masses of low-income or poor racial minorities, immigrants, and many women; and (4) full-rights-bearing citizens who again vary widely in capacities to mobilize the various resources on which effective rights-claiming agency depends (Smith 1997, 429). Again, both the constructions and applications of such categories should be understood to vary routinely on a continuum between ideal types of rights capacity and social status for different persons in different sites at different historical moments. And we also should remember the core promises of citizen rights for most persons: "freedom" to unequal political and economic participation along with highly variable subjection to the alienating, harsh terms of capitalist market competition, responsibilizing discipline, and hierarchical corporate rule.

Recognizing the wide degree of formal rights standing, social status, and rights-claiming capacities hardly exhausts our understanding about the variability of subject position for different persons in racial capitalist orders, however. It follows directly from the previous discussion that large segments of people—especially low-wage, poor, and disposable people of color; immigrants; women; queers—in racial capitalist America consequently have been governed by illiberal penal, fiscal, and bureaucratic practices that de facto eschew or relax due process, equal protection, free speech, and other rights claimable by full citizens, much less substantive social justice. Law may be "king" in America, as Thomas Paine famously proclaimed. But the types of law experienced by differently situated citizens has varied widely. In particular, law's inherent violence is channeled disproportionately and through different institutional forms and practices, directly and indirectly, toward particular groups in racial capitalist orders. For most of US history there have been legions of "Americans without (liberal) law" (Weiner 2006).

This demonstrable pattern of variable legal governance has been theorized by scholars in multiple ways. In the classic realist perspective, the history of exclusionary hierarchy and uneven liberal legal administration has been portrayed as a gap between the written rules and symbolic promises of law, on the one hand, and the wildly variable practices of rights enforcement, sustained by the allure of the legalistic "myth of rights," on the other (Gould and Barclay 2012; Scheingold 1974). The explanation turns on collective, or at least elite, hypocrisy or "beguilement" that obscures or denies the observable reality of unequal treatment and uneven implementation (Lovell 2012).

Yet another framework draws on Carl Schmitt (2005) and Giorgio Agamben (2005), among others. It recognizes historically unique "states of exception" during which the sovereign determines that law is indefinitely suspended without being abolished. In such circumstances, certain groups, either generically or in identified institutional settings, are excluded from treatment as full-rights-bearing subjects, including fundamental rights to due process, equal protection, and the like. The result, Agamben says, is banishment from political life as citizens and condemnation to the status of a refugee's "bare life" exemplified in "the (concentration) camp" outside of the normal juridical order. Such states of exception are often justified by responses to emergency, although many theorists in this tradition underline that provisional conditions of emergency often become normalized. Hardt and Negri (2000) argue that contemporary international politics rests on deployments of military power to sustain empire, thus enacting "permanent" exceptions in both foreign relations and the homeland (see Neocleous 2006).

We find merit in both explanations. However, we question the common premise of both frameworks that a single, unitary, uniform, identifiable mode of liberal law and law enforcement *ever* structured—in principle or in practice—the logic of official governance for all persons in racial capitalist regimes. We instead build on other contemporary scholars who posit that the hegemonic American legal inheritance has always been multiple in its *forms, functions, and targeted subjects*. Paralleling the variable rights standing and subject status of different populations, this pluralistic system of legal governance has been more of a variant on than a transcendent alternative ("exception") to European racialized, classed, and gendered colonial regimes (Frymer 2017; King and Smith 2005; Merry 1988, 2000; Rana 2012; Smith 1997). Critical scholars have often staked out similar positions underlining the "dual" dimensions of the American legal system—one legal form reserved for governing free, white, educated, male, property-owning "haves" or insiders, and another more brutal and exclusionary form of law for unfree, racialized and gendered "others," outsiders, and marginal many who perform wageless or low-wage labor and are subjected to more arbitrary, often brutal, and locally governed forms of social control. This conceptualization makes sense, giving the enduring dualisms of class (free/unfree), race (white/nonwhite), gender (masculine/feminine), sexuality (straight/queer), and citizenship (citizen/noncitizen) that structure the inherited political economies and cultural life in the United States.

We recall, for example, that political theorists Charles W. Mills (1997;

see also Kelley 2017) and Carole Pateman (1988; see also Gordon 2006) have powerfully made the case that such dualistic hierarchies of legal rule—between fully deserving citizens and those less than citizens, such as those constructed as nonwhite and female—were inscribed into the constitutional order of liberal contract-based societies from the very start. Aziz Rana's historical argument about the "two faces of American freedom" in the settler and postsettler eras explicitly draws historical parallels to European colonial and postcolonial legal legacies. In the United States he portrays

> a constitutional politics built on two distinct accounts of sovereign power: one of democratic consent and internal checks, and another of external and coercive discretion. In the United States, such a dual sovereign framework served to separate free settler insiders from a patchwork of ethnically excluded groups, who found themselves subject to a complicated structure of overlapping hierarchies. These hierarchies provided each colonized community distinct modes of governance and levels of rights, depending on internal economic needs and the dictates of political order. (Rana 2012, 1022)

Mae Ngai provides a powerfully provocative analysis regarding the legal status of Asian American immigrants, and Filipinos in particular, as legally "impossible subjects" needed for their labor but condemned to an "imported colonial" relationship during the twentieth century and into the present. "Modern, imported colonialism produced new social relations based on the subordination of racialized foreign bodies who worked in the United States but who remained excluded from the polity by both law and social custom" (Ngai 2004, 129; see also Weiner 2006).[11] This account does not necessarily imply that imported workers received no lawful treatment but that the coercive law treating them was different in form and function than the law accorded to dominant groups. We invoke again King and Smith's (2005) influential, parallel argument about the different, competing "racial orders"—one "white supremacist," the other "egalitarian"—that have shaped governance and been reflected in law throughout American political history.

Political historians who have studied the changing forms of racialized legal rule in the American South have offered parallel accounts. After all, the "law of slavery," while variable over time and space, defined a coercive legal system separate from that which governed white property owners and free labor at least as far back as the passage of the Virginia Code in 1705 (Tushnet 1981). Other scholars identify the systematic divergence from celebrated liberal constitutional principles in the subsequent Jim Crow era after African Americans were accorded formal legal equality (Francis 2014). A good example is Daniel Kato's (2012, 146) distinction between spatial spheres governed by national constitutional rule and those "anomalous zones . . . in which certain legal rules, otherwise regarded as embodying fundamental policies of the larger legal system, are locally suspended." These zones, he argues, were illiberal, highly violent, and "lawless" but still ordered and lawlike. Kato compares this dualism identified in the Jim Crow South specifically to postcolonial settings where rule by secular civil law over rights-bearing citizens coexists with authoritarian local tribal rule over subjects in the absence of rights (see Chatterjee 2006).

Another evocative parallel for our argument is Robert Mickey's (2015) compelling, thoroughly evidenced argument regarding the subnational "authoritarian enclaves" of wealthy white supremacy that dominated, in politics and by law, the South from the Reconstruction era through at least the 1950s. Karen Orren's (1991) influential argument that employment law was, even for white wage earners, grounded in illiberal, authoritarian, feudal principles of master-servant relations until at least the 1930s is similarly relevant. Before World War II, moreover, most women in the United States, including white women but especially women of color, were subjected to arbitrary, coercive, often violent male rule in the domestic sphere of household economy as well as, for some, at paid work outside the home, all authorized by the patriarchal and propertied differences embedded in official law (Hartmann 1976; Hartsock 1983).

These historical examples suggest the need for a generalized reconceptualization about the multiple interdependent forms of law that have governed differently situated subject groups in different institutional sites at different historical moments. Because we underline the different processes of authorizing coercion as well as the different modes of violent enforcement applied to subjects of varying legal status, we have adopted Nonet and Selznick's (2001) classic distinction between social orders governed by *autonomous*, or liberal, law and that of *repressive* law.[12] In that framework, autonomous law operates with some measure of independence from direct instrumental control by dominant social groups, and it is grounded in liberal principles of procedurally constrained legal violence, independent judicial checks on political rule, and formal respect for individual civil rights and due process of self-governing citizens. It is thoroughly embedded in and constitutive of exchange-based, contractual market logics of capitalism and corporate hierarchies. Repressive "rule by law," in contrast, more directly exercises or delegates "police powers" on behalf of dominant economic and racial groups to "manage order" among subordinate groups. It is more command oriented and administrative or managerial in form, more paternalistic, more discretionary in character, more reliant on violent force for social control, and less bound to respect the claims of liberal rights by individuals it subjugates. Indeed, de facto relative rightslessness of subjects and their subjection to repressive (rather than liberal) law are two sides of the same mutually constitutive legal relationship.

We again add that the coercive power of repressive law emanates from both its direct imposition by state officials and their permissiveness or delegation regarding various forms of arbitrary, violent social control practiced by privileged groups in civil society, including employers and corporate managers, landlords and bankers, debt collectors, security guards, and men (over women and children) generally in the domestic sphere (Henderson 1991). Our historical narrative regarding the first generation of Filipino migrant workers evidenced many of these institutionalized repressive law forms. The de facto criminalization of Filipinos authorized local police, national law enforcement, and vigilante groups to hunt down, detain, incarcerate, torture, and even kill colonial national subjects with few nods to due process. Border patrol officers and immigration officials regularly harassed, intimidated, and attempted to deport Filipinos with only occasional procedural restrictions and often under pressure from white workers, employers, and media moguls. Much of this activity was joined by FBI officials aiming to quash political dissidence, speech, and association viewed as subversive, thus discounting drastically the supposed protections of the First Amendment. And all this despite the promises of equal protection for all persons by the Fourteenth Amendment.

Finally, but hardly least, we recall the repressive discipline and violent social control imposed by corporate managers at and around work. Previous pages documented how migrant workers endured segregated labor camps resembling concentration camps, urban ghettoes, and lives on the run from hostile lynch mobs and vigilantes permitted and even supported by local law enforcement. Work was organized on a quasi-slave "plantation model" in the canneries as well as in the "factories in the field." Migrant agricultural workers were subjected to rule by what McWilliams (1939) called "fascist farms"—with absentee owners, centralized bank financiers, hierarchical control of production processes, harsh discipline for laborers, elaborate mechanisms of "espionage" and "propaganda" to supplement direct control, and strong-arm, brutal repression of unionizing efforts and dissidents. In sum, like many members of the racialized underclass, Filipinos were subjected to various forms of repressive law that were highly violent and focused on managing hierarchical order. Legal practices tended to be highly discretionary, variable, uncoordinated, and arbitrary in manifestation even as they were systematic in effect. Filipinos were subjects of repressive law because they were constructed as rightsless, racialized, disposable foreigners, which in turn limited their capacity to contest such legal rule. The overall legal order in the racial capitalist America they found was not uniformly liberal but rather was by design a patchwork of liberal and illiberal or overtly repressive legal forms.[13]

Reconstructed Forms of Repressive Law in the Racial Liberal Era

American civil rights and immigration reform in the 1960s ended public segregation and banned employer discrimination on the basis of race, religion, sex, and national origin, ushering in a second Reconstruction that advanced further the liberal constitutional project. King and Smith (2005, 83) are correct to note that the balance between competing racial orders "shifted" and principles of "egalitarian transformative order" became "authoritative in American law and many governing agencies." It is undeniable that the ascendant racially liberal political order institutionalized important restraints on violent legal practices that long had been harmful to many people. Nevertheless, egalitarian transformation was severely limited in fundamental ways and not just because political forces committed to white class privilege persisted (King and Smith 2005; Melamed 2011). For one thing, the civil rights and due process revolutions provided few ideological or institutional resources for leveraging redistribution of economic, social, and political power denied for centuries to racialized, gendered, poor, and other exploited persons, even those granted formal rights and freedom. As a result, extreme socioeconomic inequality and material marginalization persisted and even worsened in various ways. Moreover, advances in liberal rights did not end the long-standing manifestations of repressive legal governance targeting semifree and unfree subaltern subjects, especially persons of color, in the disposable laboring classes and designated surplus populations.

That said, the manifest *institutionalized forms* of repressive law sustaining order management of noncitizens and second-class citizens generally did undergo palpable changes in the era of racial liberalism. Nonet and Selznick's classic sociological theory again is evocative in this regard. Situating their various models in different stages of historical development, the authors nevertheless recognized that residue from older orders typically persists as new forms of social organization and corresponding legal institutions emerge. Indeed, they suggested that developed polities, including contemporary American society, operate through a *hybrid* system that "mixes" elements of old and new, repressive and autonomous, or liberal, legal forms in an interdependent and interactive if variegated whole (Nonet and Selznick 2001, 17). These mosaics of varied legal forms, we add, have constantly adapted and grown in response to the exigencies of class relations in racial capitalism. And that is the case in the post–World War II era. In short, the older informal, discretionary, decentralized modes and practices of repressive law were reorganized into new more bureaucratic, facially neutral, systematically coordinated, procedurally legalistic—that is, "liberalized"—administrative systems to produce order management among unruly, racialized, mostly poor and disposable or surplus populations. These legalistic developments arguably have not tamed so much as routinized, rationalized, and normalized state-administered discriminatory violence targeting subaltern groups (Cover 1986; Melamed 2011; Reddy 2011; Spade 2015; but see Epp 2010). The due process revolution reined in the overt racism of old repressive law through procedural administrative reforms, but, at the same time, it reinforced innocence among dominant groups about the continuing role of law in coercively sustaining *systematic* race, class, gender, sexual, and religious hierarchies.

One good example is federal and state urban development, highway construction, and zoning policies starting in the 1940s that systematically expanded safe, affordable housing for white people in the suburbs while systematically moving people of color (especially black and brown people) out of integrated neighborhoods into increasingly marginal, jobless, poor, and violence-plagued slums and ghettoes. As Richard Rothstein has documented in his aptly titled book *The Color of Law*, these policies implemented intentional, knowing state violence targeting racialized, semifree, second-class citizens emblematic of continued white supremacy but embedded in elaborate technocratic planning processes authorized by abstractly framed race-neutral legislation and legally underwritten by a long string of federal court rulings over many decades (Rothstein 2017; Thorpe 2016). The Fair Housing Act prohibited housing programs that compounded previous segregation of protected minority groups without a legitimate state interest. However, the evidentiary rules for proving discriminatory impact have been highly constraining, and the act has not limited multiple types of discriminatory nonhousing government programs that reinforce segregation, including especially transportation policies (Rothstein 2017, 188–91; Schwemm and Bradford 2016).

Perhaps the most dramatic and obvious hybrid manifestation of the new repressive law system has been the complex web of policing, surveillance, and mass incarceration practices often called the "New Jim Crow" penal caste system. Michelle Alexander (2012) shows how millions of racialized "second-class" citizens and unfree persons have been "trapped in a parallel social universe, denied basic and human rights." Political scientist Marie Gottschalk (2008, 245) echoes the characterization: "The carceral state has helped to legitimate the idea of creating a separate political universe for whole categories of people" who have been described as "partial citizens" and "internal exiles," disenfranchised from many forms of civil engagement. As in earlier eras, prison conditions are harsh and inhumane, while prison labor, voluntary for some but mandatory for many others, continues to be even far less compensated and far more degrading than low-paying work outside in civil society. Meanwhile, the elaborate web of costly monetary sanctions—fines, fees, bonds, wage garnishing, asset forfeiture, etc.—extracted disproportionately from low-income people of color multiplies greatly the punitiveness of the system (A. Harris 2016).

Although similar to the older Jim Crow in its harshly punitive, violent modes of order management targeting lower-class persons of color, however, the contemporary criminal justice system is more bureaucratic in organization, professionalized, and legalistically structured around a maze of facially neutral rules than earlier forms of repressive law (Murakawa 2014). For example, numerous studies have confirmed the palpable patterns of racial profiling by police while making investigatory stops of African American and Hispanic drivers, but these invasive, authoritarian practices are shrouded in a host of ostensibly color-blind protocols, rights-respecting procedures, and even rituals of courtesy that confer a semblance of undifferentiated legal treatment (Epp, Maynard-Moody, and Haider-Markel 2014). Contemporary police also are better trained in standard procedures, but their "militarized" capacity for coordinated legal violence against alleged street criminals and political protestors far surpasses that of earlier eras (Balko 2013). Yet more dramatic are the differences between volatile, racist mob lynchings in the Jim Crow era and procedurally legalistic, judicially authorized, and technocratically administered state killings today (Ogletree and Sarat 2006). It is highly relevant once again that statistically evidenced claims of racially disparate impact absent a showing of explicit intent have been defiantly rebuffed by the Supreme Court, directly for capital cases and generally for the entire carceral state apparatus (*McClesky v. Kemp*, 1987).

The contemporary carceral state to some degree reflects changes in the racial capitalist political economy as well. Modern "hyper-incarceration" (Wacquant 2010) serves increasingly to manage an impoverished surplus labor force in a postindustrial era of neoliberal welfare state rollback, surplus capital and state capacity, and accelerating technological obsolescence that is different from the preindustrialized, agriculturally based, quasi-slave foundation of Southern agrarian political economy during the Jim Crow era (Gilmore 2007; C. Johnson 2017; Western and Beckett 1999). Even so, housing segregation, poverty, and incarceration of racial minorities continue to be closely interrelated, much as was the case over a century ago. "If incarceration had come to define the lives of men from impoverished black neighborhoods, eviction was shaping the lives of women," writes Matthew Desmond (2016, 98) in his important study. In short, the machinery of contemporary criminal justice is more procedurally legalistic and facially deracialized than in the distant past, but the "ghosts" of slavery and past violent practices still haunt the repressive system of "governing through crime" that overwhelmingly targets racialized, lower-class persons (Dayan 2013; Murakawa 2014; Simon 2006).

The modern American complex of immigration regulation is, as in the past, closely intertwined with the security state and criminal justice systems regulating poor, dark-skinned, racialized migrant workers, most conscripted or escaping from Mexico and Latin America (De Genova 2010; Hernandez 2018). The estimated population of undocumented migrants grew from around a million in the early 1970s to well over ten million in the 2000s, around 3 percent of the US population. The contemporary "crimmigration" apparatus, as it is often labeled, is built on policies and practices developed over the last century and evidenced in our historical narrative regarding Filipino migrants and bracero workers. It escalated rapidly in punitiveness with new laws, policies, and bureaucratic coordination during the Reagan administration's War on Drugs and continued to expand during subsequent administrations, especially with the Clinton era 1996 Illegal Immigration Reform and Immigrant Responsibility Act (IIRAIRA) and Antiterrorism and Effective Death Penalty Act (AEDPA). Brutal immigration control practices have been politically justified by inflated fears of criminal gangs, human trafficking, and foreign terror-ists in the post-9/11 era—all identifying the ranks of undocumented migrants in racialized terms as dangerous, much as in the past (Provine and Doty 2011).

"Improper entry" into the United States can be prosecuted as a criminal offense, while undocumented status is a civil violation, but those branded "illegals" in both cases have continued to be treated generally like, or worse, than criminals. Immigration control is administered by an elaborate, Kafkaesque network of interlocking federal, state, local, and privately contracted agents. The key protocols still include surveillance, detention, deportation, and incarceration. Pretrial and mandatory detention by Immigration and Customs Enforcement officials is highly discretionary and relies on rituals of civil confinement that mimic criminal detention but fall short on actual due process, including Fourth, Fifth, and Sixth Amendment rights, again constructing a veneer of bureaucratic legalism to mask routinely discriminatory, often brutal treatment (Hernandez 2018; Venkatesh 2016). Deportation condemns migrants, like felons, to a form of civic or social death, sometimes leading to physical death (Cacho 2012). Indeed, the highly discretionary terms of deportability underline the ultimate disposability of imported, commodified laborers (De Genova 2004, 2010). Imprisonment is the other routine social control practice of crimmigration. The 1996 laws expanded categories of "aggravated felony" for noncitizens that could lead to incarceration as well as deportation. From 1992 to 2012, the number of immigrants sentenced for criminal offenses in federal court more than doubled to nearly 76,000, while unlawful entry convictions increased by nearly thirty times to almost 20,000, the latter (overwhelmingly Hispanic) representing 26 percent of all federal offenders (Light, Lopez, and Gonzales-Barrera 2014). For undocumented immigrants, including longtime residents in the United States, law's violence thus reigns as a condition of constant state terror. "This is not an area of law characterized by harsh edges or the one-off example of excessiveness. Its very core is damaging. People, institutions, and the legal system itself suffer from crimmigration law's fundamental precepts" (Hernandez 2018, 200; see also Gleeson 2010)

Media analyst Chris Hayes has captured the plural legal order in metaphorically evocative terms recognizing contemporary America's "internal" or domestic colonial legacy, an idea long invoked by black, Native, Latino, and other egalitarian scholar-activists (Carmichael and Hamilton 1967; Allen 1970; Gutierrez 2004).[14] His book focuses on criminalization and police violence, but the images can easily be extended to other dimensions of legal violence directed toward subaltern populations generally. "Different systems of justice are a centuries-old American tradition, indeed a foundational one," Hayes argues. The "terrifying truth" is that, as the book title conveys, the modern legal order has institutionalized a "colony in a nation" (Hayes 2017, 24, 32).

> In the Nation, there is law; in the Colony, there is only a concern with order. In the Nation, citizens call the police to protect them. In the Colony, subjects flee the police, who offer the opposite of protection. In the Nation, you have rights; in the Colony, you have commands. In the Nation, you are innocent until proven guilty; in the Colony, you are born guilty. . . . On the ground . . . the Bill of Rights seemed to have no force. (Hayes 2017, 37–38, 73)

Hayes's key claim deserves qualification, to be sure. Many (but not all) modern manifestations of repressive law, we have noted, at least ostensibly follow protocols attentive to minimal constitutional due process rights of free and semifree citizens (but far less so for noncitizens). Such procedural legalism is undeniably significant for moderating some degree of arbitrary abuses and providing minimal resources for contestation (Epp 2010). But we again suggest that the primary motivation and effect is to impart the *appearance* of liberal legality to the administration of racially and class-targeted legal violence (Murakawa 2014).

First-generation Filipino labor activists in our historical narrative were, we have seen, conscripted from the external colony into the violently racist Jim Crow–era internal colony. A second generation of defiant political activists mostly became semifree citizens caught up in the neocolonial order management complex of the postwar racial capitalist legal regime. The only Filipino American workers in our post-1950s historical narrative who ended up with substantial prison sentences, of course, were the Tulisan gang members and union boss convicted for murdering civil rights activists Domingo and Viernes. However, the conventional police and media framing of the murders as ordinary Filipino criminal gang violence importantly *diverted* attention away from the larger international assassination conspiracy involving Philippine President Marcos, his security establishment, the corrupt union boss, and US official complicity. Achieving justice for murdered martyrs required creative civil litigation and sustained political action to deflate the generic racialized immigrant criminalization narrative and expose the coordinated violence of two national security states directed against political dissidents.

By contrast, nearly all second-generation progressive Filipino American labor activists and their allies at the core of our historical narrative managed to avoid the long-term criminal imprisonment common among other racialized groups.[15] That said, many of the social justice activists, including especially Tyree Scott and his Central Contractors Association (CCA) allies (Griffey 2011), were routinely harassed by the police and often found themselves in local jails usually following their exercise of presumptive political rights to protest against racism and for civil rights. Even when "free," moreover, activists were often subjected to sophisticated, well-coordinated, covert campaigns of surveillance and harassment by federal officials. Freedom of Information Act inquiries by scholars have produced records of increasingly sophisticated forms of surveillance by the FBI, CIA, and Department of State targeting Filipino activists in both the Philippines and the metropole from the 1920s through the 1980s, including Carlos Bulosan, Chris Mensalvas, Silme Domingo, and Gene Viernes, among others (Alquizola and Hirabayashi 2012; Baldoz 2014; Griffey 2018a, 2018b). The murders of Domingo and Viernes almost surely were conducted while they were under surveillance by US government officials complicit in Ferdinand Marcos's violent attempts to quell opponents to his regime (Withey 2018). We have seen that the border patrol and other Immigration and Naturalization Services (INS) officials similarly surveilled, harassed, and attempted to deport scores of Filipino activists over several decades after World War II, including some in the post-1965 era connected to radical democratic politics in the Philippines.[16]

But governing through the expanding mechanisms of criminalization (Simon 2006) and direct state violence hardly exhausts modern repressive law. Equally important to our specific historical story is the continuing role of official law in authorizing repressive practices and policies by employers at work. In fact, the US legal system long has been notable among capitalist regimes in its restrictions on workers' substantive rights to organize and act to represent their interests (Getman 2016; Hattam 1993; Hogler 2015; Kolin 2016; Orren 1991; Vinel 2013). Earlier chapters documented how New Deal–era advances in empowering statutory labor laws were soon undercut by the Taft-Hartley Act, subsequent federal legislation, "deradicalizing" judicial decisions, state "right-to-work" laws, and routine use of police violence to crush worker dissent and basic political freedoms—all of which crippled unions and the potential for collective political power of workers both within workplaces and in public life during the postwar era (Fisk 1994; Getman 2016; Klare 1978). As a result, employers can discipline, demote, terminate, or blacklist employees at will, including for exercising political rights to speech and association. As we cited earlier, the prospects for even a modestly liberal democratic "workplace Constitution" guaranteeing basic rights for employees "all but vanished" by the 1980s (Lee 2014, 257–58), as did the statutory civil rights resources that ACWA activists embraced to challenge racially and gendered disparate impacts of employer policies and practices. Importantly, strikes—so important to early immigrant labor activists—by federal employees and most state public-sector workers also are subject to severe penalties. During 1981, the same year that Domingo and Viernes were assassinated, President Reagan fired eleven thousand striking federal air traffic controllers and decertified their union, PATCO, searing an enduring lesson about state violence into the collective memories of many union workers around the nation (McCartin 2011). A "capitalist society is a class society . . . that has needed not just the occasional enforcement of the law but the regular application of force . . . and a wide range of repressive interventions" against workers, writes political scientist Alex Gourevitch (2015, 763).

The persistent patterns of legalized workplace exploitation of low-wage laborers, including both citizens and noncitizens, in the private sector provided a central focus of our historical narrative. Alaska salmon canneries (and agricultural factories in the field) remained organized on the racially segregated, harshly administered plantation model into and beyond the 1980s, a model that a majority the US Supreme Court found to be legally acceptable under its cramped reading of civil rights law. We showed how this finding was consistent with the patterns of legally authorized forms of race and gender discrimination, including sexual harassment, that remain pervasive in modern corporate production processes (Berrey, Nelson, and Nielsen 2017; A. M. Marshall 2016). While the archaic salmon canneries did not develop the complex in-house processes of civil rights cooptation like those thoroughly documented by Edelman (2016), the *Wards Cove* decision became an important part of the elaborate rules and procedural-rights-based, ostensibly neutral complex of modern "working law" institutionalized to immunize racial and gender hierarchy from challenge (see also Lee 2014). As in other spheres we have surveyed, de jure procedural rights hold little power to challenge systematic, de facto racial hierarchy and class exploitation. This is largely the case for a great many female workers generally and especially women of color (Ehrenreich and Hochschild 2003; McCann 2014a) as well as for minority and immigrant male workers (Apostolidis 2018; Gleeson 2010; Venkatesh 2016), who tend to be concentrated in low-wage, dead-end, temporary, contingent, precarious work with few protections or benefits (Weil 2014).[17]

We thus summarize the logic of the repressive racial liberal and neoliberal American administrative order illustrated by our historical narrative. Legal options for challenging the inherited, systemic injustices suffered by most racialized (and gendered and queered) lower-class, underemployed and unemployed, free and unfree, disposable persons have been reduced to increasingly narrow terms of private, mostly individualized litigation by have-nots against powerful repeat-players representating haves and their state supporters. As long as no explicit intentional prejudice by public or private actors is clearly demonstrated and some semblance of formal due process has been granted, formally antiracist liberal law both insulates historically institutionalized inequalities from challenge and proscribes most affirmative remedies. Even when successful, moreover, such legal contestation rarely has yielded substantial remedial resource redistribution (Farhang 2010; Rosenberg 1991). Meanwhile, the administrative state has developed into a complex, professionalized bureaucratic machine of hybrid liberal and repressive law that directly and indirectly sustains violent order management of subaltern populations—both second-class free citizens and "illegal" or unfree noncitizens—and political dissidents for the benefit of dominant, mostly white property-owning groups in an increasingly hierarchical corporate capitalist society. Subaltern groups concurrently suffer from both a *deficit* of resources to access liberal legal rights and an *excess* of violent, illiberal law regulating their lives. Cultural scripts of innocence and ignorance regarding continued domination have been fortified by color-blind neoliberal legalism, evidencing once again that universal legal equality is at best a very limited or even empty promise in the racial capitalist order (Baldwin 1963; Cover 1986; Charles W. Mills 2017).

We realize that this overview of contemporary repressive law mechanisms has been incomplete, far more suggestive than conclusive, and deserving of much more empirical development than we can offer in this text, especially regarding examples that transcend our historical study in previous pages. But our fundamental point should be clear. In short, hierarchies of race, class, ethnicity, gender, sexuality, and the like remain baked into the structural socioeconomic dynamics and constituted by the hybrid legal order of American empire, at home and abroad. For all the changes in technological capacity, military power, aggregate wealth, and organizational sophistication of the empire, these features of American domestic and global legal development have remained as persistent in consequence as they are mutable in the specific institutional forms. The fact that "everybody knows" these ordinary social facts confirms the willful evasions of dominant groups. And all of this developed during the second half of the Twentieth Century, well before the brazen rhetoric and arbitrary practices and policies defying once conventional liberal legal pretenses by the revanchist Trump regime.

The key implication at stake is that legal mobilization studies must go further than simply identifying imbalances in the immediate instrumental resources, organizational constraints, and biases of contending policy positions in making sense of struggles over rights entitlements, status, and programs. It is not enough just to document the differential access to, or impact of, law on different demographic groups. In addition, the deeper, historically grounded institutionalized and ideological dimensions of hierarchical power as well as the different formations of the variegated legal order require serious attention and analysis. One might say that these forces are critical to understanding fully the larger opportunity structures for contestation or possible interest convergences between dominant and subaltern groups. But those analytical conceptualizations are rather narrower and less robust than what we endorse here. The promise of legal mobilization research directly depends on taking seriously that law is inherently and fundamentally both a product and producer of radical social inequality. And that is one reason why our story of legal contestation culminating in *Wards Cove* expanded substantially the temporal and spatial scope of inquiry—to map more fully the deep historical racial capitalist context of legally constituted hierarchical power dynamics in which struggles for rights-based empowerment emerged.

Conclusion: Legal Contestation amid Hegemony

We now return to the fundamental question that began this chapter: What are the prospects for continued and future legal contestation "from below" amid the long-standing, recently recrudescent manifestations of racial capitalist hierarchy and privilege? Our answer may be surprising to some readers, as it significantly complicates the starkly critical portrayal of law and hegemony developed in the preceding pages. In our view, it would be a mistake to dismiss the possibilities for political and legal mobilization as empty quests, to accept fully Marx's image of citizen rights status and participation in the public sphere as just a feeble political lion's skin. We warily join other legal mobilization scholars in underlining that, even in the current era of retrenchment in the racial capitalist order, law still provides one of the most important institutionalized sites and discursive resources for subaltern group resistance to and contestation over hegemonic policies, practices, and relationships in both state and society. After all, our historical study chronicled not just the legally authorized exploitation of immigrant and nonwhite workers but, equally important, the latter's persistent, creative struggles to challenge many forms of legally constituted hierarchy and to advance institutional change in more egalitarian, democratic, even socialist directions. It is important to recognize that most of the activists described in previous pages remained committed reformers all their lives, and many in the second generation remain so through the present period. Indeed, most of them continued to be progressive leaders in unions, local government, community organizations, immigrant and women's rights groups, low-cost housing development, journalism, education, and the like. They all have continued to fight against the interconnected manifestations of repressive law—the penal-industrial complex, crimmigration, workplace injustice, inadequate and segregated housing, and more—and for transformative causes of social justice and human rights. And they have done so with clear-eyed understanding about the limits and costs of litigation as well as the most promising, if contingent, strategies of political action beyond litigation.

Our general intellectual approach to understanding these quests again has taken its cue from the analysis offered by the sage historian E. P. Thompson (1975; Cole 2001). We agree with Thompson that law can be identified with both specific *institutions*, such as courts, and with specialized *personnel*, such as judges and lawyers, all of which may be closely linked to ruling classes or groups. But "law may also be seen as *ideology*, or as particular rules and sanctions which stand in a definite and active relationship (often a field of conflict) to social norms; and, finally, it may be seen simply in terms of its own logic, rules and procedures—that is, simply as law" (E. P. Thompon 1975, 263). Legal norms and ideas, we noted earlier, saturate society and the state alike, constituting relations at many levels of practice. Law as ideology can be viewed both instrumentally, as "mediating and reinforcing" as well as challenging hierarchical power relations, and structurally, as a metalevel intersubjective terrain for constructing and justifying those relations. Legal justification should not, Thompson insisted, be viewed primarily as mystification, as a mask obscuring material relations in the consciousness of ordinary subjects. Rather, legal ideology is routinely on display in the (racialized and gendered) "class theatre" but rife with contradictions, and it is law's ideological tensions and indeterminacy that provide spaces and resources for contestation. To cite Thompson's very famous but arguably underappreciated words,

> The rhetoric and the rules of a society are something a great deal more than sham. In the same moment they may modify, in profound ways, the behavior of the powerful, and mystify the powerless. They may disguise the true realities of power, but, at the same time, they may curb that power and check its intrusions. And it is often from within that very rhetoric (of law) that a radical critique of the practice of the society is developed. (265)[18]

We add, however, that the possibilities for and modes of strategic legal contestation tend to vary with the forms of law (discussed earlier) that govern specific institutional contexts and constructions of contending subjects. Much legal contestation takes place among recognized rights-bearing citizen subjects and groups, usually represented by legal or political elites, over means and degrees of legal enforcement or the authoritative meaning of general, often clashing, liberal legal principles, for example, between property rights and equal protection, between religious freedom and invidious racial or sexual discriminaton, between free speech and police power, or over the proper scope of police violence. This is the stuff of routine "liberal" legal mobilization policy analysis, and it is important. Scholarly study of variable institutional opportunities and unequal instrumental group resources thus makes sense, the legal analog of analyzing interest group politics (Epp 1998, 2010; Paris 2010). Yet other struggles are less over competing constructions of liberal principles than over challenges to practices that depart from or undermine officially promulgated liberal principles and rules. This is closer to Scheingold's classic argument about how the "myth of rights" often is deployed through an aspirational "politics of rights" to close the gaps between principle and practice (Scheingold 1974; Epp 1998; Gould and Barclay 2012; Paris 2010).

But much contestation instead involves efforts by subaltern semifree or unfree groups to mobilize liberal legal principles of equal treatment to challenge the overtly repressive forms of institutionalized social control and domination in various zones of society, thus endeavoring to expand the promises of liberal legal equality to historically marginalized subjects and illiberally governed institutional spaces. The history of workers' class struggles to supplant the feudal remnants of American employment law fit this characterization (Orren 1991). Contests over repressive legal management targeting minority racial, gender, sexual, immigrant, and other marginalized populations at work, in housing arrangements or in the carceral state, routinely take this more ambitious, systematically reform-oriented character as well (Smith 1997). For example, liberal equality principles have provided useful if limited resources for challenges to de facto as well as de jure racial segregation in public and workplace institutions as well as racially targeted police violence—a classic manifestation of repressive law—over the last century, from the early NAACP through the Black Lives Matter movement (Francis 2014; see also Epp 2010). Similarly, the appeals to liberal principles of equal rights provided unfairly compensated women in gender-segregated occupations grounds for potentially transformative challenges in the wage-equity movement during the 1970s and 1980s (McCann 1994). Efforts to expand and fortify rights for victims of domestic violence fit the tradition of activism as well (A.-M. Marshall 2016; Merry 2000, 2003). Finally, our historical story about how unfree, noncitizen Filipino nationals struggled to expand basic equal-protection rights and to challenge multiple manifestations of repressive law at and beyond work provides an especially important, if complex, historical model for rights "mobilization under illegality" today by undocumented immigrants (including DREAMers), day laborers, asylum seekers, deportees, felons, the homeless and generally poor, and other struggling working-class and devalued people (Venkatesh 2016).

The types of struggles against hierarchy noted above are each different but important, and they all deserve sober, critical attention devoid of romance about law's inherent principled inclusiveness. Most of these modes of contestation tend to privilege efforts to advance "resonant rights claims that stick close to familiar legal constructions and meanings in an effort to 'win . . . popular support and elite allies'" (Ferree 2003, 305–6; see also Godoy 2013, 19; McCann 1994).[19] We underline further, though, that while enforcement of prevailing neoliberal ideology may be a formidable constraint, legal mobilization in practice does not require subaltern groups to completely accept prevailing liberal, process-based legal norms sustaining hierarchical order. After all, moderate claims that may be resonant at one moment can become more radical and potentially transformative at another juncture, and vice versa. This was E. P. Thompson's core theoretical point. And it has been illustrated by our historical narrative regarding both generations of Filipino labor activists who persistently mobilized conventional rights for reconstructive purposes and reconfigured familiar rights into new, substantively radical visions for action. Indeed, previous pages have shown that struggles on behalf of transformative rights claims by defiant activists—including migrant noncitizens, semifree black labor activists, female workers, and their allies in our narrative study who eventually were granted citizen status and yet persisted in their transformative quests—have been commonplace in US history. In particular, legions of committed leftist activists in and beyond the United States have embraced the liberal principle of egalitarian citizenship to contest the proprietarian, profit-based principles of capitalism and to challenge the directly unequal material resource distribution and intersectional race/class/gender exploitation at the heart of the liberal legal system (W. Brown 2002; Smith 1997; also Kelley 2015). Such "novel" egalitarian rights claims (Polletta 2000) express "radical ideas [that] are attractive to movement actors who seek a restructuring of hegemonic ideas and the interests they express and support" (Ferree 2003, 305–6).

The latter types of novel egalitarian, class-based rights claims most often develop from a nomos born of cultural experiences distant from national legal institutions and centers of power (Polletta 2000). They may emanate from minority group experiences "below," at local peripheries removed from central state power, as Cover imagined (Spade 2015). Or they may migrate from other national, transnational, or international traditions, including those committed to human rights. Immigrants and marginal communities thus are often the source of such potentially transformative visions (Apostolidis 2009; Cummings 2018). Filipino activists in particular, we have seen, drew on a mix of traditional Filipino cultural norms, appropriation of Spanish Catholic ideas, Marxist philosophical sources, Popular Front intellectual resources, and international human rights logics, plus more. Their hybrid oppositional legal consciousness was grounded fundamentally in experience-based understandings about the workings of class, race, and gender inequality. We reiterate that the authors of these claims were not privileged elites but were "ordinary" working-class activists enacting aspirations born of long-standing oppression and marginalization.

At the same time, we should only expect various types of both preemptive and reactive countermobilization by dominant groups against such rival claims from below. Historical study, including this book, confirms that most advances for social equality are episodic, inherently constrained, and followed by periods of inertia and retrenchment (Klarman 2007; Klinkner and Smith 1999). As Nemesio Domingo put it, historical reconstructions of civil rights routinely have been followed by "deconstruction." It bears repeating that worker mobilization of both New Deal labor law and 1960s civil rights laws for egalitarian change were followed by "deradicalizing" judicial decisions and legislation.

Each of the different modes of rights contestation outlined above, and especially radical egalitarianism, typically are met with a standard repertoire of countermobilization maneuvers by dominant groups in the racial capitalist order (Dudas, Goldberg-Hiller, and McCann 2015). First, privileged elites routinely challenge the social status or identity of those *who* raise rights claims, invoking disqualifications such as race, ethnicity, religion, gender, sexual preference, wealth, education, character, and other criteria of deficient merit. Again, "identity politics" is usually anchored in imperatives imposed by dominant groups. Filipino migrants before World War II were denied legal standing on all of these bases, which compounded the intersectional process of stigmatization. Restrictions on "group rights" and trimming of class action status is another version of violence against legal identity reconstruction. Second, dominant groups habitually challenge the content of contending visions of rights and law, especially those that migrate from resonant claims toward radicalism (Ferree 2003). The substantive terms of *what* is being proposed is simply not part of "our" official legal rights tradition, it is often said. The claims do not qualify as "real" or legitimate equality rights but rather are illegitimate "special rights." This was the gist of court rulings about early Filipino property-rights claims and the subsequent generation of workers' egalitarian disparate impact theory in *Wards Cove*, not to mention the activists' democratic socialist ethos.

Finally, dominant groups and their official representatives often decry *how* challenging groups wage their rights campaigns. Radical workers' associations and Left unionism, for example, were frequently identified as improper, even criminal organizations, a veritable danger to democratic government and reason for rights denial in our historical story of Filipino labor activists. Moreover, even appeals to courts are often selectively decried as inadequately democratic, majoritarian, or representative (Haltom and McCann 2004). This dynamic again is exemplified by Justice White's express reluctance in the *Wards Cove* ruling to impose judicial will supporting minority workers against private corporate prerogatives. All of these rhetorical gambits by dominant groups, enforced by state legal violence, work to contain the various sorts of rights claims, either resonant or radical, by differently situated marginal groups.[20]

That said, these distinctions among different types of rights claiming and counterclaiming repertoires also help to explain why alternative normative commitments among dissident groups often survive epistemic violence wrought by courts and other legal elites. Jurispathic rulings and organized countermobilization may attempt to kill off discrete alternative legal constructions by denying them status as official law, as Cover puts it. But judges and other representatives of dominant groups are often unable to destroy an underlying nomos that develops across generations of social interaction and narrative construction among marginalized communities. Official law speaks its own insistent dialect of normativity that enforces racial capitalist relations, but legal meaning develops within many groups from a different and equally resilient array of historically forged ideational and solidaristic resources.

These insights help to make sense of why empirical sociolegal scholars have so often found that ordinary people's understandings of rights are more fragmented and diverse than expected by critical scholars who worry about the totalizing effects of legal ideological constraint, including especially the tendency of litigation strategies to narrow or co-opt the political aspirations of movements (e.g., McCann 1994; Lovell 2012). The persistence of those broader normative commitments among various communities means that defiant and even radical (Kelley 2015; Santos and Rodriguez-Garavito 2005) aspirations[21] emanating from alternative visions may surface again at different times and in new jurisgenetic forms to challenge the official legal order, forcing judges and other officials repeatedly to make choices about grants of legal status. The concept of episodic legal maiming—rather than killing—by Whac-A-Mole[22] officials fits easily with social movement groundings of legal mobilization theory that recognize the endurance of many rights claims and legal visions despite the relatively short life cycles of discrete historical social movements (Melucci 1989; Tarrow 1993). And that premise very much has been the case in our story of Filipino workers over several generations.

The latter type of intense contestation over law often imposes high costs on defiant activists, of course, further marginalizing their status and putting bodies on the line for violent reprisal and even death (Cover 1986). As we have argued, it is the institutionalized violence, disciplinary controls, and coercive incentive systems enacted, or at least threatened, by official law that most sustain hegemonic hierarchical order. Practical assessments of material cost and loss, often routinized into resignation, generally constrain defiant action far more than does restricted aspirational imagination, especially for the most marginal segments of society. As such, it was the persistent involvement of Filipino labor activists in rebellious action, including in many forms of contentious group politics, that made the legal mobilization framework relevant for our historical narrative. Our account of Filipino cannery workers documented many casualties of legal contestation, including the state harassment and detention, the civic death of deportation, and murders of two young rights activists in the early 1980s. At the same time, while subsequent state prosecution in the latter case quickly pinned the murder on two gang thugs, a prolonged civil trial over nearly a decade traced the conspiracy to convict a corrupt union boss and draw reparation from Philippine president Ferdinand Marcos.

To some degree, our historical narrative thus illustrates that, as Scheingold (like Thompson) famously argued, "law cuts both ways," for and against egalitarian social justice (Scheingold 1974, 91; McCann 1994). As such, rights entitlements are constantly renegotiated through both macrohistorical and individual micropolitical struggles. When, how, and to what degree legal discourse and institutions provide resources for challenge and change benefiting subaltern groups such as Filipino labor activists depends largely on the mix of legal and, especially, extralegal contextual factors. Our study thus devoted considerable attention to analyzing the changing cultural and institutional terrain of racial capitalist empire that delimited the possibilities and forms of contestation within and against law.

However, we underline again that it is law's reliance on overwhelming force that most supports hierarchical order and facilitates control of law's official constructions by powerful organized interests in white, heteropatriarchal, capitalist society. Our historical narrative regarding minority labor activists thus includes moments of triumph but, predictably, far more often mixed achievements and tragic defeats, setbacks, and routine subjugation. The concessions that the official, if variegated and hybrid, legal order at any point make to egalitarian challenges tend to be few, compromised, limited in scope, and slow in development (Bell 1980). Moreover, the proliferation of nomothetic visions is hardly limited to inclusionary, expansive, egalitarian aspirations; we recognize the many reactionary, exclusionary legal claimants that have persisted to uphold hierarchy, often in highly influential ways, throughout our history. The preceding historical narrative is a testament to all of these general positions.

Our focus on these complexities of power in a host of different struggles over rights has led us to sidestep attempts to develop or deploy systematic assessments regarding the balance of gains and setbacks that specific episodes of legal contestation generated for the working-class minority subjects at the heart of our story. An abundant and rich scholarly literature has been dedicated to evaluating winning and losing in legal battles, including the propensity for "backlash" (Albiston 2010; Cummings 2018; Keck 2009; Lobel 2003; NeJaimes 2011); we have contributed to these inquiries elsewhere. But we are not inclined here to endorse judging rights-based group activism by the standards of wins and losses in discrete disputing episodes, as if the quest for justice was a sports event. Rather, we follow Gramsci in imagining campaigns for social justice as ongoing trench battles in larger, sustained historical struggles (McCann 1994). As such, one of the primary criteria by which each aspirational act should be judged is the degree to which it becomes a resource and inspiration for subsequent contentious action. Public contests over legal principles and practices, whether within or outside of official legal institutions, often generate "forums of protest" that can keep alive alternative ideas and ideals, inspire and hotwire mobilization for new forms of advocacy, keep pressure on dominant groups to reassess their interests in conceding changes that benefit marginalized people, and thus sometimes alter at least slightly the balance of power among social groups. Even losing a battle in an official legal court, or in the court of public opinion, can leave a positive, potentially catalyzing legacy (Depoorter 2013). As Jules Lobel (2003, 2006) has argued repeatedly and eloquently, struggle for more just alternative worlds is often a Sisyphean quest, an expression of faith and courage, sometimes but not always attended by hopeful expectation. But such quests are also can be "prophetic," in that they imagine possibilities that provide the inspiration and templates for transformations that others act on in future times or other places.

The previous pages accounted for several generations of Filipino-led cannery workers engaged in such aspirational political contests over and through law. These jurisprudential struggles have been, in Guinier and Torres's (2014) evocative terms, "demosprudential" in that they introduced "new forms of representation" that disrupted the dominance of narrowly divided elite groups and actually worked to "bring the voices and bodies of non-elites into the discourse" (Torres 2007, 142). It is important in this regard not to equate official legal maiming, taming, and even killing of such rival nomoi with simple affirmation of the status quo. When judges or other legal officials reject some claims and uphold others, the preexisting dominant legal community is generally sustained. At the same time, though, the larger community's discursive conventions and institutional forms are often transformed in the process. When new groups are recognized as rights-bearing members, or demands for new types of rights entitlement are at least acknowledged, the community nomos and legal ordering are to some degree reconstituted. This is especially true in the types of struggles over citizenship, civil rights, civil liberties, and fundamental social relations that we have addressed in this book. Documenting this aspirational, demosprudential form of politics has been our core quest, while assessing the complex ways that the activists did and did not succeed in changing hegemonic relations has remained an important but secondary task (e.g., Cummings 2018). Both analytical projects are vital for scholars interested in calling attention to movements striving for more democratic, substantively just political orders, including the campaigns of activists who deemphasize or eschew rights-claiming and legal mobilization strategies.

Comparative Cross-National, Historical, Global Applications

Our analytical narrative has been grounded in US history, but racial capitalism at once emanates from and transcends the American empire. Much of the story we have told was built in various ways through colonial experiments that left deep imprints in postcolonial regimes and has been reproduced by the dynamics of what often is referred to as *globalism*. What is globalism but the expansion of racial capitalism, at once advanced and sustained by varieties of intersecting legal orders and producing increasing inequality within and among nations and people? Undeniable differences persist between the Global North and South, but the interdependencies also have continued to grow. A wide range of comparative study has explored different historical trajectories of racialization, capitalism, and racial capitalism (e.g., Winant 2001, 2004).

Legal mobilization theory has been employed by scholars for study of political struggles in nearly all parts of the world and in a variety of more and less authoritarian contexts (e.g., Ahmed Zaki 2018; Belge 2006; Chua 2014; Cichowski 2007; Gallagher 2017; Kahmaran 2017; Kurban 2017; Lake 2018; Moustafa 2009; Santos and Rodriguez-Garavito 2005; Whiting 2017). This is not surprising, because struggles to claim equal rights, to increase inclusion and empowerment through invoking creative rights claims, have become commonplace, nearly ubiquitous. Both the promises and limits of that politics of rights have been evidenced in most parts of the globe (Haglund and Stryker 2015). Studies by many leading scholars have provided reason to think that legal mobilization theory can continue to help to make sense of these developments. But inclusion of the deeper analysis about the roots of social inequality, institutionalized hierarchy, and the role of law in sustaining those inequalities within differing contests is essential to making analytical advances.

Our aim has not been to nurture either pessimism or optimism so much as to promote understanding and appreciation of how unequal social power shapes the possibilities of legal contestation in these historical processes. As Robert Cover exhorted, "just as it is our distrust for and recognition of the state as reality that leads us to be constitutionalists with regard to the state, so it ought to be our recognition of and distrust for the reality of the power of social movements that leads us to examine the *nomian* worlds they create." In sum, the vast plurality of "legal meaning is a challenging enrichment of social life, a potential restraint on arbitrary power and violence. We ought to stop circumscribing the nomos; we ought to invite new worlds" (Cover 1983, 68). This book has not aimed to advocate the specific rights-based, democratic socialist nomos espoused by the Filipino American labor activists whose legacy we document, although our affinity has been clear. Rather, our primary normative aim has been simply to celebrate their aspirations to produce a more democratic, egalitarian, just, and free world. We exhort scholars to document yet other histories of subaltern aspirational legal mobilization and political struggle generally around the globe (Darian-Smith 2013).

APPENDIX

Official Legal Texts

Legislative Acts

1790 Naturalization Act of 1790
1882 Chinese Exclusion Acts
1888 Scott Act of 1888
1892 Chinese Exclusion Acts
1892 Geary Act of 1892
1902 Chinese Exclusion Acts
1904 Chinese Exclusion Acts
1906 Naturalization Law
1914 Act of June 30, 1914 (service member naturalization)
1916 Jones Act 1916
1917 Immigration Act of 1917
1918 Act of May 9, 1918 (service member naturalization)
1924 Immigration Act of 1924 (also known as the Johnson Reed Act)
1934 Tydings-McDuffie Act of 1934
1940 Nationality Act of 1940
1945 War Brides Act
1950 McCarran Internal Security Act
1952 Immigration and Nationality Act of 1952 (McCarran-Walter Act)
1954 Communist Control Act
1964 Civil Rights Act of 1964 (Pub.L. 88-352, 78 Stat. 241) (including Title VII)
1965 Immigration and Naturalization Act of 1965 (also known as the Hart-Celler Act)
1976 Foreign Sovereign Immunities Act of 1976
1991 Civil Rights Act of 1991

Court Rulings

Bradwell v. State of Illinois, 83 U.S. (16 Wall.) 130 (1873)
Yick Wo v. Hopkins, 118 U.S. 356 (1886)
Chae Chan Ping v. United States, 130 U.S. 581 (1889)
Fong Yue Ting v. United States, 149 U.S. 698 (1893)
In re Saito, 62F (D. Mass, 1894)
Lem Moon Sing v. United States, 158 U.S. 538 (1895)
U.S. v. Wong Kim Ark (1898)
Lone Wolf v. Hitchcock, 187 U.S. 553 (1903)
United States v. Ju Toy, 198 U.S. 253 (1905)
In re Kumagai, 163 F. 922 (W.D. Wash. 1908)
In re Knight, 171 F. 299 (E.D.N.Y. 1909)
Bessho v. United States, 178 F. 245 (4th Cir. 1910)
In re Alverto, 198 F. 688 (E.D. Pa. 1912)
In re Mallari, 239 F. 416 (D. Mass. 1916)
In re Lampitoc, 232 F. 382 (S.D.N.Y. 1916)
In re Bautista, 245 F. 765 (N.D. Cal. 1917)
In re Rallos, 241 F. 686 (E.D.N.Y. 1917)
In re Para, 269 F. 643 (S.D.N.Y. 1919)
In re Charr, 273 F. 207 (W.D. Mo. 1921)
In re Song, 271 F. 23 (S.D. Cal. 1921)
United States v. Toyota, 290 F. 971 (D. Mass. 1923)
Terrace v. Thompson, 263 U.S. 197 (1923)
California v. Yatko, No. 24795, Superior Court of Los Angeles County, May 11, 1925
Toyota v. United States, 268 U.S. 402 (1925)
United States v. Javier, 22 F.2d 879 (D.C. Cir. 1927)
Robinson v. Lampton, County Clerk of Los Angeles County, No. 2496504, Superior Court of Los Angeles County (1930).
Visco v. Los Angeles County, No. 319408, Superior Court of Los Angeles County (1931).
Roldan v. Los Angeles County, 18 P.2d 706 (Cal. Ct. App. 1933)
De La Ysla v. United States, 77 F.2d 988 (9th Cir. 1935)
Schecter Poultry v. United States, 295 U.S. 495 (1935)
North Whittier Heights Citrus Ass'n v. N.L.R.B., 97 F. (2d) 1010 (C.C.A. 9th 1938)
Santa Cruz Fruit Packing Co. v. National Labor Relations Board, 303 U.S. 453 (1938)
De Cano et al. v. State of Washington, 110 P.2d 627 (Wash. 1941)
Suspine v. Compania Transatlantica Centroamericana, 37 F. Supp. 268 (S.D.N.Y. 1941)

State ex rel. Cannery etc. v. Sup. Ct, 193 P.2d 362 (Wash. 1948)
Perez v. Sharp, 32 Cal.2d 711 (Cal. 1948)
Ex Parte Mangaoang, 87 F. Supp. 932 (W.D. Wash. 1949)
Mangaoang v. Boyd, 186 F.2d 191 (9th Cir. 1950)
Harisiades v. Shaughnessy, 342 U.S. 580 (1952)
Mangaoang v. Boyd, 205 F.2d 553 (9th Cir. 1953)
Boyd v. Mangaoang, 346 U.S. 876, cert. denied (1953)
Barber v. Gonzales, 347 U.S. 637 (1954)
U.S. ex rel. Alcantra v. Boyd, 222 F.2d 445 (9th Cir. 1955)
Hazel Wolf v. John Boyd, 238 F.2d 249 (9th Cir. 1957)
Caughlan v. International Longshoremen's and Warehousemen's Union, Local No. 37-C, 52 Wn.2d 656 (Wash. 1958)
Garza v. Patnode, 65 Lab. Cas. (CCH) 52 (1971)
Griggs v. Duke Power Co., 401 U.S. 424 (1971)
State v. Fox, 82 Wn.2d 289 (Wash. 1973)
Domingo v. New England Fish Company, Case No. 713-73 C2 (W.D.Wa. filed 1973)
Carpenter v. NEFCO-Fidalgo, Case No. C74-4074S (W.D.Wa. filed 1974)
Washington v. Davis, 426 U.S. 229 (1976)
Hazelwood School District v. United States, 433 U.S. 299 (1977)
International Brotherhood of the Teamsters v. United States, 431 U.S. 324 (1977)
Domingo v. New England Fish Co., 445 F. Supp. 421 (W.D. Wash. 1977)
In re New England Fish Co., Bankruptcy No. 80-00864, ADV NO 08-0649. 19 B.R. 323 (1982)
Carpenter v. NEFCO-Fidalgo, 727 F.2d 1429 (9th Cir. 1984)
State v. Guloy, 104 Wn.2d 412 (Wash. 1985)
McClesky v. Kemp, 481 U.S. 279 (1987)
Watson v. Fort Worth Bank & Trust, 487 U.S. 977 (1988)
City of Richmond v. J.A. Croson Co., 488 U.S. 469 (1989)
Wards Cove Packing Co. v. Atonio, 490 U.S. 642 (1989)
Trajano v. Marcos, Nos. 86-2448, 86-15039, 1989 WL 76894, at 1 (9th Cir. July 10, 1989)
In re Estate of Marcos Human Rights Litigation, 910 F. Supp. 1460 (D. Haw. 1995)

Insular Cases (1901)

De Lima v. Bidwell, 182 U.S. 1
Goetze v. United States, 182 U.S. 221
Dooley v. United States, 182 U.S. 222
Armstrong v. United States, 182 U.S. 243
Downes v. Bidwell, 182 U.S. 244

Huus v. New York and Porto Rico Steamship Co., 182 U.S. 392
Dooley v. United States, 183 U.S. 151
Fourteen Diamond Rings [Pepke] v. United States, 183 U.S. 176

Summaries of Trial Proceedings

Files I–V. All verbatim summaries provided by the legal team headed by Mike Withey and on file with authors.

Notes

Introduction

1. Blackmun's use of the term *immunize* (at 662) is suggestive. He no doubt had in mind the greatly increased "immunity" against legal claims challenging racial (and gender) discrimination that the court's reasoning provided to employers. But the medicalized use of the term also connotes protection against a disease. This reading links the majority's dismissive portrayal of the cannery workers as undeserving plaintiffs assaulting legitimate business interests to the widely publicized allegations by conservative elites about an imagined epidemic of excessive, frivolous litigation in late twentieth-century America. See Haltom and McCann (2004).

2. "The essence of proletarianization is the loss of control over one's labor process and the alienation of the product of that labor" (Lewontin 1998, 76).

3. Bulosan wrote elsewhere in greater detail: "My father was a small farmer, but when I was five or six years old his small plot of land was taken by usury; and usury was the greatest racket of the ilustrado, and it still is although it is now the foreigners who are fattening on it. My father had a big family to support, so he became a sharecropper, which is no different from the sharecroppers in the Southern States. Years after, because of this sharecropping existence, my father fell into debts with his landlord, who was always absent, who had never seen his tenants—and this was absentee landlordism, even more oppressive than feudalism. Then my father really became a slave—and they tell me there is no slavery in the Philippine Islands!" Quoted in San Juan (2008).

4. The union changed its name to gender-neutral terms in 1997, dropping the "men's" from "longshore" and "warehouse," responding to rank-and-file delegate Lila Smith's proposal.

5. Fraser helpfully distinguishes the "exploited" labor of "free" citizen contract

workers from "expropriated" labor of noncitizens and semifree second-class citizens. The latter labor is conscripted rather than contracted, dependent rather than independent (Fraser 2016, 165). See also Singh (2016).

6. It is worth underlining political scientist Karen Orren's (1991) argument that American labor law, including for white waged workers, was grounded in authoritarian feudal principles of master-servant relations until the 1930s era of liberalization.

7. Melamed distinguishes among the general logic of antiracist racial liberalism and varieties of liberal multiculturalism and neoliberalism. Our study focusing on workers gives most attention to the first and third ideological currents.

8. Arguably, therefore, *racial heteronormative patriarchal capitalist* order may be a more apt term for most studies. Most critical scholars tend to think that history supports use of the term *capitalist* as inherently signaling intersectional racial, gender, and sexual hierarchies. See the conclusion.

9. We fully acknowledge that our particular focus on, and understanding of, law is not the angle that many of the activist subjects of our study tend to emphasize in their own storytelling.

Prologue to Part One

1. The gendered logic of "manliness" propelling the imperialist project is analyzed by Hoganson (1998).

2. "White love holds out the promise of fathering, as it were, a 'civilized people' capable of asserting its own character. But it also demands the indefinite submission to a program of discipline and reformation requiring the constant supervision of a sovereign master" (Rafael 2000, 23).

3. The term *race war* and discussion in this section draw heavily on Kramer (2006). Edmund Wilson's 1962 book ([1962] 1994) focuses on the Civil War, but his introduction extends the theme to subsequent bloody empire building in the Philippines.

4. This account, including the labels, draws on Weiner (2006) and Smith (1997, 433–39).

5. Justice Edward Douglass White's reasoning harbingered another Justice White (Byron) ninety years later in *Wards Cove Packing Co. v. Atonio* (1989). Both Whites similarly joined support for both capitalist business interests and racial hierarchy, although the latter was of a less explicit and slightly more "innocent" form of color-blind racism.

6. For an interesting argument about how the American commitment to constructing constitutional self-government in the Philippines marked the beginning of a newly imagined commitment to constitutionalism that animated US politics for the following century, see Rana (2010).

Chapter One

1. *Pinoy* is the term used for self-identification by the first wave of Filipinos to the continental United States before World War II. It has been used both in a pejorative sense and as a positive term of endearment.

2. Manilatowns became havens for a host of indulgences—alcohol, drugs, prostitution, gambling, petty violence—that were unsavory to discipline-based white-capitalist society but that were, ironically, learned amid the exploitative new circumstances of America quite unlike in their native land. Carlos Bulosan often lamented the learned habits of Filipinos in America.

3. The nightclub attracted America's greatest jazz musicians and became the inspiration for Duke Ellington's short film and tune *Black and Tan Fantasy* (Faltys-Burr 2009).

4. The juxtaposition of markets and law in this quote implies that markets are independent forces, which obscures the fact that all markets are constructed to some extent by law and unequal social power. We thus restate the point by noting that the laws that structured Southern markets were driven by goals of sustaining white control and subordination of African Americans rather than racially neutral ends of efficiency.

5. The exploitation of Chinese immigrants paralleled and primed the treatment of Filipinos. The political struggles of Chinese workers, especially in the American South during Reconstruction, also harbingered and provided organizational and legal precedents for Filipino activists. See Jung (2006).

6. The relative freedom of movement was not a "right." It was, paradoxically, inherent in the subjugated condition of conscripted or expropriated labor. See De Genova (2010).

7. Much of this section was initially prompted by our reading of Baldoz (2011, 38–43), but Rydell's (1983, 1984, 2012) extensive analysis expanded our understanding greatly. See also Kramer (2006), Silva (1994), and the powerful collection of images and text in Galang (2003).

8. The University of Washington itself owes a great deal to US military and economic empire building around the Pacific Rim. Many campus monuments—such as the bust of railroad mogul, Philippines annexation supporter, and "Empire Builder" James J. Hill—honor that history.

9. Violence against the Chinese in earlier decades was common. For example, in February 1886, a white mob invaded Chinatown in Seattle and ransacked the homes of three hundred denizens, forcing over two hundred Chinese to embark on a ship headed for San Francisco. Although local King County authorities and militiamen attempted to impose order on the chaos, the event was violent and bloody. A week later, 154 of the remaining Chinese were forced on to two more ships departing the city (Gillmer 2012, 403). "In one week, virtually the entire Chinese population of

Seattle was deported and the city's original Chinatown became history" (Taylor 1994, 112).

10. Vigilante violence by KKK and related white supremacist groups against African American and Japanese workers was common in the 1920s and 1930s as well. See Griffey (2007).

11. It is relevant that Bulosan often brands Filipinos as naive "innocents" but does not turn the migrants into saints. In fact, at many points in *America Is in the Heart*, Allos is saddened, ashamed, frustrated, even horrified by the ugly, unruly, violent behavior of some Filipino men. At one point, he questions what happened to these men, who were not prone to such behavior back home. But he rarely "responsibilizes" such uncivil or destructive behavior. Instead, he increasingly comes to understand that it is America—where greed, self-interested exchange relations, and brutal race and class exploitation abound—that has transformed his fellow countrymen into something worse than before they arrived. This insight is part of Bulosan's political awakening.

12. Du Bois frequently labeled the lawless violence imposed on Negroes in the Reconstruction South as "terror." "Lawlessness and violence filled the land, and terror stalked abroad by day, and it burned and murdered by night," he wrote in his epic *Black Reconstruction in America* ([1935] 1998, 694).

13. As a result of American administration and colonial education in the Philippines, Filipino immigrants were indoctrinated in United States history and culture. Baldoz (2011, 89) thus writes, "Filipinos regarded themselves as 'Americanized' because of their colonial education and took the egalitarian rhetoric propagated by U.S. officials and teachers in the islands at face value." See also Taylor (1994, 123).

14. In re Buntaro Kumagai, 163F. at 924. This position was consistent with earlier cases, especially In re Saito, 62F (D. Mass, 1894), and it was affirmed in other subsequent cases. See Sohoni and Vafa (2010). Once again, our discussion parallels Baldoz (2011), but draws also on other authors' more detailed legal analysis.

15. In re Song, 271 F. 23 (S.D. Cal. 1921).

16. This section draws on many sources, but most important is the excellent study by Nomura (1986–1987).

17. Carlos Bulosan defended against antimiscegenation by showing that love between brown male bodies and white women was antiracist and antipatriarchal, part of the revolutionary vision of radical community. See Amorao (2014).

18. Primary documents for this history can be accessed at http://depts.washington.edu/civilr/images/antimisceg/. Secondary sources include Gillmer (2012), S. Johnson (2005), and Strandjord (2009).

19. This is not to deny that Filipino migrant laborers were diverse and divided in their views. Subsequent chapters will make some of the divisions very clear. We continue to focus, though, on the radical activists, their leaders, and their aspirational projects.

Chapter Two

1. We draw heavily in these paragraphs on the characterization of the salmon canning industry written by the 1970s cannery worker leader Gene Viernes in his seven-part 1977 newspaper series (Viernes 2012). We will draw on his history throughout this chapter and then reflect on it more analytically in chapter 4.

2. The fish butchering machine was developed by a Canadian living in Seattle during the early 1900s after Chinese butchers repeatedly demanded higher wages (Mawani 2010, 49–50).

3. In many regards the labor contractor system presaged what David Weil (2014) has called "the fissured workplace" in the neoliberal era of corporate management through exploitative subcontracting.

4. For a sampling of the copious scholarly literature, see also Forbath (1991), Frymer (2008), Hattam (1993), Rogers (1990), Stone (1981), and Tomlins (1985a).

5. The International Longshoremen's Association was affiliated with the AFL until it affiliated with the CIO in 1937 as the International Longshoremen's and Warehousemen's Union (ILWU). The union later changed to a more gender-neutral name, the International Longshore and Warehouse Union, in 1997 following a resolution by Lila Smith from the ILWU's marine division, the Inland Boatmen's Union.

6. Multiple interpretations of the events and the motives of Patron emerged from the period. See Friday (1994,: 145–48). See also Mislang (n.d. [UWSC]).

7. Casaday (1938, 156) notes that "the L. V. M. Trading Company, Inc." in Seattle "occupied approximately the same role as that of Young and Mayer in San Francisco." The historian documents lower but still high levels of grievances in Seattle during the 1930s.

8. North Whittier Heights Citrus Ass'n v. N.L.R.B., 97 F. (2d) 1010 (C.C.A. 9th 1938), Santa Cruz Fruit Packing Co. v. National Labor Relations Board, 303 U.S. 453 (1938).

9. The FTA refers to the Food, Tobacco, Agricultural, and Allied Workers. Chapter 3 will document how that union replaced the UCAPAWA in 1944. Donald Henderson, an economics professor at Columbia University, advocate for racialized low-wage workers, and member of the Communist Party, led the transition as president of both unions. Red Scare witch hunts destroyed the FTA by the late 1940s. See Ruiz (1987).

Chapter Three

1. ILWU Local 37, 1952, 7.

2. ILWU Local 37, 1952, lead editorial.

3. Labor historian Howard Kimeldorf (1988, 5) writes, "Combining militancy and radical politics, the ILWU was widely recognized as the strongest bastion of Communist unionism on the West Coast, if not the entire country."

4. In re Lagunilla, 30 Wn.2d 777 (1948)

5. This account of the Mangaoang legal battles draws heavily on presentations at the AILA Immigration Law Professor Committee presentations titled *Seattle: The McCarthy Era* on June 12, 1999. Ernesto's daughter, Juana Mana'o, and attorneys Hazel Wolf and Barry Hatten provided the accounts. The Barry Hatten papers in UW Special Collections, box 2, also were very useful. See also De Vera 1994. The texts of all the cited court rulings provide excellent data for the historical narrative.

6. Wolf described her experience years later: "It was during the hysteria of the McCarthy period in the '50s that I . . . was arrested for earlier membership in the Communist Party and held for deportation to Canada. . . . I have good reasons to believe that were it not for pro bono lawyers, I would not be here today. . . . My attorneys were John Caughlan, assisted by C. T. (Barry) Hatten. They worried my case for fifteen years through innumerable administrative hearings and to the U.S. Supreme Court twice on certiorari. . . . [They] did the major work for all of the 14 deportees in Washington State."

7. We do not make the facile claim that this portrait captures the uniform oppositional legal consciousness of *all* Filipino labor activists, much less the entire rank and file. The internal factionalism documented in earlier pages underlines that they did not march in lockstep or embrace a singular ideology, so we surely recognize a diversity of views among them. Our portrait is of a select but large and influential group of Left activists who constructed the yearbook. That said, even "moderates" and "liberals" identified in our study did not seem to vary greatly from the radicals in their aspirational rights commitments; divisions owed to other factors more than did abstract ideals.

8. We carefully used the words "alleged" to characterize Bridges's Communist leanings and even affiliations. No membership in the Communist Party was ever proven in court, and no evidence of direct ties to the Soviet Union, arguably the "real" security threat, was ever presented. We do not doubt that Bridges was committed to democratic socialism, praised the "workers' state" of the Soviet Union, and interacted with Communist groups in the United States, but his "communism" was a familiar American sort during the post-1934 Popular Front era.

9. Contrary to what social movement scholars might expect, the lawyer's essay differs little in substance, style, or strategic logic from other essays in the collection. Hatten portrays the deportation cases as racial "discrimination against . . . working class leaders" and a violation of "fundamental human rights." One of the more interesting lines is a quote from Supreme Court Justice Hugo Black in a ruling concerning a persecuted "Greek progressive leader" who had been a member of the Communist Party (*Harisiades v. Shaughnessy* 1952): "Punishment through banishment from the country may be placed . . . not for what he did, but for what his political views were or are."

10. Indeed, Bulosan was repeatedly grilled for joining W. E. B. Du Bois and others in corresponding with and helping to publish the autobiography of Luis Taruc,

a leader of the communist rebellion in the Philippines. "Committee to Sponsor Luis Taruc's Autobiography letter," ca. 1953. See also Baldoz (2014); Griffey (2018b).

11. "The defense of trade union rights becomes an issue wherever there is a sharpening of the permanent conflict between the mass of workers and the capitalist State, between the wage-earners and those who draw their wealth from the exploitation of others . . . in the capitalist and colonial countries. . . . The capitalist State increasingly introduces violence into these relations which correspond to the most reactionary political methods of imperialism" (31).

12. We note that contact between Filipino labor activists and radicalized Mexican Americans was influential as well and grew in the 1960s through the alliance of Philip Vera Cruz and Cesar Chavez. Scharlin and Villanueva (2000); see the prologue to part 2.

Prologue to Part Two

1. Vera Cruz and the UFW leadership split in the 1970s over the former's insistence that the union should organize undocumented workers and his opposition to US support for Ferdinand Marcos.

2. For further incisive discussion, see Rafael (1997) and Tadiar (1997).

3. We add "integrity" to the list because widespread corruption that undercut agency commitments and effectiveness while lining the pockets of administrative elites, including black neoliberals, proliferated in this period, beginning especially with the Reagan administration. See, for example, H. Johnson (2003).

Chapter Four

1. Tyree Scott, interview by Michael McCann. March 17, 1998.

2. Michael Fox, interview by Michael McCann and Doug Baker, 1998.

3. For example, Sue Williams (1978 [UWSC]) and a dozen other workers filed grievances concerning contractual violations of "working and living conditions" at the Peter Pan Diamond E facility. Williams specifically charged Local 37 president Tony Baruso in 1976–1977 for lack of responsiveness to her claims and then assistance in changing facilities. An administrative law judge, Jerrold H. Shapiro, found that Baruso and the union failed in its duty under the NLRA to fairly represent the workers and ordered the union to provide remedies. In 1977 over forty workers angrily petitioned Baruso for inaction on violations of their "basic rights to live and work under adequate conditions" at the Uganik Processing Plant.

4. Michael Woo, interview by Michael McCann, March 13, 1998.

5. Andy Pasqua, speaking in the film "Cannery Row," by Sharon Maeda (n.d.).

6. Michael Woo, interview by Michael McCann. March 13, 1998.

7. Ibid.

8. Terri Mast, interview by Michael McCann and Doug Baker, March 17, 1998.

9. Occena participated in classes led by Asian graduate students at the Univer-

sity of California, Berkeley, in the late 1960s. He was a leader in the struggle to save the San Francisco International Hotel and traveled to Cuba with the Venceremos Brigade.

10. On Scott's innovative early campaigns, see Griffey (2011; n.d.) and Gould (1977). Our account relies primarily on Tyree Scott, interview by Michael McCann, March 17, 1998.

11. Scott rejected labels for his brand of pragmatic radical politics. In a December 1969 interview in *Seattle Magazine*, Scott expressed his reaction to those who tried to label him: "People like labels. They're easier to deal with, but labels don't mean a thing. I talk to church people and they call me radical. The Panthers call me an Uncle Tom. Union people call me a communist and a guy at the University called me a fascist. It must mean I am doing something right." American Friends Service Committee (n.d.).

12. Tyree Scott, interview by Michael McCann, March 17, 1998.

13. Ibid.

14. Michael Woo told us that the UCWA "was successful at raising money. I mean, funding organizations had read about the success of this group in Seattle, Washington, and they were like throwing money at it. I remember doing a couple of fundraising trips myself back to Chicago. And in 15 minutes you'd literally send thirty or forty thousand dollars out to Seattle. . . . As a result of the lawsuits . . . we had some money, and, the vision was 'So how can we help other folks'"? Michael Woo, interview by Michael McCann, March 13, 1998.

15. In many ways, the window of opportunity began to close as quickly as it opened. In 1972 Congress passed a number of amendments limiting the EEOC's freewheeling tactics, and retrenchment against affirmative action and civil rights politics began to gain momentum at a national level (Mulroy 2018).

16. Tyree Scott, interview by Michael McCann, March 17, 1998.

17. Ibid.

18. Ibid.

19. A great example of the working philosophy is Fox's (1980, 1) essay "Some Rules for Community Lawyers". He quotes the classic lines by Stephen Wexler (1970, 1): "The object of practicing poverty law must be to organize poor people, rather than to solve their legal problems. The proper job for a poor people's lawyer is helping poor people to organize themselves to change things."

20. Tyree Scott, interview by Michael McCann, March 17, 1998.

21. Michael Fox, interview by Michael McCann and Doug Baker, 1998. The strategy of joining radical lawyering and creative litigation to grassroots organizing and protest paralleled and drew on movement-building experiences with the UFW in the 1960s and 1970s. See Gordon (2005).

22. Michael Woo, interview by Michael McCann, March 13, 1998.

23. Ibid.

24. Nemesio Domingo Jr., interview by Michael McCann and George Lovell, 2014.

25. Michael Woo, interview by Michael McCann, March 13, 1998.

26. Nemesio Domingo Sr., interview by Michael McCann, and Doug Baker, 1998.

27. Tyree Scott, interview by Michael McCann, March 17, 1998.

28. Michael Woo, interview by Michael McCann, March 13, 1998.

29. As LELO attorney Michael Fox told us, "The lawsuits were central to mobilizing support among workers in the union. It showed 'what we can do for you.'" Michael Fox, interview by Michael McCann and Doug Baker, 1998.

30. This is one of many manifestations of how the Asian "model minority" stereotype, which depicted Asians as valued for their economic productivity and political quiescence, made the young activists' radicalism divisive in the Filipino community. See Keum (2016).

31. David Della, interview by Michael McCann, March 8, 1998.

32. Abraham Arditi, interview by George Lovell and Michael McCann, February 5, 2015.

33. Ibid.

34. Michael Woo, interview by Michael McCann, March 13, 1998.

35. Ibid.

36. The KDP was ideologically diverse and contentious. The Marxist-Leninist Education Project was formative for many, and the commitment to "democratic centralism" won much support. See Cruz, Domingo, and Occena (2017). More broadly, the terms *democratic* and *socialist* most often surface in the discourse of the second as well as the first generation, so that is our primary characterization.

37. The call for unity in struggles for justice in many ways recalled the IWW and ILWU chants that "An Injury to One Is an Injury to All." Both underlined the global dimensions and targets of solidaristic local struggle.

38. Bruce Occena, interview by George Lovell and Michael McCann, 2011.

39. Terri Mast, interview by Michael McCann and Doug Baker, March 17, 1998; Bruce Occena, interview by George Lovell and Michael McCann, 2011. As such, the ACWA did not succumb to the pattern of tensions between civil rights litigation strategies and union power common in the era (Frymer 2008).

40. David Della, interview by Michael McCann. March 8, 1998.

41. Another reason that it was important to return to work is that Baruso continually tried to discredit the reformers as outsiders. RFC election pamphlets countered by emphasizing that the people on the RFC slate were actively working in the canneries.

42. Bruce Occena, interview by George Lovell and Michael McCann, 2011.

43. Terri Mast, interview by Michael McCann and Doug Baker, March 17, 1998.

44. Ibid.

45. Michael Woo, interview by Michael McCann, March 13, 1998.

46. David Della, interview by Michael McCann, March 8, 1998. See Chew (2012, 28).

47. Again, Baruso, like Marcos, drew considerable support among Seattle's Filipino Americans who shared their origins in Ilocos Norte province with him. He was also a prominent leader in the Filipino Community Center in Seattle and in the Caballeros de Dimas-Alang.

48. The cannery owners considered the work too delicate for Filipino men.

49. L. Domingo (2010) provides a detailed account of the RFC's strategies in the elections.

50. Terri Mast, among others, later lamented that decision as a tactical error. Terri Mast, interview by Michael McCann and Doug Baker, March 17, 1998.

51. As noted previously, the term *Tulisan* means "bandits" in Tagalog, and originally it was used by imperial leaders to characterize peasant resisters, quite unlike the later criminal thugs. The gang had been held responsible for the infamous "China Gate" shootings in Seattle's Chinatown during the 1970s. It went underground for several years and reemerged under the leadership of Tony Dictado; its primary activity was offering protection for gambling houses in the International District of Seattle, with whom the gang split profits in a classic "racket."

52. The term *revolutionary* comes up frequently in 1970s activist discourse. The collection of essays on the KDP often invokes the adjective. Domingo, Occena, and Cruz (2017). ACWA ally and attorney Mike Withey, who looms large in the subsequent chapter, underlines that Silme Domingo was a "revolutionary" and references several times revolutionary alliances in his book (Withey 2018). We nevertheless stick to our label of *radicalism* to capture the undeniable range of defiant and transformative goals of the activists.

53. Toribio (1998, 159) underlines the point about the dual challenge to racial capitalism: "What set the KDP apart from its national democratic counterparts in the Philippines was more than geographic given its location in the racially-conscious U.S.A. The decades long Civil Rights Movement which finally grew into massive proportions by the early 1960s underscored this consciousness. The question of race was the core issue in the other half of the KDP's program it labeled socialist."

54. Michael Fox, interview by Michael McCann and Doug Baker, 1998. See also Fox (1980).

Chapter Five

1. Our narrative in this chapter is based on evidence that was uncovered and presented in the three local criminal trials and the federal civil suit, a large body of archived records of the CJDV and union reform movements, and media stories on the murders. Lead attorney Mike Withey's detailed, verbatim summaries for all of the trials and the records of the various trials were invaluable. We also incorporate

details from three published book sources: one by a journalist (Churchill 1995) and two by activists (Chew 2012, and Withey 2018). We drafted this chapter long before receiving Withey's (2018) book, which tells the story in personal terms; we checked our facts with that narrative.

2. For a discussion of contemporary scholarship regarding American "empire" and imperial designs, see Coward (2005); Harvey (2003); Mann (2003).

3. The fact that Domingo, despite multiple gunshot wounds, was sufficiently rational and lucid to spell the names for Urpman became relevant at several points in the trials.

4. Michael Withey, interview by Michael McCann, June 9, 1998. See also Withey (2018). As we were completing this book in late 2018, Withey filed a lawsuit against the FBI for refusing to respond after several years of FOIA filings seeking to reopen the Domingo and Viernes murder case to determine FBI complicity. The Seattle office of the FBI has admitted that Forsythe was a confidential FBI informant.

5. David Della, interview by Michael McCann, March 8, 1998.

6. Michael Withey, interview by Michael McCann, June 9, 1998.

7. Vincent Warren is executive director of the Center for Constitutional Rights. His familiar mantra is "If you have an activist, a lawyer, and a storyteller, you can change the world." https://ccrjustice.org/home/blog/2017/11/10/if-you-have-activist-lawyer-and-storyteller-you-can-change-world.

8. This label shows up throughout materials in the Cindy Domingo Papers, UWSC. Withey (2018, 158–167) devotes a chapter to the alleged plan.

9. Trial time line, Domingo/Viernes murders (authors' files).

10. Trial time line, July 14, 1983 (authors' files).

11. Ibid.

12. This is the same Paul Manafort who served as campaign chair for President Trump in 2016 and whose long history of shady practices eventuated in convictions for tax evasion and bank fraud in 2018. See Al-Hiou and Kerr (2018).

13. Malabed deposition, read at trial. "Summaries of Proceedings," file IV, vol. 1, p. 76 (on file with authors).

14. Hibey testimony at trial. "Summaries of Proceedings," file IV, vol. 13, pp. 3–4 (on file with authors).

15. Manglapus testimony at trial. "Summary of Proceedings," file IV, vol. 3, November 22, 1989, pp. 10–14 (on file with authors).

16. Psinakis testimony at trial. "Summary of Proceedings," file IV, vol. 4, November 27, 1989, pp. 19–25 (on file with authors).

17. Gillego testimony at trial. "Summary of Proceedings," file IV, vol. 14, December 11, 1989, pp. 77–79 (on file with authors).

18. Avila testimony at trial. "Summary of Proceedings," file IV, vol. 4, November 27, 1989, pp. 25–31 (on file with authors).

19. Silme purportedly was the first Filipino to attain Phi Beta Kappa status at the University of Washington.

20. After Marcos escaped to Hawaii, a class of 9,541 members filed complaints for human rights abuses against Filipinos by the Marcos regime. In Trajano v. Marcos (1989), the Ninth Circuit consolidated appeals to previous dismissal in district courts and certified a class action, which became In re Estate of Marcos Human Rights Litigation (1995). A jury trial found for the claimants and awarded $1.2 billion in damages. The court found facially valid 5,193 claims of torture, 3,404 claims of summary execution, and 944 disappearance claims. See Lutz (1994) and Schreiber and Weissbach (1998).

21. Norm Maleng, Correspondence. Cindy Domingo Papers II, box 1, folder 3.

Chapter Six

1. Tyree Scott, interview by Michael McCann, March 17, 1998.

2. The term *deconstruction* clearly refers to acts of "destroying or taking apart . . . disassembly" or "undoing." The first deconstruction was the Reconstruction era following the Civil War; the second was the dismantling of robust conceptions of civil rights advanced in the 1960s and 1970s. *Wards Cove* was a major case that contributed to and symbolized this disassembly and disabling of civil rights law in the 1980s and beyond.

3. We draw on Charles W. Mills's (2017, 1) compelling interrogation of white ignorance as a form of "systematic group-based miscognition" that has prevailed in racial capitalist regimes. Mill's study examines "White ignorance as it plays itself out in the complex interaction of Eurocentric perception and categorization, white normativity, social memory and social amnesia, the derogation of non-white testimony, racial group interests, and motivated irrationality". This ignorance is not passive, but one "that resists, . . . fights back," (11) and is "militant, aggressive" (2).

4. Nemesio Domingo Jr., interviewed by Michael McCann and George Lovell, 2014.

5. Tyree Scott, interview by Michael McCann, March 17, 1998.

6. We underline that what follows is not a conventional or neutral jurisprudential account but rather an account of the legal narrative that the activists developed to bridge their egalitarian nomos and official law. See, for example, a range of expert views on the legal issues: Brest (1976), Carle (2011), Eisenberg (1977), Farhang (2010), Freeman (1998), Karst (1978), Runkel (1994), and Spann (2010).

7. Many of the practices in the cannery that could be challenged as disparate treatment are addressed in the following paragraphs as also matters of disparate impact, underlining the vague conceptual differences generally. The lawsuit focused on a range of practices, including hiring decisions that relied on racial labeling, differential advertisements, word of mouth among favored groups, nepotism, and vague subjective criteria; separate, inferior housing for "nonwhites" provided as part of the wage arrangement; inferior provision of food; and overall plantation-model organization.

8. Michael Fox, interview by Michael McCann and Doug Baker, 1998.

9. For the lawyerly version, see Bagenstos (2006) and Sturm (2001). The ACWA activists' argument about the sources of institutional racism parallels the sociological analysis of Nelson (1995; Nelson and Bridges 1999).

10. Michael Woo, interview by Michael McCann, March 13, 1998.

11. All these points are evident in the court rulings as well as in interviews with activists.

12. Michael Woo, interview by Michael McCann, March 13, 1998.

13. Tyree Scott, interview by Michael McCann. March 17, 1998.

14. David Della, interview by Michael McCann, March 8, 1998.

15. Michael Fox (interview by Michael McCann, March 13, 1998) made the same point to us: "Civil discovery in class action litigation can leave a real impact in building an organization among plaintiffs."

16. The activists did seek clear "goals" and "targets" in job opportunity and mobility, but the term *quota* misstates the requested remedies; the term was invoked by opponents to stigmatize more than accurately describe.

17. Abraham Arditi, interview by George Lovell and Michael McCann. February 5, 2015.

18. Tyree Scott, interview by Michael McCann, March 17, 1998.

19. Abraham Arditi, interview by George Lovell and Michael McCann, February 5, 2015.

20. By National Labor Relations Board precedent, an employer deemed to be a "successor" "must recognize and bargain with any union that represented the predecessor's employees. . . . An employer is considered a 'successor' if: (1) there is substantial continuity in the predecessor's and successor's business operations . . . , and (2) the predecessor's employees constitute a majority of the new employer's work force in a separate and appropriate bargaining unit" (Jenero 2017, 355).

21. We noted earlier why the salmon cannery industry declined steadily in midcentury and dramatically in the 1970s. The reasons for bankruptcy were in part specific to NEFCO.

22. Abraham Arditi, interview by George Lovell and Michael McCann, February 5, 2015.

23. The plaintiffs' names were Samuel Cabansag Jr., Joseph C. Ancheta, Thomas G. Carpenter, Silme G. Domingo, Nellie Kookesh, Audrea A. Merculief, Frank Paul, Mary Paul, Tony Evon Sr., and Samuel Strauss. After his 1981 assassination, Silme Domingo was represented by Terri Mast, administrator of his estate, cannery worker, and spouse.

24. We heard estimates that the award was $70,000 for nearly 7,000 hours of services.

25. Quote from the opening of the Ninth Circuit en banc ruling in Atonio v. Wards Cove Packing Company, 10 F.3d 1485 (1992). After studying this case for many

years, we acknowledge that the facts of its history are complex, often elusive, and much contested. Our abridged summary of rulings along the way relies heavily on the succinct summary in the Ninth Circuit's 1992 ruling on the appeal of the plaintiffs following the trial court's judgment on remand from the Supreme Court.

26. The other plaintiffs were Alan Lew, Curtis Lew, Eugene Bacliq, Joaquin Arruiza, Randy Del Fierro, Clarke Kido, Lester Kuramoto, and Margaret Baclig.

27. The presentation of the plaintiffs' case in court was arguably awkward, sometimes by defiant design of the plaintiffs and sometimes by inexperience. The judge repeatedly displayed annoyance about violations or fumbling of process. The plaintiffs were more like one-shotters (Galanter 1974) at the high level of appellate court, while the defense attorneys were experienced repeat players. Even more important, the plaintiffs were pushing the boundaries of race and class discrimination law, while the defense was adept at playing to traditional white, propertied legal protections for hierarchy. For the confident view of very capable corporate counsel, see Fryer (2016).

28. The panel included Blaine Anderson, Thomas Tang, son of a Chinese immigrant who ran a grocery store in Phoenix, and Herbert Choy, the Korean American judge who had participated in the *Domingo* case.

29. An en banc panel in the Ninth Circuit enlists eleven of the twenty-nine judges—the chief judge and ten others randomly drawn.

30. Abraham Arditi, interview by George Lovell and Michael McCann, February 5, 2015.

31. The attorneys for Wards Cove, supported by Judge McGovern, tried to settle the case several times early in the proceedings, but the plaintiffs' attorneys resisted, buoyed by victories in the other two cases.

32. Justice White wrote the majority opinion, joined by Justices Rehnquist, O'Connor, Scalia, and Kennedy—all Republican appointees. The dissenters—including Brennan and Marshall—were Democratic appointees. Justice Stevens was appointed to the US Court of Appeals for the Seventh Circuit in 1970 and to the Supreme Court by President Gerald Ford. He notably moved leftward during his time on the court, or, as he insisted, he stayed steady as the court moved rightward. Blackmun also was a Nixon appointee who moved toward more liberal positions over his time as judge as the overall court moved in the contrary direction. It is relevant that Justice Lewis F. Powell Jr. retired in 1987 before the court ruled in *Wards Cove*. However, the court's ruling paralleled and resembled closely Powell's majority position in *McCleskey v. Kemp* (1987), where the court refused to find systematic racial disparities in death penalty cases as creating no constitutional or statutory violation. Powell's decision and the logic of his famous 1971 Memorandum, which outlined an aggressive probusiness, neoliberal political strategy to contest those who "attack the American Free Enterprise System," resonates powerfully in Justice White's majority opinion in *Wards Cove*.

33. Again, we view our project as closer to what Guinier and Torres (2014) call

"demosprudence" in that we grant respect to minority worker democratic mobilization around a transformative rights narrative. We will cite in coming pages from Blackmun and Stevens, who offered "demosprudential dissents" challenging the majority's arbitrary rejection of ACWA claims (Guinier 2008).

34. Abraham Arditi, interview by George Lovell and Michael McCann, February 5, 2015.

35. For example, Samuel Cabansag's deposition in the NEFCO case stipulated that based on what his father had told him and his own "personal experience" in the canneries, he had reason to believe there was an "oral" and a "written" policy at NEFCO prohibiting hiring of minorities for that superintendent and other "certain jobs."

36. Tyree Scott, interview by Michael McCann, March 17, 1998.

37. This move from empirical grounding to abstract deductive reasoning was characteristic of "law and economics" approaches that attended Reagan-era neoliberal policy logics and judicial as well as administrative appointments.

38. Justice Stevens did notice the relevant part of the case record and noted in his dissent that three of the allegedly "unskilled" minority cannery workers had gone on to become, separately, an architect, an Air Force officer, and a graduate student in public administration. 490 U.S. 642, 675. Again, designations of "skill" were routinely conflated with race.

39. This was a period when a cultural narrative existed about excessive, frivolous-litigation-saturated American society because of concerted efforts of big business and complicity by the mass media. See Haltom and McCann (2004).

40. Tyree Scott, interview by Michael McCann,. March 17, 1998.

41. Belton (2014, 282–90) identifies *City of Richmond v. J.A. Croson Co.* as the "first judicial salvo in the massacre," while it was *Wards Cove v. Atonio*, along with *Lorance v. AT&T Technologies* and *Martin v. Wilks*, all issued between May 1 and June 22 in 1989, that "sounded the death knell for disparate impact." We call attention to how Belton's allusions to judicial killing of egalitarian principles echo both activist Tyree Scott and legal scholar Robert Cover.

42. Nemesio Domingo (2003) summarized the same judgment. "The Wards Cove case has a history unto its own, because at the time the Supreme Court had, actually the whole political system, turned conservative under Reagan and Bush . . . So the clock for civil rights had essentially run out in terms of Wards Cove . . . and for modern civil rights in this country."

43. If quotas became a leading narrative of backlash against civil rights, then it seems apt to identify "neoliberalism" and color-blind "racial innocence" as the ascendant establishment nomos informing official law (Omi and Winant 1994; Bonilla-Silva 1997).

44. Abraham Arditi, interview by George Lovell and Michael McCann. February 5, 2015.

45. Ibid.

46. Section 105 did stipulate that a policy linked to disparate impact but that is consistent with business necessity is still unlawful if the plaintiffs demonstrate the respondent refuses a less discriminatory alternative that serves the employer's needs. See Livingston (1993).

47. Tyree Scott, interview by Michael McCann, March 17, 1998.

48. Justice White was quoting from *Watson v. Fort Worth Bank & Trust* at 992. He was referring also to the very old case, discussed earlier in this book, of *Downes v. Bidwell*, 182 U.S. 244, 292, 1901.

49. Abraham Arditi, interview by George Lovell and Michael McCann, February 5, 2015.

50. To note just one small example, in 2017–2018, Cindy Domingo served as co-organizer, joined by Mike Withey and others in the former CJDV, in the "Washington Alliance for Resistance and Power" fighting for local transformative politics in the Puget Sound area and against Trumpist revanchism.

Conclusion

1. This is not to say that critical theorizing about race, class, gender, and the like is not incorporated into sociolegal studies generally. See Barnes (2016) for a review. But legal mobilization studies have not led the way in critical theorizing about intersectional hierarchies (but see Adam 2017).

2. The term *litigation* often refers to lawsuits that proceed to a formal adjudicatory proceeding and ruling. But litigation more broadly refers to processes of disputing between claimants, especially over rights, which may take place in many settings outside of courts, including in mass media or localized contexts of work, neighborhood, families, and the like. Most rights claims are dropped or settled rather than terminated by authorized third parties (Miller and Sarat 1981; see also Barclay, Jones, and Marshall 2011; McCann 2008; Zemans 1983).

3. The term *legal subject* is used "to describe how law or legal culture constructs how we think about people—how law and legal culture ascribe particular identities and features to people, defining some characteristic as salient and others as irrelevant. The 'legal subject,' in this sense, is a subject as seen (and dealt with) through the eyes of the law or legal culture" (Balkin 1993, 2n1). In this regard, subjects are controlled by law and yet are potentially agents who can resist or contest the terms of that control.

4. Most legal mobilization scholars endeavor to distinguish among different "manifestations" of what we routinely identify with law—especially legal *institutions*, legal *actors*, and *legal norms, discourses, and symbols*. See McCann (2007) and E. P. Thompson (1975).

5. Wendy Brown (1995, 87) makes the point well: "The paradox is . . . expressed well in the irony that rights sought by a politically defined group are conferred on depoliticized individuals: at the moment a particular 'we' succeeds in obtaining

rights, it loses its we-ness and dissolves into individuals. . . . When does identity articulated through rights become production and regulation of identity through law and bureaucracy." For contrasting views, see McClure (1995) and Williams (1992).

6. We underline that race is not a fixed, "readily measurable, dichotomous (black/white) variable" anchored in biology. Rather, race is a contingent, dynamic construction imposed by dominant groups and routinely contested by subaltern racialized groups, often on legal terrain. See Gomez (2012).

7. We recognize that "ruling groups" are often divided among themselves, which increases the degree to which law is always indeterminate, contested, and volatile over time. Our historical narrative has underlined divisions among dominant groups at many points, especially regarding the racial status of Filipinos, in the colonial context and beyond.

8. Anticipating the later "model minority" trope for Asian Americans generally, disciplinary qualifications for Filipinos highlighted hard work in "private" economic life and political quiescence. See Daniel Keum (2016) and Nadal et al. (2010).

9. As noted in chapter 1, heronormative patriarchy is a foundational aspect of racial capitalist hierarchy. Our original manuscript included a substantial theoretical section on this theme. However, because our narrative case study does not develop that theme and the manuscript is long, we reluctantly cut it. We underline that our intent is not to minimize attention to patriarchy and heteronormativity, though. See W. Brown (1995), Gordon (2006), Hartmann (1976), Hartsock (1983), Kandaswamy (2008), McCann (1994, 2016), Nakano Glenn (1992), Stychin (1998), and Tadiar (2009).

10. "Everybody Knows" is the title of a Leonard Cohen song: "Everybody knows the dice are loaded. . . . Everybody knows the fight is fixed, the poor stay poor, the rich get richer. That's how it goes. Everybody knows."

11. One sensible way to analyze such dynamics is to say that some subjects are "inside" the law and others are "outside" of, or excluded from, law's promises and constraints. Instead, we find the alternative theorization of different modalities of law, on a continuum from liberal to repressive, most useful to understand the systematic enforcement of inequality by American law.

12. We acknowledge that we take liberties in adapting Nonet and Selznick's provocative concepts in ways and for purposes quite different from what the authors intended. We are also influenced in these directions by Fraenkel's (1941) theory of the "dual state."

13. The forceful relocation and incarceration of Japanese Americans in concentration camps during World War II was less exceptional in these regards than is often appreciated.

14. "Internal colonialism offered minorities an explanation for their territorial concentration, spatial segregation, external administration, the disparity between their legal citizenship and *de facto* second-class standing, their brutalization by the police, and the toxic effects of racism in their lives" (Hayes 2017, 282).

15. Filipino Americans generally are incarcerated at moderate rates relative to other ethnic and racial groups. See Rumbaut et al. (2009).

16. Even those undocumented Filipinos who, like Jose Antonio Vargas, more recently managed to slip through the restrictive immigration net and "make it" in America have testified to the terror of relentless "running" from state violence, much as Carlos Bulosan portrayed long ago (Vargas 2011; Gleeson 2010).

17. We again note our inadequate attention to the "private" patriarchal rule over unwaged, dependent female reproductive labor which remains well entrenched socially despite liberal legal adjustments.

18. We underline that we do *not* agree with E. P. Thompson's (1975, 296) claim that the "rule of law" thus is an "unqualified good," however. Our study focuses on law simply because its power is real and consequential, both for worse and for better, including not least among subaltern and resistant populations like those whose history we narrate in this book.

19. It is important to underline in this regard that demands for liberal inclusionary and egalitarian reforms often recognize the systemic need for low-wage and even poor or surplus working classes in racial capitalist orders, producing episodic convergences of subaltern and privileged interests, even if resisted by some dominant groups (Bell 1980).

20. We do not agree with many scholars such as Rosenberg (1990) and Klarman (2007) that litigation or rights claiming provokes greater "backlash" than issue advocacy in other forums or institutional forums. We find no conceptual or empirical reason to support such claims. See Keck (2009).

21. It would be conventional to refer to "counterhegemonic" aspirations and movements in this regard. As we see it, though, hegemonic orders by definition preclude truly counterhegemonic imagination. Challengers may derive resources from sources external to a hegemonic order and thus help to change radically the terms of order without qualifying as wholly counterhegemonic. Hence our choice of the term *rights radicalism*, which connotes both a very serious investment in rights and an alchemical reconstruction of rights claims into novel, transformative political projects, which were relatively radical in the historical US context.

22. On violence in Whac-A-Mole, see https://en.wikipedia.org/wiki/Whac-A-Mole.

References

Books and Articles

Abinales, Patricio N. 2003. "Progressive-Machine Conflict in Early Twentieth Century US Politics and Colonial State Building in the Philippines." In *The American Colonial State in the Philippines: Global Perspectives*, edited by Julian Go and Anne L. Foster, 148–81. Durham, NC: Duke University Press.

Adam, Erin. 2017. "Intersectional Coalitions: The Paradoxes of Rights-Based Movement Building in LGBTQ and Immigrant Communities." *Law and Society Review* 51 (1): 132–67.

Adams, Brooks. 1895. *The Law of Civilization and Decay*. New York: Macmillan.

Adams, John. 2004. *The Portable John Adams*. Edited by John P. Diggins. New York: Penguin Classics.

Afrasiabi, Peter R. 2017. *Burning Bridges: America's 20-Year Crusade to Deport Labor Leader Harry Bridges*. Brooklyn, NY: Thirlmere Books.

Agamben, Giorgio. 2005. *State of Exception*. Translated by Kevin Attell. Chicago: University of Chicago Press.

Ahmed Zaki, Hind. 2018. "In the Shadow of the State: Gender Contestation and Legal Mobilization in the Context of the Arab Spring in Egypt and Tunisia." PhD diss., University of Washington.

Akiboh, Alvita. 2015. "The 'Massacre' and the Aftermath: Remembering Balangiga and the War in the Philippines." *U.S. History Scene*, April 10. http://ushistoryscene.com/article/balangiga/.

Albiston, Catherine. 2010. *Institutional Inequality and the Mobilization of the Family and Medical Leave Act: Rights on Leave*. New York: Cambridge University Press.

Alexander, Michelle. 2012. *The New Jim Crow: Mass Incarceration in the Age of Colorblindness*. New York: New Press.

Al-Hiou, Yossur, and Sarah Stein Kerr. 2018. "Paul Manafort's Trail of Scandals." *New York Times*. August 21. https://www.nytimes.com/video/us/politics/100000005524412/paul-manafort-fraud-laundering-scandal.html.

Allen, Robert L. 1970. *Black Awakening in Capitalist America*. New York: Doubleday.

Alquizola, Marilyn, and Lane Ryo Hirabayashi. 2012. "Carlos Bulosan's Final Defiant Acts: Achievements during the McCarthy Era." *Amerasia Journal* 38 (3): 29–50.

Altman, Clara. 2013. "The International Context: An Imperial Perspective on American Legal History." In *A Companion to American Legal History*, edited by Salley Hadden and Alfred L. Brophy, 543–61. New York: Blackwell.

American Friends Service Committee. N.d. "Tyree Scott—History Link." https://www.afsc.org/resource/tyree-scott-history-link.

Amorao, Amanda Solomon. 2014. "The Manong's 'Songs of Love': Gendered and Sexualized Dimensions of Carlos Bulosan's Literature and Labor Activism." *Kritika Cultura* 23:221–35.

Amoroso, Donna J. 2003. "Inheriting the 'Moro Problem': Muslim Authority and Colonial Rule in British Malaya and the Philippines." In *The American Colonial State in the Philippines: Global Perspectives*, edited by Julian Go and Anne L. Foster, 118–47. Durham, NC: Duke University Press.

Anastacio, Leia Castaneda. 2016. *The Foundations of the Modern Philippine State: Imperial Rule and the American Constitutional Tradition, 1898–1935*. New York: Cambridge University Press.

Ancheta, Angelo N. 2006. "Filipino Americans, Foreigner Discrimination, and the Lines of Racial Sovereignty." In *Positively No Filipinos Allowed: Building Communities and Discourse*, edited by Antonio T. Tiongson Jr, Edgardo V. Gutierrez, Ricardo V Gutierrez, and Lisa Lowe, 90–107. Philadelphia: Temple University Press.

Anderson, Benedict. 1988. "Cacique Democracy in the Philippines: Origins and Dreams." *New Left Review* 1, no. 169 (May/June): 3–31.

———. 1991. *Imagined Communities: Reflections on the Origin and Spread of Nationalism*. London: Verso.

Anderson, Carol. 2003. *Eyes off the Prize: The United Nations and the African American Struggle for Human Rights, 1944–1955*. New York: Cambridge University Press.

Apostolidis, Paul. 2009. "Immigration, Liberal Legalism, and Radical Democracy in the U.S. Labor Movement." *Historical Reflections* 35 (1): 137–62.

———. 2018. *A Fight for Time: Migrant Day Laborers and the Politics of Precarity*. New York: Oxford University Press.

Arendt, Hannah. 1973. *The Origins of Totalitarianism*. New York: Houghton Mifflin Harcourt.

Asis, Maruja M. B. 2017. "The Philippines: Beyond Labor Migration, toward Development and (Possibly) Return." *Migration Information Source*, July 12. https://www.migrationpolicy.org/article/philippines-beyond-labor-migration-toward-development-and-possibly-return.

Atleson, James B. 1983. *Values and Assumptions in American Labor Law*. Amherst: University of Massachusetts Press.

Bagenstos, Samuel R. 2006. "The Structural Turn and the Limits of Antidiscrimination Law." *California Law Review* 94 (1): 1–47.

Baker, Doug. 1997. "Cannery Union Chronology." Narrative overview for unfinished PhD diss., University of Washington. (Manuscript on file with authors.)

Balbus, Isaac D. 1977. "Commodity Form and Legal Form: An Essay on the 'Relative Autonomy' of the Law." *Law and Society Review* 11 (3): 571–88.

Balce, Nerissa S. 2006. "Filipino Bodies, Lynching, and the Language of Empire." In *Positively No Filipinos Allowed: Building Communities and Discourse*, edited by Antonio Tiongson Jr., Edgardo V. Gutierrez, Ricardo V. Gutierrez, and Lisa Lowe, 43–60. Philadelphia: Temple University Press.

Baldoz, Rick. 2004. "Valorizing Racial Boundaries: Hegemony and Conflict in the Racialization of Filipino Migrant Labor in the United States." *Ethnic and Racial Studies* 27 (6): 969–86.

———. 2011. *The Third Asiatic Invasion: Empire and Migration in Filipino America, 1989–1946*. New York: New York University Press.

———. 2014. "'Comrade Carlos Bulosan': U.S. State Surveillance and the Cold War Suppression of Filipino Radicals." *Asia-Pacific Journal* 11 (33): 3–18.

Baldwin, James. 1963. *The Fire Next Time*. New York: Dial Press.

Balisacan, Arsenio, and Hal Hill. 2003. *The Philippine Economy: Development, Policies, and Challenges*. New York: Oxford University Press.

Balkin, J. M. 1993. "Understanding Legal Understanding: The Legal Subject and the Problem of Legal Coherence." *Yale Law Journal* 103:1–69.

Balko, Radley. 2013. *Rise of the Warrior Cop: The Militarization of America's Police Forces*. New York: Public Affairs.

Barclay, Scott, Lynn C. Jones, Anna-Maria Marshall. 2011. "Two Spinning Wheels: Studying Law and Social Movements." In *Studies in Law, Politics and Society*, edited by Austin Sarat, 5:1–16. Bingley, West Yorkshire: Emerald.

Barnes, Jeb. 2004. *Overruled? Legislative Overrides, Pluralism, and Contemporary Court-Congress Relations*. Palo Alto, CA: Stanford University Press.

Barnes, Mario. 2016. "Empirical Methods and Critical Race Theory: A Discourse on Possibilities for a Hybrid Methodology." *Wisconsin Law Review* 2016 (3): 443–76.

Baunach, Leo. 2013. "The International Fishermen and Allied Workers of America: Chapter 4—World War II." *Waterfront Workers History Project*. http://depts.washington.edu/dock/IFAWA_pt4.shtml.

Belew, Kathleen. 2018. *Bring the War Home: The White Power Movement and Paramilitary America*. Cambridge, MA: Harvard University Press.

Belge, Ceren. 2006. "Friends of the Court: The Republican Alliance and Selective Activism of the Constitutional Court of Turkey." *Law and Society Review* 40 (3): 653–92.

Bell, Derrick A., Jr. 1980. "*Brown vs. Board of Education* and the Interest-Convergence Dilemma." *Harvard Law Review* 93 (3): 518–33.

———. 1987. *And We Are Not Saved*. New York: Basic Books.

Bello, Walden. 1998. "U.S. Imperialism in the Asia-Pacific." *Peace Review* 10 (3): 367–73. https://focusweb.org/content/us-imperialism-asia-pacific.

Belton, Robert. 2014. *The Crusade for Equality in the Workplace: The Griggs v. Duke Power Story*. Lawrence: University of Kansas Press.

Belz, Herman. 1991. *Equality Transformed: A Quarter-Century of Affirmative Action*. New York: Transaction.

Berrey, Ellen, Robert L Nelson, and Laura Beth Nielsen. 2017. *Rights on Trial: How Workforce Discrimination Law Perpetuates Inequality*. Chicago: University of Chicago Press.

Beveridge, Alfred. 1900. *Speech to the U.S. Senate on the Philippine Question*. January 9. https://china.usc.edu/us-senator-albert-j-beveridge-speaks-philippine-question-us-senate-washington-dc-january-9-1900.

Blackmon, Douglas A. 2008. *Slavery by Another Name: The Re-enslavement of Black Americans from the Civil War to World War II*. New York: Anchor.

Blumrosen, Alfred W. 1987. "The Legacy of Griggs: Social Progress and Subjective Judgments—The Kenneth M. Piper Lecture." *Chicago-Kent Law Review* 63 (1): 1–42.

Boggs, Carl. 1977. "Marxism, Prefigurative Communism, and the Problem of Workers' Control." *Radical America* 6 (Winter): 99–122.

Bonilla-Silva, Eduardo. 1997. *Racism without Racists: Color-Blind Racism and the Persistence of Inequality in America*. New York: Rowan and Littlefield.

Bonner, Raymond. 1987. *Waltzing with a Dictator: The Marcoses and the Making of American Policy*. New York: Times Books.

Bonus, Rick. 2000. *Locating Filipino Americans: Ethnicity and the Cultural Politics of Space*. Philadelphia: Temple University Press.

Borstelman, Thomas. 2001. *The Cold War and the Color Line*. Cambridge, MA: Harvard University Press.

Boudreau, Vince. 2003. "Methods of Domination and Modes of Resistance: The U.S. Colonial State and Philippine Mobilization in Comparative Perspective."

In *The American Colonial State in the Philippines: Global Perspectives*, edited by Julian Go and Anne L. Foster, 256–90. Durham, NC: Duke University Press.

Brest, Paul. 1976. "Foreword: In Defense of the Antidiscrimination Principle." *Harvard Law Review* 90:1–55.

Bridges, Harry. 1952. *ION: Official Newspaper of the International Longshoremen's and Warehousemen's Union*, January 4. http://webcache.googleusercontent.com/search?q=cache:IoUr1ClqqNEJ:archive.ilwu.org/wp-content/uploads/2015/02/19520104.pdf+&cd=6&hl=en&ct=clnk&gl=us.

Brigham, John. 1991. *The Cult of the Court*. Philadelphia: Temple University Press.

———. 1996. *The Constitution of Interests: Beyond the Politics of Rights*. New York: New York University Press.

Brisbin, Richard. 2002. *A Strike like No Other Strike: Law and Resistance during the Pittson Coal Strike of 1989–1990*. Baltimore: Johns Hopkins Press.

Brown, Michael S. 2007. *Victorio Acosta Velasco: An American Life*. Lanham, MD: University Press of America.

———. 2012. "Intra-Ethnic Politics and the Emasculation of Filipino Labor Union Politics: The 1947 Founding of the Seafood Workers Union." *Journal of Intercultural Disciplines* 10:112–24.

Brown, Wendy. 1995. *States of Injury: Power and Freedom in Late Modernity*. Princeton, NJ: Princeton University Press.

———. 2002. "Suffering the Paradoxes of Rights." In *Left Legalism/Left Critique*, edited by Wendy Brown and Janet Halley, 208–29. Durham, NC: Duke University Press.

———. 2003. "Neoliberalism and the End of Liberal Democracy." *Theory and Event* 7 (1): 15–18.

Bulosan, Carlos. 1943. "Freedom from Want." *Saturday Evening Post*, March 6, 12

———. 1973. *America Is in the Heart*. Seattle: University of Washington Press.

———. 1995. *On Becoming Filipino: Selected Writings of Carlos Bulosan*. Edited by E. San Juan, Jr. Philadelphia: Temple University Press.

Burbank, Stephen B., and Sean Farhang. 2017a. "Class Actions and the Counterrevolution against Federal Litigation." Penn Law Legal Scholarship Repository, Faculty Scholarship, 1555. http://scholarship.law.upenn.edu/faculty_scholarship/1555.

———. 2017b. *Rights and Retrenchment: The Counterrevolution against Federal Litigation*. Cambridge: Cambridge University Press.

Burnett, Lucy. 2009. "Communist Civil Rights: Seattle Civil Rights Congress, 1948–1955." Seattle Civil Rights and Labor History Project. http://depts.washington.edu/civilr/CivilRightsCongress.htm.

Burstein, Paul. 1991. "Legal Mobilization as a Social Movement Tactic: The

Struggle for Equal Employment Opportunity." *American Journal of Sociology* 96 (5): 1201–25.

Bynum, Cornelius L. 2010. *A. Philip Randolph and the Struggle for Civil Rights*. Urbana: University of Illinois Press.

Cabotaje, Michael A. 1999. "Equity Denied: Historical and Legal Analyses in Support of the Extension of U.S. Veterans' Benefits to Filipino World War II Veterans." *Asian American Law Journal* 6 (67): 67–97. http://scholarship.law.berkeley.edu/aalj/vol6/iss1/2.

Cacho, Lisa Marie. 2012. *Social Death: Racialized Rightslessness and the Criminalization of the Unprotected*. New York: NYU Press.

Calavita, Kitty. 1992. *Inside the State: The Bracero Program, Immigration, and the INS*. New York: Routledge.

———. 2005. "Law, Citizenship, and the Construction of (Some) Immigrant Others." *Law and Social Inquiry* 30 (2): 401–20.

Carle, Susan. 2011. "A Social Movement History of Title VII Disparate Impact Analysis." *Florida Law Review* 63:251–300.

Carmichael, Stokely, and Charles V. Hamilton. 1967. *Black Power: The Politics of Liberation*. New York: Vintage Books.

Casaday, Lauren Wilde. 1938. "Labor Unrest and the Labor Movement in the Salmon Industry of the Pacific Northwest." PhD diss., University of California, Berkeley.

Castañeda, Anna Leah Fidelis T. 2001. "The Origins of Philippine Judicial Review, 1900–1935" *Ateneo Law Journal* 46:121–56.

———. 2009a. "Creating Exceptional Empire: American Liberal Constitutionalism and the Construction of the Constitutional Order of the Philippine Islands, 1898–1935." SJD diss., Harvard University.

———. 2009b. "Spanish Structure, American Theory: The Legal Foundations of a Tropical New Deal in the Philippine Islands, 1898–1935." In *Colonial Crucible: Empire in the Making of the Modern American State*, edited by Alfred McCoy and Francisco A. Scarranon, 365–74. Madison: University of Wisconsin Press.

Castaneda, Michael Schulze-Oechtering. 2009. "Fighting for Transnational Justice: The Activism of the Union of Democratic Filipinos." *McNair Scholars Journal of the University of Washington* (Spring): 65–84.

Caughlan, John. 2009. "Oral History." Communism in Washington State: History and Memory. http://depts.washington.edu/labhist/cpproject/caughlan_interview.shtml.

Celoza, Albert F. 1997. *Ferdinand Marcos and the Philippines: The Political Economy of Authoritarianism*. Westport, CT: Praeger.

Chatterjee, Partha. 2006. "Civil Liberties, Terrorism and Difference." Paper presented at Columbia University, February 4.

Chen, Anthony S. 2006. "'The Hitlerian Rule of Quotas': Racial Conservatism and the Politics of Fair Employment Legislation in New York State, 1941–1945." *Journal of American History* 92 (4): 1238–64.

Chen, Chris. 2013. "The Limit Point of Capitalist Equality: Notes toward an Abolitionist Antiracism." *Endnotes* 3. https://libcom.org/library/limit-point-capitalist-equality-notes-toward-abolitionist-antiracism-chris-chen.

Cherny, Robert, William Issel, and Kiernan Walsh Taylor, eds. 2004. *American Labor and the Cold War: Grassroots Politics and Postwar Political Culture*. Camden, NJ: Rutgers University Press.

Chew, Ronald. 1984. "Cannery Workers Win Lawsuit Appeal." *International Examiner*, April 4, 3.

———. 2012. *Remembering Silme Domingo and Gene Viernes: The Legacy of Filipino American Labor Activism*. Seattle: University of Washington Press.

———. 2014. "Carlos Bulosan Continues to Inspire Legacy of Activism." *International Examiner*, November 14. http://www.iexaminer.org/2014/11/carlos-bulosan-continues-to-inspire-legacy-of-activism/.

Chin, Douglas, et al. 1975. "Editorial: Who We Are." *No Separate Peace* 1 (1): 2. http://depts.washington.edu/civilr3/pdf/nsp/NSP0575.pdf.

Chua, Lynette J. 2014. *Mobilizing Gay Singapore: Rights and Resistance in an Authoritarian State*. Philadelphia: Temple University Press.

Churchill, Thomas. 1995. *Triumph over Marcos*. Seattle, WA: Open Hand.

Cichowski, Rachel A. 2007. *The European Court and Civil Society: Litigation, Mobilization and Governance*. New York: Cambridge University Press.

Clarke, Gerard. 1998. *The Politics of NGOs in South-East Asia: Participation and Protest in the Philippines*. London: Routledge.

Clayton, Cornell, and Howard Gillman, eds. 1999. *Supreme Court Decision Making: New Institutionalist Approaches*. Chicago: University of Chicago Press.

Clemens, Samuel [Mark Twain, pseud.]. 1900. "A Greeting from the 19th Century to the 20th Century." *New York Herald*, December 30.

———. 1901. "To the Person Sitting in Darkness." *North American Review*, February.

———. 1906. "Comments on the Moro Massacre." March 12. History Is A Weapon. http://www.historyisaweapon.com/defcon1/clemensmoromassacre.html.

Coates, Ta-Nehisi. 2015. *Between the World and Me*. New York: Spiegel and Grau.

Cole, Daniel H. 2001. "'An Unqualified Human Good': E.P. Thompson and the Rule of Law." Maurer School of Law, Articles by Maurer Faculty 403. http://www.repository.law.indiana.edu/facpub/403.

Colt, Steve. 2000. "Salmon Fish Traps in Alaska: An Economic History Perspective." Alaskool, ISER Working Paper 2000.2. http://www.alaskool.org/projects/traditionalife/fishtrap/fishtrap.htm.

CQ Almanac. 1991. 102nd Cong., 1st Sess. http://library.cqpress.com/cqalmanac/document.php?id=cqal91-1110520.

Cooley, Richard A. 1963. *Politics and Conservation: The Decline of the Alaska Salmon*. New York: Harper and Row.

Cordova, Fred. 1983. *Filipinos: Forgotten Asian-Americans*. Dubuque, IA: Kendall/Hunt.

Cover, Robert. 1983. "Forward: Nomos and Narrative." *Harvard Law Review* 97:4–68.

———. 1984. *Justice Accused: Antislavery and the Judicial Process*. New Haven, CT: Yale University Press.

———. 1986. "Violence and the Word." *Yale Law Journal* 95:1601–22.

Coward, Martin. 2005. "The Imperial Character of the Contemporary World Order." *Theory and Event* 8 (1). https://muse.jhu.edu/article/180065.

Cramton, Roger C. 1995. "Individualized Justice, Mass Torts, and Settlement Class Actions: An Introduction." *Cornell Law Review* 80:811–36.

Crenshaw, Kimberle Williams. 1989. "Demarginalizing the Intersection of Race and Sex: A Black Feminist Critique of Antidiscrimination." *University of Chicago Legal Forum* 1989, art. 8. https://chicagounbound.uchicago.edu/uclf/vol1989/iss1/8.

———. 1991. "Mapping the Margins: Intersectionality, Identity Politics, and Violence against Women of Color." *Stanford Law Review* 43 (6): 1241–99.

Crowe, Justin. 2012. *Building the Judiciary: Law, Courts, and the Politics of Institutional Development*. Princeton, NJ: Princeton University Press.

Cruz, Rene Ciria, Cindy Domingo, and Bruce Occena. 2017. *A Time to Rise: Collective Memoirs of the Union of Democratic Filipinos (KDP)*. Seattle: University of Washington Press.

Cummings, Scott L. 2018. *Blue and Green: The Drive for Justice at America's Ports*. Cambridge, MA: MIT Press.

Dade, Nicole. 2009. "The Murders of Virgil Duyungan and Aurelio Simon and the Filipino Cannery Workers' Union." The Great Depression in Washington State, Pacific Northwest Labor and Civil Rights Projects, University of Washington. http://depts.washington.edu/depress/cannery_workers_union_murders.shtml.

Daley, Patrick J., and Beverly Ann James. 2004. *Cultural Politics and the Mass Media: Alaska Native Voices*. Urbana: University of Illinois Press.

Danelsky, David J. 1971. "The Chicago Conspiracy Trial." In *Political Trials*, edited by Theodore L. Becker, 134–80. New York: Bobbs-Merrill.

Daniels, Roger. 2004. *Guarding the Golden Door: American Immigration Policy and Immigrants since 1882*. New York: Hill and Wang.

Darian-Smith, Eve. 2012. "Rereading W. E. B. Du Bois: The Global Dimensions of the U.S. Civil Rights Struggle." *Journal of Global History* 7:483–505.

———. 2013. *Law and Societies in Global Contexts: Contemporary Approaches*. Cambridge: Cambridge University Press.

David, E. J. R. 2016. "Why Are Filipinos Still Forgotten and Invisible?" *Psychology Today*, April 6. https://www.psychologytoday.com/us/blog/unseen-and-unheard/201604/why-are-filipino-americans-still-forgotten-and-invisible.

Davidson, Natalie R. 2017. "Shifting the Lens on Alien Tort Statute Litigation: Narrating US Hegemony in *Filartiga* and *Marcos*." *European Journal of International Law* 28 (1): 147–72.

Davis, David Brion. 2006. *Inhuman Bondage: The Rise and Fall of Slavery in the New World*. New York: Oxford University Press.

Dayan, Colin. 2013. *The Law Is a White Dog: How Legal Rituals Make and Unmake Persons*. Princeton, NJ: Princeton University Press.

Dawson, Michael C., and Megan Ming Francis. 2016. "Black Politics and the Neoliberal Racial Order." *Public Culture* 28 (1): 23–62.

De Cano, Pio, Jr. 2016. "Resident's Podium: Pio De Cano." *Ghosts of Seattle Past: The Future is the Past*. http://www.seattleghosts.com/tag/pio-decano/.

De Genova, Nicholas. 2004. "The Legal Production of Mexican/Migrant 'Illegality.'" *Latino Studies* 2:160–85.

———. 2010. "The Deportation Regime: Sovereignty, Space, and the Freedom of Movement." In *The Deportation Regime*, edited by Nicholas De Genova and Nathalie Peutz, 33–65. Durham, NC: Duke University Press.

Delgado, Richard. 1989. "Storytelling for Oppositionists and Others: A Plea for Narrative." *Michigan Law Review* 87:2411–41.

———. 2003. "Crossroads and Blind Alleys: A Critical Examination of Recent Writing about Race." *Texas Law Review* 82:121–52.

———. 2014a. "Law's Violence: Derrick Bell's Next Article." *University of Pittsburgh Law Review* 75:435–55.

———. 2014b. "Rodrigo's Equation: Race, Capitalism and the Search for Reform." *Wake Forest Law Review* 49:87. https://ssrn.com/abstract=2527967.

Delmendo, Sharon. 2004. *The Star Entangled Banner: 100 Years of America in the Philippines*. Camden, NJ: Rutgers University Press.

Denning, Michael. 1998. *The Cultural Front: The Laboring of American Culture in the Twentieth Century*. London: Verso.

Depoorter, Ben. 2013. "The Upside of Losing." *Columbia Law Review* 113: 817–62.

Desmond, Matthew. 2016. *Evicted*. New York: Broadway Books.

De Tagle, David P. 1930. "Justice of the Peace Rohrback of Pajaro Insults the Filipinos." *Torch*, January, no. 2. http://www.commonwealthcafe.info/wp-content/uploads/2015/02/The-Torch-from_Abe_Ignacio-Collection.pdf.

De Vera, Arleen. 1994. "Without Parallel: The Local 7 Deportation Cases, 1949–1955." *Amerasia Journal* 20 (2):1–15.

Devins, Neal. 1993. "Reagan Redux: Civil Rights under Bush." William and Mary School of Law, Faculty Publications, 429. http://scholarship.law.wm.edu/facpubs/429.

De Witt, Howard A. 1979. "The Watsonville Anti-Filipino Riot of 1930: A Case Study of Depression and Ethnic Conflict in California." *Southern California Quarterly* 61 (3): 291–302.

Dezalay, Yves, and Bryant Garth. 2010. *Asian Legal Revivals: Lawyers in the Shadow of Empire*. Chicago: University of Chicago Press.

Domingo, Cindy. 2001. "The Historic Wards Cove Discrimination Case: Separate and Unequal." *Filipinas* (October): 43–46.

———. 2004. "Cindy Domigo" (interview), Seattle Civil Rights and Labor History Project, August 9 and October 29. http://depts.washington.edu/civilr/cindy_domingo.htm.

———. 2013. "The Wards Cove Case: Separate and Unequal." Positively Filipino, October 25. http://www.positivelyfilipino.com/magazine/the-wards-cove-case-separate-and-unequal.

———. 2016. Speech at Human Rights Abuses: Expose the Cover-Ups, University of Washington School of Law, October 14. https://www.youtube.com/watch?v=9JplOqGWO28.

Domingo, Cindy, Bruce Occena, and Rene Cruz, eds. 2017. *A Time to Rise*. Seattle: University of Washington Press.

Domingo, Ligaya. 2010. "Building a Movement: Filipino American Union and Community Organizing in Seattle in the 1970s." PhD diss., University of California, Berkeley.

———. 2011. "Ebb and Flow: The Rank and File Movement in the Alaska Cannery Workers ILWU Local 37." Paper presented at the American Political Science Association, Seattle, September 1–4.

Domingo, Nemesio, Jr. 2003. "Oral History." Cindy Domingo papers, Seattle Civil Rights and Labor History Project, February 28. http://depts.washington.edu/labpics/zenPhoto/Filipino/Cindy%20Domingo/NemesioInterview/.

Dubofsky, Melvyn. 1966. "The Origins of Western Working Class Radicalism, 1890–1905." *Labor History* 7 (2): 131–54.

———. 1994. *The State and Labor in Modern America*. Chapel Hill: University of North Carolina Press.

Du Bois, W. E. B. (1900) 1996. "The Present Outlook for the Dark Races of Mankind." In *The Oxford W.E.B. Du Bois Reader*, edited by Eric Sundquist. 47–54. New York: Oxford University Press.

———. (1903) 2007. *The Souls of Black Folk*. Edited by Henry Louis Gates Jr. New York: Oxford University Press.

———. (1935) 1998. *Black Reconstruction in America: An Essay toward a History of the Part Which Black Folk Played in the Attempt to Reconstruct Democracy in America 1860–1880*. Edited by David Levering Lewis. New York: Free Press.

Dudas, Jeffrey, Jon Goldberg-Hiller, and Michael W. McCann. 2015. "The Past, Present and Future of Rights Scholarship." In *The Wiley Handbook of Law and Society*, edited by Austin Sarat and Patricia Ewick, 367–81. West Sussex: John Wiley.

Dudziak, Mary L. 2000. *Cold War Civil Rights: Race and the Image of American Democracy*. Princeton, NJ: Princeton University Press.

Dumindin, Arnaldo. 2006. Philippine-American War, 1899–1902. http://www.filipinoamericanwar.com/.

Edelman, Lauren B. 2016. *Working Law: Courts, Corporations, and Symbolic Civil Rights*. Chicago: University of Chicago Press.

Edsall, Thomas Byrne, and Mary D. Edsall. 1992. *Chain Reaction: The Impact of Race, Rights, and Taxes on American Politics*. New York: W. W. Norton.

Ehrenreich, Barbara, and Arlie R. Hochschild, 2003. *Global Woman: Nannies, Maids, and Sex Workers in the New Economy*. New York: Metropolitan Books.

Einolf, Christopher J. 2016. *America in the Philippines, 1899–1902*. New York: Palgrave MacMillan.

Eisenberg, Theodore. 1977. "Disproportionate Impact and Illicit Motive: Theories of Constitutional Adjudication." *New York University Law Review* 52:36–171.

Ellison, Micah. 2005. "The Local 7/Local 37 Story: Filipino American Cannery Unionism in Seattle 1940–1959." Seattle Civil Rights and Labor History Project. http://depts.washington.edu/civilr/local_7.htm.

Engel, David M. 2016. *The Myth of the Litigious Society: Why We Don't Sue*. Chicago: University of Chicago Press.

Engel, David M., and Frank W. Munger. 2003. *Rights of Inclusion: Law and Identity in the Lives of Americans with Disabilities*. Chicago: University of Chicago Press.

Engeman, Cassandra. 2015. "Social Movement Unionism in Practice: Organizational Dimensions of Union Mobilization in the Los Angeles Immigrant Marches." *Work, Employment, and Society* 29 (3): 444–61.

Epp, Charles. 1998. *The Rights Revolution: Lawyers, Activists, and Supreme Courts in Comparative Perspective*. Chicago: University of Chicago Press.

———. 2010. *Making Rights Real: Activists, Bureaucrats, and the Creation of the Legalistic State*. Chicago: University of Chicago Press.

Epp, Charles, Steven Maynard-Moody, and Donald P. Haider-Markel. 2014. *Pulled Over: How Police Define Race and Citizenship*. Chicago: University of Chicago Press.

Esguerra, Maria Paz Gutierrez. 2013. "Interracial Romances in the American Empire: Migration, Marriage, and Law in Twentieth Century California." PhD diss., University of Michigan.

Eskridge, William N. 1991. "Overriding Supreme Court Statutory Interpretation Decisions." *Yale Law Journal* 101:331–455.

Espiritu, Yen Le, and Diane L. Wolf. 1999. "The Paradox of Assimilation: Children of Filipino Immigrants in San Diego." In *Ethnicities*, edited by Ruben Rumbaut and Alejandro Portes, 157–86. Berkeley: University of California Press. https://migration.ucdavis.edu/rs/more.php?id=50.

Evangelista, Susan P. 1982. "Carlos Bulosan and Third World Consciousness." *Philippine Studies* 30 (1): 44–58.

Evans, Peter S., Dietrich Rueschemeyer, and Theda Skocpol. 1985. *Bringing the State Back In*. New York: Cambridge University Press.

Ewick, Patricia, and Susan S. Silbey. 1998. *The Common Place of Law*. Chicago: University of Chicago Press.

Fabros, Alex S., Jr. 1995. "When Hilario Met Sally: The Fight against Anti-miscegenation Laws." *Filipina Magazine*, February. Reprinted in Positively Filipino. http://www.positivelyfilipino.com/magazine/when-hilario-met-sally-the-fight-against-anti-miscegenation-laws.

Faltys-Burr, Kaegan. 2009. "Jazz on Jackson Street: The Birth of a Multiracial Musical Community in Seattle." The Great Depression in Washington State, Pacific Northwest Labor and Civil Rights Projects, University of Washington. http://depts.washington.edu/depress/jazz_jackson_street_seattle.shtml.

Falzon, Mark-Anthony, ed. 2016. *Multi-Sited Ethnography: Theory, Praxis, and Locality in Contemporary Research*. New York: Routledge.

Farhang, Sean. 2010. *The Litigation State: Public Regulation and Private Lawsuits in the U.S.* Princeton, NJ: Princeton University Press.

Fast, Jonathan. 1973. "Imperialism and Bourgeois Dictatorship in the Philippines." *New Left Review* 28 (March/April): 69–96.

Faulkner, William. 1951. *Requiem for a Nun*. New York: Random House.

Feldman, Leonard. 2004. *Citizens without Shelter: Homelessness, Democracy, and Political Exclusion*. Ithaca, NY: Cornell University Press.

Ferree, Myra Marx. 2003. "Resonance and Radicalism: Feminist Framing in the Abortion Debates of the United States and Germany." *American Journal of Sociology* 109 (2): 304–44.

Fisk, Catherine. 1994. "Still 'Learning Something of Legislation': The Judiciary in the History of Labor Law." *Law and Social Inquiry*. 19 (1): 151–86.

Foner, Eric. (1970) 1995. *Free Soil, Free Labor, Free Men*. New York: Oxford University Press.

Forbath, William E. 1991. *Law and the Shaping of the American Labor Movement*. New York: Cambridge University Press.

Foster, Anne L. 2003. "Models for Governing: Opium and Colonial Policies in Southeast Asia, 1880–1910." In *The American Colonial State in the Philippines:*

Global Perspectives, edited by Julian Go and Anne L. Foster, 92–117. Durham, NC: Duke University Press.

Foster, Nellie. 1932. "Legal Status of Filipino Intermarriages in California." *Sociology and Social Research*. 16 (1931/1932): 441–454.

Fox, Michael. 1980. "Some Rules for Community Lawyers." *Clearinghouse Review* (May): 1–7.

Fraenkel, Ernst. 1941. *The Dual State: A Contribution to the Theory of Dictatorship*. Translated by E. A. Shils. New York: Oxford University Press.

Francis, Megan Ming. 2014. *Civil Rights and the Making of the Modern American State*. New York: Cambridge University Press.

Francisco, Luzviminda. 1973. "The First Vietnam: The U.S.-Philippine War of 1899." History Is a Weapon. http://www.historyisaweapon.com/defcon1/franciscofirstvietnam.html.

Fraser, Nancy. 2000. "Rethinking Recognition." *New Left Review* 3 (May/June). https://newleftreview.org/II/3/nancy-fraser-rethinking-recognition.

———. 2014. "Behind Marx's Hidden Abode: For an Expanded Conception of Capitalism." *New Left Review* 86: 55–72.

———. 2016. "Expropriation and Exploitation in Racialized Capitalism: A Reply to Michael Dawson." *Critical Historical Studies* 3, no. 1 (Spring): 163–78.

Freeman, Alan D. 1998. "Antidiscrimination Law from 1954 to 1989: Uncertainty, Contradiction, Realization, Denial." In *The Politics of Law: A Progressive Critique*, edited by David Kairys, 285–311. 3rd ed. New York: Basic Books.

Fresco, Crystal. 1999. "Cannery Workers' and Farm Laborers' Union 1933–39: Their Strength in Unity." Seattle Civil Rights and Labor History Project. http://depts.washington.edu/civilr/cwflu.htm.

Friday, Chris. 1994. *Organizing Asian American Labor*. Philadelphia: Temple University Press.

Fried, Charles. 1991. *Order and Law: Arguing the Reagan Revolution—A First Hand Account*. New York: Simon and Schuster.

Fryer, Douglas M. 2016. *Justice for Wards Cove*. Bloomington, IN: Xlibris.

Frymer, Paul. 2008. *Black and Blue: African Americans, the Labor Movement, and the Decline of the Democratic Party*. Princeton, NJ: Princeton University Press.

———. 2017. *Building American Empire: The Era of Territorial and Political Expansion*. Princeton, NJ: Princeton University Press.

Fujita-Rony, Dorothy B. 2003. *American Workers, Colonial Power: Philippine Seattle and the Transpacific West, 1919–1941*. Berkeley: University of California Press.

Galang, Evelina. 2003. *Screaming Monkeys: Critiques of Asian American Images*. Minneapolis, MN: Coffee House Press.

Galanter, Marc. 1974. "Why the Haves Come Out Ahead: Speculations on the Limits of Legal Change." *Law and Society Review* 91 (1): 95–160.

———. 1983. "The Radiating Effects of Courts." In *Empirical Theories of Courts*, edited by K. D. Boyum and L. Mather, 117–42. New York: Longman.

Gallagher, Mary. 2017. *Authoritarian Legality in China: Law, Workers, and the State*. Cambridge: Cambridge University Press.

Gamboa, Ernesto. 1990. *Mexican Labor and World War II: Braceors in the Pacific Northwest, 1942–1947*. Austin: University of Texas Press.

Garrow, David J. 1978. *Protest at Selma: Martin Luther King, Jr., and the Voting Rights Act of 1965*. New Haven, CT: Yale University Press.

Gee, Shannon, dir. 2014. "One Generation's Time: The Story of Silme Domingo and Gene Viernes." Labor Film Database. https://laborfilms.com/tag/labor/.

Getman, Julius. G. 2016. *The Supreme Court on Unions: Why Labor Law Is Failing American Workers*. Ithaca, NY: Cornell University Press.

Gillmer, Jason. 2012. "Crimes of Passion: The Regulation of Interracial Sex in Washington, 1855–1950." *Gonzaga Law Review* 47 (2): 393–428.

Gilmore, Ruth Wilson. 2007. *Golden Gulag: Prisons, Surplus, Crisis, and Opposition in Globalizing California*. Berkeley: University of California Press.

Gleeson, Shannon. 2010. "Labor Rights for All? The Role of Undocumented Immigrant Status for Worker Claims Making." *Law and Social Inquiry* 35 (3): 561–602.

Go, Julian 2003. "Introduction: Global Perspectives on the U.S. Colonial State in the Philippines." In *The American Colonial State in the Philippines: Global Perspectives*, edited by Julian Go and Anne L. Foster, 1–42. Durham, NC: Duke University Press.

Go, Julian, and Anne L. Foster, eds. 2003. *The American Colonial State in the Philippines: Global Perspectives*. Durham, NC: Duke University Press.

Godoy, Angelina. 2013. *Of Medicines and Markets: Intellectual Property and Human Rights in the Free Trade Era*. Palo Alto, CA: Stanford University Press.

Goldberg, David Theo. 2002. *The Racial State*. London: Blackwell.

Goldwin, Robert A., and William A. Schambra, eds. 1982. *How Capitalistic Is the Constitution?* Washington, DC: American Enterprise Institute.

Goluboff, Risa L. 2007. *The Lost Promise of Civil Rights*. New York: Cambridge University Press.

Gomez, Laura. 2012. "Understanding Law and Race as Mutually Constitutive." *UCLA Journal of Scholarly Perspectives* 8 (1): 487–505.

Gordon, Jennifer. 2005. "Law, Lawyers, and Labor: The United Farm Workers' Legal Strategy in the 1960s and 1970s and the Role of Law in Union Organizing Today." *University of Pennsylvania Journal of Labor and Employment Law* 8:1–72.

Gordon, Linda. 2006. "Internal Colonialism and Gender." In *Haunted by Empire: Geographies of Intimacy in North American History*, edited by Ann Stoler, 427–51. Durham, NC: Duke University Press.

Gottschalk, Marie. 2008. "Hiding in Plain Sight: American Politics and the Carceral State." *Annual Review of Political Science* 11: 235–60.

Gould, Jon B., and Scott Barclay. 2012. "Minding the Gap: The Place of Gap Studies in Sociolegal Scholarship." *Annual Review of Law and Social Science* 8:323–35.

Gould, William. 1974. "The Seattle Building Trades Order: The First Comprehensive Relief against Employment Discrimination in the Construction Industry." *Stanford Law Review* 26:773–813.

———. 1977. *Black Workers in White Unions: Job Discrimination in the United States*. Ithaca, NY: Cornell University Press.

Gourevitch, Alex. 2015. "Police Work: The Centrality of Labor Repression in American Political History." *American Political Science Review* 13 (3): 762–73.

Graber, Mark A. 1993. "The Nonmajoritarian Difficulty: Legislative Deference to the Judiciary." University of Maryland, Francis King Carey School of Law, Faculty Scholarship 518. http://digitalcommons.law.umaryland.edu/fac_pubs/518.

Grant, Nicole. 2008. "White Supremacy and the Alien Land Laws of Washington State." Seattle Civil Rights and Labor History Project. http://depts.washington.edu/civilr/alien_land_laws.htm.

Greenberg, Edward S. 1983. "Class Rule under the Constitution." In *How Capitalistic Is the Constitution?*, edited by Robert A. Goldwin and William Schambra, 22–48. Washington, DC: American Enterprise Institute.

Gregor, James A. 1984. "Report: The Key Role of U.S. Bases in the Philippines." Heritage Foundation, Report, January 10. https://www.heritage.org/report/the-key-role-us-bases-the-philippines.

Gregory, James N. 2004. "The West and Workers, 1870–1930." In *A Companion to the American West*, edited by William Deverell, 24–55. Malden, MA: Blackwell.

———. 2005. *The Southern Diaspora: How the Great Migrations of Black and White Southerners Transformed America*. Chapel Hill: University of North Carolina Press.

Griffey, Trevor. 2007. "The Washington State Klan in the 1920s." Seattle Civil Rights and Labor History Project. https://depts.washington.edu/civilr/kkk_politicians.htm.

———. 2011. "Black Power's Labor Politics: The United Construction Workers Association and Title VII Law in the 1970s." PhD diss., University of Washington.

———, ed. 2018a. "FBI Documents Related to Carlos Bulosan." https://archive.org/details/FBI-Carlos-Bulosan Obtained.

———, ed. 2018b. "FBI Files on 'Communist Activities in the Philippine Islands.'" https://archive.org/details/FBI-Communist-Activities-Philippines/page/n25.

———. N.d. "Tyree Scott and the United Construction Workers Association: History." Seattle Civil Rights and Labor History Project. http://depts.washington.edu/civilr/ucwa_history.htm.

Guinier, Lani. 2008. "Foreword: Demosprudence through Dissent." *Harvard Law Review*. 122(4): 574–740.

———, and Gerald Torres. 2014. "Changing the Wind: Notes toward a Demosprudence of Law and Social Movements." *Yale Law Journal* 123:2740–804.

Gurtiza, Rich. 2015. "The Legend of Carlos Bulosan." *ILWU Dispatcher* (December 2014). https://www.ilwu.org/the-legend-of-carlos-bulosan/.

Gutierrez, Ramon. 2004. "Internal Colonialism: An American Theory of Race." *Du Bois Review* 1 (2): 281–95.

Guyotte, Roland L., and Barbara M. Posadas. 1995. "Celebrating Rizal Day: The Emergence of a Filipino Tradition in Twentieth-Century Chicago." In *Feasts and Celebrations in North American Ethnic Communities*, edited by Ramon A. Gutierrez and Genevieve Fabre, 111–27. Albuquerque: University of New Mexico Press.

Hacker, Jacob S., and Paul Pierson. 2010. *Winner-Take-All Politics*. New York: Simon and Schuster.

Haglund, LaDawn, and Robin Stryker, eds. 2015. *Closing the Rights Gap: From Human Rights to Social Transformation*. Berkeley: University of California Press.

Haltom, William, and Michael McCann. 2004. *Distorting the Law: Politics, Media, and the Litigation Crisis*. Chicago: University of Chicago Press.

Haney-López, Ian. 1997. *White by Law: The Legal Construction of Race*. New York: New York University Press.

Hardt, Michael, and Antonio Negri. 2000. *Empire*. Cambridge, MA: Harvard University Press.

Harris, Alexes. 2016. *A Pound of Flesh: Monetary Sanctions as Punishment for the Poor*. New York: Russell Sage Foundation.

Harris, Cheryl. 1993. "Whiteness as Property." *Harvard Law Review* 106 (8): 1707–91.

Harrison, John. 2011. "Canneries." Northwest Power and Conservation Council. https://www.nwcouncil.org/history/Canneries.

Hart, Melissa. 2004. "Will Employment Discrimination Class Actions Survive?" *Akron Law Review* 37:813–46.

———. 2011. "From Wards Cove to Ricci: Struggling against the 'Built-In Headwinds' of a Skeptical Court." *Wake Forest Law Review* 46:261–79.

Hartmann, Heidi. 1976. "Capitalism, Patriarchy, and Segregation by Sex." *Signs* 1 (3): 137–69.

Hartsock, Nancy. 1983. *Money, Sex, and Power: Toward a Feminist Historical Materialism*. New York: Longman.

Harvey, David. 2003. *The New Imperialism*. New York: Oxford University Press.

Hattam, Victoria C. 1993. *Labor Visions and State Power: The Origins of Business Unionism*. Princeton, NJ: Princeton University Press.

Hayes, Chris. 2017. *A Colony in a Nation*. New York: W. W. Norton.

Haynie, Stacia. 1998. "Paradise Lost: Politicization of the Philippine Supreme Court in the Post Marcos Era." *Asian Studies Review* 22 (4): 459–73.

Hedden, Andrew. 2013. "Filipino Americans and the Making of Seattle's Dr. Jose P. Rizal Bridge and Park." Seattle Civil Rights and Labor History Project. http://depts.washington.edu/civilr/rizal_report.htm.

———. 2018. "The Divided World of Tomorrow: Seattle and the Remaking of Global Capitalism, 1962–1984. Unpublished dissertation prospectus, Department of History, University of Washington.

Henderson, Lynne. 1991, "Authoritarianism and the Rule of Law." University of Nevada Las Vegas, William S. Boyd School of Law, Scholarly Works 867. http://scholars.law.unlv.edu/facpub/867.

Hensler, Deborah R., and Erick Moller. 2000. *Class Action Dilemmas: Pursuing Public Goals for Private Gain*. Santa Monica, CA: Rand Institute for Civil Justice.

Hernandez, Cesar Cuauhtemoc Garcia. 2018. "Deconstructing Crimmigration." *UC Davis Law Review* 52:1978–253.

Hinnershitz, Stephanie. 2013. "'We Ask Not for Mercy, but for Justice': The Cannery Workers and Farm Laborers' Union and Filipino Civil Rights in the United States, 1927–1937." *Journal of Social History* 47 (1): 132–52.

———. 2015. *Race, Religion, and Civil Rights: Asian Students on the West Coast, 1900–1968*. Camden, NJ: Rutgers University Press.

Hoganson, Kristin. 1998. *Fighting for American Manhood: How Gender Politics Provoked the Spanish-American and Philippine-American Wars*. New Haven, CT: Yale University Press.

Hogler, Raymond L. 2015. *The End of American Labor Unions*. Santa Barbara: Praeger.

Holbrook, Justin G. 2009. "Legal Hybridity in the Philippines: Lessons in Legal Pluralism from Mindanao and the Sulu Archipelago." SSRN, October 9. https://ssrn.com/abstract=1486169.

Hollis-Brusky, Amanda. 2015. *Ideas with Consequences: The Federalist Society and the Conservative Counterrevolution*. New York: Oxford University Press.

Horwitz, Morton. 1977. *The Transformation of American Law, 1870–1960*. Cambridge, MA: Harvard University Press.

Hussin, Iza. 2016. *The Politics of Islamic Law: Local Elites, Colonial Authority, and the Making of the Muslim State*. Chicago: University of Chicago Press.

Ileto, Raymond Clemena. 1979. *Pasyón and Revolution: Popular Movements in the Philippines, 1840–1910*. Manila: Ateneo de Manila University Press.

ILWU Local 37. 1952. *1952 Yearbook, Local 37, International Longshoremen's and Warehousemen's Union*. Seattle, WA: ILWU. https://content.lib.washington.edu/exhibits/bulosan/ilwu.html.

ILWU Local 142. 1996. *1946 Sakada Filipinos and the ILWU*. Honolulu: ILWU Local 142.http://thesakadaseries.com/images/1946_Sakadas.pdf.

ILWU Ninth Biennial Convention.1951. April 2–6. Honolulu. http://cdn.calisphere.org/data/28722/67/bk000400d67/files/bk000400d67-FID1.pdf.

Jenero, Kenneth A. 2017. "The NLRB's Successorship Doctrine, Perfectly Clear Successors, Executive Order 13495, and Worker Retention Laws: What the Trump Administration Has Inherited." *ABA Journal of Labor and Employment Law* 32:353–79.

Johnson, Cedric. 2017. "The Panthers Can't Save Us Now." *Jacobin* 1 (1). https://catalyst-journal.com/vol1/no1/panthers-cant-save-us-cedric-johnson.

Johnson, Haynes. 2003. *Sleepwalking through History: America in the Reagan Years*. New York: Anchor Books.

Johnson, Kevin R. 2005. "The Forgotten Repatriation of Persons of Mexican Ancestry and Lessons for the War on Terror." *Pace Law Review* 26:1–26.

Johnson, Stefanie. 2005. "Blocking Racial Intermarriage Laws in 1935 and 1937: Seattle's First Civil Rights Coalition." *Seattle Civil Rights and Labor History Project*. http://depts.washington.edu/civilr/antimiscegenation.htm.

Johnson, Walter. 2018. "To Remake the World: Slavery, Racial Capitalism, and Justice." *Boston Review*, February 20. http://bostonreview.net/forum/walter-johnson-to-remake-the-world.

Jung, Moon-Ho. 2006. *Coolies and Cane: Race, Labor, and Sugar in the Age of Emancipation*. Baltimore: Johns Hopkins University Press.

Kahmaran, Filiz. 2017. "Claiming Labor Rights as Human Rights: Legal Mobilization at the European Court of Human Rights." PhD diss., University of Washington.

Kandaswamy, Priya. 2008. "State Austerity and the Racial Politics of Same-Sex Marriage in the US." *Sexualties* 11 (6): 706–25.

Karnow, Stanley. 1989. *In Our Image: America's Empire in the Philippines*. New York: Random House.

Karst, Kenneth L. 1978. "The Costs of Motive-Centered Inquiry." *San Diego Law Review* 15:1163–66.

Kato, Daniel. 2012. "Constitutionalizing Anarchy: Liberalism, Lynching, and the Law." *Journal of Hate Studies* 10:143–72.

Katznelson, Ira. 2006. *When Affirmative Action Was White: An Untold History of Racial Inequality in Twentieth-Century America*. New York: W. W. Norton.

Kawar, Leila. 2015. *Contesting Immigration Policy in Court: Legal Activism and Its*

Radiating Effects in the United States and France. New York: Cambridge University Press.

Keck, Thomas. M. 2009. "Beyond Backlash: Assessing the Impact of Judicial Decisions on LGBT Rights." *Law and Society Review* 43:151–86.

Keel, Roneva. 2018a. "Colonizing Landscapes: Colonial Development and the Making of a Transpacific Proletariat." Paper presented at the Harry Bridges Center Workshare, University of Washington, February 28.

Keith, Joseph. 2013. *Unbecoming Americans: Writing Race and Nation from the Shadows of Citizenship, 1945–1960*. Camden, NJ: Rutgers University Press.

Kelley, Robin D. G. 2002. *Freedom Dreams: The Black Radical Imagination*. Boston: Beacon.

———. 2015. *Hammer and Hoe: Alabama Communists during the Great Depression*. 2nd ed. Chapel Hill: University of North Carolina Press.

———. 2017. "What Did Cedric Robinson Mean by Racial Capitalism?" *Boston Review*, January 12. http://bostonreview.net/race/robin-d-g-kelley-what-did-cedric-robinson-mean-racial-capitalism.

Keum, Daniel. 2016. "The Model to Marginality." Paper presented at the University of Washington Undergraduate Research Symposium, May 20.

Kimeldorf, Howard. 1988. *Reds or Rackets? The Making of Radical and Conservative Unions on the Waterfront*. Berkeley: University of California Press.

King, Desmond S., and Rogers M. Smith. 2005. "Racial Orders in American Political Development." *American Political Science Review* 99 (1): 75–92.

Kingle, Matthew W. 2008. *Emerald City: An Environmental History of Seattle*. New Haven, CT: Yale University Press.

Klare, Karl. 1978. "Judicial Deradicalization of the Wagner Act and the Origins of the Modern Legal Consciousness, 1937–1941." *Minnesota Law Review* 62:265–339.

Klarman, Michael J. 2007. *Brown v. Board of Education and the Civil Rights Movement*. New York: Oxford University Press.

Klein, Herbert, and Carey McWilliams. 1934. "Cold Terror in California." *Nation*, July 24.

Klinkner, Philip A., and Rogers M. Smith. 1999. *The Unsteady March: The Rise and Decline of Racial Equality in America*. Chicago: University of Chicago Press.

Kolin, Andrew. 2016. *Political Economy of Labor Repression in the United States*. Lanham, MD: Lexington Books.

Kolko, Gabriel. 1963. *The Triumph of Conservatism: A Reinterpretation of American History, 1900–1916*. New York: Free Press.

Korstad, Robert. 2003. *Civil Rights Unionism: Tobacco Workers and the Struggle for Democracy in the Mid-Twentieth Century South*. Chapel Hill: University of North Carolina Press.

Kowalski, Dan. 2000. "Hazel Wolf Remembers the McCarthy Era." HistoryLink, essay 2274, January 1. http://www.historylink.org/File/2274.

Kramer, Paul A. 2006. *The Blood of Government: Race, Empire, the United States, and the Philippines*. Durham: University of North Carolina Press.

Kurashige, Scott. 2010. *The Shifting Grounds of Race: Black and Japanese Americans in the Making of Multiethnic Los Angeles*. Princeton, NJ: Princeton University Press.

Kurban, Dilek. 2017. "The Limits of Transnational Justice: The ECtHR, Turkey and the Kurdish Conflict." PhD diss., Maastricht University.

LaFeber, Walter. (1963) 1998. *The New Empire: An Interpretation of American Expansion, 1860–1898*. Ithaca, NY: Cornell University Press.

Lake, Milli. 2018. *Strong NGOs and Weak States: Pursuing Gender Justice in the Democratic Republic of Congo and South Africa*. New York: Cambridge University Press.

Lee, Sophia. 2014. *The Workplace Constitution from the New Deal to the New Right*. New York: Cambridge University Press.

Leong, Nancy. 2013. "Racial Capitalism." *Harvard Law Review* 126 (8): 2151–226.

Lewontin, Richard C. 1998. "The Maturing of Capitalist Agriculture: Farmer as Proletarian." *Monthly Review* 50 (July/August): 72–84.

Lichtenstein, Nelson. 2002. *State of the Union: A Century of American Labor*. Princeton, NJ: Princeton University Press.

Light, Michael T., Mark Hugo Lopez, and Ana Gonzalez-Barrera. 2014. *The Rise of Federal Immigration Crimes: Unlawful Reentry Drives Growth*. Washington, DC: Pew Research Center.

Livingston, Donald R. 1993. "The Civil Rights Act of 1991 and EEOC Enforcement." *Stetson Law Review* 23:53–100.

Lobel, Jules. 2003. *Success without Victory: Lost Legal Battles and the Long Road to Justice in America*. New York: New York University Press.

———. 2006. "Courts as Forums for Protest." *UCLA Law Review* 52:477–561.

Lovell, George. 2003. *Legislative Deferrals: Statutory Ambiguity, Judicial Power, and American Democracy*. New York: Cambridge University Press.

———. 2012. *This Is Not Civil Rights: Discovering Rights Talk in 1939 America*. Chicago: University of Chicago Press.

Lovell, George, and Michael McCann. 2005. "A Tangled Legacy: Federal Courts and the Politics of Democratic Inclusion." In *The Politics of Democratic Inclusion*, edited by Christina Wolbrecht and Rodney Hero with Peri E. Arnold and Alvin B. Tillery, 257–320. Philadelphia: Temple University Press.

Lovell, George, Michael McCann, and Kirstine Taylor. 2015. "Covering Legal Mobilization: A Bottom-Up Analysis of *Wards Cove v. Atonio*." *Law and Social Inquiry* 41 (1): 61–99.

Lustig, R. Jeffrey. 1986. *Corporate Liberalism: The Origins of Modern American Political Theory, 1890–1920*. Berkeley: University of California Press.

Lutz, Ellen L. 1994. "The Marcos Human Rights Litigation: Can Justice Be Achieved in U.S. Courts for Abuses that Occurred Abroad?" *Boston College Third World Law Journal* 14 (1): 43–51. http://lawdigitalcommons.bc.edu/twlj/vol14/iss1/3.

Lynch, Owen J. 2009. "The U.S. Constitution and Philippine Colonialism: An Enduring and Unfortunate Legacy." In *Colonial Crucible: Empire in the Making of the Modern American State*, edited by Alfred McCoy and Francisco A. Scarano, 353–64. Madison: University of Wisconsin Press.

Mabalon, Dawn Bohulano. 2013. *Little Manila Is in the Heart: The Making of the Filipina/o American Community in Stockton, California*. Durham, NC: Duke University Press.

———. N.d. "The Significance of 1946 for Filipina/o Americans." Filipino American National Historical Society. http://fanhs-national.org/filam/about-fanhs/the-significance-of-1946-for-filipinao-americans/.

Mabanag, Mark. 2005. "The Filipino Forum: The Founding Years 1928–1930." Seattle Civil Rights and Labor History Project. http://depts.washington.edu/civilr/news-mabanag.htm.

Macabenta, Greg B. 2015. "Should There Be a Moro Nation?" *Asian Journal*, March 11. http://www.asianjournal.com/features/opinion-editorial-columnists/should-there-be-a-moro-nation/.

MacArthur, Arthur. 1901. *Annual Report of Major General MacArthur, U.S. Army, Commanding, Division of the Philippines*. Manila.https://archive.org/details/annualreportofma01unituoft.

MacKenzie, John P. 1991. "Editorial Notebook: An Exception to Civil Rights." *New York Times*, November 8. http://www.nytimes.com/1991/11/08/opinion/editorial-notebook-an-exception-to-civil-rights-rules.html.

MacLean, Nancy. 2006. *Freedom Is Not Enough: The Opening of the American Workplace*. Cambridge, MA: Harvard University Press.

Madison, James. (1787) 1961. "Federalist Paper #10." In *The Federalist Papers*. New York: New American Library.

Maeda, Sharon. N.d. "Cannery Row." Documentary film shown at the Human Rights Abuses: Expose the Cover-Ups conference, University of Washington, School of Law, October 14. https://drive.google.com/file/d/0B70gkmQHwZl9M2FMTFdvVHp5emM/view?u.

Magdalena, Federico V. 2017. "Managing the Muslim Minority in the Philippines." *Disarat* 29:5–30.

Mahan, Alfred Thayer. 1900. *The Problem of Asia and Its Effect upon International Policies*. Boston: Little, Brown.

Maltby, Lewis. 2010. *Can They Do That? Retaking Our Fundamental Rights in the Workplace*. New York: Portfolio.

Mann, Michael. 2003. *Incoherent Empire*. London: Verso.

Mansbridge, Jane J., and Aldon Morris, eds. 2001. *Oppositional Consciousness: The Subjective Roots of Social Protest*. Chicago: University of Chicago Press.

Marable, Manning. 1996. *Beyond Black and White: Transforming African American Politics*. New York: Verso.

Marquardt, Steve. 1992. "The Labor Activist as Labor Historian: Reforming the Alaska Cannery Workers Union." Paper presented at the American Historical Association Annual Meeting, August 13–16.

Marshall, Anna-Maria. 2016. *Confronting Sexual Harassment: The Law and Politics of Everyday Life*. New York: Routledge.

Marshall, T. H. 1950. *Citizenship and Social Class, and Other Essays*. New York: Cambridge University Press.

Marx, Karl. (1844) 1978. "On the Jewish Question." In *The Marx-Engels Reader*, edited by Robert Tucker, 26–52. New York: W. W. Norton.

———. (1846) 1982. "Letter from Marx to Pavel Vasilyevich Annenkov. December 28, 1846." In *Marx and Engels Collected Works*, edited and translated by Peter Ross and Betty Ross, 38:95. New York: International. http://hiaw.org/defcon6/works/1846/letters/46_12_28.html.

———. (1875) 1978. "Critique of the Gotha Programme." In *The Marx-Engels Reader*, edited by Robert Tucker, 525–41. New York: W. W. Norton.

Masson, Jack K., and Donald L. Guimary. 1981a. "Asian Labor Contractors in the Alaskan Canned Salmon Industry." *Journal of Labor History* 22 (3): 377–97.

———. 1981b. "Filipinos and Unionization of the Alaskan Canned Salmon Industry." *Amerasia* 8 (2): 1–30.

Mawani, Renisa. 2010. *Colonial Proximities: Crossracial Encounters and Juridical Truths in British Columbia, 1871–1921*. Seattle: University of Washington Press.

May, Glenn. 1980. *Social Engineering in the Philippines*. Westport, CT: Greenwood.

McAdam, Doug. 1982. *Political Process and the Development of Black Insurgency, 1930–1970*. Chicago: University of Chicago Press.

———. 1996. "Conceptual Origins, Current Problems, Future Directions." In *Comparative Perspectives on Social Movements: Political Opportunities, Mobilizing Structures, and Cultural Framings*, edited by Douglas McAdam, John D. McCarthy, and Mayer Y. Zald, 23–40. Cambridge: Cambridge University Press.

McCann, Michael. 1986. *Taking Reform Seriously: Perspectives on Public Interest Liberalism*. Ithaca, NY: Cornell University Press.

———. 1989. "Equal Protection for Social Inequality: Race and Class in American Constitutional Ideology." In *Judging the Constitution: Critical Essays on Judicial*

Lawmaking, edited by Michael McCann and Gerald Houseman, 191–224. Boston: Little, Brown.

———. 1994. *Rights at Work: Pay Equity Reform and the Politics of Legal Mobilization*. Chicago: University of Chicago Press.

———. 1996. "Causal versus Constitutive Explanations (or, On the Difficulty of Being So Positive . . .)" *Law and Social Inquiry* 21 (2): 457–82.

———. 2007. "Dr. Strangelove, Or How I Learned to Stop Worrying and Love Methodology." In *Studies in Law, Politics, and Society*, edited by Austin Sarat, 19–60. Boston: JAI/Elsevier.

———. 2008. "Litigation and Legal Mobilization." In *The Oxford Handbook of Law and Litigation*, edited by Keith Whittingon, Daniel Keleman, and Gregory Caldiera, 522–40. New York: Oxford University Press.

———. 2014a. "Money, Sex, and Power: Gender Discrimination and the Thwarted Legacy of the 1964 Civil Rights Act." *University of Denver Law Review* 91 (4): 779–802.

———. 2014b. "The Unbearable Lightness of Rights: On Sociolegal Inquiry in the Global Era." *Law and Society Review* 48 (20): 245–73.

McCann, Michael, and Tracey March. 1996. "Legal Tactics and Everyday Resistance: A Political Science Assessment." *Studies in Law, Politics, and Society* 15:207–36.

McCartin, Joseph A. 2011. *Collision Course: Ronald Reagan, the Air Traffic Controllers, and the Strike That Changed America*. New York: Oxford University Press.

McClure, Kirstie M. 1995. "Taking Liberties in Foucault's Triangle: Sovereignty, Discipline, Governmentality, and the Subject of Rights." In *Identities, Politics, and Rights*, edited by Austin Sarat and Thomas R. Kearns, 149–92. Ann Arbor: University of Michigan Press.

McCoy, Alfred. 1995. *An Anarchy of Families*. Quezon City: Ateneo de Manila University Press.

———. 2009. *Policing America's Empire: The United States, the Philippines, and the Rise of the Surveillance State*. Madison: University of Wisconsin Press.

———. 2017. *In the Shadows of the American Century: The Rise and Decline of U.S. Global Power*. Chicago: Haymarket Books.

McCoy, Alfred, and Francisco A. Scarano, eds. 2009. *Colonial Crucible: Empire in the Making of the Modern American State*. Madison: University of Wisconsin Press.

McKenna, Thomas M. 1998. *Muslim Rulers and Rebels: Everyday Politics and Armed Separatism in the Southern Philippines*. Berkeley: University of California Press.

McKinley, William. 1898. "Benevolent Assimilation Proclamation." In James A. Blount, *American Occupation of the Philippines 1898–1912*. New York: G. P. Putnam's Sons, 1913. http://www.msc.edu.ph/centennial/benevolent.html.

McWilliams, Carey. 1939. *Factories in the Field: The Story of Migratory Farm Labor in California*. Boston: Little, Brown.

Mejia-Giudici, Cynthia. 1998. "Filipino Americans in Seattle." HistoryLink, essay 409. http://www.historylink.org/File/409.

———. 2003. "Bulosan, Carlos (1911?–1956)." HistoryLink, essay 5202. http://www.historylink.org/File/5202.

Melamed, Jodi. 2011. *Represent and Destroy: Rationalizing Violence in the New Racial Capitalism*. Minneapolis: University of Minnesota Press.

———. 2015. "Racial Capitalism." *Journal of the Critical Ethnic Studies Association* 1 (1): 76–85.

Melo, Tania. 2018. "'We're Not Breaking the Law. We are Exercising our Citizen's Right to Enforce it.'" Paper presented as part of the dissertation project "Social Movements and the Mobilizing of Private Citizens as Law Enforcement," University of Washington.

Melucci, Alberto. 1989. *Nomads of the Present: Social Movements and Individual Needs in Contemporary Society*. Philadelphia: Temple University Press.

Merk, Frederick. 1995. *Manifest Destiny and Mission in American History*. Cambridge, MA: Harvard University Press.

Merry, Sally Engle. 1988. "Legal Pluralism." *Law and Society Review* 22 (5): 869–96.

———. 1990. *Getting Justice and Getting Even: Legal Consciousness among Working Class Americans*. Chicago: University of Chicago Press.

———. 1998. "The Criminalization of Everyday Life." In *Everyday Practices and Trouble Cases*, edited by Austin Sarat, 14–39. Evanston, IL: Northwestern University Press.

———. 2000. *Colonizing Hawaii: The Cultural Power of Law*. Princeton, NJ: Princeton University Press.

———. 2003. "Rights Talk and the Experience of Law: Implementing Women's Human Rights to Protection from Violence." *Human Rights Quarterly* 25 (2): 343–81.

Mickey, Robert. 2015. *Paths Out of Dixie: The Democratization of Authoritarian Enclaves in America's Deep South, 1944–1972*. Princeton, NJ: Princeton University Press.

Migdal, Joel. 1988. *Strong Societies and Weak States: State-Society Relations and State Capabilities in the Third World*. Princeton, NJ: Princeton University Press.

———. 2001. *State in Society: Studying How States and Societies Transform and Constitute One Another*. Cambridge: Cambridge University Press.

Mijares, Primitivo. 1976. *The Conjugal Dictatorship of Ferdinand Marcos and Imelda Marcos*. Manila: Union Square.

Miller, Richard E., and Austin Sarat. 1981. "Grievances, Claims, and Disputes: Assessing the Adversary Culture." *Law and Society Review* 14 (3/4): 525–66.

Miller, Stuart Creighton. 1982. *"Benevolent Assimilation": The American Conquest of the Philippines, 1899–1903*. New Haven, CT: Yale University Press.

Mills, C. Wright. 1940. "Situated Actions and Vocabularies of Motive." *American Sociological Review* 5(6): 904–13.

Mills, Charles W. 1997. *The Racial Contract*. Ithaca, NY: Cornell University Press.

———. 2008. "Racial Liberalism." *PMLA* 123 (5): 1380–97.

———. 2017. "White Ignorance." Chap. 4 in *Black Rights/White Wrongs: The Critique of Racial Liberalism*. New York: Oxford University Press.

Moran, Rachel. 2003. *Interracial Intimacy: The Regulation of Race and Romance*. Chicago: University of Chicago Press.

Moustafa, Tamir. 2009. *The Struggle for Constitutional Power: Law, Politics, and Economic Development in Egypt*. Cambridge: Cambridge University Press.

Mullenix, Linda S. 2014. "Ending Class Actions as We Know Them: Rethinking the American Class Action." *Emory Law Journal* 64:399–449.

Mulroy, Quinn. 2018. "Approaches to Enforcing the Rights Revolution: Private Civil Rights Litigation and American Bureaucracy." In *The Rights Revolution Revisited: Institutional Perspectives on the Role of Private Enforcement of Civil Rights in the U.S.*, edited by Lynda G. Dodd, 27–45. New York: Cambridge University Press, 2018.

Murakawa, Naomi. 2014. *The First Civil Right: How Liberals Built Prison America*. New York: Oxford University Press.

Murakawa, Naomi, and Katherine Beckett. 2010. "The Penology of Racial Innocence: The Erasure of Racism in the Study and Practice of Punishment." *Law and Society Review* 44 (3/4): 695–730.

Myrdal, Gunnar. 1944. *An American Dilemma: The Negro Problem and Modern Democracy*. New York: Harper.

Nadal, Kevin L., Stephanie T. Pituc, Marc P. Johnston, and Theresa Esparrago. 2010. "Overcoming the Model Minority Myth: Experiences of Filipino American Graduate Students." *Journal of College Student Development* 51 (6): 694–706.

Nader, Laura A. 1984–1985. "A User Theory of Law: Fourth Annual Alfred P. Murrah Lecture." *Southwestern Law Journal* 38:951–63.

Nakano Glenn, Evelyn. 1992. "From Servitude to Service Work: The Historical Continuities of Women's Paid and Unpaid Reproductive Labor." *Signs: Journal of Women in Culture and Society* 18 (1): 1–44.

———. 2002. *Unequal Freedom: How Race and Gender Shaped American Citizenship and Labor*. Cambridge, MA: Harvard University Press.

National Labor Relations Board. N.d. "Pre-Wagner Act Labor Relations." https://www.nlrb.gov/who-we-are/our-history/pre-wagner-act-labor-relations.

Nedelsky, Jennifer. 1990. *Private Property and the Limits of American Constitutionalism*. Chicago: University of Chicago Press.

NeJaimes, Douglas. 2011. "Winning through Losing." *Iowa Law Review* 96: 941–1012.

Nelson, Robert. 1995. "Law, Markets, and Gender Inequality in Pay." *Berkeley Journal of Gender, Law and Justice* 10 (1): 61–69.

Nelson, Robert, and William P. Bridges. 1999. *Legalizing Gender Inequality: Courts, Markets and Unequal Pay for Women in America*. Cambridge: Cambridge University Press.

Neocleous, Mark. 2006. "The Problem with Normality: Taking Exception to 'Permanent Emergency.'" *Alternatives* 31:191–213.

Ngai, Mae M. 2003. "The Strange Career of the Illegal Alien: Immigration Restriction and Deportation Policy in the United States, 1921–1965." *Law and History Review* 21 (1): 69–107.

———. 2004. *Impossible Subjects: Illegal Aliens and the Making of Modern America*. Princeton, NJ: Princeton University Press.

Nielsen, Laura Beth, Robert L. Nelson, and Ryon Lancaster. 2010. "Individual Justice or Collective Legal Mobilization: Employment Discrimination in the Post-Civil Rights United States." *Journal of Empirical Legal Studies* 7:175–201.

Nietzsche, Friedrich. 1874. "On the Use and Abuse of History for Life." Translated by Adrian Collins. Wikisource. https://en.wikisource.org/wiki/ On_the_Use_and_Abuse_of_History_for_Life.

Nomura, Gail. 1986–1987. "Within the Law: The Establishment of Filipino Leasing Rights on the Yakima Indian Reservation." *Amerasia* 13 (1): 99–117.

Nonato, John D. 2016. "Finding Manilatown: The Search for Seattle's Filipino American Community, 1898–2016." History Undergraduate Thesis 24, University of Washington, Tacoma. https://digitalcommons.tacoma.uw.edu/history_theses/24/.

Nonet, Philippe, and Philip Selznick. 2001. *Law and Society in Transition: Toward Responsive Law*. Piscataway, NJ: Transaction.

Novkov, Julie. 2008a. "The Miscegenation/Same-Sex Marriage Analogy: What Can We Learn from Legal History?" *Law and Social Inquiry* 33 (2): 345–86.

———. 2008b. *Racial Union: Law, Intimacy, and the White State in Alabama, 1865–1954*. Ann Arbor: University of Michigan Press.

Obasogie, Osagie K. 2013. "Foreword: Critical Race Theory and Empirical Methods." *UC Irvine Law Review* 3: 183–86.

Oberg, Kalervo. 1973. *The Social Economy of the Tlingit Indians*. Seattle: University of Washington Press.

Ogletree, Charles J., Jr., and Austin Sarat, eds. 2006. *From Lynch Mobs to the Killing State: Race and the Death Penalty in America*. New York: New York University Press.

Oh, Reginald. 2005. "Mapping a Materialist Latcrit Discourse on Racism."

Cleveland State Law Review 52: 243–53. http://engagedscholarship.csuohio.edu/clevstlrev/vol52/iss1/16.

Okada, Taihei. 2012. "Underside of Independence Politics: Filipino Reactions to Anti-Filipino Riots in the United States." *Philippine Studies* 60 (3): 307–35.

Omi, Michael, and Howard Winant. 1994. *Racial Formation in the United States: From the 1960s to the 1990s*. 2nd ed. New York: Routledge.

Ong, Aihwa. 2006. *Neoliberalism as Exception: Mutations in Citizenship and Sovereignty*. Durham, NC: Duke University Press.

Orren, Karen. 1991. *Belated Feudalism: Labor, the Law and Liberal Development in the United States*. Cambridge: Cambridge University Press.

———. 1995. "The Primacy of Labor in American Constitutional Development." *American Political Science Review*. 89:377–88.

O'Toole, G. J. A. 1984. *The Spanish War: An American Epic 1898*. New York: W. W. Norton.

Pante, Michael D., and Leo Angelo Nery. 2016. "Migration, Imagination, and Transformation: Revisiting E. San Juan's Carlos Bulosan and the Imagination of the Class Struggle." *Kritika Kultura* 26: 344–62.

Paris, Michael. 2010. *Framing Equal Opportunity: Law and the Politics of School Finance Reform*. Palo Alto, CA: Stanford University Press.

Parker, Christopher. 2009. *Fighting for Democracy: Black Veterans and the Struggle against White Supremacy in the Postwar South*. Princeton, NJ: Princeton University Press.

Parreñas, Rhacel Salazar. 1998. "'White Trash' Meets the 'Little Brown Monkeys.'" *Amerasia Journal* 24 (4): 115–34.

———. 2000. "Migrant Filipina Domestic Workers and the International Division of Reproductive Labor." *Gender and Society* 14 (4): 560–80.

Pascoe, Peggy. 2009. *What Comes Naturally: Miscegenation Law and the Making of Race in America*. New York: Oxford University Press.

Pashukanis, Evegny. 1987. *The General Theory of Law and Marxism*. London: Pluto.

Pateman, Carole. 1988. *The Sexual Contract*. Palo Alto, CA: Stanford University Press.

Philippines Exposition Board. 1904. "Report of the Philippine Exposition Board to the Louisiana Purchase Exposition and Official List of Awards Granted by the Philippine International Jury at the Philippine Government Exposition World's Fair, St. Louis, MO." St. Louis, MO: Greeley Printery. https://archive.org/details/reportofphilippi00philrich.

Pierce, Jennifer. 2012. *Racing for Innocence: Whiteness, Gender, and the Backlash against Affirmative Action*. Palo Alto, CA: Stanford University Press.

Piketty, Thomas. 2014. *Capital in the Twenty-First Century*. Cambridge, MA: Belknap Press of Harvard University Press.

Pitkin, Hanna. 1972. *Wittgenstein and Justice: On the Significance of Ludwig Wittgenstein for Social and Political Thought*. Berkeley: University of California Press.

Polletta, Francesca. 2000. "The Structural Context of Novel Rights Claims: Southern Civil Rights Organizing, 1961–1966." *Law and Society Review* 34 (2): 367–406.

———. 2006. *It Was Like a Fever: Storytelling in Protest and Politics*. Chicago: University of Chicago Press.

Pomeroy, William. 1970. *American Neo-Colonialism: Its Emergence in the Philippines and Asia*. New York: International.

Posadas, Barbara M. 1999. *The Filipino Americans*. Westport, CT: Greenwood.

Post, Robert C. 2005. "Who's Afraid of Jurispathic Courts? Violence and Reason in Nomos and Narrative." Yale Law School Legal Scholarship Repository, Faculty Scholarship Series 176. http://digitalcommons.law.yale.edu/fss_papers/176.

Provine, Doris Marie, and Roxanne Doty. 2011. "The Criminalization of Immigrants as a Racial Project." *Journal of Contemporary Criminal Justice* 27(3): 261–77.

Qin, Yucheng. 2009. *The Diplomacy of Nationalism: The Six Companies and China's Policy toward Exclusion*. Honolulu: University of Hawaii Press.

Rabin-Margalioth, Sharon. 2010. "The Market Defense." *University of Pennsylvania Journal of Business Law* 12 (3): 807–48.

Rafael, Vincente L. 1993. "White Love: Surveillance and Nationalist Resistance in the U.S. Colonization of the Philippines." In *Cultures of United States Imperialism*, edited by Amy Kaplan and Donald E. Pease, 185–218. Durham, NC: Duke University Press.

———. 1997. "'Your Grief Is Our Gossip": Overseas Filipinos and Other Spectral Presences." *Public Culture* 9: 267–92.

———. 2000. *White Love and Other Events in Filipino History*. Durham, NC: Duke University Press.

———. 2009. "The Afterlife of Empire: Sovereignty and Revolution in the Philippines." In *Colonial Crucible: Empire in the Making of the Modern American State*, edited by Alfred McCoy and Francisco A. Scarano, 342–52. Madison: University of Wisconsin Press.

Ragin, Charles C., and Howard S. Becker. 1992. *What Is a Case? Exploring the Foundations of Social Inquiry*. Cambridge: Cambridge University Press.

Rana, Aziz. 2010. *The Two Faces of American Freedom*. Cambridge, MA: Harvard University Press.

———. 2012. "Freedom Struggles and the Limits of Constitutional Continuity." Scholarhip@Cornell Law, Cornell Law Faculty Publications 1071. http://scholarship.law.cornell.edu/facpub/1071.

Rashke, Richard L. 2000. *The Killing of Karen Silkwood: The Story Behind the Kerr-McGee Plutonium Case*. 2nd ed. Ithaca, NY: Cornell University Press.

Reddy, Chandan. 2011. *Freedom with Violence: Race, Sexuality, and the US State*. Durham, NC: Duke University Press.

Roback, Jennifer. 1984. "Southern Law in the Jim Crow Era: Exploitative or Competitive?" *University of Chicago Law Review* 51: 1161–92.

Robinson, Cedric J. 2000. *Black Marxism: The Making of the Black Radical Tradition*. 2nd ed. Chapel Hill: University of North Carolina Press.

Robinson, Michael, and Frank Schubert. 1975. "David Fagen: An Afro-American Rebel in the Philippines, 1899–1901." *Pacific Historical Review* 44 (1): 68–83.

Robles, Raissa. 2016. *Marcos Martial Law: Never Again*. Quezon City: Filipinos for a Better Philippines.

Rodriguez, Dylan. 2006. "'A Million Deaths?' Genocide and the 'Filipino American' Condition of Possibility." In *Positively No Filipinos Allowed: Building Communities and Discourse*, edited by Antonio T. Tiongson Jr., Edgardo V. Gutierrez, Ricardo V. Gutierrez, and Lisa Lowe, 145–61. Philadelphia: Temple University Press.

Roediger, David R. 1991. *Wages of Whiteness: Race and the Making of the American Working Class*. New York: Verso.

———. 2005. *Working toward Whiteness: How America's Immigrants Became White*. New York: Basic Books.

Rogers, Joel. 1990. "Divide and Conquer: Further 'Reflections on the Distinctive Character of American Labor Laws.'" *University of Wisconsin Law Review*, 1–147.

Rogin, Michael Paul. (1975) 1991. *Fathers and Children: Andrew Jackson and the Subjugation of the American Indian*. New York: Random House.

———. 1987. *Ronald Reagan the Movie: And Other Episodes in Political Demonology*. Berkeley: University of California Press.

Romney, Charles W. 2016. *Rights Delayed: The American State and the Defeat of Progressive Unions*. New York: Oxford University Press.

Rosenberg, Gerald N. 1991. *The Hollow Hope: Can Courts Bring About Social Change?* Chicago: University of Chicago Press.

———. 2009. "Romancing the Court." *Boston University Law Review* 89:563–79.

Rosenblum, Jonathan. 2017. *Beyond $15: Immigrant Workers, Faith Activists, and the Revival of the Labor Movement*. New York: Beacon.

Rosenfeld, Jake. 2014. *What Unions No Longer Do*. Cambridge, MA: Harvard University Press.

Rothstein, Richard. 2017. *The Color of Law: A Forgotten History of How Our Government Segregated America*. New York: Liveright.

Ruiz, Vicki. 1987. *Cannery Women, Cannery Lives: Mexican Women, Unionization, and the California Food Processing Industry, 1930–1950*. Santa Fe: University of New Mexico Press.

Rumbaut, Ruben G., Roberto G. Gonzales, Golnaz Kamaie, and Rosaura Tofoya-Estrada. 2009. "Immigration and Incarceration: Patterns and Predictors of Imprisonment among First and Second Generation Young Adults." In *Immigration and Crime: Ethnicity, Race, and Violence*, edited by Ramiro Martinez Jr. and Abel Valenzuela Jr, 64–89. New York: New York University Press.

Runkel, Philip S. 1994. "The Civil Rights Act of 1991: A Continuation of the Wards Cove Standard of Business Necessity." *William and Mary Law Review* 35: 1177–1239.

Rydell, Robert. 1983. "Visions of Empire: International Expositions in Portland and Seattle, 1905–1909." *Pacific Historical Review* 52 (1): 37–65.

———. 1984. *All the World's a Fair: Visions of Empire at American International Expositions, 1876–1916*. Chicago: University of Chicago Press.

———. 2012. "Soundtracks of Empire: 'The White Man's Burden,' the War in the Philippines, the 'Ideals of America,' and Tin Pan Alley." In "Wars and New Beginnings in American History." Special issue, *European Journal of American Studies* 7 (2). http://journals.openedition.org/ejas/9712.

Saito, Natsu Taylor. 2003. "The Enduring Effect of the Chinese Exclusion Cases: The Plenary Power Justification for Ongoing Abuses of Human Rights." *Asian American Law Journal* 10 (1): 13–36.

Salman, Michael. 2009. "'The Prison That Makes Men Free': The Iwahig Penal Colony and the Simulacra of the American State in the Philippines." In *Colonial Crucible: Empire in the Making of the Modern American State*, edited by Alfred McCoy and Francisco A. Scarano, 116–28. Madison: University of Wisconsin Press.

Salyer, Lucy. 2004. "Baptism by Fire: Race, Military Service, and U.S. Citizenship Policy, 1918–1935." *Journal of American History* 91 (3): 847–76.

San Buenaventura, Steffi. 1996. "Hawaii's '1946 Sadaka.'" *Social Process in Hawaii* 37:74–90. http://www.efilarchives.org/pdf/social%20process%20vol%2037/sp37_steffi_sakada.pdf.

San Juan, Epifano, Jr. 1972. *Carlos Bulosan and the Imagination of Class Struggle*. Manila: University of Philippines Press.

———, ed. 1995. *On Becoming Filipino: Selected Writings of Carlos Bulosan*. Philadelphia: Temple University Press.

———. 2005. "From Race to Class Struggle: Re-Problematizing Critical Race Theory." *Michigan Journal of Race and Law* 11 (1): 75–98. https://repository.law.umich.edu/mjrl/vol11/iss1/5.

———. 2008. "Carlos Bulosan: Between Imperial Terror and Worker-Peasant Revolution." Philippines Matrix Project, September 6. https://philcsc

.wordpress.com/2008/09/06/carlos-bulosan-between-imperial-terror-and-worker-peasant-revolution/.

———. 2009. *Toward Filipino Self-Determination: Beyond Transnational Globalization*. Albany: State University of New York Press.

Santos, Boaventura de Sousa, and Cesar Rodriguez-Garavito, eds. 2005. *Law and Globalization from Below: Towards a Cosmopolitan Legality*. New York: Cambridge University Press.

Sarat, Austin. 1990. "'The Law Is All Over': Power, Resistance, and the Legal Consciousness of the Welfare Poor." *Yale Journal of Law and the Humanities* 2 (2), art. 6. http://digitalcommons.law.yale.edu/yjlh/vol2/iss2/6.

Sargent, Daniel. 2013. "The Cold War and the International Political Economy in the 1970s." *Cold War History* 13 (3): 393–425.

Scalise, Joseph. 2009. "Pasyón, Awit, Legend: Reynaldo Ileto's *Pasyón and Revolution* Revisited, a Critique." MA thesis, University of California, Berkeley.

Schaefer, Kurt. 2005. "The Black Panther Party in Seattle: 1968–1970." Seattle Civil Rights and Labor History Project. http://depts.washington.edu/civilr/Panthers1_schaefer.htm.

Scharlin, Craig, and Lilia V. Villanueva. 2000. *Philip Vera Cruz: A Personal History of Filipino Immigrants and the Farmworkers Movement*. Seattle: University of Washington Press.

Scheingold, Stuart A. 1974. *The Politics of Rights: Lawyers, Public Policy, and Social Change*. New Haven, CT: Yale University Press.

Schmitt, Carl. 2005. *Political Theology: Four Chapters on the Concept of Sovereignty*. Translated by George Schwab. Chicago: University of Chicago Press.

Schrecker, Ellen. 1994. *The Age of McCarthyism: A Brief History with Documents*. Boston: St. Martin's Press.

———. 1996–1997. "Immigration and Internal Security: Political Deportations during the McCarthy Era." *Science and Society*. 60 (4): 393–426.

———. 1998. *Many Are the Crimes: McCarthyism in America*. New York: Little, Brown.

Schreiber, Sol, and Laura D. Weissbach. 1998. "*In Re Estate of Ferdinand E. Marcos Human Rights Litigation*: A Personal Account of the Role of the Special Master." *Loyola Law Review Los Angeles* 31 (2). http://digitalcommons.lmu.edu/llr/vol31/iss2/8.

Schwemm, Robert G., and Calvin Bradford. 2016. "Proving Disparate Impact in Fair Housing Cases after Inclusive Communities." *New York University Journal of Legislation and Public Policy* 19 (4): 685–770.

Scott, Tyree. 1975. "The Album Is 'Body Heat': Record Review and Editorial Comment." *No Separate Peace* 1 (1): 4–5. http://depts.washington.edu/civilr3/pdf/nsp/NSP0575.pdf.

Selmi, Michael. 2011. "The Supreme Court's Surprising and Strategic Response to the Civil Rights Act of 1991." *Wake Forest Law Review* 46:281–307.

Seron, Carroll, and Frank Munger. 1996. "Law and Inequality: Race, Gender . . . and, of Course, Class." *Annual Review of Sociology* 22 (1): 187–212.

Sezgin, Yüksel. 2013. *Human Rights under State-Enforced Religious Family Laws in Israel, Egypt and India*. New York: Cambridge University Press.

Shalom, Stephen R. 1980. "Philippine Acceptance of the Bell Trade Act of 1946: A Study of Manipulative Democracy." *Pacific Historical Review* 49 (3): 499–517.

Shapiro, Martin. 1986. *Courts: A Comparative Political Analysis*. Chicago: University of Chicago Press.

Sharma, Preeti, Mayra Jones, and Sophia Cheng. 2016. "The Grape Boycott." In *Nonviolence and Social Movements: The Teachings of Rev. James. M. Lawson, Jr.*, edited by Kent Wong, Ana Luz Gonzalez, and Rev. James M. Lawson Jr., 71–86. Los Angeles: UCLA Center for Labor Research and Education.

Shklar, Judith. 1998. *American Citizenship: The Quest for Inclusion*. Cambridge, MA: Harvard University Press.

Shoben, Elaine W. 2004. "Disparate Impact Theory in Employment Discrimination: What's Griggs Still Good For? What Not?" *Brandeis Law Journal* 42:597–622.

Sidel, John T. 1999. *Capital, Coercion, and Crime: Bossism in the Philippines*. Stanford, CA: Stanford University Press.

Silbey, David J. 2007. *A War of Frontier and Empire: The Philippine-American War, 1899–1902*. New York: Hill and Wang.

Silva, John L. 1994. "Little Brown Brothers' St. Louis Blues: The Philippine Exposition, 1904 St. Louis World's Fair." *Filipinas Magazine*, October. Positively Filipino. http://www.positivelyfilipino.com/magazine/2013/6/little-brown-brothers-st-louis-blues-the-philippine-exposition-1904-st-louis-worlds-fair.

Simon, Jonathan. 2006. *Governing through Crime*. Oxford: Oxford University Press.

Singh, Nikhil Pal. 2005. *Black Is a Country: Race and the Unfinished Struggle for Democracy*. Cambridge, MA: Harvard University Press.

———. 2016. "On Race, Violence, and So-Called Primitive Accumulation." *Social Text* 34 (3): 27–50.

Sisk, John. 2005. "The Southeastern Alaska Salmon Industry: Historical Overview and Current Status." In *Southeast Alaska Conservation Assessment*, chap. 9.5. https://www.conservationgateway.org/ConservationByGeography/NorthAmerica/UnitedStates/alaska/seak/era/cfm/Documents/9.5_SalmonIndustry.pdf.

Skowronek, Stephen. 1982. *Building a New American State: The Expansion of Na-*

tional Administrative Capacities, 1877–1920. Cambridge: Cambridge University Press.

Smith, Rogers. 1997. *Civic Ideals: Conflicting Visions of Citizenship in U.S. History*. New Haven, CT: Yale University Press.

Sohoni, Deenesh, and Amin Vafa. 2010. "The Fight to Be American: Military Naturalization and Asian Citizenship." *Asian American Law Journal* 17 (4): 119–51.

Southworth, Ann. 2008. *Lawyers of the Right: Professionalizing the Conservative Coalition*. Chicago: University of Chicago Press.

Spade, Dean. 2015. *Normal Life: Administrative Violence, Critical Trans Politics, and the Limits of Law*. Durham, NC: Duke University Press.

Spann, Girardeau A. 2010. "Disparate Impact." *Georgia Law Journal* 98: 1133–63.

Staszak, Sarah. 2017. *No Day in Court: Access to Justice and the Politics of Judicial Retrenchment*. New York: Oxford University Press.

Stefancic, Jean, and Richard Delgado. 1996. *No Mercy: How Conservative Think Tanks and Foundations Changed America's Social Agenda*. Philadelphia: Temple University Press.

Stone, Katherine Van Wezel. 1981. "The Post-War Paradigm in American Labor Law." *Yale Law Journal* 90 (7): 1509–80.

Stotts-Johnson, Rache. 2009. "Philippine-American Chronicle." Labor Press Project, Pacific Northwest Labor and Radical Newspapers, Pacific Northwest Labor and Civil Rights Projects, University of Washington. http://depts.washington.edu/labhist/laborpress/Philippine-American_Chronicle.htm.

Strandjord, Corinne. 2009. "Filipino Resistance to Anti-Miscegenation Laws in Washington State." The Great Depression in Washington State, Pacific Northwest Labor and Civil Rights Projects, University of Washington. http://depts.washington.edu/depress/filipino_anti_miscegenation.shtml.

Strong, Josiah. 1885. *Our Country: Its Possible Future and Its Present Crisis*. New York: American Home Missionary Society.

Stryker, Robin. 2001. "Disparate Impact and the Quota Debates: Law, Labor Market Sociology, and Equal Employment Policies." *Sociological Quarterly* 42 (1): 13–46.

Stryker, Robin, Martha Scarpellino, and Mellissa Holtzman. 1999. "Political Culture Wars 1990s Style: The Drum Beat of Quotas in Media Framing of the Civil Rights Act of 1991." In *Research in Social Stratification and Mobility: The Future of Affirmative Action*, edited by Kevin Leicht, 33–106. Stamford, CT: JAI.

Sturm, Susan. 2001. "Second Generation Employment Discrimination: A Structural Approach." *Columbia Law Review* 101 (2): 458–568.

Stychin, Carl. 1998. *A Nation by Rights: National Cultures, Sexual Identity Politics, and the Discourses of Rights*. Philadelphia: Temple University Press.

Tadiar, Neferti Xina M. 1997. "Domestic Bodies of the Philippines." *Sojourn: Journal of Social Issues in Southeast Asia* 12 (2): 153–91.

———. 2009. *Things Fall Away: Philippine Historical Experience and the Makings of Globalization*. Durham, NC: Duke University Press.

Tapia, Ruby C. 2006. "Just Ten Years Removed from a Bolo and a Breech-Cloth: The Sexualization of the Filipino 'Menace.'" In *Positively No Filipinos Allowed: Building Communities and Discourse*, edited by Antonio T. Tiongson Jr., Edgardo V. Gutierrez, Ricardo V. Gutierrez, and Lisa Lowe, 61–70. Philadelphia: Temple University Press.

Tarrow, Sidney. 1993. "Cycles of Collective Action: Between Moments of Madness and the Repertoire of Contention." *Social Science History* 17 (2): 281–307.

Tashiro, Cathy J. 2015. *Standing on Both Feet: Voices of Older Mixed-Race Americans*. New York: Routledge.

Tate, C. Neal. 1993. "Courts and Crisis Regimes: A Theory Sketch with Asian Case Studies." *Political Research Quarterly* 46 (2): 311–38.

Taylor, Kieran Walsh. 2007. "Turn to the Working Class: The New Left, Black Liberation, and the U.S. Labor movement (1967–1981)." PhD diss., University of North Carolina, Chapel Hill.

Taylor, Kirstine. 2015. "Untimely Subjects: White Trash and the Making of Racial Innocence in the Postwar South." *American Quarterly* 67 (1): 55–79.

Taylor, Quintard. 1994. *The Forging of a Black Community: Seattle's Central District from 1870 through the Civil Rights Era*. Seattle: University of Washington Press.

Teles, Steven. 2008. *The Rise of the Conservative Legal Movement*. Princeton, NJ: Princeton University Press.

Teodoro, Noel V. 1999. "*Pensionados* and Workers: The Filipinos in the United States, 1903–1956." *Asian and Pacific Migration Journal* 8 (1/2): 157–78.

Thompson, E. P. 1975. *Whigs and Hunters: The Origin of the Black Act*. New York: Pantheon.

Thompson, Mark. 1995. *The Anti-Marcos Struggle: Personalistic Rule and Democratic Transition in the Philippines*. New Haven, CT: Yale University Press.

Thorpe, Rebecca. 2016 "Democratic Politics in an Age of Mass Incarceration." In *Democratic Theory and Mass Incarceration*, edited by Albert Dzur, Ian Loader, and Richard Sparks, 18–32. New York: Oxford University Press.

Tilly, Charles, and Sidney Tarrow. 2006. *Contentious Politics*. New York: Oxford University Press.

Tiongson, Antonio T., Jr., Edgardo V. Gutierrez, and Ricardo V. Gutierrez. 2006. *Positively No Filipinos Allowed: Building Communities and Discourse*, edited by Antonio T. Tiongson Jr., Edgardo V. Gutierrez, Ricardo V. Gutierrez, and Lisa Lowe. Philadelphia: Temple University Press.

Tocqueville, Alexis de. 1969. *Democracy in America*. Garden City, NY: Anchor Books.

Tomlins, Christopher L. 1985a. "The New Deal, Collective Bargaining, and the Triumph of Industrial Pluralism." *Industrial and Labor Relations Review* 39 (1): 19–34.

———. 1985b. *The State and the Unions: Labor Relations, Law and the Organized Labor Movement in America, 1880–1960*. New York: Cambridge University Press.

Toribio, Helen C. 1998. "We Are Revolution: A Reflective History of the Union of Democratic Filipinos (KDP)." *Amerasia Journal* 24 (2): 155–77.

Torres, Gerald. 2007. "Legal Change." *Cleveland State Law Review* 55: 135–46.

Trachtenberg, Alan. (1982) 2007. *The Incorporation of America: Culture and Society in the Gilded Age*. New York: Hill and Wang.

Trafford, Emily. 2015. "Hitting the Trail: Live Displays of Native American, Filipino, and Japanese People at the Portland's World Fair." *Oregon Historical Quarterly* 116 (2): 158–95.

Truxillo, Charles A. 2001. *By the Sword and the Cross: The Historical Evolution of the Catholic World Monarchy in Spain and the New World, 1492–1825*. Westport, CT: Greenwood.

Turner, Frederick Jackson. (1893) 1921. *The Frontier in American History*. New York: Henry Holt. http://www.gutenberg.org/files/22994/22994-h/22994-h.htm.

Turner, Lowell, and Richard W. Hurd. 2001. "Building Social Movement Unionism: The Transformation of the American Labor Movement." In *Rekindling the Movement: Labor's Quest for Relevance in the Twenty-First Century*, edited by L. Turner, H. C. Katz, and R. W. Hurd, 9–26. Ithaca, NY: Cornell University Press. http://digitalcommons.ilr.cornell.edu/articles/313/.

Tushnet, Mark. 1981. *The American Law of Slavery, 1810–1860: Considerations of Humanity and Interest*. Princeton, NJ: Princeton University Press.

Ueda, Reed. 1994. *Postwar Immigrant America: A Social History*. Boston: Bedford Books of St. Martin's Press.

Unjieng, Nicole Cu. 2009, "Ferdinand Marcos: Apotheosis of the Philippine Historical Political Tradition." Paper 14 in Undergraduate Humanities Forum 2008–09: Change. http://repository.upenn.edu/uhf_2009/14.

Vargas, Jose Antonio. 2011. "My Life as an Undocumented Immigrant." *New York Times*, June 20. https://www.nytimes.com/2011/06/26/magazine/my-life-as-an-undocumented-immigrant.html.

Vargas, Zaragosa. 2007. *Labor Rights Are Civil Rights: Mexican American Workers in Twentieth-Century America*. Princeton, NJ: Princeton University Press.

Venkatesh, Vasanthi. 2016. "Mobilizing under 'Illegality': The Arizona Immigrant Rights Movement's Engagement with the Law." *Harvard Law Review* 19:165–201.

Ventura, Theresa. 2016. "From Small Farms to Progressive Plantations: The Trajectory of Land Reform in the American Colonial Plantations, 1900–1916." *Agricultural History* 90 (4): 459–83.

Vidal, Gore. 1981. "Death in the Philippines." *New York Review of Books*, December 17. http://www.nybooks.com/articles/1981/12/17/death-in-the-philippines-3/.

———. 1986. "Requiem for the American Empire." *Nation*, March 11. https://www.thenation.com/article/requiem-american-empire/.

Viernes, Gene. 1978. "Chris Mensalvas: Daring to Dream." *International Examiner* 5 (4): 6–7.

———. 2012. "Alaskeros History: Reprint of Seven-Article Series in the *International Examiner*, 1977." In *Remembering Silme Domingo and Gene Viernes: The Legacy of Filipino American Labor Activism*, edited by Ron Chew, 120–45. Seattle: University of Washington Press.

Vinel, Jean-Christian. 2013. *The Employee: A Political History*. Philadelphia: University of Pennsylvania Press.

Vogel, Kenneth P. 2016. "Paul Manafort's Wild and Lucrative Philippine Adventure." *Politico*, June 10. https://www.politico.com/magazine/story/2016/06/2016-donald-trump-paul-manafort-ferinand-marcos-philippines-1980s-213952.

Volpp, Leti. 1999–2000. "American Mestizo: Filipinos and Antimiscegenation Laws in California." *UC Davis Law Review*. 33: 795–854.

Wacquant, Lois. 2010. "Class, Race, and Hyperincarceration in Revanchist America." *Daedalus* 139 (3): 74–90.

Weekely, Kathleen. 2006. "The National or the Social? Problems of Nation Building in Post–World War II Philippines." *Third World Quarterly* 27 (1): 85–100.

Weil, David. 2014. *The Fissured Workplace: Why Work Became So Bad for So Many and What Can Be Done to Improve It*. Cambridge, MA: Harvard University Press.

Weiner, Mark S. 2006. *Americans without Law: The Racial Boundaries of Citizenship*. New York: New York University Press.

Wertz, Daniel. 2008. "American Imperialism ad the Philippine War." Senior thesis, Wesleyan University.

West, Cornel. 1982. *Prophesy Deliverance! An Afro-American Revolutionary Christianity*. Louisville, KY: Westminster John Knox Press.

Western, Bruce, and Katherine Beckett. 1999. "How Unregulated Is the U.S. Labor Market? The Penal System as a Labor Market Institution." *American Journal of Sociology* 104 (4): 1030–60.

Wexler, Stephen. 1970. "Practicing Law for Poor People." *Yale Law Journal* 79 (6):

1049–67. https://digitalcommons.law.yale.edu/cgi/viewcontent.cgi?referer=https://www.google.com/&httpsredir=1&article=6035&context=ylj.

White, Lynn T. III. 2014. *Philippine Politics: Possibilities and Problems in a Localist Democracy*. New York: Routledge.

Whiting, Susan. 2017. "Authoritarian 'Rule of Law' and Regime Legitimacy." *Comparative Political Studies* 50 (14): 1907–40.

Wiebe, Robert. 1967. *The Search for Order, 1877–1920*. New York: Hill and Wang.

Williams, Eric. 1994. *Capitalism and Slavery*. Chapel Hill: University of North Carolina Press.

Williams, Patricia. 1992. *The Alchemy of Race and Rights*. Cambridge, MA: Harvard University Press.

Williams, Walter L. 1980. "United States Indian Policy and the Debate over Philippine Annexation: Implications for the Origins of American Imperialism." *Journal of American History* 66 (March): 810–31.

Wilson, Edmund. (1962) 1994. *Patriotic Gore: Studies in the Literature of the American Civil War*. New York: W. W. Norton.

Wilson, Woodrow. 1893. "Mr. Goldwin Smith's 'Views' on Our Political History." *Forum* 16 (December): 489–99. http://www.unz.org/Pub/Forum-1893dec-00489.

———. 1903. *A History of the American People*. New York: Harper and Brothers.

Winant, Howard. 2001. *The World Is a Ghetto: Race and Democracy since World War II*. New York: Basic Books.

———. 2004. *The New Politics of Race: Globalism, Difference, Justice*. Minneapolis: University of Minnesota Press.

Withey, Michael. 2016. Speech at Human Rights Abuses: Expose the Cover-Ups, University of Washington School of Law, October 14. https://www.youtube.com/watch?v=CbHIcnmQ_cI.

———. 2018. *Summary Execution: The Seattle Assassinations of Silme Domingo and Gene Viernes*. Denver, CO: Wildblue.

Wurfel, David. 1988. *Filipino Politics: Development and Decay*. Ithaca, NY: Cornell University Press.

Young, Cynthia A. 2006. *Soul Power: Culture, Radicalism, and the Making of a US Third World Left*. Durham, NC: Duke University Press.

Zemans, Frances Kahn. 1983. "Legal Mobilization: The Neglected Role of the Law in the Political System." *American Political Science Review* 77 (3): 690–703.

Zia, Helen. 2000. *Asian American Dreams: The Emergence of an American People*. New York: Macmillan.

Zong, Jie, and Janne Batlova. 2018. "Filipino Immigrants in the United States." Migration Policy Institute, Migration Information Source, March 14. https://www.migrationpolicy.org/article/filipino-immigrants-united-states.

Newspaper Articles

Anderson, Jack. 1979. "Foreign Agents' Crimes Ignored." *Washington Post*, June 30. https://www.cia.gov/library/readingroom/docs/CIA-RDP91-00561R000100070031-0.pdf.

Bailey, Gil. 1981a. "Dying Man's Clues Lead to Union Slaying Arrests." *Seattle Post-Intelligencer*, June 3.

———. 1981b. "Union Reform: And Then Gunfire." *Seattle Post-Intelligencer*, June 3.

Drogin, Bob. 1986. "Seattle Case Focuses on Agents of Marcos: Relatives of 2 Slain Unionists Contend U.S. Knew of Covert Operations." *Los Angeles Times*, April 20. http://articles.latimes.com/1986-04-20/news/mn-1055_1_intelligence-operation.

Gough, William. 1981. "Job Dispatching Hinted as Death Motive." *Seattle Times*, June 3.

Guillen, Tomas. 1981. "2 Union Officials Shot, 1 Fatally." *Seattle Times*, June 2.

Guillen, Tomas, and Dave Birkland. 1981. "Union Official Slain, Another Hurt: Hiring Dispute Probed." June 2.

Hanson, Christopher. 1991. "Senate Exempts *Wards Cove* from Civil Rights Bill." *Seattle Post-Intelligencer*, November 6.

Insigne, Manuel. ed. 1934. "Filipinos Ask Protection or Repatriation." *Philippine-American Chronicle*, September.

Laranang, Julia. 1977. "The Conviction of Ferdinand Marcos for Human Rights Violations." *International Examiner*, November 6.

Large, Jerry. 2016. "First Filipino Family Is a Rainbow." *Seattle Times*, January 20. http://www.seattletimes.com/seattle-news/first-filipino-family-is-a-rainbow/.

Mangaoang, Ernesto A. 1931. "Filipinos Want Equal Rights or Independence." *Oregonian*, September 21. https://oregonhistoryproject.org/articles/historical-records/filipinos-want-equal-rights-or-independence/#.WYJDAWeWyUk.

Miletich, Steve. 2018. "How Did Mystery Man Go from Howard Hughes Hoax to Being Witness at One of Seattle's Biggest Murder Cases?" *Seattle Times*, March 15. https://www.seattletimes.com/seattle-news/crime/how-did-mystery-man-go-from-howard-hughes-hoax-to-being-witness-at-one-of-seattles-biggest-murder-cases/.

New York Times. 1989. "Trial on in Seattle in Deaths of Marcos Foes." November 23. http://www.nytimes.com/1989/11/23/us/trial-on-in-seattle-in-deaths-of-marcos-foes.html.

Philippine-American Chronicle. 1935a. "Intermarriage Dilemma." February 15, 2.

———. 1935b. "Filipino Labor Union Local Sends Delegates to Olympia: Report Findings on Bill 301." March 1, 1.

———. 1935c. "Unamericanism." March 1, 2.

Philippine Review. 1931. "Editorial: Filipino Tragedy Continues." February. http://depts.washington.edu/civilr/images/velasco/The%20Philippine%20Review2-1931b.jpg.

Rojo, Trinidad. 1935. "The Philippine Uprising." *Philippine Advocate*, May.

Seattle Star. 1929. "Filipinos under Fire." January 15. http://depts.washington.edu/civilr/images/mabanag/FF-1-15-29-800.jpg.

Seattle Times. 1909. "Igorrotes to Have Dog Feast." July 11.

Stamets, John. 1982. "The Cannery Murders." *Seattle Weekly*, August 4–10.

Taubman, Philip. 1979. "U.S. Denies Report It Gave Foreign Agents Free Reign." *New York Times*, August 10. https://timesmachine.nytimes.com/timesmachine/1979/08/10/issue.html.

Viado, Gatalino. 1937. "No Race Deterioration in Mixed Marriages Says Filipino Writer." *Philippine Advocate*, March.

Wicker, Tom. 1982. "The Manila Connection." *New York Times*, May 21. http://www.nytimes.com/1982/05/21/opinion/in-the-nation-a-manila-connection.html.

University of Washington Special Collections

The following items are identified by UWSC in text citations.

ACWA Incorporation Papers. 1973. Tyree Scott Papers, 5245-001, box 13, folder 36.

ACWA Lawsuits. 1974. Cindy Domingo Papers, 5651-001, box 9, folder 31.

ACWA Newsletter. 1973. "Local 37—For or Against the Members." http://depts.washington.edu/labpics/zenPhoto/albums/Filipino/album_002/domingo%20and%20woo%20report/domingo%20and%20woo%20report_Page_40.jpg.

———. 1974. *The New Tide* 1, no. 2 (May 1974). http://depts.washington.edu/labpics/zenPhoto/Filipino/album_002/NTMay74_ocr/NTMay74_ocr_Page_1.jpg.

ACWA Proposal. 1973. "Proposal to Combat Employment Discrimination in the Alaska Salmon Industry." Tyree Scott Papers, ACWA Files. Box 13, folder 36. ACC NO. 245-1. http://depts.washington.edu/labpics/zenPhoto/Filipino/album_002/ACWA%20proposal/.

ACWA Report. 1973. "Report by Domingo and Woo on Observation Trip to Alaska Canneries." September 10. http://depts.washington.edu/labpics/zenPhoto/Filipino/album_002/domingo%20and%20woo%20report/.

Alaskero News. 1979. "Leadership Launches Work." Vol. 1, no. 1, April. Cannery Workers and Farm Laborers Union Local 7 papers, 3927-0001, box 33, folder 43.

Bulosan, Carlos. 1950. "I Want the Wide American Earth." PNW04510, no. 0581-012, box 3/17.

Chomley Spectator. 1929. "Natural Rights in Danger." Editorial, July 29. Victorio Velasco Papers, 1435-003, box 3, folder 24.

CJDV Newsletter. 1981a. "Anti-Marcos Labor Activists Murdered: Marcos Linked to Seattle Slayings." July 21. Cindy Domingo Papers, 5651-002, box 3, folder 25.

———. 1981b. August 3. Cindy Domingo Papers, 5651-002, box 4, folder 41.

———. 1981c. August 21. Cindy Domingo Papers, 5651-002, box 4, folder 41.

———. 1981d. September. Cindy Domingo Papers, 5651-002, box 4, folder 41.

———. 1981e. October. Cindy Domingo Papers, 5651-002, box 4, folder 41.

———. 1981f. "Dictado Trial Set for April 1st." December 1. Cindy Domingo Papers, 5651-002, box 4, folder 41.

———. 1982a. June 1. Cindy Domingo Papers, 5651-002, box 4, folder 41.

———. 1982b. "Civil Suit Filed: Marcos and the U.S. Named in the Murder of Seattle Activists." September/October. Cindy Domingo Papers, 5651-002, box 4, folder 41.

———. 1984. Spring, Cindy Domingo Papers, 5651-002, box 4, folder 41.

———. 1985. "Philippines to Stand Trial for Domingo/Viernes Murders." November. Cindy Domingo Papers, 5651-002, box 4, folder 41.

———. 1986. Spring, Cindy Domingo Papers, 5651-002, box 4, folder 41.

"Committee to Sponsor Luis Taruc's Autobiography letter." [1953], box 4, folder 8, Carlos Bulosan Papers, Pacific Northwest Historical Documents. Accessed June 13, 2017. http://digitalcollections.lib.washington.edu/cdm/singleitem/collection/pioneerlife/id/21768/rec/18.

Domingo, Cindy. 1982–1983. Correspondence with Norm Maleng. Cindy Domingo Papers II, 5651-002, box 1, folder 3.

Domingo, Nemesio. 2000. "*Wards Cove* Press Packet," August 7. Cindy Domingo Papers, 5651-001, box 4, folder 13.

Filipino Labor Journal. 1932. "Our Platform." The Filipino American National Historical Society Archives, Seattle WA.

ILWU Local 37 Trial Committee. 1955. "Minutes of the Trial Committee." January 17. John Caughlan Papers, 0704-001, box 23/15-24/10.

Landau, Saul. 1985. Speech at the 1985 Memorial for Domingo and Viernes given in Seattle. Cindy Domingo Papers, 1973-2010, box 2, folder 9.

Local 7 News. 1947. "Briones, Velasco, Pilien Swamped in Election." Vol. III, No. 9. Victorio A. Velasco papers, 1435-003, box 6, folder 32.

Maleng, Norman. "Correspondence." Cindy Domingo papers, 2917-2010. box 1, folder 3.

Mensalvas, Chris et al. 1954. Letter to Lou Goldblatt, ILWU Secretary-Treasurer. December 1. John Caughlan Papers, 0704-001, box 23/15-24/10.

Mislang, Margaret. N.d. "Who Murdered Virgil S. Dunyungan?" Cannery Workers and Farm Laborers Union Local 7 Records, 3927-001, box 9, folder 15.

National Industrial Recovery Administration (NIRA) Hearing on Code of Fair Practices and Competition. 1934. San Francisco. February. 22-25. Cannery Workers and Farm Laborers Union Local 7 Records, 3927-001, box 36, folder 24.

Northwest LELO. 1987. "Press Release: Statement of Nemesio Domingo, named plaintiff and class representative in *Domingo v. New England Fish Co.*" Authors' files.

———. 2000. "Letter to Attorney Abraham Arditi." Cindy Domingo Papers, Box 4, Folder 4 ("Wards Cove").

RFC Election Slate Pamphlet. 1978. Box 33 folder 28. CWLFU-UW. Accessed May 29, 2018. http://digitalcollections.lib.washington.edu/cdm/compoundobject/collection/pioneerlife/id/18146/rec/10

Rojo, Trinidad A. 1947. "Birth of CIO Local 7." Trinidad Rojo Papers, 3586-002, Box 1, Folder 5.

———. 1952. "Birth and Growth of Local 37." *ILWU Local 37 1952 Yearbook*. Chris Mensalvas Papers, 2361-001, Box 1, Folder 14. 14-15.

———. N.d., ca. 1985. "Food Tobacco and Allied Workers of America, CIO Local 7, Now, International Longshoremen and Warehouse Union (ILWU), Local 37," 1. Trinidad Rojo Papers, 3586-002, box 1, folder 9.

Schenk, Maria. 1975, "Birds of Passage: Perspectives on the Filipino Experience in North America." Maria Schenk papers, accession no. 3045-002.

Scott, Tyree. 1989. Press Statement. June 8. Cindy Domingo Papers, 5651-001, box 9, folder 31.

Viernes, Gene. 1980. "No 'Pot of Gold' for Transient Workers." July. http://digitalcollections.lib.washington.edu/cdm/ref/collection/pioneerlife/id/18039.

Williams, Sue. 1978. Grievance. JD-(SF)-124-78. June 28. Cannery Workers and Farm Laborers Union Local 7 Records, 3927-001, box 30, folders 42–44.

Interviews

Some interviews do not have exact dates, as these were conducted in the first phase of research long before academic publication was imagined. All interviews are on file with authors.

Arditi, Abraham. Interview by George Lovell and Michael McCann, February 5, 2015.

———. Interview by Stuart Scheingold, n.d.

Avila, Geline. Interview by Michael McCann, June 22, 1998.

Caughlan, John. Interview by Michael McCann and Doug Baker, July 16, 1998.
Della, David. Interview by Michael McCann, March 8, 1998.
Domingo, Cindy. Interview by Michael McCann, March 8, 1998.
Domingo, Nemesio, Jr. Interview by Michael McCann and Doug Baker, 1998.
Domingo, Nemesio, Jr. Interview by Michael McCann and George Lovell, 2014.
Fox, Michael. Interview by Michael McCann and Doug Baker, 1998.
Gurtiza, Rich. Interview by Michael McCann, 1998.
Ko, Elaine. Interview by Michael McCann. September 1998.
Mast, Terri. Interview by Michael McCann and Doug Baker, March 17, 1998.
Occena, Bruce. Interview by Michael McCann, June 22, 1998.
———. Interview by George Lovell and Michael McCann, 2011.
Scott, Tyree. Interview by Michael McCann, March 17, 1998.
Tactaquin, Cathey. Interview by Michael McCann, June 1998.
Tomayo, Bill, Interview by Michael McCann, September 19, 1998.
Von Bronkhurst, Emily. Interview by Michael McCann, 2011.
Withey, Michael. Interview by Michael McCann, June 9, 1998.
Woo, Michael. Interview by Michael McCann, March 13, 1998.

Index

Page numbers followed by "f" refer to figures

The Chicago Series in Law and Society
Edited by John M. Conley, Charles Epp, and Lynn Mather

Series titles, continued from front matter:

FAILING LAW SCHOOLS *by Brian Z. Tamanaha*

EVERYDAY LAW ON THE STREET: CITY GOVERNANCE IN AN AGE OF DIVERSITY *by Mariana Valverde*

LAWYERS IN PRACTICE: ETHICAL DECISION MAKING IN CONTEXT *Edited by Leslie C. Levin and Lynn Mather*

COLLATERAL KNOWLEDGE: LEGAL REASONING IN THE GLOBAL FINANCIAL MARKETS *by Annelise Riles*

SPECIALIZING THE COURTS *by Lawrence Baum*

ASIAN LEGAL REVIVALS: LAWYERS IN THE SHADOW OF EMPIRE *by Yves Dezalay and Bryant G. Garth*

THE LANGUAGE OF STATUTES: LAWS AND THEIR INTERPRETATION *by Lawrence M. Solan*

BELONGING IN AN ADOPTED WORLD: RACE, IDENTITY, AND TRANSNATIONAL ADOPTION *by Barbara Yngvesson*

MAKING RIGHTS REAL: ACTIVISTS, BUREAUCRATS, AND THE CREATION OF THE LEGALISTIC STATE *by Charles R. Epp*

LAWYERS OF THE RIGHT: PROFESSIONALIZING THE CONSERVATIVE COALITION *by Ann Southworth*

ARGUING WITH TRADITION: THE LANGUAGE OF LAW IN HOPI TRIBAL COURT *by Justin B. Richland*

SPEAKING OF CRIME: THE LANGUAGE OF CRIMINAL JUSTICE *by Lawrence M. Solan and Peter M. Tiersma*

HUMAN RIGHTS AND GENDER VIOLENCE: TRANSLATING INTERNATIONAL LAW INTO LOCAL JUSTICE *by Sally Engle Merry*

JUST WORDS, SECOND EDITION: LAW, LANGUAGE, AND POWER *by John M. Conley and William M. O'Barr*

DISTORTING THE LAW: POLITICS, MEDIA, AND THE LITIGATION CRISIS *by William Haltom and Michael McCann*

JUSTICE IN THE BALKANS: PROSECUTING WAR CRIMES IN THE HAGUE TRIBUNAL *by John Hagan*

RIGHTS OF INCLUSION: LAW AND IDENTITY IN THE LIFE STORIES OF AMERICANS WITH DISABILITIES *by David M. Engel and Frank W. Munger*

THE INTERNATIONALIZATION OF PALACE WARS: LAWYERS, ECONOMISTS, AND THE CONTEST TO TRANSFORM LATIN AMERICAN STATES *by Yves Dezalay and Bryant G. Garth*

FREE TO DIE FOR THEIR COUNTRY: THE STORY OF THE JAPANESE AMERICAN DRAFT RESISTERS IN WORLD WAR II *by Eric L. Muller*

OVERSEERS OF THE POOR: SURVEILLANCE, RESISTANCE, AND THE LIMITS OF PRIVACY *by John Gilliom*

PRONOUNCING AND PERSEVERING: GENDER AND THE DISCOURSES OF DISPUTING IN AN AFRICAN ISLAMIC COURT *by Susan F. Hirsch*

THE COMMON PLACE OF LAW: STORIES FROM EVERYDAY LIFE *by Patricia Ewick and Susan S. Silbey*

THE STRUGGLE FOR WATER: POLITICS, RATIONALITY, AND IDENTITY IN THE AMERICAN SOUTHWEST *by Wendy Nelson Espeland*

DEALING IN VIRTUE: INTERNATIONAL COMMERCIAL ARBITRATION AND THE CONSTRUCTION OF A TRANSNATIONAL LEGAL ORDER *by Yves Dezalay and Bryant G. Garth*

RIGHTS AT WORK: PAY EQUITY REFORM AND THE POLITICS OF LEGAL MOBILIZATION *by Michael W. McCann*

THE LANGUAGE OF JUDGES *by Lawrence M. Solan*

REPRODUCING RAPE: DOMINATION THROUGH TALK IN THE COURTROOM *by Gregory M. Matoesian*

GETTING JUSTICE AND GETTING EVEN: LEGAL CONSCIOUSNESS AMONG WORKING-CLASS AMERICANS *by Sally Engle Merry*

RULES VERSUS RELATIONSHIPS: THE ETHNOGRAPHY OF LEGAL DISCOURSE *by John M. Conley and William M. O'Barr*